IFIP Advances in Information and Communication Technology

534

Editor-in-Chief

Kai Rannenberg, Goethe University Frankfurt, Germany

IFIP – The International Federation for Information Processing

IFIP was founded in 1960 under the auspices of UNESCO, following the first World Computer Congress held in Paris the previous year. A federation for societies working in information processing, IFIP's aim is two-fold: to support information processing in the countries of its members and to encourage technology transfer to developing nations. As its mission statement clearly states:

IFIP is the global non-profit federation of societies of ICT professionals that aims at achieving a worldwide professional and socially responsible development and application of information and communication technologies.

IFIP is a non-profit-making organization, run almost solely by 2500 volunteers. It operates through a number of technical committees and working groups, which organize events and publications. IFIP's events range from large international open conferences to working conferences and local seminars.

The flagship event is the IFIP World Computer Congress, at which both invited and contributed papers are presented. Contributed papers are rigorously refereed and the rejection rate is high.

As with the Congress, participation in the open conferences is open to all and papers may be invited or submitted. Again, submitted papers are stringently refereed.

The working conferences are structured differently. They are usually run by a working group and attendance is generally smaller and occasionally by invitation only. Their purpose is to create an atmosphere conducive to innovation and development. Refereeing is also rigorous and papers are subjected to extensive group discussion.

Publications arising from IFIP events vary. The papers presented at the IFIP World Computer Congress and at open conferences are published as conference proceedings, while the results of the working conferences are often published as collections of selected and edited papers.

IFIP distinguishes three types of institutional membership: Country Representative Members, Members at Large, and Associate Members. The type of organization that can apply for membership is a wide variety and includes national or international societies of individual computer scientists/ICT professionals, associations or federations of such societies, government institutions/government related organizations, national or international research institutes or consortia, universities, academies of sciences, companies, national or international associations or federations of companies.

More information about this series at http://www.springer.com/series/6102

Luis M. Camarinha-Matos · Hamideh Afsarmanesh
Yacine Rezgui (Eds.)

Collaborative Networks of Cognitive Systems

19th IFIP WG 5.5 Working Conference
on Virtual Enterprises, PRO-VE 2018
Cardiff, UK, September 17–19, 2018
Proceedings

 Springer

Editors
Luis M. Camarinha-Matos ⓘ
Nova University of Lisbon
Monte Caparica
Portugal

Yacine Rezgui ⓘ
Cardiff University
Cardiff
UK

Hamideh Afsarmanesh ⓘ
University of Amsterdam
Amsterdam
The Netherlands

ISSN 1868-4238   ISSN 1868-422X (electronic)
IFIP Advances in Information and Communication Technology
ISBN 978-3-030-07568-2   ISBN 978-3-319-99127-6 (eBook)
https://doi.org/10.1007/978-3-319-99127-6

This Springer imprint is published by the registered company Springer Nature Switzerland AG
The registered company address is: Gewerbestrasse 11, 6330 Cham, Switzerland

Preface

Collaborative Networks and Cognition

Recent advances in artificial intelligence, specifically in the areas of machine learning, sensorial perception, reasoning, communication capabilities, and human–machine interaction, have led to a new generation of cognitive systems that fundamentally challenge the foundations of past information systems. Cognition becomes distributed across networks of smart things, smart systems, organizations, and people. Simultaneously, users are increasingly becoming connected and proactive participants in cyber-physical ecosystems as opposed to being passive recipients of various top–down optimization regimes, thus paving the way to a new generation of "user-in-the-loop" cognitive systems, leveraging on domain semantics and higher-order intelligence. With the explosion of available data, cognitive systems can therefore learn, reason, and more effectively interact with each other, the users, and their surrounding environments, hence enabling higher levels of collaboration in networks of humans and systems.

Furthermore, the growing levels of hyper-connectivity among people, organizations, smart things, systems, and machines offer new perspectives on user experience, collective awareness, collective intelligence, and even collective emotions. This emerging reality challenges the way collaborative networks and systems are designed and operate with an increasing need to factor in a user-driven perspective. New forms of collaborative cognitive problem-solving can be devised, while the network's evolutionary nature and its resilience and sustainability perspectives become the key issues. On the other hand, there is a need to better understand the potential for value creation through collaborative approaches in this context.

The 2018 IFIP Working Conference on Virtual Enterprises (PRO-VE 2018) provided a forum for sharing experiences, discussing trends, identifying challenges, and introducing innovative solutions aimed at fulfilling the vision of goal-oriented collaboration in networks of cognitive systems. Understanding, modeling, and proposing solution approaches in this area require contributions from multiple and diverse areas, including computer science, industrial and electrical engineering, social sciences, economy, organization science, and technologies, among others, which are well tuned to the interdisciplinary spirit of the PRO-VE Working Conferences.

PRO-VE 2018, held in Cardiff, UK, was the 19th event in this series of successful conferences, including:

PRO-VE 1999 (Porto, Portugal), PRO-VE 2000 (Florianopolis, Brazil), PRO-VE 2002 (Sesimbra, Portugal), PRO-VE 2003 (Lugano, Switzerland), PRO-VE 2004 (Toulouse, France), PRO-VE 2005 (Valencia, Spain), PRO-VE 2006 (Helsinki, Finland), PRO-VE 2007 (Guimarães, Portugal), PRO-VE 2008 (Poznan, Poland), PRO-VE 2009 (Thessaloniki, Greece), PRO-VE 2010 (St. Etienne, France), PRO-VE

2011 (São Paulo, Brazil), PRO-VE 2012 (Bournemouth, UK), PRO-VE 2013 (Dresden, Germany), PRO-VE 2014 (Amsterdam, The Netherlands), PRO-VE 2015 (Albi, France), PRO-VE 2016 (Porto, Portugal), and PRO-VE 2017 (Vicenza, Italy).

This proceedings book includes selected papers from the PRO-VE 2018 Conference. It provides a comprehensive overview of major challenges that are being addressed, and recent advances in various domains related to the collaborative networks and their applications. There was therefore a strong focus on the following areas related to the selected main theme for the 2018 conference:

- Blockchain in Collaborative Networks
- Industry Transformation and Innovation
- Semantics in Networks of Cognitive Systems
- Cognitive Systems for Resilience Management
- Collaborative Energy Services in Smart Cities
- Cognitive Systems in Agribusiness
- Building Information Modeling
- Industry 4.0 Support Frameworks
- Health and Social Welfare Services
- Risk, Privacy, and Security
- Collaboration Platform Issues
- Sensing, Smart, and Sustainable Enterprises
- Information Systems Integration
- Dynamic Logistics Networks
- Collaborative Business Processes
- Value Creation in Networks
- Users and Organizations Profiling
- Collaborative Business Strategies

We are thankful to all the authors, from academia, research, and industry, for their contributions. We hope this collection of papers represents a valuable tool for those interested in research advances and emerging applications in collaborative networks, as well as identifying future open challenges for research and development in this area. We very much appreciate the dedication, time, and effort spent by the members of the PRO-VE international Program Committee who supported the selection of articles for this conference and provided valuable and constructive comments to help authors with improving the quality of their papers.

July 2018   Luis M. Camarinha-Matos
                                                                                            Hamideh Afsarmanesh
                                                                                                    Yacine Rezgui

Organization

 PRO-VE 2018 – 19th IFIP Working Conference on VIRTUAL ENTERPRISES
Cardiff, UK, September 17–19, 2018

Conference Chair

Yacine Rezgui, UK

Program Committee Chair

Luis M. Camarinha-Matos, Portugal

Program Committee Co-chair

Hamideh Afsarmanesh, The Netherlands

Program Committee

Antonio Abreu, Portugal
Hamideh Afsarmanesh, The Netherlands
Cesar Analide, Portugal
Beatriz Andres, Spain
Dario Antonelli, Italy
Américo Azevedo, Portugal
Frédérick Bénaben, France
Peter Bernus, Australia
Peter Bertok, Australia
Xavier Boucher, France
Jeremy Bryans, UK
Luis M. Camarinha-Matos, Portugal
Wojciech Cellary, Poland
Naoufel Cheikhrouhou, Switzerland
Rob Dekkers, UK
Filipa Ferrada, Portugal
Adriano Fiorese, Brazil

Rosanna Fornasiero, Italy
Gary Fragidis, Greece
Cesar Garita, Costa Rica
Ricardo Gonçalves, Portugal
Ted Goranson, USA
Paul Grefen, The Netherlands
Jairo Gutierrez, New Zealand
Dmitri Ivanov, Germany
Tomasz Janowski, Portugal
Eleni Kaldoudi, Greece
Dimitris Karagiannis, Autria
Adamantios Koumpis, Germany
Leandro Loss, Brazil
António Lucas Soares, Portugal
Laura Macchion, Italy
Patricia Macedo, Portugal
Nikolay Mehandjiev, UK

Thomas Meiren, Germany
Kyrill Meyer, Germany
Istvan Mezgar, Hungary
Arturo Molina, Mexico
Ovidiu Noran, Australia
Paulo Novais, Portugal
Adegboyega Ojo, Ireland
Ana Inês Oliveira, Portugal
Eugenio Oliveira, Portugal
Martin Ollus, Finland
Angel Ortiz, Spain
A. Luis Osório, Portugal
Hervé Panetto, France
Iraklis Paraskakis, Greece
Adam Pawlak, Poland
Jorge Pinho Sousa, Portugal
Raul Poler, Spain
Ricardo Rabelo, Brazil

Yacine Rezgui, UK
João Rosas, Portugal
Hans Schaffers, The Netherlands
Jens Schütze, Germany
Weiming Shen, Canada
Volker Stich, Germany
Chrysostomos Stylios, Greece
Stefania Testa, Italy
Klaus-Dieter Thoben, Germany
Lorna Uden, UK
Paula Urze, Portugal
Katri Valkokari, Finland
Rolando Vallejos, Brazil
Agostino Villa, Italy
Antonio Volpentesta, Italy
Lai Xu, UK
Christian Zinke, Germany
Peter Weiß, Germany

Special Session Organizers

Special Session on Cognitive Systems for Resilience Management
Yacine Rezgui, UK
Wanqing Zhao, UK

Special Session on Semantics in Networks of Cognitive Systems
Yacine Rezgui, UK
Thomas Beach, UK

Special Session on Collaborative Energy Services in Smart Cities
Gari Fragidis, Greece
Martina Occelli, Germany

Special Session on Cognitive Systems in Agribusiness
Mareva Alemany, Spain
Angel Ortiz, Spain
Jorge Hernandez, UK
Lynne Butel, UK

Organizing Committee

Thomas Beach (OC chair), UK
Yacine Rezgui (OC chair), UK
Muhammad Ahmad, UK
Jean-Laurent Hippolyte, UK

Andrei Hodorog, UK
Ioan Petri, UK
Wanqing Zhao, UK

Technical Sponsors

IFIP WG 5.5 COVE
Co-Operation infrastructure for Virtual Enterprises
and electronic business

Society of Collaborative Networks

Organizational Co-Sponsors

Nova University of Lisbon

UNINOVA

UNIVERSITY OF AMSTERDAM

Contents

XII   Contents

Collaborative Business Processes

Collaboration Platform Issues

Information Systems Integration

Collaborative Business Strategies

Industry 4.0 Support Frameworks

Health and Social Welfare Services

Semantics in Networks of Cognitive Systems

Dynamic Logistics Networks

Blockchain in Collaborative Networks

The Relevance of Blockchain for Collaborative Networked Organizations

Hans Schaffers[✉]

Adventure Research, 7231 GL Warnsveld, The Netherlands
hs@adventureresearch.nl

Abstract. Blockchain, a distributed secure digital ledger technology, is a relatively recent development with potentially transformational implications for economy and society. Its specific characteristics enable new decentralized models of distributed and trusted transactions. This position paper explores the implications of blockchain for collaborative networked organizations. In particular we aim at understanding the implications for companies in various economic sectors, and how new forms of networked organizations and new business models will be enabled. We also will focus on enablers of blockchain innovations, in particular with respect to governance of blockchain-based platforms and business networks. The paper results in a discussion of research challenges in the field of blockchain-enabled collaborative networked organizations.

Keywords: Blockchain · Organizations · Collaboration · Networks
Governance

1 Introduction

Over the last years, blockchain technology and its applications received a lot of attention in business, academia and society at large [1]. According to a recent survey, 77% of FinTech companies expect to adopt blockchain as part of a production system or process by 2020 [2]. A lot of innovation is going on, mostly in the domain of financial services and payments systems, however use case experimentation and piloting is proceeding in many other sectors including logistics and supply chains, education, healthcare, government services and energy.

Key players in the blockchain ecosystem are diverse [3]. Blockchain platforms such as Ethereum, Hyperledger, NEO, Coinbase, the R3 consortium and Ripple enable developers to develop smart contract and distributed applications. Large financial institutions are involved, including large banking and insurance companies, as well as accountancy firms, venture capitalists, and computing firms such as IBM who offer blockchain platform and enterprise solutions. Increasingly there is interest from the side of national and global regulators, governments and standardization organisations.

Blockchain technologies and current developments are explained in many publications such as [1, 3–5]. In addition, there exist a variety of lively blogs discussing blockchain technological developments, use cases, governance issues and more. Blockchain technology is based on distributed digital ledger technology, recording

Published by Springer Nature Switzerland AG 2018. All Rights Reserved
L. M. Camarinha-Matos et al. (Eds.): PRO-VE 2018, IFIP AICT 534, pp. 3–17, 2018.
https://doi.org/10.1007/978-3-319-99127-6_1

cryptographic secured transactions in chains of chronologically connected, stored and timestamped blocks. As such blockchain is based on a new form of distributed consensus of transactions and in principle enables peer-to-peer economies. Its importance goes far beyond its most prominent application, the cryptocurrency called Bitcoin. Blockchain has the wide-ranging potential to enable radically new decentralized forms of organization and radically new business models.

Based on a review of literature, this paper aims to explore, examine and discuss how blockchain affects forms of collaborative networked organisations and to understand the determinants of adoption and transition towards blockchain economies. The precise impacts of blockchain on economy and society are still unclear. Internationally a range of blockchain pilots are being carried out to understand these impacts as well as their business models, governance frameworks and other key factors for adoption, scaling up and success. Section 2 presents an overview of blockchain technology and impacts.

At the intersection of blockchain technology and organizational change several challenging issues come together. Section 3 therefore aims to understand the underlying conditions for blockchain-enabled forms of collaborative organizations. Section 4 takes a closer look at the relevance of blockchain for collaborative networked organizations and how these are enabling new ways of working and doing business. A central adoption issue, addressed in Sect. 5, is the governance and decision-making mechanisms in blockchain-enabled decentralized organizations. Finally, challenges and research opportunities for the future are being discussed in Sect. 6.

2 Blockchain Technology and Impacts

2.1 Blockchain as Technological Innovation

The origin of blockchain technology lies in a protocol for peer-to-peer transactions developed by Satoshi Nakamoto, a pseudonym [4]. Nakamoto describes the digital currency bitcoin as 'peer-to-peer electronic cash system, allowing online payments to be sent directly from one party to another without going through a financial institution'. The underlying blockchain technology is based on applying peer-to-peer distributed timestamps to generate computational proof of the chronological order of transactions. As [4] explains, blockchain is a collection of blocks which are chronologically linked and cryptographically secured, and its data are stored immutable in a shared database, the digital ledger. The software system enables the validation of transactions by consensus mechanisms within the network of all participants. This way blockchain technology allows parties to engage in transactions directly, whereas the integrity of the data involved in the transactions is ensured without the need for a trusted third party. All participants to a blockchain have access to and can store and modify a copy.

A key innovation for blockchain has been the possibility of smart contracts, which are based on software rules for execution of blockchain transactions, contingent on events or conditions, as explained in [6, 7]. Such smart contracts can be stored as transactions in the distributed ledger. This principle has a wide range of application possibilities varying from automated execution of contingent claims (insurance and finance [8]) to, in the future, industrial applications in the scope of Internet of Things and big data. Smart contract tools are offered for example by the Ethereum and Hyperledger Fabric platforms. A related development pursued by Ethereum is that a set of smart contracts creates a so-called Decentralized Autonomous Organization [9]. An example is The DAO crowdfunding platform created in 2016 upon the Ethereum blockchain, functioning as investment fund for start-ups where funding comes from the Ether cryptocurrency functioning as shares. The DAO subsequently experienced an infamous hack, which reminds us of the complexities of such systems and of the vulnerabilities in using the in itself extremely secure blockchain and smart contracts technology.

2.2 Blockchain Platforms

Blockchain applications normally require collaboration among parties involved e.g. for trading and supply chain management. Blockchain applications can be implemented through existing blockchain platforms; alternatively, parties can decide to build and operate their own blockchain system [10]. The different options available are connected to the operating models and governance frameworks of existing blockchain platforms [11]. In addition, these choices are dependent on the business model and trade-offs in terms of control and ownership on the side of the application owner (user).

In this context, the distinction between private and public blockchain platforms is essential and a lot of debate is going on regarding this issue [12]. A public ('permissionless') blockchain platform such as Bitcoin and Ethereum is completely open in terms of participation and access agreements. However, Ethereum is also an infrastructure which enables building distributed organizations based on smart contracts [8]. A private ('permissioned') blockchain builds on permission for modifying the ledger and access agreements. Examples of permissioned blockchains are Ripple and Hyperledger Fabric (hosted by The Linux Foundation).

A specific form of private blockchain is consortium blockchain, where participants for a consortium which is governed by consortium agreements. For example, IBM Blockchain Platform, making use of Hyperledger technologies, is a service for companies to help creating, operating and governing their private blockchain applications. Setting up private consortium blockchains implies a variety of important issues, such as the process of consortium building, partner selection, consortium composition and extension, dispute settling, rules for network governance, and legal and regulatory aspects. There is an interesting relationship with the field of collaborative networked organizations where comparable type of issues are in discussion [13].

2.3 Blockchain Applications and Business Models

As such, blockchain goes far beyond cryptocurrency bitcoin payments as it records and keeps track of all kinds of transactions and mutations. Think of use cases in financial transactions, insurance claim process, transfer of all kinds of asset ownership, and making changes in complex contracts and records. Given its emphasis on value ownership and exchange, blockchain is sometimes called the 'Internet of Value' [1].

The first and most prominent application of blockchain technology has been the Bitcoin blockchain, which has a wide range of implications for the economy and financial system as explained in [14, 15]. The precise reasons why bitcoin as digital currency system represents value are analysed in [16], although there is definitely some controversy in this matter. However, the underlying blockchain technology is of wider relevance for the economy [17] as it provides a platform for decentralized secure economic transactions in general, affecting the financial industry, insurance, supply chain management, energy markets, healthcare and many more. Interestingly, blockchain applications are often crossing the borders of sectors and probably it is there where the most attractive and innovative use cases lie. Some examples of potential blockchain applications discussed in literature are the following:

- Financial transactions. New financial instruments such as micro-payments, peer-to-peer lending, trading records and smart contracts can be built upon blockchain [18].
- Business process management. Applications of blockchain technology for business process management are described in [19], demonstrating its application potential in interorganizational transaction settings and discussing governance and accountability aspects and how smart contracts may provide solutions. In [20], a prototype blockchain application for cross-organizational workflow management in a financial institution is presented applied to document workflow for letter of credit. The prototype was implemented on a private Ethereum blockchain enabling smart contracts. The paper concludes that blockchain increases auditability, trust, efficiency and improves workflow management. However, remaining challenges include process and document standardization and regulation.
- Insurance. Given the event-driven nature of insurance use cases, blockchain and smart contracts may have considerable implications. Examples presented in [8] include claim processing and automatic refund, crop insurance in relation to weather data, identity verification and fraud prevention, and pay-per-use insurances.
- Auditing. Blockchain technology provides much opportunity for auditing. [21] discusses automated audits based on correctness analysis of statements. Given the opportunities for fraud in the software environment the paper states that security of the underlying environment and IT systems controls is critical for adoption.
- Education. A Joint Research Centre study provides an overview of blockchain education opportunities [22]. Examples are the issuing of certificates, storing verified e-portfolios, and managing intellectual property rights. An interesting use case is storage of qualifications on a blockchain. An example, elaborated in the report, is how the Open University in the UK is working on standards for badging, certification and reputation with the use of blockchain as a trusted ledger. The report also states that educational business models might very well change in using blockchain technology, as administration costs will decrease and fraud reduced. In the future, students could benefit from increased flexibility in selecting courses á la carte.
- Supply chain management. Blockchain technology may increase transparency and traceability of supply chains. In [23], blockchain adoption bottlenecks are addressed both on the supplier and consumer sides. In [24] a case study of supply chain integration based on blockchain is presented, concluding that functionalities such as

timestamps and smart contracts were beneficial. The paper also identifies a need for standards and interoperability, which blockchain itself does not offer.

- Assets sharing. Blockchain technology combined with Internet of Things creates interesting application opportunities in the sharing economy [25]. Blockchain could avoid dominance of dominant platform players such as Airbnb and Uber [3].
- Real estate transactions. Many intermediary parties are involved, and blockchain is supposed to transform the role of intermediaries such as notaries and cadastre. These actors are looking for new roles and services in the blockchain-enabled value chain.
- Open innovation, co-creation and IP management. Blockchain could support the tracking, management and exchange of intellectual property rights. This has also been an issue since long in the Collaborative Networked Organizations community.

Of high interest is the potential of blockchain within the domain of Industry 4.0. Industry 4.0 focuses on applying the concept of Internet of Things within the smart factory and emphasizes how smart factories are connected within a wider business ecosystem [26]. Different layers of applying smart technologies can be distinguished: the smart plant built around autonomously operating and interconnected cyber-physical systems, the smart factory enabling responsive and adaptive manufacturing automation and the smart business network or ecosystem enabling demand-driven flexible supply chain management. Industry 4.0 enables network-centric production methods, smart product and service concepts and responsive business models in collaborative ecosystems.

Blockchain and smart contracts fits well into the network-centric Industry 4.0 paradigm. Applications to supply chain management, product tracking and auditing are currently being worked on. [27] describes a number of applications, including a pilot in which IBM and Maersk tested the application of blockchain in logistics and supply chain management focusing on the tracking of containers during shipping movements. Foreseen are also applications of blockchain smart contracts in combination with data analytics and smart sensor systems (Internet of Things). The paper also identifies technical and organizational issues to be resolved, such as scalability and latency, lack of standards, and establishing the appropriate legal and regulatory conditions.

Probably the most interesting applications of blockchain in Industry 4.0 will be found in logistics, asset management and supply chain management. A particular interesting possibility could be how blockchain technology could support the response to unexpected disturbances within the supply chain. Given the lack of satisfactory interoperability among enterprise systems manual interventions are often required. Application of blockchain and smart contracts technology could facilitate rescheduling, replanning and contracting, making supply chains more resilient, responsive and adaptive.

Adoption of blockchain technologies will have profound impacts on the company business model, including the structure of partnerships, the corporate governance model, the financial model and the technical infrastructure and there is a growing literature in this field. For example [28] examines the different ways how key elements of corporate business models are affected. For example, the support of micropayments and the increased transaction security alters the revenue model, simplifies delivery processes and facilitates extension of the business network.

As a conclusion so far, blockchain will not only affect the business models of individual corporations but will require modified business models at the level of collaborative networks. Blockchain changes the coordination of economic activities in business networks, and blockchain applications require new forms of partnerships and collaboration networks established in consortia or other forms of networked organization. This also implies the need to establish appropriate governance models not only at the level of individual organizations but at the level of collaborative networks.

3   Blockchain and Economics of Governance

3.1   Blockchain as Governance

We now turn to understanding the nature of blockchain-enabled organizations. Blockchain can be understood as one form of governance, the same way markets, hierarchies and networks are forms of governance suitable in different situational contexts. This perspective originates mostly from the influential paradigms of transaction cost economics [29] and theory of the firm [30], where organizations are seen as 'nexus of contracts'. Williamson's organizational failures framework [29] looks at economics of organization from the perspective of contracts and transaction costs and analyses how both environmental factors (uncertainty and complexity, small numbers exchange relations) and human factors (bounded rationality and opportunism, also in relation to exploitation of trust) require 'governance'. Situationally different generic governance mechanisms can be identified with generic forms, markets, hierarchies and relational contracts. This has been explored not only in finance but also in organizational science studies in relation to network governance [31].

Of interest is the relation of these concepts to the characteristics of blockchain technology. In [32], building on transaction cost economics and public choice economy, blockchain is presented as alternative governance model, a specific type of decentralized organization. Given its transformational potential [32] considers blockchain not just as a new type of information technology but more institutional as a 'technology of governance' The paper argues that blockchain-enabled smart contracts and Decentralized Autonomous Organization will, through their transparency and decentralization characteristics, modify transaction costs. However, blockchain relates to complete contracts in the sense of anticipating to all potential future states, whereas in reality organizations address incomplete contracts characterized by uncertainties, so that most organizations are built upon governance arrangements to provide incentives and trust for cooperation. Clearly this implies that there are limits to blockchain-enabled decentralized autonomous organizations.

Interestingly [32] also addresses the role of collective decision-making rules and procedures. Blockchain is considered as 'trustless commons' where rules are embedded in smart contacts. This discussion bridges to the concept of peer production and sharing as developed in [33] and one direction for future innovation could be to understand the potential of blockchain for such commons-based models. [32] also refers to the importance of the governance of common pool resources as explored by Eline Ostrom, who proposed 'design rules' for successful commons self-governance. It can be expected that insight in how these governance-related issues are relevant for blockchain will be highly relevant for wider scale adoption of blockchain.

3.2 Impact on Intermediaries

Blockchain enables companies to decrease their transaction costs, with profound effects on the nature of companies: how they are funded and managed, how they create value and how they perform basic functions such as marketing, accounting, human resources, procurement, legal affairs [1]. Blockchain's technological characteristics enable extremely decentralized and self-organised forms of organization, aimed at creating, executing and managing transactions. Given the blockchain impact on transaction costs, blockchain-enabled organizational networks constitute an alternative with respective to traditional structures such as firms, supply chains and markets [34].

This may lead to disintermediation: intermediaries such as financial institutions and lawyers might no longer be needed in the future [32] and are exploring different roles and business models, as business networks based on blockchain could be better suited for creating products and services than traditional vertical integration [35]. For example, the role of intermediary platform organizations such as banks, insurance companies, auditors will be strongly affected, in particular through blockchain-enabled smart contracts, as blockchain enables bypassing such intermediaries through enabling peer-to-peer transactional relations.

Whereas these intermediaries will be affected structurally, the business models of many other organizations, supply chains and business networks will be affected due to the mentioned new technical opportunities for trustless secure transactions enabled by blockchain technology. Also, traditional platform models where large intermediaries owning the platforms capture the vale may become affected by blockchain applications [17]. Blockchain-based applications such as the OpenBazaar marketplace are able to coordinate the common activities of a large number of individuals without the help of a third party, in a secure and decentralized manner [17]. New cooperative models are emerging where users are contributors as well as shareholders.

4 Blockchain and Collaborative Networked Organizations

4.1 Collaborative Networked Organizations

The previous section looked into the fundamentals of blockchain-enabled organizations. We now take a closer look to how blockchain relates to collaborative networked organizations. The latter concept focuses on collaboration for value creation across the boundaries of teams and organizations and within communities and associated forms of distributed collective intelligence. In [36], a collaborative network is defined as 'a network consisting of a variety of entities (e.g. organizations and people) that are largely autonomous, geographically distributed, and heterogeneous in terms of their operating environment, culture, social capital and goals, but that collaborate to better achieve common or compatible goals, thus jointly generating value, and whose interactions are supported by a computer network'. A diversity of forms exists; examples of types of collaborative networks are the professional virtual community, the extended enterprise, a business ecosystem, a virtual team, a virtual enterprise a supply chain. Key issues determining the success of collaborative networks are the building and maintaining of trust [37], the system of incentives, rules of fairness and sharing benefits, transparent governance principles [38], and alignment of values of participants [13].

Since long, issues such as trust, governance and culture have been important in connection with collaboration-oriented technological innovations. Over time, discussion has moved from technologies enabling collaborative working and e-business to technologies, business models and governance principles for business networks and more recently platform-based ecosystems [39].

4.2 Blockchain-Enabled Collaborative Organizations

The issue is now how blockchain could contribute innovative elements to collaborative networked organizations, and how blockchain applications could benefit from collaborative networks organizations. This is an area which is open for new research, and the below aims to provide some initial views based on some available studies.

As regards trust and governance mechanisms, blockchain technology pursues trustless transaction environments. The fundamental approach of public, open blockchain technology developed by Nakamoto [4] is to enable secure peer-to-peer transactions, and in this perspective, 'blockchain is governance'. Still, blockchain has some security challenges as mentioned in Sect. 2. However, these vulnerabilities seem to be part of the technical and organizational environment of blockchain applications rather than to the blockchain and smart contracting technologies.

Within collaborative networked organizations research, mechanisms to build and maintain trust among participants and to create governance mechanisms have received attention [36, 38, 40]. Also, ownership and control issues as well as business models are important to address, otherwise partnering will fail. Consortium formation, definition of governance principles, partner selection and role definition are important activities in setting op and evolution of such networks. For example, [13] discusses the alignment of values of participants in the formation and evolution of collaborative networks. Therefore, an interesting research issue would be how tools for partner selection and other aspects of governance could be designed applicable in the lifecycle management of blockchain-enabled collaborative networks.

Trust, control and governance mechanisms remain particularly relevant at the level of private and consortium blockchains, where business networks and consortia are building and operating a blockchain application. Blockchain solutions require a collaboration among many different players in a viable ecosystem. Selection of participants and establishing a clear governance model is therefore important, already in the development phase [10]. Here comes in a number of the same issues as in collaborative networked organizations: participant selection, consortium sizing, joining and leaving procedures, consortium goals agreement, consensus building, liability, KPI's, platform management and decision making.

Blockchain could have implications not only for e-business transaction processes but also for human-oriented collaboration environments and virtual teams. Think of collaboration platforms which support distributed teams, such as shared workspace BSCW, having a wide range of functionalities such as document sharing, versioning, calendaring, presence, project management, conferencing and many more. Blockchain technology provides the opportunity to facilitate groupwork in terms of immutable project-related transactions to be registered on a blockchain. Here we see the distinction between blockchain as a formal procedural solution and the social trust-based system of group collaboration.

The view of organizations as sets of transactional contracts has great value but also its limits. Organizations are complex socio-technical systems, where we see a variety of formal and informal, even spontaneous, structures and processes mediated through human interactions, team work, organizational procedures and rules, governance structures, leadership, and organizational culture. Organizations understood as nexus of contracts is a valuable perspective, focusing on transaction processes between parties that can be automated based on data such as orders, reservations and payments, on the other hand, the context of such transactions is human, social and cultural.

5 Governance of Blockchain Ecosystems

Governance is an issue to be considered in different contexts and at different levels of abstraction. Blockchain as a structural form of governance (as alternative for markets and hierarchies) was discussed in Sect. 3. This should be distinguished from governance as a process, to be applied to blockchain applications, platforms and ecosystems and at the global level comparable with internet governance, as discussed in [1, 3].

At a fundamental, global level [3] takes a point of departure in how governance of the internet is currently arranged (with entities such as ICANN, IETF, the WWW Consortium and other) in order to learn about implications for global blockchain governance. This level of governance agrees on general rules, is setting standards, agrees on and maintains policies, engages in knowledge development, implements watchdog functions, and builds out the global infrastructure. In [3] a self-organised multi-stakeholder governance structure for blockchain as a global resource – Internet of Value - is discussed, made up of various types of networks and institutions. The vision is that as a global resource, and from the need to protect consumers, citizens and companies in relation to the involved risks, blockchain requires global 'stewardship', which also includes legal frameworks and standardization.

Besides at the global ecosystem level, [1] envisions governance at the level of platforms and applications. At the level of blockchain platforms such as Ethereum, Ripple and Hyperledger, governance challenges include issues such as scaling, the creation of shared views within the blockchain community, the incentives for mass collaboration on innovations, how to agree on standards enabling interoperability, and how to address threats such as The DAO hack. At the level of blockchain applications, [1] proposes governance mechanisms in relation to assets and tools that run on platforms such as digital currencies and smart contracts, and applications such as payments, smart contracts, insurance which raise specific governance issues. Also, attention to platform and application interoperability will be important according to [1].

In this context, a debate is ongoing in relation to the need for blockchain control and governance. One of the controversies is whether governance should be implemented through blockchain code, or whether blockchain is part of a wider socio-technical system requiring governance and legislation. Given the apparent legal challenges and risks of blockchain-enabled transactions in the societal domain, such as liability, responsibility and enforceability, governance and regulatory challenges will require more attention [1]. This vision is also shared in [41], stating that blockchain technology operates independently from any centralized institutions or trusted authorities and implements their own internal system of rules, almost exclusively governed by the rules of code. This discussion actually raises the fundamental debate about autonomy and self-organization vs control and regulation, about whether individual freedoms are restrained rather than enhanced, and whether regulation constrains innovation opportunities, as raised in [32, 42].

For example, [43] asserts that although blockchain governance is encoded in the blockchain protocols, it is still necessary to trust the functioning of the code as expected. We already referred to the hack of The DAO, where a vulnerability allowed for diverting a large amount of funds, while this did not violate Ethereum's of The DAO's rules or legal frameworks itself. In words of [46]: 'Code is law for machines, law is code for people'. A related view is [44], stating that when rules embedded in blockchain software could favour some companies at the expense of others, the authority to change the underlying rules becomes critically important. Governance mechanisms in order to agree on software changes, including dispute resolutions, sanctions, and enforcement of penalties will be needed. In a private or permissioned blockchain this could be similar to agreeing on a partnership agreement. In the same line of argument [45] states that the vision of 'Blockchain as governance' which indeed can lead to completely different ways of organizing economies has its limits: blockchains are part of a development and change process of a social nature, and thus are complex socio-technical systems. It is asserted that blockchains, by regulating human exchange, have serious distributional, ethical, and political consequences. Governance rules will be needed and this will raise difficult issues.

There is also ongoing work to resolve governance issues through technical mechanisms. In [46] an interesting blockchain-powered blueprint for a shared and public programmable economy is presented focusing on digital identities, blockchain-based trust, programmable money and marketplaces. Interestingly, some researchers working on blockchain applications for business process management are aware of governance issues. In [19] agency problems and incentives are found of high importance. The paper states that smart contracts could establish new governance models such as in decentralized Autonomous Organizations. However, in the light of our discussion it remains to be seen whether this approach is appropriate in terms of overcoming agency issues in business networks.

Governance in Blockchain platforms may learn from governance of network governance and governance of platform ecosystems in general. [39] discusses platform governance in terms of decision rights partitioning, control, and ownership, and identifies a central governance challenge in retaining sufficient control to ensure the platform integrity while relinquishing enough control to encourage innovation by developers. It would be an interesting topic for research to study the mechanisms of platform governance and governance in collaborative networked organisations and examine what is relevant for blockchain governance, given the situational context and the specific architectural and technological system embedded in the blockchain ecosystem.

6   Challenges of Blockchain in Collaborative Environments

Clear benefits of blockchain technology are the highly secure transactions made possible by blockchain technology. However, many literature sources point to challenges in terms of vulnerabilities, scale and performance, interoperability and standardization, new business models, governance mechanisms, legal and regulatory issues, and associated with all these issues, adoption, upscaling and acceptance of blockchain.

Interoperability and standards across different blockchain platforms and applications will be required. ITU, ISO and other organizations are working on standards terminology, reference architecture, identity management, security and many other topics. The Blockchain Interoperability Alliance has been set up in 2017 as a collaboration between parties aiming to connect various blockchain protocols and establish industry standards. Interoperability could help creating a richer ecosystem of and enable the creation of cross-blockchain smart contracts.

Now that blockchain technology has become more mature, also academic research has addressed various aspects of blockchain. Several publications have highlighted the new research issues associated with blockchain. For example, [47], in their introduction to a special issue of Business & Information Systems Engineering, emphasizes the relevance of blockchain technology for information systems research. Potential challenging research areas are disruption of existing and creation of new business models; technical, economic and environmental sustainability of blockchain applications; standards and interfaces related to blockchain; organizational implications and legal issues. Also, [18] point to research needs regarding trust and collaboration in blockchain platform ecosystems. Research questions include how both trust and anonymity can be guaranteed in blockchain-mediated networks, how risks can be identified and mitigated, and how organizational and managerial issues in blockchain platforms such as financial structure, business models and pricing strategies can be resolved, how blockchain platforms function without central authority, how open these platforms are for contributions and participation, and which incentives are effective for participating developers. In [20], a research agenda for blockchain applications to business process management is proposed, including the development of appropriate execution and monitoring systems, the feasibility of using blockchain for process-aware information systems, the application of design science approaches combined with software engineering; and the impact on strategy and governance of blockchains.

There is also attention for legal and regulatory issues in relation to blockchain. Apart from the issues addressed by [1, 3] in this respect, and the very useful overview of legal and regulatory issues in [6, 48] studied the legal aspects of smart contracts as a specific application of blockchain. It appears that complex legal questions surround blockchain and smart contracts in the sense of liability, applicable law, jurisdiction, proper governance, dispute resolution and privacy. One of the key legal issues is the establishment of proper governance mechanisms. In this discussion, the distinction between private (permissioned) and public (permissionless) blockchains is crucial as governance models will be different.

Given the emergence of networked organizations, network governance – as opposed to governance through markets and hierarchies - has emerged as an area of interest [31]. Research in this field seems to focus mostly on understanding and explaining the reason of existence and the viability conditions of such forms. This means there is a lack of research oriented towards organizational (re-)design of networks and platforms. in particular very little is known about redesign of blockchain platforms ecosystems including governance mechanisms. Issues that can be raised are: which forms of network governance match specific characteristics of blockchain systems? How effective are current forms of governance in blockchain ecosystems? How can effective forms of network governance and organizational routines be designed and validated? An interesting area of research would be to investigate the applicability of collaborative network design principles and governance frameworks as described in [49] to blockchain-enabled organizational forms. In addition, we should keep an eye on the limits of the extremely decentralized organizations enabled by blockchain technologies [50] and find out what the new principles for blockchain-enable collaborative organizations are.

The issue of adoption and acceptance, and readiness (mastering a wide range of capabilities), is of prime importance. There is a clear challenge of transition towards blockchain-enabled collaborative networks based on the view of blockchain applications as complex socio-technical systems. Adopting blockchain implies engaging in a systemic transition process. Studies such as [32, 34] state that blockchain is a foundational technology and not just a disruptive technology. The impact might be transformational but will take decades to become clear as with the internet, and the process of adoption will not be radical but gradual and steady [34].

Research of blockchain in relation to organizational innovation and collaborative networks is in the early stages. Especially there is a need for insights in organizational change and redesign during the process of blockchain adoption and in the context of business model innovation. Design and change management approaches will be useful. Collaborative networked organizations and network governance perspectives could learn from each other and apply to blockchain. Blockchain applications must be considered in the context of socio-technical systems, and the transition towards such blockchain systems provides a challenging area of research.

References

1. Tapscott, D., Tapscott, A.: Realizing the potential of blockchain. a multi-stakeholder approach to the stewardship of blockchain and cryptocurrencies. White Paper, World Economic Forum (2017)
2. Kashyap, M., Shipman, J., Garfinkel, H.: PwC Global FinTech Report. Price Waterhouse Cooper (2017). www.pwc.com/fintechreport

3. Tapscott, D., Tapscott, A.: Blockchain Revolution. How the Technology Behind Bitcoin is Changing Money, Business and the World. Penguin, London (2016)
4. Nakamoto, S.: Bitcoin: a peer-to-peer electronic cash system (2008). https://bitcoin.org/bitcoin.pdf
5. Swan, M.: Blockchain. Blueprint for a New Economy. O'Reilly Media, Sebastopol (2015)
6. Rikken, O., et al.: Smart Contracts as a specific application of blockchain technology. Dutch Blockchain Coalition (2017)
7. Prinz, W., Schulte A.T.: Blockchain und Smart Contracts. Technologien, Forschungsfragen und Anwendungen. Fraunhofer-Gesellschaft (2017)
8. Gatteschi, V., Lamberti, F., Demartini, C., Pranteda, C., Santamaría, V.: Blockchain and smart contracts for insurance: is the technology mature enough? Future Internet **10**, 20 (2018)
9. Buterin, V.: A next-generation smart contract and decentralized application platform (2014). https://github.com/ethereum/wiki/wiki/White-Paper
10. Deloitte: Taking blockchain live. The 20 questions that must be answered to move beyond proofs of concept. Deloitte Development LLC (2017)
11. Deventer, O., Brewster, C., Everts, M.: Governance and business models of blockchain technologies and networks. TNO White Paper, June 2017
12. Buterin, V.: On public and private blockchains. ethereum blog, 7th August 2015. https://blog.ethereum.org/2015/08/07/on-public-and-private-blockchains/
13. Macedo, P., Camarinha-Matos, L.: Value systems alignment analysis in collaborative networked organizations management. Appl. Sci. **7**, 1231 (2017). www.mdpi.com/2076-3417/7/12/1231/pdf
14. Böhme, R., Christin, N., Edelman, B., Moore, T.: Bitcoin: economics, technology, and governance. J. Econ. Perspect. **29**(2), 213–238 (2015)
15. De Filippi, P., Loveluck, B.: The invisible politics of Bitcoin: governance crisis of a decentralized infrastructure. Internet Policy Rev. **5**, 3 (2016)
16. Van Alstyne, M.: Why Bitcoin has value. Commun. ACM **57**(5), 30–32 (2014)
17. De Filippi, P.: What blockchain means for the sharing economy. Harvard Bus. Rev. 15 March 2017. https://hbr.org/2017/03/what-blockchain-means-for-the-sharing-economy
18. Lindman, J., Rossi, M., Tuunainen, V.K.: Opportunities and risks of blockchain technologies in payments – a research agenda. In: Proceedings of the 50th Hawaii International Conference on System Sciences (2017)
19. Mendling, J., et al.: Blockchains for business process management – challenges and opportunities. In: ACM Transactions on Management Information Systems (2018, in press)
20. Fridgen, G., Radszuwill, S., Urbach, N., Utz, L.: Cross-organizational workflow management using blockchain technology – towards applicability, auditability and automation. In: 51st Hawaii International Conference on Systems Sciences (HICSS 2018), January 2018. https://www.fim-rc.de/Paperbibliothek/Veroeffentlicht/696/wi-696.pdf
21. Psaila, S.: Blockchain: a game changer for audit processes? Deloitte Malta Article (2017)
22. Grech, A., Camilleri, A.F.: Blockchain in education. In: dos Santos, A.I. (ed.) EUR 28778 EN (2017)
23. Francisco, K., Swanson, D.: The supply chain has no clothes: technology adoption of blockchain for supply chain transparency. Logistics **2**(1), 2 (2018). http://www.mdpi.com/2305-6290/2/1/2
24. Korpela, K., Hallikas, J., Dahlberg, T.: Digital supply chain transformation toward blockchain integration. In: Proceedings of the 50th Hawaii International Conference on System Sciences, pp. 4182–4191 (2017)

25. Huckle, S., Bhattacharya, R., White, M., Beloff, N.: Internet of Things, blockchain and shared economy applications. Procedia Comput. Sci. **98**, 461–466 (2016)
26. Thoben, K.-D., Wiesner, S., Wuest, T.: Industry 4.0 and smart manufacturing. A review of research issues and application examples. Int. J. Autom. Technol. **11**(1), 4–16 (2017)
27. Dieterich, V., Ivanovic, M., Meier, T., Zäpfel, S., Utz, M., Sandner P.: Application of blockchain technology in the manufacturing industry. Working Paper, Frankfurt School Blockchain Center (2017)
28. Nowinski, W., Kozma, M.: How can blockchain technology disrupt the existing business models? Entrep. Bus. Econ. Rev. **5**(3), 173–188 (2017)
29. Williamson, O.E.: Markets and Hierarchies. Analysis and Antitrust Implications. The Free Press, New York (1976)
30. Jensen, M.C., Meckling, W.: Theory of the firm, managerial behaviour and ownership structure. J. Financ. Econ. **3**(4), 305–360 (1976)
31. Provan, K.G., Kernis, P.N.: Modes of network governance: structure, management and effectiveness. J. Public Adm. Res. Theor. **18**(2), 479–516 (2008)
32. Davidson, S., de Filippi, F., Potts, J.: Economics of blockchain (2016). https://ssrn.com/abstract=2744751 or http://dx.doi.org/10.2139/ssrn.2744751
33. Benkler, Y.: The Wealth of Networks. How Social Production Transforms Markets and Freedom. Yale University Press (2007)
34. Iansiti, M., Lakhani, K.R.: The truth about blockchain. Harvard Bus. Rev. **95**(1), 118–127 January–February 2017
36. Camarinha-Matos, L., Afsarmanesh, H., Galeano, N., Molina, A.: Collaborative networked organizations – concepts and practice in manufacturing enterprises. Comput. Ind. Eng. **57**(1), 46–60 (2009)
37. Camarinha-Matos, L., Afsarmanesh, H.: A comprehensive modeling framework for collaborative networked organizations. J. Intell. Manuf. **18**, 529–542 (2007)
38. Msanjila, S.S., Afsarmanesh, H.: Modeling trust relationships in collaborative networked organisations. Int. J. Technol. Transf. Commer. **6**(1), 40–55 (2007)
39. Tiwana, A.: Platform Ecosystems. Aligning Architecture, Governance and Strategy. Morgan Kaufman, Waltham (2014)
40. Loss, L., Schons, C.H., Neves, R.M., Delavy, I.L., Chudzikiewicz, I.S., Vogt, A.M.C.: Trust building in collaborative networked organizations supported by communities of practice. In: Camarinha-Matos, L.M., Afsarmanesh, H., Novais, P., Analide, C. (eds.) PRO-VE 2007. ITIFIP, vol. 243, pp. 23–30. Springer, Boston, MA (2007). https://doi.org/10.1007/978-0-387-73798-0_3
41. De Filippi, P., Wright, A.: Blockchain and the law: the rule of code (2018)
42. Atzori, M.: Blockchain technology and decentralized governance: is the state still necessary? J. Gov. Regul. **6**(1), 46–62 (2015)
43. Murck, P.: Who controls the blockchain. Harvard Bus. Rev. 19 April 2017. https://hbr.org/2017/04/who-controls-the-blockchain
44. Yermack, D.: Corporate governance and blockchains. Rev. Financ. **21**(1), 7–31 (2017)
45. Sclavounis, O.: Understanding public blockchain governance, 17 November 2017. https://www.oii.ox.ac.uk/blog/understanding-public-blockchain-governance/
46. Pouwelse, J., De Kok, A., Fleuren, J., Hoogendoorn, P., Vliegendhart, R., De Vos, M.: Laws for creating trust in the blockchain age. Eur. Prop. Law J. **6**(3), 321–356 (2018)
47. Beck, R., Avital, M., Rossi, M., Thatcher, J.B.: Blockchain technology in business and information systems research. Bus. Inf. Syst. Eng. **59**(6), 381–384 (2017)

48. Maupin, J.: Mapping the global legal landscape of blockchain and other distributed ledger technologies. Centre for International Governance Innovation, CIGI Papers Nr. 149, October 2017
49. Shuman, J., Twombly, J.: Collaborative networks are the organization: an innovation in organization design and management. Vikalpa J. Decis. Mak. **35**(1), 1–14 (2010)
50. McAfee, A., Brynjolfsson, E.: Machine Platform Crowd. Harnessing our Digital Future. W.W. Norton & Company, New York (2016)

Industry Transformation and Innovation

Collaborative Transformation Systems - Path to Address the Challenges Around the Competitiveness of Mature Countries

Americo Azevedo[✉]

INESC TEC and Faculty of Engineering, University of Porto,
Rua Doutor Roberto Frias, 4200-465 Porto, Portugal
ala@fe.up.pt

Abstract. In mature countries manufacturing is one of the most significant sources of economic development and growth. In those countries, manufacturing transformation systems will be grounded on seamless collaborative environments and will have a high degree of flexibility in production, in terms of product needs (specifications, quality, design), volume, timing, resource efficiency and cost, being able to adapt to customer needs and make use of the entire network chain for value creation. Future transformations systems will be massively collaborative and will be enabled by a network-centric approach, making use of multidimensional data analytics, driven by advanced ICT and the latest available proven manufacturing technologies.

Keywords: Transformation systems · Advanced manufacturing · Maturity

1 Introduction

We understand transformation system as the combination of assets and processes required to deliver a product (e.g. a manufactured product by a manufacturing industry). By assets we consider the main resources, these include human and capital resources, required for the processing and delivery of goods or services. By processes we consider the set of structured activities, interrelated coherently and forming a network of activities and originating several flows, that transform inputs into outputs and maximizing the value to the different stakeholder's organization.

Mature countries are here understood as established countries with stable, robust and strong economies, advanced capital markets and developed but older infrastructure. Example of such countries include United States, Western Europe, and Japan. Risk factors include aging population, limited economic growth, high national debt, and high pension obligations. These countries seek to continue to be competitive and relevant in today's economy [1].

In the context of transformation systems and mature countries. the importance of advanced manufacturing is being increasingly recognized by policy-makers around the world. The contribution of manufacturing to national economies today is emphasized

L. M. Camarinha-Matos et al. (Eds.): PRO-VE 2018, IFIP AICT 534, pp. 21–32, 2018.
https://doi.org/10.1007/978-3-319-99127-6_2

in national policy documents in terms of delivering well-paid jobs, attracting foreign direct investment, increasing productivity and improving other economic variables [2]. In line with this, Europe 2020 strategy underlines the role of 'technology' as the key solution for addressing the challenge of increasing Europe's economic competitiveness and consequently guaranteeing economic growth and job creation. The rationale behind is investing in key enabling technologies, which will help innovative ideas to be transformed *"into new products and services that create growth, high-skilled adding-value jobs, and help address European and global societal challenges"*. In fact, manufacturing is considered a key enabler for Europe's grand societal challenges [3].

Nowadays, in a globalized and increasingly complex world, it is fully recognized that manufacturing industries are under a strong competitive pressure. A proper balance between new collaborative manufacturing strategies, comprehensive organization, management, optimization tools, and cost-efficient automation will provide the basis for building a strong competitive position in the global market. Furthermore, there is a consensual need to create and implement development strategies that can ensure, in a competitive and sustainable way, a growing economy aligned for job creation and solving societal challenges.

In fact, and looking for European Union, the European Council set the objective of making the EU *"the most competitive and dynamic knowledge-based economy in the world, capable of sustainable economic growth with more and better jobs and greater social cohesion"*. It is consensual that is essential to develop a knowledge based industrial system, integrating collaborative dynamic networks of different entities and hiring the competences required to manufacture and deliver custom made products with a time to market able to answer properly to an ever-changing global customer demand. Recognizing the crucial role of industry in the recovery and development of the European economy, a number of European and national programs and initiatives have been launched in recent years around so-called Factories of the Future and Industry 4.0. In this context of change and technological development, the competitiveness of the national industries goes through the modernization of their transformation systems. These should be flexible in adapting to change, responsive to the satisfaction of variable and diversified demand profiles, and efficient both in terms of energy and material consumption and in the use of productive resources. On the other hand, the adoption of collaborative solutions by companies, ensuring greater interaction and integration upstream and downstream, will allow the creation of dynamic and digitally integrated value chains with global efficiency gains.

Manufacturing industries are rapidly adopting a new customer-focused manufacturing paradigm in order to deal with the increasing demand for personalized products. The adjustment from low product variety and high production volume to high mix and low volume poses many important challenges.

Considering the above, we intend in this paper to discuss most relevant critical issues and challenges that we consider crucial in future transformation systems, namely, in advanced high-value manufacturing business environments.

The remaining of the paper is organized as follows: Sect. 2 presents the main critical issues to address in manufacturing transformation systems. Section 3 delves on highlighting key enabling technologies supporting technological solutions for flexibility.

Section 4 is about decision support systems in dynamic environments and Sect. 5 highlights key point concerning organization and operations strategies. Section 6 raises the idea of promoting the adoption of a technology roadmap strategy, and the paper ends in Sect. 7, with final remarks.

2 Critical Issues to Address in Manufacturing Transformation Systems

Nowadays, manufacturing transformation systems are adopting a new paradigm: from low variety and volume-oriented environments (mass production) to high variety and on-demand personalized, customer-driven and knowledge-based production. Furthermore, advanced manufacturing leads to an increasingly automated world that will continue to rely less on labor-intensive processes and more on evolutive information-technology and adaptive intensive processes that enable flexibility. Moreover, advanced manufacturing will become increasingly linked at global level as automation and digital supply-chain management become the backbone across enterprise systems. This new value creation environment is an encouraging approach to significantly improve the competitiveness of the manufacturing industry. Manufacturing, as the core of growth and development of mature economies, must become increasingly high added value, competitive and sustainable, by building on competences and knowledge coming from higher education and R&D [4].

Delivering high value-added customized products, assessing the performance of the manufacturing systems, managing the operational complexity induced by the product variety, and dealing with different levels of decisions from strategic to tactical and operational, taking into account the impact of disturbances and unplanned events over the plan execution, are issues of great practical relevance that still need to be solved. In that context, it is relevant to address different critical issues, namely:

- To develop new methodological tools and reference models to support the improvement of visibility of collaborative value chains networks, and to anticipate the risks and opportunities of production networks models and of flexible manufacturing strategies.
- To contribute to the enrichment of state-of-art of Digital Factory and Digital Manufacturing (Virtual Manufacturing) through the integration of prediction modelling approaches oriented to the quantifying of the impact of operational decisions in the future system's performance.
- To leverage the decision-making processes in the specific case of high mix and low volume production. To attain such goal, optimisation tools to determine optimized factory designs concerning the utilization of the resources and energy consumption, while enhancing the role of human capabilities in the manufacturing systems will be developed.
- To enhance existing knowledge regarding the performance of Product Service Systems (*servitization of manufacturing*), throughout the development of an analytical framework that incorporates lifecycle assessment and cost modelling methodologies.

- To contribute to a better understanding of the complex modelling issues that appears when different models and methods, either quantitative or qualitative, are combined to solve problems within the transformation systems.
- To contribute to the advancement of the Internet of Things (IoT) in the context of Collaborative Transformation Systems which emphasizes the idea of consistent digitization and linking of all value-chain's resources in an economy. In fact, in our view the merging of the virtual and the physical worlds through cyber-physical systems (which provide the basis for the creation of an IoT in manufacturing) and through enhanced multimedia approaches and the resulting fusion of technical processes and business processes are leading the way to a new industrial age where production processes are fine-tuned, adjusted or set up differently in real time.
- To promote the sustainability and competitiveness of collaborative manufacturing transformation systems. Organizational strategies and tools for advanced manufacturing management systems are crucial objects of research and application for reengineering the future economic tissue of goods and services: (i) Efficient and reliable collaborative transformation systems: "address sustainability, integrating the full social, environmental and economic costs and benefits at local, regional and national levels. The quality, reliability and maintainability of products should be incorporated in the development phase and assured during the production process"; (ii) Flexible Industries: "Manufacturing industries worldwide are experiencing increasing demands of higher product complexity and diversity from their markets, which require continuous and dynamic change of product design tools, production planning and control approaches, supply chain strategies, logistics and total quality management practices".
- To develop models and methods which can support the design of sustainable high-value chains collaborative networks and innovative strategies in order to face increasing dynamic supply and deliver requirements, increasing pressure for cost optimization and total quality management and business excellence approaches implementation.

Digital Value Chains

It is recognized around the globe that effective use of digital technologies is key to competitiveness in the modern world. In fact, Collaborative Transformation Systems use massively ICT along with intelligent software applications to optimize the use of material, labor, and energy to produce customized, high-quality products for on-time delivery, and to quickly respond to changes in market demands and supply chains.

Mastery of digital technologies and platforms in high-value chains across all industry sectors – and the consequent "ability to create a digital thread that connects all operations involved in producing goods and services – offers very significant opportunities to create value for the customer and to strengthen the competitiveness of organizations".

The change associated with this digitization of industry is driven by the convergence of three key technological trends related to:

- Connecting "things" to the digital space (driven by IoT – embedded software, sensors, actuators, connectivity, low power ICT etc.);

- Creating value from knowledge (driven by (Big) Data Science, HPC, cloud computing etc.);
- Deploying autonomous systems (driven by robotics, automation, machine learning, etc.).

The above technologies form the core of an emerging, information-centric, Collaborative Transformation System that "maximizes the flow and re-use of data throughout the enterprise. The ability of disparate systems, however, to exchange, understand, and exploit product, production, and business data rests critically on information standards" [5]. The role of standards will be unavoidable for enabling collaborative transformation systems.

Human-Centred Manufacturing

A key strategic priority is to consider Human capital as the most valuable resource of the collaborative transformation systems, namely considering high added-value manufacturing environments. Thus, future transformation systems will consider the human in focus, being more supportive and friendly to the human operator. Within manufacturing enterprises, the human-centred workplaces, where the technical equipment and tools support the humans, make their job attractive and eventually improve their performance, will enable the employee's full talent and capability to be unfolded. Additionally, even if older skilled jobs may disappear during the envisioned manufacturing renaissance, human-centred manufacturing will create new positions and promote wider inclusion of people to be employed in manufacturing, considering the actual societal challenges, such as ageing workforce. Special focus will be given in making manufacturing more attractive, featuring the harmonisation of the job's quality with operator's satisfaction and commitment.

Knowledge-Based Manufacturing

The quality and availability of a highly skilled workforce and its ability to lead innovation constitute the most important factor for manufacturing competitiveness. Skill gaps and shortages hinder the industry's innovation performance world-wide. On top of that, the employment pattern in the manufacturing industry is changing towards more knowledge - and skills - intensive jobs. New education and training approaches for developing skills and building competences are required.

Taking into account this strategic priority, collaborative transformation systems will focus on the human employee and provide him/her with novel educational/training platforms to build competences for efficiently utilizing the latest, advanced manufacturing equipment. Introducing emerging paradigms for the seamless integration of manufacturing research, innovation, education and training activities, such as the Teaching and Learning Factory paradigms, provide brand new approaches to enrich manufacturing knowledge. Technology-enabled (e.g. ICTs, high-grade industrial didactic equipment etc.), real-life and life-long learning "environments" for building competence and catalysing product and process innovation (for blue and white-collar workers/employees) will be employed.

Teaching and Learning Factories will be real factories in which trainees can learn by using innovative machines, simulate manufacturing tasks and situations, and perform innovation tasks in a real industrial environment bringing training and education closer to industrial needs. The dual approach to knowledge transfer, the factory in the classroom and the classroom in the factory, assure both initial and continuous skill improvement of human capital. New business models, emerging with new knowledge transfer technologies, will lead to job creation and economic growth in the education/training business as well.

Sustainable Manufacturing
A key point in competitiveness is how a firm intends to create and sustain value without compromising the ability of the future generations to meet their own needs. Thus, leading resource efficiency will be a decisive competitive factor for manufacturing, also contributing to the people's wellbeing around factories. In that context, Circular Economy is expected to constitute an extraordinary strategic opportunity for mature countries, also in terms of jobs creation and economic growth since new profitable products and business models can be established by manufacturing companies founded to take care of End-of-Life processes.

Circular economy in manufacturing transformation systems, defining practices that allow to maximise value from products and materials and to minimise the environmental impact via re-using, remanufacturing and recycling, will allow manufacturing to become more competitive and, at the same time, to harmonically coexist with healthy living areas, respecting the landscape and preserving natural resources. Therefore, mature countries can become the leading of the integrated manufacturing/de-manufacturing industrial technologies and also contributing to a global sustainable growth.

3   Technological Solutions for Flexibility - Key Enabling Technologies

The competitiveness of transformation systems depends largely on their productivity, flexibility and responsiveness to market demands. Advances in production technologies, such as robotics and collaborative technologies, will play a very important role in the future of the industry. However, their impact on decision support systems is an open question.

One of the main goals in the coming years is the integrated development of advanced robotics with the decision-making process methodologies to increase the productivity of the factories of the future. In the near future the robots will be able to cooperate with humans at their workstation and will receive the production orders in a highly flexible manufacturing scenario. In this way, the best of each partner, robot and human, is exploited, on the one hand, the cognitive abilities and human dexterity that can be concentrated in tasks that add added value to the product and, on the other, the capacity of the robot in performing repetitive tasks accurately.

Continuing this vision in terms of impact on industry requires not only the obvious technological development in terms of robotics but also an integrated development of decision support techniques and tools so that they can incorporate highly flexible production technologies capable to adapt to different tasks with a minimum of reprogramming, with high capacities of perception and of work in environments more designed for human use. This new paradigm represents a challenge for the modelling techniques of production processes where machines/robots are traditionally static and flexibility was only guaranteed by human operators. It is thus fundamental to integrate the technological, organizational and social components, developing human-centred automation systems that allow to define the level of optimal automation, guaranteeing efficiency and quality in the work for the operators.

The expected impact through this new approach is reflected in the social, economic and scientific dimensions. The social and economic impact will result from the appreciation of industrial activity, increased productivity, greater flexibility and better working conditions. At the scientific level, a high impact is expected from the innovative approach that investigates robotic and automation technology in combination with management and decision-making processes. Thus, the integrated development of decision tools aligned with the efficient use of advanced production technologies will have to meet the recent challenges of custom and low volume production. To take advantage of the potential of advanced robotics in these scenarios requires a flexible management system that can make real-time decisions and be integrated into an adaptive production system.

4   Decision Support Systems in Dynamic Environments

As mentioned, the recent emergence of disruptive technologies may revolutionize advanced production systems in all types of industries, particularly those with high mix and customization, as long as they are accompanied by general management practices and analytical tools that adjust to this new reality.

Transformation activities are typically characterized by high levels of variability (for example, operating income, quantities ordered, variety, delivery dates, demand, etc.) and disturbances (such as equipment breakdowns). These uncertainties trigger a significant deviation between production and maintenance programs and their implementation. Consequently, it is critical that in these dynamic environments the production scheduling and maintenance and maintenance procedures are both proactive and reactive. Dealing with uncertainty poses a significant challenge, especially since the problems of resource scaling and maintenance policy optimization, even when treated without uncertainty (i.e., deterministically) are already intractable. It should be noted that new technologies require greater sophistication in handling scheduling and production control issues, and maintenance management. Thus, it is imperative to define intelligent ways of modelling and solving the complex systems that emerge from this reality. A proactive approach deals with uncertainty in order to produce robust (production or maintenance) programs that can accommodate variability and disturbances. In turn, the reactive approach should promote a rescheduling or a set of real-time maintenance actions that respond in the most effective (and timely) way possible to the uncertainties of the productive environment.

The agile and real-time decision-making process, in addition to incorporating conditions and constraints generated by the use of technology (e.g., robotics), should be supported by a number of advanced analytical methods that promote system efficiency, flexibility and agility adaptive production. These methods have different objectives and are employed in different environments, promoting:

- Better information - building on large datasets to get a clear picture of the past/present (identifying patterns and trends);
- Better forecasting - obtaining predictions/careful simulations of events/results and risk estimates to illuminate management challenges at the level of advanced production systems;
- Better decision - supporting complex decisions to improve performance in multiple industries and domains.

These three objectives relate to different types of analytical methods that are not mutually exclusive, but rather collectively exhaustive, namely methods of descriptive analytics, predictive analytics, and prescriptive analytics.

Descriptive analytics uses business intelligence and data mining. Performance data from production schedules can be exploited to provide information on current or past trends of events, revealing details and previous performance. In addition, the treatment and statistical analysis of overall equipment efficiency (OEE) data may reveal factors that are impacting the different types of losses (associated with availability, performance and quality).

Predictive analytics uses a set of algorithms and modelling techniques (such as prediction and simulation) to understand future trends in data. It helps managers anticipate likely scenarios, enabling better informed planning and decision making. However, it does not recommend actions. Exemplifying its role in the case of predictive maintenance, when monitoring and predicting/determining the condition of the machine/production equipment in service, allows to anticipate where and when the failures will occur, as well as the respective causes. Real-time access to multiple sources of information to monitor the condition of the equipment, combined with predictive analytical techniques, allows us to estimate the evolution of asset reliability and take appropriate actions to avoid the consequences of the failure.

Finally, the prescriptive analytics allows to generate optimized and intelligent recommendations and to estimate the future results of decisions, based on descriptive and predictive analyses of structured and unstructured data. Together with risk matrices, cost indicators and estimates of equipment condition evolution, maintenance policies are optimized, maximizing asset availability and improving product quality, leading to increased operating income at an appropriate cost.

Of course, the analytical maturity of industrial firms varies considerably with respect to an organization's ability to use advanced analytical data and methods to support key decision-making processes in the planning of its operations. Companies are trying to progress from the world of descriptive analytics to predictive analytics, and from this to prescriptive. New technological opportunities will accelerate the readiness for this movement.

5 Organization and Operational Strategy

The adoption of technologies and solutions that allow in dynamic environments the necessary adaptability and real-time decision making, must be accompanied by organizational models and operational strategies oriented to the operational excellence of the value chain. The challenge is to design organizational and management models that promote the alignment of the operational strategy, involving the entire chain, namely its resources and processes, with the organization's own competitive strategy.

In this context there are some key issues, such as:

- How to formulate and evaluate the transformation system, in a logic of value maximization and alignment with the organization's competitive strategy?
- How to choose and adapt the resources and processes that best guarantee the organization's competitive priorities?
- How to sustainably improve operational performance toward excellence?
- How to organize and manage the dynamics of change in a short and medium-term horizon?

The answer to these questions is not self-evident. In fact, it is very difficult to predict the effects that the decisions and actions taken on the set of resources and processes will have on the future performance of the production system, and on the skills that can guarantee cost, quality, response and flexibility. This is due not only to the technological complexity of the production systems themselves, but to the fact that increasingly environments are characterized by increasingly complex products, low volume and high variety, and demand variability.

The existence of trade-offs and restrictions in the operations system implies that no operational decision can be universally appropriate; instead, each operational strategy implies a "tailor-made" organization and operating system: its resources and processes are configured so that the competencies they generate best fit the customer value proposition specified by the company's competitive strategy. Thus, strategy decisions imply choices in operational competencies.

As environments, competitive strategy, and operations evolve, organizations must strive to maintain the necessary alignment over time. In order to meet a new customer need, the company may need to develop new skills as well as develop and implement new capabilities and processes that may lead to the creation of new products, services and markets. This "dynamic alignment" assumes a continuous process of adaptation to ensure that operations and competitive strategy remain aligned over time.

6 The Importance of a Technology Strategic Roadmap

The changes brought about by the digital revolution in the process of transformation and creation of value are radical and represent a real challenge for companies [6]. The digital transformation of current enterprises, namely through Industry 4.0 initiatives, promises to revolutionize their transformation systems, namely concerning reducing costs and expanding business opportunities.

A number of macroeconomic effects and operational benefits are announced. Increasing productivity in more flexible environments, reducing time-to-market, reducing resource unavailability and non-quality are just a few of the gains that are expected to be guaranteed. In addition, in a job creation and destruction balance sheet, it is expected that when maturity is achieved (a period of 10–15 years is expected for industry 4.0 to reach maturity). Other benefits include the creation of new value creation networks and the exploitation of new business models, which in turn will lead to new professions. With regard to the envisioned Fourth Industrial Revolution (industry 4.0), *"we understand maturity of an industrial enterprise as the state of advancement of internal and external conditions that support Industry 4.0's concepts and fundamentals"* [7].

Digital transformation is not just about advanced machines and robotics, smart products and Internet of Things. The use of new technologies and the acquisition of new knowledge, through the selective treatment of information, will inevitably lead to new types and ways of working. The ability to analyze the prevailing organizational culture and the existing patterns of operation will therefore be fundamental to the successful implementation of a Digital Transformation Strategy.

Therefore, within a framework evolving around the principles and concepts of Industry 4.0, the main challenges for companies include understanding what Digital Transformation actually means. A structured approach is a key point. One of the first actions is to evaluate the maturity (digital readiness) of manufacturing companies. Assessing maturity means to conceptualize and measure maturity of an organization regarding some specific target state [8, 9]. It is particularly important to define a vision in this context and necessarily aligned with the overall strategy of the company. Identifying priorities and targets to be tackled in the coming years and developing pilot projects (proof of concept) will be the next steps.

Industry 4.0 will have a significant benefit for companies that internalize well what the Fourth Industrial Revolution means and, in particular, how they can operate and develop their business, in a logic of looking at the entire value chain, that is, far beyond the traditional frontier of the company. Moreover, collaborative networks [10, 12, 13] will have a key role in enabling future industrial's competitiveness. As stated by Camarinha-Matos et al. [11], *"collaboration is at the heart of most challenges in Industry 4.0 and thus the area of Collaborative Networks shall be considered as an enabler – although certainly not the only one – for this industrial transformation"*. In fact, some important concepts in Industry 4.0 include "networking", "value chains", "vertical and horizontal integration", and "co-engineering/through engineering", which very well match the issues addressed for the Collaborative Networks.

7   Final Remarks

Looking at the future of the manufacturing industry, as a complex collaborative transformation system, requires understanding of the past. It is full recognized that technologies can quickly change the economic landscape of a country and the world. This occurred in the 18th Century, through the first Industrial Revolution and again in the beginning of 20th Century with the development of *taylorism* and the mass production paradigm. In the late 20th Century, the rapid development of consumer electronics was followed by the massification of personal computers and later the internet. Although these latter developments, they have already changed the lives and working habits of a generation. Countries willing and capable of taking advantage of these new technologies prosper, where others fall behind [12].

It used to take a very long 'time-to-market' for new research results and discoveries to be commercialized. However, nowadays this has changed radically between countries to bring new technologies and solution to market in a faster way, to gain a differentiation "advantage and establish a dominant market position in the following years. This was achieved by the US through the rapid commercialization of technologies such as semiconductors, computers, and the internet". Looking at the past, the history of industrialization shows us that from a relationship of personalization centered on the craftsman, it has evolved into a mass production environment where "power" has passed to the side of the producer and simultaneously all the productive activity is decoupled from consumers. In this evolutionary line, another relevant fact has to do with the growth of services weight in the economy and the consequent loss of importance in the society of the manufacturing activity. However, today we are seeing a real paradigm shift. The exponent of this change will materialize with the implantation of what is meant by "factory of the future", in the environment of what is understood to be the fourth industrial revolution. There will be, in this context, the active and collaborative participation of the consumer in the processes of creation and transformation processes. Increasingly, the transformation system will be full distributed, forming a true collaborative ecosystem, autonomous and adaptive in the processes of value creation.

Nowadays in manufacturing here are still many unresolved issues, uncertainties and challenges. In fact, European industry in particular has been facing substantial economic challenges stemming not only from the increased pace of technological development, the decline in the availability of natural resources, rising energy prices, but also the aging of the working class and, of course, the globalization of markets. It is therefore in this demanding and challenging context that Industry 4.0 promotes a vision in which developments in information technologies are expected to enable new forms of design and production. We will see an increasingly active consumer participation in the creation and production processes.

The "brand image" of this fourth industrial revolution is undoubtedly the consonance of internet technologies, namely with the massification of the "internet of things", with the exponential increase of computational capacity and in particular of the so-called "cloud computing". Therefore, a new generation of industrial systems based on innovative services will emerge whose functionalities reside in intelligent factories and machines, cyberphysical systems, natural man-machine integration, autonomy and adaptability, product and service systems, virtualization, augmented reality and the "cloud".

In particular. in the context of collaborative manufacturing and logistics, digital marketplace platforms have not yet moved completely from supporting simple collaboration approaches [15]. Indeed, the design, development, implementation and use of future Collaborative Transformation Systems require an ever-increasing knowledge on enabling technologies and business and operational practices. Moreover, the digital and networked world will surely trigger new business and operational practices in manufacturing. Therefore, this is relevant and current research issue to guarantee an effective and efficient performance. In this context, competitive and sustainable development is emerging as the core global strategic vision to be deployed so as to meet the economic, social, environmental and technological challenges that most societies are facing today and in particular in mature countries.

Acknowledgements. This work is part of the Project "TEC4Growth - Pervasive Intelligence, Enhancers and Proofs of Concept with Industrial Impact/NORTE-01-0145-FEDER-000020" is financed by the North Portugal Regional Operational Programme (NORTE 2020), under the PORTUGAL 2020 Partnership Agreement, and through the European Regional Development Fund (ERDF).

References

1. The Five Country Classifications. http://timmccarthy.com/the-five-country-classifications/
2. Links, P.: Emerging trends in global advanced manufacturing. University of Cambridge (2013)
3. EFFRA: Factories of the Future - Multi-annual roadmap for the contractual PPP under Horizon 2020 (2013)
4. Azevedo, A. (ed.): Advances in Sustainable and Competitive Manufacturing Systems. Springer Science & Business Media, Switzerland (2013). https://doi.org/10.1007/978-3-319-00557-7
5. Lu, Y., Morris, K.C., Frechette, S.: Current Standards Landscape for Smart Manufacturing Systems, vol. 8107, pp. 22–28. National Institute of Standards and Technology, NISTIR, Gaithersburg (2016)
6. Schwab, K.: The global competitiveness report 2016–2017. WE Forum (2016)
7. Schumacher, A., Erol, S., Sihn, W.: A maturity model for assessing industry 4.0 readiness and maturity of manufacturing enterprises. In: Procedia CIRP, vol. 52, pp. 161–166 (2016)
8. Ganzarain, J., Errasti, N.: Three stage maturity model in SME's toward industry 4.0. J. Ind. Eng. Manag. **9**(5), 1119 (2016)
9. De Carolis, A., Macchi, M., Negri, E., Terzi, S.: A maturity model for assessing the digital readiness of manufacturing companies. In: Lödding, H., Riedel, R., Thoben, K.-D., von Cieminski, G., Kiritsis, D. (eds.) APMS 2017. IFIPAICT, vol. 513, pp. 13–20. Springer, Cham (2017). https://doi.org/10.1007/978-3-319-66923-6_2
10. Camarinha-Matos, L.M., et al.: Collaborative networked organizations–concepts and practice in manufacturing enterprises. Comput. Ind. Eng. **57**(1), 46–60 (2009)
11. Camarinha-Matos, L.M., Fornasiero, R., Afsarmanesh, H.: Collaborative networks as a core enabler of industry 4.0. In: Camarinha-Matos, L.M., Afsarmanesh, H., Fornasiero, R. (eds.) PRO-VE 2017. IFIPAICT, vol. 506, pp. 3–17. Springer, Cham (2017). https://doi.org/10.1007/978-3-319-65151-4_1
12. Hauser, H.: The Current and Future Role of Technology and Innovation Centres in the UK: A Report. Department for Business Innovation and Skills (2010)
13. Appio, F.P., et al.: Collaborative network of firms: antecedents and state-of-the-art properties. Int. J. Prod. Res. **55**(7), 2121–2134 (2017)
14. Durugbo, C.: Collaborative networks: a systematic review and multi-level framework. Int. J. Prod. Res. **54**(12), 3749–3776 (2016)
15. Cisneros-Cabrera, S., Ramzan, A., Sampaio, P., Mehandjiev, N.: Digital marketplaces for industry 4.0: a survey and gap analysis. In: Camarinha-Matos, L.M., Afsarmanesh, H., Fornasiero, R. (eds.) PRO-VE 2017. IFIPAICT, vol. 506, pp. 18–27. Springer, Cham (2017). https://doi.org/10.1007/978-3-319-65151-4_2

Need and Solution to Transform the Manufacturing Industry in the Age of Industry 4.0 – A Capability Maturity Index Approach

Volker Stich[1], Gerhard Gudergan[1(✉)], and Violett Zeller[2]

[1] Institute for Industrial Management (FIR) at RWTH Aachen University,
Campus-Boulevard 55, 52074 Aachen, Germany
gerhard.gudergan@fir.rwth-aachen.de
[2] i4.0MC – Industrie 4.0 Maturity Center,
Campus-Boulevard 55, 52074 Aachen, Germany

Abstract. Digitalization is changing the industrial landscape in a way we did not anticipate. The manufacturing industries worldwide are working to develop strategies and concepts for what is labelled with different terms such as the Industrial Internet of Things in the USA or Industrie 4.0 in Germany. Many industrialized economies are driven by the production sector and this sector needs specific approaches and instruments to take up other than those approaches we know from start-ups and ventures coming from Silicon Valley and other places. In this paper, we demonstrate an appropriate approach to transform producing companies in a systematic and evolutionary approach.

In particular, the objective of this paper is to provide results from two initiatives which conceptually build upon each other and are of particular relevance for the production industry. First, we present a global survey on the state of implementation and the future perspectives of the concept Industrie 4.0 from 2016. Findings from this study have forced parts of the German industry to heavily invest into a common approach to accelerate change towards Industry 4.0 in order to stay competitive in worldwide economy. This approach is presented in a second part.

Keywords: Digital transformation · Industrie 4.0 · Maturity model
Manufacturing industry

1 Introduction

Concept and vision of Industrie 4.0 is often defined as "real-time, high data volume, multilateral communication and interconnectedness between cyber-physical systems and people", in order to realize self-optimizing business processes [3]. This depiction of Industrie 4.0 concentrates primarily on a technological understanding with the objective that manufacturing companies achieve a competitive advantage. However, the fundamental economic lever of Industrie 4.0 lies in stimulating business processes through necessary decisions and real-time adaptations [2].

L. M. Camarinha-Matos et al. (Eds.): PRO-VE 2018, IFIP AICT 534, pp. 33–42, 2018.
https://doi.org/10.1007/978-3-319-99127-6_3

Combined with adequate organizational conditions, companies are able to react faster to growing market dynamics, to develop new products more quickly and precisely [4, 9].

Many results presented in this paper were gained within the context of a conceptual reference framework developed by german Government for Industry 4.0. The initial study is from 2016 and polled 433 industrial manufacturing executives in five regions – China, France, German speaking countries, the United Kingdom and the United States. We applied a specific capability maturity model for our analyses. The results provide an understanding of industry preparedness for Industrie 4.0. The huge potential of Industrie 4.0 is clearly pointed out but there are significant differences between countries. These differences in turn initiated a significant investment of resources by a consortium driven by the German industry and the German academy of science and engineering ACATECH. The later revealed a reference model and open standard and was successfully applied to transform manufacturing companies towards Industry 4.0 [3].

2   Background and Motivation: Global Benchmark of Industry 4.0 Maturity

In 2015 and 2016, a comprehensive global research study assessed industry attitudes towards Industrie 4.0 in the aerospace, automotive, electronics, machinery and process industries in China, France, German speaking countries, the United Kingdom, and the United States. There was a focus defined on asset efficiency because this is considered an important performance indicator for the success of all kind of manufacturing innovation programmes including Industrie 4.0 programs. The study polled 433 executives through an online survey as well as telephone interviews. FIR at RWTH Aachen and the independent research firm Vanson Bourne conducted the study for the leading information systems provider Infosys [4, 5].

For the purpose of analysis, enterprises were categorized as "Early Adopters" or "Followers". The actual status from 2015 and the aspiration for 2020 was analysed by asset efficiency levers, industry and production type, and country. Respondents were asked to outline their current maturity levels on these levers and their target for 2020 on a four point scale. The research used the Industrie 4.0 framework, conceptualized by the German government and developed by industry leaders.

In 2015, the vast majority (85%) of companies were aware of the high potential in implementing Industrie 4.0, Only 15% of enterprises surveyed had already implemented dedicated strategies for asset efficiency. An additional 39% had partially implemented these strategies.

Nearly half of the respondents surveyed (48%) wanted to implement Industrie 4.0 solutions systematically by 2020 (see Fig. 1). Conversely, by 2020 still one fifth of the respondents indicated that they will have made at best piecemeal progress.

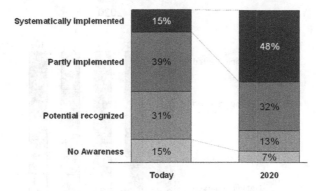

Fig. 1. Use of Industrie 4.0 concepts to manage assets

The survey further found significant variance in the adoption levels in different markets. Figure 2 below, shows that in 2015 68% of respondents from China had partially or systematically implemented Industrie 4.0 in asset management programs, estimated to increase to 89% by 2020. Comparable numbers for France are 27% and 58% respectively (Fig. 3).

Across the five countries surveyed - China, France, Germany, the United Kingdom and the United States – the level of maturity in Industrie 4.0 varied significantly. While no country could claim to be the global early adopter in implementing Industrie 4.0, the percentage of companies in China that claimed to be early adopters was significantly higher than anywhere else (see Fig. 4).

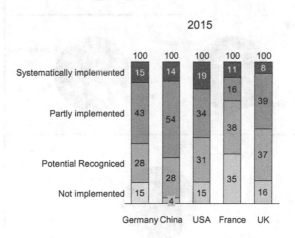

Fig. 2. Country comparison of Industrie 4.0 concepts to manage assets in 2015

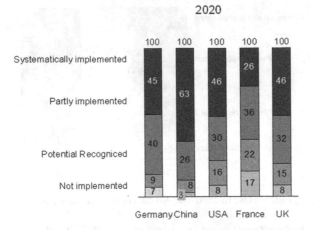

Fig. 3. Country Country comparison of Industrie 4.0 concepts to manage assets in 2020

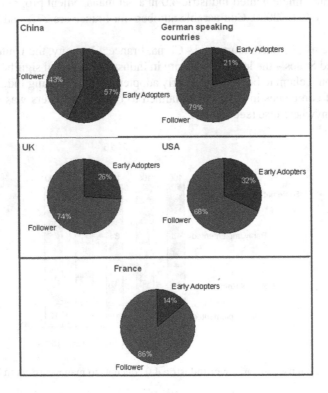

Fig. 4. Early adopter and follower analysis by country

It is expected that a number of factors were and still are driving this; notably the focused initiatives and investment from the Chinese Government to develop more sustainable industry growth. Also manufacturing is core for China and the market is accustomed to rapidly implementing new technology, especially in green field sites free of legacy infrastructures. Germany (21%), the United Kingdom (36%) and the United States (32%) have similar maturity footprints both in terms of 2015 status and 2020 ambition. This could be because of their historical leadership in manufacturing. In France (14%), the Industrie 4.0 implementation was comparatively less mature. The economic downturn phase in 2015 and unsuccessful digitization programs could have been contributing factors.

3   Objective and Goal: Development of the Acatech Industrie 4.0 Maturity Index

The global benchmark on Industrie 4.0 maturity presented earlier clearly indicated an urgent need to act. Before this background, we present the approach and model developed by an industry consortium with the support of acatech in Germany. The model's approach is based on a succession of maturity levels, i.e. *value-based development stages* (see Sect. 3.1) that help companies navigate their way through every stage in the digital transformation. To ensure that all aspects of manufacturing companies are taken into account, the model's structure is based on the "Production and Management Framework" by [6]. The framework's four *structural areas* enable a comprehensive analysis and set out a number of guiding principles that allow companies to identify which Industrie 4.0 capabilities they still need to develop. In the following, the underlying concepts and model of the acatech Industrie 4.0 Maturity Index are illustrated.

3.1   Value-Based Development Stages – Industrie 4.0 Maturity Levels

As a first step, a general awareness is necessary that Industrie 4.0 can be achieved step-wise and according to individual company benefits. The basic structuring of Industrie 4.0 into successive stages is presented below in Fig. 5.

The development path is based on computerization (1), which is the starting point for digitization and refers to the targeted use of information technologies. It enables cost-effective production with low error rates and generates the necessary precision, which is indispensable for the production of many modern products [3, 9].

Achieving the *connectivity* level (2), the targeted or isolated use of IT is replaced by networked components. A complete integration between IT (information technologies) and OT (operative technologies) levels has not yet taken place; however, interfaces to business IT are provided by parts of implemented OT [3, 11, 12].

Based on this, a digital *visibility* (3) is established with the help of sensors, which enable recording of processes from start to finish with a high amount of captured data. Processes states are no longer limited to individual areas, such as in a production cell, but can be extended to a production system or the entire company in real time in order to create a digital model, also known as the "digital shadow" [3, 7, 9].

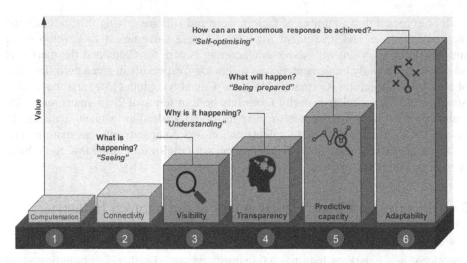

Fig. 5. Value-based development stages of Industrie 4.0 – Industrie 4.0 Maturity Levels [3]

For a better causal understanding of processes, it is necessary to create further *transparency* (4) about the correlations in data stocks. Process knowledge is more and more required to support more complex decisions, which are based on semantic connections and aggregation of data.

Building up, the *predictive* capability level (5) enables simulation of different future scenarios and identification of those that are most likely. To this end, the digital shadow is projected into future-based scenarios and evaluated according to probability of occurrence. The ability to *adapt* (6) can enable an automatic reaction to expected machine failures or delays in delivery through a modified sequence in production planning.

3.2 Required Capabilities for a Company's Structural Areas

The skills that are relevant for the transformation of a manufacturing company into a learning, agile organization are assessed through the *four structural areas* of resources, information systems, culture and organizational structure (see Fig. 6). All of them characterize the structure of an organization and are examined over the six levels of the Industrie 4.0 development path, which is represented by six concentric circles in Fig. 6.

Each structural area is divided by two *principles*, each of which - depending on the benefit-oriented development levels - successively builds up skills. These skills guide the further development of the manufacturing company. The degree to which the abilities are implemented determines the maturity level of each principle. The maturity levels of the two principles are summarized and together they represent the evaluation of the structural area, which is oriented on the development levels.

The structural area *resources* includes all physical, tangible resources. This contains, for example, employees of a company, machinery and systems, the tools and materials used and the final product.

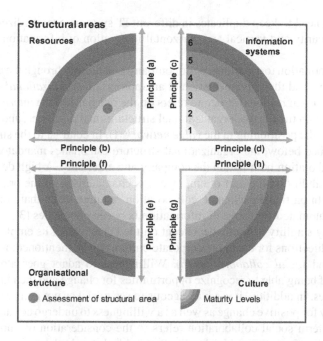

Fig. 6. Structure of the structural areas [3]

The two principles dividing this structural area are differentiated into *digital competence* and *structured communication*. "Digital competence" (a) characterizes the generation of data and its target-oriented independent processing into information by resources with corresponding technical components. This facilitates an information-driven way of working, based on feedback from the process environments and not on forecast-based planning specifications. The skills of digital competence also include the use of embedded systems and the retention of digital competence, which can only be successful, if attention is paid to promoting interdisciplinary thinking and action by employees - if they are increasingly integrated into the innovation process. Through "structured communication" (b) collected information is linked and creates an overall picture. An efficient communication can be defined and interface designed in order to support decision-makers [3, 7, 8].

With the help of employees, information technologies and data information is available within *information systems* in accordance to economic criteria. Many manufacturing companies do not make sufficient use of data. The decisive factor is the insufficient processing of the collected data into information and its subsequent provision to the employees, which is why the first principle includes the *processing and preparation of data* (c) for decision support. This requires, among other things, context-based information provision, data storage and application-oriented interfaces in order to provide a technical infrastructure for real-time use of data and information ultimately [10]. In the context of the second principle, it is a question of *integration for optimized data (d)* use and increased agility under the primary aspect of data sharing within the value chain. However, this is only possible through the use of one leading information system that eliminates the need to keep duplicates in different IT systems. Standardized interfaces, detailed IT security and vertical and horizontal integration of information systems are required.

The transformation to a learning, agile company is achieved through the technologies explained above and the implementation of an appropriate *organizational structure*. In this model, the organizational structure refers on the one hand to the *internal corporate organization* (e) in the form of organizational structures and processes, and on the other hand describes the positioning in the *value network* (f). In contrast to the structural area *culture* described below, the organizational structure establishes mandatory rules that organize collaboration both within the company and externally. A high degree of individual responsibility on the part of employees is characteristic of the organic internal organization. In particular, dynamic collaboration requires skills that contribute to a smooth and automated exchange of information between companies [3].

A company's agility is highly dependent on the behaviour of its employees. In this context, two directions for changing corporate culture can be mentioned: *willingness to change (g)* and *social collaboration (h)*. Willingness to adapt goes along with the prerequisite of being able to recognize opportunities for change and then initiate appropriate measures. In addition, it is advantageous to see mistakes not as a problem, but as an opportunity for positive change as well as a willingness to undergo continuous further training. The term social collaboration refers to the consideration of knowledge as a decisive guideline for action, which implies that an ideal state is characterized by making decisions based on knowledge [8].

The benefit levels presented allow companies to better assess their own Industrie 4.0 development and determine the next stage on their transformation path [2, 3].

4   Application of the Acatech Industrie 4.0 Maturity Index

The application of the acatech Industrie 4.0 Maturity Index consists of three successive phases (see Fig. 7) [3] illustrated in the following.

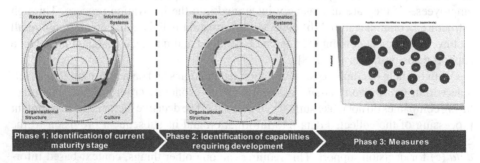

Fig. 7. Application of the acatech Industrie 4.0 Maturity Index [3]

4.1 Phase 1: Identifying the Current Industrie 4.0 Development Stage

The company's location results from the six value-based development stages for Industrie 4.0 (see Sect. 3.1) and the skills dedicated to them. For an appropriate assessment, the consortium has developed a questionnaire, with approx. 600 questions for the business processes *engineering, production, logistics, service, sales* and *marketing*. An inspection of a production plant can give a first impression of the processes, followed by a detailed evaluation of the business processes. The as-is analysis and the questionnaire is conducted based on the order processing process, which forms the framework situation for the evaluation of existing skills. With the help of a questionnaire evaluation the Industrie 4.0 Maturity Index and Levels can be identified for each structural area.

4.2 Phase 2: Capabilities to be Acquired

For the evaluation, the answers to the questionnaire shape the basis for the evaluation of the current situation of the company by the radar image (see Fig. 7). The dependencies of the structural areas determine consistent development in all structural areas as an essential goal. This is the basis for the recommendation for companies to approach the resulting areas of action and to strive for a consistent maturity stage across all four structural areas and in this way to use the maturity stage (achieve maturity stage consistency).

4.3 Phase 3: Identifying Concrete Measures

The next step is to derive measures addressing areas identified as requiring action. Necessary measures can be deduced from the missing capabilities evaluating the four structural areas. By evaluating individual processes, many individual measures can be dedicated, which makes it easier for companies to create a digital roadmap.

In defining strategic objectives for a company, identified measures are worked out precisely. Achieving the targeted stages of development, in turn, aims to support the realization of the strategic objectives formulated at the outset. This enables decision-makers in manufacturing companies not only to identify at a glance the measures needed to achieve a higher maturity level, but also the interdependencies between identified measures. The purpose of this presentation is also to simplify the creation of a digitization roadmap by determining the order in which measures are implemented in terms of time and costs [3].

5 Conclusion and Outlook

The acatech Industrie 4.0 Maturity Index provides companies a supporting tool for transformation into a learning, agile company. This approach has proven in many cases to be of particular relevance for producing companies which has an outstanding role for more traditional structured, manufacturing based economies such as the European economy. It is important to differentiate this against more disruptive perspectives we know from venture capital driven and greenfield innovation in the IT-industry with its focus on end consumer offerings. The methodology describes six benefit-oriented development stages for four key areas. Each stage corresponds with additional, achievable benefits. This approach can be applied to develop a digital roadmap tailored to the needs of individual company in order to help them master the digital transformation if – as mostly in the case of the existing manufacturing and production industry – an evolutionary and structured transformation approach is the best choice. In this cases, the approach presented supports companies to guide their transformation in a very structured and most efficient and fast process.

References

1. Schuh, G., Jordan, F., Maasem, C., Zeller, V.: Industrie 4.0: Implikationen für produzierende Unternehmen. In: Gassmann, O., Sutter, P. (eds.) Digitale Transformation im Unternehmen gestalten. Geschäftsmodelle, Erfolgsfaktoren, Handlungsanweisungen, Fallstudien, pp. 39–58. Hanser, München (2016)
2. Schmitz, S., Wenger, L.: Acatech Industrie 4.0 Maturity Index: Welche Fähigkeiten sind im Wandel entscheidend? IT Prod. 5, 54–55 (2017)
3. Schuh, G., Anderl, R., Gausemeier, J., ten Hompel, M., Wahlster, W. (eds.): Industrie 4.0 Maturity Index. Managing the Digital Transformation of Companies (acatech STUDY), p. 21. Herbert Utz Verlag, Munich (2017)
4. Infosys: Industry 4.0. The state of the nations. 1. Aufl. Hg. v. Infosys Ltd. Bangalore (2015)
5. Gudergan, G., Stich, V., Schmitz, S., Buschmeyer, A.: The global evolution of the industrial Internet of Things – a cross country comparison based on an international study on Industrie 4.0 for asset efficiency management. In: Proceedings of the International Conference on Competitive Manufacturing, Coma 2016, Stellenbosch, February 2016
6. Boos, W., Völker, M., Schuh, G.: Grundlagen des Managements produzierender Unternehmen. In: Schuh, G., Kampker, A. (eds.) Strategie und Management produziernder Unternehmen (VDI-Buch), pp. 1–61. Springer, Heidelberg (2011). https://doi.org/10.1007/978-3-642-14502-5_1
7. Bauernhansl, T., Krüger, J., Reinhart, G., Schuh, G.: WGP-Standpunkt Industrie 4.0. Hg. v. Wissenschaftliche Gesellschaft für Produktionstechnik Wgp e. V
8. Zühlke, D.: Die Cloud ist Voraussetzung für Industrie 4.0. Präsentation. VDI. VDI-Pressegespräch anlässlich des Kongresses. In: AUTOMATION 2013, Baden-Baden, 25 June 2013
9. Schuh, G., Potente, T., Thomas, C., Hauptvogel, A.: Steigerung der Kollaborationsproduktivität durch cyber-physische Systeme. In: Bauernhansl, T., ten Hompel, M., Vogel-Heuser, B. (eds.) Industrie 4.0 in Produktion, Automatisierung und Logistik, pp. 277–295. Springer, Wiesbaden (2014). https://doi.org/10.1007/978-3-658-04682-8_14
10. Hering, N., et al.: Smart Operations. Hg. v. FIR an der RWTH Aachen. Aachen (2015)
11. Vogel-Heuser, B.: Herausforderungen und Anforderungen aus Sicht der IT und der Automatisierungstechnik. In: Bauernhansl, T., ten Hompel, M., Vogel-Heuser, B. (eds.) Industrie 4.0 in Produktion, Automatisierung und Logistik, pp. 37–48. Springer, Wiesbaden (2014). https://doi.org/10.1007/978-3-658-04682-8_2
12. Kaufmann, T., Forstner, L.: Die horizontale Integration der Wertschöpfungskette in der Halbleiterindustrie – Chancen und Herausforderungen. In: Bauernhansl, T., ten Hompel, M., Vogel-Heuser, B. (eds.) Industrie 4.0 in Produktion, Automatisierung und Logistik, pp. 359–367. Springer, Wiesbaden (2014). https://doi.org/10.1007/978-3-658-04682-8_18

Collaborative Networks and the 'Five Regions of the Future'

Andrew Crossley[1,2]($\boxtimes$)

[1] University of Bristol, Bristol, UK
Andrew.Crossley@Bristol.ac.uk
[2] ServQ Alliance, Chepstow, Wales, UK

Abstract. 'Five Regions of the Future' was written in 2005 by two Futurists, Joel A. Barker and Scott W. Erickson, before the rise of social media, smartphones, and the advent of Industry 4.0. They proposed a framework for technological development based around five 'regions': Super Tech; Limits Tech; Local Tech; Nature Tech; and Human Tech, which they called TechnEcologies. The paper examines how collaborative networks can either complement or potentially disrupt this framework and sets out some areas that could form the basis of future collaborative research in Barker and Erickson's TechnEcologies.

Keywords: Collaborative networks · Future technologies · Industry 4.0

1 Introduction

In 2005 two Futurists, Barker and Erickson published a book called *"Five Regions of the Future: Preparing Your Business for Tomorrow's Technology Revolution"* [1]. For over twenty-five years they studied and catalogued tens of thousands of articles, and held hundreds of meetings, leading up to their book's release. They proposed a new framework based around five 'regions', each of which they termed a TechnEcology. These were:

1. Super Tech (ST): Bigger, better, more. (e.g. fusion power)
2. Limits Tech (LMT): Use what you've got. (e.g. aerogel insulation)
3. Local Tech (LOT): Smaller and local. (e.g. electric wind turbines)
4. Nature Tech (NT): At one with nature. (e.g. organic plastics)
5. Human Tech (HT): What lies within us. (e.g. stem cells)

They described a TechnEcology as a *"complex ecosystem of technology. The individual elements are made up of the tools and techniques invented by humans that interact in both mutualistic and competitive manners to increase the variety of technologies and the complexity of interaction."* [1]. HT cocoons the other four regions, because humans exploit them or coexist with them. Finally, Universal Technologies (UTs) live at the heart of Barker and Erickson's model (Fig. 1). Their proposed UTs were: Aerogel (super light insulation); Thermal Depolymerization (carbon-based waste recycling); Advanced computers; Chronobiology (mapping human patterns over time); 3-D printing for manufacturing; Hydrogen fuel cells; Holography; Lab on a chip; Nanotubes; Space satellites; Computer simulations; and E-books.

© IFIP International Federation for Information Processing 2018
Published by Springer Nature Switzerland AG 2018. All Rights Reserved
L. M. Camarinha-Matos et al. (Eds.): PRO-VE 2018, IFIP AICT 534, pp. 43–52, 2018.
https://doi.org/10.1007/978-3-319-99127-6_4

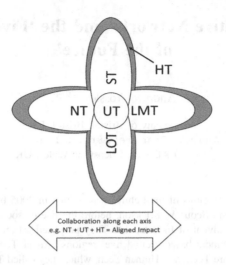

Fig. 1. Barker and Erickson's model updated for the aligned impact of collaboration

Several of their UTs are viable in 2018, including the 3-D printing of houses. With the benefit of hindsight some of these UTs may appear obvious. However, they were not when the original research was being developed. Their original UT predictions pre-dated the latest technologies such as smart phones, high powered graphical tablets, and e-books, by over a decade. Some of these UT's are having a profound impact on personal activity, such as highly accurate time-based GPS tracking, digital imaging and photography, crowd-sourcing of data and internet search activity. This has also created a politically charged environment on data security, data management, abuse, and governance.

Barker and Erickson's research indicated that the United States and Japan were heavily reliant on, and advocates of, Super Tech and predicted that Denmark was migrating towards Local Tech. This was in the pre social media and Industry 4.0 era, when basic shared platforms and intranets were the dominant collaboration technologies. This paper examines how collaborative networks can either complement or potentially disrupt Barker and Erickson's model and sets out some areas that could form the basis of future collaborative research within the respective TechnEcologies.

2 Collaboration Futures

Table 1 shows the approximate segmentation of papers by TechnEcology from the Proceeding of PRO-VE 2014 (Collaborative Systems for Smart Networked Environments) [2], PRO-VE 2015 (Risks and Resilience of Collaborative Networks) [3], PRO-VE 2016 (Collaboration in a Hyperconnected World) [4], and PRO-VE 2017 (Collaboration in a Data-Rich World) [5]. The conferences' dominant themes related to software, systems, and processes in support of Super Tech. These were typically in manufacturing, transportation, and logistics. There were relatively few publications on social/healthcare, food/agriculture, and the green/circular economy.

Table 1. Classification of the PRO-VE proceedings from 2014 to 2017 by TechnEcology

Proceedings	ST	LMT	LOT	NT	HT	Totals
PRO-VE 2014	61	4	5	0	3	73
PRO-VE 2015	47	7	5	0	2	61
PRO-VE 2016	46	7	0	0	4	57
PRO-VE 2017	52	10	2	1	3	68
Totals	**206**	**28**	**12**	**1**	**12**	**259**

At the PRO-VE 2016 Conference [4], ten younger researchers were asked to propose one or two future collaborative scenarios and the potential challenges they could anticipate with their proposals [6]. Of the ten researchers who presented:

- Five selected Super Tech scenarios: customized 'smart' production for limited run items such as legacy parts; globally democratized manufacturing and assembly; virtual and augmented reality in e-participation; regulation of 5G mobile technologies; and, smart personal assistance for elderly care.
- Three chose Limits Tech scenarios: collaborative sharing of vehicle capacity in self-organizing supply networks; constraints on the future employment options for millennials, if traditional large employers reduce in numbers; and, the co-creation and management of disaster relief services.
- One chose a Local Tech scenario: localized power generation using renewables, with local energy storage and decentralized power grids.
- One chose a Human Tech scenario: mapping emotions in collaborative networks.
- None chose a Nature Tech scenario.

Their predictions were weighted towards Technology and Computing related collaboration. This is a similar segmentation of research published in the recent PRO-VE conferences. Given the conference titles and thematic topics [2–5], this may not be a surprise. However, it does give the expert collaboration community a chance in the short to medium term (now to 20 + years), to steer towards a more multi-disciplinary and integrated approach to collaboration research and development.

2.1 Collaboration Within Super TechnEcologies

As at 2018, Industry 4.0 is dominantly located within the Super Tech region and the UT hub. In 2017 Camarinha-Matos et al. [7] described the position of collaborative networks as core enablers for Industry 4.0. They looked at collaboration issues and proposed some outline solutions to six dimensions within Industry 4.0, namely: vertical integration of smart production systems; horizontal integration through global value chain networks; through engineering across value chains; accelerating manufacturing; digitization; and new business models. They also listed a series of related research challenges for collaborative networks. These mainly related to the Super Tech region, covering some aspects of Universal Technologies, except for *"seek inspiration in nature, towards optimized solutions"*. This is Nature Tech, which is discussed in 2.4 below.

Barker and Erickson cited possibilities for Super Tech such as: mile high cities with 90% of the world's population living in them; smart homes that order food, cook meals, and water plants; 3-D TV and holography; hybrid sports with real and robot athletes. These are all highly aligned to the current trends in construction; smart buildings and Building Information Management (BIM) [8]; occupancy management; smart white goods; smart entertainment and leisure systems; people tracking; security and 'crowd' management, such as the 'Bristol is Open' project [9].

Industry 4.0 and the interconnectedness of living and working environments can support this 'vision' if people are prepared to live this way. However, there are significant risks to this TechnEcology that need more collaborative research. The risks illustrate the principal challenges on human vulnerabilities, especially in highly concentrated ecosystems and environments, as highlighted by a recent World Health Organization report [10]. In planning and managing life in this 'region', more research and solutions will be needed for: fire risk; drought; famine; contagious and airborne diseases; civil unrest and crime; along with the likely polarization of wealth and power. Super Tech also needs to address collaboration in agriculture; food storage and distribution; energy; water security; and, social wellbeing as highlighted by Montgomery [11].

Evidence from China, where supercities have sprung up in the past two decades, already illustrates some of the challenges with airborne pollution; traffic congestion and some polarization of wealth and related personal wellbeing. Planning for a new supercity in the Pearl River Delta, with a population of 42 million, has highlighted these issues [12]. Hence, more research is needed into: social inclusiveness; community and individual healthcare; the psychological benefits of green spaces within buildings; fitness; leisure; and, personal space management as proposed by Montgomery [11]. Whilst collaborative networks as enablers are already established within expert communities, more research is going to be needed for the establishment and protection of critical infrastructure, hazards and disaster relief, food security and material supply. Risks and threats can become concentrated. It is recommended that these be investigated over the short to medium term (now to 10 + years). A paper by the Institute of Technology summarizes these hazards [13].

2.2 Collaboration Within Limits TechnEcologies

One of the most controversial propositions within Limits Tech is the potential need for population management to enable conservation of critical resources. In 2009 Lovelock [14] assessed the implications of unrestrained population growth and the effect on the earth as an ecosystem. The political and humanitarian implications of this are far reaching and beyond the scope of this paper. However, future collaborative research into the impact and consequences of rapid population growth has validity in the medium to longer term (10 to 20 + years).

On the positive side, Limits Tech promotes the benefits of: durable clothing; the revival of handicrafts, giving both personal satisfaction and saving transport; earth restoration; energy reduction and efficiency; highly efficient and insulated homes; the revival of trains and public transport, in preference to cars and lorries; and, the importance of the UT – hydrogen fuel cells.

Within the PRO-VE community there has been some well-targeted research into Green Virtual Enterprise Breeding Environments by Romero et al. [15] in 2015. By 2017 Romero et al. [16] had developed this concept and linked it to a Limits Tech related framework called RESOLVE [17]. Additional research by Shamsuzzoha et al. [18] on waste reuse, Falsafi and Fornasiero [19] on waste electronics and Jansson [20] on ship refurbishment have all contributed to this theme. This whole area of mapping circular economies and promoting a culture of scarcity, sustainability, reuse, and repurposing is likely to provide dividends as highlighted by the UK based WRAP organization [21]. In the author's technical fields of asset management, engineering and infrastructure maintenance, there are three growing trends that have potential for the future promotion of collaboration within Limits Tech: the need to extend the useful life of critical infrastructure for financial or scarcity reasons [22]; the need for repurposing of former offices and commercial buildings into habitable environments for people [23]; and, the large increase in knowledge and enthusiasm for sustainable futures driven by younger people's desire to live in a healthier environment [24]. The author believes that fruitful areas for research and the practical application of Collaborative Networks and Virtual Enterprises are:

- The design and management of circular economies with SMART environmental performance targets on a macro and micro scale (micro economies can also be designed for Local Tech);
- Greater modularization with reuse options built in (container-based housing);
- Better Building Information Management (BIM) systems and reporting [8];
- The adoption of BREEAM for master planning and sustainability measurement for both large and small-scale development [25];
- Integrated and energy efficient transport systems;
- Renewable energy, recycling, low carbon design and product distribution;
- Sustainable procurement linked to carbon/mileage;
- Modelling intergenerational resource usage and fairness more effectively, as highlighted by Lloyd in his case study on the City of Hamilton [26]; and,
- A significantly greater focus on durability and critical asset management [22].

This is a long list with major global opportunities for the collaborative research community in the short to medium term (now to 10 + years).

2.3   Collaboration Within Local TechnEcologies

For many advocates of Super TechnEcology, Local Tech could be viewed as either archaic or potentially post-apocalyptic. Indeed, some of the scenarios envisaged are a fruitful source for the fiction and film industries. However, humans have survived and thrived for millennia based around physical and locally sustainable, communities where people know and trust each other, especially in times of scarcity and conflict, as highlighted by Dent [27]. So how can Local Tech based communities make best use of Universal Technologies, where they are available, and what are the implications for collaborative research?

Barker and Erickson referred to the work of Schumacher [28] and the choice of appropriate technology that could be most effectively supplied and used locally with the concept that *"production from local resources for local needs is the most rational way of economic life"*. They then pointed out the importance of appropriate scale – not too big to be dehumanizing and not too small to miss the 'variety of life'. A market town or larger village has many of the relevant facets of Local Tech, especially when combined with local supply chains and effective low or even net zero carbon forms of transportation and energy use.

Some communities are forced down this route through access challenges, driven by geography such as island, valley, mountain, or fjord based communities. Others have elected to live this way, such as the Lammas project. It is based at the ecovillage Tir y Gafelin in West Wales. Lammas *"combines the traditional smallholding model with the latest innovations in environmental design, green technology and permaculture. The ecovillage was granted planning permission in 2009 by the Welsh Government and is currently part-way through the construction phase. At its heart it consists of 9 smallholdings positioned around a Community Hub building, and it is supported by a range of peripheral projects and networks."* [29]. Whilst being a prototype, this is typical of small scale Local TechnEcology.

Local TechnEcology does not mean primitive living and collaboration is a critical facet of success. Hence, more people-centered systems such as Dent's partnering [27] and Covey's trust-based models [30] are important to a community's success. Their adoption for business based collaborative communities is also described by the Welsh Government's Joint Bidding Guide [31]. Local market modelling is also useful, such as the system proposed by Dupont et al. [32], especially when dealing with fairness of trade and risk spreading. Hernandez et al. [33] looked at links between location, risk and the agricultural value chain and Taurino described the use of resources for SME based clusters [34]. All of these give a useful collaborative context for Local Tech.

More research into collaboration within the context of Local TechnEcologies will be useful, especially for the developing world, to help the maintenance of local and village communities and related agriculture and craft. It is recommended that this be more thoroughly researched in the short to medium term (now to 10 + years) as a potential response to the pull of the supercities in 2.1 above.

2.4   Collaboration Within Nature TechnEcologies

Camarinha-Matos et al. [7] briefly mentioned this region. Nature TechnEcology is a very fertile 'region' for future collaborative research and development, as highlighted by Thompson [35] in his Bioteams models and Benyus [36] in the book on Biomimicry. As more bioscience is explored, the links between humans and their natural environment are becoming more symbiotic.

One recent example, that demonstrates how Nature Tech can work with Universal Technologies and ingenuity, is the research into the production of Galantamine which reduces the acceleration of dementia in humans. The drug is extracted from Daffodils. It has been found that harsh growing conditions for Daffodils, due to cold and altitude, create more of the valuable compound. Hence a hill farmer in Wales has changed the use of much of his estate from animal farming to grow Daffodils from which he abstracts the drug. He collaborates with two universities, and the UK Government Department DEFRA, to research the optimum time to plant and harvest his Daffodils, to maximize the Galantamine yield [37]. A second example is the research by a team at the University of Leeds into the substitution of synthetic and potential carcinogenic hair dyes by anthocyanins extracted from the solid waste stream of a major blackcurrant drinks manufacturer in the UK [38].

Working in true collaboration with nature to mimic and enhance natural processes, reduce aspects of pollution, develop medicines and new products is a very positive way forward. This will be fruitful in the medium and longer term (5 to 20 + years) but needs far more collaboration between scientists, biologists, botanists, zoologists, the agricultural communities, virtual learning and collaboration experts to succeed.

2.5   Collaboration Within Human TechnEcologies

As stated in the introduction, Human Tech cocoons the other four regions. It combines the physiological and psychological aspects of humans (body and mind). Barker and Erickson pointed out that *"only recently have we begun to understand the scope and power of these technologies in any conscious way.* Their four primary rules of HT are:

1. *The real needs of humans are not material needs;*
2. *Science is only now learning how to measure human technology;*
3. *God or mother nature or evolution, depending on your point of view, has endowed us with extraordinary capabilities; and,*
4. *Our true work is to know ourselves."*

In their book they refer to a series of developments in the understanding of Human Tech such as: bilateral symmetry (natural selection); earwax (linkages to breast cancer); tears (toxin reduction); pheromones (chemical communication); gene therapy (long before recent advances in mapping and treatment); chronobiology (body clock and ageing); stem cells; and antibiofilm secretions (lactoferrin to prevent bacterial infections). These are rich areas for research using collaboration systems and theories, data modelling, large scale experiments and statistical validation but more likely for the medium to longer term (5 to 20 + years). The author has classified this as HTa.

On the wellbeing side, Barker and Erickson promoted collaborative traits such as organizational management, creating and using microloans (promoting self-sufficiency), teamwork and leadership. These are more developed up to and including an international standard on collaborative working [39]. However, the standard needs more research into the classic areas of trust, mutual benefit, and mapping of inputs and outcomes. This needs short-term research (within 5 years) to get more grounding in human 'reality' as opposed to collaboration systems theory. The author is researching in this area, aligned to overall competencies and system integration and has classified this as HTb.

3   Conclusion and the Way Forward

At the outset, this paper set out to examine how collaborative networks can either complement or potentially disrupt the Barker and Erickson model and identify some areas that could form the basis of future collaborative research in the respective

TechnEcologies. Each TechnEcology was described in the overall context of collaboration research, applications, and linkages to both Industry 4.0, where appropriate, or human factors. The overall proposed timelines for research consideration were also proposed. These are summarized in Table 2.

Table 2. Potential timelines for collaboration research into TechnEcologies

TechnEcology	Timeline for Potential Research		
	Within 5 Years	5 to 10 + Years	10 to 20 + Years
Super Tech (ST)			
Limits Tech (LMT)			
Local Tech (LOT)			
Nature Tech (NT)			
Huma Tech (HTa) Physiology			
Human Tech (HTb) Behaviors			

Over a decade of changes and developments in technologies, societies and collaboration systems have impacted Barker and Erickson's original predictions and propositions. Many of their predictions are appearing as reality, especially in the areas of Super Tech and Limits Tech. One of their final recommendations was that humans need to strike a balance between the capitalist and resource hungry world of Super Tech and the other TechnEcologies. This paper has proposed how the collaborative research and development community can support the various regions, with some potential timelines.

As a final offering, in his major work on Partnering Intelligence, Stephen M. Dent opens with the statement that *"For as long as humans have populated the planet, we have struggled to survive. Along the way we have learned that prosperity comes from banding together, determining what is in our best mutual interest, and moving forward in partnership."* [27]. This is still the driving force for human advancement and social stability. This paper has raised potential areas for research into advanced collaboration system and some ideas of which TechnEcology regions the research community can productively support and some recommended timescales.

References

1. Barker, J.A., Erickson S.W.: Five Regions of the Future: Preparing your Business for Tomorrow's Technology Revolution, p. 12. Porfolio (Penguin Group) (2005). ISBN 1-59184-089-9
2. Camarinha-Matos, L.M., Afsarmanesh, H. (eds.): Collaborative Systems for Smart Networked Environments. Springer, Heidelberg (2014). https://doi.org/10.1007/978-3-662-44745-1. IFIP Series 434/2014

3. Camarinha-Matos, L.M., Bénaben, F., Picard, W. (eds.): Risks and Resilience of Collaborative Networks. IAICT, vol. 463. Springer, Heidelberg (2015). https://doi.org/10.1007/978-3-662-44745-1

4. Afsarmanesh, H., Camarinha-Matos, L.M., Lucas Soares, A. (eds.): Collaboration in a Hyperconnected World. IAICT, vol. 480. Springer, Hidelberg (2016). https://doi.org/10.1007/978-3-319-45390-3

5. Camarinha-Matos, L.M., Afsarmanesh, H., Fornasiero, R. (eds.): Collaboration in a Data-rich World. IAICT, vol. 506. Springer, Cham (2017). https://doi.org/10.1007/978-3-319-65151-4

6. Young Researchers Panel at PRO-VE 2016, Porto, Portugal, 3–5 October 2016

7. Camarinha-Matos, L.M., Fornasiero, R., Afsarmanesh, H.: Collaborative networks as a core enabler of Industry 4.0. In: Camarinha-Matos, L.M., Afsarmanesh, H., Fornasiero, R. (eds.) PRO-VE 2017. IAICT, vol. 506, pp. 3–17. Springer, Cham (2017). https://doi.org/10.1007/978-3-319-65151-4_1

8. Arthur, S., Li, H., Lark, R.: A collaborative unified computing platform for building information modelling (BIM). In: Camarinha-Matos, L.M., Afsarmanesh, H., Fornasiero, R. (eds.) PRO-VE 2017. IAICT, vol. 506, pp. 63–73. Springer, Cham (2017). https://doi.org/10.1007/978-3-319-65151-4_6

9. University of Bristol. https://www.bristolisopen.com/

10. Health as The Pulse of the New Urban Agenda. United Nations Conference on Housing and Sustainable Urban Development, Quito 2016 (2016). WHO http://www.who.int/phe/publications/urban-health/en/, ISBN 978 92 4 151144 5

11. Montgomery, C.: Happy City: Transforming our Lives through Urban Design. Macmillan, London (2015). ISBN-13 978-0141047546

12. Moore, M., Foster, P.: China to create largest mega city in the world with 42 million people. The Daily Telegraph, 24 Jan 2011 (2011)

13. IET: Infrastructure Risk and Resilience: Managing Complexity and Uncertainty in Developing Cities (2014). IET https://www.theiet.org/sectors/built-environment/managing-complexity.cfm? ISBN 978-1-84919-920-9

14. Lovelock, J.: The Vanishing Face of Gaia: A Final Warning. Basic Books, New York City (2009)

15. Romero, D., Noran, O., Afsarmanesh, H.: Green virtual enterprise breeding environments bag of assets management: a contribution to the sharing economy. In: Camarinha-Matos, L. M., Bénaben, F., Picard, W. (eds.) PRO-VE 2015. IAICT, vol. 463, pp. 439–447. Springer, Cham (2015). https://doi.org/10.1007/978-3-319-24141-8_40

16. Romero, D., Noran, O., Bernus, P.: Green virtual enterprise breeding environments enabling the RESOLVE framework. In: Camarinha-Matos, L.M., Afsarmanesh, H., Fornasiero, R. (eds.) PRO-VE 2017. IAICT, vol. 506, pp. 603–613. Springer, Cham (2017). https://doi.org/10.1007/978-3-319-65151-4_53

17. McKinsey's Centre for Business and the Environment, Ellen MacArthur Foundation: Growth Within: A Circular Economy Vision for a Competitive Europe. Report (2015)

18. Shamsuzzoha, A., Helo, P., Sandhu, M.: Green virtual business network for managing and reusing waste between partner organizations. In: Afsarmanesh, H., Camarinha-Matos, L.M., Lucas Soares, A. (eds.) PRO-VE 2016. IAICT, vol. 480, pp. 639–651. Springer, Cham (2016). https://doi.org/10.1007/978-3-319-45390-3_55

19. Falsafi, M., Fornasiero, R.: Establishing networks for the treatment of WEEE components. In: Afsarmanesh, H., Camarinha-Matos, L.M., Lucas Soares, A. (eds.) PRO-VE 2016. IAICT, vol. 480, pp. 652–660. Springer, Cham (2016). https://doi.org/10.1007/978-3-319-45390-3_56

20. Jansson, K.: Circular economy in shipbuilding and marine networks – a focus on remanufacturing in ship repair. In: Afsarmanesh, H., Camarinha-Matos, L.M., Lucas Soares, A. (eds.) PRO-VE 2016. IAICT, vol. 480, pp. 661–671. Springer, Cham (2016). https://doi.org/10.1007/978-3-319-45390-3_57
21. WRAP organization. http://www.wrap.org.uk/about-us/about/wrap-and-circular-economy
22. UK Gov.: Strategic Framework and Policy Statement on Improving the Resilience of Critical Infrastructure to Disruption from Natural Hazards UK Government March 2010 (2010)
23. Wheeler, B.: The rush to turn offices into flats. http://www.bbc.com/news/uk-politics-25107646. Accessed 19 Dec 2013
24. Construction Youth. https://www.constructionyouth.org.uk/
25. Building Research Establishment Environmental Assessment Method. https://www.breeam.com/
26. Lloyd, C.: International Case Studies in Asset Management, pp. 155–164. ICE Publishing (2012). ISBN 978-0727757395
27. Dent, S.M.: Partnering Intelligence: Creating Value for Your Business by Building Strong Alliances, 2nd Edition. Davies-Black Publishing (2004). ISBN 0-89106-181-9
28. Schumacher, E.F.: Small Is Beautiful: Economics as If People Mattered: 25 Years Later, with Commentaries. Hartley & Marks Publishers; Subsequent edition (December 1, 1999), ISBN 0-88179-169-5
29. The Lammas Project. http://lammas.org.uk/en/welcome-to-lammas/
30. Covey, S.M.R., Merrill, R.R.: The Speed of Trust: The One Thing that Changes Everything. Simon & Schuster, New York City (2008). ISBN 1416549005
31. Welsh Government's Joint Bidding Guide. https://gov.wales/topics/improvingservices/bettervfm/publications/jointbidding/?lang=en
32. Dupont, L., Lauras, M., Yugma, C.: How to maintain the network resilience and effectiveness in case of resources reduction? A covering set location approach. In: Camarinha-Matos, L.M., Bénaben, F., Picard, W. (eds.) PRO-VE 2015. IAICT, vol. 463, pp. 136–145. Springer, Cham (2015). https://doi.org/10.1007/978-3-319-24141-8_12
33. Hernandez, J.E., et al.: Challenges and solutions for enhancing agriculture value chain decision-making. a short review. In: Camarinha-Matos, L.M., Afsarmanesh, H., Fornasiero, R. (eds.) PRO-VE 2017. IAICT, vol. 506, pp. 761–774. Springer, Cham (2017). https://doi.org/10.1007/978-3-319-65151-4_68
34. Taurino, T.: Evaluating collaboration and governance in SME clusters. In: Camarinha-Matos, L.M., Bénaben, F., Picard, W. (eds.) PRO-VE 2015. IAICT, vol. 463, pp. 388–397. Springer, Cham (2015). https://doi.org/10.1007/978-3-319-24141-8_35
35. Thompson, K.: Bioteams: High Performance Teams Based on Nature's Most Successful Designs. Meghan Kiffer Pr (2008), ISBN 0929652428
36. Benyus, J.M.: Biomimicry: Innovation Inspired by Nature. William Morrow (edition 1) is May 1997 (1998) ISBN-10: 0688136915
37. Country Living. https://www.countryliving.com/uk/wellbeing/a20099679/welsh-daffodils-combat-dementia/
38. Rose, P.M., Cantrill, V., Benohoud, M., Tidder, A., Rayner, C.M.: Blackburn, R.S: Application of anthocyanins from blackcurrant (Ribes nigrum L.) fruit waste as renewable hair dyes. J. Agric. Food Chem. **66**, 6790–6798 (2018)
39. British Standards Institute: ISO 44001:2017, Collaborative business relationship management systems - Requirements and framework (2017)

Promoting SME Innovation Through Collaboration and Collective-Intelligence Network in SMEs: The PMInnova Program

Agostino Villa[1], Teresa Taurino[1(✉)], Gianni Piero Perrone[2],
Andrea Villa[2], and Enrico Borgo[3]

[1] Department of Management and Production Engineering, Politecnico di Torino,
Corso Duca degli Abruzzi 24, 10129 Torino, Italy
{agostino.villa,teresa.taurino}@polito.it
[2] Kiron Organization Secretariat, Via Napoli 40, 15121 Alessandria, Italy
gp@perrone.it, andrea.villa@istoreto.it
[3] Cassa di Risparmio di Asti S.p.A., Piazza Libertà 23, 14100 Asti, Italy
borgo.enrico@virgilio.it

Abstract. The necessity of SMEs of collaborating together to be competitive again, is mandatory in any European country. Two main perspectives for SMEs to become stronger and stronger: force their collaboration in the project, test and obtain products of high technological level and sophisticated style; inhabit managers to share knowledge, skills and abilities, in order to create a collective intelligence. This is the objective of the PMInnova Program (that means: SME innovation), a strategic agreement between Politecnico di Torino and Gruppo Bancario Cassa di Risparmio di Asti, Biella and Vercelli, dedicated to supporting SMEs both in their innovation projects and in participating in European projects. The work will present some results of the PMInnova Program, for companies in which the use of IoT, AI, and Big Data has been the condition for the creation of the aforementioned collective-intelligence.

Keywords: Small and Medium Enterprises · Supporting innovation
SME collaboration · PMInnova Program · Technology transfer

1 Introduction

The European industrial reality is constituted by 95% by Small and Medium Enterprises (SMEs) [1]. The main characteristics of SMEs are essentially two: egocentrism, especially in the owners and founders of small enterprises that, over time, have designed high value products; their high consideration of the company and the quality of its products, associated with the fear that the qualifying aspects of their production techniques will be copied by competitors especially of larger dimensions [2].

These two characteristics encourage many managers of SMEs to manage the business in conditions of great confidentiality, imposing on employees the obligation not to

L. M. Camarinha-Matos et al. (Eds.): PRO-VE 2018, IFIP AICT 534, pp. 53–58, 2018.
https://doi.org/10.1007/978-3-319-99127-6_5

disseminate their work, and sometimes neither by patenting their innovations to avoid their future re-use by third parties [3, 4].

Such behavior is found in a high percentage of SME managers met under the PMInnova Program, a strategic agreement between Politecnico di Torino and the banking group of the Cassa di Risparmio di Asti, Biella and Vercelli (in Piedmont and part of Lombardy regions, in North-West Italy).

This program is dedicated to promoting innovation and development in SMEs, encouraging collaborations, as will be described in later parts of the work.

Therefore, this work is organized as follows. Section 2 briefly illustrates the objectives of the PMInnova Program, indicating its first results. Section 3 describes how some of the brightest SMEs, in terms of product quality or in terms of technological level work (for reasons of confidentiality names are disguised, however, they will be communicated to each interested reader). Section 4 will present the proposals for technological and/or organizational innovation that are presented to the SME manager. These proposals encourage him to collaborate with other companies in the same sector or in the sectors of machinery manufacturers and ICT services from one side and to promote internal growth with a gradual transfer of knowledge from older operators to younger people on the other side.

2 Objectives and Activities of the PMInnova Program

Politecnico di Torino - Department of Management and Production Engineering - and Bank of Asti group have signed a convention to implement a program of consulting, research and training, dedicated to promoting development technology and organization of Micro, Small and Medium Enterprises (SMEs). The agreement is called PMInnova Program - Promoting Innovation and Development in SMEs.

In this context it is expected that the actors of the agreement can support the enterprises in pursuing their innovation goal:

- studying the feasibility of projects and alternative options;
- identifying funding opportunities in European, national or regional context;
- defining the necessary training programs.

More precisely, the activities that are developed in favor of SMEs, especially if customers of Banca di Asti group, are the following:

(a) Information on funding programs. The banks in the group, after consulting the Polytechnic, select the SMEs that present innovation plans of particular interest and place them in the PMInnova communication list in order to receive, under an annual subscription, information on open calls in European, national and regional funding programs. It follows that an SME on the PMInnova list may request to take advantage of the activities referred to in the following points.

(b) Innovation of SMEs [5]. Once received requests for the implementation of innovation projects sent by SMEs belonging to the aforementioned PMInnova list, the Politecnico di Torino will be able to provide consulting, research and training activities as indicated below:

b.1. Consulting to meet the needs of innovation or training of SMEs, in terms of feasibility study of the innovation plan, search for funding opportunities both European and national, support for the formulation and development of a specific project, with particular attention to the plan "Industry 4.0" [6, 7];

b.2. Consultancy to support the SME in its participation in a consortium linked to a European project or a national or regional funding program, in order to define, together with the SME itself, the contribution it can provide to the project consortium, the activities to be performed, and the costs to be covered through the financing.

(c) Evaluation of the technical-managerial-financial status of an SME belonging to the PMInnova list, which will be jointly developed by Politecnico di Torino and the banks of the group, on the basis of detailed data of the requesting SME, with one or more visits to the company for a deep analysis of its most relevant characteristics and its main strengths and weaknesses [8, 9].

Every communication between the SMEs, Politecnico di Torino and the banks will be managed by the Organizing Secretariat of the PMInnova Program, entrusted by the Bank of Asti to the Non-profit Association "KIRON - Studies on Communication and Organizational Mediation", with operational headquarters in Asti.

About the main fields to which the PMInnova program is dedicated, the following points provide some suggestions:

- problems of industrial security and cyber security;
- requirements of energy saving, reduction of consumption, use of renewable energy sources;
- the need for "lean industrial organizations" to allow real-time control of quality, costs and waste;
- the need for innovative logistics management, to maximize the level of customer service [10, 11];
- the growing need to apply efficient automation, information and communication technologies, even in small production and/or service systems, within the "Industry 4.0" program, also with attention to the needs of effective communication and company promotion.

As regards SME support for European projects proposals, the PMInnova program's objective is to support Italian SMEs that could contribute as a partner in the project consortium, to help them to provide input for the proposal and contributions to the project itself.

It is also expected that banks of the group Banca di Asti and Politecnico di Torino will promote, within the PMInnova program, events and/or conferences on specific topics of innovation and development of SMEs, as well as "invitations for new ideas" for graduating students of Politecnico di Torino and other European universities.

3   Brief Analysis of Some Smart SMEs

As can be understood from Sect. 2, the agreement of one of the four collaboration activities between Politecnico and the enterprise requires a preliminary meeting (brief and dedicated to mutual knowledge) between a professor of the Polytechnic and the manager/owner of the SME asking for support to innovate. From this meeting derives very useful knowledge not only of the type of management but also of the PMI and its limits.

In one month and a half, more than 25 enterprises had a meeting in Politecnico.

The first example of smart SMEs met is an enterprise specialized in the design and prototyping of special hydraulic lifting systems for any type of machine or large objects. Its activity ranges from self-propelled cranes to aerial platforms, to special lifting structures. On the basis of information and requirements of the clients, they start a complete process starting from the project of the system to its construction and implementation, by giving an answer to the customer needs. Typical examples are the large molds for mechanical production.

The company, which employs 15 people, has been repeatedly awarded the gold medal at the International Grand Prize for Inventions.

It is evident that in this SME an internal collective intelligence is very developed, thanks to its small size and to a young staff with strong individual motivations. However, it suffers from two critical issues: on the one hand it presents serious difficulties of interaction with other companies, mainly suppliers to which a specific component is requested; on the other hand, while wishing to participate in European projects, it fears the dissemination of its ideas.

The second company plans and builds for over twenty years electronic products for safety within each production company (especially mechanical), using precision measurement sensors and technologies for the application of infrared and ultrasound. It has recently decided to design and produce optoelectronic equipment for safety barriers. This SME, producing for mechanical production companies related to the automotive sector in the Turin area, has suffered much from the recent economic-financial crisis and has been forced to halve its staff.

The third company deals with the production of special bolts, dedicated almost exclusively to safety systems in the automotive sector. About thirty years ago, the company was founded by the current owner who is still "the technological soul". With each acquisition of a new order for a new product to be printed, the organization of the work begins with the study of the mold based on the design of the product itself (executed in co-design with the large automotive company to which the product is designated), to move on to the production phase of the new mold and the best production cycle of the final product.

The company consists of three departments:

- first molding department with two machines consisting of 6 presses to form a circle plus eight single presses, some threading machines and one washing unit;
- a finishing department that includes lathes and tappers;
- a special department consisting of two multiple presses during installation.

Excluding the latter, the average age of the other machines exceeds 18 years.

4   Proposals for Technological-Organizational Innovation

The most interesting PMI, for an analyst who intends to develop a feasibility study for a company innovation project, is the third one described.

In it, the molding and finishing department have machines with simple but efficient automatisms. They do not have any data collection, analysis and transfer tool to the management system.

The simplest and most effective innovation consists, therefore, in the following interventions:

- to equip the pallets of material and products, both semi-finished and finished, of RFID for their easy recognition;
- to arrange RFID readers in correspondence with the loading/unloading systems of each machine and along the paths of the pallets from one machine to another, thus obtaining a network for collecting data and transferring information to the management system, in analogous form to an IOT network [12].

Regarding the design of each new mold, it is necessary to organize a project group that includes, in addition to the current (few) experts, line operators who can provide indications on defects found in production.

It would also be useful, but in a subsequent step, to equip the group with "collective intelligence" on the aforementioned S/W tools that facilitate proposals and modifications of molds by using Augmented Intelligence tools for an a-priori evaluation of the effects of certain forms on the compression process of the material.

The response of an analyst to the innovation request of the second of the three SMEs mentioned is simpler and more complex at the same time.

More complex as the manager of the PMI lives in a situation of progressive and strong contraction of his business. To this, it can only be remedied by a strong decision, linked to an equally robust innovation initiative.

It is also true that the company has recently decided to invest in the design and production of optoelectronic equipment for safety barriers for machine tool operators.

For this system two possible developments could be obtained:

- In the IOT optics, by using the equipment not only as "screens" for security, but also as "sensors" of production flows;
- by creating, with the use of low-frequency lasers, a network of linear sensors in the entire factory through which there could be a continuous monitoring of a large number of "state variables" of the plant.

The first company mentioned in Sect. 3 is, at the same time, the best from the technological point of view, the most structured in terms of collective intelligence but also very "closed" with respect to possible collaborations.

This characteristic is the consequence of its way of working, of its internal organization and of its way of interacting with the clients.

Moreover, its strength lies precisely in its "collective intelligence" which is also the motive of its excellent image towards a client park that includes all the best multinationals, from aeronautics to automotive, from gas to tires.

In this case, the analyst has only one suggestion: carefully take care of a gradual rejuvenation of the "collective intelligence".

5 Conclusions

In this work, we wanted to present a new (and perhaps only) initiative: the agreement between a technical university (the Polytechnic of Turin) and a Banking Group (Cassa di Risparmio of Asti, Biella and Vercelli) to develop an initiative which sees both of them as providers of knowledge, advice, research and training for SMEs.

SMEs have been, for a long time, forgotten by the great national and European programs since the goal was to support big enterprises to allow Europe to compete globally. Now, we realize that over 60% of employed people work in micro, small and medium-sized enterprises: a workforce that demands attention from governments and economic and cultural institutions.

References

1. Muller, P., Jenna, J., Herr, D., Koch, L., Peycheva, V., McKiernan, S.: Annual report on European SMEs 2016/2017. Editor Karen Hope (2017). https://doi.org/10.2873/742338
2. Bititci, U.S., Martinez, V., Albores, P., Parung, J.: Creating and managing value in collaborative networks. Int. J. Phys. Distrib. Logist. Manag. **34**(3–4), 251–268 (2004)
3. Camarinha-Matos, L.M., Afsarmanesh, H.: Collaborative Networked Organizations—A Research Agenda for Emerging Business Models. Kluwer Academic Publishers, Boston (2004)
4. Camarinha-Matos, L.M., Afsarmanesh, H.: Collaborative networks: a new scientific discipline. J. Intell. Manuf. **16**(4–5), 439–452 (2005)
5. Tsai, K.-H.: Collaborative networks and product innovation performance: toward a contingency perspective. Res. Policy **38**, 765–778 (2009)
6. Huxham, C.: Creating Collaborative Advantage. Sage Publications, London (1996)
7. McLaren, T., Head, M., Yuan, Y.: Supply chain collaboration alternatives: understanding the expected cost and benefits. Internet Res. Electron. Netw. Appl. Policy **12**(4), 348–364 (2000)
8. Taurino, T., Villa, A.: From SMEs networks towards collaborative management. Procedia Manuf. **13**, 1297–1304 (2017)
9. Ollus, M., Jansson, K., Karvonen, I.: On the management of collaborative networks. In: Symposium Cost Oriented Automation, La Habana, Cuba (2017)
10. Taurino, T., Villa, A.: Developing collaborative manufacturing in small and medium-sized enterprises. In: 24th International Conference on Production Research – New challenges for Production Research, 30 July–3 August 2017, Poznan, Poland (2017)
11. Taurino, T., Villa, A.: From industrial districts to SME collaboration frames. Int. J. Prod. Res. (2017)
12. Wortmann, F., Fluchter, K.: Internet of Things – technology and value added. Bus. Inf. Syst. Eng. **57**(3), 221–224 (2015). https://doi.org/10.1007/s12599-015-0383-3

Risk, Privacy and Security

Bank Branches as Smart Environments: Introducing a Cognitive Protection System to Manage Security and Safety

Salvatore Ammirato[1], Francesco Sofo[2], Alberto Michele Felicetti[1]([✉]),
and Cinzia Raso[1]

[1] Department of Mechanical Energy and Management Engineering,
University of Calabria, Via P.Bucci, 87036 Rende, CS, Italy
{salvatore.ammirato,alberto.felicetti,
cinzia.raso}@unical.it
[2] Faculty of Education, University of Canberra, Canberra, ACT 2601, Australia
francesco.sofo@canberra.edu.au

Abstract. Protection of Bank Branches (BBs) represents an interesting setting where potential benefits deriving from the introduction of IoT technologies can give best results in terms of operational performances. In this paper we present main results of an ERFD funded project aimed to redesign BBs as smart environments. First, we summarize main results of a multiple case study among Italian banking groups aimed to characterize the problem. Second, we propose main characteristics of a *cyber-physical-social space (CPSS)* specifically designed to facilitate the rise of a *smart BB*. Third, we introduce the architecture of a *cognitive protection system* designed to manage a network of BB CPSSs belonging to a banking group in order to improve both the degree of security and safety inside the branch environment, and the operational performances of security management processes.

Keywords: Internet of Things · Intelligent Protection System
Cyber-physical-social space · Cyber-physical security · Case study

1 Introduction

Over recent years, the "Internet of Things" (IoT) concept is gaining more and more popularity. Since Ashton first introduced this term in 1999, dealing with the introduction of RFiD sensors in supply chain management [1], the concept has been evolving representing a new paradigm in which the Internet extends into the real world embracing everyday objects [2].

At the core of the IoT there are the *smart objects* (SOs), which are physical things enhanced by electronic devices providing them with local intelligence and connectivity to the cyberspace [3]. Local intelligence means that SOs are able to sense/log/interpret what's occurring within the surrounding environment. SOs are building blocks for a *smart environment* where different kinds of SOs continuously work to make human interactions more comfortable and safer [4]. New research directions argue that sensing and connection is not enough: SOs should have the capability to learn, think, and

© IFIP International Federation for Information Processing 2018
Published by Springer Nature Switzerland AG 2018. All Rights Reserved
L. M. Camarinha-Matos et al. (Eds.): PRO-VE 2018, IFIP AICT 534, pp. 61–73, 2018.
https://doi.org/10.1007/978-3-319-99127-6_6

understand both physical and social worlds [5]. This emerging need to empower IoT with a "brain" for a higher level of intelligence leads to a new paradigm named *Cognitive Internet of Things* [5]. Cognition refers to the ability to be aware of the environment and the human interactions, be able to learn from the past actions and use it to make future decisions that benefit the network [6]. Thus a *cognitive information system* is able to modify its behaviour on the basis of experience, data analysis and interaction of smart and not SOs. This approach challenges the way networks and systems are designed and operate with humans. Current industrial trends and initiatives aim to "connect the unconnected", changing the way people and companies act every day in many key sectors, such as communications, health care, finance, education, transportation, manufacturing and agriculture [7]. An area that is becoming "a domain of major economic and social interest for the introduction of IoT" is the security domain [8]. Security of is a cutting edge issue gaining growing attention in recent years. Today, millions of connected devices are used to enhance protection levels of many types of infrastructures under the IoT paradigm [9].

Bank Branches (BBs) represent an interesting setting where potential benefits deriving from the introduction of IoT technologies can be best exploited. In fact, a BB can be seen as a worksite where humans interact among them and smart objects to carry out multiple banking activities (operational, economic and financial). The presence of such characteristics enables, in principle, the shaping of a BB as a smart environment and its devices controlled by a cognitive information system. Unfortunately, the lack of sensible efforts in improving the BB protection system represents the main hindrance to a full transformation of a BB in a smart environment [10].

This paper reports results from the BaSS (Bank Security and Safety) project, funded under the EU ERFD program, which was aimed to support banking groups to design a *Cognitive Information System* able to improve:

- the degree of security and safety inside the branch environment
- the operational performances of security management processes

2 Theoretical Background

2.1 The BB Security Context

Bank branches are physical spaces that, traditionally, represent the contact points between banks and their customers. Even if the growth of on-line banking is an undoubtable trend, consumers being still more likely to use on-line channels for basic operations continuing to rely on bank branches for more complex financial transactions [11]. Money transactions are moving from bank counter to remote controlled platforms which are accessible via web (Internet/mobile banking) or placed close to the branch (ATMs) [12]. At the same time, the branch's physical layout is changing. Traditional "hard" security measures as visible security cameras, armour windows and metal detectors are going to be removed from customers' sight. Although such measures are important to give protection to structures and people, they can generate a bad feeling of impending danger that can persuade customers to avoid entering in the branch or to stay within the branch the shortest possible time. It is evident that the aim to reduce the sense of anxiety in customers, is in contrast with the need to guarantee protection of people and properties against criminal attacks.

A criminal attack can be viewed as a sequence of actions happening in an interaction space, with the aim to obtain an unfair benefit and/or damage people or organizations [13]. The following table describes the categories of illegal actions (or *threats*) against BBs (Table 1).

Table 1. Threats against BBs.

Threat	Description
T_1: Robbery	Stealing from a bank while bank employees and customers are subjected to force, violence, or the threat of violence, putting the victim in fear
T_2: Theft	The illegal taking of another's property
T_3: Fraud	Is the use of potentially illegal means to obtain money, assets, or other property owned or held by a bank institution
T_4: Damage	Intentional or unintentional harm to somebody's property

FBI and EBF reports agree that criminal attacks against BBs are a problem that continues to take a toll on financial institutions and communities across the U.S. and Europe [14, 15]. Indeed, the growing number of attacks and their high rate of success prove that current protection measures are still not so efficacy and overall protection systems are far from the global security concept.

The occurrence of terroristic and criminal attacks at the international level, emphasized the role of security and strengthened the importance to monitor and control critical.

To improve degree of security and safety of people and goods inside a space an effective protection system is required. Conrath [16] defined protection as the set of measures that prevent or deter attackers from accessing to physical and logical resources and guidelines on how to design structures to withstand hostile acts. While in the past the emphasis was primarily addressed to the security of physical assets, today, businesses and public institution of all sizes and industries perceive a growing need to protect people and intangible assets, to preserve the continuity of their business processes. In this sense, new approaches in designing protection systems need to combine the security needs with those of operational freedom.

2.2 Smart Environment as Cyber-Physical-Social Systems

SOs are able to detect and interpret what is occurring in the surrounding environment (through an embedded sensor), interacting with other SOs, exchanging information with people and perform one or more actions through an actuator [17]. The integration of SOs within physical processes, by means of computation and networking features, shapes the so-called "cyber-physical system" (CPS) [18]. A CPS, which represents the technological layer of a smart environment, is able to acquire and apply knowledge to offer context-based services to the environment [19]. A CPS integrates two main aspects:

- a cyberspace, that refers to the generalized information resources, including virtual and digital abstractions to achieve interconnections among cyber entities;
- and a physical space, that refers to the real world, in which physical objects are respectively perceived and controlled by sensors and actuators to establish interactions via the communication channels, remote collaboration, real-time localization, and autonomy maintenance [20].

Two main functional elements characterize a CPS [21]:

- Advanced connectivity ensuring real-time data acquisition from the physical world and information from the cyber space;
- intelligent data management, analytics and computational capability that construct the cyberspace

Basing on the CPS paradigm, applications have been developed to assist people activities in many domains which become smart environments: transportation and logistics [21], smart buildings [22], smart health [23], etc.

New approaches tend to consider human factors as an integrant part of the CPS instead of placing them outside its boundaries. In this sense, many authors proposed the concept of Cyber-Physical-Social System (CPSS) [24, 25]. CPSS extends the concept of CPS, including the so-called "social space" domain, featuring human participation and interaction among humans as well as human-computer interaction. Hence, it is possible to characterize a CPSS as comprising the following components:

- Social Space (SS): the human space containing human actors, relationships and user's interconnected device (Internet of People – IoP)
- Cyberspace (CS): the software based systems and the underlying infrastructures and platforms providing services to the users (Internet of Services – IoS)
- Physical Space (PS): the physical world of interconnected SOs, including sensors, actuators and gateways (Internet of Object – IoO).

When coupled, the above-mentioned components led to the definition of the following subsystems characterizing a CPSS:

- Human Computer Interaction (HCI): The human is not just an operator in a smart environment, but he/she continuously interact with SOs/devices to get mobiquitous services.
- Cyber social space (CSS): virtual worlds, social networks and internet based services allowing synchronous and asynchronous relationship among humans.
- Cyber Physical Space (CPS): integration of software based systems, platforms, networking infrastructures and interconnected SOs and devices providing context based services.

As stated in [25], CPSS appears to be an advanced version of the IoT paradigm where social attributes are considered to address the integration of computation, networking and physical processes aching the interfusion of the cyber–physical space and social space.

From an operational point of view, the design of a CPSS can benefit of the recent advances in mechatronics which led to a new generation of multipurpose sensors, known as *indirect or synthetic sensors* [26]. According this approach, single physical sensor can detect different characteristics from the same signal, instead of requiring the use of many sensors. The ultimate embodiment of this approach would be a single general-purpose sensor able to digitize an entire building. This kind of sensors can be attached to a variety of objects, and without modification, sense many facets [27, 28]. Synthetic sensors overcome traditional limitations of limited sensing functionality, limited large scale interoperability and failure to provide complex interpretations of implicit assumptions [29].

3 Methodology

With the aim *"to develop technology-based solutions to important and relevant business problems"*, the present study follows the design research paradigm proposed in [30]. As stated in [31], a design science research process can be summarized on the following three steps: problem identification, solution design and validation.

The first step was aimed to highlight characteristics and weaknesses of the protection systems currently adopted by banking groups to protect security and safety of their branches. The framework methodology we have used at this step is based on a multi-methodological development approach that include a systematic literature research and review and interviews with experts. Literature review was intended to create a complete understanding of the BB security domain and IoT field of study. Moreover, we performed semi-structured interviews with a sample of convenience of six respondents who were working for primary Italian banking groups as security managers at the time of the study. The data gathering for the case study has been carried out in Italy during the last three months of 2016. The interviews were based on pre-defined open questions dealing with organizational and technological characteristics of the current protection systems. The second step of the methodology was aimed to propose an architecture for a *cognitive protection system* for BBs able to manage protection through a redesign of the BBs. In particular, we introduce a logical model of BB under a CPSS perspective and the architecture the architecture of the *Intelligent Protection System – IPS*, a cognitive platform designed to manage BB security. Third step consisted in testing activities in order to experiment it inside a BB context.

4 The Italian BB Case Study

4.1 The BB Protection Systems

Measures to protect the BB environment can be classified according to the desired effect to a criminal attack: prevention and reaction.

Prevention measures are static measures intended to prevent/obstacle harms to bank assets discouraging the potential criminals by doing the attack. Three typologies belong to this category: traditional "hard" measures (structural measures such as armour windows, armed guards, armour-plated doors, time lock doors); "soft" or psychological measures (i.e.: transparent glasses or display panels which gives information about the presence of security controls, etc.), and "technological" measures used to identify and enable/hinder people entering BB environment or interacting with ATMs, (e.g., secure ID generator, credit card; biometric data) [16].

Reaction measures require the activation (automatic or human driven) of a countermeasure further to a risky event (i.e.: sound alarm, systems for tracing money, emergency calls to law-enforcement, etc.) [32]. Traditional ways to recognize suspect behaviours comes from perimetric/volumetric sensors and from two "analogic" systems that continuously monitor the environment: the armed guards and video-surveillance system. In both cases humans, directly (the armed guards) or indirectly (the security guard looking at the video streaming from the control room) present on the scene are charged to pay attention to suspect behaviours of people who could attack the BB.

Unfortunately, interviews agreed that security measures are characterized by low efficacy and by outdated and stand-alone mechanisms. Traditional "hard" security measures clash with commercial purposes of BBs. Protection measures currently adopted cannot constantly monitor the environment properly: traditional camera surveillance systems are characterized by low effectiveness due to the tiredness and the alienation of operators because of the repetitive nature of the job. Moreover, protection measures are incapable of retaining, storing and communicating data about their state in order to examine the contexts of BB. If available, contextual information could be used to support and enhance the ability to execute specific countermeasures by providing information and services tailored to the security needs.

4.2   Towards a New Concept of BBs as CPSSs

As emerges from interviews, the growing interest of criminals in attacking BB is directly related to the persistent use of obsolete security technologies that, moreover, are a source of organizational inefficiencies, high costs and are characterized by long reaction times and scarce level of effectiveness.

The transformation of a BB in a smart environment can allow, in principle, to overcome these critical issues, improving security process performances and effectiveness against criminal attacks. In the following sections we summarize main characteristics of a CPSS specifically designed to facilitate the rise of a *smart BB*. In the so-called *BB CPSS*, protection measures, both smart and non-SOs, are capable of interacting among them and with humans through a digital network, to improve the BB security and safety management. Inside the BB CPSS, the cyber domains of communication and computing are combined with the dynamics of physical objects and their interaction with human actors proper of a BB setting [19]. After, we introduce the architecture of the *IPS - Intelligent Protection System* – which is the cognitive protection system designed to manage a network of BB CPSSs belonging to a banking group in order to improve both the degree of security and safety inside the branch environment, and the operational performances of security management processes.

4.2.1   The Logical Model of a BB CPSS

Each BB environment is characterized by the presence of a set of context entities, intended as physical or conceptual objects which interact among them [33]. According to Ning's view [25], it is possible to identify the subsystems which compose the BB CPSS and, for each of them, types of context entities interact inside:

- Social Space (SS): all the human actors which interact inside a BB. Four category of human entities are identified: customers, employees, attackers and guards.
- Cyberspace (CS): the local component of the IPS, that is a software based systems able to manage the security and safety operational process which happen inside a BB.
- Physical Space (PS): physical SOs and non SOs involved in security and safety processes.

The following table provide a description of the main context entities of a BB modelled as a CPSS (Table 2).

Table 2. Main context entities of a BB modelled as a CPSS.

Space	Entity	Entity detail	Description
SS	People	P_1: Customer	A person who is utilizing one or more of the services provided by the bank
		P_2: Employee	A person who works for a bank institution under a contract of employment
		P_3: Attacker	A person who is performing a criminal action to obtain an unfair benefit and to damage someone or something
		P_4: Guard	Outsourced contractor monitoring for potential threats to BB, on-site (e.g. armed guard) and remotely (security guard inside the control room)
CS	IPS		A web platform based on a client-server architecture able to manage security and safety process within a BB
PS	Bank assets	BA_k	The set of tangible and intangible goods that are threatened by criminal attacks
	Weapons		Any device used with intent to inflict damage or threaten people, structures, or systems
	Safety and security systems	Non SOs	Static measures intended to prevent/obstacle harms to bank assets discouraging the potential criminals by doing the attack (e.g. structural measures such as armour windows, armed guards, armour-plated doors, time lock doors)
		SOs	SOs that leverage on IoT features to provide security and safety services. These systems require the activation (automatic or human driven) of a countermeasure further to a risky event. Such systems are based on HCI or machine-to-machine interactions

Volpentesta et al. [34] proposed that every action performed by context entities inside a smart environment affects their state. Interactions between entities can be sensed, interpreted and mediated through IoT based protection systems. In certain cases, a subset of actions performed by humans in a BB can be recognized as threatening and may trigger a sequence of security service actions (e.g. a counter-measure) involving people (attackers, customers, employees) physical goods, as well safety and security systems. We define "security patterns" the sequence of actions involving context agents within a bank branch in order to detect of a threat.

In order to model security pattern, we used the following formalism. Let us con-sider S_k the set of all possible statuses of a Bank Asset BA_k and A_k a non-empty set of actions that can be performed on BA_k. We assume that any action $a \in A_k$, performed by an actor P_i, determines a status change (from $s_{i,k}$ to $s_{j,k}$, $i \neq j$, $s_{i,k} s_{j,k} \in S_k$) of a Bank Asset BA_k. Each actor P_i is allowed to perform a set of activities $A_{k,i}$, where $A_{k,p} \subseteq A_k$.

The triple BA_k $(S_k, A_k, P(A_k))$ univocally identifies the interaction graph $G_{BAk}(N(S_k), E(A_k, P(A_k)))$, where $N(S_k)$ is the set of nodes, and $E(A_{k,p})$ is the set of arcs determining the transaction from a node to another, due to an action a $\in A_k$, performed by an actor P. A dangerous situation is detected when a transaction from a node n_x to n_y is due to an action A_k such that a $\in A_k$ and $a \notin A_{k,p}$. A security pattern for a resource is a path p on the graph G_{BAk}. Continuous interactions along the graph shape the logical model of the BB CPSS. Security patterns constitute the building blocks of a security infras-tructure, in the sense that any security infrastructure comes out from a combination of some security patterns. Unlike traditional security systems, where sensors are only capable of detecting simple actions in an environment (e.g. motion sensors), the IPS allows security management procedures based on complex and structured events. For example, traditional sensors are able to sense simple events like "a strongbox is open" or "a human with a metal object is crossing the BB entering door" recognizing them as dangerous events. The IPS sensors are able to sense primary events and learn, reason, and more effectively interact with humans inside a BB, leveraging on machine learning algorithms to process the data collected and recognize only real dangerous situations. Appropriate machine learning algorithms enable the IPS to combine security patterns to infer secondary events. More formally, let P_{BAk} be the set of admissible patterns on G_{BAk}, (i.e. a sequence of actions considered not dangerous for BA_k's safety and security), the IPS recognizes a threat when it identifies an interaction such that $p \notin P_{BAk}$. In the previous example, the IPS recognizes that strongbox is open due to authorized scheduled refilling activities (p_1) and the armed human is a guard already authorized to enter the BB (p_2). Since both p_1 and $p_2 \in P_{BAk}$, both are "false positives" threats and the IPS do not activate any reaction measure.

4.2.2   The Architecture of the IPS

The IPS is able to manage many BBs as remote controlled CPSSs in order to both increase the degree of security and safety of the branches and reduce operational and management costs of the banking group protection system. We defined a logical and technological model allowing the remote management of the BB CPSSs, able to handle data coming from synthetic sensors, video surveillance (passive safety), and real-time reports from employees and sensors (active safety). The network architecture of the IPS is described below.

- Local Nodes: A local node is a local protection unit of a BB charged to manage and control the BB CPSS. Local nodes make use of computer vision and synthetic sensors technologies, able to carry out the local management of the signaling, comprising the correlation with the state of other software subsystems. Any local nodes interact with the central node.
- Central Node: A control room that collects signals from each CPSS (local node), and is able to implement prevention or reaction risk protocols [35]. The central node uses embedded technologies in order to recognize each kind of threat.

The IPS is a cognitive system since it is able to recognize the types of ongoing events in each BB and suggest (or automatically adopt) in real time a set of appropriate countermeasures. The IPS continuously updates and upgrades its security patterns since it is able to learn from past criminal attacks, adopted countermeasures and effects of such adoption. The IPS integrates efficient models and algorithms allowing the "unstructured events" video surveillance, in order to minimize the number of *false positive* alarms and to minimize the number of not identified risky situations. Smart cameras can be equipped with computer vision able to recognize human behaviour.

The IPS data-processing architecture is based on a web-based multi-tier solution which makes use of an interprocess communication mechanisms typical of enterprise-type solutions.

Figure 1 shows the different components of the IPS and how information flows occur from the BB CPSSs to the control room.

- **Sensor gateway**: a network device able to collect heterogeneous data from sensors.
- **Alert management**: represent all the alarm warnings generated by the sensors (break-in, intrusion, etc.) that are sent as a textual list to the control panel.
- **Data Communicator**: transmission communication protocol among the recognition systems (which filter the alarms by assigning them a level of danger) and the platform that will display them on the control panel. This communication is based on XML/RPC web services.
- **Technical Operator Panel**: web interface for technical operators in order to manage security activities at an operational level.
- **Operator Manager Panel**: Management interface to analyse statistical data and setting up change to the security platform.
- **DB**: is the Data Base where will be saved all the events and decisions taken. Naturally it contains the whole knowledge base of the system on the security measures, security patterns and the risk model.

The human interaction with security services is mediated by a ubiquitous computing system and every smart object in the environment can potentially give either an input to the IPS or an output to each person inside the smart environment. In fact, the interaction is not centralized in a single device, but it involves a person, a potentially huge set of smart objects distributed in the real world, and many security services running on the system.

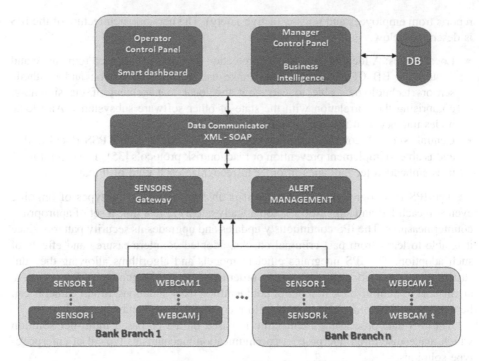

Fig. 1. The network architecture of the IPS

5 Conclusions

Several authors highlighted the need for an integrated approach to managing physical security [36]. Physical protection systems leverage not only on technologies, but integrate people, procedures and equipment for the protection of goods or services against theft, sabotage or any action aimed at harming people or property, implying the need for an integrated methodological approach. Physical security of people and spaces (e.g. workplace, private and public areas), is becoming increasingly important, and requires comprehensive and integrated solutions, characterized by ease of configuration and immediacy of use.

The availability of a new generation of multipurpose and low-cost sensors enabled the opportunity to easily redesign physical spaces as smart environments. In order to exploit this opportunity, there is a need to design appropriate platforms able to manage and process data deriving from sensors. Thanks to the recent technological developments, it has become possible to integrate physical networks of SOs with cognitive systems where applications can use such an intelligent infrastructure to carry out data analytics, process optimization and decision support. In particular, we propose to deal with the traditional physical security issue of BBs under a CPSS perspective. The technological infrastructure of a BB can be modelled as a CPSS where smart and non-SOs used as protection measures, can interact among them and with humans through a digital network. Moreover, the introduction of an effective and tailored Intelligent Protection System is responsible to manage an analyze data acquired to synthetic sensors.

The IPS we proposed combines a high level of security and safety within a bank branch to a more rapid access to the physical structure and an increased positive feeling requested by the customers. The non-invasive sensor network designed within the platform realizes a more comfortable environment through the elimination from the customer's sight of protective elements of a crime, such as bars, revolving doors, gunmen, etc., which, although currently necessary to prevent robberies, increase the sense of anxiety. This is in line with the changing of commercial banking needs, whose marketing functions are pushing to let bank branches be more and more similar to selling point of other industries.

Ongoing studies are testing a prototype of the IPS in order to experiment it inside a BB context.

References

1. Ashton, K.: That "Internet of Things" thing. RFID J. **22**(7), 97–114 (2009)
2. Mattern, F., Floerkemeier, C.: From the Internet of Computers to the Internet of Things. In: Sachs, K., Petrov, I., Guerrero, P. (eds.) From Active Data Management to Event-Based Systems and More. LNCS, vol. 6462, pp. 242–259. Springer, Heidelberg (2010). https://doi.org/10.1007/978-3-642-17226-7_15
3. Kopetz, H.: Real-time Systems: Design Principles for Distributed Embedded Applications. Springer, Heidelberg (2011). https://doi.org/10.1007/978-1-4419-8237-7
4. Cook, D., Das, S.K.: Smart Environments: Technology, Protocols and Applications, vol. 43. Wiley, Hoboken (2004)
5. Wu, Q., et al.: Cognitive Internet of Things: a new paradigm beyond connection. IEEE Internet Things J. **1**(2), 129–143 (2014)
6. Al-Turjman, F.M.: Information-centric sensor networks for cognitive IoT: an overview. Ann. Telecommun. **72**(1–2), 3–18 (2017)
7. Sadeghi, A.R., Wachsmann, C., Waidner, M.: Security and privacy challenges in industrial Internet of Things. In: Proceedings of the 52nd Annual Design Automation Conference, p. 54. ACM (2015)
8. Del Giudice, M.: Discovering the Internet of Things (IoT) within the business process management: a literature review on technological revitalization. Bus. Process Manag. J. **22**(2), 263–270 (2016)
9. Alvi, S.A., Afzal, B., Shah, G.A., Atzori, L., Mahmood, W.: Internet of multimedia things: vision and challenges. Ad Hoc Netw. **33**, 87–111 (2015)
10. Tinnilä, M.: Efficient service production: service factories in banking. Bus. Process Manag. J. **19**(4), 648–661 (2013)
11. Bank Seta: THE BANK OF THE FUTURE: innovative solutions to meet the challenges of the new environment. Technical report, Wits Business School (2014)
12. Sofo, F., Berzins, M., Ammirato, S., Volpentesta, A.: Investigating the relationship between consumers' style of thinking and online victimization in scamming. JDCTA **4**(7), 38–49 (2010)
13. Matthews, R., Pease, C., Pease, K: Repeated bank robbery: themes and variations (2001)
14. EBF: Physical security report 2015. Technical report, European banking federation (2016)
15. FBI: BANK CRIME STATISTICS – 2015. Technical report, U.S. Department of justice federal bureau of investigation Washington (2016)

16. Conrath, E.J.: Structural Design for Physical Security: State of the Practice. ASCE Publications, New York (1999)
17. García, C.G., Meana-Llorián, D., G-Bustelo, B.C.P., Lovelle, J.M.C.: A review about smart objects, sensors, and actuators. Int. J. Interact. Multimed. Artif. Intell. **4**, 7–10 (2017)
18. Lee, E.A.: Cyber physical systems: design challenges. In: 11th IEEE International Symposium on Object Oriented Real-Time Distributed Computing (ISORC), pp. 363–369. IEEE (2008)
19. Monostori, L.: Cyber-physical production systems: roots, expectations and R&D challenges. Procedia CIRP **17**, 9–13 (2014)
20. Volpentesta, Antonio P., Muzzupappa, M., Ammirato, S.: Critical thinking and concept design generation in a collaborative network. In: Camarinha-Matos, Luis M., Picard, W. (eds.) PRO-VE 2008. ITIFIP, vol. 283, pp. 157–164. Springer, Boston (2008). https://doi.org/10.1007/978-0-387-84837-2_16
21. Lee, J., Bagheri, B., Kao, H.A.: A cyber-physical systems architecture for industry 4.0-based manufacturing systems. Manuf. Lett. **3**, 18–23 (2015)
22. Felicetti, C., De, R., Raso, C., Felicetti, A.M., Ammirato, S.: Collaborative smart environments for energy-efficiency and quality of life. Int. J. Eng. Technol. **7**(2), 543–552 (2015)
23. Zhang, Y., Qiu, M., Tsai, C.W., Hassan, M.M., Alamri, A.: Health-CPS: healthcare cyber-physical system assisted by cloud and big data. IEEE Syst. J. **11**, 88–95 (2015)
24. Zeng, J., Yang, L.T., Lin, M., Ning, H., Ma, J.: A survey: cyber-physical-social systems and their system-level design methodology. Future Gener. Comput. Syst. (2016). https://www.sciencedirect.com/science/article/pii/S0167739X1630228X
25. Ning, H., Liu, H., Ma, J., Yang, L.T., Huang, R.: Cybermatics: cyber–physical–social–thinking hyperspace based science and technology. Future Gener. Comput. Syst. **56**, 504–522 (2016)
26. Lloret, J., Canovas, A., Sendra, S., Parra, L.: A smart communication architecture for ambient assisted living. IEEE Commun. Mag. **53**(1), 26–33 (2015)
27. Grill, T., Polacek, O., Tscheligi, M.: Conwiz: the contextual wizard of oz. J. Ambient Intell. Smart Environ. **7**(6), 719–744 (2015)
28. Laput, G., Zhang, Y., Harrison, C.: Synthetic sensors: towards general-purpose sensing. In: Proceedings of the 2017 CHI Conference on Human Factors in Computing Systems, pp. 3986–3999. ACM (2017)
29. Tripolitsiotis, A., Prokas, N., Kyritsis, S., Dollas, A., Papaefstathiou, I., Partsinevelos, P.: Dronesourcing: a modular, expandable multi-sensor UAV platform for combined, real-time environmental monitoring. Int. J. Remote Sens. **38**(8–10), 2757–2770 (2017)
30. Hevner, R.H., March, S.T., Park, J., Ram, S.: Design science in information systems research. MIS Q. **28**(1), 75–105 (2004)
31. Offermann, P., Levina, O., Schönherr, M., Bub, U.: Outline of a design science research process. In: Proceedings of the 4th International Conference on Design Science Research in Information Systems and Technology. ACM (2008)
32. Baker, P.R.: Physical protection systems. In: Baker, P.R., Benny, D. (eds) The Complete Guide to Physical Security. CRC Press (2012)
33. Wojciechowski, M., Xiong, J.: A user interface level context model for ambient assisted living. In: Helal, S., Mitra, S., Wong, J., Chang, Carl K., Mokhtari, M. (eds.) ICOST 2008. LNCS, vol. 5120, pp. 105–112. Springer, Heidelberg (2008). https://doi.org/10.1007/978-3-540-69916-3_13

34. Volpentesta, A.P., Felicetti, A.M., Ammirato, S.: Intelligent food information provision to consumers in an internet of food era. In: Camarinha-Matos, Luis M., Afsarmanesh, H., Fornasiero, R. (eds.) PRO-VE 2017. IAICT, vol. 506, pp. 725–736. Springer, Cham (2017). https://doi.org/10.1007/978-3-319-65151-4_65

35. Volpentesta, A.P., Ammirato, S., Palmieri, R.: Investigating effects of security incident awareness on information risk perception. Int. J. Technol. Manag. **54**(2/3), 304–320 (2011)

36. Garcia, M.L.: Design and Evaluation of Physical Protection Systems. Butterworth-Heinemann, Oxford (2007)

A Proposal for Risk Identification Approach in Collaborative Networks Considering Susceptibility to Danger

Jiayao Li[1(✉)], Frédérick Bénaben[2], Juanqiong Gou[1], and Wenxin Mu[1]

[1] School of Economics and Management, Beijing Jiaotong University, Beijing, China
{jiayaol,jqgou,wxmu}@bjtu.edu.cn
[2] Mines Albi, University of Toulouse, Albi, France
frederick.benaben@mines-albi.fr

Abstract. The paper proposes a research framework for risk identification approach in collaborative networks dedicated to develop a formalizing, structured reference for risk identification and risk mitigation and explore an effective mechanism that can motivate diverse partners to manage risks collaboratively. The approach is based on a formalized vision of Danger/Risk/Consequence chain that is defined as the primary schema of the proposed methodology. The DRC chain indicates five risk-related concepts and their interrelationships, which is able to well describe risk-related collaborative contexts. Cascading effect in the concept chain are presented for further interpreting. Furthermore, a supply chain scenario of three use cases is given to illustrate the proposed framework.

Keywords: Risk identification · DRC chain · Susceptibility to danger
Cascading effect · Collaborative network

1 Introduction

A collaborative network is an alliance constituted by a variety of entities (e.g. organizations and people) that are largely autonomous, geographically distributed, and heterogeneous in terms of their operating environment, culture, social capital and goals, but that collaborate to better achieve common or compatible goals, and whose interactions are supported by a computer network [1]. Collaborative networks such as virtual organizations, dynamic supply chains, professional virtual communities, collaborative virtual laboratories, etc. are complex systems associated with uncertainties in dynamic business environments [2]. It is noted that the collaboration increases the dependences among enterprises, which makes enterprises more susceptible to risks. It is critical for collaborative networks to take systematic approaches to identify risks as early as possible, and implement appropriate strategies to manage the risk propagation throughout the evolution of collaboration [3].

While the above discussion shows the importance of risk identification, however, it is worthy to note that there appears to be no overarching typology to delineate exactly what constitutes risk and how to understand risk [4]. [5] argues that risk management consists

L. M. Camarinha-Matos et al. (Eds.): PRO-VE 2018, IFIP AICT 534, pp. 74–84, 2018.
https://doi.org/10.1007/978-3-319-99127-6_7

of four key management aspects: (i) assessing the risk sources; (ii) defining the adverse consequences; (iii) identifying the risk drivers; and (iv) mitigating risks. [6] indicates that risk is at least made up of three essential components: (i) a driver or drivers which trigger the risk to happen; (ii) an event with probability that signifies the occurrence of the risk; and (iii) a consequence or consequences resulted from the risk. [7] presents a three-dimensional framework dedicated to structure the domain of crisis management based on the Danger/Risk/Consequence chain (DRC chain). In summary, the risk-related concepts could be concluded as *danger*, *stake*, *risk*, *event* and *consequence*.

Anyway, risk management is a very complex domain with a lot of constraints. Consequently, it is very difficult to get a global overview of such a domain. This article is mainly dedicated to present a proposal for risk identification approach to support collaborative networked organizations. The proposed approach is based on the DRC chain (as shown in Fig. 1), which is not so far from FTA (Fault Tree Analysis) principles [8]. Furthermore, *danger*, *risk* and *consequence* may be considered as causal sources (in a waterfall structure) that must be formalized as models to help decision makers [7].

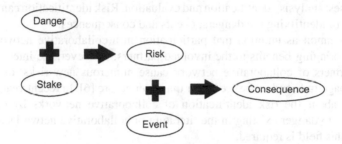

Fig. 1. A framework for risk identification approach

More specifically, the research methodology is proposed:

- A danger typology and a stake typology are developed for collaborative networked organizations based on the review of present related literatures.
- The interconnections rules between *dangers* and *stakes* and their impacts on *risks* could be summarized, which aims to build a risk typology as a static reference model of risk knowledge.
- In addition to *danger*, *stake* and *event*, *risk* and *consequence* can be also considered in a *cascading effect* structure [9]. Their interrelationships could be analyzed and summarized.
- A risk knowledge base with a risk typology and interrelationships is used for the deduction of risk identification rules based on previous research works.
- A metamodel connected with a risk knowledge base will be defined based on the research of collaborative situation metamodel [10, 11].

The research should contribute to a deeper and broader understanding risk based on the schema of DRC chain. Besides, the risk identification research based on such an understanding will contribute to better practices by suggesting collaborative responses from multiple partners in collaborative networks.

This article is structured according to the following sections: Sect. 2 presents a literature review; Sect. 3 describes the DRC chain considering susceptibility to danger and interrelationships of the five risk-related concepts; in Sect. 4, a supply chain scenario is given to illustrate the part of proposed methodology; Sect. 5 concludes this research work and gives some perspectives for future works.

2 Literature Review

According to [12], risk is the combination of the frequency, or probability, of occurrence and the consequence of special hazardous events.

Risk Management corresponds to a set of activities that organizations use to control the many risks, which may undermine their ability to achieve objectives. Considering international standards on entrepreneurial management process risk, [13] organizes a reference risk taxonomy, which shows that risk management includes two principal dimensions, namely, assessment and treatment. Risk assessment could be summarized as three phases: analysis, identification and evaluation. Risk identification can be defined as a process of identifying the dangers, events and consequences.

It is a common assumption that participation in a collaborative network has the potential of bringing benefits to the involved partners. However, the interconnections between partners of collaborative network cause numerous new risks, of which the impacting magnitude and scope are larger than ever before [6]. In recent years, there are few studies about the risk identification of collaborative networks by considering susceptibility to danger existing in the literature of collaborative networks and further research in this field is required.

Regarding the approach of risk identification in collaborative context, it focuses on literature review, semi-structured interviews and questionnaire. They can be called as the experienced-based methods. [14] directly takes advantage of the risks identified by project manager to determine the events with negative impacts. [15] identifies the stakeholder-associated risks through the previous risk identification literatures, and classified them into seven categories. [16] identifies the risks caused by customer collaboration in product development through relevant literatures by domain experts and questionnaire in the enterprises. [17] analyzes the research paradigms regarding risk and stakeholder analysis in green buildings through literature review. [18] undertakes a systematic literature review on risks sources and resilience factors in agri-food supply chains. [19] successively uses literature review, semi-structured interviews and questionnaires to identify a list of human safety risk factors and also the cause–effect relationships among those risks.

Regarding the application of risk identification results, most results of identified risks are used to further risk evaluation and propose risk response or risk mitigation strategies. In order to investigate those risk interactions, the focus of risk evaluation methods has gradually been shifting from individual risks to networks of risk [6, 19]. It considers nodes in the network and their relationships, focusing on the structure and patterning of these relationships and seeking to identify both their causes and effects [20, 21].

We conclude the following:

- A systematic approach to the identification and categorization of risks in collaborative context is lacking.
- The current risk identification methods mainly focus on review, expert interview and questionnaire.
- More future works are attentive to the identification of risk interconnections.
- The present research of the application of risk identification result also lacks of a sharing-based risk response mechanism considering capabilities and resources of partners to contribute to their collaboration.

3   Understanding Risk

Risk can be seen as combination of the probability of an *event* and its *consequence*. However, *danger* and *stake* are also closely related to *risk* with the exception of the concepts of *event* and *consequence*. DRC chain is a concepts schema that is able to describe risk-related contexts.

3.1   General Illustration of DRC Chain

In this schema, the five risk-related concepts could be defined as follows:

- *Danger* can be defined as any specific dangerous characteristic of the environment, which is a signal word used to indicate an imminently hazardous situation [22].
- *Stake* or *assets* can be seen as item, thing or entity that has potential or actual value to an organization [23] and potential susceptibility to dangers.
- *Risk* is a potential manifestation of the *danger* onto some concerned *stakes* [7].
- *Event* is defined as a change or outcome that triggers *risks*. If one *risk* might occur it would be due to some *events* [24].
- *Consequence* generally means a set of negative impacts of the risk occurrence.

The general illustration of DRC chain could be described as follows: Each of those negative facts is due to one (or several) *event*(s) that trigger(s) one (or several) *risk*(s); This (or these) *risk*(s) occur(s) because the considered area/system is concerned by one (or several) *danger*(s) that affect(s) one (or several) *stake*(s) [7].

Furthermore, the DRC chain could indicate the *susceptibility to danger*, which means the state of being very likely to be influenced or affected by danger. The following example in enterprise collaborative context illustrates *susceptibility to danger* (see Fig. 2).

Company C is the only one able to produce *Product P* for the *core company CC*, which is a *danger* for the *stake CC* because its *Product PP* must be produced by using *P*. Consequently, the *risk* is that *PP* may not be produced. It would be triggered if C decides not to produce *P* anymore (an *event* occurs), then cause a *consequence* as which *CC* cannot sell *PP* to its customers. For this general illustration of DRC chain, the demand side *CC* is susceptible to the danger of which there is no alternative provider regarding its required product. Different *stakes* have different degrees of susceptibility to danger while some *stakes* are not susceptible to danger.

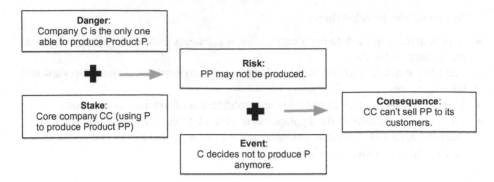

Fig. 2. An illustration of "susceptibility to danger" in DRC chain

3.2 Interconnections in DRC Chain

In the schema of the DRC chain, *risk* is created by *danger* and *stake* while *consequence* is created by *risk* and *event*. It can be seen that *risk* and *consequence* are the "generated" elements. Therefore, they are the ones which directly impact the considered system. Accordingly, it is worth to focus on what effects that they might create. One of perspective that can indicate it is *cascading effects* that could be described as multiple connections initiated by *risk* and *consequence* in the DRC chain.

A *cascading effect* is an inevitable and sometimes unforeseen chain of *events* due to an act affecting a system [25]. If there is a possibility that the *cascading effect* will have a negative impact on the system, it is probable to analyze the effects with a *risk* or *consequence* analysis. Figure 3 shows six connections initiated from *consequence* (see connections (1) (2) (3)) and *risk* (see connections (4) (5) (6)), in order to present the *cascading effect* as follows: *consequence* and *risk* are regarded as the causal sources that target at *danger*, *stake* and *event*.

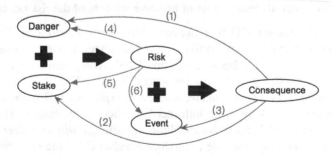

Fig. 3. Interconnections in DRC chain

To illustrate the *cascading effect* further, three use cases are presented in Fig. 4, which are the real ones from a cosmetic French company. The interconnections between the first two use cases (see connections (1) (2) (3) of Fig. 4) could indicate *consequence* as the causal source. The first use case is already described in previous section, the *consequence* of which is that *CC* cannot sell *PP*. It is worth mentioning that this *consequence* could bring about the next use case.

The second use case is described as follows: *CC* has to contract with another company *C'* that can produce *P*, however, which is a *danger* for the new provider *C'*. Concerning this *stake*, the *danger* could be manifested as a *risk* that its *Product P* may decline in quality. Under this circumstance, if there is a big demand for *P* from *CC*, the *risk* would be triggered and cause a *consequence* as which *C'* produces lower quality products and its image might be degraded.

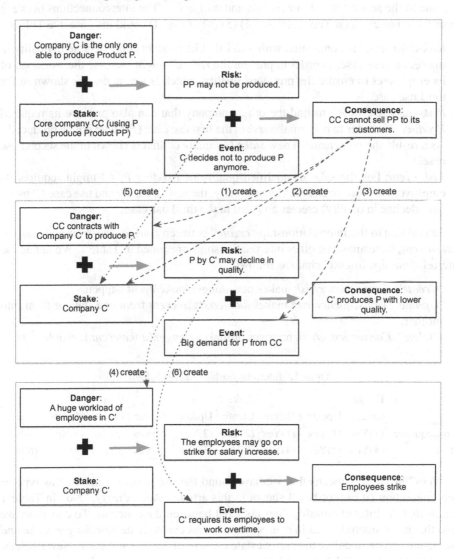

Fig. 4. An illustration of cascading effect in DRC chain

In summary, it can be seen that one *consequence* in a scenario could create a new *danger* (*CC* contracts with *C'*), also a new *stake* (*company C'*) and even an *event* (big demand from *CC*), which lead to another risk-related scenario.

The third use case is described as follows: A huge workload of employees in *Company C'* is a *danger* for the *stake C'*, because it could create a *risk* that the employees may go on strike for salary increase. The *risk* would be triggered if *C'* requires them to work overtime (an *event*), then a *consequence* of employees' strike might be caused.

Regarding *risk* as the causal source, the creation of *danger*, *stake* and *event* is generally due to the actions of risk prevention and mitigation. The interconnections between these three use cases (see connections (4) (5) (6) of Fig. 4) could indicate it as below:

- *Risk-danger*: *C'* is confronted with a *risk* that its products may decline in quality in the second use case. In order to prevent the *risk*, *C'* might increase the workload of its employees to ensure the products' quality, which is a new *danger* shown in the third use case.
- *Risk-stake*: *CC* needs to find the other company that can also produce its required *Product P* in order to prevent the *risk* in the first use case (*PP* may not be produced). As a result, the *risk* creates a new *stake Company C'* that is shown in the second use case.
- *Risk-event*: For the sake of qualified quality of *Product P*, *C'* might requires its employees to work overtime. Consequently, the *risk* in the second use case (*P* by *C'* may decline in quality) creates an *event* in the third use case.

In addition to the interrelationship "*create*" between *consequence/risk* and *danger/stake/event*, there are some other interrelationships presented in Table 1. We define the interrelationships in DRC chain as follows:

- "*Create*": *Consequence/risk* makes new *danger/stake/event* happen.
- "*Update*": *Consequence/risk* makes *danger/stake/event* from one state or form into another.
- "*Delete*": *Consequence/risk* removes or makes *danger/stake/event* invisible.

Table 1. Interrelationships in DRC chain

	Danger			Stake			Event		
	Create	Update	Delete	Create	Update	Delete	Create	Update	Delete
Consequence	(1)Yes	(1)Yes	(1)Yes	(2)Yes	(2)Yes	(2)Yes	(3)Yes	(3)No	(3)No
Risk	(4)Yes	(4)Yes	(4)Yes	(5)Yes	(5)Yes	(5)Yes	(6)Yes	(6)No	(6)No

"Yes" in Table 1 means that we have found the use cases to support this type of interconnection (it cannot be all shown in this article). Accordingly, "No" in Table 1 means that the interrelationship does not exist between the concepts. To conclude, we hold that in considered scenario *consequence or risk* could create new *danger, stake and event*, and update or delete the current state or form of *danger* and *stake*. Nevertheless, *event* could not be updated or deleted because we cannot change what has happened before.

4 Supply Chain Scenario Illustration

Supply chain is considered as a specific form of collaborative network. It is a stable long-term network of enterprises each having clear roles in the value chain, covering all steps from initial product design and the procurement of raw materials, through production, shipping, distribution, and warehousing until a finished product is delivered to a customer [26].

In order to further illustrate the proposed DRC chain, three use cases of the supply chain scenario (presented in Fig. 5) would be given to be used to perform the progress of current work. Two partners are involved in this simple scenario: the *core enterprise* is the demand side, which submits orders to buy its required materials from the *suppliers*. Furthermore, the three use cases are described as follows:

- The first use case: Labor strike of suppliers is a *danger* for the core enterprise (a *stake*), because it would create the *risk* of the shortage of its required products. If the production disruption (an *event*) happens, the *risk* could be triggered. Then the *consequence* of overdue delivery cannot be avoided.
- The second use case: Shortage of products required by the core enterprise is a *danger* for the supplier who provides them (a *stake*). The *risk* is that the core enterprise might give a negative feedback in the evaluation of this supplier, and the *risk* occurs if overdue delivery from the supplier (an *event*) happens for several times. The core enterprise might consider to change the supplier to ensure its normal operation of business (a *consequence*).
- The third use case: Overdue delivery of supplier for long time is a *danger* for the core enterprise (a *stake*). It would create a *risk* that the core enterprise has to change the supplier. If many negative comments from the evaluation of the supplier (an *event*) are given to the decision-maker, the *risk* could be triggered. Consequently, the core enterprise needs to reselect the other suppliers to replace the tasks of the original supplier as soon as possible (a *consequence*).

By comparing with the three use cases (presented in Fig. 5) and referring to the *cascading effect* in DRC chain (presented in Fig. 3), it can be seen that a target or outcome in one situation could be the causal source to connect another situation. Accordingly, several interconnections could be concluded:

- *Consequence-danger* and *Consequence-event*: The *consequence* of overdue delivery in the first use case could create a *danger* in the third use case (see connection (1)), and also create an *event* in the second use case (see connection (3)).
- *Risk-danger*: The *risk* of shortage of required products in the first use case could create a *danger* in the second use case (see connection (4)).
- *Risk-event*: The *risk* of negative evaluation in the second use case could create an *event* in the third use case (see connection (6)).

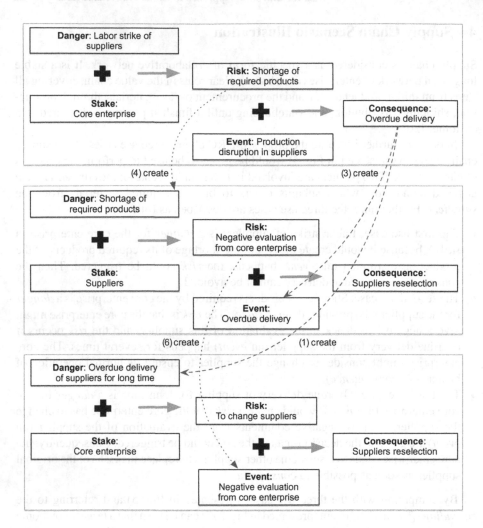

Fig. 5. Use cases illustration of supply chain scenario

5   Conclusion

The presented framework of risk identification approach might be considered as a formalizing reference dedicated to identify and mitigate risk in collaborative networks. The proposed approach is compliant with the schema of Danger/Risk/Consequence chain that helps to formalize the risk-related knowledge that includes five concepts (*danger, stake, risk, event* and *consequence*) and their interrelationships. Cascading effect could be indicated in DRC chain, which could contribute to a deeper understanding of risk-related collaborative contexts. Besides, the devised danger typology and stake typology can be further used to develop a risk knowledge base for risk identification of collaborative networks. Furthermore, the risk knowledge base combined with the current methodology of metamodeling could contribute to further explore the ways in which an effective mechanism that can motivate diverse partners in collaborative networks to manage risks collaboratively.

The future works would use System Dynamics [27] to develop the proposed approach, which focus on: (i) developing a danger typology and a stake typology by synthesizing the growing diverse literatures; (ii) the deduction of interconnection rules of dangers and stakes in order to build a risk knowledge base for collaborative networks; (iii) developing risk identification rules based on the risk knowledge base; (iv) metamodeling with risk knowledge base that can be dedicated to support collaboration of partners, and deduce the collaborative processes of risk mitigation.

Acknowledgments. The presented research works have been supported by "the Fundamental Research Funds for the Central Universities of China". The authors would like to thank the project partners for their advice and comments.

References

1. Camarinha-Matos, L.M., Afsarmanesh, H.: On reference models for collaborative networked organizations. Int. J. Prod. Res. **46**(9), 2453–2469 (2008)
2. Jamshidi, A., Abbasgholizadeh Rahimi, S., Ait-kadi, D., Ruiz, A.: A new decision support tool for dynamic risks analysis in collaborative networks. In: Camarinha-Matos, L.M., Bénaben, F., Picard, W. (eds.) PRO-VE 2015. IFIPAICT, vol. 463, pp. 53–62. Springer, Cham (2015). https://doi.org/10.1007/978-3-319-24141-8_5
3. Wulan, M., Petrovic, D.: A fuzzy logic based system for risk analysis and evaluation within enterprise collaborations. Comput. Ind. **63**(8), 739–748 (2012)
4. Rao, S., Goldsby, T.J.: Supply chain risks: a review and typology. Int. J. Logist. Manag. **20**(1), 97–123 (2009)
5. Juttner, U., Peck, H., Christopher, M.: Supply chain risk management – outlining an agenda for future research. Int. J. Logist. Res. Appl. **6**(4), 197–210 (2003)
6. Zeng, B., Yen, P.C.: Rethinking the role of partnerships in global supply chains: a risk-based perspective. Int. J. Prod. Econ. **185**, 52–62 (2017)
7. Bénaben, F., Barthe-Delanoë, A.-M., Lauras, M., Truptil, S.: Collaborative systems in crisis management: a proposal for a conceptual framework. In: Camarinha-Matos, L.M., Afsarmanesh, H. (eds.) PRO-VE 2014. IFIPAICT, vol. 434, pp. 396–405. Springer, Heidelberg (2014). https://doi.org/10.1007/978-3-662-44745-1_39
8. Vesely, W.E., Goldberg, F.F., Roberts, N.H., Haasl, D.F.: Fault Tree Handbook. Office of Nuclear Regulatory Research (1981)
9. Turoff, M., Bañuls, V.A., Plotnick, L., Hiltz, S.R., Huerga, M.R.D.L.: A collaborative dynamic scenario model for the interaction of critical infrastructures. Futures **84**, 23–42 (2016)
10. Bénaben, F., Lauras, M., Truptil, S., Salatge, N.: A metamodel for knowledge management in crisis management. In: Hawaii International Conference on System Sciences, pp. 126–135. IEEE Computer Society (2016)
11. Lauras, M., Bénaben, F., Truptil, S., Lamothe, J., Macé-Ramète, G., Montarnal, A.: A meta-ontology for knowledge acquisition and exploitation of collaborative social systems. In: International Conference on Behavior, Economic and Social Computing, pp. 1–7. IEEE (2015)

12. Edwards, P.J., Bowen, P.A.: Risk Management in Project Organisations. Elsevier, Oxford (2005)
13. Rosas, J., Urze, P., Tenera, A., Abreu, A., Camarinha-Matos, L.M.: Exploratory study on risk management in open innovation. In: Camarinha-Matos, L.M., Afsarmanesh, H., Fornasiero, R. (eds.) PRO-VE 2017. IFIPAICT, vol. 506, pp. 527–540. Springer, Cham (2017). https://doi.org/10.1007/978-3-319-65151-4_47
14. Fang, C., Marle, F., Zio, E., Bocquet, J.C.: Network theory-based analysis of risk interactions in large engineering projects. Reliab. Eng. Syst. Saf. 106(2), 1–10 (2012)
15. Yang, R.J., Zou, P.: Stakeholder-associated risks and their interactions in complex green building projects: a social network model. Build. Environ. 73(1), 208–222 (2014)
16. Zhang, X., Yang, Y., Su, J.: Risk identification and evaluation of customer collaboration in product development. J. Ind. Eng. Manag. 8(3), 928–942 (2015)
17. Yang, R.J., Zou, P.X.W., Wang, J.: Modelling stakeholder-associated risk networks in green building projects. Int. J. Proj. Manag. 34(1), 66–81 (2016)
18. Zhao, G., Liu, S., Lopez, C.: A literature review on risk sources and resilience factors in agri-food supply chains. In: Camarinha-Matos, L.M., Afsarmanesh, H., Fornasiero, R. (eds.) PRO-VE 2017. IFIPAICT, vol. 506, pp. 739–752. Springer, Cham (2017). https://doi.org/10.1007/978-3-319-65151-4_66
19. Wang, X., Xia, N., Zhang, Z., Wu, C., Liu, B.: Human safety risks and their interactions in china's subways: stakeholder perspectives. J. Manag. Eng. 33, 5 (2017)
20. Scott, J.: Social Network Analysis: A Handbook. Sage, Thousand Oaks (2000)
21. Zhou, X., Lu, M.: Risk evaluation of dynamic alliance based on fuzzy analytic network process and fuzzy TOPSIS. J. Serv. Sci. Manag. 05(3), 230–240 (2012)
22. ISO 3864-2, Technical Committee, ISO/TC 145/SC 2, Graphical symbols - Safety colours and safety signs (2016)
23. ISO 41011, Technical Committee, ISO/TC 267, Facility management – Vocabulary (2017)
24. Lahmar, A., Galasso, F., Chabchoub, H., Lamothe, J.: Towards an integrated model of supply chain risks: an alignment between supply chain characteristics and risk dimensions. In: Camarinha-Matos, L.M., Bénaben, F., Picard, W. (eds.) PRO-VE 2015. IFIPAICT, vol. 463, pp. 3–16. Springer, Cham (2015). https://doi.org/10.1007/978-3-319-24141-8_1
25. Cascade Effect: A Dictionary of Ecology. Encyclopedia.com
26. Camarinha-Matos, L.M., Afsarmanesh, H., Galeano, N., Molina, A.: Collaborative networked organization-concepts and practice in manufacturing enterprises. Comput. Ind. Eng. 57(1), 46–60 (2009)
27. Forrester, J.: System dynamics, systems thinking, and soft OR. Syst. Dyn. Rev. 10(2–3), 245–256 (1994)

A Framework to Navigate the Privacy Trade-offs for Human-Centred Manufacturing

Sobah Abbas Petersen, Felix Mannhardt[(✉)], Manuel Oliveira, and Hans Torvatn

SINTEF Digital, Trondheim, Norway
{sobah.petersen,felix.mannhardt,manuel.oliveira,
Hans.torvatn}@sintef.no

Abstract. New technological advances can offer personalised and timely services for industry workers. Exoskeletons, HoloLens, Process Mining and Social Knowledge Networks are some of these services offered to workers by the EU HuMan project. These services could alleviate a worker's physical stress, their cognitive load or provide help based on the knowledge and experiences of their peers. The successful application of several such services depends on the availability of data about a worker's state, including their performance. This paper focusses on the design of cognitive systems that provide personalised services while respecting a worker's privacy and the needs of an organisation. We present a framework for supporting privacy by design and the risks, threats and needs of users, organisations and developers.

Keywords: Privacy · Trust · Manufacturing · Real-time support
Human centred

1 Introduction

Privacy has been defined as "the right to be left alone" [1]. It is a concept that has sparked many discussions in several domains. In 1890, Warren and Brandeis wrote an article in the Harvard Law Review, which was one of the most influential essays in the history of American Law. Privacy was considered from the perspective of a human being, e.g. if they are pursued, bothered or harmed by others. A broader perspective of affecting a human being beyond physical harm was also considered, such as if their feelings were affected or someone's private life was invaded. As we are well aware, these continue to be concerns of privacy even today.

The focus of privacy has been on the protection of data pertaining to a person; i.e. protection of personal information with an emphasis on data security and methods, frameworks and techniques for ensuring appropriate data security. However, in the age of ubiquitous computing and social networks, such a data-centric view that disregards the influence of human factors is inadequate and the need for a more person-centric view of privacy is required, e.g. [2]. In fact, with increasing accessibility to data and the technology to aggregate data and conduct sophisticated analyses at workplaces, the need to protect the data and the privacy of individuals is more important than ever

© IFIP International Federation for Information Processing 2018
Published by Springer Nature Switzerland AG 2018. All Rights Reserved
L. M. Camarinha-Matos et al. (Eds.): PRO-VE 2018, IFIP AICT 534, pp. 85–97, 2018.
https://doi.org/10.1007/978-3-319-99127-6_8

before. The area of Human Factors and Ergonomics (HFE) has focused on safety and security at the workplace, part of which is also data security; e.g. [3].

In Industry 4.0, the use of smart technologies and sensors are seen as the future of manufacturing [4]. Tomorrow's factories [5] will leverage on new and emerging technologies and digital solutions to enhance collaboration not only among the workers, but also between the human workers and technology – Human in the Loop (HITL). Technologies such as exoskeletons and other wearables promise collaboration networks between humans and technology, leading to improved health and safety at the workplace [6] and reduced physiological load. Combined with sophisticated analytics and insights, cognitive systems are developed to provide timely and relevant support to workers. Similarly, other types of technologies, such as Augmented Reality, support workers with cognitive load minimisation and performance improvement [7]. Collaborative and cognitive networks include different types of technologies, such as social and cognitive assistive technologies, enhanced data collection and potential risks for privacy and data security [3].

The attention to the privacy protection of individuals at their workplaces or in society has been a priority of many countries, the most recent of which is the European Union's General Data Protection Regulation (GDPR). GDPR defines personal data as "any information relating to an identified or identifiable natural person (data subject)". Methods such as data anonymisation or pseudonymising needs rethinking, to ensure that personal data is processed with the aim to irreversibly prevent the identification of the individual to whom the data relates to. The GDPR provides new rights to the data subjects where they now have control of their data, improving data transparency and empowerment of data subjects [10]. It focuses on the protection of personal data and not only on the privacy of personal data, increasing the need to be clear about who has access to data and how data is used. To achieve this, it is also important that the data provider trusts the data receiver to not misuse the data. Data privacy, thus, goes beyond technological solutions into the softer aspects of an organisation, such as the individual's trust in the organisation in the use of the collated data. This would mean that trusting employees would give their consent to the organisation to collect, store and process their personal data [11]. Consciously working to deliver value in exchange for personal data that is collected and highlighting and communicating the benefits to the employees can foster trust.

The introduction of GDPR raises awareness among employees, organisations and technology developers on protecting employees by protecting their personal data. At the same time, we have become used to the personalised services that are on offer, such as the personalised recommendations through online systems, often oblivious to the fact that it is the personal data collected through our digital footprint that has facilitated such services. This inconsistency between privacy attitudes and privacy behaviour of individuals is coined the privacy paradox [8].

The aim of this paper is to draw attention to the privacy concerns of operators in the manufacturing industry and support developers of technologies to adopt privacy by design as their default practice. The main research focus is on the revelations about GDPR concerns and identifying the risks, threats, and needs perceived by users and developers when dealing with the privacy-personalisation trade-offs in cognitive systems. We do this by presenting a framework for Trust and Privacy design, developed within the context of the EU H2020 HuMan [9] project. The main research activities that contributed to the HuMan Trust and Privacy Framework (TPF) were a literature review of Privacy and Trust models, a workshop with the use case partners in the HuMan project and the analysis of GDPR. The HuMan TPF was then presented to the project consortium and a second workshop was held with the end-user companies and the technology developers. This paper reports the outcomes of both these workshops from the two perspectives of both the users and the developers.

This paper is structured as follows: Sect. 2 describes the HuMan project and some of the HuMan services; Sect. 3; describes the HuMan TPF; Sect. 4 presents and overview of the users' perspectives; Sect. 5 provides an overview of the developers' perspectives; Sect. 6 presents the feedback on the framework and finally Sect. 7 summarises the paper.

2 HuMAN Project

The EU H2020 HuMAN project aims to digitally enhance the operator on the shopfloor to support them in their work, assisting them in mitigating any productivity losses resulting from both physical and cognitive fatigue whilst contributing to greater well-being. Towards this goal, the cognitive system envisioned in HuMan captures physiological data from the operator (through wearable sensors), is aware of the production context (e.g. tasks, workplace) in which the operator is embedded and uses data analytics on historical data to provide timely and contextualised support for operators. The HuMan cognitive system monitors these data streams and is able to determine when an intervention is needed, for example, due to an increased stress level that was detected for an operator. The HuMan system is organised as several loosely coupled services that exchange and consume data through a shared middleware (event bus) provided by the HuMan core solution. The data that is exchanged may be used directly in a real-time fashion or is stored for later analysis. An example for the direct usage of data is the automatic detection of whether there is need for an intervention. An example for indirect usage is the improvement of work places or work processes by analysing aggregated historical data. Some of the services that are developed in the HuMan project are Exoskeleton (EXOS), Shopfloor Insight Intelligence (SII) and Social Knowledge Network (SKN).

The EXOS service is coupled to a light-weight exoskeleton that an operator wears to distribute the physical stress on their body, reducing the likelihood of injury and allowing the operator to maintain their optimal performance levels. The HuMan solution monitors the different physiological signals, such as heart rate and galvanic skin response, to determine the onset of fatigue and thereby activate the exoskeleton. The service then adjusts the level of support in proportion to the level of physical stress until operational parameters have exceeded and the operator is advised to take a rest, as the device is unable to further assist them. EXOS monitors physiological data which may be correlated to the operator's performance to provide real-time support.

The SKN service leverages on the collective knowledge and experience of peers by using ideas from social computing and captures and stores media directly related to an operator's activity. In addition, the level of engagement and how the operator contributes to the curation of knowledge can be assessed. The SKN service uses stored data, particularly captured via Social Networks.

The SII is one of the data analytics component of the HuMan system and relies on the captured data from other services. It combines data from several sources into a coherent event log and applies process mining methods to reveal what actually happened on the shop-floor [12]. Based on aggregated data as well as individual executions of work processes, the SII aims to reveal and help identifying root causes for recurring physical and cognitive stress that cannot be alleviated automatically by the available intervention measures of the HuMan system.

3   HuMan Privacy and Trust Framework

In the HuMan project, we have developed a Trust and Privacy Framework to increase awareness of privacy and trust issues among individuals and to support developers in achieving privacy by design. Several models of Privacy in the literature emphasise the relevance of the flow of information or data (e.g. [13, 14]), the use information or data (e.g. [15, 16]) and the visibility or who has access to personal data (e.g. [17]). Trust models from literature draw attention to the role of the "trustor" and "trustee" and the interaction between them [18], and how trust may be learned or built over time or from situational cues [19]. Dimensions of trust identified in the literature include the trust in the device or the technology used, in how the data is dealt with and the trust in the whole system, e.g. the whole HuMan system including the technologies, services, organisations and people [20]. Most frameworks that address trust and privacy look at online systems and trust in the system. In the context of HuMan, there is a strong emphasis of trust beyond the system, but in the organisation and among individuals. Privacy networks identify the receiver of the information and the type of information shared as important precisely because a person may share some information with people they trust, but not with ones they don't trust and this central idea has influenced the design of our framework. In addition, the literature and guidelines available on complying with the GDPR regulations draw attention to transitions in the use of data such as when storing data or transferring the data from one place to another.

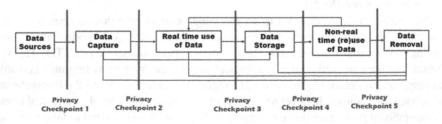

Fig. 1. HuMan trust and privacy framework

Drawing from these, we can see the relevance of analysing the data element and its lifecycle as it flows through the system, to determining how to design for privacy. The privacy requirements depend on what you do with the data and who does what. Hence, depending on what the HuMan system or the service does with which data, the privacy design has implications. Thus, we have analysed a data element, from the source and the capture of the data to the end of its lifecycle, illustrated in Fig. 1. We have examined closely what happens when data transitions from one phase to another, and the implications for ensuring privacy across each of the transitions. We have called these Privacy Checkpoints. An early version of the framework was presented in [21].

3.1 Privacy Checkpoints

The Privacy checkpoints provide guidelines for designers and developers to take the necessary precautions and actions for ensuring IT systems and services that protect privacy of individuals and organisations, and foster trust among the workers and in the organisation. The Privacy Checkpoints and how they can support the design of privacy through the data transitions are explained in the following paragraphs. Detailed guidelines have been developed for each checkpoint and we refer to examples of these in Sect. 3.2.

Privacy Checkpoint 1 – enhances awareness of specific things that need to be ensured every time a data element is captured by any means. The data originates at a source, which may be a workplace, a human worker, or other; e.g. environment. Data may be captured from any source, by a variety of ways. Data may be captured without the source being aware of it or with the consent of the source, automatically by technology (e.g. sensors or cameras) or manually.

Privacy Checkpoint 2 – helps to identify the guidelines that are relevant for the real-time or near real-time use of data (e.g. to provide support to a worker or to provide personalised and timely feedback), store data without being used real-time or removed from the system.

Privacy Checkpoint 3 – identifies the guidelines that are relevant when storing data and for ensuring the security of the stored data. If the data is stored, it may be used for a different purpose. Data storage requires attention in many ways such as informing the data subject and obtaining consent, how long it will be stored for and who may have access to it. Most importantly, the anonymisation and indeed ensuring that the data source or data subject cannot be identified through the data. Particularly, the abundance of third party data storage services, such as the cloud-based storage services, has called for increased awareness of privacy and data security issues.

Privacy Checkpoint 4 – provides guidelines when stored data is used. Stored data may be used as single data elements or/and aggregated with other data elements, perhaps from different sources, to make sense of various contexts and situations. Use of stored data calls for a careful evaluation of what data is used, how, for what purpose and by whom, to ensure privacy and to foster trust in the organisation(s) that collect, use and store the data.

Privacy Checkpoint 5 – provides guidelines on how data should be removed from a system. Data may be removed due to various reasons; e.g. by someone, it may have expired or be ported to another storage system. An important criterion when data is captured or stored is to obtain consent, which encompasses many dimensions such as for how long a data element can be kept in storage. As such, a data element may have a date that determines when the data is not valid any more (or expires) or should be deleted from the system. Deletion or removal of a data element has requirements beyond just deleting data element as to respect privacy; it means all traces of that data element and its links to other entities must also be removed.

As seen from Fig. 1, every single data element does not always follow the complete sequence or all the transitions that have been identified for the lifecycle. For example, the data may be stored with being used real-time or the data may be removed at any point in the lifecycle of a data element; it may be deleted right after it's captured, after real-time use, after storing and without reuse or at any time while it's in storage. Thus, the Privacy Checkpoints provide awareness and guidelines for developers that should be followed prior to any activity on the data; e.g. Privacy Checkpoint 1 applies before any data is captured and similarly, Privacy Checkpoint 5 applies before any data is removed. So, independent of when the data is removed (e.g. after capture or from storage), the guidelines should be considered.

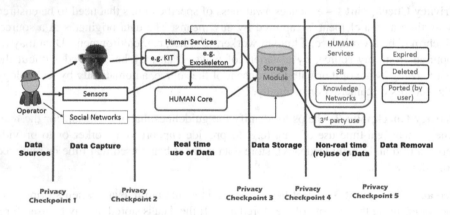

Fig. 2. HuMan TPF and services

3.2 Applying the Framework to HuMan Services

The HuMan cognitive system and the services address personal data through all the transitions that are captured in the HuMan TPF, illustrated in Fig. 2. We will focus on two of the services to illustrate the diversity of the type of data the HuMan services require and how the HuMan TPF could be used to support privacy by design.

The Exoskeleton service captures and uses collated data related to a worker's performance of a physical task and physiological conditions and provide real-time support. Physiological data about a worker performing a physical task are captured and monitored to determine if the worker is tired or experiencing physical exertion. Based on the condition of the worker, the exoskeleton intervenes to provide appropriate and timely support for the worker. In this service, real-time data is captured and used real-time. Thus, the guidelines presented in the Privacy Checkpoints 1 and 2 should be considered; e.g. inform the user of data capture, obtain consent, etc. If data is deleted after the work shift, guidelines presented in the Privacy Checkpoint 5 are relevant; but Checkpoints 3 and 4 are not relevant. If the data is stored for secondary use, the guidelines presented in the Privacy Checkpoints 3 and 4 are relevant; e.g. inform the user, obtain consent, ensure data security, etc.

The data that is captured may be stored and used in various ways for supporting workers or improving organisational processes at a later time. This may be done by using single data elements, aggregating data elements and sources, doing correlations or conducting other processes. The SII is a service that processes secondary data to gain insights into the workplace, by applying process mining methods. This framework was first presented in the context of process mining and the SII service in [21]. The guidelines presented in Privacy Checkpoint 4 are extremely important for the SII service; e.g. ensure that consent is obtained for secondary use of data, inform how data will be used, appropriate data security measures, ensure that an individual cannot be identified, etc. For example, a worker's performance against the shift information for the shop floor could help identify an individual. Thus, designing the right privacy in the light of how the data is used is of utmost importance. The HuMan TPF provides support to isolate the specific transitions that the data elements undergo and thus, helps to draw attention to the important and specific design issues at hand for any situation.

4   Threats, Opportunities and Needs: Users' Perspectives

The users were represented by either middle managers that understood the workers' and the organisation's perspectives and/or researchers working with them. The data presented in this section was collected from two separate events; the threats and opportunities workshop and the workshop where the HuMan TPF was used. In the threats and opportunities workshop, the data was gathered using post-it notes, on two large sheets of paper; one for threats and one for opportunities. For the workshop where the HuMan TPF was used, a list of risks was gathered on a large sheet of paper.

The threats and opportunities identified by the use case partners and others were diverse and spanned over several dimensions: e.g. individual/personal and organisational; internal (within the organisation), which could be among peers or between employer and employee, and external (or third parties, such as insurance companies or trade unions); technical and non-technical such as organisational processes or cultural and short and long term perspectives. An important observation was the perception of people and how the workers perceived their privacy and threats to them. This is no surprise as supported by the studies by Adam and Sasse (e.g. [16]). It has to do with their perceived value of the data and how it is used by the organisation. Interesting discussions took place on how things that are initially perceived as threats could be turned around to opportunities, by both technical and non-technical solutions. The discussions resulted in the identification of several opportunities and benefits that could be leveraged from data collection, as shown in Table 1.

Table 1. Users' perspectives: threats and opportunities of data collection

	Threats	Opportunities
Individual	• Misuse of data and information • Health and safety • Security • Vulnerability • Intrusion (by technology)	• Enhanced knowledge • Knowledge sharing • Accelerated learning and performance improvements • Personalised support and services • Recognition from others and the organisation • Benefits of new analyses of data
Organisation (within)	• Misuse of data and information • Data Security	• Process improvements • Benefits of new analyses of data • Proactive action • Improved company image
Organisation (external)	• Misuse of data by 3rd parties • Data Security	• Increased awareness in the unions on benefit of data collection

In addition to the explicit threats and opportunities, some of the contents from the workshops can be interpreted as needs which can be translated as technical and organisational requirements. These needs are summarised below:

- The workers would like to have control of their data; e.g. decide if they want the data to be collected and who has access to their data.
- The workers perception of the value of the data as well as risks associated with data collection need to be managed.
- The workers' concerns on how the data will be used by others and the organisation need to be managed. A major part of this is fostering and managing the trust between the worker and the organisation.
- The workers' feelings, attitudes and perceptions, which is related to cultural and social aspects. This also requires attention to trust building and managing trust.

The list of needs identified from the workshop where the HuMan TPF was used are listed below. In contrast to the above needs, references to the specific uses of the data and the transitions, e.g. capture, storage or deletion, possibly indicate the participants' awareness of privacy issues with regard to how the data may be treated and used.

- Choice of which information is recorded (captured) about them, before use and while the service is used.
- Pre-set privacy profiles for the different stages in the lifecycle, such as for storage, to ease them to select one from an existing set.
- Possibility to erase data.
- Clear distinction between personal/individual data and company data.
- It should not be possible to identify an individual by linking data.
- Data should only be used for the benefit of the user; not for managerial purposes.

5 Privacy by Design: Developers' Perspectives

The data from the developers were collected from the workshop where the HuMan TPF was used. The developers were split into three groups, ranging from 4-6 participants in each group. The groups were formed around the different HuMan services, e.g. the KIT, EXOS or SII. Their tasks were to identify the personal information the services require from workers or the workplace and to discuss solutions by actively practising privacy by design. They were asked to do this by using the HuMan TPF. They were provided a large printout of the framework, illustrated in Fig. 1.

There were a lot of concerns and discussions within the groups. There was a natural cause for concern as many of the HuMan services focus on personalised, timely support, which require personal information (e.g. physiological data) as well as the identification of the individual that receives the support. Solutions that comply with GDPR and meet the privacy and trust needs of the workers require careful attention and detailed insights into how the data will be treated.

Two of the groups used the printouts of the framework that were provided to make notes. The data capture phase focused on identifying the personal data as well as other data that were captured or used from sources other than the workers; e.g. task related data. For the EXOS service, personal data is captured from the exoskeleton as well as from a smart watch. For the real-time use of this data, there were discussions around which data elements were real-time and which were reused from storage and from the results of processing and analyses of other services such as the SII. These discussions raised awareness about the design of the consent from the user, how to make the data usage transparent to the user and how to provide the appropriate choices to the user. It also increased awareness of the design of the service in the case of limited consent from users; i.e. if and when some of the data were not available. This was a reason to address data minimisation and designing the services to be as effective as possible while respecting the GDPR requirement of data minimisation. Drawing attention to the real-time and secondary use of data encouraged developers to think of the data that is required real-time, perhaps for short-term reasoning. It stimulated discussions around which data is necessary to be stored for supporting long-term reasoning or other types of analyses. This may often require making trade-offs with data capturing and the benefits from the services. Awareness of such issues stimulated discussions around the design of consent, privacy settings and profiles.

One of the groups had noted "login" for all the Privacy Checkpoints, indicating that the user should be informed about the use of the data across all transitions and therefore the need for obtaining the appropriate consent from the user. When talking to the developers, it became evident that the login functionality by the user may not be trivial. There may be different use cases or scenarios where a user logs into the system; e.g. to perform work, using the EXOS service, or to look at the data that is stored to see how s/he performed after the work shift. Thus, from a usability perspective, the design of the consent, privacy profile and login functionality did not necessarily appear as discrete functionalities. Another point of discussion was the GDPR requirement on the right to be forgotten when a user requests his/her data to be removed from the system. Furthermore, there were a no. of other design related discussions, triggered both by the nature of the personal information and the personalised services as well as the data transitions and the potential multiple use of data, both real-time and secondary. A detailed discussion of these is beyond the scope of this paper.

6   Feedback on the Framework

After the HuMan Trust and Privacy workshop using the framework, which lasted 1.5 h, participants were asked to complete a short questionnaire, to obtain feedback about the HuMan TPF and the workshop itself. There were 18 respondents. The questionnaire included statements and the users were asked to indicate how much they agreed with the statements, using a likert scale (Strongly agree, Agree, Neither agree or disagree, Disagree and Strongly disagree). The responses to the 5 statements about the HuMan TPF are shown in Fig. 3.

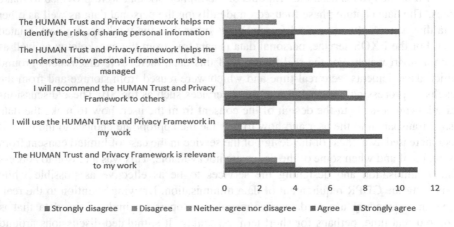

Fig. 3. Feedback on the framework

The feedback to the statements that the HuMan TPF is helpful are generally positive; i.e. most participants either agreed or strongly agreed to the statements. However, the responses to the two statements about using and the relevance of the HuMan TPF, indicate that more than half the participants strongly disagreed. For the statement "I will recommend the HuMan TPF to others", 7 out of 18 responded "neither agree nor disagree", but no one disagreed. A possible explanation for the negative results may be the short duration of the workshop and the lack of experience of the participants in using the HuMan TPF.

7 Summary and Future Work

The advent of industry 4.0, with its emphasis on smart factories, relies on the digitisation of the organisation where everything can be measured and tracked, including the human operator on the shopfloor. The advances of technology have opened up new opportunities in decision making and support based on the data that has become accessible. Along with such opportunities, one is faced with the many challenges associated rooted in the privacy paradox where the operator needs to assess what value is conveyed in exchange of loss of privacy.

It is precisely because of the concerns on how personal data is accessed, processed and utilised that has led to legislation on personal data protection, of which GDPR represents the most recent response from the EU to address the abuse and violations on the use of personal data with particular focus on the consumer. However, the difficulty of balancing the concerns associated to the privacy paradox is evidenced in the large number of service providers that are unable to comply with the new regulation and consequently have terminated their service entirely or block service access to Europeans.

The HuMan cognitive system relies on the capture and processing of personal data in order to provide best level of assistance of its services for the operator to carry out their work. To support handling the privacy paradox and encourage the trust of operators in the HuMan solution, a trust and privacy framework was developed. The purpose of the framework is to provide a structured approach to develop the HuMan solution by ensuring that one is aware of the different privacy checkpoints along the lifecycle of personal data, from the point of capture to the removal from the system. By providing a framework, a dialogue with different stakeholders within an organisation can be supported and the developers, all of whom may not be aware of the implications of collecting, processing and storing personal data. Not all the associated guidelines and recommendations have a direct impact on software being developed, with many addressing new processes that are required to be put in place by the organisation. In addition to the guidelines, the framework provides support to the analysis of risks, threats and needs from the users' perspectives.

The paper presented the HuMan TPF, which is being used within the HuMan project to support the developers to identify areas where design trade-offs may help to achieve privacy by design. Some of these trade-offs can be summarised as the value and benefit of the service vs. the data that is captured, the quality of the service vs. data minimisation, the level of control given to the user vs. transparency and flexibility and step-wise consent design vs. usability. The framework is used to facilitate a structured dialogue between the users and developers towards building a solution that delivers value with the users being in control of their personal data.

A workshop was organised to evaluate the HuMan TPF by both the end-user organisations and the development team. The discussions during the workshop and the results demonstrate that privacy by design still remains an afterthought by the development team, with very few being even aware of the concerns on privacy beyond having appropriate terms of service with consent, which in many cases would be implied and not explicit. This lack of understanding is no longer compatible with regulation initiatives such as GDPR, which is addressed by the HuMan TPF.

The feedback from using the framework in a workshop is described. Additional workshops are planned to include the operators and workers from the use case partner companies. The feedback will be used to see how the framework could be improved to support both users and developers. Future work will include using the framework actively to raise awareness and to design and develop both technology and organisational services to achieve privacy by design and comply with GDPR regulations.

Acknowledgements. This research is funded by the EU's H2020 research and innovation programme, grant agreement no. 723737 (HUMAN). We thank all participants of the trust and privacy workshops conducted within the context of the HuMan project.

References

1. Warren, S.D., Brandeis, L.D.: The right to privacy. Harv. Law Rev. **4**(5), 193–220 (1890)
2. Adams, A., Sasse, M.A.: Users are not the Enemy. Commun. ACM **42**(12), 40–46 (1999)
3. Carayon, P.: Human factors of complex sociotechnical systems. Appl. Ergonom. **37**(4), 525–535 (2006)
4. Thoben, K.-D., Weisner, S.A., Wuest, T.: "Industrie 4.0" and smart manufacturing–a review of research issues and application examples. Int. J. Autom. Technol. **11**(1), 4–19 (2017)
5. EFFRA European Factories of the Future Research Association, Factories 4.0 and Beyond: Recommendations for the work programme 18-19-20 of the FoF PPP under Horizon 2020 (2016)
6. Looze, M.P., et al.: Exoskeletons for industrial application and their potential effects on physical work load. Ergonomics **59**(5), 671–681 (2015)
7. Blattgerste, J., et al. Comparing conventional and augmented reality instructions for manual assembly tasks. In: PETRA 2017, Rhodes, Greece (2017)
8. Kokolakis, S.: Privacy attitudes and privacy behaviour: A review of current research on the privacy paradox phenomenon. Comput. Secur. **64**, 122–134 (2017)
9. HUMAN Project (2017). https://www.sintef.no/en/projects/human/. Accessed 1 May 2018
10. EU GDPR Portal. GDPR Key Changes: An overview of the main changes under GPDR and how they differ from the previous directive. https://www.eugdpr.org/key-changes.html. Accessed 23 Nov 2017
11. The Nordic Cognizant Blog - The Business Journal of Cognizant Nordic, GDPR is more than just rules - it's about trust
12. van der Aalst, W.M.P.: Process Mining - Data Science in Action, 2nd edn. Springer, Heidelberg (2016)
13. Nissenbaum, H.: Privacy in Context: Technology, Policy, and the Integrity of Social Life. Stanford University Press, Stanford (2010)
14. Ziegeldorf, J.H., Morchon, O.G., Wehrle, K.: Privacy in the Internet of Things: threats and challenges. Secur. Commun. Netw. **7**(12), 2728–2742 (2014)
15. Solove, D.J.: A taxonomy of privacy. Univ. PA Law Rev. **154**(3), 477–560 (2006)
16. Adams, A., Sasse, M.A.: Privacy in multimedia communications: protecting users, not just data. In: Blandford, A., Vanderdonckt, J., Gray, P. (Eds) People and Computers XV—Interaction without Frontiers (Joint Proceedings of HCI 2001 and IHM 2001), pp. 49–64. Springer, London (2001)

17. Barker, K., et al.: A data privacy taxonomy. In: Sexton, A.P. (ed.) BNCOD 2009. LNCS, vol. 5588, pp. 42–54. Springer, Heidelberg (2009). https://doi.org/10.1007/978-3-642-02843-4_7
18. Riegelsberger, J., Sasse, M.A., McCarthy, J.D.: The mechanics of trust: a framework for research and design. Int. J. Hum.-Comput. Stud. **62**(3), 381–422 (2005)
19. Dibben, M.R., Morris, S.E., Lean, M.E.J.: Situational trust and co-operative partnerships between physicians and their patients: a theoretical explanation transferable from business practice. QJM: Int. J. Med. **93**(1), 55–61 (2000)
20. Daubert, J., Wiesmaier, A, Kikiras, P.: A view on privacy & trust in IoT. In: IEEE ICC workshop on security and privacy for Internet of Things and cyber-physical systems. IEEE (2015)
21. Mannhardt, F., Petersen, S.A., Oliveira, M.:. Privacy challenges for process mining in human-centered industrial environments. In: Intelligent Environments. Springer, Rome (2018)

Cognitive Systems for Resilience Management

Optimizing Humanitarian Aids: Formulating Influencer Advertisement in Social Networks

Nastaran Hajiheydari$^{(\boxtimes)}$, Masoud Salehi, and Arman Goudarzi

Faculty of Management, University of Tehran, Tehran, Iran
{nhheidari,masuod.salehi,goodarzi_arman}@ut.ac.ir

Abstract. In order to solve problems encountered during natural disasters, in addition to NGOs and relief teams, various individuals intend to help the injured. Although the cooperation of people has remarkable advantages, the disparity between the needs of the injured and the people's donations can cause problems such as trouble for relief teams and wasting the substantial resources. In generic, the influencer selection in the marketing endeavors is mainly aimed to maximize people's awareness and attention, but this research proposes a method for influencer selection, using Social Network Analysis (SNA) and optimization techniques, by which it is possible to establish an adaptation between the public attention and the type of injured necessities. The proposed method is applied to a real sample network of Facebook friends, to evaluate the efficiency and validity of the formulated method.

Keywords: Disaster management · Humanitarian Aid · Advertisement
Influencer selection · Social Network Analysis · Optimization
Influence maximization

1 Introduction

Natural disasters always have been one of the human concerns. The statistics show that between 1980 and 2004 two million people were killed and 5 billion people affected by natural disasters in total [1]. To solve the problems encountered during natural disasters, various people and organizations such as local and International Humanitarian Organizations (IHO), government and military get involved in helping the injured [2, 3]. Meanwhile, the benevolent people are also willing to contribute to solving the problems by providing different kinds of donations. This cooperation alongside its various benefits, can increases the complexity of coordination and implementation of disaster relief programs, especially when donations be unsolicited [2, 4]. This unrequested supplies and donations can cause troubles such as waste relief teams' time, resources, congest the relief chain and create bottlenecks [5]. On the other hand, previous researches have emphasized the role of media attention on increasing these issues [2, 3]. It has been explained that increasing media attention will increase unsolicited donations and consequently, the problems created for relief teams will be intensified [2]. Also, it is completely significant for donors to perceive that their donations are used in a way that has the greatest possible benefit for the injured [2]. In fact, donors are somehow the customers of relief organizations and thereupon, they

© IFIP International Federation for Information Processing 2018
Published by Springer Nature Switzerland AG 2018. All Rights Reserved
L. M. Camarinha-Matos et al. (Eds.): PRO-VE 2018, IFIP AICT 534, pp. 101–110, 2018.
https://doi.org/10.1007/978-3-319-99127-6_9

must be satisfied to continue their co-operation [4]. Besides, it is proven that the media's attention, especially online social networks, can be used as a powerful platform to attract more donations [4, 6]. For example, After the Haiti earthquake during 48 h Red Cross received around 8 million dollars of charity through people's texts in social media [7].

The role and importance of social media in attracting help and donations in one side and the obstacles of receiving undemand aids on the other hand, highlights the need for managing and directing the media attention in the event of natural disasters. This research aims to propose a method for influencer selection, using the Social Network Analysis (SNA) and optimization techniques, through which it would be possible to establish an adaptation between the public attention in social media and the type of injured necessities. In this way, current research would come up with a solution to prevent mentioned problems in relief programs. In this paper, Influencer refers to individuals who have some personal or network desirable attributes such as expertise, credibility, and connectivity enabling them to persuade people in their network [8]. Influencers can shape others attitudes by their power of authenticity and reach [9].

2 Social Media in Disaster Relief Management

With the development of online social networks, a variety of applications of these networks for disaster relief management also are emerged. Crisis management organizations, are using data extracted from social networks to determine where aid are needed and to broadcast their own needs [10]. As instance, Ushahidi (www.Ushahidi.com) is an open source platform providing crisis map to show the different needs of injured by their locations [7]. A great deal of research has been made in this regard. A survey showed that Twitter activity after a hurricane has a strong correlation with per-capita economic damages, and it suggested that the online social networks could be used for rapid assessment of damage caused by a large-scale natural disaster [11]. Based on Zhu et al. (2011) the understanding of the factors that influence the behavior of Twitter users in retweeting tweets on natural disasters will make it easier for disaster managers to choose optimal messages to propagate in the network. In other words, they focused on how to choose the best content to speed up the information propounding the disaster to help injured [12]. In a comprehensive review, Landwehr et al. (2014) divided the social network analysis and efforts in crisis management into four categories, keyword-based labeling, crowdsourcing-based labeling, sentiment based labeling and network analysis for relevance [10]. Based on literature analysis, the social media have been considered as an influential channel to engage people and donors in crisis management during natural disasters.

3 Method

In order to develop a method for influencer selection, using the Social Network Analysis (SNA) and optimization techniques to choose the best set of influencers in a complex network is necessary. In this way, an adaption between actual injured needs and public awareness of each kind of the needs through an online social network would be possible. This will be done in three subsections: in the first step, the diffusion model of a message through a social network is discussed. In the second subsection, our subject is differentiated from a typical influence maximization problem and then the problem is formulated to obtain the cost function. And finally in the last section, the optimization algorithm to make the adaptation is applied.

3.1 Diffusion Model

As discussed, a social network can be a powerful tool for spreading information among individuals. So far, many scholars have studied the information diffusion model in a social network [13], including researches on the diffusion process in "word of mouth" [14] and "viral marketing" [15]. Influence maximization is also considered as an attractive topic of research in the marketing field, which researchers are trying to maximize the distribution of a message on a network by finding the most influential nodes [16–19]. Meanwhile, David Kempe et al. (2003) formulated this issue by presenting two stochastic diffusion models [17], which have become a basis for many researchers in this field [16]. In this paper, one of Kempe et al. (2003) diffusion models, called Independent Cascade, is used as the basis for our model.

Let's assume $G = (N, E)$ as a directed social network where N represents the set of nodes (individuals) and E represents set of edges (relationships between individuals). In this network, each node is considered as being active or inactive (active nodes have received the message). Now we start with a set of initial active nodes A_0. In the first step $t = 0$ each active node like V has a single chance to activate its inactive neighbor W, with probability P_{VW}. At the end of this step if any of the active nodes succeed to activate any of its neighbors, diffusion process will continue in the step $t = 1$ with the set of newly activated nodes A_1, otherwise the entire diffusion process model will be stopped. It should be noted that in this case, each node could only activate the neighbors who follow him (followers), and can be activated by his neighbors whom he follows (following). Therefore, it is necessary to consider the direction of the edges. For example in Fig. 1, node V can be activated by node Y with probability P_{YV} and can activate node W and U respectively with probability P_{VW} and P_{VU}.

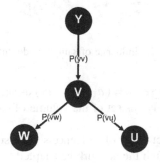

Fig. 1. A sample graph with 4 nodes

In this paper, a real data set of 347 friends on Facebook is utilized to test and run algorithms. This data set is free and available on www.snap.stanford.edu/data.

3.2 Formulating Problem

Again, let's assume $G = (N, E)$ as our network where $N = (n_1 \quad \cdots \quad n_i)$ represents set of nodes. In this network, each node like Y can activate all other nodes in t steps with different probabilities. For example in Fig. 1, Y can activate W in two steps with probability $P_{YW} = P_{YV}.P_{VW}$. In this way, matrix G_P illustrates the chance of each node to activate any other one.

$$G_P = \begin{matrix} & \begin{matrix} n_1 & n_2 & \cdots & n_i \end{matrix} \\ \begin{matrix} n_1 \\ n_2 \\ \vdots \\ n_i \end{matrix} & \begin{bmatrix} P_{n_1 n_1} & P_{n_1 n_2} & \cdots & P_{n_1 n_i} \\ P_{n_2 n_1} & P_{n_2 n_2} & & P_{n_2 n_i} \\ \vdots & & \ddots & \vdots \\ P_{n_i n_1} & P_{n_i n_2} & \cdots & P_{n_i n_i} \end{bmatrix} \end{matrix} \tag{1}$$

Figure 2 represents an example of the probability of activating other nodes by initially activated node n_{56} in the network of Facebook friends.

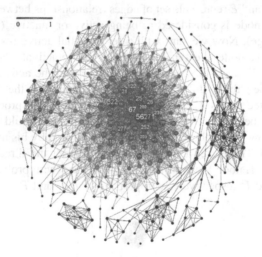

Fig. 2. Influence of sample node "n56"

Now we need to consider set $A = (a_1 \quad \cdots \quad a_j)$ as set of different needs of injured (items), and $V = (v_1 \quad \cdots \quad v_j)$ as set of the volume of each item, which is estimated by relief teams.

The objective is to select a set of influencers S in such a way that the level of awareness of each item through the network be adapted to the volume of actual needs.

$$S = \begin{pmatrix} n_{a_1} & n_{a_2} & \cdots & n_{a_j} \end{pmatrix} \qquad (2)$$

In above set of influencers, each element like n_{a_1}, represents the influencer who is in charge for influence item a_1. As argued, each influencer (each node) can activate all other nodes, so it is considered that there is a possibility for all nodes to donate any item. Matrix G_A represents this issue:

$$G_A = \begin{matrix} & \begin{matrix} n_1 & n_2 & \cdots & n_i \end{matrix} \\ \begin{matrix} n_{a_1} \\ n_{a_2} \\ \vdots \\ n_{a_j} \end{matrix} & \begin{bmatrix} P_{n_{a_1} n_1} & P_{n_{a_1} n_2} & \cdots & P_{n_{a_1} n_i} \\ P_{n_{a_2} n_1} & P_{n_{a_2} n_2} & & P_{n_{a_2} n_i} \\ \vdots & & \ddots & \vdots \\ P_{n_{a_j} n_1} & P_{n_{a_j} n_2} & \cdots & P_{n_{a_j} n_i} \end{bmatrix} \end{matrix} , \; j \le i \qquad (3)$$

In above matrix, $P_{n_{a_1} n_1}$ is the probability for n_1 to be activated by n_{a_1} regardless to the presence of other influencers. But n_1 can be activated by other influencers as well. It means that the influence boundaries of influencers may overlap in some nodes. So, the probability that n_1 will be going to donate a_1 in presence of other influencers, is calculated as below:

$$P_{a_1 n_1} = P_{(n_1 \text{ be activated})} . P_{(n_1 \text{ choose } a_1)} \qquad (4)$$

$$P_{(n_1 \text{ be activated})} = 1 - \prod \left(1 - P_{n_{a_j} n_1} \right) \qquad (5)$$

$$P_{(n_1 \text{ choose } a_1)} = \frac{P_{n_{a_1} n_1}}{\sum P_{n_{a_j} n_1}} \qquad (6)$$

By repeating the above for all nodes, it is possible to calculate the probability for each node who will donate a_1 in presence of other influencers. These calculations can be again repeated for other items to obtain matrix GD.

$$GD = \begin{matrix} & \begin{matrix} n_1 & n_2 & \cdots & n_i \end{matrix} \\ \begin{matrix} a_1 \\ a_2 \\ \vdots \\ a_j \end{matrix} & \begin{bmatrix} P_{a_1 n_1} & P_{a_1 n_2} & \cdots & P_{a_1 n_i} \\ P_{a_2 n_1} & P_{a_2 n_2} & & P_{a_2 n_i} \\ \vdots & & \ddots & \vdots \\ P_{a_j n_1} & P_{a_j n_2} & \cdots & P_{a_j n_i} \end{bmatrix} \end{matrix} , \; j \le i \qquad (7)$$

$$P_{(\text{Total probability of donating } a_j)} = \sum_1^i P_{a_j n_i} \qquad (8)$$

To clarify the difference between this matrix and the previous one, it should be noted that in the previous matrix the effect of the presence of other influencers was not taken into account. So any change in influencer set S may cause a change in all elements of the matrix GD and consequently change in total probability for donating all items. Therefore, it is complicated to choose the best set of influencers in such a way that total probability of donating different needs in the network, adapt to the actual volume of each item. This issue necessitates deploying optimization algorithms in the next section.

3.3   Optimization Algorithm

The first step to solve an optimization problem is calculating the cost function. The cost function is defined as the distance from the current state to the optimal condition. Therefore, the more this function gets closer to zero, the more favorable the situation is. In this case, the favorable situation is the equality of the actual amount of demand per item with the total probability of donating that item. So, the cost function is as below:

$$CostFunction : \sum_{1}^{j} \left| v_j - \sum_{1}^{i} P_{a_j n_i} \right| \tag{9}$$

In above function, $V = (v_1 \cdots v_j)$ is the actual needed amount of each item, which is estimated by the relief teams. Now by employing an optimization algorithm, we can find the best set of influencers to minimize the difference between the actual need of an item and total probability for donating that item (minimizing cost function).

3.4   Quantum Genetic Algorithm (QGA)

This study deployed an evolutionary Genetic Algorithm, QGA, which is based on quantum computing and quantum theory concepts to minimize the cost function. Researchers have already shown a variety of positive features for this algorithm, including low computing time, powerful search capability and fast convergence [20].

Considering the complexity of the network of Facebook friends and the fact that the ID of the nodes in the dataset does not follow a particular order, which made the network more complicated, this algorithm, QGA, is used for optimization. For the initial random population, after several trials and errors, we have chosen 50 chromosomes and 100 iterations as it leads the results to an acceptable level of convergence and efficiency. Each chromosome contains 5 genes, which in this case represents a set of 5 influencers. So, each gen can get an integer number between 1 and 347 (Population).

4   Results

As explained, in solving influencer maximization problems, researchers are trying to select the most influential set of influencers, whereas, this research intended to solve another type of problem. Therefore, the result of this study is compared with two other methods of selecting the influencers. The first method is simple random selection, which can be considered as the result of decision making without having the network information (Random Selection). In the second method, the criteria for selecting influencers are the influential power of the individuals in the absence of the other influencers. It means that if we need the awareness of item a1 to be v1, we will simply choose the node with influential power equal to v1 (Fast Selection).

To compare the result of the methods, a set of 5 needs as $V = (10 \quad 30 \quad 14 \quad 23 \quad 8)$ is considered for the population of network = 347. So, 22.7 percent of the network needs to get activated, tailored to the needs. In Table 1, the results of the proposed method is compared with two other ones. We repeated QGA selection method 100 times to get better results and also to check the reliability of this method. Additionally, for the random selection method, 100 different sets of influencers have been chosen randomly. But regarding the fast selection method, only one set of influencers, which is the closest set based on the influential power to the set of injured needs V, was picked up.

Table 1. Results

Selection method	Results				
	Min. Cost	Average Cost	St. Dev.	RMSE	Efficiency
QGA Selection	1.013	3.585	1.744	3.99	95.78%
Fast Selection	14.089	14.089	0	14.098	83.42%
Random Selection	55.308	68.601	6.511	67.65	19.29%

In Table 1, the term Efficiency shows how much a method is successful to make the adaption between the awareness in the network and the set of injured necessities and is calculated as below:

$$Efficiency : 1 - \frac{Cost}{\sum_1^j V_j} \qquad (10)$$

Table 1 illustrates a significant 12.3% difference between the efficiency of QGA selection method and the Fast Selection method. This difference emphasizes the impact of presence of different influencers in the same network which can cause conflict of information diffusion boundaries.

4.1 Decision-Making Framework

Based on the aforementioned, it is assumed that each nodes could potentially be an influencer, therefore accessing and communication with them is not a serious problem. Therefore, in the results section, the algorithm only shows the best results. But in a more realistic approach in a network like G, some nodes may be not available or might be not willing to spread the information on the network. Therefore, the results of the current optimization may be inadequate for decision makers to choose the best set of influencers. In such circumstances, decision makers can check all network nodes in term of availability before running the algorithm. As checking the availability of all the nodes in a big network can take a long time, it is not recommended especially in crisis situations, Another solution is that decision makers be able to pass on to the next best answer in the case of unavailability of any of influencers in the first best set.

On the other hand, in disaster management, "time" is always a key factor. The relief teams estimation of the volume of different items is mainly time related. Therefore, their schedule to expand awareness of the necessities through the network has some time boundaries. To formulate our problem, it is considered that each node's diffusion process is reached to its final state and cannot extend more. But it could take several days for a node as an influencer to reach to its final state (see Fig. 3).

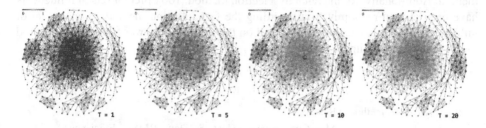

Fig. 3. Information diffusion over time

Hence, adding the issue of time to the problem and the availability of nodes are also important for the optimal result. It means that best set of influencers may be different from a time boundary to another one, and the best set of influencers in a time boundary may be not available. Therefore, the results should be made available to decision-makers in a way so that they can make better decisions according to different circumstances. In Fig. 4, a chart that helps decision makers make flexible decisions in specific circumstances is proposed, where each circle represents a distinct set of

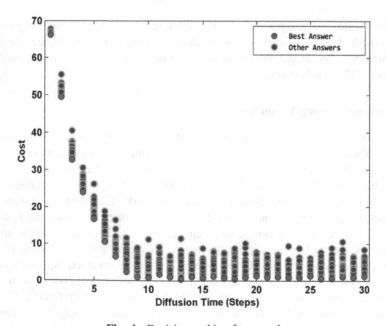

Fig. 4. Decision making framework

influencers. Decision makers can choose the best set of influencers according to time constraints, and if any of influencers was not available, they will easily pass on to the next best set.

5 Conclusion

In this paper, the importance of managing people's awareness of the injured necessities was presented as one of the challenges of disaster management. In the case of inappropriate information diffusion of needs, philanthropists with inappropriate donations, in addition to wasting their donations, might congest the relief chain. Formulating message propagation on social networks in order to create adaptive awareness is the main contribution of this paper. Time constraints in crisis management and influencers' willingness to collaborate on spreading of the messages, were considered as two important issues to find the best answer, which well answered using a decision making framework.

Determining the actual set of nodes and edges that shapes network structure, till now, is the substantial limitation for this type of research. For further research, the proposed model could be validated in a real disaster context. Also, it is suggested that the impact of the presence of influencers in other social networks and effect of traditional media be considered in formulating this problem.

References

1. Strömberg, D.: Natural disasters, economic development, and humanitarian aid. J. Econ. Perspect. **21**(3), 199–222 (2007)
2. Besiou, M., Stapleton, O., Van Wassenhove, L.N.: System dynamics for humanitarian operations. J. Humanit. Logist. Supply Chain Manage. **1**(1), 78–103 (2011)
3. Van Wassenhove, L.N.: Humanitarian aid logistics: supply chain management in high gear. J. Oper. Res. Soc. **57**(5), 475–489 (2006)
4. Balcik, B., et al.: Coordination in humanitarian relief chains: practices, challenges and opportunities. Int. J. Prod. Econ. **126**(1), 22–34 (2010)
5. Russell, T.E., The humanitarian relief supply chain: analysis of the 2004 South East Asia earthquake and tsunami. Massachusetts Institute of Technology (2005)
6. Martin, J.A.: Disasters and donations: the conditional effects of news attention on charitable giving. Int. J. Public Opin. Res. **25**(4), 547–560 (2013)
7. Gao, H., Barbier, G., Goolsby, R.: Harnessing the crowdsourcing power of social media for disaster relief. IEEE Intell. Syst. **26**(3), 10–14 (2011)
8. Bakshy, E., et al.: Everyone's an influencer: quantifying influence on twitter. In: Proceedings of the Fourth ACM International Conference on Web Search and Data Mining. ACM (2011)
9. Freberg, K., et al.: Who are the social media influencers? A study of public perceptions of personality. Public Relat. Rev. **37**(1), 90–92 (2011)
10. Landwehr, P.M., Carley, K.M.: Social media in disaster relief. In: Chu, W.W. (ed.) Data Mining and Knowledge Discovery for Big Data. SBD, vol. 1, pp. 225–257. Springer, Heidelberg (2014). https://doi.org/10.1007/978-3-642-40837-3_7
11. Kryvasheyeu, Y., et al.: Rapid assessment of disaster damage using social media activity. Sci. Adv. **2**(3), e1500779 (2016)

12. Zhu, J., et al.: Statistically modeling the effectiveness of disaster information in social media. In: Global Humanitarian Technology Conference (GHTC). IEEE (2011)
13. Goldenberg, J., Libai, B., Muller, E.: Using complex systems analysis to advance marketing theory development: modeling heterogeneity effects on new product growth through stochastic cellular automata. Acad. Mark. Sci. Rev. **2001**, 1 (2001)
14. Goldenberg, J., Libai, B., Muller, E.: Talk of the network: a complex systems look at the underlying process of word-of-mouth. Mark. Lett. **12**(3), 211–223 (2001)
15. Richardson, M., Domingos, P.: Mining knowledge-sharing sites for viral marketing. In: Proceedings of the Eighth ACM SIGKDD International Conference on Knowledge Discovery and Data Mining. ACM (2002)
16. Mohammadi, A., Saraee, M.: Finding influential users for different time bounds in social networks using multi-objective optimization. Swarm Evol. Comput. **40**, 158–165 (2018)
17. Kempe, D., Kleinberg, J., Tardos, É.: Maximizing the spread of influence through a social network. In: Proceedings of the Ninth ACM SIGKDD International Conference on Knowledge Discovery and Data Mining. ACM (2003)
18. Barbieri, N., Bonchi, F.: Influence maximization with viral product design. In: Proceedings of the 2014 SIAM International Conference on Data Mining. SIAM (2014)
19. Liu, B., et al.: Influence spreading path and its application to the time constrained social influence maximization problem and beyond. IEEE Trans. Knowl. Data Eng. **26**(8), 1904–1917 (2014)
20. Zhang, G.-X., et al.: Novel quantum genetic algorithm and its applications. Front. Electr. Electron. Eng. China **1**(1), 31–36 (2006)

Supporting SOA Resilience in Virtual Enterprises

Roque O. Bezerra[1(✉)], Ricardo J. Rabelo[1], and Maiara H. Cancian[2]

[1] Department of Automation and Systems Engineering,
Federal University of Santa Catarina, Florianopolis, SC, Brazil
{roque.bezera, ricardo.rabelo}@ufsc.br
[2] Estácio Florianopolis, Rodovia SC401 Km 01, Florianopolis, SC, Brazil
maiara.cancian@estacio.br

Abstract. Computing systems are essential nowadays for the execution of companies' business processes and should keep operating permanently. Modern approaches, as Service Oriented Architecture (SOA), have been gradually adopted by companies to implement their systems. This paper exploits a Virtual Enterprise (VE) scenario where its members' systems are available as services and are selected to support the VE operation itself. Regarding VE properties and inspired in the autonomic computing paradigm, a resilience architecture and system have been designed and implemented to help VE's supporting system to recover from services' faults, respecting the business processes' QoS in place. Results are presented and discussed in the end.

Keywords: Reference business processes · Service Oriented Architecture
Resilience · Fault tolerance · Virtual Enterprises

1 Introduction

Computing systems have become essential for the execution of companies' business processes. As such, keep them permanently operating is one of their major concerns [1]. SOA (Service Oriented Architecture) has been increasingly adopted by SMEs to foster newer business models, based on larger scale provision and offering of software services that are distributed over the Internet and that can be accessed on demand, from everywhere, anytime from pervasive providers from digital ecosystems [2].

This paper deals with Virtual Enterprises (VE). One of VE's properties refers that its members share resources and working principles as well as they have enough IT preparedness to participate in VEs. In this sense, this work exploits the scenario where VE members can share their software services assets, and a SOA/services-based and cross-boundary system is temporarily and dynamically created to support the execution of the VE's business processes throughout the VE life cycle [3].

This created system is therefore composed of (loose-coupling) services from the currently VE members and, eventually, also from their IT supporting business partners, creating a large-scale distributed system. In this scenario, several faults (e.g. services unavailability) can happen during the system execution so causing problems in the VE and related businesses if proper measures are not applied [4].

© IFIP International Federation for Information Processing 2018
Published by Springer Nature Switzerland AG 2018. All Rights Reserved
L. M. Camarinha-Matos et al. (Eds.): PRO-VE 2018, IFIP AICT 534, pp. 111–123, 2018.
https://doi.org/10.1007/978-3-319-99127-6_10

This paper addresses this issue from the IT resilience perspective. IT resilience generally refers to guaranteeing the operation of the system under control and its recovery in the presence of faults or high degradation within acceptable costs [5].

VEs bring up additional resilience requirements and research opportunities regarding their collaborative, dynamic and open natures. However, it hasn't been tackled much in specific in the literature. Despite the complexity of the problem, most of the evaluated works on SOA resilience doesn't consider much the intrinsic VE dynamics in terms of members composition, and they usually assume a too simplistic IT reality of SOA problems when applied in real business cases [1, 6].

This paper presents a resilience architecture and supporting system to deal with the VE scenario where a heterogeneous SOA-based system should remain operating when the involved services have problems or the VE's composition change (hence the respective services should be replaced as well). It is an ongoing work and has been developed under the action-research methodology.

This article is organized as following. Section 1 has introduced the problem and the objectives of the work. Section 2 summarizes the requirements of a resilience architecture for SOA in VEs. Section 3 presents the proposed architecture. Section 4 describes the prototype and the achieved results. Section 5 presents some preliminary conclusions and the next main steps of this work.

2 Literature Review and VE Resilience Aspects

Resilience and fault tolerance terms are sometimes used as synonyms or just used differently depending on the scientific 'community'. Some authors, like [7, 8], take resilience as a wider perspective for systems reliability. They consider that fault tolerance term is more appropriate to be used in the cases where faults treatment is handled at system's design, while resilience would be more suitable in more flexible, open, dynamic, evolving and less prescriptive architectures, which is the case of the proposed work in this paper. Adaptive fault tolerance is another term found out in the literature and it seems equivalent to resilience [7].

After an extensive review on theoretical foundations of collaborative networks and VEs as well as of computing resilience and fault tolerance, a number of aspects were identified as important to be taken into account when a resilience architecture/system is going to be developed for dealing with VE.

A systematic literature review (SLR) [9] was done upon five international scientific repositories looking for works combining the areas of SOA/services, resilience/fault tolerance and VE (and its other equivalent terms). Almost three thousand papers were found out in the search, and 27 were preliminary selected. Due to space limitation to mention them in the references, only the nine taken as the most relevant ones (for the purpose of this work) are listed.

Table 1 summarizes these works against the identified VE-related aspects as well as highlights the envisaged contribution of this work. By "supported" it is meant at least *some* level of guarantee. By "not (yet) supported" it is meant that the given feature is not currently supported but it is planned to be in the next version of the work. By "not supported" that the given feature is not anyhow supported in this proposal.

Table 1. Summary of the literature review

VE-related aspect	Works [10–18]	Proposed work
1. Newcomers can join a VE and current members can leave it during its execution. This means that the composed SOA/services-based supporting system should be also dynamically recomposed accordingly in order to keep the VE operating gracefully	−Most of them support dynamic discovery and re-composition	Supported
	−These works only consider previously defined alternative services, and a discovery and execution in local & intra-enterprise environments	Supported
	−None works consider the dynamics and scalability of members' composition	Supported
	−Only one work considers the dynamics and scalability of existing services provision	Supported
2. VE members are independent companies and usually adopt different models in their BP modeling, impacting the services' functional requirements and the way SOA layer interacts with the Business and Infrastructure layers This relates to very well defined scope of responsibilities (and hence the actions) of each layer	−Only one work offers some level of integration with the Business layer	Supported
	−All works support integration with the Infrastructure layer	Supported
	−Only four works adopt standard BP models, but none of them make use of this to facilitate services discovery and interop	Supported
3. VE members implement their services in different technologies, IT standards & patterns, security mechanisms, granularities, deployed in different servers, and registered using different signatures and repositories. The effective system (re)composition and execution require syntactic or semantic interoperability mediation	−Most of works assume a homogeneous environment, basically composed of web services, XML and SOAP	Not (yet) supported
	−Only three works use some mediation (via ESB [*Enterprise Service Bus*]) to support larger interoperability	Supported
	−Only two works offer some security support	Not Supported
4. Companies (and so their services) can be linked to several VEs simultaneously in their different stages, meaning that a given service can have several instances/tenants in execution responding to different VEs' QoS metrics and multiple SLAs	−Most of works deal with end-to-end QoS	Supported
	−Three works also monitor and handle temporal restrictions of the individual services	supported
	−None works support multi-tenancy	Not supported
5. Companies' services are in theory permanently running. However, services can become unavailable or fail during different VE phases: before getting bound to given VEs; before being invoked by a given VE's business processes (BP); and during their execution in given VEs	−All works checks services only in the execution phase	Supported

(*continued*)

Table 1. (*continued*)

VE-related aspect	Works [10–18]	Proposed work
6. Each business a VE is related to can have different priorities (i.e. weights) in terms of the most critical QoS metrics to pursuit, impacting the general costs and hence the feasibility of the resilience policy in place	−Only four works support some level of parametrization, weighting or prioritization	Supported
7. The access to VE members' services should follow the VE governance model and possibly the gov model of the long-term alliance the members belong to	−Not supported	Not supported
8. The general computing infrastructure to support the execution of the VE resilience system should ideally be deployed in servers that are not dependent of any given VE member as it can leave the VE anytime. The own resilience system should ideally be resilient in order to mitigate its complete fail in the case of problems	−All works have developed centralized architectures/systems to handle resilience	Supported
	−All works do not support self-resilience	Not (yet) supported
9. The VE's legal obligations only end after all the contracted aspects have been fulfilled. This means that the VE members' services should be kept 'connected' even after the final 'product' (which originated the creation of a VE) has been delivered	−Not supported	Not supported
10. The replacement of a given VE member (and its services) by another members (and its services) should consider implementation issues, like the service's components lock-in and business duties. Yet, the creation of services' replicas may imply replicating other components as well (e.g. a database)	−Not supported.	Not (yet) supported
11. VE members are dealing with real businesses, carried out collaboratively and in a distributed way. Resilience supporting systems should ideally act pro-actively close to the involved members' services in order to prevent the VE from generally failing because given members' services have got down	−Half of works do it pro-actively	Supported

3 The Proposed SOA-Based Resilience Architecture and System

This section presents the proposed resilience architecture for VEs.

Considering (i) this is an ongoing work; (ii) the complexity of some aspects related to VE resilience (Table 1); and (iii) that some of them involve issues that are not even totally or well solved in the distributed systems area; the proposed architecture showed in this paper has been designed to handle (at different levels of depth) only the aspects pointed out in Table 1.

3.1 The Resilience Architecture's Rationale

A number of general design principles have been considered in the architecture:

(a) All VE members belong to a long-term collaborative alliance of type VBE (*Virtual organization Breeding Environment*), which is grounded on trust and members' autonomy, and whose members intrinsically have the willingness to collaborate and share resources [4]. This means that, as a general rule, their services can be made available to be accessed by other VBE members and hence VEs [6]. This assumption relies on the fact that any VBE member must respect a number of common principles of work and introduce them in their companies so that their general differences get hidden to other companies. This all refers to the so called members' preparedness [4].

(b) IT preparedness is one of the pre-conditions for a company to be member of a VBE and VE [4]. This means that their services and computing infrastructure should be previously prepared (at several levels) and duly wrapped so as to be also used by other client systems, including the resilience system. This, however, does not mean forcing all companies to adopt the same IT or standards, although this actually happens in plenty of cases in real life SMEs when integrating with larger enterprises.

(c) When a given company leaves a VE its services keep available to be accessed by the resilience system so as to replace problematic services, regarding the collaborative nature of VBEs (as in [6]). However, their effective use depends on BP's activities restrictions and/or technological factors;

(d) The architecture separates the whole resilience actions into three inter-dependent actors ('responsibility' layers, as in [18]), relating to the model, runtime and deployment views: (1) the planning layer (as a BPM-like environment, where business processes and activities are defined and services are discovered and bound to); (2) the SOA/services layer (where services are deployed, made available, also discovered and executed); and (3) the middleware/operating system layer (responsible to support the execution and communication of all services – and of the own resilience system). A number of assumptions are taken within each layer. One of the most important ones is the adoption of a given reference model for BP modeling (as a VBE/VE common neutral model for internal interoperation), based on which all VBE members would have their services developed according to, although implemented in different technologies, semantics and granularities, as in [19];

(e) The resilience actions can require human intervention (e.g. QoS relaxation) in the case of unsolvable situations so as to keep the VE operating (as in [6]);

(f) The resilience architecture/system has to be decentralized and distributed so as to prevent central points of faults, as in [8];

(g) Each new system's reconfiguration/re-composition has a cost, which should be measured and evaluated before being set up, as in [16].

In this current version of the prototype only services' *faults* are treated. No services' *degradation* analysis is performed.

Five types of general *faults* can be treated by a resilience system for SOA-based systems [14]: *publication, discovery, composition, binding,* and *execution*. A number of very concrete faults are associated to each one. *Publication* and *Binding* faults are actually not considered as necessary to be treated in the proposed architecture. It is assumed that *publication*-related faults (e.g. *wrong publication, wrong interface* and *lookup faults*) are resolved at VBE level when every company properly register its services in their repositories and make them available in the VBE's services federation. In terms of *binding*, it is assumed that the related faults (*wrong binding, binding denied* and *access denied*) are resolved at BPM level when the BPMN and BPEL process are generated, and that services are 'naturally' available as their owners belong to the given VE and VBE (or to their IT business partners).

In terms of *Discovery* and *Composition*, the faults to be treated by the resilience system [14] refer to *services inexistence, services unavailability, services inadequacy* (e.g. inadequate QoS) and *discovery fail*. This can happen when services are being bound to BPs' activities. In terms of *Execution* faults, these three faults can also happen when services are going to be *invoked by the BPEL* process and when *services get crashed*. Yet, as the resilience system also monitors the BPEL process another possible fault is the *BPEL process crash*.

Two other SOA-related faults [14] are treated in other layers: the *reserved communication port* fault, which is not up to the SOA layer/resilience system to solve as ports are automatically defined by the infrastructure and middleware layer/systems. The *incorrect result* fault is resolved by the high-level applications, which understand the business logic associated to the BPs' activities.

3.2   The Architecture

The architecture has been devised to support both VE-related aspects (Table 1) and the core design principles, previously described. In order to facilitate its explanation and due to space restrictions, only a general description will be provided, besides mixing some general aspects of implementation and execution.

IT resilience can be addressed from different approaches. Regarding that the desired resilience architecture should monitor its own state and adapt itself in the presence of faults, the autonomic computing approach has been chosen. The *self-inspection* and *self-adaptation* techniques [20] are used to implement that.

The architecture is designed to cope with the discovery, composition and execution faults applying two approaches: *services replaceability* (replacement of the faulty service by an equivalent one [10]) and *services provision and migration* (creation of replicas or dynamic migration of the faulty service to other servers [20]).

The architecture is organized into three layers regarding their role (Fig. 1). Their components work in two different moments: when the VE is being created (Project Phase) and when the supporting service-based system is composed and set up; and when it is executed (Execution Phase). The resilience system will then take care of this VE system.

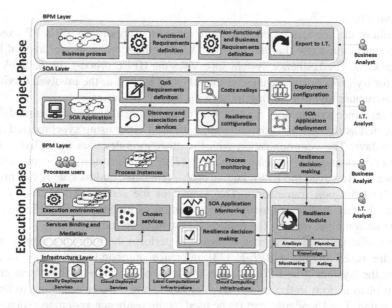

Fig. 1. The proposed architecture and resilience phases

Project Phase:

A VE is created after some steps [4], including the one where the so-called VE's coordinator indicates, in the planning/BPM layer, the actual BPs each VE member will be responsible for. In the implemented prototype, the open standard *UBL* BP Reference Model [21] has been adopted regarding its target on supply chains. Each of its 68 BPs has a number of pre-defined activities and documents to be exchanged between members. As services are dynamically discovered and bound to the involved BPs' activities, only a functional reference of the required services are provided, as in [22]. This provides higher flexibility to the resilience system in its search for equivalent services when it decides to replace the unavailable ones. The VE coordinator's business analyst also specifies the non-functional requirements (as QoS attributes) for each BP's activity, which are used by the resilience system both to control the time constraints of each BP's activity and the BP's end-to-end QoS, as in [6]. All this has been developed using the *Eclipse* and *IBM Websphere*'s APIs.

Once the VE's services are finally discovered and bound, a BPEL (*BP Execution Language*) file is generated as the result of the VE planning, previously modeled (in BPMN). This BPEL is deployed as a SOA application and put into the execution environment (a BPEL engine based on the *Apache ODE*). This is done interacting with the supporting infrastructure (via a *REST API* and *Docker*) and deploying the required services: the execution environment, the involved VE members' services and the own resilience services-based system. Each deployed service may have different numbers of replicas (not implemented yet in this prototype). The replication level and deployment policies can be defined by IT analysts, meaning that the resilience "level" of the own resilience system can be configured.

Execution Phase:
In this phase the services-based system generated to support the VE's BP execution starts to run in the sense that the involved VE members' services are invoked by the BPEL process. The resilience system supervises the BPEL process (in the SOA layer, mainly for trying to guarantee the end-to-end QoS) as well as the involved services (in the infrastructure layer, for trying to keep up the VE operating).

The resilience system does not take care of its own resilience at all. Its modules are implemented as *threads* and communicate with each other using synchronized queues coded in Java. The communication with the other modules uses the SOAP protocol (*point-to-point*) and the *Apache ActiveMQ* (*JMS publish-subscribe* communication middleware). However, the BPEL engine is also replicated and its state is synchronized (using the *Infinispan* framework). This is part of the self-resilience strategy of the model as another replica can assume the execution of the process in the case a given one gets unavailable, making the resilience system more reliable.

The resilience system has been designed to perform the following main activities, which are based on the *MAPE-K* [23] reference autonomic computing model: it *m*onitors the "system" (the BPEL process and services); it *a*nalyses the system entities' status; it *p*lans actions in the case of services faults; and it *e*xecutes actions to keep the VE operating. The *k*nowledge part (to be used by the resilience system to evolve) is not supported in the current prototype.

Services availability is monitored using *endpoint monitoring* via heartbeat requests/ "ping" [24], using two techniques: a *fail fast* every 500 ms to check if services are listening to their ports and, complementarily, a *timeout* of 1000 ms [25].

The resilience system performs an 'expansion cycle' of services discovery (and further composition and binding) during its execution in the case a given service has a problem: it starts by searching for a new service in the respective VE member's repository. If no equivalent service is discovered then the search is expanded to the other VE's members. It ends with a wider search in the VBE's and IT business partners' repositories (i.e. the services replaceability approach). In the case no services are found out then the system will try to deploy the faulty service in another (previously defined) computing infrastructure (i.e. the services provision approach).

An ESB (*Camel ESB*) is used as a complementary entity to help in the services binding and mediation avoiding point-to-point and tight-coupling communication. It pro-actively checks if the invoked services keep being available and responding to the required QoS, and sends this information to the monitoring module. The ESB is kept permanently updated when new services are bound to given BPs or when members composition change. Besides that, in spite of the implemented prototype has only considered WS-* services, the use of the ESB allows supporting "any" other services' implementation technologies.

4 Results

This section presents the VE scenario and computing prototype implemented in a controlled environment to quantitatively assess the proposed resilience architecture.

This scenario refers to a hypothetic customer who asks for a given product close to a given VBE's company. This product is basically composed of three parts, being one part produced by this company. This company then triggers the process of VE creation, ending up by forming the following VE: this company ('Partner 1') is the *VE Coordinator* and interacts with the customer; and 'Partner 2' and 'Partner 3', which manufacture the other two product's parts. These two partners should send their parts directly to Partner 1 once they have been finished for the final product assembly.

This VE's plan is showed in the Fig. 2, which is the graphical representation of the BPEL file generated from the respective BPM/BPMN modeling. This plan reflects the standard flow of activities specified in the UBL process *'Ordering Process'*.

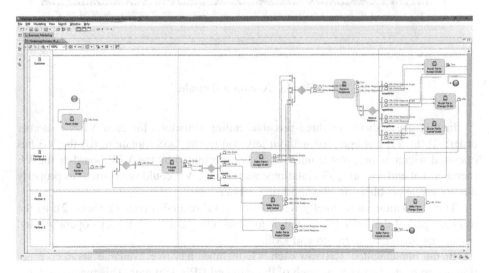

Fig. 2. The business process scenario and related BPEL file

It was simulated a scenario where 100 customer orders arrives to the VE and then the resilience system should try to keep the supporting VE system running and attending the BP's end-to-end QoS in the presence of several services' faults.

Due to space restrictions only the *discovery* and *execution* faults will be showed in this section, i.e. it is assumed that *binding* faults (in the BPEL file) will not happen, although being supported by the developed resilience system.

A number of performance indicators would have to be used to measure the many aspects of resilience in the implemented model. Considering the goals of the current stage of the work, two reference performance indicators [26] are so far used to measure the "quality" of the resilience system: the *"resilience time"* (the time spent to recover from a local fault without violating the global end-to-end QoS, including all the communication, latency and processing times – *'reaction time'* in Fig. 3, line "≡"); and *"End-to-End violation"* (the number of times and process' instances the end-to-end QoS has been violated - *'process instance duration'* in Fig. 3, line "■").

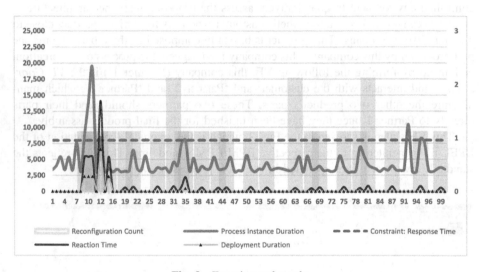

Fig. 3. Experimental results

In this sense, there are three possible ending situations for each VE's customer order: (i) the VE has operated without any end-to-end QoS violation; (ii) the VE has operated within an acceptable number (to be determined by the VBE board or the VE members) of end-to-end QoS violations; and (iii) the VE could not operate as properly due to severe problems in its supporting services.

These situations are actually related to the VE-related aspect 11 (Sect. 2), as the ultimate goal of the resilience system is to "guarantee" that the VE keeps operating and respecting the required end-to-end QoS.

In the implemented scenario each VE member has five available services functionally equivalent to execute each of the standard BP's activities. This means that any of them can be used by the resilience system to automatically replace a faulty service. The services unavailability is randomly set up in the prototype. The replacement strategy is performed via the 'expansion cycle', as previously explained.

The end-to-end QoS value for the UBL process 'Ordering Process' was set up as 8 s (line "■ ■" in Fig. 3), so it should be observed by the resilience system when summing the individual response times of all the involved services (line "●"). The *y* axis represents the time, whereas the *x* axis represents the VE' instance. *Y* axis is also used to represent the number of services replacements (shaded bars - *'reconfiguration count'*) necessary to recover from services unavailability in the 100 VE's instances.

One thousand services were deployed in the so-called VBE's services federation, being their signatures and QoS attributes also randomly generated when registered. Their response time was randomly assigned with a sleeping time when services are invoked. The computing infrastructure was deployed in three distributed Intel servers in a link of 100 Mbps and a mean latency time of 2 ms.

The resilience system starts monitoring the involved services as soon as the VE is created and services are bound to its BPs. In this experiment, the (simulated) faults start to happen from instance 7 on, when services get unavailable. The resilience system then performs its 'expansion cycle'. The shaded bars indicate the number of services replacement per BP's composition per VE's instance.

The process' instance duration (line "■") is quite variable. This is due both to the natural variability of services availability/re-composition time and to the variable execution flows of the BP activities (Fig. 2).

The 'deployment duration' (line "▲") shows when the services provision strategy steps in after all the attempts to search for a substitute service in the 'expansion cycle' have failed (*discovery fault*), which took 6.000 ms. This provision took about 2.500 ms to be executed. However, it is necessary to wait for the services initiation in the server and for the re-composition completion. Summing all the other related actions this ended up taking about 20.000 ms, which violates the required global QoS.

As a final average, the resilience system could maintain the VE operating well in 93% of its instances, which can be considered as quite acceptable in general terms.

In terms of computational complexity, the main variables involved in the system execution (e.g. number of services and number of instances) had a *linear* complexity, which seems to be also quite reasonable for a VE scenario.

This prototype and achieved results tried to show at which extent the VE-related aspects 1-2-3-4-5-6-8-11 listed in Table 1 (Sect. 2) were somehow supported.

5 Final Considerations

This paper has presented preliminary results of an ongoing research that, at last, aims at conceiving and implementing an autonomic resilience architecture and system to sustain the Virtual Enterprise (VE) operation in the presence of diverse faults in its SOA/services-based supporting systems.

A core assumption of this architecture is that VE members all belong to a long-term business alliance grounded on trust, collaboration and resources sharing, including software assets. IT preparedness is one of the pre-conditions for a company to be member of a VBE and VE, being its systems properly wrapped as services. Therefore, the VE supporting system is formed by a composition of members' services involved in the diverse business processes related to the given VE' business and it is the one that the resilience system supervises.

VE brings up a number of particular requirements to be supported when compared to a resilience system for "any" distributed system. The devised architecture has been designed to cope with most of them although adopting some assumptions. Issues that are not supported by the architecture and system were also identified, to be highlighted security, governance and the *Knowledge* part of the MAPE-*K* model.

A system prototype was implemented and assessed using open source tools and IT standards, in a controlled environment. Three types of services faults were tested. In general, it can be said that the system showed a good potential to support resilience actions within feasible costs as well as in terms of computing complexity.

The mean result of 93% of recovery could be actually better. The simulated environment has actually "forced" each service to get unavailable many times during the VE's instances execution, which is not realistic in minimally robust infrastructures. This number also shows the importance of a resilience system for VEs. Almost all VE instances would have had problems to keep operating within the required QoS level if the diverse detected services' faults were not properly treated.

Next main steps of this research include: the consideration of services *degradation faults*; a self-resilience model; the implementation of services in multiple technologies and protocols; and a support for stateful services' replicas, which brings tough issues to be coped with in terms of services coordination and of evolution of system's state.

References

1. Rabelo, R.J., Baldo, F., Alves-Junior, O.C., Dihlmann, C.: Virtual enterprises: strengthening SMES competitiveness via flexible businesses alliances. In: North, K., Varvakis, G. (eds.) Competitive Strategies for Small and Medium Enterprises, pp. 255–272. Springer, Cham (2016). https://doi.org/10.1007/978-3-319-27303-7_18
2. Brzeziński, J., et al.: Dependability infrastructure for SOA applications. In: Ambroszkiewicz, S., Brzeziński, J., Cellary, W., Grzech, A., Zieliński, K. (eds.) Advanced SOA Tools and Applications. Studies in Computational Intelligence, vol. 499, pp. 203–260. Springer, Heidelberg (2014). https://doi.org/10.1007/978-3-642-38957-3_5
3. Bezerra, R.O., Cancian, M.H., Rabelo, R.J.: Enhancing network collaboration in SOA services composition via standard business processes catalogues. In: Camarinha-Matos, L. M., Afsarmanesh, H., Fornasiero, R. (eds.) PRO-VE 2017. IAICT, vol. 506, pp. 421–431. Springer, Cham (2017). https://doi.org/10.1007/978-3-319-65151-4_38
4. Afsarmanesh, H., Camarinha-Matos, L.M., Ermilova, E.: VBE Reference Framework. In: Camarinha-Matos, L.M., Afsarmanesh, H., Ollus, M. (eds.) Methods and Tools for Collaborative Networked Organizations, pp. 35–68. Springer, Boston (2008). https://doi.org/10.1007/978-0-387-79424-2_2
5. Annarelli, A., Nonino, F.: Strategic and operational management of organizational resilience: current state of research and future directions. Omega **62**, 1–18 (2015)
6. Vernadat, F.B.: Technical, semantic and organizational issues of enterprise interoperability and networking. IFAC Proc. **42**(4), 728–733 (2009)
7. Strigini, L.: Fault tolerance and resilience: meanings, measures and assessment. In: Wolter, K., Avritzer, A., Vieira, M., van Moorsel, A. (eds.) Resilience Assessment and Evaluation of Computing Systems, pp. 3–24. Springer, Heidelberg (2012). https://doi.org/10.1007/978-3-642-29032-9_1
8. Banatre, M., Pataricza, A., Moorsel, A., Palanque, P., Strigini, L.: From Resilience-Building to Resilience-Scaling Technologies: Directions - ReSIST NoE Deliverable D13. Technical reports (2007). http://hdl.handle.net/10451/14107

9. Kitchenham, B., Charters, S.: Guidelines for performing Systematic Literature Reviews in Software Engineering. Technical report EBSE-2007-01 (2007). https://www.elsevier.com/__data/promis_misc/525444systematicreviewsguide.pdf
10. Cardellini, V., et al.: MOSES: a framework for QoS driven runtime adaptation of service-oriented systems. Softw. Eng. 38(5), 1138–1159 (2012)
11. He, Q., et al.: Localizing runtime anomalies in service-oriented systems. IEEE Trans. Serv. Comput. 10(1), 94–106 (2017)
12. Weidong, W., Liqiang, W., Wei, L.: A resilient framework for fault handling in web service oriented systems. In: IEEE International Conference Web Services (2015)
13. Calinescu, R., Grunske, L., Kwiatkowska, M., Mirandola, R., Tamburrelli, G.: Dynamic QoS management and optimization in service-based systems. IEEE Trans. Softw. Eng. 37(3), 387–409 (2011)
14. Ardagna, D., Baresi, L., Comai, S., Comuzzi, M.: A service-based framework for flexible business processes. IEEE Softw. 28(2), 61–67 (2011)
15. Menascé, D., Gomaa, H., Malek, S., Sousa, J.: SASSY: a framework for self-architecting service-oriented systems. IEEE Softw. 28(6), 78–85 (2011)
16. Stein, S., Payne, T.R., Jennings, N.R.: Robust execution of service workflows using redundancy and advance reservations. IEEE Trans. Serv. Comput. 4(2), 125–139 (2011)
17. Hummer, W., Leitner, P., Michlmayr, A., Rosenberg, F., Dustdar, S.: VRESCo – vienna runtime environment for service-oriented computing. Service Engineering, pp. 299–324. Springer, Vienna (2011). https://doi.org/10.1007/978-3-7091-0415-6_11
18. Friedrich, G., Fugini, M.G., Mussi, E.: Exception handling for repair in service-based processes. IEEE Trans. Softw. Eng. 36(2), 198–215 (2010)
19. Schratzenstaller, W.M.K., Baldo, F., Rabelo, R.J.: Semantic integration via enterprise service bus in virtual organization breeding environments. In: Nguyen, N.T., Trawiński, B., Fujita, H., Hong, T.-P. (eds.) ACIIDS 2016. LNCS (LNAI), vol. 9622, pp. 544–553. Springer, Heidelberg (2016). https://doi.org/10.1007/978-3-662-49390-8_53
20. Pääkkönen, P., Pakkala, D.: Mechanism and architecture for the migration of service implementation during traffic peaks. Serv. Oriented Comput. Appl. 9(2), 193–209 (2015)
21. OASIS.: Universal Business Language Version (UBL) 2.1. 2013 (2016). http://docs.oasis-open.org/ubl/UBL-2.1.html
22. de Souza, A.P., Rabelo, R.J.: A dynamic services discovery model for better leveraging BPM and SOA integration. Int. J. Inf. Syst. Serv. Sect. (IJISSS) 7(1), 1–21 (2015)
23. Kephart, J.O., Chess, D.: Dm.: the vision of autonomic computing. Computer 36(1), 41–50 (2003)
24. Homer, A., Sharp, J., Brader, L., Narumoto, M.: Cloud design patterns: prescriptive architecture guidance for cloud applications. Microsoft Pattern Pract. 238 (2014)
25. Nygard, M.T.: Release it!: design and deploy production-ready software. In: Raleigh, N.C. (ed.) Pragmatic Bookshelf (2007)
26. Liu, D., Deters, R., Zhang, W.J.: Architectural design for resilience. Enterp. Inf. Syst. 4(2), 137–152 (2010)

Formalization and Evaluation of Non-functional Requirements: Application to Resilience

Behrang Moradi[(⌧)], Nicolas Daclin[(⌧)], and Vincent Chapurlat[(⌧)]

LGI2P, IMT Mines Ales, 7, rue Jules Renard, 30100 Ales, France
{Behrang.Moradi, Nicolas.Daclin,
Vincent.Chapurlat}@mines-ales.fr

Abstract. This paper introduces the development of a method for the specification, formalization and evaluation of resilience. The developed method is based on two working approaches. First, we study and analyze several resilience metrics and indicators as well as the relationship between resilience and other non-functional requirements namely "*-ilities*". Concepts for evaluation are identified and defined. Further, we map out these "*-ilities*" by positioning them according to the dynamic of the resilience represented as a set of zones. A set of indicators to evaluate the resilience and particularly indicators that are associated with these "*-ilities*" to each zone of the resilience has to be selected. The expected benefit of such method is to allow to evaluate resilience in order to master and improve it.

Keywords: System of systems engineering · Resilience
Non-functional property · "*-ilities*"

1 Introduction

To fulfil its mission adequately, a collaborative system must satisfy functional and non-functional requirements. Among the non-functional requirements a set is called "*-ilities*" [1] and represents "*the desired properties of systems, […] that often manifest themselves after a system has been put to its initial use*" [2]. For instance, let's mention the *Flexibility, Robustness, Safety, Interoperability or Survivability*. Figure 1 presents the network of "*-ilities*" correlations and their relationships as defined in [2]. The work proposed attempts to study and analyze "*-ilities*" as a whole rather than to study an "*-ility*" in isolation and focuses on the resilience assessment. Resilience is an important property because it must be mastered and maximized [3] to effectively cope with disruptive events and maintain acceptable levels of services and performance (*e.g.* loss of an organization in a collaborative network, fire requiring the engagement and collaboration of different organization…). There exist several definitions of resilience. Generally speaking, it is defined as "*the ability of the system to resist, absorb, recover or adapt to disturbances and diminish the consequences as well as to recover quickly and effectively*" [4]. Lastly, resilience is practiced in various application area *e.g.*, critical infrastructure monitoring, security, transport [5–7].

L. M. Camarinha-Matos et al. (Eds.): PRO-VE 2018, IFIP AICT 534, pp. 124–131, 2018.
https://doi.org/10.1007/978-3-319-99127-6_11

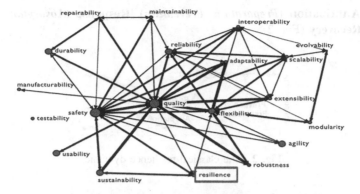

Fig. 1. Correlation network of "*-ilities*" [2]

The research question deals with the evaluation of the resilience. The prevention, preparation and management of negative perturbations for the security and protection of systems have become a major concern. Indeed, a disturbance may lead to heavy loss of performance and affect a system, so that the evaluation resilience can participate to the improvement of a performance of a system. The purpose is to study the resilience with the consideration of its ecosystem that means including the possible relationships with other non-functional requirements. Currently, resilience is evaluated without considering possible impacts coming from other requirements but also possible impacts generated by resilience as well. As a consequence, the targeted objective is to develop a metric to evaluate resilience numerically and sufficiently generic to be practicable to any networked system subject to any type of disruption. The paper is structured as follows. After this brief introduction, the concept of resilience is presented as well as different methods to evaluate it. The next section presents the concepts which act as foundation for the development of our approach to analyze and evaluate resilience. The final section presents the conclusion and the future perspective for this research.

2 Resilience Definition and Evaluation

2.1 Definition

There are numerous definitions of resilience. Let's mention the following ones:

- "*the intrinsic ability of a system to adjust its functioning prior to, during, or following changes and disturbances, so that it can sustain required operations under both expected and unexpected conditions*" [8];
- "*the ability to anticipate, prepare for, respond to, adapt to disruptions and to mitigate the consequences as well as to recover in timely and efficient manner including preservation restoration of services*" [9];

They all suggest that resilient systems are able to manage disastrous situation due to several capacities requested throughout the classical phases of the disaster management lifecycle: **Anticipation** (*Preparation*, *Prevention*), **Response** (*Absorption*, *Adaptation*) and **Recovery** (Fig. 2).

Fig. 2. The classical resilience dynamic

Anticipation (*Prevention* and *Preparedness*) aims at identifying and minimizing the risks of the occurrence of an event. This zone concerns also the preparation to face up an event [10]. *Response* (*Absorption* and *Adaptation*) expresses the absorptive capability (**robustness**), *i.e.*, the ability to reduce the negative impacts caused by disruptive events and minimize consequences with less efforts [3, 4]. The adaptive capability (**adaptability**) refers to the ability to adapt to disruptive events through self-organization (**flexibility**, **interoperability**) to minimize consequences and it can be enhanced by using emergency systems. *Recovery* is defined as a return to a qualified acceptable condition. The restorative capability refers to the ability of the system to rapidly be repaired (**maintainability**, **repairability**) and return to a, as much as possible, normal and a reliable functioning mode that meets the requirements for an acceptable and desirable level of quality of service and expected control [3]. The study and synthesis of different definitions shows that the authors believe resilience is characterized by zones such as Anticipation, Recovery and Response; each author considers more or less zones in their study (*e.g.* for [18] resilience is a problem of response and recovery) (Fig. 3). As part of resilience assessment, we consider the three areas of dynamic of resilience, as defined by [19].

Anticipation	Response	Recovery	Reference
✔	✔	✔	[20]
✖	✔	✔	[19]
✖	✔	✔	[11]
✖	✔	✔	[5]
✖	✔	✔	[21]
✖	✖	✔	[15]

Fig. 3. Resilience dynamic

2.2 Resilience Metric

Resilience can be assessed in different ways. It can be evaluated by measuring the performance or loss of performance of a system before and after the disruptive event, the potential loss of functionality, the loss of quality of service, the effectiveness of the security barriers, as well as the activities recovery. Numerous works related to the evaluation of the resilience are provided in the literature *e.g.* [5, 12, 14, 15] that evaluates resilience with different points of view. [12] proposes a metric of resilience that can be associated in two types such as the *focus* attribute parameters, which usually consist of indices based on subjective assessments and the *indicators* built on data-bases, which quantify the system attributes that contribute to resilience. The performance-based methods, which measure the consequences of system disturbances and the impact that system attributes have on mitigating these consequences. [5] states the measurement of resilience is a function of the 3 capacities (absorption, adaptation and recovery) as well as recovery time, through the measurement of the performance and its evolution. The method is based on a resilience analysis framework and a metric for measuring resilience. The analysis framework consists of system identification, resilience objective setting, vulnerability analysis, and stakeholder engagement. Lastly, [15] provides a quantitative measure of resilience in the face of multiple disaster-related events. It extends the concepts of the resilience triangle and predictive resilience in disaster by considering the trade-offs between several criteria. Its work is based on sudden disasters and the initial impact of each event as well as the recovery time of the system before the next event. In this work (Fig. 4), robustness is used to increase the resilience so that it recovers its performance and returns to an acceptable state. Thus, there is a link between resilience and robustness.

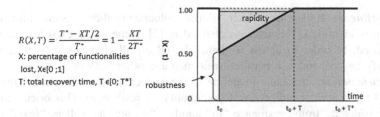

$$R(X,T) = \frac{T^* - XT/2}{T^*} = 1 - \frac{XT}{2T^*}$$

X: percentage of functionalities lost, $X \in [0 ; 1]$

T: total recovery time, $T \in [0; T^*]$

Fig. 4. The predicted resilience triangle as a proportion of T^* [15]

These works show three approaches to assess resilience (Fig. 5). Let's note that [15] highlights the link between resilience and another "*-ility*" (robustness in the Zone2-response). Its measurement shows the importance of considering the link between "-ilities" since the more the robustness, the more the resilience can be efficient. However, each metric treats the resilience in isolation, *i.e.*, they do not consider the possible relationship with other "*-ilities*". In this sense, stakeholders don't have any information about the possible impact of the resilience onto other "*-ilities*" and *vice versa*. Thus, the ecosystem of "*-ilities*" and their relationship can be used and study to evaluate a given "*-ility*", here, the resilience.

Reference	Ecosystem of '-ilities'	Method/ approach	Zone
[5]		Resilience factor	Response, Recovery
[15]		Potential losses	Recovery
[16]	(Robustness)	Loss of features	Response, Recovery

Fig. 5. Synthesis of different resilience assessment methods

3 Research Work Proposal

The assessment of resilience relies on defining and analyzing the set of "-*ilities*", *i.e.*, the analysis and formalization of the relationship between resilience and other "-*ilities*" (Fig. 6). In this hypothesis, we focus on the analysis of the resilience and its environment and highlight the various components to consider to evaluate resilience. The four components considered are (in red and numbered on Fig. 6):

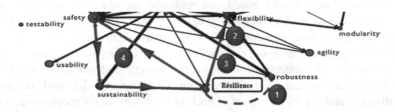

Fig. 6. Partial correlation network of "-*ilities*" including components for evaluation. (Color figure online)

1. **The influence.** It identifies which "-*ilities*" influence resilience. Some influences are currently identified. However, as claimed in [2], some might exist but are not yet identified. In order to assess resilience based on all elements, it is necessary to identify any dependence between resilience and other "-*ilities*".
2. **The orientation.** It means to define if the influence is unidirectional (ex. quality → resilience) or bidirectional (ex. quality ↔ resilience). This orientation must be considered "from" resilience "to" another "-*ilities*" as well as "from" another "-*ilities*" to resilience.
3. **Dependence.** It defines the intensity of the variation between two "-*ilities*". For instance a high variation (positive or negative) of an "-*ility*" leading to a high variation (positive or negative) of the impacted "-*ility*" expresses a high dependence.
4. **The propagation.** The chain represents a relation "starting from" the resilience and returning to the resilience via another "-*ilities*" (resilience → safety → sustainability). In this work we consider and limit a chain to a path with 3 "-*ilities*".

In this hypothesis, we present the "-*ilities*" that have links with the resilience and thus we analyze their relations based on the four components (influence, orientation, dependence, and propagation). Figure 7 shows the set of "-*ilities*" in relation with the resilience. Some links stem from [2], and some are added following the study of the "-*ilities*" and their possible relationships. For instance, interoperability is linked with resilience, since it enables a collaborative system to collaborate coherently to achieve the desired operational effect, so the relationship with resilience – *e.g.* to mitigate crisis situation - is needed and important. Adaptability is an "-*ility*" expected in the dynamic of resilience (response zone – ability to adapt), so it has a direct link to resilience, which helps to minimize a negative impact. Then a given link must be characterized by the four components defining a relation. For instance, the sustainability influences (component 1 – influence) the resilience that means a variation of sustainability leads a variation of the resilience. Then, the direction (component 2 - orientation) of this influence is directed from sustainability to resilience, because sustainability allows the system to withstand shocks (Zone 2 – response). The force (component 3 – dependence) is defined such as the high increase of sustainability leads to a high increase of the resilience. Lastly, the propagation (component 4 – propagation) represents the chain - limited to three path - starting from the sustainability *via* the resilience. In this example the chain is characterized by the path sustainability – resilience – safety (with a last feedback to sustainability). Figure 8 summarizes the relation between resilience and sustainability in agreements with the four items of the first hypothesis. In this end, each relationship between resilience and other "*-ilities*" (which impact resilience) have to be identified and formalized. In the same way, the components, such as dependence and propagation, must formally established to allow the evaluation of the resilience (*e.g.* quantification or qualification of dependence and definition of effect in the propagation chain).

Fig. 7. Network of correlation of "*-ilities*" and resilience

Based on these first components presented, we will define resilience indicator that will measure and manage the capacity of a collaborative system to recover from an event. The indicator considers the capacity to cope with the consequences of disturbances. In addition, the indicator explains the impact of anticipation, response and recovery activities that could be taken after the disruption to reach the acceptable level of service (performance).

Moreover, the resilience dynamic must be considered. Indeed, the aim is to know the level of resilience for each zone to implement adapted solution to improve resilience. To this purpose, "*-ilities*" and their influences are mapped in each zone (*e.g.* flexibility can be expected during the prevention, Fig. 9). This positioning is relative to the analysis of resilience and "*-ilities*" that have identified links in each area. The objective is to get a resilience indicator for each zone. In the end, the aggregation of each indicator will provide an evaluation of the resilience. Thus, each "*-ilities*" related to resilience is analyzed to be re-located precisely on the corresponding phase of resilience. This analysis is mainly related to the study of the intrinsic characteristics and

Influence	Orientation	Dependence	Propagation
Resilience-Sustainability	S → R	Strong	Resilience, Safety, Sustainability

Fig. 8. Characterization of the relation between resilience and sustainability

their understanding of a given "*-ility*" with regards to characteristics expected during a given phase of the resilience. It is to note that a given "*-ility*" can cover several phases of resilience life-cycle. For instance, robustness is interpreted as a measure of performance change. It is positioned in anticipation zone, because the effect of robustness allows the system to increase the readiness to deal with disruptive events. It is also positioned in the response zone, which makes it possible to absorb the negative effects of a disturbing event and increase the level of resilience of the system. Adaptability is the ability of a system to change to perform its basic work in uncertain or changing environments. Thus, adaptability is positioned in the response zone (Fig. 9), by minimizing the negative impact by protection against shocks. As last example, flexibility can be defined as the ability of a system to comply with its core mission that is not included in the definition of system requirements in disrupted or changing environments. This can be conceptualized as minimizing the consequences with less effort [17]. Thus, the flexibility is positioned on response and recovery zones. Figure 9 shows the mapping of the "*-ilities*" with the different resilience zones (*e.g.* flexibility is positioned in zone 2, zone 3 and robustness in zone 1, zone 2, zone 3). Mapping makes possible to establish the resilience indicators associated with these "*-ilities*" and for each zone. These indicators ultimately enable the level of resilience to be accurately identified and assessed, so aggregation of all these indicators will provide an assessment of the overall resilience.

Fig. 9. Resilience Dynamic and "*-ilities*" mapping

4 Conclusion

The here presented work aims, in the end, to evaluate the resilience relying on the dynamic of the resilience and on its study as an "*-ilities*" belonging to an ecosystem of "*-ilities*". The purpose is to support a collective of actors - for instance involved in a collaborative network - to manage their resilience based on the knowledge of its level and to improve it. First, several resilience metrics are studied and analyzed as well as the relationship between resilience and other "*-ilities*". Then, the components that defines the relationship between "*-ilities*" are defined and "*-ilities*" linked to the resilience are mapped by positioning them according to its dynamic. Future work is related to the formalization of the components of relationship to get metric and to evaluate the resilience.

References

1. ISO/TC 184/SC 5: Advanced automation technologies and their applications — Part 1: framework for enterprise interoperability (2011)
2. De Weck, O.L., Ross, A.M., Rhodes, D.H.: Investigating relationships and semantic sets amongst system lifecycle properties (Ilities). In: Third International Engineering Systems Symposium, CESUN 2012, Delft University of Technology, 18–20 June 2012
3. Chin, K.S., Yau, P.E.E.E., Wah, S.I.M.K., Khiang, P.C.: Framework for managing system-of-systems ilities, pp. 56–65 (2013)
4. Haimes, Y.Y.: On the definition of resilience in systems. Risk Anal. **29**(4), 498–501 (2009)
5. Francis, R., Bekera, B.: A metric and frameworks for resilience analysis of engineered and infrastructure systems. Reliab. Eng. Syst. Saf. **121**, 90–103 (2014)
6. Berkeley III, A.R., Wallace, M.: National infrastructure advisory council a framework for establishing critical infrastructure resilience goals final report and recommendations by the council (2010)
7. Andrews, Z., Bryans, J., Payne, R., Kristensen, K.: Fault modelling in system-of-systems contracts (2014)
8. Hollnagel, E.: Resilience engineering in practice: a guidebook (2013)
9. Cutter, S.L., et al.: Disaster resilience: a national imperative, pp. 25–29 (2013)
10. UNESCO: Disaster planning: prevention, response, recovery (2017)
11. Nan, C., Sansavini, G.: A quantitative method for assessing resilience of interdependent infrastructures. Reliab. Eng. Syst. Saf. **157**, 35–53 (2017)
12. Henry, D., Ramirez-Marquez, J.E.: Generic metrics and quantitative approaches for system resilience as a function of time. Reliab. Eng. Syst. Saf. **99**, 114–122 (2012)
13. Zobel, C.W.: Representing perceived tradeoffs in defining disaster resilience. Decis. Support Syst. **50**, 394–403 (2011)
14. Henry, D., Ramirez-Marquez, J.E.: Generic metrics and quantitative approaches for system resilience as a function of time (2012)
15. Zobel, C.W.: Comparative visualization of predicted disaster resilience. In: Seventh International ISCRAM Conference, pp. 1–6 (2010)
16. Fricke, E., Schulz, A.P.: Design for changeability (DfC): principles to enable changes in systems throughout their entire lifecycle. Syst. Eng. (2005)
17. Bordoloi, S.K., Cooper, W.W., Matsuo, H.: Flexibility, adaptability, and efficiency in manufacturing systems. Prod. Oper. Manag. **8**(2), 133–150 (1999)
18. Nogal, M., O'Connor, A., Caulfield, B., Martinez-Pastor, B.: Resilience of traffic networks: from perturbation to recovery via a dynamic restricted equilibrium model. Reliab. Eng. Syst. Saf. **156**, 84–96 (2016)
19. Cox, A., Prager, F., Rose, A.: Transportation security and the role of resilience: a foundation for operational metrics. Transp. Policy **18**(2), 307–317 (2011)
20. Filippone, E., Gargiulo, F., Errico, A., Di, V., Pascarella, D.: Resilience management problem in ATM systems as a shortest path problem (2016)

Nurturing Virtual Collaborative Networks into Urban Resilience for Seismic Hazards Mitigation

Giulia Cerè[✉], Wanqing Zhao[✉], and Yacine Rezgui[✉]

BRE Trust Centre for Sustainable Engineering, Cardiff School of Engineering,
Cardiff University, Cardiff CF243AB, UK
{cereg, zhaow9, rezguiy}@cardiff.ac.uk

Abstract. A holistic analysis of the resilience of the built environment in relation to natural disasters needs to consider multidimensional parameters being interactive and mutually influencing each other as a collaborative network, including the physical side of the urban framework (e.g., structures and infrastructures) and the socio-organizational system (e.g., stakeholders, designers and governments). In this paper, an analysis is conducted to first provide a categorization of several dimensions that characterize the urban context, such as damage and structural typology, urban connectivity, building functionality. These factors have been then related to the resilience of the built environment in the context of the urban system considered as a collaborative network in order to point out the relevant interdependencies between its components. Particularly, this is meant to identify the relevant socio-organizational nodes, their interaction and how their collaboration can reflect on the physical network. The analysis is based on the real data from Old Beichuan, a town severely destroyed in the 2008 Wenchuan earthquake in China.

Keywords: Resilience · Collaborative networks · Built environment

1 Introduction

Collaborative networks (CNs) consist of a set of autonomous entities geographically distributed, jointly working for the achievement of a shared goal and value creation [1]. The level of integration achieved in CNs is a characterizing factor that differentiate them from other virtually networked structures. In fact, this leads to data-rich collaboration where information are owned by the different entities with a continuous mutual exchange bringing more value than the simple sum of the knowledge contribution produced by the individual members [2]. The underlying idea behind CNs is then the enhanced value chain process resulting from the shared knowledge and high interconnectivity level between all the network components.

A CN is therefore constituted by a series of nodes that can be either considered as socio-organizational or physical. Examples of socio-organizational nodes can be private and public stakeholders, regulatory institutions and governmental authorities whereas physical nodes refer to structural and infrastructural elements, such as buildings, roads and energy-related institutions. Each node of the CN entails a specific

L. M. Camarinha-Matos et al. (Eds.): PRO-VE 2018, IFIP AICT 534, pp. 132–143, 2018.
https://doi.org/10.1007/978-3-319-99127-6_12

function, hence for instance the regulatory one is in charge of devising the legislative standards that the planning and design nodes must comply to. Grounding of that, the response to a specific disruption provides an immediate indication of the level of collaboration between the different figures involved in the prevention, design and post-disaster management phases that should be iteratively be adapted according to the evolving nature of disasters [3].

Existing researches mainly combine the concepts of resilience and CNs to natural hazards separately while dealing with disaster risk management. On a large scale, several researches focus on the contribution of the individual entities involved in the resilience planning or they adopt a more governmental-based approach [4]. Interactive online mapping technologies are already in place where the historical patrimony of the building stock is significant [5], providing sectorial mapping of rural and urban areas, historical nucleuses and consolidated territorial planned zones. On a building level, the work proposed by Uzielli et al. [6] is a representative example of how to quantify resilience on a urban scale in face of soil-related disruptions and involving a multi-domain mapping for the characterization of the building stock. Cerè et al. [7] conversely presented an overview of resilience in face of natural hazards examining both qualitative and quantitative approaches.

On the other side, there is a growing trend in considering the concept of CNs together with resilience in face of natural hazards, although concrete applications have not been considered extensively. For example, the work devised by Jassbi et al. [2] draws the attention to the multifaceted nature of resilience and the need of overcoming traditional risk-based approaches in favor of a methodology enriched by the interrelations between the entities constituting the system, hence as a CN. Jung and Song [8] strengthened the existing linkage between CNs, resilience and disaster management, highlighting how the entities' fragmentation hinders the overall post-disaster response and it is not financially beneficial. The authors also underline the case-specificity of the "bonding and bridging effect" between the diverse network components, consisting in the inter-organizational connectivity within a specific CN [8]. Andrew and Carr [9] strengthen the underpinning concepts of trust and information-sharing between the actors of a CN, calling for a collective recognition of the risk scenario and stronger consensus on the strategy to adopt.

The existing body of knowledge regarding CNs and resilience is therefore consistent and extensive, but not in terms of their practical implementation relatively to urban scenarios in face of natural hazards. The presented work aims at contextualizing the concept of CNs and resilience while dealing with seismic scenarios, considering the whole urban framework as a CN and identifying the relevant connections between both the physical (e.g., buildings and infrastructures) and virtual (e.g., stakeholders) components. The analysis focuses in particular on the county of Old Beichuan, in the aftermath of the 2008 Wenchuan Earthquake. Besides, the proposed research highlights the consequences of the fragmentation in CNs, leading to an insufficient resiliency level and resulting in poor preventive and post-disaster recovery measures [10].

The paper is structured into five sections, starting with an overview regarding the methodology devised for the research and followed in the third section by a detailed description of the mapping. Subsequently, the outcome of the mapping will be discussed in the fourth section followed by the conclusions in the fifth one.

2 Methodology and Study Area

In this section the county of Old Beichuan is adopted as a case study aimed at contextualizing the presented research. Old Beichuan is located in the Wenchuan province in China, and has also been accounted amongst the most significantly damaged sites in the aftermath of the 2008 earthquake. The methodology adopted for the scope of the presented analysis is outlined in Fig. 1 and entails three main phases (i.e., A, B and C). In first instance, the data-collection phase has been carried out throughout two field trips in December 2016 and July 2017, and the richest dataset has been gathered relatively to the central portion of Old Beichuan, since the remaining areas of the city (i.e., the northern and southern ones) were not directly accessible. The whole dataset included 3D laser scanning, photographic material and satellite imageries that allowed the comparison between pre and post site-conditions. These imageries have been gathered from the Google Earth database and particularly for the years 2001 and 2010. As part of the first work thread a preliminary site analysis has been carried out by manually mapping the whole building stock of the area in order to then compare it with the satellite imageries and photos. A schematic of the area available at the entrance of the Old Beichuan site allowed to identify the institutional buildings (e.g., transportation bureau, schools), while specific information regarding the functionality were gathered from panels spread in the site. It has to be pointed out that it is likely for some buildings to be lacking in the analysis because they have been completely destroyed and in the meantime the debris have been removed.

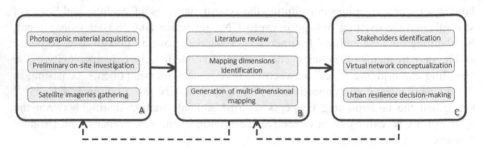

Fig. 1. Methodology overview

The second stage involved a literature review of existing qualitative damage scales for seismic-related hazards and the identification of the dimensions to include in the mapping. Following to that, the information regarding each dimension have contextually been added to the overlapped satellite imageries to characterize the physical network. Eventually, the third part of the work entailed the interpretation of the produced material considering the whole urban framework as a CN and implementing resilience in order to evaluate the response to the hazard. The mapping is therefore functional to the identification of the socio-organizational elements (i.e., nodes) of the CN and how their decision-making processes can influence the physical nodes in case of disruption.

3 Incorporating Collaborative Networks for Urban Resilience Analysis

Scope of this work is to adopt the concept of CNs for the understanding of resilience in the context of a real case scenario in the aftermath of a seismic hazard and this section in particular focuses on the interrelations between the different nodes of the urban network. The focus is on how the socio-organizational ones can be related to resilience management and their influence on the physical network in the context of the urban framework as a CN.

Figures 2, 5 and 6 show different levels of mapping as a result of the data-set analysis results overlapping to the 2010 post-earthquake satellite imagery gained from the Google Earth database, as previously described in Sect. 2. Mainly, the multi-dimensional mapping involves the following:

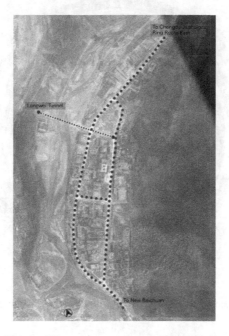

Fig. 2. Urban connectivity of Old Beichuan

- Road network system and connectivity with other urban centers, as in Fig. 2;
- Damage level according to the qualitative site-specific scale, as in Fig. 5a;
- Damage typology, as in Fig. 5b;
- Building functionality, as in Fig. 6a;
- Construction material (i.e., reinforced concrete framed buildings or masonry load bearing structures) as in Fig. 6b.

Figure 3 highlights the specific influence of each mapped dimension on the main phases of resilience as identified by the literature [11] in mainly: disaster prevention, damage propagation, assessment and recovery. In particular, it is outlined how different factors can influence certain phases rather than others and this entails the involvement of specific socio-organizational nodes that have an influence on the physical network, as represented in Fig. 4. For instance, stakeholders and clients have an influence on the technical and planning nodes, imposing financial constraints that therefore reflect on the construction technology and overall quality of the structure in the preventive phase. At the damage occurrence, this translates into specific damage levels and typologies which cannot be influenced anymore but they can be functional for post-disaster and recovery strategies for insurance companies, regulatory nodes and constructors. Given the cyclic nature of this process, information from previous disaster are vital for improving preventive strategies, as it can be seen in Fig. 3 where it is highlighted that damage-related mapping have a significant impact on this phase.

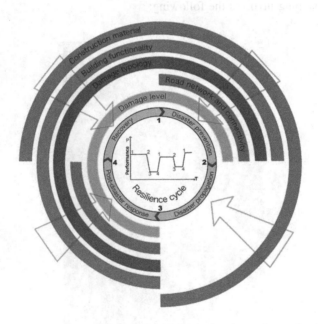

Fig. 3. Interdependencies between multi-dimensional mapping and resilience

The building functionality is a key aspect given its strong interrelations between the regulatory nodes and stakeholders. In fact, regulations establish specific categories of building defined as "strategic" (e.g., hospitals and schools) that are requested to comply higher performance levels. Normally these buildings are financed by public stakeholders, which should translate into more effective preventive measures and construction technologies, influencing both damage level and typology. The building functionality is also relevant for post-disaster and recovery phases. In fact, depending on damage level and typology, the technical nodes (e.g., planners, designers and engineers) have to collaborate with insurance companies to assess the financial entity of

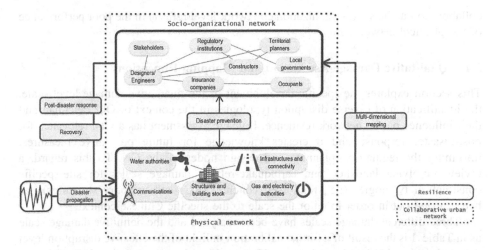

Fig. 4. Collaborative urban network conceptualization

the damage and then inform occupants and stakeholders in respect to the required interventions for performance recovery.

Figure 4 also shows how the different phases of resilience interlace with the CN structure and how they specifically influence each other. In particular, the mapping is the instrument functional for the socio-organizational nodes to characterize the physical network and understand where to intervene, since each dimension (e.g., damage type and level, construction technology) can be qualified and classified. Post-disaster response and recovery are mainly unidirectional actions resulting from decisions taken at the socio-organizational network level and impacting the physical nodes. Conversely, preventive strategies are mutually affected by both socio-organizational and physical nodes, since their development is nurtured by previous disruption information, as in Fig. 3.

As it can be observed both from Figs. 3 and 4, the disaster propagation cannot actively be dumped other than intervening on preventive measures, which are key for a good resilient performance of the system and they are highly influenced by lessons learnt from previous disruptions. That is why damage level and typology mapping are vital to categorize the vulnerability of the physical system in face of potential future hazards, in a cyclic process as in Figs. 3 and 4. Being the whole urban framework a highly interconnected network and considering the mutual influences of the different components as in Fig. 3, it becomes clear that to improve the system's resilience it is required to intervene on the level of collaboration. Figure 3 shows in fact that a simultaneous coincidence of several domains in the same phase translates in a higher demand for collaboration. This means involving socio-organizational nodes with different domains of expertise in order to cover all the requested dimensions of analysis.

The consideration of the urban framework as a CN leads to understand that each network component (i.e., component of the network) is meant to be influenced by the others and at the same time it has an effect on other features. A scarce level of collaboration at the socio-organizational network level reflects in the poor performance of the physical network.

3.1 Qualitative Damage Assessment and Mapping Dimensions

This section explores the specific development of the qualitative damage level scale, the identification of diverse disruption typologies in the context of Old Beichuan and their influence on the network resilience. Damage assessment has a vital relevance for post-disaster response and it creates knowledge for future preventive measures, informing the regulatory, planning and design nodes of the CN. To this regard, a review involving landslide and earthquake-related damage scales for site-specific construction typologies (i.e., reinforced concrete (RC) and masonry structures) has been carried out in order to tailor the scale to the specific Chinese context.

Three different damage scales have been analyzed and the definitive damage scale as in Table 1 is the result of a further calibration in light of the effective disruption level detected during the field investigations. The resulting damage scale involves structural and non-structural elements and concerns mainly two structural technologies (i.e., RC frames and masonry buildings) being the most popular types in mountainous Chinese areas [12] and in light of the field investigations in Old Beichuan. The first scale of damage analyzed was developed by Okada and Takai [13] and mainly deals with seismic hazards addressing RC structures, wooden frames and masonry buildings. The scale proposed by Mavrouli et al. [14] has been included given its consideration of structural and non-structural elements (e.g., infills and openings), in addition to its applicability to landslide scenarios. The author also involved the development of fragility curves, which cannot be adopted in the context of Old Beichuan site, given the predominantly qualitative dataset of information. The choice of the damage scale developed by Hu et al. [12] was motivated by their analysis of buildings damaged by debris flow occurred in Zhouqu (China) in 2010 and grounds on the China's Classification System of Earthquake Damage to Buildings [15].

The classification based on construction materials, as in Fig. 6b, has been obtained based on the works devised by [12–14, 16], which involved mainly analysis conducted in the context of debris flows and seismic events. Lieping [16] and Hu [12] proposed overviews of the Chinese construction background in the aftermath of respectively a debris flow and the 2008 Wenchuan earthquake, allowing a deeper understanding of the most frequent structural typologies. The final classification is based on the field investigations carried out in December 2016 and July 2017, since they represent directly the materials effectively adopted in that area, mainly RC frames and masonry buildings.

The typology of damage summarized as in Fig. 5b has been assessed qualitatively combining the on-site investigations with the overview provided by Lieping et al. [16] regarding building disruptions detected in the aftermath of the Wenchuan Earthquake. Namely, the damage typologies are the following:

- Foundation system failure: consisting mainly in the incapability of the foundation of withstanding the soil deformation and hence leading to differential displacements in the superstructure;

Table 1. Adapted damage scale for seismic hazard for the Chinese context.

Damage index	Damage description for RC frames with masonry infills	Damage description for masonry load-bearing walls buildings
D0	No damage	
D1	Negligible damage, building preserves its functionality with no need for repair	
D2	Structural elements show thin cracks, more visible cracks on infill and non-structural walls; building functionality not affected	Secondary walls damaged; building functionality not affected; minor repairs are needed
D3	Visible cracks on structural elements, severe cracks on non-structural elements and detachment of concrete from columns and beams; infill walls collapsed partially; building functionality compromised	Minority of load-bearing walls damaged, extensive cracks on load bearing walls and roof. Overall functionality compromised
D4	Minority of load-bearing walls damaged, extensive cracks on load bearing walls and roof. Overall functionality compromised	Majority of load-bearing walls damaged and failure of pitched roofs. Functionality severely compromised. Building might not worth to be repaired
D5	Severe collapse of structural elements, less than 50% of the building survives or it is totally collapsed	Majority of load bearing walls severely damaged, building stability jeopardized or complete structural failure

- Soft-storey collapse-mechanism: primarily ascribed to a lack of stiffening elements at the ground level (e.g., infill walls). This collapse mechanism mainly affects RC frames;
- Overall torsional behavior: this is usually due to a wrong placement of stiffness and mass centers in the structure leading to the development of torsional actions given a torque generated between the two centers;
- Development of plastic hinges: this mechanism happens when in particular sections of the structure the solicitation forces the section to exploit its deformational plastic abilities.

4   Discussion

The strong interconnection between the socio-organizational and physical networks constituting the overall urban CN and how this interlaces with resilience is showed in both Figs. 3 and 4. The devised multi-dimensional mapping shows how the gathered information are complimentary to the demand for a strong level of cooperation particularly needed prior to the hazard occurrence (i.e., disaster prevention) and in its aftermath (i.e., post-disaster response). These phases consists in fact in the ones that can influence the most the response of the physical system to the hazard and entail the highest level of planning and a horizontal collaboration across the different actors of the virtual system.

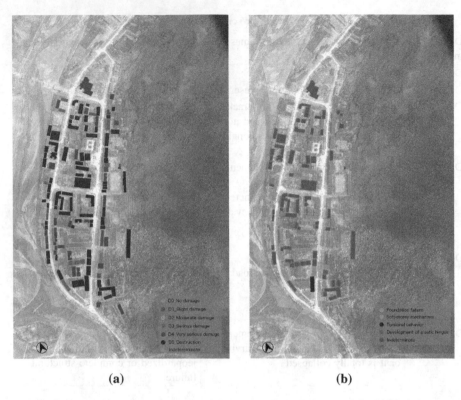

(a)   (b)

Fig. 5. Level (a) and typology (b) of damage to the building stock in Old Beichuan

The mapping appears to be consistent with the conceptualization proposed in Fig. 3 and also with the information gathered in site in relation to the post-disaster response. In fact, Fig. 1 shows that the road network has not been designed to be redundant, implying both a poor level of strategic planning in the preliminary phase and a scarce site-analysis. This lack of foresight and interrelation between the CN components lead to the incapability of emergency rescue systems to access the area once the three main access points have been compromised, forcing civilians to compensate the absence of emergency plans. It has been in fact acknowledged from the site investigation that in the aftermath of the seismic event the Water and Agricultural Machinery Bureau of Old Beichuan provided numerous public water emergency points in order to supply water to the survivors also repairing damaged water points that prevented people from accessing potable water. On a different note, it is worth pointing that no fire brigade headquarter has been detected in the investigated area of Old Beichuan.

Figure 3 shows that construction materials and in general the structural nature and its design influence the whole resilience cycle, apart from the post-response phase. In particular, this dimension is the only one that can damp the disaster propagation because it is impossible to intervene on a structure during an ongoing hazard. Considering also the mapping provided in Fig. 6b and the overall level of disruption registered as in Fig. 5a, it becomes clear that this dimension tightly interlace with the level and typology of the damage, which consequently have the function to inform designers, stakeholders and decision-makers nodes in general about new potential constructions and preventive strategies following to the recovery. Therefore, the information acquired from the multi-dimensional mapping have scope of transferring information from the physical to the socio-organizational network in order to prioritize post-response and recovery strategies but also nurturing the knowledge for future preventive strategies.

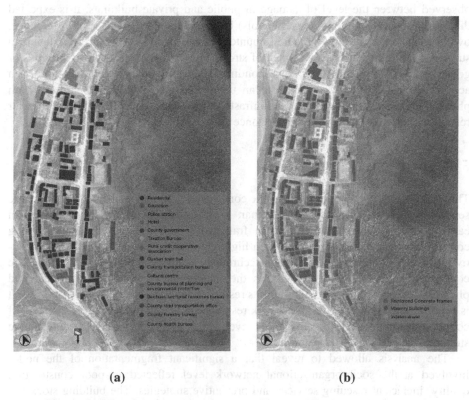

(a)   **(b)**

Fig. 6. Building functions (a) and construction materials (b) in Old Beichuan

With particular regard to the context of Old Beichuan County, an overall fragmentation of the different CN entities has been registered, showing a lack of preventive strategies for post-response planning and a poor resilience achieved at the physical network level. This led to a negative chain of events in which the non-collaborative nature of this particular urban network resulted in a complete incapability of response and recovery from the event, despite the significant efforts of local emergency services. As pointed out in Sect. 3 and shown in Figs. 4a and b, a strong correlation between the seriousness of the damage and its geotechnical-based nature has been detected. In particular it has been observed a predominant soft-storey behavior failure mechanism induced by vertical differential settlements at the foundation level. This reveals an evident fragmentation between the nodes involved in the preliminary design phase of the different buildings. In particular, this applies to all the technical entities involved in site analysis and design (e.g., geologists, engineers, territorial planners, local authorities) and their interaction with budget-holder nodes, such as stakeholders and governmental nodes. As a matter of fact, in most cases stakeholders and clients are reluctant to invest significant amount of money to devise preventive measure in face of events with a probabilistic occurrence [7], such as seismic hazards.

On the other side and in light of the mapping, no particular correlation has been observed between the level of damage in public and private buildings. It is expected that public-owned buildings (e.g., schools) have undergone a lower level of damage, owing to more performing structural countermeasure thanks to the stronger financial support coming from the involvement of strong investors such as public authorities or governments. Despite that, a corresponding level of collaboration has not been achieved and this clearly reflected in an unsuitable planning with regards to both physical elements (e.g., structures and infrastructures) and strategies (e.g., post-disaster response), affective the overall performance of the network.

5 Conclusions

This paper presented an integration of the concepts of CNs and resilience in the specific seismic hazard scenario of Old Beichuan in the aftermath of the 2008 Wenchuan earthquake. To characterize the urban framework and highlight the underpinning connections, five dimensions have been highlighted and mapped (i.e., urban connectivity, building function, construction technology, damage typology and level). The conceptualization of the urban CN as the integration of socio-organizational and physical networks allowed to highlight its resiliency level in face of a seismic hazard. It is been outlined how the overall network resilience is highly influenced by the level of collaboration at the socio-organizational level, which particularly reflects in preventive strategies and post-disaster response.

The analysis allowed to reveal that a significant fragmentation of the nodes involved at the socio-organizational network level reflected in poor construction quality, inefficient rescuing services and preventive strategies. The building stock has been incapable of damping the disaster propagation due to unsuitable design choices, making impossible any type of recovery. Stakeholders and designers have to be sensitized about the long-term consequences of the decisions taken prior to any actions, considering that the high level of interdependency of urban network leads to proportionate likelihood for disaster chains. A consideration of the urban framework as a CN embedding resilience can provide a comprehensive overview of the different nodes composing the socio-organizational network. This aspect is crucial in order to achieve a targeted planning of how to address the urban CN's resilience in each of its phases and for each of the dimensions that have an effect on it.

Acknowledgements. This research is supported by the Building Research Establishment (BRE) and the National Environment Research Council (NERC) under grant NE/N012240/1.

References

1. Camarinha-Matos, L.M., Afsarmanesh, H.: Collaborative networks. In: Wang, K., Kovacs, G.L., Wozny, M., Fang, M. (eds.) PROLAMAT 2006. IIFIP, vol. 207, pp. 26–40. Springer, Boston (2006). https://doi.org/10.1007/0-387-34403-9_4
2. Jassbi, J., Camarinha-Matos, L.M., Barata, J.: A framework for evaluation of resilience of disaster rescue networks. In: Camarinha-Matos, L.M., Bénaben, F., Picard, W. (eds.) PRO-VE 2015. IFIP, vol. 463, pp. 146–158. Springer, Cham (2015). https://doi.org/10.1007/978-3-319-24141-8_13
3. Barthe-Delanoë, A.-M., Bénaben, F., Carbonnel, S., Pingaud, H.: Event-driven agility of crisis management collaborative processes. In: 9th International ISCRAM Conference 2012, Vancouver, pp. 1–5 (2012)
4. Shim, J., Kim, C.-I.: Measuring resilience to natural hazards: towards sustainable hazard mitigation. Sustainability 7, 14153–14185 (2015)
5. Comune di Bologna Iperbole. http://dru.iperbole.bologna.it/cartografia. Accessed 13 Apr 2018
6. Uzielli, M., Catani, F., Tofani, V., Casagli, N.: Risk analysis for the Ancona landslide-II: estimation of risk to buildings. Landslides 12(1), 83–100 (2015)
7. Cerè, G., Rezgui, Y., Zhao, W.: Critical review of existing built environment resilience frameworks: directions for future research. Int. J. Disaster Risk Reduct. 25, 173–189 (2017)
8. Jung, K., Song, M.: Linking emergency management networks to disaster resilience: bonding and bridging strategy in hierarchical or horizontal collaboration networks. Qual. Quant. 49(4), 1465–1483 (2015)
9. Andrew, S.A., Carr, J.B.: Mitigating uncertainty and risk in planning for regional preparedness: the role of bonding and bridging relationships. Urban Stud. 50(4), 709–724 (2013)
10. Mischen, P.A.: Collaborative network capacity. Public Manag. Rev. 173(3), 380–403 (2015)
11. Ouyang, M., Dueñas-Osorio, L.: Time-dependent resilience assessment and improvement of urban infrastructure systems. Chaos Interdiscip. J. Nonlinear Sci. 22(3), 033122 (2012)
12. Hu, K.H., Cui, P., Zhang, J.Q.: Characteristics of damage to buildings by debris flows on 7 August 2010 in Zhouqu, Western China. Nat. Hazards Earth Syst. Sci. 12(7), 2209–2217 (2012)
13. Okada, S., Takai, N.: Classifications of structural types and damage patterns of buildings for earthquake field investigation. In: 12th World Conference on Earthquake Engineering, Auckland (2000)
14. Mavrouli, O., et al.: Vulnerability assessment for reinforced concrete buildings exposed to landslides. Bull. Eng. Geol. Environ. 73(2), 265–289 (2014)
15. Classification of earthquake damage to buildings and special structures. National Standard of China, GB/T 24335-2009 (2009)
16. Lieping, Y., Xinzheng, L., Zhe, Q., Peng, F.: Analysis on building seismic damage in the Wenchuan earthquake. In: The 14th World Conference on Earthquake Engineering, Beijing (2008)

Sensing, Smart and Sustainable Enterprises

Sensing, Smart and Sustainable S^3 Enterprises: Principles, Goals and Rules

Fábio Müller Guerrini[✉], Thales Botelho de Sousa, and Juliana Suemi Yamanari

São Carlos School of Engineering, University of São Paulo, São Carlos, SP, Brazil
{guerrini,thalesbotelho,jusuemi}@usp.br

Abstract. Currently, traditional companies need of models, skills, processes and technologies to face the challenges imposed by the highly competitive market, which requires constant innovations. Through the concepts of detection and monitoring, intelligence and sustainability, Sensing, Smart and Sustainable (S^3) enterprises exert an important role in the digitization of strategies, decisions and operations, and are efficient to face the challenges intrinsic to the digital economy and intelligent manufacturing. Literature presents the need of development of methods and enterprise models that portray reality of the S^3 Enterprises. In this context, to facilitate the formalization of S^3 Enterprises and understand the dynamics of their operations, this paper aims to develop an enterprise model of such organizations. Through the For Enterprise Modeling method, the enterprise model documents the goals, business rules, processes and concepts of S^3 Enterprises. The contribution of this paper is the identification of guiding principles that allow companies interested in applying the S^3 concepts have a reference as base, once it has been mapped through perspectives of different domains of knowledge.

Keywords: Sensing enterprise · Smart enterprise · Sustainable enterprise Enterprise modeling · Intelligent manufacturing

1 Introduction

Weichhart et al. [1] introduced the concept of Sensing, Smart and Sustainable (S^3) enterprise system, presenting the challenges and current developments of digital age companies. This concept its quite new, therefore, there are a lot of challenges around this novel theme. Like the Industries 4.0, Made in China 2025, Internet Industrial, Advanced Manufacturing, Internet +, Society 5.0, among other similar initiatives developed in many countries, S^3 Enterprise can be seen as one of the industrial approaches for achieving the intelligent manufacturing.

The concept of sensing enterprise was created with the advent of the Augmented Internet, representing an attempt of reconciling traditional non-native "Internet-friendly" organizations with the stupendous possibilities offered by the cyber worlds [2]. Sensing enterprise is characterized by the anticipation of future decisions through of capture of multidimensional information, and it enables that a company reaches and

L. M. Camarinha-Matos et al. (Eds.): PRO-VE 2018, IFIP AICT 534, pp. 147–155, 2018.
https://doi.org/10.1007/978-3-319-99127-6_13

knows different scenarios. In addition, sensing enterprise develops proactivity and dynamism for quick and efficient decision-making in a short time [3]. According to Filos [4], smart enterprise is an interconnected, knowledge-driven organization. Smart enterprise is able to adapt quickly to changes and challenges of the current competitive market, and also is agile enough to create and exploit knowledge, in response to the opportunities of the digital age [4]. Sustainable enterprise concept is associated with the implementation of good manufacturing practices, reducing the use of inputs for production, optimizing plant operations and improving products in order to minimize the inherent environmental impacts arising from its use and life cycle. Thus, in addition to environmental concerns, the sustainable enterprise must include social, economic and ethical aspects [5].

S^3 enterprises aim to meet the challenges of the digital age, requiring proper formalization [1]. Enterprise modeling is fundamental to understand the connection between companies, as well as the dynamics, robustness and fragility of the activities developed [6]. So, this paper aims to model the main elements related to S^3 enterprises through For Enterprise Modeling (4EM) method. The enterprise models aim to stimulate the application of sensing, smart and sustainable concepts.

2 Guiding Principles of the Modeling

According to Weichhart et al. [1], the sensing, smart and sustainable concepts are based on eight principles: agility, transparency, empowerment, sharing, collaboration, resilience, innovation and self-organization.

Agility is a temporal concept, associated with the response time and cycle of identification of opportunity, configuration, operation/reconfiguration and dissolution [7]. Transparency ensures access to information and cloud-based processing for enabling community response [1]. Empowerment refers to the influence and control of individuals and communities on the decisions that affect them. Sharing information and knowledge encourages innovation and collaboration processes [1]. Collaboration occurs when several autonomous and geographically distributed entities with a heterogeneous operating environment, culture, goals and social capital collaborate to achieve better results and common goals. Collaboration among companies is present in several studies involving: network of collaborative companies, alliances, partnerships, cooperation, collaborative supply chain, among others [8]. Resilience is the association of 3 essential components: notion of trauma, adversity and risk to the human development; positive adaptation and overcoming adversity; and process that considers the dynamics among emotional, sociocultural and cognitive mechanisms that influence human development [9]. Innovation is the successful use of new ideas in terms of products, processes, services and business practices [10]. Self-organization is the ability of reorganization of networks into more complex structures, as well as the use of more complex processes without a detailed and centralized management guideline [11].

This paper aims to stimulate the application of S^3 systems in companies, aid its formalization and processing of large amount of information, and pursuing this purpose, the principles have been incorporated into the modeling.

3   Methodology

3.1   Research Method

For modeling S^3 enterprises, papers published in Scopus and Web of Science databases were analyzed, and specialists of companies that are targeting the sensing, smart and sustainable concepts were interviewed. The professional interviewed was part of the staff of a technology company in the field of optoelectronics (working in the medical, industrial, optical, aerospace and defense components). In 2009, the company received the FINEP Innovation Award, in the category Medium-Sized Company. The professional was responsible by the departments and processes of import, export, purchasing, planning and control of production, warehousing, receiving and shipping.

3.2   Enterprise Modeling

For Loucopoulos and Kavakli [12], enterprise modeling is a set of conceptual modeling techniques to describe the structure and business processes of a company, its missions and objectives. For Sandkuhl et al. [13], 4EM provides systematic support for analyzing, understanding, and documenting a business, its objectives, business processes, and support systems. 4EM is based on organizational modeling, in order to clarify all current corporate functions, present requirements and necessary reasons for possible and certain organizational changes, expose alternatives to those requirements, and provide criteria for the evaluation of these alternatives.

4   Results

Based on the interview conducted and the information of the literature related, the Concepts, Goals, Business Rules, and Processes models were developed.

4.1   Concepts Model

S^3 enterprise is a digital company. The learning environment is necessary for efforts to bring benefits to companies. In this learning environment, teamwork refers to the flexibility, versatility, creativity and intelligence, essential concepts to S^3 enterprises. Sensing system includes orientation towards change and smart system involves the concepts of human and technological system and virtual organization. Sustainable system covers the concepts of reuse, reduction, recycling and consumer orientation, where the first three refer to the environmental aspects and the fourth to the economic and social aspects. Architectures and languages divided in enterprise architecture and service-oriented architecture serve as support for the system sustainability. Architecture is a description of a basic arrangement and connectivity of parts of a system and usually has several meanings, depending on its use. Guiding principles of S^3 enterprises are: agility associated with dynamic configuration, transparency, empowerment, sharing, collaboration, resilience, innovation and self-organization. Figure 1 presents the Concepts Model.

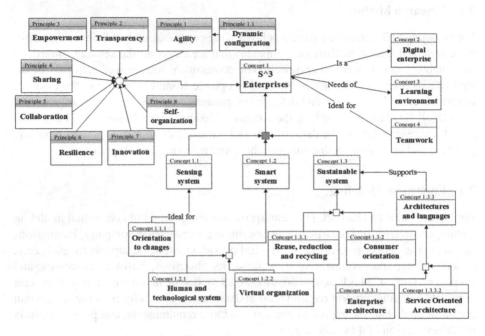

Fig. 1. Concepts model.

4.2 Goals and Business Rules Models

Figure 2 presents the Goals and Business Rules of S^3 enterprises. The main goal is to stimulate the application of S^3 systems, and it is directly supported by two goals: to strengthen competitiveness and to process large amount of information. S^3 system seeks to stimulate the sensing, smart and sustainable philosophies, create mechanisms for stimulating innovation, and to ensure collaboration, cooperation and a holistic vision. The threats related to this goal are conceptual, organizational and technological barriers. Some business opportunities are identified, such as improving digital competencies and decision-making. To strengthen the company competitiveness, it is necessary to invest periodically in intellectual assets. Processing large amounts of information requires strategic use of Information and Communication Technologies (ICTs) for real-time information gathering, integrated ICTs platforms, and adaptation to the increase in the volume of transactions. Stimulating the sensing philosophy requires the use of convergent ITs, and dynamism to meet market expectations. Stimulating smart philosophy makes continuous use of smart services. Stimulating sustainable philosophy requires the constant incorporation of elements of self-organization. Creation of mechanisms to stimulate innovation requires the continuous reappraisal of traditional paradigms and actors with complementary cognitive distances. To ensure collaboration and cooperation and a holistic view, it is essential to invest in Research and Development (R&D)

throughout the product life cycle. In addition, we can mention some rules that support this last goal, such as: stakeholder involvement throughout the product life cycle, development of an overview of the supply chain, and systematic monitoring of the product development process. Lastly, of course, there is a need to periodically audit the S^3 system, to ensure that it remains fully operational and that the main goals and all other goals are effectively achieved.

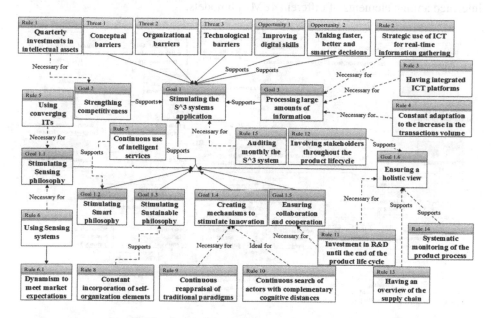

Fig. 2. Goals and business rules model.

4.3 Processes Model

The Processes Model of the 4EM interacts with Goals, Business Rules, and Technical Components and Requirements models. Figure 3 illustrates the Processes Model of S^3 enterprises. The process of sensing systems development is supported by the stimulus to this philosophy, capture of multidimensional information and proactivity and agility in decision making. Process 1 is triggered by five business rules: use of converging ITs; strategical use of ICTs to collect information in real time; establishment of collaborative links for innovation transfer; sharing of skills and resources; alignment and compatibilization of interorganizational goals. The process of smart systems development is supported by the stimulus to smart philosophy, adaptability to market needs, creation and exploitation of knowledge and responsiveness to the opportunities of the digital age. continuous use of intelligent services, integrated ICT platforms, establishment of collaborative links for innovation transfer; sharing of skills and resources; alignment and compatibilization of interorganizational goals are rules that trigger this process. The process of sustainable systems development is supported by stimulus to the sustainable philosophy and operations optimization of facility that receives support of a best practices bank. The process of sustainable systems development has eight associated rules: constant adaptation to the increase in the volume of transactions, incorporation of elements of self-organization, periodic audit of the S^3 system, reduction of productive inputs, improvement of products to minimize environmental impacts, establishment of collaborative links for innovation transfer, sharing of competencies and resources, and alignment and compatibility of interorganizational goals. Dashed lines indicate the interface among elements of different 4EM submodels.

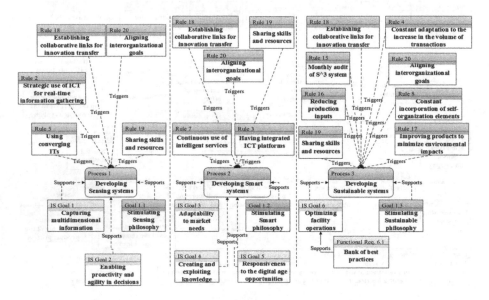

Fig. 3. Processes model.

5 Discussion of the Results

Using the 4EM methodology it was possible to obtain the following results:

- The Concepts Model presented the main definitions and principles of the S^3 enterprises, as well as some supporting concepts (architectures and languages) and its needs (orientation to change, teamwork and learning environment).
- The Goals and Business Rules Models presented the main goals of S^3 enterprises, the opportunities that can be reached with this new business paradigm, threats that hinder these opportunities, as well as the guidelines that, in addition to being closely related to the goals and processes, indicate the main considerations to be analyzed in its formalization.
- The Processes Model associates goals, rules, technical components and requirements, however, due to restriction of information, this model does not present in detail the main activities carried out for the formalization of S^3 enterprises. Even so, it is possible to observe the main rules that trigger each necessary process, as well as the information system goals and functional requirements that support certain processes.

6 Conclusions

This research presented concepts related to the S^3 enterprises, whose goals are directly related to the new trends and needs of the market. Through a literature review and consultation with specialist in the field, this study sought to provide an overview of the sensing, smart and sustainable concepts, with the purpose of developing enterprise models based on 4EM method. In this way, the models presented an initial view on the main requirements necessary for the formalization of S^3 enterprises. These models also allowed researchers, entrepreneurs and interested in the development of such organizations to analyze them from other perspectives.

6.1 Practical and Scientific Contributions of the Research

The main practical and scientific contributions of the research were:

- Provide stakeholders with an overview of S^3 enterprises, its foundations, concepts, expected goals, as well as the processes and rules necessary for its execution.
- Representation of S^3 enterprises in an enterprise model that was developed and systematized with the Concepts, Goals, Business Rules, and Processes models of the 4EM method. Such representation allows its analysis and orientation from different perspectives.
- Contributions for the literature of sensing, smart and sustainable enterprises, by filling research gaps identified in previous works, and presenting a new analytical approach for such organizations.

6.2 Critical Positioning

In our vision, collaborative networks have been identified as a major vehicle for consolidation of S^3 enterprises. Collaboration is an inherent principle to the S^3 enterprises, as the definition of its domain and use of the enterprise modeling as language allows to understand more clearly how the relationship among companies occurs. Regarding the development of the Processes Model, despite the difficulty in modeling the processes to the point of identifying specific steps, the modeling in high level allows to understand how the rules, goals and principles are correlated with the processes. Finally, the enterprise model is an initial step towards the construction of a formal and well-recognized framework of S^3 enterprises.

6.3 Limitations of the Approach and Future Research

It is important to point that not all steps defined by the 4EM method have been met. The method reinforces the need to gather a group of people to perform the enterprise modeling of the process in question, however this not occurred, as S^3 enterprises is still a future perspective, and consequently there are not many experts in the field with consolidated knowledge to provide consistent information.

Another important limiting factor to be mentioned is the fact that there are few papers applied on this subject in the literature, which complicates the collection of consolidated data and information. As S^3 enterprises are not yet properly formalized, the models of Actors and Resources, and Technical Components and Requirements of the 4EM method were not developed. Thus, future research can thoroughly examine the main agents and supporting information systems of these organizations, to incorporate them into the abovementioned enterprise submodels of the 4EM and join them to the other models presented in this paper. Another suggestion for future works is the execution of a case study to apply the models developed in this work, as according to Voss et al. [14], this is the most appropriate research method to conduct investigations in which experience is rare and contextual conditions are unknown, and for Runfola et al. [15], case study offers the opportunity of understanding a phenomenon that is particularly important in the field of management.

References

1. Weichhart, G., Molina, A., Chen, D., Whitman, L.E., Vernadat, F.: Challenges and current developments for sensing, smart and sustainable enterprise systems. Comput. Ind. **79**, 34–46 (2016)
2. Agostinho, C., Jardim-Gonçalves, R.: Sustaining interoperability of networked liquid-sensing enterprises: a complex systems perspective. Annu. Rev. Control **39**, 128–143 (2015)
3. Ferro-Beca, M., Sarraipa, J., Agostinho, C., Gigante, F., Jose-Nunez, M., Jardim-Gonçalves, R.: A framework for enterprise context analysis based on semantic principles. Comput. Sci. Inf. Syst. **12**(3), 931–960 (2015)
4. Filos, E.: Smart organizations in the digital age. In: Mezgar, I. (ed.) Integration of ICT in Smart Organizations. Idea Group Publishing, London (2006)
5. Mauricio-Moreno, H., Miranda, J., Chavarría, D., Ramírez-Cadena, M., Molina, A.: Design S3-RF (Sustainable x Smart x Sensing - Reference Framework) for the future manufacturing enterprise. IFAC-PapersOnLine **48**(3), 58–63 (2015)
6. Braha, D., Stacey, B., Bar-Yam, Y.: Corporate competition: a self-organized network. Soc. Net. **33**(3), 219–230 (2011)
7. Goranson, H.T.: The Agile Virtual Enterprise: Cases, Metrics and Tools. Quorum Books, Westport (1992)
8. Camarinha-Matos, L.M., Afsarmanesh, H.: On reference models for collaborative networked organizations. Int. J. Prod. Res. **46**(9), 2453–2469 (2008)
9. Luthar, S.S., Cicchetti, D., Becker, B.: The construct of resilience: a critical evaluation and guidelines for future work. Child Dev. **71**(3), 543–558 (2000)
10. Christopherson, S., Kitson, M.: Innovation, networks and knowledge exchange. Camb. J. Reg. Econ. Soc. **1**(2), 165–173 (2008)
11. Kash, D., Rycroft, R.: Emerging patterns of complex technological innovation. Technol. Forecast Soc. Change **69**(6), 581–606 (2002)
12. Loucopoulos, P., Kavakli, V.: Enterprise knowledge management and conceptual modelling. In: Goos, G., Hartmanis, J., van Leeuwen, J., Chen, P.P., Akoka, J., Kangassalu, H., Thalheim, B. (eds.) Conceptual Modeling. LNCS, vol. 1565, pp. 123–143. Springer, Heidelberg (1999). https://doi.org/10.1007/3-540-48854-5_11
13. Sandkuhl, K., Stirna, J., Persson, A., Wißotzki, M.: Enterprise Modeling: Tackling Business Challenges with 4EM Method. Springer, Heidelberg (2014)

14. Voss, C., Tsikriktsis, N., Frohlich, M.: Case research in operations management. Int. J. Oper. Prod. Manag. **22**(2), 195–219 (2002)
15. Runfola, A., Perna, A., Baraldi, E., Gregori, G.L.: The use of qualitative case studies in top business and management journals: a quantitative analysis of recent patterns. Eur. Mang. J. **35**(1), 116–127 (2017)

Open Innovation Laboratory for Rapid Realisation of Sensing, Smart and Sustainable Products: Motives, Concepts and Uses in Higher Education

Arturo Molina Gutiérrez[1(✉)], Jhonattan Miranda[1], Dante Chavarría[1],
Julieta Noguez[1], Miguel Ramírez[1], Manuel E. Macías[1],
Edgar O. López[1], Martín R. Bustamante[1], Martín Molina[1],
Pedro Ponce[1], Daniel Cortés Serrano[1], and José Ramírez[2]

[1] School of Engineering and Sciences, Tecnológico de Monterrey,
Monterrey, Mexico
{armolina, jhonattan.miranda, dante.chavarria, jnoguez,
miguel.ramirez, mmacias, edlopez, rbustama, jose.molina,
pedro.ponce, a01655708}@itesm.mx
[2] Instituto Tecnologico de Tlahuac, Mexico City, Mexico
pep_antonio@hotmail.com

Abstract. Open Innovation is not a new concept and it is been actively used by different entities to cope with new challenges posed by the evolving society in business, science and education. However, for this last one seems to be poor documentation about how higher education institutions are dealing with it. It is evident that universities are applying concepts like Open Innovation Laboratories, however it is not clear the methodologies or resources they are using. Tecnologico de Monterrey recently created its own laboratory and in this article we present the motives, concepts and uses of it in the context of higher education. Different approaches are made, from the development of core competences concepts to the physical and virtual tools used in the lab. Two study cases are briefly presented in order to illuminate how external actors are collaborating with internal actors in an Open Innovation process.

Keywords: Open Innovation · Open Innovation Lab
New product development · Sensing smart and sustainable products
Collaborative Networks · Higher education

1 Introduction

The globalized world in which we live is getting increasingly competitive and there is the need to solve fast and in a novelty way the challenges that arise in business, science and education [1]. Evolution of Communication and Information Technologies (ICTs) broke geographic barriers and allowed the expansion of Collaborative Networks (CN) and the transformation of Open Innovation (OI). The OI assumes that innovation process is an action where not only internal actors within an institution or and enterprise participate

L. M. Camarinha-Matos et al. (Eds.): PRO-VE 2018, IFIP AICT 534, pp. 156–163, 2018.
https://doi.org/10.1007/978-3-319-99127-6_14

meaning that, "internal ideas can also be taken through external channels" [2]. During the last years, OI paradigm has been using especially by firms and they consider "The Open Innovation as a distributed innovation process based on purposively managed knowledge flow across organisational boundaries, using pecuniary and non-pecuniary mechanisms in line with the organisation's business model" [3, 4].

Due to this process of OI, higher education institutions play an increasingly important role and have a closer relationship with the industry creating new research agendas [5]. In this new collaboration scheme ICTs play a fundamental part so in 2013, Tecnologico de Monterrey launched TEC21 educational model targeting a new generation of students who are digital native and demand the use of innovative learning methods and modern technological equipment. For this reason, Tecnologico de Monterrey is evolving in order to provide adequate infrastructure to face current requirements by adopting new learning methods, technologies, and redesigning its learning physical and virtual spaces. In 2017, an Open Innovation Laboratory (OIL) was established to provide innovative resources that will support the exchange of knowledge and experiences during innovation process of new product development that in its core are Sensing, Smart and Sustainable (S^3) [6].

This paper is structured as follows. The second part is the exposition of the motives that drove the creation of this laboratory and the advantages that are obtained. In the third part it is explained the concepts in which is based including an elaboration of the three pillars that support it. Finally a brief description of the uses of the laboratory in higher education as well as some study cases for further insight of its utilization in real life scenarios.

2 Motives

The OIL provides the necessary tools, technological platforms and methodologies to higher education students, therefore they experiment integrated learning and collaboration skills, which in turn will provide them with the most employable profile in global professional market. These characteristics are desired worldwide thus, there are three main motives to build and implement this OIL in higher education.

(i) This OIL aims to develop desirable competencies in digital native students. Diverse researchers and institutions have defined a set of core competencies and skills [7, 8]. In this sense, product innovation research group at Tecnologico de Monterrey designed a program based on five main competencies. These competencies are named '5Cs' and they are listed below.

- **Critical Thinking.** Student is able to analyse, synthesise and evaluate problems in order to provide solutions. This is achieved by being involved in real scenarios where they reflect critically and are able to interpret information, and draw conclusions.
- **Creativity and Innovation.** Students must demonstrate originality and inventiveness in work and understand real world limits by adopting new ideas [9] and are requested to provide solutions through the development of new products.

- **Communication.** Improving communication skills will allow students to express ideas clearly in oral, nonverbal and written way so they will be able to participate in complex communication contexts such as negotiations, elevator pitches, and project explanation.
- **Collaboration.** This competence is essential for a project development. Students must demonstrate the ability to interact and work with different actors, which participate in an OI process. Also, they assume shared responsibility for collaborative work and value the individual contributions made by each team member [10].
- **Cooperation.** The development of this competence allows the student to share information, knowledge and personal strengths. Cooperation is used as a strategy in group work where there are common objectives, and the success of the group performance will depend on the cooperation between the members of the team.

(ii) Provide necessary infrastructure to support professional training of students with dynamic learning experiences addressing the needs of modern learners. This includes rapid realisation platforms for rapid prototyping with physical places and virtual resources like makerspaces and remote laboratories where users can interact with internal and external communities. By doing this is possible to develop novel and innovative S^3 products with high social impact on priority sectors, hence students are encouraged to promote the generation of new business models and companies' incubation.

(iii) This OIL aims to improve traditional engineering courses and to contribute to the generation and exchange of knowledge by incorporating new learning methods and design methodologies to stimulate innovation and creativity. Therefore, differences between using traditional learning methods and using the OIL in courses related to new product development (NPD) are listed in Table 1.

Table 1. Traditional courses vs. Open Innovation Laboratory

Traditional courses	Using Open Innovation Lab
The learning process focuses on develop traditional competencies	The learning process is aimed at developing desirable competencies in the 21st-century student
The product development process is linear. Therefore the product development process is delayed	Shorten the product development process by incorporating philosophies such as Concurrent Engineering (CE)
The product development process is carried out in the classroom without specific infrastructure to develop prototypes	Provide the right tools for a rapid prototype realisation
The course is carried out without considering current social problems	Use of specific methodologies for current social problems identification
Solutions are proposed without reaching desirable aspects of society	Proposed solutions are based on the concept 'sensing, smart and sustainable (S^3)'
The problem is fictitious	Address real-life problem scenarios
The innovation process is close. Therefore it is not considering multidisciplinary and external collaborative groups	Promote the interactive collaboration between internal and external actors
There are no programs to monitor the transfer of technology	Support the maker movement to stimulate an entrepreneurship culture and foster companies incubation and economic development

3   Concepts

OIL is an arrangement of different concepts between specific knowledge and platforms hence it is necessary to structure them in a well-designed fashion. To do this the OIL is presented in three main pillars:

- Learning Techniques. Consist in an specific set of learning techniques and courses aimed to develop in students competences that are desirable to the today's engineer profile but also to aid in the propose of innovative solutions to real-life problems
- Design Methodologies. They are well developed frameworks and models used to bring structure to the ideas of products and services developed during the continuous iteration and use of the learning techniques.
- Rapid Product Realisation Platform. These modern technologies (software and hardware) are used to support the innovation process by providing the resources to design, manufacture and test the solutions obtained from the previous pillars.

Each one of the pillars of the OIL is further analysed in Table 2.

Table 2. Three major pillars of the open innovation laboratory

Pillars	Resources to be used
Learning techniques	• Active Learning ○ Problem-Based Learning (PBL) ○ Case-Based Learning (CL) ○ Project Oriented Learning (POL) • Blended Learning ○ MOOCs ○ Online Courses • Hybrid Learning ○ Face to Face Learning ○ Distance Learning
Design methodologies	• Sensing, Smart and Sustainable Product Development Reference Framework (S^3-RM) • Integrated Product, Process and Manufacturing System Development Reference Model (IPPMD -RM) • Decision-making strategies • Creative Thinking Model • I-Corps • Agile Software Development/ Mobile Development • Ontologies/ Taxonomies/ Process Planning Design • Rapid prototyping techniques

(continued)

Table 2. (*continued*)

Pillars	Resources to be used
Rapid product realisation platform	• Makerspace (Sensing, Smart and Sustainable technologies) • Reconfigurable Micro Machine Tools • Micro-Factory (Fabrication of Prototypes) • Artificial Intelligent Toolkit • Haptics Technology • Bio-Instrumentation Lab • Remote Laboratories/ Virtual Reality/ Augmented Reality • Robotics NAO Laboratory • Lab on a CHIP • Decision Centre • PLM software platform

The OIL focuses on developing new products and services that are S^3 by analysing products from the viewpoints of the sensing, smart and sustainable concepts. With these descriptions, the designers will obtain suitable information to consider during the product development process. These concepts are further explained in Table 3.

Table 3. The sensing, smart and sustainable concepts

S^3	Description
Sensing	The sensing concept refers to the capability that a system has to detect events, acquire data, and measure changes that occur in a physical environment [11]
Smart	The smart concept incorporates sensing, actuation, and control functionalities in order to describe and analyse situations and make decisions based on the available data in a predictive or adaptive manner [12]. In addition, the concept could be applied to design and enable products to work in an interconnected environment and could be applied to improve decision-making processes to enhance product performance
Sustainability	The sustainable concept is related to design of products and manufacturing processes that are ethical, as well as operationally, robust; sustainability is conceived multi-dimensionally, in environmental, social and economic terms [13]

4   Uses in Higher Education

At Tecnologico de Monterrey, OIL as a Collaborative Network has been used in different environments where external and internal actors can interact to develop new S^3 products and services to support innovation process and development of high impact engineering projects. The implementation of the OIL enroll the participation of multidisciplinary professionals from universities, companies, and government as a Collaborative Network [14]. In this sense, the Collaborative Network is responsible of (Fig. 1):

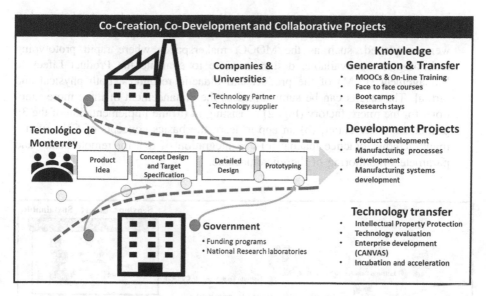

Fig. 1. Open Innovation Laboratory used by companies and the government

- Supporting knowledge generation through research stays and training programs using face-to-face courses and MOOCs (Mass On-Line Open Courses).
- Developing Research projects (e.g. new product development, manufacturing processes development and manufacturing systems development).
- Supporting technology transfer in order to generate enterprise incubation and acceleration, promote intellectual property and participate in technology testing programs.

4.1   Case Studies

It is important to highlight how these concepts are being applied in higher education at Tecnologico de Monterrey with the purpose of encourage its adoption in other institutions around the world thus, here are exposed 2 case studies to illustrate real life scenarios.

(i) Design Methodologies (M2017) and Integrated Manufacturing System Course where students are encouraged to develop real commercial products using methodologies like IPPMD and S^3 thus, they apply different techniques, methods, thinking and engineering tools for the different product development stages during the academic period (16 weeks, 3 h per week). For the materialization of the idea specific tools are provided like makerspaces, the Micro-Factory where the essential manufacturing processes for prototyping are available and different types of programs like CAD/CAM [14].

(ii) Summer research boot camp 2017 where interdisciplinary students from different universities joined efforts to solve specific problems exposed by the Product Innovation Research Group of Tecnologico de Monterrey. Teams of two people were formed and assigned a specific challenge that had to be solved through 8 weeks of research. Throughout the development of the project, different tools were employed, such as the MOOC, makerspaces where rapid prototyping technologies are available, design software to evaluate the Product Lifecycle Management (PLM) of the product and didactic resources, both physical and virtual. The results can be summarized as the enhancement of three more functions for the micro factory (Fig. 2) consisting in (a) the implementation of the 3d printer and laser cutter, (b) an app to learn the basics concepts of CNC with a manufacturing practice manual (c) the integration of IoT for remote health and parameters monitoring of the micromachine.

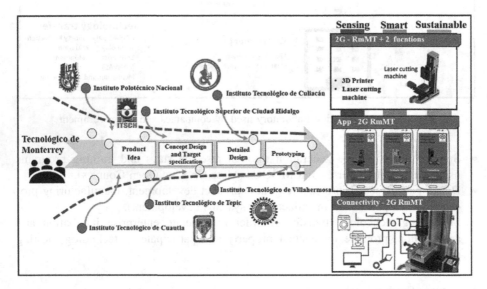

Fig. 2. OI in the summer research boot camp

5   Conclusions

The use of Open Innovation Laboratory in higher education has provided valuable experience for students, companies and government involved in this concept of open and collaborative network approach. Several projects have materialized and are being implemented using this concept. Its use in engineering courses as well as specific projects like research summer boot camps demonstrate the development of critical skills exposed in this work by challenging the students to adapt new forms of collaboration and as a result several innovative products have passed from the divergence to the convergence of the idea and in most cases achieving the manufacturing stage. Also numerous improvements have been made to traditional courses thus, enhancing them to better suite digital natives.

Future work will focus on benchmarking learning improvements in an analytical way thus, providing hard data about the benefits of the OIL in higher education. It is also necessary to evaluate students to provide data about usability of the laboratory, suggestions and possible improvements. In addition, technologies presented will be updated, more technologies, methodologies and techniques will be proposed to be integrated in the Open Innovation Laboratory. Finally, new resources and research lines will be identified and included in order to support innovation in this space.

References

1. Camarinha-Matos, L.M., Afsarmanesh, H.: Collaborative networks: a new scientific discipline. J. Intell. Manuf. **16**(4–5), 439–452 (2005)
2. Chesbrough, H.W.: Open Innovation: The New Imperative for Creating and Profiting From Technology. Harvard Business School Press, Harvard (2003)
3. Laursen, K., Salter, A.: Open for innovation: the role of openness in explaining innovation performance among UK manufacturing firms. Strat. Manag. J. **27**(2), 131–150 (2006)
4. Chesbrough, H.W., Bogers, M.: Explicating open innovation: clarifying an emerging paradigm for understanding innovation". In: Chesbrough, H., Vanhaverbeke, W., West, J. (eds.) New Frontiers in Open Innovation. Oxford University Press, Oxford (2014)
5. Perkmann, M., Walsh, K.: University–industry relationships and open innovation: towards a research agenda. Int. J. Manag. Rev. **9**(4), 259–280 (2007)
6. Miranda, J., et al.: Open innovation laboratory for rapid realization of sensing, smart and sustainable products (S3 Products) for higher education. Int. J. Educ. Pedagogical Sci. World Acad. Sci. Eng. Technol. **11**(5), 1194–1200 (2017)
7. Binkley, M., Erstad, O., Herman, J., Raizen, S., Ripley, M., Miller-Ricci, M., Rumble, M.: Defining twenty-first century skills. In: Griffin, P., McGaw, B., Care, E. (eds.) Assessment and Teaching of 21st Century Skills, pp. 17–66. Springer, New York, NY (2012)
8. Häkkinen, P., Järvelä, S., Mäkitalo-Siegl, K., Ahonen, A., Näykki, P., Valtonen, T.: Preparing teacher-students for twenty-firstcentury learning practices (PREP 21): a framework for enhancing collaborative problem solving and strategic learning skills. Teach. Teach. Theory Pract. **23**, 25–41 (2016). https://doi.org/10.1080/13540602.2016.1203772
9. Adamidi, F., Paraskeva, F., Bouta, H., Gkemisi, S.: Problem-based learning in language instruction: a collaboration and language learning skills framework in a CSCL environment. In: Uden, L., Liberona, D., Liu, Y. (eds.) LTEC 2017. CCIS, vol. 734, pp. 133–146. Springer, Cham (2017). https://doi.org/10.1007/978-3-319-62743-4_12
10. Hall, P.: Interprofessional teamwork: professional cultures as barriers. J. Interprof. Care **2005** (Supplement 1), 188–196 (2005)
11. Porter, M.E., Heppelmann, J.E.: How smart, connected products are transforming competition. Harvard Bus. Rev. **92**(11), 64–88 (2014)
12. Nebylov, A., Sharan, S., Arifuddin, F.: Smart control systems for next-generation autonomous wing-in-ground effect vehicles. IFAC Proc. Vol. **43**(15), 112–117 (2010)
13. Haapala, K.R., Zhao, F., Camelio, J., Sutherland, J.W., Skerlos, S.J., Dornfeld, D.A., Jawahir, I.S., Clarens, A.F., Rickli, J.L.: A review of engineering research in sustainable manufacturing. J. Manuf. Sci. Eng. **135**(4), 041013 (2013)
14. Miranda, J., Chavarría-Barrientos, D., Macías, M., Molina, M., Ponce, P., Wright, P.K., Molina, A.: Experiences in interactive collaborative learning using an open innovation laboratory, the design methodologies course as case study. In: 2017 IEEE International Conference on Engineering, Technology and Innovation/International Technology Management Conference (ICE/ITMC) (2017)

In-Store Proximity Marketing
by Means of IoT Devices

Jarogniew Rykowski[(✉)], Tomasz Chojnacki[(✉)], and Sergiusz Strykowski[(✉)]

Department of Information Technology, Poznan University of Economics and Business,
Niepodległości 10, 61-875 Poznań, Poland
{rykowski,chojnacki,strykow}@kti.ue.poznan.pl

Abstract. Recently we observe a boom of e-shopping and e-marketing, with
plenty of tools, systems, and improvements to encourage customers to purchase
more goods and services and to cut off the costs. One may enumerate here the
recommendation systems, JIT strategy, instant shopping channels connected to
the advertisement, personal targeting, and many more. To facilitate the implementation and operation of such systems, we collect several data related to users'
behavior by means of cookies, server logs, link and timing analysis, etc. Up to
now, limited attention has been paid to apply all of these mechanisms to real stores
and marketplaces. To fill the gap, in this paper we propose a multi-level system
to (1) contextually analyze customer behavior at a shopping space by means of
Internet-of-Things devices and services, (2) process this information at server-
side to compute some instant purchasing recommendations and incentives, and
(3) immediately send these recommendations to the customers, either in a form
of classical marketing message, or as a personal advice, possibly linked with a
discount, "special offer", etc. In such a way, each customer is served personally
and thus has more motivations to buy the recommended or discounted items.

Keywords: In-store marketing · Proximity marketing · Internet of Things

1 Introduction

Characterized by continuous progress and covering more and more domains and application areas, new communication and information technologies (ICT) changed our life
completely. Nobody is now surprised by new proposals to solve everyday problems and
to make life easier, just by applying a new device or automated service. Recently we
observe this trend also for the activities related to the mass market, from surveys on
social opinions and acceptance, via traditional marketing, to recommendation systems.
The general trend is to encourage customers to buy more goods and services and to cut
off the costs. To facilitate an implementation and operation of such systems, we collect
several data related to users' behavior by means of cookies, server logs, link and timing
analysis, etc. This trend is especially visible for network-based versions of classical
market processes, such as those related to e-shopping and e-marketing. Plenty of ICT-
based solutions have been proposed towards modern channels of the advertisement [1],

L. M. Camarinha-Matos et al. (Eds.): PRO-VE 2018, IFIP AICT 534, pp. 164–174, 2018.
https://doi.org/10.1007/978-3-319-99127-6_15

including personal and instant marketing and targeting (nearly approaching famous *Minority Report* movie [2]), facilitating the shopping process – recommendation systems [3], just-in-time [4] orders and deliveries, and many more.

Up to now, most of the efforts were put on improving the electronic channels and e-* versions of traditional processes. For example, e-shops extensively use recommendation systems based on users' activity logs, personal targeting based on history and recent decisions. E-marketing tools, such as Google AdWords [5], are concentrating on the network and computers/smartphones for searching and accessing the items. However, so far limited attention has been paid to apply all of these mechanisms to real stores and marketplaces. This situation was caused by a limited possibility of gathering the personal information of the same quality at physical places and in a real situation, in comparison with their e-* counterparts. For example, it is quite trivial to analyze server log to filter out some information about previous "shelves" (i.e., Web pages) visited by the user to guess primary interests of this user. However, in a real store, similar information is not so easy to achieve, as the users are not individually tracked across the shopping area. Undoubtedly, one may point out that a customer could be tracked by human personnel, but this approach seems to be much too expensive and as such is usually reserved only for a limited number of stores and situations, such as selling the jewelry or similar luxury items.

With the introduction of the Internet of Things [6] (IoT) and Services (IoS), these limitations seem to be relaxed. Automatic cameras, equipped with face recognition and behavior analysis, may play a role of human personnel and continuously track customers in a shopping space [7]. Intelligent shelves may detect the fact of taking some goods, even temporary, and guess what the client is looking for [8]. Smart shopping carts, counting the items, may recommend buying some more products, supplementing the current shopping [9]. And last but not least, personal smartphones with such utilities as "a list to buy," medical contraindications and recommendations, or even some keywords "not to forget" may facilitate the choice for undecided and dis-oriented customers [10].

To our best knowledge, so far limited efforts have been reported joining the above-depicted technologies and systems into one consistent proposal, to facilitate shopping in the real stores and marketplaces. Among the most recent proposals, we should point out the work on off-line recommendation system for the real stores and customers based on Oracle tools [11]. However, this one and similar proposals operate on nice diagrams and ideas only, leaving apart the technical solutions and more in-depth research on system requirements and functionality. Also, the proposals are usually addressed to large supermarkets and general stores, bypassing the needs of small stores specialized in certain types of the items such as shoes or clothes. Little work is also done on pre-requisites' analysis related to the set of necessary local devices and services, organizational changes, possible profits, etc. Instead, the proposals concentrate on the traditional way of usage of mobile phones – scanning the barcodes or RFID tags and browsing the product ratings and opinions [12], so-called on-shelf-availability ("temporary out-of-stock") feature [13], supply chain management [14, 15], etc.

To fill the gap, in this paper we propose a multi-level system to (1) contextually analyze customer behavior at a shopping space by means of Internet-of-Things devices and services, (2) process this information at server-side to compute some instant recommendations and purchasing incentives, and (3) immediately send these recommendations to the customers, either in a form of classical marketing, or as a personal advice, possibly linked with a discount, "special offer", etc. In such a way, each customer is served personally and thus has more motivations to buy the recommended or discounted items.

The recommendation/advertisement is computed in a cloud, thus enabling cooperation of several small marketplaces towards a common sales strategy. Separately, none of the small stores is able to implement and utilize such complicated system. However, all these stores together may elaborate a common solution, based on the past analysis of many customers and their final decisions. For example, one may compute the time a customer is standing in front of a shelf with some items, sending the "special offer" only to the hesitating customers, different strategy may be applied to a person with or without a child, to a person cruising across the shopping area vs. the one concentrating on specific item, color, type, etc.

To facilitate information exchange for local context and customer behavior among several shopping points, we propose to apply so-called virtual IoT devices, thus normalizing the local information to be processed at the server side. To this goal, we propose an ontology of IoT devices, as well as a way to group the devices into conglomerates with enhanced functionality. Normalization makes it also possible to enrich the local context by some external information, in case some necessary local devices are missing. For example, data about air quality, humidity, etc. may be generated for the whole shopping mall, assuming these parameters are similar for all the places and thus easily shared. Similarly, personal information about the customers, generated as a result of observation at given location, may be further used elsewhere.

The remainder of the paper is organized as follows. First, in Sect. 2 we shortly describe current state-of-the-art for instant marketing in real stores by means of ICT. Section 3 is devoted to a proposal of a new system architecture aimed in collecting the personal information at the place, standardizing it and enhancing by a local context, and sending to the cloud to compute personal shopping incentives at real-time. In Sect. 4 we discuss possible ways of standardization and virtualization of local IoT/IoS utilities, followed by a discussion of remote server-side functionality. Finally, Sect. 5 summarizes the proposal and depicts the future work.

2   Current Usage of ICT in Real Stores and E-Shops

At the moment, the usage of ICT technologies for shopping and marketing may be divided into two disjointed areas: those used in real stores, and those specific for e-shopping. The first area is usually related to the following proposals: loyalty cards, alert systems and security services, customer-flow analysis and tracking, RFID for supply chain management, and, as for the scientific proposals rather than the reality: "intelligent" shopping carts and shelves, and personal advertising and filtering.

Loyalty Cards. A loyalty card is a discount/payment card offered to a customer. With such card, a customer may count on lowering a price for "special offers", cyclic and single discounts, exchanging collected "points" to "gifts" or price reduction, etc. Instead, the customer is obliged to register their shopping details, such as timings, prices, choices, etc. Such information is then used to improve the organization of the store, to determine rates and discounts, to assess the marketing effects, etc.

Alert and Security Systems. Several technologies are used against crime and theft, to mention magnetic and radio tags for expensive items, security gates, monitoring systems based on cameras and detailed inspection, etc. Most of these techniques require direct human control. Thus they are usually restricted in usage by delays and the law (e.g., in order to catch a thief one must call the police forces).

Customer-Behavior Analysis and Tracking. Tracking systems, based on automatization of monitoring of some characteristic features of the customers, such as positions, movements, stops, delays while making a choice, etc., are usually based on cameras and video analysis. As it is almost impossible to track each individual customer separately, except for very artificial conditions (such as a single customer for the whole store), usually the videos are analyzed only statistically, e.g., to point out a place frequently visited by the customers to establish a marketing point, to detect if the organization of the shelves is correct, etc.

RFID. Radio-operated tags are used mainly to facilitate supply-chain management [16]. Due to several restrictions of the technology, related mostly to the physics of radio-signal propagation, it is usually not possible to track individual goods unless they are big enough or separated of each-other [17]. As a consequence, RFID tags are mainly used for large containers and packages, and for the shelves rather than individual items and goods. As for the latter, traditional bar codes are applied, however, with limited tracking possibilities due to the need of line-of-sight (LOS) inspection [18]. Even if there are some attempts to track RFID tags of individual items, not only inside the store but also after shopping (to mention the analysis of wastebaskets near homes to get the popularity of a product at given area), this technology seems to be quite specialized and hardly applied for direct and personalized marketing.

"Intelligent" Shopping Cart. Shopping carts are used in larger stores to temporary collect the items to be later paid in total at the cashing point. There were some proposals to include a display at the top of a cart to enumerate all the items and to count the total price for the contents of the cart. Such carts were tested by several market leaders, however, never gaining significant attention, for several reasons. First, due to technology restrictions, it is hard to detect the contents of a cart automatically – either a customer is forced to scan a barcode/RFID tag manually, or some tags are omitted because of screening of radio signals or above-mentioned LOS restriction. Second, as the customer was aware of the price at any moment, frequently they decided to remove too expensive items from the cart. Also, the accumulators for the displays to operate were heavy and needed frequent recharging. Recently, there were some attempts to replace the displays by personal smartphones; however, this approach was hardly accepted by the public mainly due to the concerns on privacy.

On-Site Personal Recommendations. Similar to advice provided by a human assistant from store's staff, one may imagine similar assistance given by computers, preferably personal smartphones. An imagination of how it may look like is given in famous "Sixth Sense" presentation at one of the TED conferences [19]. For example, a customer is scanning a tag or taking a photo of an item, and after a short time, they are notified with a red or green light if the product is suitable to buy or not, due to customers' opinions, medical recommendations, or simply a previous choice and individual/family experience. Similarly, the smartphone may guide the customer to complete the list of items to buy, navigating across the shopping area. However, as it may be seen for the "Sixth Sense" project, such assistance is very restricted according to the place and situation, and, without the support of complex external systems and services computing the recommendations, seems to be impractical.

Note that none of the above-mentioned techniques is able to detect and analyze personal information about a given customer at real-time, i.e., at the moment of choosing particular items by this customer. All these techniques are based on collecting some information and processing this information off-line, mostly for statistical purposes. Such experiments as "intelligent shopping carts" and "Sixth Sense" project are very interesting, however, quite restricted and impractical.

On the other hand, for e-shops one may enumerate several online technologies, to be used to assist the customer in taking the purchasing decisions at (near) real-time. These techniques include log analysis, personal targeting and recommendations, instant, and individual offers both for the items and their pricing.

Log Analysis. Log analysis is a very useful tool for gathering the information what a user was doing while visiting a website, which pages they saw, for how long, how they navigated, etc. In general, analyzing this information statistically may enable targeting a specific user, i.e., linking this user with a well-defined group of "similar" users. Then it is possible to predict the future customer activities, and even to facilitate some desired activities by below-discussed personal marking and recommendations.

Personal Targeting and Instant Offer. A customer, identified by a statistical member of a group of "similar" customers, may be treated in the way related to the group. For example, once a customer watched some action movies only, it is quite probable that they will get another action movie. And if they are about to leave the system or hesitating for a longer time, it is valuable to offer them a personal discount, e.g., 5%, for the next action movie to be realized within a few minutes.

On-Line Personal Recommendations. Everybody knows a bit of advice while buying some items in an e-shop: "customers who bought this item also bought items X, Y, and Z". The choice of such recommended items is based on the statistical analysis of shopping of the past customers [4, 20]. For some applications areas, this simple approach is quite valuable, such as for computer games, electronics, furniture, etc. Recently, a specialization of this approach for mobile devices and services took attention of the researchers – the specifics for the mobile world is a base of huge expectations towards the automatization of this market.

Collaboration of Several Stores at the Base of a Common Customer. The above-described personal recommendations are not necessarily addressed to a single store and/or type of an item to be purchased. Instead, it would be much more useful to determine a global profile of a customer, to be used for several item types and store locations. To this goal, cooperation is needed of several stores, based on the store-independent identification of the customer. The latter might be implemented as a common loyalty card/application, e.g., the one issues by a shopping mall. Note that such identification is not obligatorily linked to processing personal data of the customer. Instead, it is enough to generate a unique number being a representative of the customer – this task may be performed as a part of the subscription procedure. It is, however, an open question how to determine the set of marketing rules to cover different types and domains at once (such as "a customer who bought red shoes will be probably interested in red blouses").

Note that, on the contrary to the real-store technologies, e-shopping techniques are based on online analysis and instant recommendations. However, they are built on the information that is not available for automatic treatment at a real place, such as timings and presence of given person at given place and time, careful inspection of the items before shopping, returning to the place/item after some time, choosing a product from a group of similar ones, hesitating before final decision, etc. The question is if we really cannot get such information in real time and place, to shift the profits of e-shopping analysis to the area of real stores and marketplaces. We think that gathering such information is now possible with the recent advances in the field of Internet of Things and Services. Our idea is described in the next chapters.

3 Proposed System Architecture

The proposal is based on two fundamental assumptions, these are the following:

- there is a local system of IoT devices (both real and virtual) for each place, such as a store or a market/exhibition place; in general, IoT devices gather some information about local context (HVAC – heating, ventilating, and air-climatization conditions, positions and movements of customers and visitors of the store, characteristic features of humans and their activities - staying, fast/slow moving, watching, listening, etc.);
- the local contextual information is sent to the cloud to be processed at server-side and to compute some shopping incentives, which in turn is sent back to be presented locally to customers.

As a result, we obtain a solution based on the cooperation among several, possibly small or medium-sized stores, to attract the customers with JIT marketing information, incentives, and offers. Locally gathered information about the context and customer activities is processed in a centralized way, thus making it possible to share the costs among all the business partners involved. As the cost of local IoT devices is reasonably small (c.f., further discussion on a set of possible hardware/software to be used for monitoring the customers), and the cost of quite complicated server-side analysis of the data gathered locally is shared, from the point of view of a single shopping point the whole system is effective and not very expensive.

In a natural way, the system is divided into two primary layers:

- *local IoT network*, responsible for collecting the information of a different kind, nature, and meaning. To this goal, we propose to use: (1) smartphones with a loyalty application, working according to BYOD (bring you own device) idea and acting as a broker between the system and a customer, (2) geolocation beacons, to identify a place inside a store, such as a single shelf or a stand, (3) Near-Field-Communication (NFC), Radio-Frequency-Identification (RFID) and QR-code tags, to enable information exchange at the distance of centimeters, for example to realize the payments or identify given item, (4) local WiFi or global GSM-related network (such as LTE) to contact the cloud and obtain marketing information, and (5) local sensors of different purpose, to collect the data of the local context (such as HVAC conditions, but also visual and acoustic background, weather forecast, image analysis towards the detection of presence and activities of humans, etc.). All this information is multiplexed by specialized hardware (based on Raspberry Pi and AVR processors/ modules), standardized according to specific ontology and sent at the request to the cloud, to form a local context.
- *remote server operating in the cloud*, to process the context to compute JIT advertising, to be sent back to the customers to their BYOD devices. The server is using several artificial-intelligence tools, such as neural networks and reasoning systems, to (1) possibly automatically extract the important information from the local context, and (2) process a set of predefined (expert-generated) and dynamic rules to choose the most appropriate marketing information or a personalized offer, to be presented to the customer.

The nodes exchange the information in a standardized way. To this goal, we plan to prepare an extendable ontology of virtual IoT devices. Each virtual device is based on an arbitrary chosen set of physical IoT devices operating locally and remotely, and is characterized not only by some information collected (such as a temperature, air pressure, a number of customers in a store, their positions and distance from a shelf, timings related to the customers and choosing/regarding the items, etc.), but also by the accuracy of the data. The latter parameter is used to express the trust and the importance of the sensor. This approach makes it possible to report some external sensors/information as a part of the local context, however, with limited accuracy. For example, there may be a thermometer reporting the temperature close to a shelf – the accuracy is then represented as 100% maximum value. If, however, the store is equipped with only a single global thermometer, such centrally measured temperature is accompanied by the accuracy limited to 70%. Further, if the store has no own thermometer, but there is a global temperature sensor for the whole shopping mall, the information from such global sensor is reported with the accuracy at the level of 50%. Moreover, the accuracy may also be used to share some information among several locations. For example, it may be assumed that the temperature in each store in the same shopping mall is similar – then one spot may get the data from the neighbor, with the accuracy at the level of, e.g., 60%. Anyway, the information from the virtual sensor is always available, differing only in the accuracy and trust. This idea is applied to all the virtual sensors, shared by the stores if needed and always reported in a standardized way to the remote server.

One should note that the presented approach preserves the anonymity and the privacy of the customer. The system knowns and is able to identify only the smartphone, more precisely, the loyalty application, by its registration (serial) number. Name and surname, address, e-mail, any other identification information – none of such information is needed by the system to operate. In the matter of fact, the system tracks past and current activities of the customer to better adjust marketing information and personal offers, and send appropriate messages in real-time during shopping activities. But this is exactly the way human shopping assistants act – they identify the customers visually, they come closer and offer their help to facilitate the choice. So, one may expect that the level of acceptance of the automated assistance will be similar as for nowadays human staff.

Note also that the shared database of the customers is a base for efficient collaboration of several stores towards a common customer. While concentrating the knowledge on customer's habits and choices at a single place, we obtain a possibility to apply this knowledge at many places and coincidental interactions. This way of the cooperation is especially useful for small and medium enterprises such as the small shops in a shopping mall, as typically the customers are going to visit a store by coincidence, from time to time, also searching for something not usual and planned.

4   Typical Scenario of System Usage

A store is equipped with several physical sensors: HVAC conditions, RFID/NFC sensors to localize the items on shelves, devices registering an interaction of a customer with an item (such as getting an item from the shelf, unpacking it, testing, verifying the size in a fitting room, comparing fashion, colors, etc.), camera-based analyzers (person locators, crowd detectors, localizers, movement detectors, timers, size/position estimators, such as cameras able to distinguish a mother and a child based on the growth, etc.), and similar sensors. Some information may be also provided manually by shopping assistants, such as the mood of a client, ambiance, impression, etc. All this information is standardized and collected by a local multiplexer.

At the moment, a customer is approaching a place marked by a geolocation beacon – a stand, a shelf, or, in the simplest case, main entrance to the store. Once fetched by the customer's smartphone, beacon signal pops up a loyalty application. The application contacts the server in a cloud and reports beacon identifier. The server localizes the store and detailed place and asks local multiplexer of this store to send all the information regarding the virtual sensors. Then, the data is processed to compute a JIT advertising or personal offer and further sent back to the customers.

Note that the virtual sensors are chosen based on customer's location, but they are not necessarily operating precisely at this location. Due to the standardization and virtu-alization of the sensors, the server may operate in the same way for any other place, taking only into consideration, if needed, the accuracy for the sensors reported at this location. Note also that the smartphone itself may extend the context, for example, to report favorite color, size, fashion, etc., of the "most wanted" item. This information may also be sent to the store staff, to better assist the customer at the moment. For example, by scanning a beacon installed close to an entrance to the shopping mall at an exhibition place with some mannequins and clothes, a customer will be given by a map how to get to the store, and inside the store a ready-to-test item will be waiting for them, just prepared by the store staff, fitting customer's size and favorite color. This is also a good point to start cooperation among several stores. For example, one may point out a case of shopping the trekking shoes at one location and providing there some more information to complete the rest of the equipment in the other stores near-by.

It is an open question how to generate the marketing information in JIT manner on the server side. At the very beginning, the system will be based on a set of fixed marketing rules, prepared by the human experts and parameterized by the information coming from virtual sensors. For example, if a customer is standing in front of a shelf with some clothes for more than 30 s, hesitating what to buy, the store may offer them a 10% discount on condition they will complete the choice and report to the cash register in the next five minutes. The discount will be automatically deducted from the price during the payment via the smartphone and further registering this fact by the loyalty application. Such the set of fixed rules may be also improved by a dynamic analysis realized with some artificial-intelligence tools, such as neural networks or extendable expert systems. However, this aspect of system functionality needs further research, and probably such improvements will be introduced step by step after some experiments with real customers and situations.

5   Conclusions and Future Work

The proposal depicted in this paper is a new approach to generate marketing information and purchasing incentives in real-time and for real locations (stores, exhibitions, marketplaces, etc.). The advertisement will be selected based on the sensors located near the place where the customer is currently located, their behavior and current activity, appearance (e.g., an adult or a child), and the general context. The location of the customer will be determined by their personal device after detecting a geolocation beacon or after scanning an NFC/RFID/QR code. The location will be used by a remote server to determine the store and possibly also a detailed place inside this store. Then, a set of IoT devices will be contacted to provide the information about the local context, describing not only traditional parameters such as the temperature, air pressure and flow, noise, etc., but also customer activities in a shopping area such as positions, movements, gestures, actions (e.g., getting an item from a shelf, unpacking it, walking with it to the fitting room, etc.). The contextual info will be sent to the cloud in a standardized way. Based on this information, an advertisement or a personalized offer will be generated and sent back to the customer.

The system is a chance for small and medium-size stores to cooperate to attract the customers, with the promising technology and the costs shared by all the business partners. The proposal is an adaptation of existing tools related to digital marketing to the level of the real store and a specific purchasing situation. A customer subjected to such a marketing stream will probably treat and feel it in the same way as assistance provided by the human staff – one should expect a high degree of acceptance of the marketing messages and shopping incentives and an increase in customer satisfaction with the service.

There are several aspects of the proposal not covered by this paper, mainly due to the lack of space. One should mention here security and privacy issues, anonymity, a possibility of abusing detailed information about a customer for non-local purposes, how to encourage and reward the customers for entering to the system, and many more. All these aspects should be discussed, also addressing the recent European regulations on data privacy. This is our general plan for the future work. Also, we would like to study the economic base for the cooperation of several stores, taking into account the fact that some of them are possible competitors on the same market (area, shopping mall, city, etc.). Regarding the above-mentioned anonymity, some would claim that in case of a single store anonymous access is possible; however, when dealing with cooperation of several stores and a common customer, the customers are anyway no more anonymous as they have to register for the system. This claim is only partially valid. As it was pointed out earlier in the text, there is no need to identify the customers by their personal data. Instead, a serial number of the loyalty application may be used to this goal. Thus, as a decision to keep the application or uninstall (reinstall) it is left to the customer, we fully conform to the accordance of "a right to forget" and similar rules.

References

1. Adams, R.: Intelligent advertising. AI & Soc. **18**(1), 68–81 (2004)
2. Minority Report - Personal Advertising in the Future (2002). https://www.youtube.com/watch?v=7bXJ_obaiYQ
3. An Introduction to Recommender Systems (2018). https://www.springer.com/cda/content/document/cda_downloaddocument/9783319296579-c2.pdf
4. Just In Time – JIT (2018). https://www.investopedia.com/terms/j/jit.asp
5. Get your ad on Google today (2018). https://adwords.google.com/intl/en_cy/home/
6. Ashton, K.: That 'Internet of Things' Thing (2009). www.rfidjournal.com/articles/view?4986
7. Mullin, G.: Amazon launches supermarket with NO checkouts and uses cameras to track what shoppers remove from shelves (2018). https://www.thesun.co.uk/money/5394671/amazon-supermarket-no-checkouts-seattle-camera-technology/
8. Intelligent Shelf Label Solution: Blueprint (2012). https://www.intel.pl/content/dam/www/public/us/en/documents/solution-briefs/intel-blueprint-intelligent-shelf-label-final-r.pdf
9. Yewatkar, A., Inamdar, F., Singh, R., Bandal, A.A.: Smart Cart with Automatic Billing, Product Information, Product Recommendation Using RFID & Zigbee with Anti-Theft (2016). https://www.sciencedirect.com/science/article/pii/S1877050916002386
10. Park, M.-H., Hong, J.-H., Cho, S.-B.: Location-based recommendation system using bayesian user's preference model in mobile devices. In: Indulska, J., Ma, J., Yang, Laurence T., Ungerer, T., Cao, J. (eds.) UIC 2007. LNCS, vol. 4611, pp. 1130–1139. Springer, Heidelberg (2007). https://doi.org/10.1007/978-3-540-73549-6_110
11. Passinger, P.: What Happens When IoT, Big Data and Real-Time Location Systems Meet? (2018). https://www.cmswire.com/digital-experience/what-happens-when-iot-big-data-and-retail-location-systems-meet/
12. von Reisechach, F., Guinard, D., Michahells, F.: A mobile product recommendation system interacting with tagged products. In: 2009 IEEE International Conference on Pervasive Computing and Communications, Galveston, TX, pp. 1–6 (2009)

13. Vargheese, R., Dahir, H.: An IoT/IoE enabled architecture framework for precision on shelf availability: enhancing proactive shopper experience. In: 2014 IEEE International Conference on Big Data (Big Data), Washington, DC, pp. 21–26 (2014)
14. David, Z., Gnimpieba, R., Nait-Sidi-Moh, A., Durand, D., Fortin, J.: Using internet of things technologies for a collaborative supply chain: application to tracking of pallets and containers. Procedia Comput. Sci. **56**, 550–557 (2015)
15. Sarac, A., Absi, N., Dauzère-Pérès, S.: A literature review on the impact of RFID technologies on supply chain management. Int. J. Prod. Econ. **128**(1), 77–95 (2010)
16. What is RFID? (2018). http://www.technovelgy.com/ct/technology-article.asp
17. Swedberg, C.: Decathlon Sees Sales Rise and Shrinkage Drop, Aided by RFID, RFID J. p.2, 07 December 2015. https://www.rfidjournal.com/articles/view?13815/2
18. What's the Difference Between Barcode and RFID? (2018). www.redbeam.com/rfid-vs-barcode
19. Meet the SixthSense (2008). https://www.ted.com/talks/pattie_maes_demos_the_sixth_sense
20. Pazzani, M.J., Billsus, D.: Content-based recommendation systems. In: Brusilovsky, P., Kobsa, A., Nejdl, W. (eds.) The Adaptive Web: Methods and Strategies of Web Personalization. LNCS, vol. 4321, pp. 325–341. Springer, Heidelberg (2007). https://doi.org/10.1007/978-3-540-72079-9_10

Users and Organizations Profiling

Open Innovation Participants Profiling: An Archetypes Approach

João Rosas[1,2(✉)], Paula Urze[1,3], Alexandra Tenera[1,4],
and Luis M. Camarinha-Matos[1,2]

[1] Faculty of Sciences and Technology,
NOVA University of Lisbon, Caparica, Portugal
{jrosas, cam}@uninova.pt, {pcu, abt}@fct.unl.pt
[2] Center of Technology and Systems (CTS), UNINOVA, Caparica, Portugal
[3] CIUHCT – Centro Interuniversitário de História das Ciências e da Tecnologia,
Lisboa, Portugal
[4] Research and Development Unit for Mechanical and Industrial Engineering
(UNIDEMI), Caparica, Portugal

Abstract. Organizations adopting Open Innovation seem to express slightly specific behavioral patterns, attitudes and values, which are beneficial and that can be perceptible in their interactions with outsiders. It would be useful to find a way to identify these characteristics and to perceive them in potential participants for Open Innovation consortia. This research work explores the concept of archetypes to provide an abstract way to express how companies engaging in Open Innovation look like. The adopted method applies web mining and preliminary results are presented, which show the potential of the approach.

Keywords: Open innovation · Collaboration · Organization archetypes

1 Introduction

Society has undergone profound changes, due to the progress in the varied technological, economic and social segments. Companies need to continually face new challenges, caused by new paradigms such as Social Networks, Internet of Things, and Artificial Intelligence or the convergence of technologies leading to Industry 4.0, which together yield a disruptive and fast changing environment [1]. At the manufacturing level, due to these multifaceted developments, we may be at the 4th industrial revolution. To adapt to these abrupt and unpredictable changes, companies feel the need to adopt new strategies, based on the paradigms of collaboration [2] and open innovation [3].

Open Innovation (OI) has been a strategy adopted by organizations, in which they share intellectual property and interact with outsiders (e.g. suppliers, customers, partners, research entities, retirees, etc.) which act as sources of ideas to create new and lucrative products and services. The success of OI projects depend, among other factors, on the attitudes and behaviors that each participant expresses, which are difficult to evaluate, given the variety and high-level complexity of the involved aspects. Therefore, there is a need to consider more abstract ways to characterize OI participants. In this regard, OI participants seem to express slightly specific behavioral patterns,

© IFIP International Federation for Information Processing 2018
Published by Springer Nature Switzerland AG 2018. All Rights Reserved
L. M. Camarinha-Matos et al. (Eds.): PRO-VE 2018, IFIP AICT 534, pp. 177–189, 2018.
https://doi.org/10.1007/978-3-319-99127-6_16

attitudes, and values, which can be perceptible in their interactions with customers, suppliers, partners, and society, and that appear to favor OI engagement. It is as if they have "special characteristics", which come as impressions of symbolic nature. In this research work, we pursue this idea exploring the concept of archetypes to determine how participants in OI look like, focusing on organizations.

For applying the notion of archetypes in OI, we need to address a number of questions through our research, namely: What are archetypes? How do they manifest in the context of organizations? What is the importance of archetypes in open innovation? These questions are briefly addressed in a literature review, in Sect. 2. In Sect. 3, we describe the research method used to identify the archetypes that best characterize OI participants, including an analysis of the obtained results. Section 4, the final one, contains the relevant conclusions and a suggestion for future work.

2 Background

Although the addressed topic would benefit from an analysis of different scientific areas, in this section we only emphasize the main aspects that contribute to the presented research questions.

2.1 The Notion of Archetype

The term "archetype" derives from the Greek compound word "archétupos", in which arché means "first principle" and tupos means "impression". The word refers to the creative source of things that cannot be perceived or observed directly, but which manifests itself through impressions or images [4]. Plato illustrated archetypes in his "allegory of the cave" to show that people could only see distorted shadows of objects of the real world. The original and real forms of these objects, the archetypes, are outside the perception of people [5].

Later in 1919, this idea of the archetype was used by Carl Jung in psychology. While studying ancient and actual myths and religions, he noticed recurring patterns, themes and symbols, and that these patterns also emerged in the dreams and fantasies of his patients. He proposed that there are elements in the human psyche that are pre-personal and transpersonal with the power to influence human thought and behavior, which he called archetypes [6].

Jungian archetypes represent primitive mental images inherited from our ancestors and resident in our collective unconscious. Archetypes consisted of archaic representations of primordial types and models, which are used to evaluate people, things, or situations. Examples of archetypes are the warrior, the hero, the mother… Archetypes can be represented through images, beliefs and myths. They are of indefinite nature and subject to many meanings [7]. A number of archetype structures used nowadays in people and organization realm are of Jungian origin [6, 8].

2.2   Organizational Archetypes

As stated in [9], archetypes can be used to represent organizational structures and management systems that can be better understood by analysis of overall patterns as a function of ideas, beliefs and values. These archetypes can be used inside holistic interpretive frameworks for the classification of organizational structures and systems, according to the differences and similarities in these overall patterns. Furthermore, archetypes are also seen as "qualitative patterns of strategic thought linked to predispositions towards different kinds of reactive or proactive strategy" [10].

There is already significant literature on the use of organizational archetypes to model organizations. For instance, the work described in [11] proposed the use of archetypes as a way of explaining the response of large companies to organizational challenges that affect their probability of success. Some applications of organizational archetypes are focused on the characterization of organizational culture [12, 13]. In [14], archetypes are used to categorize sustainable innovative business models.

Archetypes have been heavily studied in the construction of brands for companies [8]. These archetypes are based on the Jungian ones and we adopt them in our research method.

2.3   Archetypes in Open Innovation

Open innovation has been a strategy used by organizations to explore new commercial opportunities, which would be more difficult to achieve in a traditional organization-centric way. Empirical evidence [15] shows that companies that practice Open Innovation require a set of network capabilities, namely capacity to absorb knowledge, ability to transfer knowledge and relational capacity (openness) regarding suppliers, customers, higher education institutions, competitors, among others [16]. In this sense, "organizations allow unused and underutilized ideas to go outside the organization for others to use in their business models" [17] and, in turn, they are receptive to external knowledge to incorporate in their own developments.

Several researchers and practitioners have elaborated the approach of OI, enriching the field with research focused on the way OI occurs. It is precisely by using the interpretive framework of the archetypes and the way companies claim to practice the OI model that we will try to fit these two concepts together. We may ask what archetypes prevail in companies that adopt this innovation model. That is, what values, beliefs and ideas are embodied in the rationale that describes OI practice?

These networking capabilities relate to several aspects addressed in the area of collaborative networks [2], such as mutual trust [18, p. 11], the ability to collaborate [19], risk and benefits sharing [20], competencies fitness [21] and organizational values alignment [22]. Moreover, organizations are entities of a multi-faceted nature, encompassing several dimensions, namely structural, componential, functional and behavioral ones [23]. Due to these complexities, we may also ask whether there could be a more abstract and comprehensive approach to help characterize OI participants' networking capabilities. As such, we could rely on the organizational archetypes holistic interpretative frameworks mentioned before. Pursuing this way, we may consider an approach for evaluating the networking capability of an organization through archetypes classification. But finding these archetypes has hardly been done, and it is the focus of our research method.

Nevertheless, this idea of exploring archetypes frameworks in OI contexts has already been approached in previous research works. To our best knowledge, they are few and do not explore the rationality proposed in this research work. Table 1 illustrates some examples and scope of such research works. In this table, the example more slightly close to our approach is the one described in [24].

Table 1. Open-Innovation archetypes identified in bibliography.

Application	Archetypes examples	Reference
Innovation patterns	Outside-in process; Inside-out process & Coupled process	[25]
Profiling OI participants	Professionals, Explorers, Scouts & Isolationists	[24]
Decision making	Under Radar, The Regulated Recipe, Follow the Directions, Directed Stumbling, "A New Way To...", Explore Problem-Solving Space; Fix MY House	[26, p. 95]
OI ecosystem Management	Development, Workbench, Access, Insight	[27]
Project Management	The Supporter, The Information Manager, The Knowledge Manager, The Coach	[28]

3   Finding the Archetypes Displayed by OI Participants

3.1   Research Method Explained

As mentioned above, archetypes manifest themselves in subliminal way, through impressions, images and symbols that arise in the several ways organizations operate and interact, including the documents they put available on the web.

Therefore, one way of identifying which archetypes characterize companies, and in our case, those participating in OI projects, is to analyze the documents that they put online on their web sites. The rational is that if we can evaluate people from the way they express, through writing and speaking, using our archetypical references, it is also possible to perceive the archetypes of OI participants, from the web documents they use to "speak" with the market. By analyzing the words and expressions that are used in those documents, we can infer which archetypes lie behind them. For this, two important problems need to be resolved. The first one is how to infer that a document is connoted with certain archetypes. The second problem relates to the difficulty in associating archetypes to a large number of web documents, as usually such type of problems requires a large corpus [29]. Such an effort implies the utilization of knowledge discovery techniques, in our case Web Mining, as described in a later section.

3.2   Inferring Archetypes from the Identified Documents

As mentioned before, the question addressed here is how to infer that a document is connoted with concrete archetypes, for example, "Revolutionary" or "Sage", as these archetypes do not manifest themselves directly in the documents, because they are of latent nature [30]. To solve this problem, we adopted a technique that is used in Text Mining. When trying to infer that a document is associated to a certain class, we can specify a set of "seed words" and look for them in the document. For example, to detect whether a document relates to the concept "car", we can use the set {engine, chassis, brakes...} as "seed words" [31].

In a similar way, our approach also consisted in obtaining a set of seed words for each archetype. For choosing them, we looked for available examples of companies that were characterized through archetypes frameworks. For example, in the online document [32], it is suggested that the company with the "Ruler" archetype (e.g. Mercedes Benz) has the following characteristics: expertise, controller, leadership, and authority. Based on the suggestions from [8, 32, 33], we could identify and obtain associations between archetypes and their related terms, which are later taken as "seed words" during the text mining process. The obtained associations can be seen in Table 2.

Table 2. Association between latent archetypes and corresponding terms.

Archetype	Associated terms
Magician	synchronicity, serendipity, dreamer, visionary, coaching, consultancy, catalyst, positive, renovation
Caregiver	compassionate, loyal, generous, consistent, trustworthy, comforting, supportive, responsive, reliable
Hero	competent, courageous, responsive, directed, disciplined, focused, strong, brave, functional, productive
Explorer	independent, determined, active, exploration, adventurer, youthfulness, rebel, learner, experimenter, energetic
Innocent	peaceful, happiness, optimistic, tranquil, kindness, simplicity, consistent, altruism, unpretentious, natural, optimistic, unpretentious, supportive
Jester	playful, spontaneous, innovative, flexible, original, modern, fair
Revolutionary	radical, innovative, energy, energetic, challenging, creative, progress, transformation, growth
Ruler	leader, commanding, authoritative, expertise, controller, conservative
Sage	intelligence, knowledge, methodical, researcher, challenging, robust, devoted, trustful, thoughtful, classic
Creator	authenticity, imagination, organized, inventive, perfectionist, efficacy, persuasion, futurist, excellence, rebel
Lover	affection, emotion, hedonist, artistic, hospitality, openness, beauty, aesthetics
Every person	genuine, real, reliable, hardworking, trust, collaborate, honest, stable, sharing, democratic, authentic, peer

3.3   The Web Mining Phase

Web mining techniques comprise a particular category of Text Mining, in which the documents are available on the Web. Text Mining is usually applied in knowledge extraction, documents classification, topics modeling, opinion mining, sentiment analysis, and so on. Text Mining methods and tools are available in significant number and variety, and there is a continuous progress in this area. There are three kinds of analysis performed in Web Mining, namely web content mining, web structure mining, and Web usage mining [34]. In this work, we rely on the content analysis side of Web Mining.

Therefore, our Web Mining-based research method starts by obtaining a collection of web pages from companies that engage in open innovation projects. At an early stage, we tried to use Text Mining packages that were already available, for example the R Project for Statistical Computing [35]. But, as mentioned in the *OpenMinted* project [36], there are still issues in terms of interoperability for building more complex or more sophisticated Text Mining applications. In our case, we need that our custom-made Web Mining tool has got the following functionality: access web documents and extract their content; use the sub-links of each web document to see whether related documents are still relevant in terms of open innovation, and extract their content; process the collected documents with Text Mining techniques, as described in the next section; and use the WordNet semantic network to be able to identify synonymy and related words. The entire process is illustrated in Fig. 1. For this, we developed a tool that includes a Java application for handling steps 1 to 3; and Prolog predicates which use WordNet during step 4.

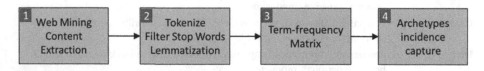

Fig. 1. Representation of the text mining process.

These phases are briefly described here:

1. Obtain a collection of web addresses with documents mentioning "open innovation". In addition, see whether sub-links contained in each document point to other documents that are also related to OI. This step resulted in a corpus of "Open Innovation related web documents" from companies. The obtained collection comprised 4675 documents.
2. The second phase consists of tokenizing the text, filtering stop words, and performing lemmatization. For each word, lemmatization is only accepted if the resulting word exists in the dictionary of English words, as we need to use WordNet in the last phase.
3. In this phase, a term-frequency matrix [37] is constructed, in which the lines of the matrix correspond to documents and the columns to words; each cell contains the frequency of occurrence a word in a particular document. Table 3 shows a partial representation of the obtained term-frequency matrix.

Table 3. Representation of Term-frequency matrix

Doc	corporate	create	energy	innovate	plan	...
1	0	0	0	13	2	...
2	9	0	1	19	0	...
3	0	5	0	3	0	...
4	1	0	0	2	0	...
...	...	...	...	...	...	...

4. This phase consists in associating the words of the documents to each archetype, which will be explained in the next section.

3.4   Discovery of the Most Important Archetypes

Our approach to discover the associations between the words contained in the web documents and the archetypes in Table 2 is based on the work described in [38]. In this work, we define the concept words(c) as representing all the words associated with a concept c, which in our case corresponds to an archetype defined in the left side of Table 2. The words returned by this predicate correspond to the elements on the right side of the table. The predicate classes(w) provides the classes to which a word w of a document is associated, that is, it consists of the set:

$$classes(w) = \{c | w \in words(c)\}. \tag{1}$$

As mentioned in [38, 39], the incidence of a class or archetype c, can be determined as follows:

$$freq(c) = \sum_{w \in words(c)} freq(w). \tag{2}$$

The determination of $freq$(w), in turn, is done as described in [31]. In such way, the terms in the right side of Table 2 are used as "seed words" of the corresponding left-side archetype. Then, each word in the documents that corresponds to the seed words is accounted. Figure 2 shows some seed words for the "Revolutionary" archetype. By using Wordnet, we can also account synonymous and related words of the seed words. For example, by asking WordNet which words are related to "innovative", which is a seed word of Revolutionary archetype, the answer includes "innovate", "invention", "innovativeness", "groundbreaking", etc.

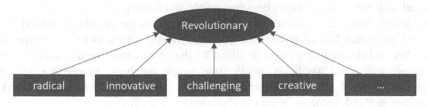

Fig. 2. Seed words of class/archetype "Revolutionary".

The determination of the frequency of each word in the documents was made using two levels of depth. At level 1, only the words that corresponded to the "seed words" are searched in the documents. At level 2, WordNet is used to consider synonyms and related words as well. With these approaches, we can find the incidence of archetypes in OI web documents.

Archetypes Determination, Search Level 1

At level 1, only the words that corresponded to the "seed words" are searched in the documents. Whenever a word matched, the value *freq* of matrix tf(*doc, word, freq*) is added to the archetype incidence. Proceeding with this search to each word of each document provides the determination of the more incident archetypes in the documents, which is illustrated in Fig. 3.

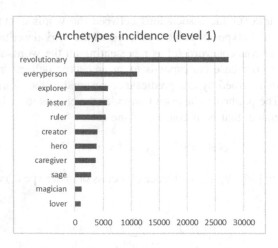

Fig. 3. Discovered archetypes, level 1.

Based on these results, we can state that the archetypes with more incidence in the documents are "revolutionary", "everyperson", "jester", and "ruler". A more detailed analysis of these results is done below.

Archetypes Determination, Search Level 2

In addition to the previous search level, we look for synonyms and related words to each seed word of each archetype, which as mentioned before, is done using WordNet. Our method is inspired in [39], which describes an approach based on the utilization of Wordnet to identify associations between words and concepts.

In search level 2, whenever a "seed word", any synonymous or related word matched, the value *freq* of matrix tf(*doc, word, freq*) is added to the archetype incidence. We add attenuation weights to adjust for the cases where the documents' words are farther from seed words, in the Wordnet graph ontology. Proceeding with this search to each word of each document provides the determination of the more incident archetypes in the documents, which is illustrated in Fig. 4.

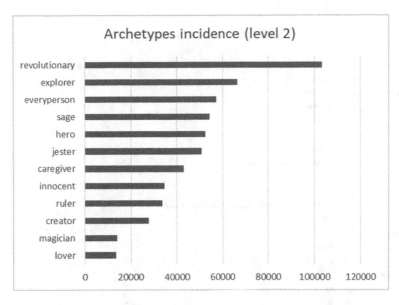

Fig. 4. Discovered archetypes, level 2

3.5   Results Discussion

The results obtained during search for level 1 show that archetypes with more incidence in the used documents are the archetypes "revolutionary", "everyperson", "jester" and "ruler". In the search for level 2, the archetype "explorer" moved from seventh to second position. This is because, in the previous search level, the seed words "determined", "exploration" and "youthfulness" did not get any hits. In level 2, correspondences were found through synonymy and derivations using wordNet, e.g., the words "ambitious", "expedition" and "juvenile", respectively.

In Fig. 5, the elements more related with the resulting archetypes are depicted. The terms with more correspondences to the revolutionary archetype are: innovate, growth, energetic and radical. This is interesting because, as suggested in [33], organizations with the revolutionary archetype spend great energy pursuing radically different things, challenge the status quo, and the developed products lead to true innovations. The companies suggested as possessing the archetype of revolutionary were: "Apple" and "Harley Davidson".

The second identified archetype, the "explorer", allows to characterize independent companies that are very active and like to learn based on the experience. A suggested enterprise with this archetype is "Starbucks" [32]. The last archetype, "everyperson", has the elements "hardworking", "reliable" and "collaborate". As suggested in [32], "everyperson" organizations provide comfortable spaces where everyone is treated equally and work in collaboration. The suggested companies with these archetypes are "Craiglist" and "The Associated Press".

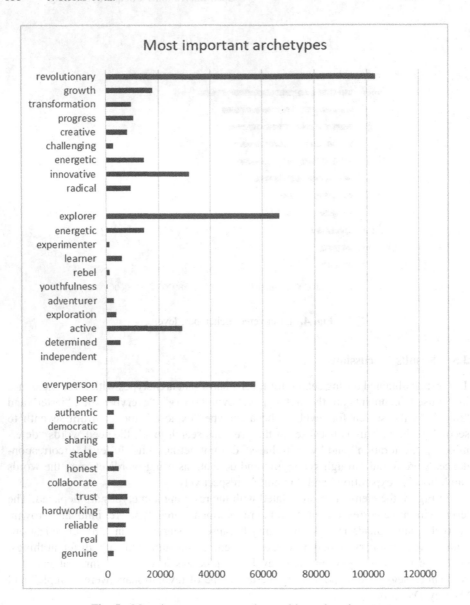

Fig. 5. More important aspects observed in each archetype.

The knowledge of these archetypes could be used to develop a holistic interpretive framework for OI participants' classification, and therefore, be used in OI projects management, for instance, in partners' engagement and assessing risk.

4   Conclusions and Future Work

This research work consisted in the discovery of the archetypes that best characterize the companies participating in OI. In Sect. 2, we highlighted the role of archetypes in representing images, impressions, myths and symbols with the ability to both characterize influence people's behavior. On the part of organizational archetypes, we highlighted their role in interpretive schemas allowing the classification of the typology, structures, strategies, values and processes of organizations. As such, these schemes would also be useful in archetype characterization of OI participants.

The followed research method is based on web mining applied to enterprises' web documents with content mentioning "open innovation". According to the obtained results, the archetypes that seem to characterize OI participants are (1) the "revolutionary" that prefer radical development and likes to overcome challenges; (2) the "explorer", which likes to learn and explore new things; and (3) the "everyperson", which is hardworking, "reliable" and gives preference to collaboration. The results obtained with this work can be used in the construction of models for risk assessment, or in the characterization and classification of candidates for IO projects.

To our knowledge, the application of archetypes in the context of OI, using the proposed approach, has not received much attention from researchers. This is an exploratory study and as such there are still various aspects and limitations that need to be addressed. A difficulty initially felt, is that it was necessary to study and cross several concepts from distinct areas, without having a good conceptual reference matrix. While we tried to fill the gap, it is nevertheless necessary to make a more systematic and in-depth conceptualization of the definitions and application of archetypes into OI contexts.

As to ensure that we were collecting web documents only from companies and enterprises, and excluding other types of content, such as papers, essays, discussion forums, etc., the documents collection had to be done manually, resulting in a relatively small set of documents, approximately 4600. This part can also be improved through a more efficient retrieving approach. The Text Mining process could also be improved with the utilization of additional steps of knowledge extraction, including, statistical inference and use of alternative Text Mining methods. In this regards, we could for instance use Inverse Document Frequency [40], to weight the importance of a word according to its frequency in the documents.

Considering these limitations, interesting points to explore in the future work include further development of a more complete conceptual reference matrix for archetypes in Open Innovation. Additionally, we could then depart from the notion of archetype of the general context of organizations, to a more specific one in the OI context. It is also necessary to apply distinct methods of knowledge discovery and to improve the web documents retrieving process.

Acknowledgments. This work has been partially supported by the Center of Technology and Systems (CTS) – Uninova, by the Portuguese FCT-PEST program UID/EEA/00066/2013, by CIUHCT - Interuniversity Center for the History of Science and Technology and by UNIDEMI - Research and Development Unit for Mechanical and Industrial Engineering by the Portuguese FCT-PEST program UID/EMS/00667/2013.

References

1. Camarinha-Matos, L.M., Fornasiero, R., Afsarmanesh, H.: Collaborative networks as a core enabler of industry 4.0. In: Camarinha-Matos, L.M., Afsarmanesh, H., Fornasiero, R. (eds.) PRO-VE 2017. IFIP AICT, vol. 506, pp. 3–17. Springer, Cham (2017). https://doi.org/10. 1007/978-3-319-65151-4_1
2. Camarinha-Matos, L.M., Afsarmanesh, H.: Collaborative networks: Value creation in a knowledge society. In: Wang, K., Kovacs, G.L., Wozny, M., Fang, M. (eds.) Knowledge Enterprise: Intelligent Strategies in Product Design, Manufacturing, and Management. PROLAMAT 2006. IFIP International Federation for Information Processing, vol 207. Springer, Boston (2006)
3. Chesbrough, H.: Open innovation: Where we've been and where we're going. Res. Technol. Manag. **55**(4), 20–27 (2012)
4. What are Archetypes? (2016). https://aras.org/about/what-are-archetypes. Accessed 2018/ 04/05
5. Plato, Book VII of The Republic, The Allegory of the Cave (2009). http://webspace.ship. edu/cgboer/platoscave.html. Accessed 15 Apr 2018
6. Papadopoulos, R.K. (ed.): The Handbook of Jungian Psychology: Theory, Practice and Applications. Psychology Press, New York (2006)
7. Jung, C.G.: The Archetypes and the Collective Unconscious. Routledge, New York (2014)
8. Mark, M., Pearson, C.S.: The Hero and the Outlaw: Building Extraordinary Brands Through the Power of Archetypes. McGraw Hill Professional, New York (2001)
9. Greenwood, R., Hinings, C.R.: Understanding strategic change: the contribution of archetypes. Acad. Manag. J. **36**(5), 1052–1081 (1993)
10. Miller, D., Friesen, P.H.: Archetypes of strategy formulation. Manag. Sci. **24**(9), 921–933 (1978)
11. Fleck, D.L.: Archetypes of organizational success and failure. BAR-Brazilian Administration Review **6**(2), 78–100 (2009)
12. Jung, T., Scott, T., Davies, H.T., Bower, P., Whalley, D., McNally, R., Mannion, R.: Instruments for exploring organizational culture: a review of the literature. Public Adm. Rev. **69**(6), 1087–1096 (2009)
13. Ouchi, W.G., Wilkins, A.L.: Organizational culture. Ann. Rev. Sociol. **11**(1), 457–483 (1985)
14. Bocken, N.M., Short, S.W., Rana, P., Evans, S.: A literature and practice review to develop sustainable business model archetypes. J. Clean. Prod. **65**, 42–56 (2014)
15. Teixeira, A.A.C., Lopes, M.: Open Innovation in Portugal. Acta Oeconómica **62**(4), 435–458 (2012)
16. Gassmann, O., Enkel, E., Chesbrough, H.: The future of open innovation. R&d Manag. **40**(3), 213–221 (2010)
17. Danneels, L., Viaene, S.: Open co-creation coming of age: the case of an open services experiment. In: Proceedings of the 51st Hawaii International Conference on System Sciences, January 2018
18. Jemielniak, D., Marks, A.: Managing Dynamic Technology-Oriented Businesses: High Tech Organizations (2012)
19. Rosas, J., Camarinha-Matos, L.M.: An approach to assess collaboration readiness. Int. J. Prod. Res. **47**(17), 4711–4735 (2009)
20. Camarinha-Matos, L.M., Abreu, A.: Performance indicators for collaborative networks based on collaboration benefits. Prod. Plann. Control **18**(7), 592–609 (2007)

21. Rosas, J., Macedo, P., Camarinha-Matos, L.M.: Extended competencies model for collaborative networks. Prod. Plann. Control **22**(5–6), 501–517 (2011)
22. Macedo, P., Camarinha-Matos, L.M.: A qualitative approach to assess the alignment of Value Systems in collaborative enterprises networks. Comput. Ind. Eng. **64**(1), 412–424 (2013)
23. Camarinha-Matos, L.M., Afsarmanesh, H., Ermilova, E., Ferrada, F., Klen, A., Jarimo, T.: ARCON reference models for collaborative networks. In: Collaborative Networks: Reference Modeling, pp. 83–112, Springer, Boston (2008)
24. Keupp, M.M., Gassmann, O.: Determinants and archetype users of open innovation. R&d Manag. **39**(4), 331–341 (2009)
25. Gassmann, O., Enkel, E.: Towards a theory of open innovation: three core process archetypes (2004)
26. Bingham, A., Spradlin, D.: The Open Innovation Marketplace: Creating Value in the Challenge Driven Enterprise. Ft Press, Upper Saddle River (2011)
27. Tamoschus, D., Hienerth, C., Lessl, M.: Developing a framework to manage a pharmaceutical innovation ecosystem: collaboration archetypes, open innovation tools, and strategies. In: 2nd World Open Innovation Conference, pp. 19–20, November 2015
28. Desouza, K.C., Evaristo, J.R.: Project management offices: a case of knowledge-based archetypes. Int. J. Inf. Manag. **26**(5), 414–423 (2006)
29. Fast, E., Chen, B., Bernstein, M.S.: Empath: understanding topic signals in large-scale text. In: Proceedings of the 2016 CHI Conference on Human Factors in Computing Systems, pp. 4647–4657. ACM, May 2016
30. Maloney, A.: Preference ratings of images representing archetypal themes: an empirical study of the concept of archetypes. J. Anal. Psychol. **44**(1), 101–116 (1999)
31. Godbole, S., Bhattacharya, I., Gupta, A., Verma, A.: Building re-usable dictionary repositories for real-world text mining. In: Proceedings of the 19th ACM International Conference on Information and Knowledge Management, pp. 1189–1198. ACM, October 2010
32. The 12 Archetypes - A proven framework for understanding individual personality and organizational behavior (2017). https://www.culturetalk.com/12-archetypes/. Accessed 10 Apr 2018
33. Explorer, Hero, or Jester: What's Your Company's Cultural Archetype? (2018), https://blog.hubspot.com/agency/cultural-archetypes. Accessed 10 Apr 2018
34. Grace, L.K., Maheswari, V., Nagamalai, D.: Analysis of web logs and web user in web mining (2011). arXiv preprint arXiv:1101.5668
35. The R Project for Statistical Computing. https://www.r-project.org/. Accessed 2018/03/15
36. Open Mining Infrastructure for Text and Data. http://openminted.eu/about/. Accessed 10 Apr 2018
37. Tokunaga, T., Makoto, I., Text categorization based on weighted inverse document frequency. In: Special Interest Groups and Information Process Society of Japan (SIG-IPSJ) (1994)
38. Jiang, J.J., Conrath, D.W.: Semantic similarity based on corpus statistics and lexical taxonomy. arXiv preprint arXiv:cmp-lg/9709008 (1997)
39. Resnik, P.: Wordnet and distributional analysis: a class-based approach to lexical discovery. In: AAAI Workshop on Statistically-Based Natural Language Processing Techniques, pp. 56–64, July 1992
40. Bloehdorn, S., Cimiano, P., Hotho, A., Staab, S.: An ontology-based framework for text mining. In: LDV Forum, vol. 20, No. 1, pp. 87–112, May 2005

Research Investigation on Food Information User's Behaviour

Antonio Palmiro Volpentesta and Alberto Michele Felicetti(✉)

Department of Mechanical Energy and Management Engineering,
University of Calabria, Via P.Bucci, 87036 Rende, CS, Italy
{antonio.volpentesta, alberto.felicetti}@unical.it

Abstract. Recent advances in smart food technologies have renewed the attractiveness of those studies on human information behaviour that take the food consumer as focus of interest. In this paper, we introduce a reference framework to model the food information usage process and the interrelation between the food consumer's behaviour and the food information user's behaviour. Basing on this framework, we present a literature review that classifies research works according to research approach types and stages of the food information usage process. The aim is to present a state of art of significance to food marketing and to the development of food intelligent services with higher satisfaction and value.

Keywords: Food information · Consumer's behaviour
Information user's behaviour · Literature review · Intelligent food services

1 Introduction

The current paradigm shift towards a digital consumer society is leading new digital business to collect a big amount of food data that can be transferred and processed further with data analytics and intelligence tools. Food data are about food composition, consumer preferences, preparation and other food consumption activities (e.g., online recipes, databases of bio-molecular compounds in foods, restaurant reviews, and so on). Data management tools are based on crowdsourcing, data mining, large-scale data analysis, machine learning, and network analysis.

These trends with the continuous penetration of smart technologies are driving the emergence of intelligent food services that support food business in better understanding food consumers, improving marketing researches, and increasing food processes efficiency. For example, restaurant chains are investigating how big data can help to understand better the consumer behaviour inside a restaurant and to discover best practices to improve background processes. They look at big data analytics on menu entries and clusters of customers to optimize the drive-thru experience and to challenge spikes in demand ahead of time.

On the consumer's side, the availability of food information and intelligent services can give the food consumer new insights into his/her choice, propose novel ingredient combinations, and identify socio-cultural, safety, nutritional and bio-molecular factors that determine which foods we enjoy and why [1]. They are already changing food

© IFIP International Federation for Information Processing 2018
Published by Springer Nature Switzerland AG 2018. All Rights Reserved
L. M. Camarinha-Matos et al. (Eds.): PRO-VE 2018, IFIP AICT 534, pp. 190–202, 2018.
https://doi.org/10.1007/978-3-319-99127-6_17

consumption activities as shaping food consumer culinary preferences, habits, and food information needs. Moreover, these services may shape new form of businesses based on platforms of collaborative food consumption.

This new context makes research studies on the relationship between the behaviours of food consumer and food information user quite important. Several studies addressed the role of food information in food consumption activities [2]. However, literature lacks of a holistic overview of the way food consumers behave in seeking, selecting and using food-related information. This paper intends to fill this gap providing a literature review of scientific research that combines knowledge on food consumer's and food information user's behaviours. Research topics are classified according to research approach types and stages of the food information usage process that is a series of consumer's food information related activities. Throughout this paper, rather than simply focusing on 'information use', in the narrowest sense of usage, we refer to it as the process that comprises all stages from the identification of a food information need through the final stage of information contextualization and use.

The aim is to present a state or art that identifies mature areas of research, areas requiring further investigation, and current and future research directions of significance for the development of new food information services with higher satisfaction and value.

2 Background and Motivations

Consumers are daily involved in food-related activities: planning what to eat, purchase, store and cook food, eating, and disposing remnants. The series of consumer's food-related activities is known as food provisioning [3] or food consumption process [4]. Over recent years, patterns of food consumption have experienced rapid change, as result of the growing interest of consumers on health, food safety, environmental and social issues. For that reason, food consumer behaviour is a widely addressed topic in scientific literature.

Consumer behaviour is defined as the set of activities directly involved in obtaining, consuming and disposing product, services or experiences, to satisfy needs and desires [5]. Basing mainly on cognitive approaches to consumer behaviour, specific behavioural models with respect to the food consumption process have been developed across the years. Such models are mainly based on social cognitive theory [6] and the theory of planned behaviour [7].

Information processing of marketing stimuli is central to explain consumer behaviour [8]. As matter of fact, information plays a crucial role in reducing uncertainty during a decision-making process [9]. Needs for information emerge from the recognition of a gap between a person's knowledge current state and his/her desirable state [10]. Due to its nature, an information need arises as an output of a more basic need. It is a part of the search for the satisfaction of a physiological, affective or cognitive need, as an individual is engaged on "*information seeking towards the satisfaction of needs*" [11]. Users' behaviour in information seeking and use is widely investigated under the concept of human information behaviour [12]. This literature stream attempts to develop generalizable explanations of human behaviour when humans acquire and process information, including selection, evaluation, and use of information contents, sources and channels [13].

Over recent years, the information behaviour of food consumers is assuming growing interest from many different perspectives (food business marketing, food information business, public food authorities, food consumers). However, from whatever perspective, the emerging request is to manage in more effective ways food information, and this can be done by leveraging on a deeper knowledge about food information user's behaviour. The main challenge of food information management is to deliver the information that enables consumers to make appropriate choices according to their own individual objectives, as they are involved in food consumption activities. Unfortunately, information asymmetry occurs all along the food chain, deeply affecting consumer decision behaviour(s) [14]. This is mainly due to the intrinsic nature of food sector, often exposed to unknown characteristics. Quality and safety issues about food are difficult to identify, and in the majority of cases recognizable only after their consumption. In fact, depending on the type of attribute, food is considered as an experience (some food attributes can be determined just after purchasing and consumption) or credence good (some food attributes that cannot be determined by consumer even after consumption) [15]. Main consequences of asymmetric information are moral hazard (a food producer takes more risks (e.g. falsely labelling, food adulteration) because consumers bear the burden of those risks), and adverse selection (producers hide some food information in a transaction, leading consumers to poor decisions making). Several scholars address the problem of asymmetries proposing solutions to overcome moral hazard and adverse selection, by means of contracts, product labelling and monitoring system (public or private), certifications [16]. However, conventional ways of food information provisioning seem not to solve the problem of asymmetries, justifying the increasing interest towards innovative solution for a more effective food information provision. On the one hand, consumers are demanding more and more relevant, reliable and appropriate food information for their decision-making. On the other hand, food information providers face the challenge of identifying what kind of food information consumers are interested in and when, where and how information should be provided [1]. Recent advances in "Internet of food" technologies (such as food sensors, cloud computing, food data analysis, and mobile app technologies) makes possible to conceive new food information services, letting consumers get more relevant food information than they usually obtain through on-product labeling, mass media or other traditional channels.

3 Food Information Usage Process

In what follows we present a reference framework to model the food information usage process and the interrelation between the food consumer's behaviour and the food information user's behaviour. Food needs are human primary needs that may come from internal stimuli, normally a physiological or emotional needs (e.g. hunger, desire for salty/sweet foods) or from external stimuli (e.g. an advertisement, the smell /the sight of yummy food, etc.). They let often arise food-related primary needs associated with a consumer's activity in a stage of the food consumption process (e.g. purchasing appropriate food products, choosing where to buy food, planning meals).

The identification of a food information need represents the first stage of the information usage process. It starts as soon as the consumer recognizes an aroused food-related primary need or a need to fill a knowledge gap. The food consumer becomes aware that food information should be acquired and collected in order to meet that need. He/she translates a food-related need or the awareness of a food knowledge gap into an information question relevant to a choice in a specific food consumption stage or to a food learning activity. This leads the food consumer to become a food information user. The clarity of the information question is crucial for the success of the rest of the process, i.e. the retrieval and use of the desired food information.

Food information seeking is the second stage of the information usage process. In this stage, the food information user is actively and purposefully involved in a conscious effort to acquire information in response to a food-related need or a need to fill a food knowledge gap. From a decisional point of view, food information users have to choose the appropriate information channel and the information source able to meet his/her food information need. A user may explore several information channels (e.g. labels, social media, mobile apps) and information sources (e.g. food producers, distributors or other food supply chain stakeholders) and ends his/her research when he/she evaluates the retrieved information as sufficiently relevant and reliable. Nowadays, collaborative food information seeking and sharing represent a recent aspect of food information consumer's behaviour. The increased availability of social media tools facilitates interactive communication among consumers, leaving a large margin for third parties to become food information providers (e.g., food bloggers, forum, recommender systems) [17]. In fact, social media make possible food consumers to group themselves in communities around a collective purpose and contribute to the production or dissemination of food information [18]. Beyond advantages deriving from collaborative food information seeking, some critical issues about the trustworthiness of the information provided are emerging in research studies [19].

The output of food information seeking is an information cue that a consumer could use to support his/her food decision-making or learning process.

Once food information is selected, consumers can use it for some food choices in a food-related activity, i.e. an activity of the food consumption process or an activity of a food learning process. How consumers interpret, give meaning to, evaluate, and use food information depends on their previous experience, expertise, and needs, as well as their current consumption context, i.e. situational and temporal conditions in which the consumer's food choice occurs [20]. Context awareness has a significant influence on the food information user, as context cues can support user to better interpret food-related information. In fact, context awareness provides the user with sensory and cognitive cues that allow him/her to refer delivered data and information to food items. An information content can be properly interpreted by taking into account other elements within the environment surrounding food products the information content is referring to (e.g. other food products), specific physical conditions (e.g. light, humidity, temperature, localization, spatial layout, package integrity) or organizational features (e.g. operation rules, shop opening). In other words, contextualization is necessary to the use of the food information for either to make an appropriate consumption choice or to enable a deliberate food learning process.

Lastly, we recall that a food learning process can be also triggered by psychobiological stimuli when the consumer is directly involved in a food consumption activity. Trial-and-error approaches, social interactions, lessons learned carrying out real-life food activities, allow consumers to acquire knowledge to create or modify their ideas and values about food.

The above food information usage process and its interrelation with the food consumption process is presented in Fig. 1.

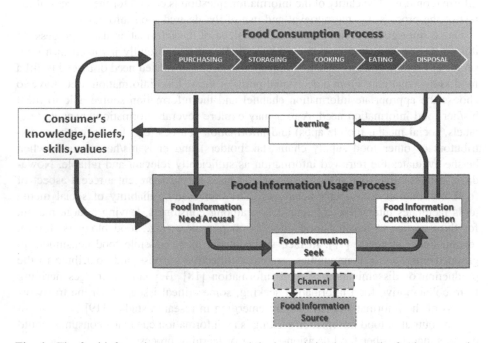

Fig. 1. The food information usage process and the interrelation between the food consumer's behaviour and the food information user's behaviour

4   Literature Review

In our work, we carried out a literature review of scientific papers on human information behaviour that take the food consumer as the focus of interest. In what follows, we present the methodology we have adopted and main results arising from the analysis of retrieved papers that are classified according to research approaches and stages of the food information usage process.

4.1   Methodology

We selected Google Scholar as scientific research engine where to perform our search. We initialized a list L of search keywords with English terms related to the above mentioned scientific domain (e.g. "information seeking", "need for information", "information need arousal", "consumer behaviour", "information behaviour", as well as synonymous, and other broader/wider terms). We performed a search on Google Scholar using keywords in the list L coupled with term "food" and other terms used for major food groups. We identified main research lines in the domain of food consumer information behaviour. Moreover, the list L was possibly extended by adjoining new terms found among the author keywords of each paper. The activity was iteratively performed until no newer keywords or new papers were found. We analysed the abstract of each paper in order to determine whether it matched our inclusion criterion: the paper deals with a phase of the food information usage process at least.

At the end of this cycle, we obtained the final set P, consisting of 64 papers to be analysed. For each paper p ∈ P we identified the research line(s) addressed in that paper and the research approach(es) adopted. To classification purposes, we selected the following research approaches [21]: literature review, empirical research (quantitative survey, case study), model.

4.2 Results

For sake of clarity, we present our results in three subsections each of which corresponds to one of the main activities of food information usage process, namely food information needs identification, food information seeking and food information contextualization. The complete list of papers we reviewed is available at: https://drive. google.com/open?id=1NGNDkVRtusIcm_C6w6cBga2DAJQlHT8X

4.2.1 Food Information Needs Identification

Extant literature in cognitive psychology and behavioural economics attempts to explain the link between the rational consumer and necessary inputs, capabilities and willingness to engage in a food decision making process. A food information need arouses as a consequence of consumer's involvement in a food consumption activity, and it is affected by some consumer's attributes (interests, attitudes, experiences, and knowledge). In fact, food information needs vary from a consumer to another and may affected from the judgement of their values and beliefs, habits, the tools available for information search and the knowledge about these tools [P7]. Some authors identify consumer interests, motivational states and habits as drivers in food information needs arousal [P1]. However, we may summarize the general research questions in literature about the identification of food information needs as follows:

- *Why do consumers need food information and what information do they need?*
- *What activates their food information need?*

These questions have been tackled under either a specific perspective reflecting a consumer's interest in a food property type or a psychological perspective related to the antecedents of a consumer's interest. We have grouped food properties in 6 broad classes, namely healthiness, safety, convenience, hedonism, culture and ethics/ sustainability which correspond to 6 specific perspectives:

Healthiness: this research direction addresses the impact of health-related consumers' values on food information user's needs. Researches are centred on the identification of consumer's interest towards health related food information, e.g. healthy food properties (e.g. anticancer) [P4], food wellness related properties (e.g. anti-ageing food, food improving skin elasticity) [P5], nutritional composition of the food (protein, carbs, fat, calories, vitamins, minerals) [P3]. Survey based research demonstrated that consumers with health related interests, have continuous and more intense information needs about food [P6] [P12].

Safety: researches are devoted to investigate the way a consumer's information need arises under a safety-related perspective, They show that this arousal is strictly entwined with the consumer's perception of risks associated to food-related hazards [P8], e.g., chemical and microbiological contaminants associated with food chains [P9], presence of preservatives, colorants, and artificial sweeteners in food products [P10].

Convenience: researches are addressed to study food information need arousal in consumers whose main interest is towards food costs and convenience. They are mostly devoted to determine what consumer's information needs are from what they depend, e.g. buying food at a lower price, finding the nearest food store, and, more in general, gaining benefits during food related activities [P14].

Hedonism: few research works, explicitly focusing on the relationship between the pleasure of food and information need arousal, have been found in scientific literature. However, some of them give some considerations about consumers' information needs, although they restricted the attention to a specific food group, e.g. meat [P15]; others have been oriented to determine the terms that consumers use to indicate and measure emotions associated with foods [P16]. Of course, these results can be of some interest for further research on identifying food information needs of consumers, mainly driven by concern for sensory quality of food products. As matter of fact, they may help to understand how consumers conceptualize and express food information needs into words.

Culture: although cultural interests and patterns of consumer's behaviour towards food have been largely studied in literature, the impact of socio-cultural interests and dispositions towards the arousal of food information needs has been scarcely investigated. Some researchers have linked up these interests with food consumers (called foodies) who recognize their food information needs in a continuous commitment to self-education (learning about food typicity, traditions and values, trying new cooking techniques, reading magazines, cookbooks, culinary history, and food blogs) [P18].

Ethic/sustainability: researches have been focused on information needs of consumers that are driven by taking social and environmental concerns of food products into account, i.e. 'ethical consumerism'. They mainly investigate consumer's preferences and needs of information about 'fair trade' aspects (e.g., fair prices to farmers, integration of handicapped people, animal welfare, preservation of biodiversity) and other food-related sustainable practices from an environmental and social point of view (e.g., reduction of greenhouse gases, protection of the tropical rainforest, prevention of child labour) [P21].

The last perspective deals with the identification of psychological factors that influence individual consumer's need for information:

Psychological: researches in this direction are devoted to investigate individual characteristics that shape the arousal of food information needs. Some of them deals with variables in the psychological domain such as uncertainty, involvement, personality and knowledge [P22].

In Table 1 we summarize results of our review, specifying the type of research approach and related references.

Table 1. Research directions on food information needs identification.

Perspective	Research type	References
Healthiness	Quantitative survey	P1, P2, P3
	Empirical research	P4, P5
	Qualitative study	P6
Safety	Review	P7
	Quantitative survey	P8, P9, P10, P11, P12
	Model	P13
Convenience	Qualitative study	P14
Hedonism/emotion	Model	P15, P16
Cultural	Quantitative survey	P17, P18
	Review	P19
	Qualitative	P20
Ethical/sustainabilty	Quantitative survey	P21
Psychological	Review	P22

4.2.2 Information Seeking

Scholars identified several patterns in food information seeking, depending on whether food consumer perceives a real need for information [P22], his/her emotional state [P23] or his/her skills [P24]. From a decisional point of view, when a user is consciously involved in an effort to acquire information about food, he/she has to choose the appropriate information channel and the information source able to meet his/her food information need. Information channel refers to a medium used by the consumer in finding food information (mobile-apps, blogs, newspapers, radio stations, television stations, and so on). Information source refers to persons or organizations (public authorities, food firms, third parties food product certifiers, educational organizations, information practitioners and other food supply chain stakeholders) from which food information comes to consumers.

Research on food information seeking attempted to understand how users behave when they search for food information, including factors affecting the selection and the evaluation of information sources and channels. We summarize the general research questions about food information seeking process as follows:

- *Which factors influence information channel selection in food information seeking?*
- *How do consumers use information channels to seek food information?*
- *Which determinants motivate consumers to choose a food information source?*

With respect to the **first question**, extant literature has been concerned with consumer's perceived channel benefits as main factors influencing the selection of a food information channel. Researches have been conducted to identify benefits that are linked up to information channel availability and accessibility as well as to consumers' effort reduction. Benefits have been investigated for many internet and mobile-based channels that can overcome some limitations of traditional channels (e.g. labels, radio, and television), as making information retrievable whenever and wherever the consumer needs for (in time and in place information). Some researches provide empirical evidences about the impact of channel availability and accessibility on the consumer's channel selection [P25] [P26] [P27] as well as time and cognitive efforts required by information searching on a given channel [P28] [P29] [P30].

The **second research question** has garnered less attention in literature on food information user's behaviour. Some scholars have tackled this question by focusing on a restricted domain of food information, pertaining to some food quality attribute (e.g., safety), and new internet and mobile-based channels. They investigated consumers' intention to use current prevalent online and offline information channels. For instance, some of them investigated the inclination of consumers, who are familiar with social media applications, to use these as a channel to seek information about safety related [P33] [P34] or health related issues [P35], compared to other more traditional mass media and Internet channels.

With reference to the **third research question**, source credibility is widely recognized as the main determinant affecting consumer's choice of a food information source. Source credibility refers to the extent to which a recipient believes that the source has considerable knowledge, skills and experiences to provide objective information without bias. Credibility of food information sources includes several aspects influencing the extent to what individuals consider a source credible. Recently, some empirical studies have been carried out to identify factors that affect the credibility of a food information source. They mainly deal with three factors:

Perceived expertise: it refers to the degree to which recipients perceive the information source as having the experience, skills, and capacity to provide accurate information. Some researchers have given empirical evidences about perceived expertise and the impact on the overall evaluation of the information sources. For example, Van Dillen et al. [P42] ranked several information sources about health and nutrition according the degree of expertise perceived by Dutch consumers. Hiddink et al. [P43] investigated some sources of nutrition information and found that perceived expertise of noncommercial sources was much higher than for commercial sources.

Trustworthiness: it deals with the confidence that the source provides objective and correct information. Most of the research aimed to determine to what extent consumers trust in food information sources and which factors affect their trust in those sources [P45]. Several researches, based on survey approach, tend to segment consumers according to their level of trust with respect to information sources [P46]. Other researchers investigated determinants of source trustworthiness as mediating effect on eWOM credibility [P49].

Attractiveness: it refers to the degree to which an information source is appealing to consumers by exerting verbal, physical, or technology-mediated communication. Few research works, explicitly focusing on information source attractiveness, have been found in scientific literature. Some of them empirically investigated the influence of food blog attractiveness on blog user's trust in blog information [P53].

In Table 2 we summarize results of our review, specifying the type of research approach and related references.

Table 2. Research directions on food information seeking.

Research line	Focus	Research type	References
Factors influencing food information channel selection	Channel benefits	Quantitative survey	P25, P26, P27, P28, P29, P30
		Model	P31
		Qualitative research	P32
Consumers motivation to use an information channel	Usefulness and familiarity with social media	Quantitative survey	P33, P34, P35
Determinants in consumer's choice of a food information source	Perceived expertise	Qualitative research	P36
		Empirical research	P37, P38
		Quantitative survey	P39, P40, P41, P42, P43
	Trustwhortiness	Quantitative survey	P8, P44, P45, P46, P47, P48, P49,
		Qualitative research	P50, P51
		Review	P52
	Attractiveness	Quantitative survey	P53

4.2.3   Information Contextualization and Use

Food information use is widely investigated under a marketing perspective in terms of impact on consumer's behaviour, e.g. nutritional information influence on the decision to buy or not a food product. Of course, many information provider organizations (public authorities, food firms, and other food supply chain stakeholders), are interested in these investigations, as they tend to shape consumers' behaviour or to redirect their food-related decision-making. From the scientific literature's perspective, several studies have been conducted on the influence of food information on consumer choices in food consumption activities, but they rather limited their scope to some aspect of the information use process. Most of them have been focused on consumers' use of nutritional labels for purchasing decisions and dietary changes, see [P54] for a review, consumers' use of information about genetically modified food, or other safety related issues. However, we may summarize that they all face the following general research question about food information use:

- *Which factors influence the information use in food consumer's choices?*

Researches from the literature reveal that these factors pertain to the three main entities involved in food decision-making: consumer (who takes the decision), context (situational and temporal conditions in which the decision should be taken), and information (input of the decision-making process).

Consumer: pertaining factors refer to consumer's attributes that influence consumer's interpretation, evaluation, and use of a food information cue. They may be grouped in *demographic characteristics* (such as age, gender, education [P54]), *motivation and interests* (e.g. health-related interests [P55], food involvement [P56],), and *food knowledge* (e.g. ability to understand food information [P57]);

Context: extant research of information systems evidences that the way users give meaning and importance to information depends on temporal and location attributes of items within the context where users make decisions. Unfortunately, contextual factors have not been prioritized in previous research related to food information use. Few studies deal with the influence of context on food consumer decision making, focusing mainly on environmental factors [P58] and socio-cultural contextual factors [P11].

Information: few studies have been directed to empirically examine how much information use depends on the quality of the information a consumer receives. Some research works have focused on the influence of information content qualities, in terms of accuracy, currency, completeness, timeless, and understandability, on consumer's online food purchasing [P59]. Some others focused on consumer preferences about information content format or presentation attributes, but most of them limited their scope to investigate nutrition label formats [P54].

In Table 3 we summarize results of our review, specifying the type of research approach and related references.

Table 3. Research directions on food information contextualization.

Research line		Research type	References
Factors influencing the information use in food consumer's choices	Consumer	Quantitative survey	P1, P63, P55, P56, P60, P61, P62, P63, P64
	Context	Quantitative survey	P11, P53, P58
	Information	Quantitative survey	P59
		Review	P54

5   Conclusions and Future Research Directions

Results arising from our literature review confirm a great interest that researchers have shown in food consumer's information behaviour over past decades. However, the identified research directions reflect a classical marketing perspective. The interrelation between the food consumer's behaviour and the food information user's behaviour has been investigated without taking into account current paradigms of Internet-of-Food and collaborative food consumption. Considering these new paradigms as part of the food consumption process, the food information usage process needs to be aligned and new research challenges need to be addressed in order to accelerate the development of the next generation of food information services with higher satisfaction and value.

In particular, capabilities of current context-sensitive technologies make urgent to open up research directions in order to investigate the role of food information contextualization in the food information usage process. As matter of fact, contextualization is absolutely essential both to let the consumer make appropriate choices in his/her food consumption activities and to enable consumer's informal learning process that is crucial for his/her future related behaviour.

References

1. Volpentesta, A.P., Felicetti, A.M., Ammirato, S.: Intelligent food information provision to consumers in an internet of food era. In: Camarinha-Matos, L.M., Afsarmanesh, H., Fornasiero, R. (eds.) PRO-VE 2017. IAICT, vol. 506, pp. 725–736. Springer, Cham (2017). https://doi.org/10.1007/978-3-319-65151-4_65
2. Van Rijswijk, W., Frewer, L.J.: Consumer needs and requirements for food and ingredient traceability information. Int. J. Consum. Stud. **36**(3), 282–290 (2012)
3. Goody, J.: Cooking, Cuisine and Class. A Study in Contemporary Sociology Cambridge University Press, Cambridge (1982)
4. Marshall, D.W.: Food choice, the consumer and food provisioning. In: Marshall, D.W. (ed.) Food Choice and the Consumer, pp. 3–17. Blackie Academic & Professional (1995)
5. Sirgy, M.J.: Self-concept in consumer behaviour: a critical review. J. Consum. Res. **9**(3), 287–300 (1982)
6. Friese, M., Hofmann, W., Wänke, M.: When impulses take over: moderated predictive validity of explicit and implicit attitude measures in predicting food choice and consumption behaviour. Br. J. Soc. Psychol. **47**(3), 397–419 (2008)
7. Arvola, A., et al.: Predicting intentions to purchase organic food: the role of affective and moral attitudes in the Theory of Planned Behaviour. Appetite **50**(2–3), 443–454 (2008)
8. Vermeir, I., Verbeke, W.: Sustainable food consumption among young adults in Belgium. Ecol. Econ. **64**(3), 542–553 (2008)
9. Citroen, C.L.: The role of information in strategic decision-making. Int. J. Inf. Manag. **31**(6), 493–501 (2011)
10. Belkin, N.J., Oddy, R.N., Brooks, H.M.: ASK for information retrieval: Part I. Background and theory. J. Doc. **38**(2), 61–71 (1982)
11. Wilson, T.D.: On user studies and information needs. J. Doc. **62**(6), 658–670 (2006)
12. Spink, A., Cole, C.: Human information behaviour: Integrating diverse approaches and information use. J. Assoc. Inf. Sci. Tech. **57**(1), 25–35 (2006)
13. Browne, G.J., Cheung, C.M., Heinzl, A., Riedl, R.: Human information behaviour. Bus. Inf. Syst. Eng. **59**(1), 1–2 (2017)
14. Starbird, S.A., Amanor-Boadu, V.: Contract selectivity, food safety, and traceability. J. Agric. Food Ind. Organization **5**(1), 1–20 (2007)
15. Grunert, K.G.: Current issues in the understanding of consumer food choice. Trends Food Sci. Technol. **13**(8), 275–285 (2002)
16. Hobbs, J.E.: Information asymmetry and the role of traceability systems. Agribusiness **20**(4), 397–415 (2004)

17. Corvello, V., Felicetti, A.M.: Factors affecting the utilization of knowledge acquired by researchers from scientific social networks: an empirical analysis. Knowl. Manag. Int. J. **13**(3), 15–26 (2014)
18. Rutsaert, P., et al.: Social media as a useful tool in food risk and benefit communication? a strategic orientation approach. Food Policy **46**, 84–93 (2014)
19. Gao, Q., Tian, Y., Tu, M.: Exploring factors influencing Chinese user's perceived credibility of health and safety information on Weibo. Comput. Hum. Behav. **45**, 21–31 (2015)
20. Booth, D.A.: Food-conditioned eating preferences and aversions with interceptive elements. Ann. N. Y. Acad. Sci. **443**(1), 22–41 (1985)
21. Volpentesta, A.P., Felicetti, A.M.: Competence mapping through analysing research papers of a scientific community. In: Camarinha-Matos, L.M. (ed.) DoCEIS 2011. IFIP AICT, vol. 349, pp. 33–44. Springer, Heidelberg (2011). https://doi.org/10.1007/978-3-642-19170-1_4

Predicting the Relationship Between Virtual Enterprises in an Agile Supply Chain Through Structural Equation Modeling

Alan Eardley[1(✉)], Ariunbayar Samdantsoodol[2], Hongnian Yu[3],
and Shaung Cang[3]

[1] Staffordshire University, Stoke-on-Trent, UK
w.a.eardley@staffs.ac.uk
[2] Mongolian University of Science and Technology, Ulaanbataar, Mongolia
[3] Bournemouth University, Poole, UK

Abstract. Virtual enterprises are formed in response to turbulent market conditions and are influenced by factors such as the changing relationship between customers and suppliers, the spread of agile supply chains and shorter product life cycles. Research suggests that successful virtual co-operation and supply chain agility are best achieved when the core capabilities of the partners are complementary. This paper examines the relationship between virtual enterprises in supply chains and provides further insights into the factors affecting agility. A hypothetical model is developed to examine the factors and a structural equation model tests the hypotheses, based on survey data from virtual enterprises in Mongolia. The model uses a simulation based on exploratory factor analysis, confirmatory factor analysis and path analysis. The results provide empirical evidence of the ability of the model to predict benefits arising from the formation of the virtual enterprise.

Keywords: Virtual enterprise · Supply chain agility
Structural Equation Modeling

1 Introduction

The business environment today is typified by rapid and unpredictable changes due to political and economic factors [1], disruptive interventions from new entrants to markets and innovative business models [2] and developments that represent a 'step change' in enabling technologies [3]. The resulting levels of environmental uncertainty, organizational instability, market turbulence and employment insecurity are making it difficult and expensive for companies to function in isolation. The traditional response of monolithic 'growth by acquisition' no longer seems appropriate where downsizing and agility are becoming the normal responses to the business environment. Instead, agile supply chains combining virtual organizations offer the necessary flexibility for supporting lean process improvements and responsive production initiatives to increase market share and sustain growth for all the participants [4]. By combining to form virtual enterprises and aligning themselves in agile supply chains, many companies are now able to develop very flexible logistics systems and supply chain networks,

L. M. Camarinha-Matos et al. (Eds.): PRO-VE 2018, IFIP AICT 534, pp. 203–214, 2018.
https://doi.org/10.1007/978-3-319-99127-6_18

supported by web and mobile technologies that as individual small and medium-sized enterprises (SME) the would not be able to afford [5]. This emerging collaborative strategy is geared to exploiting the temporary windows of opportunities offered by volatile global markets and to sharing risks and optimizing resources based on complementary core competencies and despite geographic locations [6].

To gain a better insight into the phenomenon, it is necessary to explore the factors leading to the collaboration of virtual enterprises in agile supply chains and to study the effects of such collaborations. Therefore, this paper investigates the factors involved in forming virtual enterprises and collaborating in agile supply chains. The aim of the research is the development of a framework that can be used to predict and improve the relationships in a virtual enterprise based on an agile supply chain using the structural equation modeling technique. The rest paper has the following structure; in Sect. 2 a brief overview of supply chain management, virtual enterprises and supply chain agility is given, and based on this hypotheses are developed. Section 3 explains the research methodology and design by which the hypotheses are tested. Section 4 includes the data analysis using structural equation modeling (SEM), addresses factor measurement and tests the research hypotheses using the results. Section 5 then provides conclusions and makes suggestions for future research.

2 Theoretical Basis and Development of Hypotheses

The idea of the virtual enterprise is not new. Davidow and Malone [7] define a virtual enterprise as, '...a number of independent vendors, customers, even competitors, composing a temporary network organization through information technology, in order to share the technology, cost and meet the purpose of the market demand'. Katzy and Schuh [8] state that a virtual enterprise, '...is based on the ability to create temporary co-operations and to realize the value of a short business opportunity that the partners cannot (or can, but only to lesser extent) capture on their own'. A VE is therefore defined in this research as an alliance of separate companies formed temporarily to share costs, to bring together complementary skills and to take advantage of short-term market opportunities. This concept is used to characterize the global supply chain among dynamic organizational networks containing companies with many different relationships [9]. A typical virtual enterprise is ephemeral, as the partners will seek to integrate with others in the supply chain and may take part in different virtual enterprises as opportunities arise [10]. The Internet and mobile technologies are major ingredients in forming virtual enterprises, facilitating value-building functions such as vertical and horizontal integration and flexible collaboration [11].

2.1 Definition of Virtual Enterprise

As virtual enterprises are often defined from different perspectives by different researchers, it is difficult to find a suitable definition of the phenomenon, but the literature review suggests that a typical virtual enterprise will exhibit the following properties:

- Affiliation based on the core competencies, resources and skills of selected partners;
- The objective of enhancing a business opportunity which is difficult for a single enterprise to achieve;
- Temporary collaboration until the business opportunity has passed;
- A virtual network based on the Internet and mobile technologies;
- Trusted sharing of information costs, risks and technologies;
- Participating enterprises are geographically dispersed and independent legal entities;
- In most cases, some powerful 'leading' enterprise co-ordinates, organizes and manages the supply chain;
- The virtual enterprise itself owns no resources, assets or plant.

Correspondingly, supply chain agility is the virtual enterprise's ability to react rapidly to changing market forces and to exploit them as business opportunities [12]. Research suggests that supply chain agility can most successfully be arrived at through the integration of enterprise capability factors such as highly skilled and knowledgeable people and information and communication technologies (ICT) such as the rapid and effective adoption of common systems [13]. The research that is the subject of this paper differs from a previous study in that it includes a narrower range of virtual organizations than were examined in [13], focusing on virtual organizations combining in the Mongolian Reserved Meat Program. The data in this paper was used to simulate the relationships between virtual participants in the supply chain to validate the previous study.

Binder and Clegg [14] consider that core competencies and enterprise capability are the main drivers of virtual enterprise collaboration. Yusuf *et al.* [15] consider some early examples of agility and define agility as, "…a system with exceptional internal capabilities intended to meet the rapidly changing needs of the market place with speed and flexibility. The internal capacities of the firm include 'hard and soft' technologies, human resources, and an educated and highly motivated management". Therefore, enterprise capability has a direct impact on virtual enterprises in agile supply chains. On the other hand, it is suggested that ICT was an essential foundation for the formation and management of many 'real-world' virtual enterprises [16]. Researcher suggests that information sharing can aid the effectiveness and efficiency of supply chains (SC) by streamlining the flow of information, shortening response time to customer needs, enhancing the potential for collaboration and coordination and sharing the risks as well as the benefits of virtual operation [17]. Therefore, the adoption of ICT influences virtual enterprises directly and is therefore one of the major enablers of agility.

2.2 Development of Hypotheses

Virtual enterprises seek to combine in a dynamic way the resources and competencies that form the best fit and, "…can be reshaped in different organizational forms to cope with unexpected changes and disruptions, while also seeking to take advantage of new business opportunities" [18]. Based on this and other definitions taken from the literature review (as discussed above) the factors affecting virtual enterprises and agile supply chains were developed into a conceptual model of the relationships (see Fig. 1).

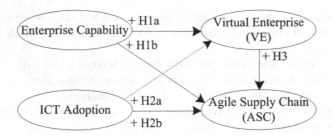

Fig. 1. Influences on virtual enterprise and supply chain agility (Samdantsoodol *et al.*, 2013)

This enables five hypotheses to be proposed, based on the identified factors of influence (H1 to H3), two of which are linked (H1a and H1b, H2a and H2b) [29]. The hypotheses are as follows:

H1a: Enterprise capabilities positively drive virtual enterprise collaboration;
H1b: Enterprise capabilities positively enable supply chain agility;
H2a: ICT adoption positively enables virtual enterprise collaboration;
H2b: ICT adoption positively influences supply chain agility;
H3: Virtual enterprise formation positively influences supply chain agility.

3   Research Methodology and Design

Virtual enterprises in the Mongolian Reserved Meat Program (MRMP) were chosen as the subject for this research as part of a simulation to validate a model of the operation of an agile supply chain. The research was conducted in Mongolia as the MRMP offered a good example of a temporary collaborative network, a phenomenon that has received attention in research [19] and for which frameworks and models have been proposed [20]. To investigate these influencing factors, many groups of measurable indicators needed to be measured in terms of their importance. A questionnaire-based survey was designed to do this and was targeted at companies having a responsibility for logistics, such as the integrated planning and control of all materials, parts and product flows and essential information flows between partners along the whole supply chain.

Five draft questionnaires were initially submitted to a focus group to check the readability of the questionnaire and to detect any unforeseen ambiguities and minor changes were made, based on this pilot survey. Hard and soft copies of the final questionnaire were then distributed to a sample of companies included in a list collected from the Mongolian Yellow Pages site[1]. These organizations are all based in Mongolia and represent a variety of industry types, sizes and levels of turnover. Table 1 presents a breakdown of the number of responding organizations of each type participating in the survey.

---

[1] Mongolian Yellow Pages available at: www.yp.mn.

Table 1. Profile of respondents (Samdantsoodol *et al.*, 2013)

Type of industry/company profile	Number	Percentage
Total	65	100.0
Type of industry		
Manufacturing	20	30.7
Transport & Freight Forwarder	8	12.3
Information & Communication	7	10.8
Wholesale & Retail trade	5	7.7
Oils & gas	1	1.5
Others	5	7.7
Number of employees		
1–9	9	13.8
10–19	15	23.1
20–49	11	16.9
50–199	10	15.4
over 200	20	30.8
Company annual turnover (tugrug)		
Less than 250 million	21	32.3
Less than 1 billion	18	27.7
Less than 1.5 billion	3	4.6
More than 1.5 billion	23	35.4
Designation of respondents		
CEO, Director	21	32.3
Manager	39	60
Others	5	7.7

The main survey used a three-part research questionnaire; Part One consisted of basic profile information of the participants. Part Two included questions related to the drivers and enablers of the virtual enterprises and the capabilities of agile supply chains. Part Three covered questions related to business successes achieved through supply chain agility. From the literature review, the questions were ranked using a five-point Likert scale (from 'very low' to 'very high') to eliminate skewing the statistics from the second and third parts of the questionnaire. In the first round 50 questionnaires were distributed and 34 responses resulted (a 58% response rate). All the questionnaires were addressed to identified senior officers of the organizations concerned. In the second round, another 50 printed questionnaires were given out, and 36 were subsequently returned. Out of the total of 70 returned questionnaires 65 were usable as five questionnaires were incomplete and did not contain sufficient data for further analysis. This was considered as an acceptable proportion upon which to base a statistical analysis of this type, although it is accepted that this number of responses cannot represent all the firms in the market.

The structural equation modeling technique (SEM) is often used to specify, analyze and test hypothetical models that describe complex relationships between sets of variables [19]. Therefore, the SEM was chosen to analyze the relationship between enterprise capability, ICT adoption, virtual enterprise affiliation and supply chain agility. The SEM was applied in two stages, first developing the measurement model and then the structural model [22]. The measurement model shows how the underlying variables or hypothetical relationships are affected by the observed variables. The exploratory and confirmatory factor analysis models are included in the measurement model which examines the reliability and validity of the modeled relationships between the observed variables. The structural model also identifies the causal relationships between the latent variables, examines the effects of these relationships and indicates the resulting variances, both explained and unexplained, using path diagrams.

4   Data Analysis and Discussion

4.1   Assessment of Measurement Quality

An analysis of factors was carried out with SPSS 20.0 for Windows (including the AMOS 20.0 software) and principle component analysis (PCA) was used to extract relevant factors. These factors were then subjected to varimax rotation to maximize the squared loading variances on all the variables in the factor matrix, to differentiate clearly the original variables. Some variables that were not correlated strongly were then eliminated from the data set and the remaining variables were then distributed into four factors for analysis. First, exploratory factor analysis (EFA) was carried out to measure the loadings of factors as shown in Table 2. In the same table, the result of reliability testing is demonstrated by Cronbach's alpha analysis, which ranges from .620 to .839, indicating acceptable internal consistency in the data. However, the alpha value of the virtual enterprise was low and although this could create a problem in further analysis, the study continued to include it in the hypothetical model, as it was felt to be so important to the research.

4.2   Evaluation and Discussion of Research Hypotheses

In this section the structural model is described as it was established and tested in the present study. The confirmatory factor analysis (CFA) was adopted to examine if the data matched a hypothetical measurement model and whether the measured latent variables correlated with the researchers' understanding of each variable. The maximum likelihood method (MLM) [22] based on covariance matrices between any two variables was employed to calculate the covariances in the structural model.

The AMOS 20.0 software (see Sect. 3.1) was used to calculate and examine the causal relationships within the hypothetical model, and to analyze the influences upon and between these causal relationships. This analysis confirmed the properties of the structural model by verifying it with the covariance analysis. Several 'goodness of fit' (GOF) indices of the measurement model are presented in Table 3. As in other studies, the chi-square *per* degree of freedom ($\chi 2/df$), the goodness-of-fit index (GFI), the normed fit index (NFI), the Tucker-Lewis index, the comparative index (CFI), and the root mean square error of approximation (RMSEA) were used to verify the

Table 2. Reliability and validity of the model (Samdantsoodol *et al.*, 2013)

Latent and measurement variables	Factor loadings	Cronbach's α
Enterprise capability		
EC1: Information capability	.876	.839
EC2: Human related competency	.773	
EC3: Technology competency	.726	
EC4: System integration competency	.670	
EC5: Strategy	.627	
ICT adoption		
ICT1: Decision support system	.870	.768
ICT2: Smart technology	.836	
ICT3: Prevent, detect, respond to and recover from a data corruption or security breach	.561	
VE		
VE1: Usage of information technology	.682	.620
VE2: Responsiveness	.665	
VE3: Ability to share information and knowledge	.558	
Agile SC		
ASC1: Quickness/speed	.833	.832
ASC2: Cost	.803	
ASC3: Time reduction	.710	
ASC4: Competency	.620	

appropriateness of the structural model. The hypothetical model was revised to improve the GOF as shown in Table 3. Two methods were initially considered for refining the model. The first method involves deleting any paths that have exceptionally low causal relationships, and the second method involves identifying additional causal relationships between factors [23]. The second method was chosen and an additional causal relationship was included in the improved hypothetical model. The GOF of the improved model was compared to the original hypothetical model and the GFI and NFI was found to be acceptable. However, both of those indices are sensitive to sample size, underestimating the fit where the number of instances is below 200 [24]. On the other hand, the non-normed fit index (NNFI) is also outside the recommended range for this size of sample [25]. Also, the relatively small sample size and the degrees of freedom have created artificially large values for the RMSEA. The other GOF measures are within in the recommended ranges as shown in Table 3.

SEM analysis was then used to evaluate the improved hypothetical model (see Fig. 2). The structural model then gives a chi-square value of 138.189 with 82 degrees of freedom (i.e. $p < 0.001$). The ratio of the chi-square value to the degrees of freedom is therefore 1.68, which is below the suggested value of 3.0 [25]. The results shown in Table 4 show that virtual enterprise factors (VE) and agile supply chain (ASC) factors are most influenced (positively and significantly) by enterprise capabilities. ICT adoption factors (ICT) have a significant and positive influence on both sets of factors, but virtual enterprise itself does not strongly influence supply chain agility.

Table 3. Indices of fit of the structural equation models (Samdantsoodol *et al.*, 2013)

GOF measure	Threshold	Hypothetical SEM	Moderated SEM
χ^2	<3.0	152.340	124.420
df	>0.90	84.000	81.000
χ^2/df	>0.90	1.810	1.540
GFI	>0.80	0.781	0.817
Normed fit index (NFI)	>0.85	0.711	0.764
Tucker–Lewis index	<0.08	0.797	0.866
Comparative fit index (CFI)	<0.08	0.838	0.897
RMR		0.059	0.053
RMSEA		0.113	0.092
Lower bound		0.084	0.058
Upper bound		0.141	0.122

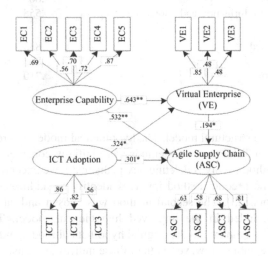

Fig. 2. Evaluation of the hypothetical model using SEM (Samdantsoodol et al., 2013)

Table 4. SEM and path analysis (Samdantsoodol *et al.*, 2013)

Paths	Path coefficient
H1a: Enterprise capability → VE	0.643**
H1b: Enterprise capability → ASC	0.532**
H2a: ICT adoption → VE	0.324*
H2b: ICT adoption → ASC	0.301*
H3: VE → ASC	0.194*

*p < 0.05; **p < 0.01; ***p < 0.001.

Table 5 shows the relationships between the factors, the total effect being arrived at by combining the direct and indirect effects [26]. Enterprise capability has the most direct effect on the ASC, as when the value of the enterprise capabilities increases by 1, the agility factor goes up by 0.532. Indirect effects involve one or more intervening (or mediator) variables [27]. Enterprise capabilities have the highest indirect effect, being the most efficient in the short term efficient for the improvement of the agility index. In the longer term, therefore, an improvement to the enterprise capabilities factors implies the achievement of greater agility [28].

Table 5. Effects of latent factors on supply chain agility (Samdantsoodol *et al.*, 2013)

Latent factor	Direct effect	Indirect effect	Total effect
Enterprise capability	0.532	0.125	0.657
ICT adoption	0.301	0.063	0.364
VE	0.194	0.000	0.194

To test the hypotheses, the squared multiple correlation (R^2) values of the dependent (or endogenous) variables were calculated [29]. Table 4 shows that enterprise capability and ICT adoption have a major positive influence on virtual enterprise collaboration although these contribute 51.8% of the total variance of the VE ($R^2 = 0.518$ as shown in Table 6). These results support the hypotheses H1a and H2a. The analytical results reveal that enterprise capability, ICT adoption and VE have a significant positive effect on supply chain agility. These predictors have 58.2% of variance of the agility factor ($R^2 = 0.582$ as shown in Table 6). Thus, the results support hypotheses H1b, H2b and H3.

Table 6. R^2 of endogenous variables (Samdantsoodol *et al.*, 2013)

Dependent variables	R^2
VE	0.518
ASC	0.582

Enterprise capability positively influences five variables: (i) The information capability (standard coefficient = 0.687); (ii) the human-related competency (standard coefficient = 0.559, p < 0.001); (iii) the technology competency (standard coefficient = 0.696, p < 0.001); (iv) the system integration competency (standard coefficient = 0.721, p < 0.001) and (v) the strategy (standard coefficient = 0.871, p < 0.001). As party of the measurement component, ICT adoption positively influences three factors: (i) the decision support system (standard coefficient = 0.856); (ii) the smart technology (standard coefficient = 0.816, p < 0.001) and (iii) the prevention, detection, response and recovering from a data corruption or security breach (standard coefficient = 0.559, p < 0.001). VE also positively influences three other measurement components: (i) the usage of information technology (standard coefficient = 0.854, p = 0.001) and (ii) the responsiveness (standard coefficient = 0.481, p = 0.006) and (iii) the ability to share information (standard coefficient = 0.475).

Finally, the results indicate that the ASC positively influences its four key measurement variables: (i) the quickness or speed (standard coefficient = 0.625); (ii) the cost (standard coefficient = 0.583, $p < 0.001$); (iii) time reduction (standard coefficient = 0.685, $p < 0.001$) and (iv) the competency (standard coefficient = 0.809, $p < 0.001$).

It is recognized that this study has the following limitations. Firstly, the relatively small sample size could affect the fit indices. Therefore, more questionnaires should be distributed and collected by the researchers in a fuller study, so that the survey validity will be improved. Secondly, the variable load on a factor could cause an increased bias in the parameter estimates.

5 Conclusion

To survive in turbulent and unstable market conditions, SMEs may seek to increase their competitiveness by collaborating to form a virtual enterprise as a supply chain. This study investigated the influence of enterprise capability and ICT adoption on affiliation, and examined causal relationships affecting supply chain agility. First, a conceptual hypothetical model was developed based on a literature review. SEM was applied to improve the relationships between the factors. Analyses were then conducted on the measurement and structural models using exploratory and confirmatory factor analysis respectively, measuring the properties of the observed variables through the reliability and validity of the data. In the second step, the structural model was set up and based on calculated GOF indices, the model was verified and the relevant hypotheses were validated by path analysis and squared multiple correlation. Enterprise capability and ICT adoption are shown to have a strongly positive and significant influence on VE affiliation to build up robust co-operation. additionally, supply chain agility is shown to be influenced positively and significantly by enterprise capabilities and ICT adoption.

The concept of supply chain agility is a complex one and has many factors affecting it, so the entire domain is difficult to cover completely in a single piece of research. Therefore, further research is recommended to expand upon the conceptual model, including additional factors to examine their relationships. In addition, the size of the sample should be increased to improve the quality and reliability of the analysis.

Acknowledgements. This work was supported by the European Erasmus-Mundus Sustainable eTourism project 2010-2359 and EU Erasmus Mundus Project-ELINK (EM ECW-ref.149674-EM-1-2008-1-UK-ERAMUNDUS).

References

1. Knoke, D.: Changing Organizations: Business Networks in the New Political Economy. Routledge, New York (2018)
2. Drucker, P.: The Age of Discontinuity: Guidelines to our Changing Society. Routledge, New York (2017)

3. Sindi, S., Roe, M.: The evolution of supply chains and logistics. In: Sindi, S., Roe, M. (eds.) Strategic Supply Chain Management, pp. 7–25. Palgrave Macmillan, Cham (2017). https://doi.org/10.1007/978-3-319-54843-2_2. ISBN 978-3-319-54842-5

4. Langston, J.: Key Performance Indicators in an Agile Supply Chain. Corescholar.libraries. wright.edu, http://corescholar.libraries.wright.edu/master_infosystems/22

5. Ribeiro, J., Barata, J., Colombo, A.: Supporting agile supply chains using a service-oriented shop floor. Eng. Appl. Artif. Intell. **22**(6), 950–960 (2009)

6. Li, Q., et al.: Business processes oriented heterogeneous systems integration platform for networked enterprises. Comput. Ind. **61**(2), 127–144 (2010)

7. Davidow, W.H., Malone, M.S.: The Virtual Corporation: Structuring and Revitalizing the Corporation for the 21st Century. Harper Business, London (1993)

8. Katzy, B.R., Schuh, G.: The virtual enterprise. In: Handbook of Lifecycle Engineering: Concepts, Models and Technologies. Kluwer Academic, Boston (1998)

9. Ghadimi, P., Toosi, F.G., Heavey, C.: A multi-agent systems approach for sustainable supplier selection and order allocation in a partnership supply chain. Eur. J. Oper. Res. **269**, 286–301 (2017). https://doi.org/10.1016/j.ejor.2017.07.014

10. van Hoek, R.I.: Logistics and virtual integration: postponement, outsourcing and the flow of information. Int. J. Phys. Distrib. Logist. Manag. **28**(7), 508–523 (1998)

11. Chituc, C.M., Azevedo, A., Toscano, C.: Collaborative business frameworks comparison, analysis and selection: an analytic perspective. Int. J. Product. Res. **47**(17), 4855–4883 (2009)

12. Fayezi, S., Zutshi, A., O'Loughlin, A.: Understanding and development of supply chain agility and flexibility: a structured literature review. Int. J. Manag. Rev. **19**(4), 379–407 (2017)

13. Samdantsoodol, A., Cang, S., Yu, H., Eardley, A., Buyantsogt, A.: Predicting the relationships between virtual enterprises and agility in supply chains. Expert Syst. Appl. **84**, 58–73 (2017)

14. Binder, M., Clegg, B.: Enterprise management: a new frontier for organisations. Int. J. Prod. Econ. **106**(2), 409–430 (2007)

15. Yusuf, Y.Y., Gunasekaran, A., Musa, A., Dauda, M., El-Berishy, N., Cang, S.: A relational study of supply chain agility, competitiveness and business performance in the oil and gas industry. Int. J. Prod. Econ. **147**, 531–543 (2014)

16. Cao, Q., Dowlatshahi, S.: The impact of alignment between virtual enterprise and information technology on business performance in an agile manufacturing environment. J. Oper. Manag. **23**(5), 531–550 (2005)

17. Li, S., Lin, B.: Accessing information sharing and information quality in supply chain management. Decis. Support Syst. **42**(3), 1641–1656 (2006)

18. Camarinha-Matos, L.M.: Collaborative networks: a mechanism for enterprise agility and resilience. In: Mertins, K., Bénaben, F., Poler, R., Bourrières, J.-P. (eds.) Enterprise Interoperability VI. IESACONF, vol. 7, pp. 3–11. Springer, Cham (2014). https://doi.org/10.1007/978-3-319-04948-9_1

19. Appio, F.P., Martini, A., Massa, S., Testa, S.: Collaborative network of firms: antecedents and state-of-the-art properties. Int. J. Prod. Res. **55**(7), 2121–2134 (2016)

20. Durugbo, C.: Collaborative networks: a systematic review and multi-level framework. Int. J. Prod. Res. **54**(12), 3749–3776 (2015)

21. Sohn, S.Y., Joo, Y.G., Han, H.K.: Structural equation model for the evaluation of national funding on R and D project of SMEs in consideration with MBNQA criteria. Eval. Program Plan. **30**(1), 10–20 (2007)

22. Su, Y., Yang, C.: A structural equation model for analyzing the impact of ERP on SCM. Expert Syst. Appl. **37**(1), 456–469 (2010)

23. Cho, K., Hong, T., Hyun, C.: Effect of project characteristics on project performance in construction projects based on structural equation model. Expert Syst. Appl. **36**(7), 10461–10470 (2009)

24. Hooper, D., Coughlan, J., Mullen, M.R.: Structural equation modelling: guidelines for determining best fit. Electron. J. Bus. Res. Methods **6**(1), 53–60 (2008). Articles 2

25. Hess, A.S., Hess, J.R.: Understanding tests of the association of categorical variables: the Pearson chi-square test and Fisher's exact test. Transfusion **57**(4), 877–879 (2017)

26. Sohn, S.Y., Kim, H.S., Moon, T.H.: Predicting the financial performance index of technology fund for SME using structural equation model. Expert Syst. Appl. **32**(3), 890–898 (2007)

27. Kline, R.B.: Principles and practice of structural equation modeling. Guilford Press, New York (2005)

28. Anderson, J.C., Gerbing, D.W.: Predicting the performance of measures in a confirmatory factor analysis with a pretest assessment of their substantive validities. J. Appl. Psychol. **76**(5), 732–740 (1991)

29. Samdantsoodol, A., Yu, H., Cang, S., Tumur-Ochir, A.: A structural equation model for predicting virtual enterprise and agile supply chain relation. In: 19th International Conference on Automation and Computing, London, U.K., 13–14 September 2013

Collaborative Business Processes

The Need for Compliance Verification in Collaborative Business Processes

John Paul Kasse[1(✉)], Lai Xu[1], Paul deVrieze[1], and Yuewei Bai[2]

[1] Computing and Informatics, Faculty of Science and Technology, Bournemouth University, Poole, Bournemouth BH12 5BB, UK
{jkasse,lxu,pdvrieze}@bournemouth.ac.uk
[2] Industry Engineering of Engineering College, Shanghai Polytechnic University, Jinhai Road 2360, Pudong, Shanghai, People's Republic of China
ywbai@sspu.edu.cn

Abstract. Compliance constrains processes to adhere to rules, standards, laws and regulations. Non-compliance subjects enterprises to litigation and financial fines. Collaborative business processes cross organizational and regional borders implying that internal and cross regional regulations must be complied with. To protect customs' data, European enterprises must comply with the EU data privacy regulation (general data protection regulation - GDPR) and each member state's data protection laws. An example of non-compliance with GDPR is Facebook, it is accused for breaching subscriber trust. Compliance verification is thus essential to deploy and implement collaborative business process systems. It ensures that processes are checked for conformance to compliance requirements throughout their life cycle. In this paper we take a proactive approach aiming to discuss the need for design time preventative compliance verification as opposed to after effect runtime detective approach. We use a real-world case to show how compliance needs to be analyzed and show the benefits of applying compliance check at the process design stage.

Keywords: Compliance · Collaborative business process · Business process verification · Virtual factory · Compliance verification

1 Introduction

Compliance is about adherence to regulations, guidelines or predefined legal requirements like norms, laws and standards. In terms of business processes, compliance relates to conformance to different process perspectives [1, 2], namely control flow, resources, data, and time. *Control flow* - strict adherence to the sequential flow of activities and their relationships, *resources* - adherence to policies for allocation and assignment of resources to perform tasks, *data* - adherence to access control and authorization, and *time* - temporal process aspects like delays. The perspectives constrain the process according to the internal organizational policies. Besides, external policies and regulations present compliance demands that must be satisfied especially for cross organizational business processes i.e. the collaborative business processes [3–5], a trend of borderless business processes subject to contractual and international regulations.

© IFIP International Federation for Information Processing 2018
Published by Springer Nature Switzerland AG 2018. All Rights Reserved
L. M. Camarinha-Matos et al. (Eds.): PRO-VE 2018, IFIP AICT 534, pp. 217–229, 2018.
https://doi.org/10.1007/978-3-319-99127-6_19

Moreover, partner organizations vary the core process to suit specific needs of their market or business environment resulting in process variants. Notably, the variants must stay compliant with the core process. Such scenarios justify compliance as a big and relevant topic of various applications.

Current compliance challenges and dynamics have led to new laws and regulations or revision of existing ones, e.g. the GDPR, Sabanese-Oxley Act 2002 (SOX), Base III, ITIL, ISO 2700, and Consumer Protection Act 2015 (CPA) inter alia. An organization's compliance is exhibited by its business processes conforming to the regulations. Non-compliance results in fines, litigations or loss of corporate image. Facebook is striving to rebuild public trust after breach of subscriber trust due non-compliance to data privacy [6].

Compliance provides means to monitor adherence to quality standards for products and services, consumer protection and operational transparence. Also, strict adherence to financial and accounting standards enables firms to maintain sound financial positions to avoid bankruptcy as was the case for Tyco, Global Crossing and Adelphia, Enron, HIH, Société Générale, AOL and Worldcom corporate scandals [7]. Furthermore, where process variants exist and entry to a new market is required, compliant variants can be selected easily for similar environments. For example, a collaborative business process is varied to suit laws and regulations of different countries, the most closely compliant process variant is chosen to save on time.

Compliance in business process management is complex and not automatic to achieve especially where end users are non-experts in modeling. As will be observed (Sect. 2), support for compliance is structured for non-collaborative processes whose interaction is limited to single organizations, and targets control flow and resource perspectives. Employed techniques like process mining are curved upon the detective after-the-effect principle seeking to monitor conformance of observed behavior with modeled behavior. A knowledge gap exists to support checking for compliance of collaborative business processes with policies beyond control flow to external regulations, laws and standards. A review of modelling and verification approaches for collaborative business processes further reveals that compliance has not received deserved attention [8, 9]. The expanded scope of constraints creates complexity and conflicts necessitating their verification e.g. need to ensure that internal and external regulations map and synchronize to avoid any conflicts that can lead to deadlocks in the process. This is preferred at design time.

To that effect, we adopt concept of compliance-by-design [10] as a paradigm to achieve design time preventive compliance of the business process models with regulatory requirements. Compliance-by-design is a process of developing a software system that implements a business process in such a way that its ability to meet specific compliance requirements is ascertained [11]. To achieve compliant processes at runtime, compliance strategies are built and checked at design time. In this paper we emphasize the need for design time compliance checking through application of formal methods to reason about business processes as system models and compliance requirements as properties to automate compliance verification.

The rest of the paper is organized as follows; Sect. 2 reviews related work and shows how this work differs, Sect. 3 presents an industry based collaborative business process case to support our analysis, Sect. 4 presents a detailed analysis of the compliance requirements and need for verification. We conclude with Sect. 5.

2 Related Work

Compliance, its checking and verification in business process management and workflow management has been widely addressed from different angles; compliancy to control flow aspects of the business process [1, 2, 12], resource allocation using role, task and attribute based approaches [13–16], security policy mechanisms [17–20] and compliance verification approaches 21]. Categorically, compliance checking is addressed from 2 fronts i.e. at design time or runtime. Some approaches however target both design time and runtime compliance.

Design time compliance checking is a preventative approach that addresses compliance of business process models to constraints before execution time i.e. constraints are enforced on models and checked before execution. On contrary, *runtime compliance* checking is a detective after-the-effect approach for monitoring compliance of business processes while in execution [10, 22]. While the runtime approach is considered flexible and declarative being able to capture compliance issues beyond design; the design approach is preferred for being proactive to deal with compliance violations before they arise and permitting early time correction during process design. Following is a discussion of some compliance approaches.

PENELOPE (Process ENtailment from the ELicitation of Obligations and PErmissions) language is based on deontic logic supporting declarative expression of control flow constraints for process events. Permission and obligation constraints to perform events are explicitly expressed as temporal deontic assignments enforced on process models at design time. A compliant control flow non-executable model is generated to support process designers to verify and validate other models by showing decision points and possible violations [12, 23, 24]. The approach's application is limited to control flow and resource related compliance checking.

Relatedly, a process fragment lifecycle technique is proposed to support consistent specification, integration and monitoring of compliance controls in business processes. A process fragment is a connected graph representing part of a business process modified to incorporate compliance requirements, which are later integrated into the original business process by means of the so called 'gluing' and 'weaving' methods to create a compliant process [25]. In this approach, compliance related to control flow and data perspectives is supported. Even then, there is no way to prove lack of deadlocks or livelocks in a constrained process model i.e. no verification is supported which renders it difficult to determine correctness of integrated compliance changes.

In [22], the concept of compliance-by-design is coined to overcome limitations of the after-the-effect approaches like process mining. It provides means to reason about compliance rules by modeling control objectives and applying formal methods to enrich business process models with annotations and visualizations [10]. The concept is supported with a formalism for expressive modeling of compliance specifications i.e. the Formal Contract Language (FCL). FCL is a deontic logic and non-monotonic based language for design time constraints specification and enforcement on BPMN business process models.

Contract Language (CL)is a also a deontic logic based language for formal automated analysis of electronic contracts. It supports detection of conflicts between service-based contracts and local contracts in SOA environments. Compliance between contract language rules and models is checked via an evaluation algorithm implemented in CLAN tool. The tool also analyses contracts for soundness and completeness [26, 27].

A compliance request language (CRL) is a design time approach for automated contractual constraint enforcement and checking on process models. It uses temporal logic for formal reasoning over formalized compliance patterns to detect violation of compliance constraints [21].

Compliancy has as well been addressed from a privacy and security angle where relevant policies are specified, enforced and checked on process models to comply with security and privacy requirements. Key in the category are the role based access control models (RBAC) [13, 20, 28–31] used for access control and authorization based on roles. Users are grouped into roles and permissions are assigned to groups e.g. Auditors assigned access to some resources in the process. In addition, task based access control models (Task-based Access Control) [14, 32, 33] provide a dynamic approach to enforcement of compliance to access and authorization policies based on the tasks executed in the process. Compared to RBAC, TBAC offers simplified, automated and self-admissible models where access to tasks is authorized following the context and progress of the process. On another hand, attribute-based access control models (ABAC) regulate access and authorization through a combination of attributes of both the subject (requester) and the object (e.g. file), and the environment [15, 16, 29, 34]. The proposed models under this category guide constraint specification, enforcement and monitoring to ensure compliance to policies related to resource allocation, authorization and access control for tasks, resources and data in workflow systems. Key constraints are based on requirements to express segregation of duty, binding of duty, need to know among others which prevent or detect fraud, errors of commission or omission. However, these proposals do not provide mechanisms for design time verification. Besides, their application to collaborative environments can be noticed so far.

Moreover, in [17] a framework for enforcement and monitoring of compliance to security policies in large autonomous information systems is proposed and implemented. SecBPMN is used to design process models while security policies are expressed using SecBPMN-Q after which the SecBPMN-Q are verified against SecBPMN specifications via an implemented query engine. A socio-technical security modeling language (STS-ml) is extended to support privacy by design i.e. to model privacy as a requirement and support verification of privacy properties for models through formal reasoning [18]. Little support is provided to address verification among the compliancy constraints. A compliance approach based on Petri-net semantics and syntax is proposed to check compliance on two fronts, i.e. checking rules restricting data attributes and rules restricting activities when a certain data condition holds. Process mining technique is employed to extract logs from the process execution and observe behavior. The approach is an after-the-effect theory tracing already executed processes, this way it differs from our proactive compliance approach [1, 35].

A formalized constrained workflow involving local and global constraints, separation of duty and binding of duty constraints is proposed to enhance administration of security information in workflow systems. The rationale is to establish necessary conditions for a set of constraints that ensure a sound constrained workflow authorization schema where, for any authorized role or user, there is at least one complete workflow instance when the user can execute the role. Constraints are checked for consistence to avoid deadlocks or security lapses at runtime [33].

Table 1 summarizes the discussed approaches categorized according to how they support compliance enforcement and checking. The categories are; structural, contractual obligations and security and privacy. Other attributes in relation to formalism, application and process perspectives supported are also summarized.

Table 1. Summary of Compliance Methods

Approach	Formalism	Application	Methods	Control flow	Resource	Data	Time
Approaches based on compliance to structural behavior							
Process Mining	Petri nets	Run time	Imperative	√	√		
Process fragment lifecycle	–	Run time	Imperative	√		√	
Compliance checking approach	Petri nets	Run time	Imperative	√		√	
Approaches based on compliance to contractual obligations behavior							
PENELOPE	Deontic logic	Design time	Declarative	√			
FCL	Deontic logic	Design time	Imperative	√	√	√	√
Contract language	Deontic logic, temporal logic	Design time	Imperative	√		√	
Compliance request language	Temporal logic	Design time	Imperative	√	√		√
Approaches based on compliance to security and privacy policies							
RBAC	Temporal logic	Design time					
TBAC	Temporal logic	Design time			√	√	√
ABAC	Temporal logic	Design time			√	√	√
SecBPMN	Temporal logic	Design time Runtime	Imperative	√	√		

(continued)

Table 1. (*continued*)

Approach	Formalism	Application	Methods	Control flow	Resource	Data	Time
STS-ml	–	Design time Runtime	Imperative	√	√		
Formal constrained workflow	Temporal logic	Design time	Imperative		√	√	

3   Motivating Case Study

This section presents a description of an industry collaborative business process that serves as a motivating case study. 'Pick and Pack' is a process from a big supermarket with a chain of stores across Europe and some parts of Asia.

To create orders, customers must register via the store's online system. Upon submission of customer order, notifications are sent to both the store and the customer as confirmation. Store staff check order details, pick and pack items. Before packing items are verified by picking staff for conformity with order, and after by handover staff. One or more staff may be assigned to an order depending on its size. For items that may be out of stock, the order is put on suspense for a period until stock is availed or staff is permitted to contact customer to seek opinion either to wait, change or cancel order. Item substitution is permissible, for instance changing a fresh vegetable item to tinned one. A customer can cancel an order delayed beyond acceptable waiting time. Ready orders are either picked by the customers, delivered by store or via a preferred courier. Figure 1 is the pick and pack process model.

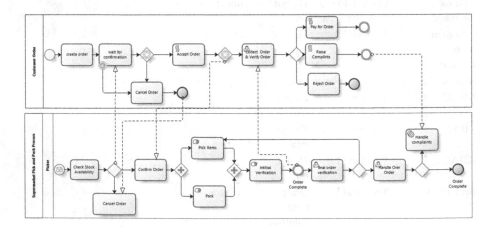

Fig. 1. Pick and pack business process

The case study serves as an example of different perspectives and compliance rules specific to a collaborative process e.g. *control flow*; order confirmation is subject to stock availability, *process data*; orders can only be handed over if they pass the verification check, *process resource*; final order verification must be done by different staff, *process time*; orders can be rejected or cancelled if beyond a specific time. Moreover, there are different stakeholders with differing interests that must be matched and satisfied. Customers buy items and they expect them to be of acceptable quality, non-defective, in right quantities and delivered on time. The store staff and managers work on customer orders; they are expected to meet customer expectations, item availability and timelines. Also, there are different companies in the supply chain like suppliers and couriers. In the background are shareholders whose interest is profit making. They expect financial fluency non-solvency of the company. Unverified compliance issues could lead to process flaws. E.g. packing non-ordered items, wrong item quantities, running out of stock, defect items etc. The business process accesses customer data during execution which raises data privacy concerns in terms of legality and legitimization i.e. who has access to data when and for what purpose.

4 Need for Compliance Checking in Collaborative Processes

Traditionally, business process design is based on business objectives expressed in the terms of control flow, resources, data and time perspectives. Similarly, checks followed the same line verifying adherence the to these perspectives for single organization processes. The new regulatory requirements coupled with changing contractual obligations in business collaborations renders existing processes non-compliant to the new rules. This creates a need to formalize the regulatory requirements and verify for conformity between them as well as the existing process models. The new rules may lead to structural changes in the control flow, e.g. when tasks are removed or added, which also affects resource allocation, data access or activity time schedules for the business. (For example, Brexit once actualized will affect many business processes across Europe and the relevant regulations). Besides, new data is created that maps into existing resources and task necessitating new forms of access control and authorization. Verification for compliance is therefore needed to support conformance checks for the existing processes to avoid reinventing the wheel, wastage of resources and time to create new processes each time regulations change.

4.1 Compliancy with Data Privacy

As described in Sect. 3, we use the case to illustrate the need for compliance verification and how it can be achieved. The process should comply with internal policies and external regulations like GDPR, SOX and BASE III, national fiscal policy, customer protection act. For space limitations, illustration is based on the GDPR to demonstrate the proposed process driven authorization as a mechanism to achieve access control. We however briefly describe all the regulations.

GDPR regulates data privacy where data controllers are responsible for data protection in the organization. It requires keeping data for individuals private, have their consent to collect and process it, notify them if there is any change, avail it to owners if needed in a required format and seek their consent before it can be transferred to third parties. In the case, customer data is collected and processed. When orders are delivered by delivery companies customer data is exchanged. Within Europe, different countries treat different kinds of customer data differently. Therefore, there are challenges even for specifying same business function process in different ways in different countries. SOX and Base III relate to financial standards to protect shareholders and the public from financial manipulations, intentional errors and fraudulence. The super market is required to maintain a stable financial position to the satisfaction of shareholders. Fiscal policy is a national law that differs per region. It demands openness and transparency of business processes to enable tax assessment, tracking and monitoring to prevent tax fraud. Table 2 lists extracted compliance scenarios, requirements sections of the regulations.

Table 2. Compliance requirements generated from the case

Req	Use case compliance scenario	Compliance requirement	Policy level/Regulation
Rq.1	Customers registers on system with private data	Inform data owners which data is collected, processed and use	Data privacy GDPR
Rq.2	Customer submits order(s). The system notifies customer of successful submission immediately	Notify customer of the order details submitted	Internal policy
Rq.3	Notify customer when order(s) will be ready. Orders are ready between 30 and 60 min	Notify customer of the waiting times	Internal policy
Rq.4	For delays notify customer. Customer can wait or cancel the order	Notify customer of delays. Right to cancel order and get a full refund	Internal policy, Consumer Rights Act 2015

Considering the discussed knowledge gaps in the previous section and the analysis from the case study, we illustrate compliance verification using the proposed design time approach.

4.2 Supporting Verification for Compliance

4.2.1 Compliance Verification Approach

Underpinning the approach is the need to support end users to specify and verify collaborative business process for adherence to regulatory constraints. This is achieved through the approach's components i.e. the rules modeler, rules verifier and rules enforcer.

i. Compliance Modeler

Compliance rule modeler supports the extraction of requirements from their sources and translates them into constraints based on defined compliance attributes (Fig. 2). Some are adopted and adapted from [21, 36, 37] while other are proposed. For automated application, the attributes are formalized to achieve formal semantics based on temporal logic languages.

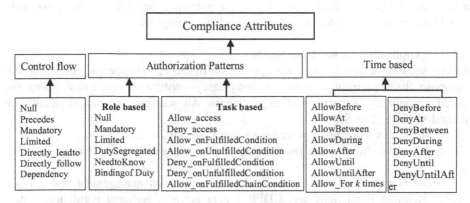

Fig. 2. Compliancy attributes meta-model

ii. Compliance Rules Verifier

To our knowledge none of the existing framework supports this capability. It is intended to ensure coherent, accurate, complete and consistent constraints. Conflicts between constraints are likely to exist and thus it is necessary to verify them before enforcement. For example, internal policies may conflict with external regulations. If unchecked, conflicts may create deadlocks or live-locks in the process. Consistency is required between; internal policies and collaboration contractual policies and between internal policies and national regulatory policies. Internal policies are translated into requirements i.e. properties to be satisfied while the external policies into system models using temporal logic, then apply formal reasoning and model checking techniques to support automatic verification amongst them. The intention is to derive an ideal state where both internally and externally derived constraints can be used to constrain a business process without inbound conflicts, ambiguities and inconsistencies. Some of the targeted error checks relate to resource authorization and access control that would otherwise be a source of flaws and insecurity in the business process; for instance Privilege leakage, locking and conflict [33]. Verification will be achieved by integrating with existing model checkers. Specifically, NuSMv [38] a version of the traditional SMV [39] model checker is preferable for its expressive power in checking models for satisfiability to constraints.

iii. The Attribute Enforcer

Verified compliance constraints are enforced on the business process activities constraining them according to requirements. For instance, to achieve privacy, access to data is controlled and authorized based on its need to accomplish a time bound activity in the business process i.e. access is legitimized. In such scenario, during runtime the task will invoke the authorization API seeking access to a specific data item. The authorization engine will then check its access policy repository built according to the access control policy. Based on the request outcome, the task will progress, halt, terminate or be skipped for the business process to progress.

4.2.2   Application to the Case Study

In this section we briefly show the application of the compliance attributes that will compose the implementation for the compliancy verification mechanism using the stated compliancy scenarios and requirements. All scenarios and requirements are related to Table 2 in Sect. 4.2.

Scenario 1: Customers register on system with private data.

Requirement: Inform data owners what data is collected, processed and intended use.

Regulation: Internal and external regulations on data management and privacy apply. Relevant regulations are; GDPR - data privacy. National regulation – data privacy. Industry specific best practice on data management principles.

Enforcement and verification: a combination of attributes is applied. In terms of control flow, the initial activity is not *preceded* by any other activity, proceeding to the next step in the process can only be allowed upon fulfillment of a condition i.e. upon successful system registration (*Allow_onFulfilledconditon*). If the condition is not fulfilled, access is denied until fulfilled (*Deny access, DenyUntil*).

Scenario 2: The customer submits order(s).

Requirement: Notify customer of (un)successful submission immediately by SMS or email about the order details submitted.

Regulation: Internal policy. In terms of control flow the next task is determined. Regarding resources, access to customer data, at what level in the process and who can communicate with the customer must be authorized. There is also constraint on structure and content of the communicated message

Enforcement and verification: Before communication, the preceding activity must have succeeded (*AllowAfter*) and requirement 1 (Rq.1 in Table 2) fulfilled. The task can execute and access (*Allow_access*) customer data (email address or contact number) to initiate the communication. Otherwise access is denied if orders are not submitted. But communication can still happen for incomplete order to establish why never completed purchase (*Allow_onUnulfilledCondition*). This can provide valuable feedback.

Scenario 3. Notify customers when orders will be ready.

Requirement: Confirm order and possible pick up/delivery times

Regulation: Internal policy. Orders are ready six (6) hours from the order submission time. Customer initiated interactive communication allowed with special category staff e.g. sales support staff only if changes must be made to the order.

Enforcement and verification: This requirement is *mandatory* and allowed access to customer data (*Allow_access*) for immediate automated communication (*NeedtoKnow*) to the customer at point when the order is submitted (*AllowAt*). Interactive communication is restricted to specific staff (*Limited*). Otherwise if the condition of successful order submission is not fulfilled access is denied (Deny access) at that moment in time (*DenyAt*).

For automated application especially for the non-expert end-users as illustrated in the preceding section, a declarative approach will be adopted for implementation where all combinations of the attributes and their executions or behavior are implicitly permissible except where explicitly forbidden i.e. by stating what is non-permissible.

5 Conclusion

Compliance is a major concern today regardless of the industrial sector to keep pace with changing regulations besides the rising concerns of security, product and service quality and data privacy. With EU revising its GDPR set to commence by May 2018; concerned organizations are working towards meeting its requirements before deadline by realigning their business processes. To support them in due course is a necessary step. In doing so, other than the detective after-the-effect compliance checking, a proactive preventive approach is preferred to identify and combat compliancy violations before they take place to avoid the costs of fines or litigations. The effort of this research is geared towards a comprehensive approach for modeling, verification and enforcement of compliance constraints on collaborative business processes with an end user perspective.

Acknowledgements. This research has been partially sponsored by EU H2020 FIRST project, Grant No. 734599, FIRST: vF Interoperation suppoRting buSiness innovaTion.

References

1. Taghiabadi, E.R., Gromov, V., Fahland, D., van der Aalst, W.P.: Compliance checking of data-aware and resource-aware compliance requirements. In: Meersman, R., Panetto, H., Dillon, T., Missikoff, M., Liu, L., Pastor, O., Cuzzocrea, A., Sellis, T. (eds.) OTM 2014. LNCS, vol. 8841, pp. 237–257. Springer, Heidelberg (2014). https://doi.org/10.1007/978-3-662-45563-0_14
2. Borrego, D., Barba, I.: Conformance checking and diagnosis for declarative business process models in data-aware scenarios. Expert Syst. Appl. 41(11), 5340–5352 (2014)
3. Ziemann, J., Matheis, T.: Modelling of cross-organizational business processes-current methods and standards. In: Proceedings of the EMISA 2007, vol. 2, no. 2, pp. 87–100, (2007)
4. Telang, P.R., Singh, M.P.: Specifying and verifying cross-organizational business models: an agent-oriented approach. IEEE Trans. Serv. Comput. 5(3), 305–318 (2012)
5. Schulz, K.A., Oklowska, M.E.: Facilitating cross-organisational workflows with a workflow view approach. Data Knowl. Eng. 51(1), 109–147 (2004)

6. Guynn, J.: Facebook CEO Mark Zuckerberg finally speaks on Cambridge Analytica: we need to fix 'breach of trust'. Tech (2018). https://www.usatoday.com/story/tech/2018/03/21/facebook-ceo-mark-zuckerberg-finally-speaks-cambridge-analytica-we-need-fix-breach-trust/445791002/. Accessed 12 Apr 2018

7. Johnson, C.: Enron's ethical collapse: lessons for leadership educators. J. Leadersh. Educ. 2(1), 45–56 (2003)

8. Kasse, J.P., Xu, L., de Vrieze, P.: A comparative assessment of collaborative business process verification approaches. In: Camarinha-Matos, Luis M., Afsarmanesh, H., Fornasiero, R. (eds.) PRO-VE 2017. IAICT, vol. 506, pp. 355–367. Springer, Cham (2017). https://doi.org/10.1007/978-3-319-65151-4_33

9. Kasse, J.P., Nabukenya, J.: Towards adoption of business process analysis and design techniques in transitional countries: design validation, vol. 2, pp. 248–256 (2012)

10. Sadiq, S., Governatori, G.: Managing regulatory compliance in business processes. In: vom Brocke, J., Rosemann, M. (eds.) Handbook on Business Process Management 2. International Handbooks on Information Systems, vol. 2008, pp. 159–175. Springer, Heidelberg (2010). https://doi.org/10.1007/978-3-642-01982-1_8

11. Kochanowski, M., Fehling, C., Koetter, F., Leymann, F., Weisbecker, A.: Compliance in BPM today - an insight into experts views and industry challenges, Inform 2014. Big Data, pp. 769–780. Komplexität meistern (2014)

12. Goedertier, S., Vanthienen, J.: Designing compliant business processes with obligations and permissions. In: Eder, J., Dustdar, S. (eds.) BPM 2006. LNCS, vol. 4103, pp. 5–14. Springer, Heidelberg (2006). https://doi.org/10.1007/11837862_2

13. Sandhu, P.R.: The RBAC96 Model (2003)

14. Thomas, R.K., Sandhu, R.S.: Task-based authorization controls (TBAC): a family of models for active and enterprise-oriented authorization management. In: vom Lin, T.Y., Qian, S. (eds.) Database Security XI. IFIP Advances in Information and Communication Technology, pp. 166–181. Springer, Heidelberg (1998). https://doi.org/10.1007/978-0-387-35285-5_10

15. Yuan, E., Tong, J.: Attributed Based Access Control (ABAC) for web services. In: The IEEE International Conference on Web Services, pp. 561–569 (2005)

16. Gautam, M.: Poster : constrained policy mining in attribute based access control, pp. 121–123 (2017)

17. Salnitri, M., Dalpiaz, F., Giorgini, P.: Modeling and verifying security policies in business processes. In: Bider, I., et al. (eds.) BPMDS/EMMSAD -2014. LNBIP, vol. 175, pp. 200–214. Springer, Heidelberg (2014). https://doi.org/10.1007/978-3-662-43745-2_14

18. Robol, M., Salnitri, M., Giorgini, P.: Toward GDPR-compliant socio-technical systems: modeling language and reasoning framework. In: Poels, G., Gailly, F., Serral Asensio, E., Snoeck, M. (eds.) PoEM 2017. LNBIP, vol. 305, pp. 236–250. Springer, Cham (2017). https://doi.org/10.1007/978-3-319-70241-4_16

19. Müller, J.: Security Mechanisms for Workflows in Service-Oriented Architectures (2015)

20. Combi, C., Viganò, L., Zavatteri, M.: Security Constraints in Temporal Role-Based. Codaspy, pp. 207–218 (2016)

21. Elgammal, A., Turetken, O., van den Heuvel, W.J., Papazoglou, M.: Formalizing and applying compliance patterns for business process compliance. Softw. Syst. Model. 15(1), 119–146 (2016)

22. Sadiq, S., Governatori, G., Namiri, K.: Modeling control objectives for business process compliance. In: Alonso, G., Dadam, P., Rosemann, M. (eds.) BPM 2007. LNCS, vol. 4714, pp. 149–164. Springer, Heidelberg (2007). https://doi.org/10.1007/978-3-540-75183-0_12

23. Goedertier, S.: Declarative techniques for modeling and mining business processes, no. 284, p. 248 (2008)

24. Goedertier, S., Vanthienen, J.: Compliant and flexible business processes with business rules. In: BPMDS, pp. 94–103 (2007)
25. Schumm, D., Leymann, F., Ma, Z., Scheibler, T., Strauch, S.: Integrating compliance into business processes process fragments as reusable compliance controls, pp. 2125–2137 (2010)
26. Fenech, S., Pace, G.J., Schneider, G.: Automatic conflict detection on contracts. In: Leucker, M., Morgan, C. (eds.) ICTAC 2009. LNCS, vol. 5684, pp. 200–214. Springer, Heidelberg (2009). https://doi.org/10.1007/978-3-642-03466-4_13
27. Fenech, S., Pace, Gordon J., Schneider, G.: CLAN: a tool for contract analysis and conflict discovery. In: Liu, Z., Ravn, Anders P. (eds.) ATVA 2009. LNCS, vol. 5799, pp. 90–96. Springer, Heidelberg (2009). https://doi.org/10.1007/978-3-642-04761-9_8
28. Ertugrul, A.M., Demirors, O.: An exploratory study on role-based collaborative business process modeling approaches. In: Proceedings of the 7th International Conference on Subject-Oriented Business Process Management - S-BPM ONE 2015, pp. 1–5 (2015)
29. Khan, A.R.: Access control in cloud computing environment. ARPN J. Eng. Appl. Sci. 7(5), 613–615 (2012)
30. Sandhu, R.: Rationale for the RBAC96 family of access control models. In: Proceedings of the First ACM Workshop on Role-based Access Control – RBAC 1995, no. 1, p. 9 (1996)
31. Alshehri, A., Sandhu, R.: Access control models for virtual object communication in cloud-enabled IoT. In: 2017 IEEE International Conference on Information Reuse and Integration (IRI) (2017)
32. Wu, M.: Role and task based authorization management for process-view. In: Proceedings of the Second International Conference Security and Cryptography, no. 707, pp. 85–90 (2007)
33. Tan, K., Crampton, J., Gunter, C.A.: The consistency of task-based authorization constraints in workflow systems. In: Proceedings of the 17th IEEE Computer Security Foundation Workshop, pp. 155–169 (2004)
34. Axiomatics, Attribute Based Access Control (ABAC) (2018). https://www.axiomatics.com/attribute-based-access-control/. Accessed 09 Apr 2018
35. Ramezani, E., Fahland, D., van der Aalst, W.M.P.: Diagnostic information in temporal compliance checking. Tech. report, BPM Cent. report no. 2 (2012)
36. Gammal, E.: Towards a comprehensive framework for business process compliance FRAMEWORK FOR BUSINESS PROCESS (2014)
37. Hall, N., Dwyer, M.B., Avrunin, G.S., Corbett, J.C.: Property specification patterns for finite-state verification 1 Introduction 2 Design and other patterns. In: Proceedings of the Second Workshop on Formal Methods in Software Practice, vol. 2, pp. 7–15 (1998)
38. Cimatti, A., et al.: NuSMV 2: an opensource tool for symbolic model checking. In: Brinksma, E., Larsen, K.G. (eds.) CAV 2002. LNCS, vol. 2404, pp. 359–364. Springer, Heidelberg (2002). https://doi.org/10.1007/3-540-45657-0_29
39. Biere, A., Cimatti, A., Clarke, E., Zhu, Y.: Symbolic model checking without BDDs. In: Cleaveland, W.Rance (ed.) TACAS 1999. LNCS, vol. 1579, pp. 193–207. Springer, Heidelberg (1999). https://doi.org/10.1007/3-540-49059-0_14

Enhancing Robust Execution of BPMN Process Diagrams: A Practical Approach

Hodjat Soleimani Malekan[✉], Mohammad Shafahi,
Naser Ayat, and Hamideh Afsarmanesh

Informatics Institute, University of Amsterdam, 1098XH Amsterdam, The Netherlands
{h.soleimanimalekan,m.shafahi,
h.afsarmanesh}@uva.nl, naser.ayat@gmail.com

Abstract. As a standard modeling language for definition of business processes and services, BPMN is used both within the organizations as well as for co-creation of joint services to run among the networked organizations. However, introducing certain constructs, such as OR-join and Complex-join in BPMN Process Diagrams (BPDs) can lead to execution problems, due to ambiguities inherent in these constructs in relation to their execution semantics. Although these constructs are often used to represent the real-world behaviors, none of the existing approaches applied by the BP management systems are practically tuned to disambiguate and support their proper execution. Rooted in workflow patterns concept, we first introduce a set of algorithms to automate the identification of ambiguous patterns (i.e., workflow patterns that include OR-join constructs). Then, we introduce a set of equivalent unambiguous BP fragments that can substitute those ambiguous patterns. To this end, we have conceptualized the identification of three OR-join ambiguous patterns by applying the RPST technique, represent a set of unambiguous solutions for their substitution, and implemented our method as the proof of concept for our approach.

Keywords: Business process execution · BPMN · OR-join · Workflow patterns
Ambiguous patterns

1 Introduction

Business Process Model and Notation (BPMN) [1] is a standard modeling language for describing Business Processes (BPs). The primary objective of BPMN is to provide a standard notation that is intuitive enough to be understood by business users (e.g., domain experts). In addition, it is expressive enough to be executed by technical users (e.g., BP analysts) [3]. To this end, BPMN Process Diagram (BPD) is an effective means for designing and executing BPs by domain experts and BP analysts, respectively.

Through its semi-concise definition, besides supporting the actors internal to each organization, BPMN adequately supports Collaborative Networked Organizations (CNO) [19] in consolidating their BPDs [20] and co-creating business services [17] that can jointly run among different organizations. In particular, the provision of relevant features, as well as the expressiveness, and understandability of the BPMN notations

© IFIP International Federation for Information Processing 2018
Published by Springer Nature Switzerland AG 2018. All Rights Reserved
L. M. Camarinha-Matos et al. (Eds.): PRO-VE 2018, IFIP AICT 534, pp. 230–243, 2018.
https://doi.org/10.1007/978-3-319-99127-6_20

assist the BPD designers in CNOs to accomplish their mission [2]. The need for definition of joint business services in CNOs is addressed in the literature in the past [17, 18]. We have also studied and reported some real-world cases in [16], which evaluates the suitability of BPMN for CNOs. In this real application case, in order to construct Eco-friendly buildings, a general contractor establishes a CNO together with its collaborators. Then the established CNO successfully defines, aligns, and consolidates independent BPs from different organizations toward delivering a number of shared business services, all represented by BPDs. During this exercise; however, we discovered several executability concerns about those defined BPDs that used "OR-join" to combine the BPs from different CNO members, as also reported in some other literature [9, 10]. In this paper, we address a number of executability problems related to BPDs.

To generate an executable BPD, the use of some problematic BPMN constructs, such as OR-join [3, 4] and Complex-join [5] makes run-time problems, because of ambiguities in their execution semantics. For instance, the existence of OR-join gateway in BPDs, which is used to capture the synchronization behaviors, causes the BP management systems (e.g., Activiti) have no idea of for how many paths of the join gateway should wait before proceeding to the next step [3, 4].

Nevertheless, one challenge to resolve the problematic constructs is well understanding the molder's intention behind the applied constructs. This, in turn, helps with offering equivalent executable BP fragments, to be substituted with the existing BP model. In this regard, we have applied the concept of *workflow patterns* [6, 7], which is designed to provide a rigorous basis for different aspects of BP technologies (e.g., BP execution). Hence, we are aimed at identifying and resolving the certain OR-join included workflow patterns, so-called *ambiguous patterns* in this paper. In practice, the ambiguous patterns are not properly executed by any of the many BP management systems that support BPMN [3].

To deal with the problem of ambiguous patterns in BPDs, we design a solution that: (i) identifies three ambiguous patterns that include OR-join (e.g., general synchronizing merge), (ii) suggests unambiguous equivalent workarounds for disambiguating by the users, and (iii) introduces a Disambiguation Support System tool to interact with business users on identifying and resolving ambiguities.

Consequently, for the rest of this paper, we first explain the BPMN notation, briefly. Second, we explain why OR-join is ambiguous, and define and exemplify the ambiguous workflow patterns. Next, the algorithm for the identification of ambiguous patterns, as well as the unambiguous workaround BP fragments are proposed. Then, the architecture of our developed Disambiguation Support System is explained. After discussing the results of our research, the conclusion is presented.

2   Business Process Modeling and Notation

BPMN (ver. 2.0.2) is a popular BP modeling language standard that targets both appropriate visualization and executive semantics [1]. Because of its rich graphical notation and XML exchange definitions, it is used pervasively by organizations [2]. To represent BP, BPDs are produced by using BPMN elements.

In Fig. 1, the main elements of BPMN are illustrated into six categories of "Events", "Activities", "Gateways", "Connectivity objects", "Swimlanes", and "Artifacts". In principle, gateways control the *split* and *join* in the flow of processes. In the *split* construct, several paths diverge from the gateway, while in the *join* construct, several paths converge into one path. Similar to XOR logical operator in programming languages, the continuation of the process flow in an XOR (exclusive) gateway is mutually exclusive. Also, in the case of having multiple incoming paths into an exclusive gateway, the flow continues only if one of the incoming paths is activated. The AND (parallel) gateway denotes the concurrent trigger of all paths that either come to or go out of the gateway.

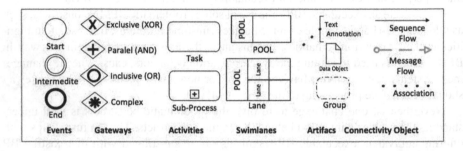

Fig. 1. A set of BPMN elements

The OR (inclusive) gateway combines the behaviors of both the exclusive gateways and the parallel gateways. Thus, the trigger of one, a certain number, or all of the outgoing path(s) is possible in a split condition. Similarly, in a merge condition, process flow continues after receiving one, a certain number, or all of the incoming activated path(s). The Complex decision gateways are suitable for expressing decision points by the BP rules (e.g., when n paths out of m existing paths can be chosen).

Activities show the tasks that are being carried out in a process. Modelers can localize a set of related activities of a process in one sub-process. Selecting the level of details about activities depends on modeler's perception [3]. Events can appear at the beginning, in the middle, and at the end of processes, called start, intermediate, and end events, respectively. Circles in BPMN notation depict event constructs (see Fig. 1). Artifacts in BPMN notation show some extra necessary explanation about a process. Depicting text annotations, data object, and group, in turn, facilitates the perception of BPDs.

Connectivity objects represent the three main flow streams in BP diagrams: "sequence flow", "message flow", and "association". Sequence flows show the execution order of activities. The direction of the exchanged message is illustrated by message flow. Association links depict the direct interactions between BPMN elements. Swimlanes denote resources such as process participants and roles in processes. Furthermore, swimlanes represent either one organizational role in a Lane or a set of business participants in a Pool.

In spite of its rich set of elements, BPMN executions face difficulties, because of unclear execution semantics. The semantics of BPMN is described textually and is not formally standardized [4]. This issue can result in ambiguities, because of either failure in formalizing some BPMN constructs (e.g., OR-join construct), or different potential interpretations of the standard (e.g., Complex-join construct). As such, the robust execution of BPDs that include OR-join [3] and Complex-join [5] can lead to inconsistencies in executability of a BPD. The BP management systems also lack the execution features for supporting the mentioned ambiguous constructs [3, 8].

Although those two ambiguous constructs are difficult to elaborate, in certain cases applying OR gateways or Complex gateways are inevitable. For instance, the OR-join is appropriate for combining two different behaviors in merging two BP models. Similarly, the complex synchronization behavior, which is captured by Complex-join gateway has no substitution with split and join constructs of other BPMN gateways [5]. In this paper, we focus on OR-join ambiguity resolution. In the next section, we take a closer look at the reasons behind the OR-join ambiguity in BPDs.

3   Why Is the OR-Join Construct Ambiguous?

In order to represent the synchronization, the OR-join constructs are used. More precisely, the OR-join synchronizes some of its incoming paths that their precise number is unknown until the execution time of a BPD.

Note that, during the execution of a BPD, the current point of execution is indicated by the concept of *the thread of control*. The execution starts, when the thread of control is located at the start point. Accordingly, the thread of control traverses from the *start* point to the *endpoint*. In the meanwhile, a thread of control can split into several distinct threads after a diverging point (see Si in Fig. 2), or multiple distinct threads are joined into a single thread of control in a converging point (see Ji in Fig. 2). Borrowed from Petri net notation [3], the BPMN standard document [1] uses the notion of "token" (the black circles on gateways in Fig. 2) to explain the states, which are traversed by different threads of control.

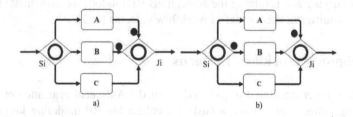

Fig. 2. An example of OR-join enablement

The OR-join serves as a converging point that waits for all tokens produced *upstream* on all its incoming paths to arrive. By reaching the state that no active token can come along a particular incoming path, the OR-join is enabled [1]. Yet, it is not clear what is considered within the range of the term *"upstream"* associated with an OR-join [9]. We describe the threads of control in an OR-join by an example, illustrated in Fig. 2.

The OR-split Si produces tokens for all or some of its outgoing paths, i.e., either one task, such as "Task A", or two tasks, e.g., "Task A and Task B", or all three tasks (i.e.,

A, B, and C) are enabled. The corresponding OR-join, Ji, is supposed to synchronize the paths, which are enabled by Si. In brief, enabling Ji depends on information of the enabled paths that lead to the OR-join, called the non-local information. Various situations of this issue are shown in parts (a) and (b) of Fig. 2.

In part (a), Ji is enabled. Yet, in part (b), Ji is supposed to wait for the upstream token until it arrives after passing the "Task B". Both parts of Fig. 2 have the same incoming paths of Ji; nevertheless, the position of remained tokens determines the activation of Ji [10]. In summary, enabling decision of OR-join requires the knowledge of the current state as well as possible future states of the process. In practice, determining all possible states of the BP becomes very complicated when other constructs, such as multiple OR-joins, cycles, or cancellation exist in a BPD [9].

The OR-join enabling decision in different proposed approaches, namely [9], is based on the information of the current state as well as the possible future states of the BP model. The formal techniques introduced; hence, seek to determine all possible states of the BP model during the execution which are computationally expensive. Accordingly, introducing a "clean semantic" for the OR-join construct is almost impossible, due to numerous configurations in BP models, e.g., vicious circle [3, 4].

Removing the OR-join poses three challenges. First, how to preserve the behavior of the OR-join included BPD, which is initially intended by the modeler. The OR-join construct is used to show the synchronized behavior; thus, the substitution of this construct should represent both the synchronization and flexible behavior of OR (i.e., the combined behavior of both AND/XOR gateways) [10]. Second, the executability of the BPD with OR-join constructs is a concern, while, no fully automated solution has been implemented [3]. Finally, the solutions should be understandable by BP modelers [10]. Consequently, we intend to identify the ambiguous fragments (i.e., OR-join included fragments) and provide equivalent workaround solutions to be substituted with thereof. Moreover, the usability of solution by the domain experts and BP analysts matters for us in offering our disambiguating solution. To provide a systematic solution for both identifying and resolving the ambiguous BP models, we investigate the occurrence of ambiguities in the context of workflow patterns [6, 7].

4 Ambiguous Workflow Patterns

The workflow pattern initiative, introduced by van der Aalst et al. is an attempt to identify the recurring patterns to provide a basis for enhancing BP modeling languages and evaluating commercial tools [6]. To support different behaviors and functions (so-called control-flow) in BPs, 43 patterns has introduced in [6], which are recently delineated in [7]. Supporting more patterns indicates the higher level of expressiveness of a modeling language. BPMN is more expressive in comparison with most of the graphical modeling languages [6], such as EPC or UML. Nevertheless, three of the BPMN-represented workflow patterns use the problematic OR-join construct to represent the *synchronizing* behavior.

The three ambiguous patterns are the variants of "synchronizing merge" control-flow pattern. Generally, in a *synchronizing merge* pattern, two or more incoming paths, which are previously diverged from a unique split point, converge into one particular join construct [6]. In BPMN, the OR-join construct controls the convergence point and passes the thread of control to succeeding element [7]. Beyond the general mentioned structure, each of the three synchronizing merge variants is distinguished by its specifications and the way it provides information for OR-join construct to pass the thread of control to the next step. Here, we explain and exemplify the three variants of: *"structured"*, *"local"* and *"general"* synchronizing merge [6].

First, the *Structured synchronizing merge* pattern is a balanced BP fragment, and no further split and join can appear in the way from divergence point (i.e., OR-split) towards convergence point (OR-join).

For example, the product line of a company is audited according to a quality management plan. In case of nonconformity, a set of preventive actions and/or corrective actions are taken to eliminate the nonconformity. The annual audit ceremony is closed when neither any nonconformity is identified, nor any preventive and/or corrective actions are left. The BPD of this example is illustrated in Fig. 3 where the structured synchronizing merge area is enclosed by dashed-line.

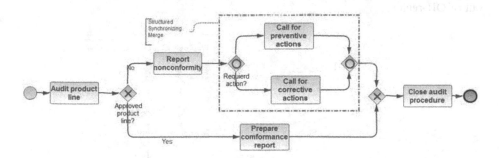

Fig. 3. Structured synchronizing merge in BPMN

Second, the local synchronizing merge pattern can decide on synchronization based on the available local information. Unlike the structured synchronizing merge, the local synchronizing merge fragments can include cycles. Although the cycle within the BP model, must either completely locate on a single path coming from the split point to the join point, or the entire OR region should be contained in a cycle [7].

For example, consider in the previous example, taking the preventive actions can is followed by a review task. This cycle is illustrated by adding two XOR-gateway in the dashed-line area in Fig. 4. In this case, the control XOR- gateway can take the thread of control out of cycle, it is decidable whether the OR-join will be enabled or not.

Finally, the general synchronizing merge is neither structured nor can be enabled without analyzing all possible future states. Although it covers more OR-join included BP models, it faces serious problems during the execution time. Besides, any cycle can exist in this pattern.

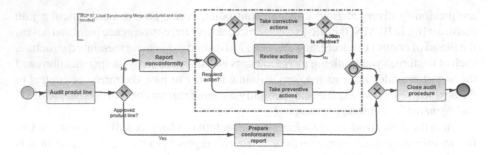

Fig. 4. Local synchronizing merge in BPMN

For example, regarding the quality auditing scenario, considering that for checking the efficiency of the preventive actions, the outsourcing is continuously checked. If it needs an external third-party for outsourcing, the "Plan outsourcing" task is performed. Otherwise, the efficiency of the preventive task is confirmed by the committee. In Fig. 5, the XOR-gateway to "required external resource" can take the thread of control out of OR-region.

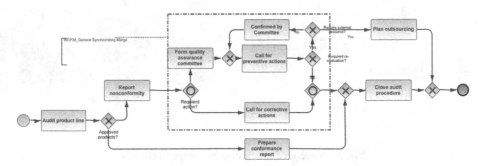

Fig. 5. General synchronizing merge in BPMN

None of the presented solutions for OR-join semantics, such as in [9, 10] are implemented and fully supported by main BP management systems, such as jBPM[1], Activiti[2], and Camunda[3] [8].

5   Algorithm for Ambiguous Pattern Identification

Let us, first, explain briefly the intuition behind our algorithm. To identify the mentioned ambiguous patterns in a given BPD, the Refined Process Structured Tree (RPST) technique is used [11]. The RPST technique hierarchically decomposes a BP model into a set of fine-grained fragments, which have "single-entry-single-exit" (SESE) boundary

---

[1] https://www.jbpm.org.
[2] https://www.activiti.org.
[3] https://www.camunda.org.

nodes. The SESE fragments provide a sound basis for recognizing an ambiguous pattern in BP models. Because, the single-exit node of the fragment facilitates the identification of OR-join constructs. Comparably, the corresponding entry point of the fragment can enclose the ambiguous pattern's region. Thus, we can precisely determine ambiguous fragments, regardless of the BP models' elements between the split and join points. Furthermore, the processing time for making the RPST is linear and the implementation of the algorithms is not computationally expensive [11]. Figure 6 shows an example of RPST decomposition.

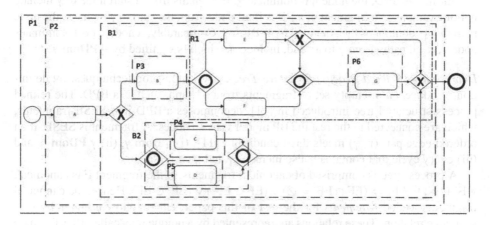

Fig. 6. An example of RPST decomposition of a BP

We consider a BPMN Process Diagram (BPD) as the input for our pattern identification purpose. The corresponding definition of the BPD model is captured, as follows:

Definition 1 (BPMN Process Diagram). A BPMN Process Diagram is a graph-based representation of a business process. BPD is a tuple of **BPD = (T, GX, GA, GO, GC, E)**; where T is a non-empty set of tasks, and G is the superset of gateways, such that **G = GX ∪ GA ∪ GO ∪ GC**, where GX is the set of XOR gateways, G is the set of AND gateways, GO is the set of OR gateways, and GC is the set of Complex gateways, these sets are all disjoint. All nodes in a BPD are defined by N = G ∪ T. The control flow, which is the set of direct edges between two nodes in a BPD, is defined by E ⊆ N × N. Each fragment (say F) is a non-empty directed sub-graph of a BPD, **F = (NF, EF)**, where, NF ⊆ N and **EF = E ∩ (NF × NF)**.

Definition 2 (Well-Structured BPD). Two ordered sets of predecessor and successor nodes are defined for each node (i.e., a task or a gateway). For instance, regarding a task $\tau \in T$, $\bullet\tau$ stands for the set of immediate predecessor nodes, i.e., $\bullet\tau = \{\eta \in N \mid (\eta, \tau) \in E\}$, and $\tau\bullet$ is the set of immediate successor nodes of τ; $\tau\bullet = \{\eta \in N \mid (\tau, \eta) \in E\}$.

In a well-structured BPD, there is at most one incoming sequence path (i.e., edge) and one outgoing sequence path for every task τ, such that $\mid \bullet\tau \mid \le 1 \wedge \mid \tau\bullet \mid \le 1$. There exists only one start node, such that $\eta \in T$ and $\mid \bullet\eta \mid = 0$, and only one end node, where $\eta \in T$, if $\mid \eta\bullet \mid = 0$. A gateway can be either a split or a join. A gateway "g_s" represents a split gateway, if $|\bullet g| = 1 \wedge |g\bullet| > 1$. In a similar way, "g_j" signifies a join gateway, if $|\bullet g| > 1 \wedge |g\bullet| = 1$; thus "go_j" is an example of OR-join gateway.

Definition 3 (Paths). There exists a path between η and η', if an ordered set of nodes are in sequence, such that $\langle (\eta 1, \eta 2), (\eta 2, \eta 3), \ldots , (\eta x - 1, \eta x) \rangle$, where $(\eta = \eta 1) \wedge (\eta' = \eta x) \wedge \forall 1 \leq i < x\text{-}1$ $(\eta i, \eta i + 1) \in E$; $i, x \in N$. The path is signified by $\boldsymbol{\eta \rightarrow \eta'}$.

There is a cyclic path, if a path exists that starts and ends at the same node. Hence, a BPD has a cycle, if $\exists \eta \in N, \boldsymbol{\eta \rightarrow \eta}$.

For $\eta, \gamma \in$ BPD, the node η is dominate γ, if all paths from a start node to γ include η. For example, in a fragment of a BPD, if all paths from the start to γ includes the node η, then "η" dominates "γ", denoted by $\boldsymbol{\eta}$ **Dom** $\boldsymbol{\gamma}$. Comparably, a node η post-dominates node γ, if all paths from γ to an end, include η, which is signified by $\boldsymbol{\eta}$ **PDom** $\boldsymbol{\gamma}$.

Definition 4 (Refined Process Structure Tree). Decomposition techniques, by definition, produce a non-empty set of fragments from a graph, such as a BPD. The refined process structured tree introduced in [11], decomposes a BPD into SESE fragments, which are connected to the rest the BP model via two nodes. A fragment is SESE, if an ordered edge pair (η, γ) meets three conditions [11]: (i) η **Dom** γ, (ii) γ **PDom** η, and (iii) every cycle that contains η also includes γ and vice versa.

A process tree is comprised of canonical fragments. If the fragment F is canonical, $\forall F' \in N, F \neq F' \Rightarrow (EF \cap EF' = \emptyset) \vee (EF \subset EF') \vee (EF' \subset EF)$. Hence, the canonical fragments, called *fragments* for the rest of this paper, either follow a hierarchy or a sequence relation. These relations are represented by a unique tree, called RPST, where the parent of each fragment is the smallest fragment that contains it [11].

The SESE region is connected to the other fragments, with two boundary nodes as the entry/exit nodes, such that no incoming/outgoing edge of them are in F. A boundary node "η" is an entry, where **entry(F)** $= \mathbf{E} \cap ((\mathbf{N\backslash NF}) \times \mathbf{NF})$, or can be an exit point, where **exit(F)** $= \mathbf{E} \cap (\mathbf{NF} \times (\mathbf{N\backslash NF}))$.

Definition 5 (RPST Fragments' Classes). Let F be a fragment of a BPD. It can appear in four classes of: "*trivial*", "*polygon*", "*bond*", and "*rigid*" [11], as follows:

F is a *trivial* fragment (T), if F is a singleton that includes only a single sequence arc, such as a sequence flow in a BPD.

F is a *polygon* fragment (P), if there is a sequence of fragments of $(z1, z2, \ldots , zn)$, and $n \in \mathbb{N}$, where the entry of z1 is the entry of F, the exit of zn is the exit of F, and for all i that $1 \leq i \leq n$ the exit of zi, is the entry of zi + 1, therefore, $\mathbf{F} = \cup_{mi = 1} \mathbf{zi}$. In Fig. 6, "P2", is a polygon that includes the sequence of: "Task A" and "B1 fragment".

F is a *bond* fragment (B), if it includes all fragments "z" that share the same entry and exit nodes with F, such that $\mathbf{F} = \cup_{z \in C} \mathbf{z}$. Where, "C" is the set of the canonical fragments with common boundary nodes (i.e., entry and exit) with "F". For instance, the two OR-gateways before and after task "C" and task "D" in Fig. 6 are the entry and exit of the bond fragment "B2". Bond fragments are thus balanced by definition.

F is a *rigid* fragment (R), if it is none of the all above classes of fragments (i.e., trivial, polygon, and bond). For instance, "R1" is a rigid fragment, shown in Fig. 6. The rigid fragments are arbitrary and unstructured [11].

The Algorithm 1 summarizes our ambiguous pattern identification approach.

Algorithm 1. Identifying OR-join included patterns

Require: BPD: A BPMN Process Diagram
Ensure: S: A set S of OR-join included patterns in BPD

```
 1: S ←∅
 2: Construct the RPST of BPD in accordance with [11]
 3: Let F be the set of all fragments in the RPST
 4: Let B be the set of bond fragments in F
 5: Let R be the set of rigid fragments in F
 6: for all b ∈ B do
 7:   if (εxit(b) ∈ GO_J) ∧ (εntry(b) ∈ GO_S) then
 8:     if ((∃ η → η) ∧ (⟨η → η⟩ ⊂ ⟨εntry(b) → εxit(b)⟩))
 9:       S ← S ∪ (b, "Local synchronizing merge")
10:     else if (∄η → η) then
11:       S ← S ∪ (b, "Structured synchronizing merge")
12:     end if
13: end for
14: for all r ∈ R do
15:   if (go_j ∈ GO_J)∧(go_s ∈ GO_S)∧(go_s Dom go_j)then
16:     if (∃ γ → γ) ∧ (⟨γ → γ⟩ ⊂ ⟨go_s → go_j⟩) then
17:       S ←S ∪ (r, "Local synchronizing merge")
18:     else
19:       S ← S ∪ (r, "General synchronizing merge")
20:   end if
21: end for
22: return S
```

---

6 Ambiguous Pattern Resolution

To substitute the ambiguous OR-join included patterns, we suggest three equivalent BP fragment represented in [12, 13], illustrated in Fig. 7. The workaround solutions are composed by "AND-"and "XOR-" gateways; thus, they are executable. Furthermore, they are structured and more understandable by users [3]. Besides, users are able to focus on specific BP fragment (selected as the ambiguous pattern) for restructuring a BPD, which greatly assists users when they work with the arbitrary structures of local and general synchronizing merge patterns.

In Fig. 7, the "suggestion I" represents the behavior of OR-join, while it also lets the situation of neither "A" nor "B". The behavior of OR-join can be also captured by using suggestions "II and III"; however, they use one task, such as "A", more than once in a BP model. Besides, the main problem of these two workarounds (i.e., II and III) is the scalability problem, in case that they are more than two tasks in the OR-region the number of paths and combinations grows exponentially.

7 Architecture of Disambiguation Support System (DSS)

To facilitate the process of disambiguation a Disambiguation Support System (DSS) is designed and partially developed. The DSS Architecture is illustrated in Fig. 8.

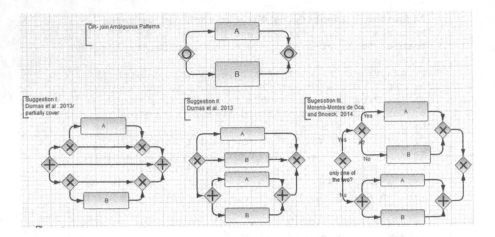

Fig. 7. The OR-join workaround solutions

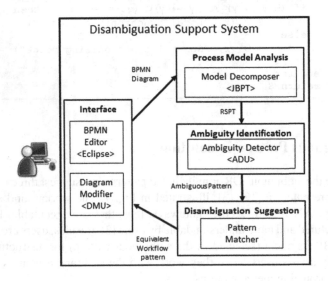

Fig. 8. Disambiguation Support System architecture

The DSS units are as follows:

(i) *Model Pre-processor.* This unit is responsible for designing and illustrating the BPMN Process Diagrams. To develop this unit, we have used Eclipse[4] BPMN 2.0 editor. Moreover, the syntactical correctness of developed BPMN models is checked in accordance with the Eclipse verification rules.

(ii) *Model Decomposer.* The RPST builder creates a structured tree from *.bpmn files. Hence, we can recognize the types of fragments (i.e., bond or rigid). For this purpose, we have used jBPT[5] and BPT-NH[6], which are two Java libraries that apply graph structures to provide a hierarchy in form of RPST for BPMN process diagrams.

(iii) *Ambiguity Identifier:* Following our proposed algorithm, we identify the OR-join ambiguous patterns. Accordingly, the ambiguous patterns their type are returned.

(iv) *Disambiguation Recommender.* According to the identified ambiguous pattern, unambiguous solutions are recommended to modelers.

(v) *Visual Representor.* This unit manages the user interactions and graphical interface, and it is also the subject of further development.

Figure 9 depicts a screenshot of ambiguity identifier unit of DSS, which its source code is available on online[7]. The algorithm performs well on the identification of OR-join patterns based on the test of different examples of ambiguous patterns.

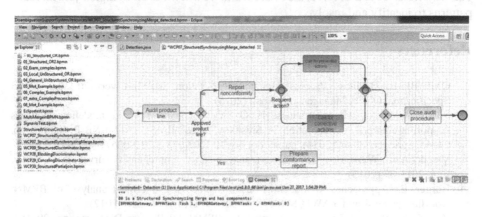

Fig. 9. A screenshot of the ambiguity identifier feature in DSS system

8   Discussion and Conclusion

In this paper, we tackled the problem of certain ambiguous and non-executable BPDs that include the OR-join constructs. Nevertheless, this construct is vastly used when combining and consolidating different BPs by independent organizations, such as those

---

[4] Eclipse : www.eclipse.org/bpmn2-modeler.

[5] Java Business Process Technology (JBPT): www.code.google.com/jbpt.

[6] BPT-NH: www.github.com/BPT-NH.

[7] BPCon : https://bitbucket.org/Hodjat/disambiguationsupportsystem .

that are members of a CNO that wish to share their BP repositories to deliver a set of consolidated business services [16].

To provide our solution, the concept of workflow patterns is applied, in order to identify the ambiguous patterns systematically and suggest equivalent unambiguous BP fragments for substituting with them. To this end, a set of formalized definitions are provided for ambiguous patterns and the corresponding algorithm is designed, implemented, and verified. No similar BPMN disambiguation solution based on ambiguous workflow identification has been addressed to the best of our knowledge, while the identification of workflow patterns is partially studies in two research works.

The study introduced in [14] proposes definitions to recognize a number of workflow, however they have excluded the OR-join included workflow patterns. Another study by Elaasar et al. in [15] introduces a MOF-based modeling language for the purpose of identifying patterns in BPMN that has taken the workflow patterns as a test case. However, they have reported difficulties in identifying the aimed patterns (i.e., structured synchronizing merge), due to the sensitivity of the method to natural language notes on gateways and the lack of provided information of gateways (e.g., conditions to follow each path emanated from a gateway). In comparison, our approach not only provided disambiguation suggestions, but also is not limited by the information of the gateway variables of a BPD. As the future work, we will focus on Complex-join included patterns to identify and resolve.

References

1. OMG/BPMI: Business Process Model and Notation (BPMN) version 2.0.2. OMG Specification, Object Management Group (2014)
2. Soleimani Malekan, H., Afsarmanesh, H.: Overview of business process modeling languages supporting enterprise collaboration. In: Shishkov, B. (ed.) BMSD 2013. LNBIP, vol. 173, pp. 24–45. Springer, Cham (2014). https://doi.org/10.1007/978-3-319-06671-4_2
3. Van der Aalst, W.M.: Business process management: a comprehensive survey. ISRN Softw. Eng. **2013**, 37 (2013)
4. Börger, E.: Approaches to modeling business processes: a critical analysis of BPMN, workflow patterns and YAWL. Softw. Syst. Model. **11**(3), 305–318 (2012)
5. Kossak, F., et al.: A Rigorous Semantics for BPMN 2.0 Process Diagrams, pp. 29–152. Springer, Cham (2014). https://doi.org/10.1007/978-3-319-09931-6_4
6. van Der Aalst, W.M., Ter Hofstede, A.H., Kiepuszewski, B., Barros, A.P.: Workflow patterns. Distrib. Parallel Databases **14**(1), 5–51 (2003)
7. Russell, N., van der Aalst, W.M., ter Hofstede, A.H.: Workflow Patterns: the Definitive Guide. MIT Press, Cambridge (2016)
8. Geiger, M., Harrer, S., Lenhard, J., Wirtz, G.: BPMN 2.0: The state of support and implementation. Future Gener. Comput. Syst. **80**, 250–262 (2018)
9. Wynn, M.T., Edmond, D., van der Aalst, W.M.P., ter Hofstede, A.H.M.: Achieving a general, formal and decidable approach to the OR-Join in workflow using reset nets. In: Ciardo, G., Darondeau, P. (eds.) ICATPN 2005. LNCS, vol. 3536, pp. 423–443. Springer, Heidelberg (2005). https://doi.org/10.1007/11494744_24
10. Völzer, H.: A new semantics for the inclusive converging gateway in safe processes. In: Hull, R., Mendling, J., Tai, S. (eds.) BPM 2010. LNCS, vol. 6336, pp. 294–309. Springer, Heidelberg (2010). https://doi.org/10.1007/978-3-642-15618-2_21

11. Polyvyanyy, A., Vanhatalo, J., Völzer, H.: Simplified computation and generalization of the refined process structure tree. In: Bravetti, M., Bultan, T. (eds.) WS-FM 2010. LNCS, vol. 6551, pp. 25–41. Springer, Heidelberg (2011). https://doi.org/10.1007/978-3-642-19589-1_2
12. de Oca, I.M.M., Snoeck, M.: Pragmatic Guidelines for Business Process Modeling. Faculty of Economics and Business, KU Leuven (2015)
13. Dumas, M., La Rosa, M., Mendling, J., Reijers, H.A.: Fundamentals of Business Process Management, vol. 1, p. 2. Springer, Heidelberg (2013). https://doi.org/10.1007/978-3-642-33143-5
14. Juan, Y.C., Yuan, K.Y.: Control flow pattern recognition for BPMN process models. Int. J. Electron. Bus. Manag. 111(2), 133 (2013)
15. Elaasar, M., Briand, L.C., Labiche, Y.: VPML: an approach to detect design patterns of MOF-based modeling languages. SoSyM 14(2), 735–764 (2015)
16. Soleimani Malekan, H., Adamiak, K., Afsarmanesh, H.: A systematic approach for business service consolidation in virtual organization. SOCA 12, 41 (2018)
17. Camarinha-Matos, Luis M., Afsarmanesh, H., Oliveira, A.I., Ferrada, F.: Cloud-based collaborative business services provision. In: Hammoudi, S., Cordeiro, J., Maciaszek, Leszek A., Filipe, J. (eds.) ICEIS 2013. LNBIP, vol. 190, pp. 366–384. Springer, Cham (2014). https://doi.org/10.1007/978-3-319-09492-2_22
18. Afsarmanesh, H., Sargolzaei, M., Shadi, M.: Semi-automated software service integration in virtual organisations. Enterp. Inf. Syst. 9(5–6), 528–555 (2015)
19. Camarinha-Matos, L.M., Afsarmanesh, H., Galeano, N., Molina, A.: Collaborative networked organizations– concepts and practice in manufacturing enterprises. Comput. Industr. Eng. 57(1), 46–60 (2009)
20. Soleimani Malekan, H., Rezazade Mehrizi, Mohammmad H., Afsarmanesh, H.: Positioning collaboration in business process model consolidation in VOs. In: Afsarmanesh, H., Camarinha-Matos, Luis M., Lucas Soares, A. (eds.) PRO-VE 2016. IAICT, vol. 480, pp. 110–123. Springer, Cham (2016). https://doi.org/10.1007/978-3-319-45390-3_10

Complex Collaborative Physical Process Management: A Position on the Trinity of BPM, IoT and DA

Paul Grefen[1(✉)], Heiko Ludwig[2], Samir Tata[2], Remco Dijkman[1], Nathalie Baracaldo[2], Anna Wilbik[1], and Tim D'Hondt[1]

[1] Eindhoven University of Technology, Eindhoven, Netherlands
p.w.p.j.grefen@tue.nl
[2] IBM Research Almaden, San Jose, CA, USA

Abstract. In the modern economy, we see complex business processes with a physical character executed collaboratively by a set of autonomous business organizations. Examples are international container logistics, integrated supply and manufacturing networks, and collaborative healthcare chains - all of which handle physical objects. Over time, these processes have become more complex, more business-critical, more time-critical, and at the same time heavily mass-customized. This implies that the processes need to be managed more explicitly in an increasingly real-time fashion, with ample attention to individual process cases. To support this kind of processes, no single existing technology class suffices. Therefore, we propose to integrate technologies from the areas of business process management (BPM - to manage the processes), internet of things (IoT - to sense and actuate the physical objects) and distributed analytics (DA - to take the right decisions at the right place in real-time) into a trinity. We illustrate our position with an example from the domain of container logistics.

Keywords: Collaborative business process · Physical business process
Business process management · Internet of Things · Distributed analytics

1 Introduction

In the modern economy, we see complex business processes with a physical character that are executed collaboratively by a set of autonomous business organizations. We find examples in many business domains. In international container logistics [14], a network of transportation and administration companies collaborate to facilitate the process of physically moving containers from a location on one continent to a location on an another continent. The containers are physical objects to be managed, but so are the transportation vehicles, such as ships, trains and trucks. In integrated supply and manufacturing networks, we see multiple companies that tightly collaborate - but in a distributed fashion - to provide services and produce complex products. These products need to be physically moved around, but also physical manufacturing resources, such as robots, need to be controlled. This development is evident in the well-known Industry 4.0 concept [1]. In collaborative healthcare chains [11], we see how patients (here the main physical objects) are treated by multiple, distributed organizations in an

L. M. Camarinha-Matos et al. (Eds.): PRO-VE 2018, IFIP AICT 534, pp. 244–253, 2018.
https://doi.org/10.1007/978-3-319-99127-6_21

overall treatment plan and their logistics need to be monitored and managed. In smart mobility solutions for people transport [15], we see comparable processes in which organizations collaborate to efficiently move people in urban contexts.

Over time, these processes have become more complex, more business-critical, more time-critical, and at the same time heavily mass-customized. Increasing process complexity is mainly created by increasing product complexity, but also by increasing rules and regulations. Increased competition in the global marketplace has made processes more business-critical. The necessity is growing to more explicitly collaborate and integrate processes with business partners to operate more efficiently. Customers expect processes to be ever faster, making them more time-critical. Given these 'pressures' on business processes, they need to be mass-customized as well - think of individual routing for single containers to meet strict delivery deadlines or highly individualized health care processes.

In this position paper, we present our view on automated support for these processes. In Sect. 2, we develop a conceptual view on the integration of three technology domains that is required for this support. In Sect. 3, we relate this conceptual view to a high-level systems view focusing on control. In this section, we also discuss an example from sea container logistics. In Sects. 4 and 5, we present a discussion of our position from the points of view of the state of the art, respectively implied challenges. We conclude this short paper in Sect. 6.

2 Towards a Trinity of BPM, IoT and DA

The developments outlined in the previous section imply that processes need to be managed more explicitly in an increasingly real-time fashion, with ample attention to individual process cases. This calls for advanced business process management (BPM) principles and technology - both within organizations and between organizations to arrive at process-oriented virtual organizations [16]. But for the processes we discuss in this paper, BPM cannot be fully executed in the digital domain - it needs to be connected to the physical world where 'the action takes place'. To deal with the time-critical and mass-customized nature of the processes, this connection must be both real-time (or at least near-real-time) and linked to all individual physical objects being handled in the process - which may be many. This connection has become possible through what is called the Internet of Things (IoT) [20], that couples the physical world to the digital world and allows individual physical objects to produce data and to be digitally actuated (i.e., to be given commands to change its state in one way or the other). The amounts of data being generated can be overwhelming in size though - think of a process managing a large container ship that transport many thousands of individual smart containers, each of which produces data in a continuous fashion, reporting its location and physical state (such as temperature). To process this flood of data, we need advanced analytics. But we do not want all data to be analyzed at a central location. This would require all data to be transported (think of all the containers, that may be linked to the internet through a satellite link), would require huge central processing facilities, and last but certainly not least, would imply great business privacy and security threats. Consequently, we want the IoT data to be processed as much as possible at its origin (i.e., at what we call 'the edge' of the Internet), leading to distributed analytics (DA).

To support this kind of processes, we therefore propose to integrate business process management (BPM - to manage the processes), internet of things (IoT - to sense and actuate the physical objects) and distributed analytics (DA - to take the right decisions at the right place in real-time) technologies into an integrated trinity. This trinity is illustrated in Fig. 1. In this figure, we see how the three technology domains are complementary to 'close the control loop' for advanced, distributed, physical business processes. In this loop, BPM is concerned with realizing business goals by managing processes implementing these goals, DA is concerned with domain-specific reasoning logic that operationalizes the business logic of the domain, and IoT is concerned with managing the physical, real-world situation - both in sensing and in actuating. As the figure shows, DA is essential to transform low-level, high-volume data and events into high-level, low-volume information and triggers that have direct meaning to decision making in process management. DA also enables learning from the behavior of "things" and processes.

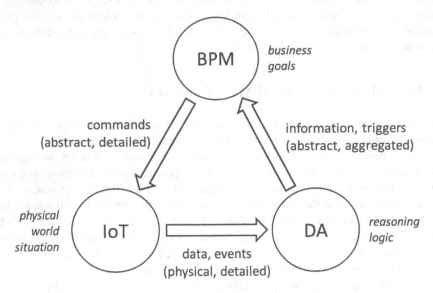

Fig. 1. Trinity view of BPM, DA and IoT

3   A Systems View

The trinity of technologies shown in Fig. 1 is of a high-level, conceptual nature - and hence not fit for systems engineering - i.e., for designing systems that combine BPM, DA and IoT to support the distributed physical processes we have discussed in the previous section. For this purpose, we have to map the trinity of technologies to a systems view. We use an adapted version of a multi-level control model for advanced, flexible information systems [2], shown in Fig. 2. This model can be seen as a highly abstracted (and hence simplified) layered architecture for a BPM+DA+IoT system. The architecture is comprised of a set of logical components that represent the processing associated with the layer's function. Each logical component can be mapped to a set of actual processing nodes in a technical architecture.

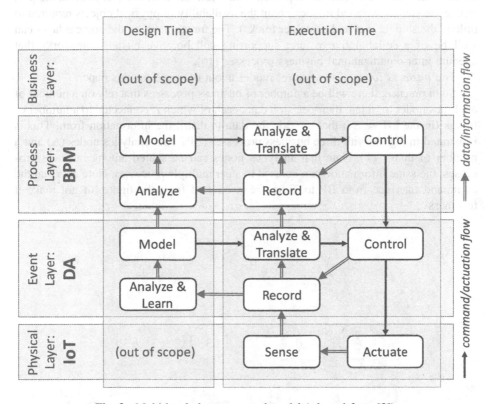

Fig. 2. Multi-level abstract control model (adapted from [2])

In the control model, we place IoT technology at the lowest of the four layers: the *physical layer*. This layer contains the physical objects, but also the low-level digital interfaces to sense and actuate them. In the processes described before in this paper, this layer is of a highly distributed nature, containing for example large numbers of smart sea containers being transported or connected patients being treated.

We place DA technology in the *event layer*. This is where data is received from the physical layer, recorded, analyzed and translated into decision information. This layer is also highly distributed - but possibly with fewer nodes than the physical layer: a single DA node may handle multiple IoT nodes. In container logistics, a DA node per container ship may process data from a set of IoT nodes (i.e., containers) on that ship to generate overall cargo characteristics of a transport order (for example, the average temperature or the average vibration measured by the sensors in the containers).

We place BPM technology in the *process layer*. This is where decisions are made about the execution of business processes, based on information from the DA layer - and information from non-physical sources, of course. In our container transport example, the process layer can receive information from a DA node on a ship about the status of the containers and the ship itself, and information from a DA node in the port where the ship is expected to dock about the availability of physical objects required to unload the ship (cranes and container trucks). The functionality in the process layer can well be of a collaborative nature, supporting collaborative business networks that execute inter-organizational business processes [16].

The *business layer* of the control model is out of scope for this paper.

So in practice, there will be a number of business processes that rely on a number of analytics nodes to obtain their decision data, each of which is connected to a number of things (in the IoT sense) that provide the data to distill the information from. This is illustrated in Fig. 3, with three business processes (BP), four analytics nodes (A) and a number of things (T). Note that analytics nodes can be shared among business processes: the same information can be used to steer multiple processes. Note also that the command interface from BP to T has been omitted from the figure, to not make it too messy.

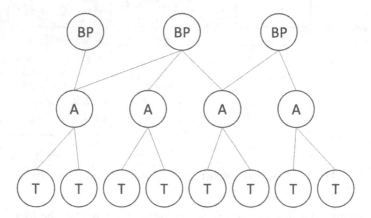

Fig. 3. Business processes, analytics nodes and things

We can make the abstract picture of Fig. 3 concrete by an application example from container transport that illustrates the complexity of a real-world situation. We have four processes: a shipping process at a freight forwarder, a transportation process at a shipping line, a trans-shipment process at a deep-sea terminal, and a transportation process at a trucking company. The involved things are: container ships, container trucks, reefer containers (transmitting information on status, including temperature), cranes at the terminal (one kind for unloading the ships, another kind for loading the trucks), and automated guided vehicles (AGVs) that take the container to/from temporary storage at the terminal. In this context, the following example analytics services can be deployed:

- Container monitoring: using data from the trucks, cranes and containers to check if the container is being handled properly (used primarily by freight forwarders);
- Location monitoring: using data from the ships and trucks to monitor the location of the container (used by shipping lines, trucking companies, freight forwarders);
- Storage monitoring: using data from cranes, AGVs, containers to monitor the status of the container in storage (used by freight forwarders, trucking companies – to check if the container can already be picked up, and terminals).

4 Discussion: State of the Art

The combination of BPM and IoT has already gained some attention in research and development [3, 6, 12, 21]. An example application domain is collaborative transport and logistics [14]. An analysis of potential benefits and important challenges has been published [3]. Analytics is mentioned in this analysis, but distributed analytics is not positioned explicitly as a third required technology domain here, however, to complement BPM and IoT. Business models for IoT have also been studied [6]. An integration of business processes, social networks, and Internet of Things into a single platform called Business-2-Social was also proposed [12].

The combination of IoT and (distributed) analytics has also received attention [17]. Platforms for the combination of the two domains are under development. The concept of *fog computing* (as a highly distributed, local version of *cloud computing*) plays a role here [18]. Making IoT-based analytics distributed in a structured way with explicit attention for BPM as required for our proposed trinity is a topic of research still, however.

The combination of BPM and analytics has received a great deal of attention already, mostly in the field of process mining [7]. Process mining, however, is mainly focused on redesigning business processes (i.e., on the *design time* column of Fig. 2), not on supporting decision making during execution of processes. Distribution aspects have not received much attention in process mining. A notable challenge in distributed process mining is the absence of a single notion of 'case' (i.e., process instance), such that it is difficult to discover the relations between process instances from different partners [8].

Supporting decision making is explicitly addressed in the machine learning (ML) field. Recent advances in deep learning methods (that can be seen as part of ML) allow building models with high predictive power from big data [4]. Transfer learning frameworks [9] can support distributed analytics. To support privacy preservation in ML, differential privacy techniques can be used [13]. Research on the link between ML and IoT is ongoing [5], but the ML field is not yet strongly connected to the BPM field.

5 Discussion: Challenges

From the discussion in the previous section, we can observe that some groundwork for our trinity is under development, but there is no complete framework yet for the entire concept. There are currently plenty of challenges, both from the application point of view, from the architecture point of view and from the technology point of view.

From the application point of view, granularity of things (again in the IoT sense) and related bundling and unbundling is an important and hard topic. Revisiting the container transport case, we can treat individual containers as things (which makes sense from say a temperature control perspective), but we can also treat a ship with 5000 containers on board as a thing (which makes sense from a location management perspective, as all containers move the same way while on board). These changes, however, once the containers get unloaded at the destination port, where they are each unloaded individually (unbundling), but may be regrouped again on trains or river barges (bundling). Another important issue is event binding: when an event is generated by a thing and processed by an analytic node, it is important to be able to relate the event to the right business process instance, and consequently to the right party in a collaborative logistics network. The exact way of event binding can be highly dependent on the application domain.

From an architecture point of view, there is an interesting question: does a three-layer model suffice? Given Fig. 3, it may make sense to have multiple analytics layers between the things and the business process layer, certainly if the number of things is very large. To illustrate numbers using our sea container example: in 2016, the Port of Rotterdam handled approximately 7.4 million sea containers [10] and a single large container ship can transport over 20,000 TEU (Twenty Foot Equivalent Unit) [19], or over 10,000 large sea containers. Using multiple DA layers in the systems view allows for computation load distribution by increasing parallelism in analytical processing. Using multiple DA layers also allows to have multiple layers of data privacy and hence more flexibility in collaborative data sharing between organizations. In the container example, we may want (i) one privacy layer in which all details of individual containers are visible (but not shared); (ii) one layer in which detailed handling data are visible (and shared between specific collaborating transport parties) but not the details on the contents of the containers (as these may be of a competitive nature for the owners of the goods); (iii) one layer in which aggregated handling data are visible on a per-ship basis (and shared with all partners in a collaborative network); and (iv) one layer in which aggregated handling data are visible only on the overall port level (and are completely public).

From the technology point of view, there are several issues to be addressed. One important issue is the dynamic deployment of analytics functionality from the process layer to the distributed analytics layer. In other words: when the BPM layer requires specific information or specific triggers, there is a need to instruct the DA layer about this. This can be done by deploying analytics code into the DA layer, which may in turn need to deploy code in the IoT layer. Certainly, in a multi-layer model as discussed above, there are plenty of questions to be answered here. Note that additional complexity is introduced if the involved BPM and DA/IoT nodes are owned by different partners in a collaborative business network: specific privacy and security issues will need to be addressed.

A final challenge that we want to briefly discuss here is the use of BPM for managing 'traditional' business processes (i.e., business processes that directly serve customers) versus the use of BPM for learning processes in our trinity framework. When we use BPM for managing customer-oriented business processes, we assume the existence of appropriate analytics models to be deployed in the DA and IoT layers. Where these models do not yet exist (i.e., the parameters of models still have to be learned), BPM can also be used to manage the distributed learning process. In this case, the complex deployment process of iterative distributed learning is managed by a process engine. Obviously, both uses of BPM can be combined in complex, collaborative application scenarios - but the ways to model, deploy and execute this imply open research questions at this point.

6 Conclusions

In this position paper, we present a view on an integration of business process management, distributed analytics and internet of things technology. This integration is required to effectively and efficiently manage complex, distributed, collaborative business processes that have a real-time, data-intensive character in handling physical objects.

We are convinced that more and more 'physical' processes will evolve in this direction, in many collaborative application domains. An example is urban mobility [15], where a business domain of 'just' operating rather isolated fixed lines of public transport (without much notion of individual travelers and real-time circumstances) is transforming into real-time, collaborative travel management on a mass-customized basis.

The conceptual trinity model of BPM, IoT and DA and its operationalization into an abstract control model are merely the start of thinking about a structural integration of the three technology domains towards the support of complex collaboration networks in various business domains. As we have pointed out, there are plenty of challenges to overcome and questions to be answered by research. We have identified the following questions in this paper:

- How can we deal with the granularity of IoT things handled in collaborative business processes, certainly in the context of bundling and unbundling?
- Is a single DA layer sufficient in the proposed control model, or should be have multiple DA layers to support multiple privacy levels and increased parallelism?
- How do we dynamically deploy analytics functionality in a structured (and standardized) way from the BPM to the DA and IoT layers? In a collaborative business network, how to do this when the involved nodes belong to different partners?
- How do we combine knowledge management processes (like advanced federated learning) with operational business processes, both in modeling and enactment?

Acknowledgments. The ideas presented in this position paper are based on current collaboration between Eindhoven University of Technology and IBM Research Almaden. The European Supply Chain Forum is acknowledged for partly financing this collaboration.

References

1. Industrie 4.0: Smart Manufacturing for the Future. Germany Trade & Invest (2014)
2. Grefen, P., Eshuis, R., Turetken, O., Vanderfeesten, I.: A Reference Framework for Advanced Flexible Information Systems. In: Matulevičius, R., Dijkman, R. (eds.) CAiSE 2018. LNBIP, vol. 316, pp. 253–264. Springer, Cham (2018). https://doi.org/10.1007/978-3-319-92898-2_21
3. Janiesch, C., et al.: The Internet-of-Things Meets Business Process Management: Mutual Benefits and Challenges. arXiv:1709.03628 (2017)
4. Schmidhuber, J.: Deep learning in neural networks: an overview. Neural Networks **61**, 85–117 (2015)
5. Mohammadi, M., Al-Fuqaha, A., Sorour, S., Guizan, M.: Deep learning for IoT Big Data and streaming analytics: a survey. arXiv:1712.04301 (2017)
6. Dijkman, R.M., Sprenkels, B., Peeters, T., Janssen, A.: Business models for the internet of things. Int. J. Inf. Manag. **35**(6), 672–678 (2015)
7. van der Aalst, W.: Process Mining: Discovery, Conformance and Enhancement of Business Processes. Springer, Heidelberg (2011). https://doi.org/10.1007/978-3-662-49851-4
8. Pourmirza, S., Dijkman, R.M., Grefen, P.W.P.J.: Correlation miner: mining business process models and causal relations without case identifiers. Int. J. Coop. Inf. Syst. **26**(2), 32 (2017)
9. Yosinski, J., Clune, J., Bengio, Y., Lipson, H.: How transferable are features in deep neural networks? arXiv:1411.1792 (2014)
10. Port of Rotterdam. Facts & Figures, A Wealth of Information, Make it Happen (2017)
11. Bhakoo, V., Chan, C.: Collaborative implementation of e-business processes within the health-care supply chain: the monash pharmacy project. Supply Chain Manag. **16**(3), 184–193 (2011)
12. Ugljanin, E., et al.: Re-engineering of smart city's business processes based on social network and internet of things. Autom. Control Robot. **16**(3), 275–286 (2017)
13. Hall, R., Rinaldo, A., Wasserman, L.: Differential privacy for functions and functional data. arXiv:1203.2570 (2012)
14. Baumgraß, A., Dijkman, R., Grefen, P., Pourmirza, S., Völzer, H., Weske, M.: A software architecture for transportation planning and monitoring in a collaborative network. In: Camarinha-Matos, Luis M., Bénaben, F., Picard, W. (eds.) PRO-VE 2015. IAICT, vol. 463, pp. 277–284. Springer, Cham (2015). https://doi.org/10.1007/978-3-319-24141-8_25
15. Grefen, P., Turetken, O., Traganos, K., den Hollander, A., Eshuis, R.: Creating agility in traffic management by collaborative service-dominant business engineering. In: Camarinha-Matos, Luis M., Bénaben, F., Picard, W. (eds.) PRO-VE 2015. IAICT, vol. 463, pp. 100–109. Springer, Cham (2015). https://doi.org/10.1007/978-3-319-24141-8_9
16. Grefen, P., Eshuis, R., Mehandjiev, N., Kouvas, G., Weichhart, G.: Internet-based support for process-oriented instant virtual enterprises. IEEE Internet Comput. **13**(6), 65–73 (2009)
17. Escamilla-Ambrosio, P.J., Rodríguez-Mota, A., Aguirre-Anaya, E., Acosta-Bermejo, R., Salinas-Rosales, M.: Distributing Computing in the internet of things: cloud, fog and edge computing overview. In: Maldonado, Y., Trujillo, L., Schütze, O., Riccardi, A., Vasile, M. (eds.) NEO 2016. SCI, vol. 731, pp. 87–115. Springer, Cham (2018). https://doi.org/10.1007/978-3-319-64063-1_4

18. Bonomi, F., Milito, R., Natarajan, P., Zhu, J.: Fog computing: a platform for internet of things and analytics. In: Bessis, N., Dobre, C. (eds.) Big Data and Internet of Things: A Roadmap for Smart Environments. SCI, vol. 546, pp. 169–186. Springer, Cham (2014). https://doi.org/10.1007/978-3-319-05029-4_7
19. World's Biggest Container Ships in 2017. Marine Insight (2017). https://www.marineinsight.com/know-more/10-worlds-biggest-container-ships-2017/ (Inspected May 2018)
20. Li, S., Da Xu, L., Zhao, S.: The Internet of Things: a survey. Inf. Syst. Front. 17(2), 243–259 (2015)
21. Meyer, S., Ruppen, A., Hilty, L.: The things of the internet of things in BPMN. In: Persson, A., Stirna, J. (eds.) CAiSE 2015. LNBIP, vol. 215, pp. 285–297. Springer, Cham (2015). https://doi.org/10.1007/978-3-319-19243-7_27

Collaboration Platform Issues

Using Chatbots to Assist Communication in Collaborative Networks

Christian Frommert(✉), Anna Häfner(✉), Julia Friedrich(✉), and Christian Zinke(✉)

Institute for Applied Informatics e.V., University of Leipzig, 04109 Leipzig, Germany
{frommert,haefner,friedrich,zinke}@infai.org

Abstract. Novel technological possibilities enable a better communication and knowledge exchange within collaborative networks. The paper indicates that the potential of enterprise social network is by far not exploited yet. Although systems are connected to each other, and the conditions for frictionless data exchange are created, there is a lack of flexible possibilities to use the data stock within the network efficiently and user-friendly. Chatbots provide a possibility to meet this challenge. Nowadays, chatbots are used to improve customer communication and simplify the daily routine in consumers' lives. Within collaborative networks, their use and benefits had not been fully discovered yet. This paper examines current chatbot technologies and implements a use case driven prototype to show the benefits of chatbots within enterprise social networks for (internal) communication by smart combining data across collaborative networks.

Keywords: Chatbot · Enterprise Social Network · Natural Language Processing
Virtual assistant

1 Introduction

The creation and extension of collaborative networks (CNs) are mainly driven by novel technologies and have various forms, like virtual organizations or virtual enterprises [1]. In general, CNs include a variety of stakeholders. Their goals and culture may differ, but their efforts are always characterized by the endeavor to improve networking and collaboration among a variety of entities, human or organizational [1, 2]. The success of such CNs is highly dependent on knowledge exchange and management, which can be technically supported by Enterprise Social Networks (ESNs) [4]. The problem is that even successfully implemented ESNs are mostly not well connected to daily work organization and work, e.g., knowledge discovery, with limited interaction and communication possibilities to other systems. As an example, a social network (e.g., HumHub), an authentication service (e.g., LDAP) and a calendar service (e.g., Google calendar) may be integrated; still, this does not necessarily mean there is a flexible interaction process between them based on unstandardized user input, e.g., in natural language (which is even prevalent in ESNs).

Natural language based assistance systems in consumer space like Siri, Alexa, Cortana and Google Assistant are actively developed and widely used [3]. Consumers

© IFIP International Federation for Information Processing 2018
Published by Springer Nature Switzerland AG 2018. All Rights Reserved
L. M. Camarinha-Matos et al. (Eds.): PRO-VE 2018, IFIP AICT 534, pp. 257–265, 2018.
https://doi.org/10.1007/978-3-319-99127-6_22

can let assistance systems take care of simple processes and automate routines using bots and smart home technologies. They offer interconnectivity with consumer services like calendar, music services or shopping. In the context of smart home, people are using these bots to have everyday tasks in their household managed, while in the business context bots are mainly used for marketing purposes and to respond customers' requests [5]. The potential of bots, concretely chatbots, for knowledge exchange and collaboration within CNs is not adequately addressed, up to now. To change this situation, the paper has three goals:

- Give an overview of current chatbot engines and their states
- Design a solution for better interaction and knowledge exchange within CNs
- Implement a chatbot into two use-cases with reference character to show the main benefits.

2 Theoretical Background

To examine how chatbots could operate inside companies, basic knowledge of the interaction platforms (ESN), the technology to let bots interact with human users in their natural language (Natural Language Processing) and the working method of chatbots themselves is required.

Enterprise Social Networks (ESN) are web-based platforms which allow users to contribute persistent objects to a shared pool. This shared pool may the technical backbone for collaboration within CNs. Company users can be allowed to respond to those objects (interaction). Also, profile information can be presented, and employees can be connected using features like a "Following" system and friendship requests. Examples of ESN include platforms like weblogs, wikis, microblogs and social networking platforms [6]. Usually, ESN does not provide public access. The access is usually limited to a company or CN via the Intranet. Integrated applications and external services extend the ESN by providing for example a survey tool (e.g. Humhub Polls [7]), a calendar (e.g. by integrating Google Calendar with Automate.io [8]), a file and document management tool (e.g. Humhub Files [9]), a project and task management system (e.g. by integrating Trello via Unito [10]), a customer relationship management system (e.g. by integrating Salesforce in Slack [11]) and many more.

"**Natural Language Processing** (NLP) is a theory-motivated range of computational techniques for the automatic analysis and representation of human language." [12] It is differentiated in Natural Language Understanding (NLU), which turns natural language into structured data, and Natural Language Generation, which creates a natural language out of structured data [13]. To create a dialogue representation, the use of NLU is needed. With the help of pruning, stemming and part-of-speech tagging a text representation is created, which can be classified to so-called intents ("intent classification"). Additionally, user-specific objects (entities) can be extracted. This process is known as Named-Entity Recognition (NER) [14].

Chatbots are text-based software systems that interact with human users in their natural language and make decisions based on predefined rules [15]. They include an interpreter, which analyzes incoming messages, and a key-value memory to store user-specific information. With the use of a chatbot scripting language [16], like AIML [17], it is possible to define the logic of the chatbot by assigning actions to input patterns. Chatbot engines are development tools used to create chatbots [18].

The use of an ESN as communication interface allows for a translation of user sentences into machine code (by using NLP). Instructions can be executed by a chatbot to automate complex tasks or give adequate answers by combining several data sources. In summary, chatbots enable a novel form of interaction within ESNs and therefore new collaboration patterns in CNs.

3 Methodology

For the presented research, a design-oriented approach [19] was chosen. The fundamental paradigm of the Design Science Research (DSR) is constructive with the aim to design, build and reflect artifacts [22][1]. Therefore, in computer science a generative procedure has been developed by Pfeffers [19], containing four steps: the problem description, the objectives' development, the design of an artifact and the evaluation of this artifact. This overall problem and the objectives (especially for this paper) are already described in Sect. 1. To design a solution for the given problem, three main tasks were faced: At first, the current state of chatbot technologies was evaluated. Secondly, two use cases, which stand prototypically for the given problem and can be assisted by using a chatbot, were defined. As the last step, a chatbot which is fulfilling the use cases was implemented.

To identify an appropriate chatbot, that is suitable for the integration into ESN current chatbot solutions were evaluated and compared to each other, using Google and Github search, Chatbots Magazine [20] and the corresponding documentation of the found chatbots. Only chatbots with a working website and activity within the last two years were listed. The evaluation had two main steps. Firstly, the bots were evaluated by the criteria architecture (on-premise/SaaS), interconnection possibilities (plugin model) and license model. As the chatbot should be used in commercial space with sensitive data, it is essential that no company data be transferred to other companies. Therefore, Software-as-a-Service and Closed-Source solutions were voted out. Since the solution should be deployed within the company's ESN, it has to be interconnectable to various services. Hence, chatbots without options to access other services via a plugin model were also excluded. In a second step open source, on-premise and extendible chatbots were compared regarding the development progress and state, availability and quality of documentation, availability of a RESTful API, NLU and chatbot scripting language support as well as context sensitivity.

After choosing a suitable chatbot solution, the use cases will be presented. The use cases are developed as exemplary showcases for the benefits of chatbots within ESNs. For the implementation, some preconditions were assumed. The initial situation is a CN which has

---

[1] These artefacts are designed to solve human problems. The aim is to develop an artefact, which is "by definition, a purposeful IT artifact created to address an important organizational problem" [23].

successfully implemented an ESN accompanied by an appropriate (internal) social media strategy. Exemplarily, we have chosen the social network Humhub, as it is a well-known open-source, modular ESN solution. The implementation uses ESN data sources, like user profiles and calendar information, as well as generic business data which are provided by other tools like an Active Directory. Because of Humhub's lack of a RESTful API, a Middleware[2] has been implemented to guarantee the communication between the chosen Chatbot and Humhub as well as the possibility to connect more data sources.

4   Evaluation of Chatbot Engines

Overall 21 chatbot solutions have been evaluated. Table 1 shows the classification of chatbots regarding their architecture (on-premise/SaaS), interconnection possibilities

Table 1. Comparison of Chatbot Engine

Chatbot Engine Name	On-Premise Architecture	Open Source	Plugin Model	Version	Last Update	NLU Support	Chatbot Scripting Language Support	REST API	Context Sensitive	Quality of Documentation
Botkit	X	X	X	0.6.13	04/2018	X	Proprietary, RiveScript	-	X	+
Botpress	X	X	X	1.1.13	03/2018	-	Proprietary	-	X	++
Bottr	X	X	X	0.1.6	11/2016	-	-	-	-	+
Chatfuel	-	-	-							
ChatScript	X	X	-							
Chatterbot	X	X	X	0.8.5	03/2018	X	Proprietary	-	X	++
Dexter	-	-	-							
Dialogflow	-	-	-							
E.D.D.I.	X	X	X	4.3.0	04/2018	-	-	X	X	+
Errbot	X	X	X	5.1.3	04/2018	-	Proprietary	-	X	+
Facebook Bots	-	-	-							
Hubot	X	X	X	3.0.1	02/2018	-	-	-	-	+
IBM Watson Conversation Service	-[1]	-	X							
IKY	X	X	X	1.0	03/2018	-	-	X	-	-
Lita	X	X	X	5.0.0	02/2018	-	-	-	-	+
Microsoft Bot Framework	-[1]	X	X							
Pandorabots	-	-	-							
Program-O	X	X	-							
Rasa Core	X	X	X	0.8.5	04/2018	X	Proprietary	X	X	++
Rebot	-	-	-							
wit.ai	-	-	X							

[1] Chatbot on-premise, Chatbot-Framework SaaS (Interpreter, Key-Value-Store)
[2] No Plugin-System, needs Middleware

Table as of: April 2018

---

2 https://github.com/DServSys/Rasahub.

(plugin model) and license model. Eleven of these solutions have been voted out in the first run. Only ten solutions were open source, on-premise, and extendible chatbots. In the second round and based on the presented requirements and conditions, Rasa Core was chosen as a suitable chatbot engine as it fits best to all conditions. It is an open source, highly developed and well-documented software. Also, Rasa Core integrates well with Rasa NLU regarding the classification of intents and the extraction of entities from input sentences.

5 Chatbot Implementation for ESN

After choosing a suitable chatbot, the concrete use cases have been developed to test if chatbots can improve the interaction within CNs.

5.1 Use Cases

Use Case One deals with the problem of finding an available appointment among multiple employees. In a conversation between two or more employees, it should be possible to trigger the bot to search for an available appointment in a specific timeframe and other conditions (like free rooms or other persons). Up to now, this case is a typical example for high-effort (manual) tasks. The most common way is to start a process of appointment finding, where one leader sets different time slots for a vote. All participants have to choose sufficient time slots. After voting, the leader needs to take action, set a calendar appointment, with integrated room booking, or needs to start the process of booking a room within the CN. The goal is to reduce these unnecessary efforts and interactions. Within the first conversation, the bot should collect all necessary information and present all available appointments. If the employee accepts the suggested time, a new calendar entry will be made for all involved persons (and rooms). The use case as it is shown in Fig. 1 illustrates the benefits of chatbots for organizational processes as it combines data from several users to make an intelligent suggestion.

Use Case Two is the search for employees with specific competences within the company network to support knowledge exchange and agile resource sourcing within CNs. Thus, the leading question of the specific use case was how to improve the discovery of competences and know-how besides a long non-interactive list of central administered (silo mentality) organigram. To search for a specific task or know-how and get a matching competence and people, it was necessary to represent the company's structure as a graph and assign synonyms. Furthermore, it was necessary to link tasks to each department. Moreover, the idea of ESNs is to empower the user, to provide their description of competencies to push individualism and motivation. In productive implementations, it would also be possible only to return colleagues who are online (for faster workflow, if privacy conditions allow that). Those and the input sentences should be stemmed to match each other using the Python NLTK package. This way, the transferring processes and permanent availability of business knowledge can be improved.

5.2   Proof of Concept

To pursue the defined goal and show the benefits of an integration of a chatbot within an ESN and the according to the connection of different data sources, the two use cases were implemented by using Rasa Core. In the domain file all user intents and entities, message templates, slots and bot actions were listed. Rasa Core needs multiple training data for input classification, meaning a minimum of ten sentence samples for each intent is needed. Also, dialogue modelling is required, which means that each possible route should be defined. Figure 2 provides a visualization of the dialogue model for use case one. User intents are painted blue, while bot actions are shown with a white background.

The implemented chatbot communicates with the user through Humhub Mail. With the calendar use-case, it is possible to ask for an appointment on a specific date or time frame, and the desired duration of the appointment. An NER tool, to extract the necessary time information, is Duckling [21]. Optional properties are additional participants and a meeting room that shall be booked. After collecting all information, the calendars of the persons in the conversation (and possible additional participants) and the room are accessed and matched together to find a suitable time frame for an appointment, which suits all participants. The first feasible time frame found, will be communicated to the conversation. If it is accepted by a participant, the chatbot is booking the appointments to all participants' calendars. If the time frame is declined, another suitable appointment proposal will be made.

The search for a colleague with desired competencies and know how who, e.g., can help regarding a specific problem, is addressed in use case two. As an example, an employee has a question regarding his paycheck, and a responsible payroll employee could help him. The common approach to identify a person that could be helpful for a

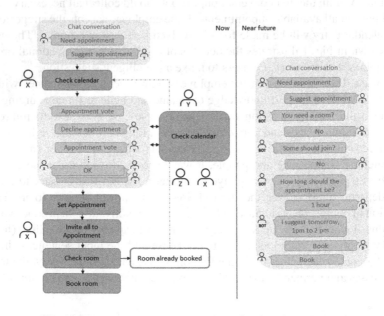

Fig. 1. The organizational process to find a shared appointment

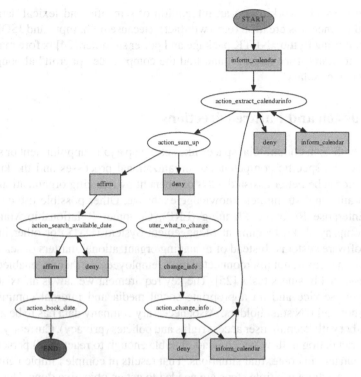

Fig. 2. Dialogue model of the implemented calendar chatbot

specific problem is to search the employee list, ask a colleague or send a broadcast message to all employees. With the help of a chatbot, the needed information could be presented immediately by connecting both employees (as it is shown in Fig. 3). The asking employee tells the chatbot: "I have a problem regarding my paycheck.". Paycheck is a synonym for payroll, and another employee is assigned the competence "payroll". The chatbot is automatically detecting "paycheck" with the synonym "payroll" and is looking for a person with this competence. If no employee with a matching competence was found, it would be possible to search a higher organizational level within the company's structure for "payroll" (like Human Resources department). This is possible as the chatbot was implemented using a JSON description and can be combined with the online-state of the employees.

Fig. 3. Use case two. Identifying competence

We are currently working on an integration of semantic and lexical databases to automate the synonyms creation (e.g., wordnet). Because both, input and JSON model, are stemmed using Python NLTK package and porter stemmer [24] before matching, it is possible to search for "salaries" and find the competence "payroll" although it was only assigned to "salary".

6 Discussion and Future Directions

By using chatbots in commercial spaces like setting up a joint appointment or searching for persons with specific competencies, organizational processes and the knowledge management can be better assisted. CNs can benefit by reducing organizational efforts of collaboration and strengthen knowledge exchange. Other possible use cases could involve Enterprise Resource Planning (ERP), Customer Relationship Management (CRM), company Wiki, Document Management System (DMS) or other internal or external software systems. Instead of managing organizational matters or searching for information in various, not interconnected tools, employees are thereby enabled to focus on more essential business tasks [25]. The key requirement we saw is an existing ESN or messaging service and an appropriate social media and internal communication strategy among all CN stakeholders. Also, necessary company data has to be accessible by the chatbot with keeping user access rights and policies (privacy). Currently, the main flaw is a strict dialogue flow which is not flexible enough to react to all person's interactions accurately in contextual situations. That results in complex implementations of essential tasks, where multiple steps are needed to get an objective done. Hence, many training data is needed to keep up a natural language message flow and enable the chatbot to react to messages which differ from the trained paths. Reinforcement learning could be a way to enable the chatbot to make more intelligent decisions [26]. In the future, using better machine learning algorithms, more company data, better interpreters and dialogue models, the user experience will improve more and more. With the rise of data producing wearables like smart glasses, it is imaginable, that future chatbots will make use of these data and at this moment help it react to individual requests in a better way. In regards to the Industrial Internet of Things (IIoT), workers need to operate with more complex machines while the cognitive performance of humans will remain consistent. As a result assistance systems like chatbots will be imperative.

References

1. Camarinha-Matos, L.M., Afsarmanesh, H.: Collaborative networks a new scientific discipline. J. Intell. Manuf. **16**(4–5), 439–452 (2005). https://doi.org/10.1007/s10845-005-1656-3
2. Camarinha-Matos, L.M., Afsarmanesh, H.: On reference models for collaborative networked organizations. Int. J. Prod. Res. **46**(9), 2453–2469 (2008). https://doi.org/10.1080/00207540701737666
3. Dale, R.: The return of the chatbots. Nat. Lang. Eng. **22**, 811–817 (2016). https://doi.org/10.1017/S1351324916000243

4. Zinke, C., Friedrich, J.: Digital social learning – how to enhance serious gaming for collaborative networks. In: Camarinha-Matos, L.M., Afsarmanesh, H., Fornasiero, R. (eds.) PRO-VE 2017. IFIPAICT, vol. 506, pp. 669–677. Springer, Cham (2017). https://doi.org/10.1007/978-3-319-65151-4_59

5. Cui, L., Huang, S., Wei, F., Tan, C., Duan, C., Zhou, M.: SuperAgent: a customer service chatbot for e-commerce websites. In: Bansal, M., Ji, H. (eds.) Proceedings of ACL 2017, System Demonstrations. Proceedings of ACL 2017, System Demonstrations, Vancouver, Canada, 01 July 2017, pp. 97–102. Association for Computational Linguistics, Stroudsburg (2017). https://doi.org/10.18653/v1/p17-4017

6. Behrendt, S., Richter, A., Trier, M.: Mixed methods analysis of enterprise social networks. Comput. Netw. **75**, 560–577 (2014). https://doi.org/10.1016/j.comnet.2014.08.025

7. HumHub Polls. https://www.humhub.org/de/marketplace/details?id=3

8. Automate.io: https://automate.io/integrations

9. HumHub Files. https://www.humhub.org/de/marketplace/details?id=25

10. unito. https://unito.io/

11. Coenraets, C.: Slack and Salesforce Integration. http://coenraets.org/blog/2016/01/slack-salesforce-integration/ (2016)

12. Cambria, E., White, B.: Jumping NLP curves: a review of natural language processing research [review article]. IEEE Comput. Intell. Mag. **9**, 48–57 (2014). https://doi.org/10.1109/MCI.2014.2307227

13. Liddy, E.: Natural language processing. In: Encyclopedia of Library and Information Science, 2nd edn. Marcel Decker, Inc, New York (2001)

14. Mohit, B.: Named entity recognition. In: Zitouni, I. (ed.) Natural Language Processing of Semitic Languages. TANLP, pp. 221–245. Springer, Heidelberg (2014). https://doi.org/10.1007/978-3-642-45358-8_7

15. Shawar, B.A., Atwell, E.: Different measurements metrics to evaluate a chatbot system. In: Proceedings of the Workshop on Bridging the Gap: Academic and Industrial Research in Dialog Technologies, pp. 89–96. Association for Computational Linguistics, Stroudsburg (2007)

16. Cahn, J.: CHATBOT: Architecture, design, and development. Ph. D. Dissertation, University of Pennsylvania (2017)

17. Marietto, M.d.G.B., et al.: Artificial Intelligence MArkup Language: A Brief Tutorial (2013)

18. Shawar, B.A., Atwell, E.: Accessing an information system by chatting. In: Meziane, F., Métais, E. (eds.) NLDB 2004. LNCS, vol. 3136, pp. 407–412. Springer, Heidelberg (2004). https://doi.org/10.1007/978-3-540-27779-8_39

19. Peffers, K., Tuunanen, T., Rothenberger, M.A., Chatterjee, S.: A design science research methodology for information systems research. J. Manag. Inf. Syst. **24**, 45–77 (2007). https://doi.org/10.2753/MIS0742-1222240302

20. Chatbots Magazine. https://chatbotsmagazine.com/

21. Duckling. https://duckling.wit.ai/

22. March, S.T., Smith, G.F.: Design and natural science research on information technology. Decis. Support Syst. **15**, 251–266 (1995). https://doi.org/10.1016/0167-9236(94)00041-2

23. Vaishnavi, V., Kuechler, W.: Design Research in Information Systems (2004)

24. Porter, M.F.: An algorithm for suffix stripping. Program **14**, 130–137 (1980). https://doi.org/10.1108/eb046814

25. Morana, S., Friemel, C., Gnewuch, U., Maedche, A., Pfeiffer, J.: Interaktion mit smarten Systemen — Aktueller Stand und zukünftige Entwicklungen im Bereich der Nutzerassistenz. Wirtsch. Manag. (2017). https://doi.org/10.1007/s35764-017-0101-7

26. Serban, I.V., et al.: A Deep Reinforcement Learning Chatbot. CoRR abs/1709.02349 (2017)

Exploring the CIMO-Logic in the Design of Collaborative Networks Mediated by Digital Platforms

Eric Costa[1,2(✉)], António Lucas Soares[2,3],
and Jorge Pinho de Sousa[2,3]

[1] Research, Innovation and Enterprise, Solent University, East Park Terrace,
Southampton SO14 0YN, UK
eric.costa@solent.ac.uk
[2] INESC TEC – INESC Technology and Science,
Campus da FEUP, Rua Dr. Roberto Frias 378, 4200-465 Porto, Portugal
als@fe.up.pt, jsousa@inesctec.pt
[3] FEUP – Faculty of Engineering, University of Porto,
Rua Dr. Roberto Frias S/N, 4200-465 Porto, Portugal

Abstract. Collaborative networks (CNs) of organizations are nowadays complex and intertwined compositions of technological, cognitive and social artifacts. The design of such compositions should be addressed as a socio-technical endeavor as a way to maximize the success probability. In despite of intensive research in this community, much has to be explored to achieve sound contributions to a design theory of CNs. In this paper, we make use of the context-intervention-mechanism-outcome logic (CIMO-logic) as a way to improve the design propositions component of a CN design theory. Variations of the concept of "mechanism" are explored with the goal of making clearer the socio-technical perspective in the design propositions. This theoretical exploration is illustrated with a case of transforming an industrial business association (IBA) in a digital collaborative network.

Keywords: Collaborative networks · Design theory · Socio-technical systems
CIMO-logic · Digital platforms

1 Introduction

Digital platforms (DPs) play a fundamental role in today's connected and data-rich society supporting information sharing, collaboration and collective action [1], in cooperation settings such as online communities or enterprise networks. In the business domain, DPs have been fundamental for organizational strategies, strongly relying on formal and informal relationships with other entities, with variations of DPs being designed and developed to improve the management of processes and activities, in particular supporting collaboration and information management [2, 3]. Notwithstanding this development, the full potential of DPs is far from being released or even acknowledged by the individual companies or business networks [4]. The reason for this lies in two interrelated challenges: on the one hand, in the intrinsic organizational

© IFIP International Federation for Information Processing 2018
Published by Springer Nature Switzerland AG 2018. All Rights Reserved
L. M. Camarinha-Matos et al. (Eds.): PRO-VE 2018, IFIP AICT 534, pp. 266–277, 2018.
https://doi.org/10.1007/978-3-319-99127-6_23

and managerial complexity in implementing collaboration-based inter-organizational structures and behaviors [5] and, on the other hand, in the lack of guidance in the design and implementation of DPs as socio-technical systems [6].

Design Science Research (DSR) is a research paradigm that has been used in research for the construction of viable and innovative artifacts [7]. An artifact can take many forms. It can be a conceptual artifact, represented by a method, model or framework [8], or it can also represent design theories and design principles [9], algorithms and guidelines. The main strengths of DSR are the focus on the creation of artifacts for addressing unsolved problems in organizations [7, 8], the rigorous evaluation of these artifacts [10], and the contribution with new knowledge to the body of scientific evidence [11].

Design propositions represent another type of artifact in DSR [12]. Design propositions are used mainly in business and management studies to obtain prescriptive knowledge and design principles, helping people and organizations to solve specific field problems [13]. The CIMO-logic is a framework that was first proposed by Denyer et al. [14] to help in the development of more rigorous design propositions. The definition of these four components in each design proposition allows for a better understanding and agreement between the design team, who wants to propose some interventions to a specific problem faced by an organization, and the practitioners, who want to have their problems solved.

The current literature of CIMO shows the applicability of this prescriptive framework in different organizational and societal contexts, such as organization and management studies [14], community building in education [15], and business models for sustainability [16]. However, the research problem that is posed now is related with the current discrepancies in previous CIMO-logic studies, where we can find different interpretations or a lack of understanding about the meaning of each component of CIMO. On the one hand, the fact of existing different interpretations of the CIMO-logic is good because it allows to obtain insightful discussions among the research community and for the sake of progression of this specific framework. On the other hand, the vastness of versions for the CIMO-logic that we can find in the literature also causes additional difficulties for both current and new researchers that want to use this framework in their research projects, creating problems as well for obtaining a more agreed and unified version.

It is not the aim of this paper to provide this unified version for the meaning of each component that integrates the CIMO-logic. The paper's goal is to instead present and discuss different interpretations and versions of the application of CIMO in various research contexts, which may contribute to a further detailed extension of this research in a different study. To achieve that, we first analyze the current CIMO literature and present some particular applications. After that, we use our own data from a previous research project to present a case study with two different interpretations/versions for the application of this prescriptive framework, having as a context, the design of CNs mediated by DPs.

With this paper we hope to provide a perceptive discussion about the CIMO-logic, helping to clarify the components that make up this prescriptive framework. Another contribution of this paper is to show the importance of using the CIMO-logic to obtain more rigorous design propositions, as innovative DSR artifacts. We also expect that the findings of this paper can support researchers to co-design more effective CNs, socio-technical systems, and cognitive systems, by using the CIMO-logic.

2 CIMO-Logic

2.1 Design Propositions and the CIMO-Logic Components

Denyer et al. [14] present an extension of the so-called CIMO-logic as a discussion of prescriptive knowledge in the form of design propositions. The CIMO-logic allows to obtain a systematic structure for the propositions, combining problematic Contexts with certain Intervention types, which follow determined generative Mechanisms, to deliver specific Outcomes. Therefore, design principles that are formulated according to CIMO-logic indicate what to do, in which situations, to produce what effect, and offer understanding of why this happens [13, 14]. Table 1 describes in detail each component of the CIMO-logic for constructing design propositions.

Table 1. Components of the CIMO-logic for the design propositions [14, 15, 17]

Component	Description
C - Context	The results that human actors aim to achieve and the surrounding (external and internal environment) factors that influence the actors
I - Interventions	Purposeful actions or measures (products, processes, services or activities) that are formulated by the designer or design team to solve a design problem or need, and to influence outcomes
M - Mechanisms	The mechanism that is triggered by the intervention, in a certain context, by indicating why the intervention produces a certain outcome. It can be an explanation of the cognitive processes (reasoning) that actors use to choose their response to the intervention and their ability (resources) to put the intervention into practice
O - Outcome	Result of the interventions in its various aspects

Design propositions represent one of the key knowledge products of DSR [13]. According to van Aken [12], rigorous design propositions need to be (i) field-tested, to allow obtaining evidence about the practicability of the design position in a specific context, and (ii) grounded, to help explaining the reasons for a determined action to origins the desired outcome in the intended context. Accordingly, van Aken et al. [18] show that the main product of DSR in operations management is the creation of innovative generic design that has been well-tested, well-understood and well-documented, to establish pragmatic validity. This generic design is supported by the design propositions, in order to understand where and how it can be used in the field.

2.2 CIMO-Logic Applications

Previous literature shows that CIMO has been applied in different contexts, mainly for performing research syntheses and for the creation of solutions to address and solve specific field problems, by developing design propositions. Table 2 presents a summary of different case applications of the CIMO-logic. Only papers that have a clear specification and separation of each CIMO component were included in this summary. These cases were selected to provide a comparison and a better understanding on how previous studies have been addressing this prescriptive framework.

3 Case Study

3.1 Case Description and Research Methodology

Our case study is focused on improving the role of industrial business associations (IBAs), with the use of DPs, to provide a better support to the internationalization of small and medium enterprises (SMEs). The ultimate goal is to transform IBAs in effective digitally enabled CNs.

A digital platform is defined by Spagnoletti et al. [1] as "*a building block that provides an essential function to a technological system and serves as a foundation upon which complementary products, technologies, or services can be developed*". Spagnoletti et al. [1] suggest that, to be effective, DPs should support the mix of three types of social interaction mechanisms for online communities: (i) information sharing, where free participation is allowed and actors make their own contents available on the internet and available to all members; (ii) collaboration, where actors follow rules and engage in activities that require group coordination, and participants adapt their behavior to others; and (iii) collective action, where a close coordination is required with actors following a common goal and standing by common rules, and decisions made by group members prevail over personal interests.

Accordingly, a digital transformation of IBAs was suggested, by proposing the adoption of DPs that can foster CNs and facilitate the three types of social interaction structures: information sharing, collaboration, and collective action. Following a DSR approach, these suggestions for improvement were defined in the form of design propositions (our artifact) with the help of the CIMO-logic. Therefore, the design propositions were developed to obtain detailed requirements and features for DPs supporting the internationalization of SMEs, situated in the specific context of IBAs.

These design propositions represent prescriptive knowledge and are regarded as mid-range theory, positioned between the case-specific and the universal [18].

To develop the design propositions, we have used both knowledge from practice and from theory, in order to obtain more robust design propositions that are field-tested and grounded [12]. The practical knowledge was obtained from different empirical studies that we have been performing in a specific research project. Results of these empirical studies can be found in [24–26]. Following a DSR approach, the aim of this project was to study and design new collaboration and information management socio-technical solutions to improve the institutional network support provided by IBAs to the internationalization of SMEs. The data collection was mainly based on interviews with IBAs and SMEs from different industrial sectors, both in Portugal and in the UK. A total of 44 interviews were performed in this project. For the theoretical part, we

Table 2. Applications of the CIMO-logic from the literature and examples of design propositions

Reference	Area	Aim	Context	Intervention	Mechanism	Outcome
[19]	Information systems	Design a portal for mapping competencies of an IT cluster	In a multi-actor cluster with a broad scope of technologies	Building a common space representation	By reinforcing the motivation of actors to exchange and combine knowledge	Serves to foster knowledge creation
[20]	Operations management	Synthesize a research program on tracking for operations management	Industrial asset management	Tracking composites of several individual products	Basis of decision-making shifted from product type to individual product	More effective and efficient asset maintenance through condition-based programs. Lifecycle management to improve products through product development
[21]	Innovation management	Develop design principles that help multinational firms to re-design their new venture development process	in the context of a new venture development process for a venture in the bottom of the pyramid markets	A team must be established by	(a) creating a small entrepreneurial focused team, (b) having local based knowledge processes, (c) having competent & serious team members;	To achieve a positive new venture performance
[22]	Supply chain management	Develop a framework for disaster relief supply chain quality management	Formulating strategy and structuring the resource portfolio	Planning for lean and quality	Design for Six Sigma; SIPOC Analysis	Economic development; environmental performance; social equity
[16]	Energy ecosystems	Explore how firms together in the energy business ecosystems develop their business models	Current business models make hay an expensive source for biogas production	Biogas production is deeply integrated with biomass production leading to the possibility of nutrient cycling and organic farming	Both farmer and biogas company achieve efficiency improvements and increased value of their offerings to customers	New business model and potential for increased total value creation through an industrial ecosystem
[23]	Open innovation	Direct SMEs in implementing, executing, and improving open innovation in their organizations	When developing an open innovation strategy	Decide on innovation goals aligned to business strategy and obtain an innovation portfolio view	Managing investment and risk	Providing a view of the innovation which will be developed

were based on theories and background on information systems, DPs, CNs, information management, international business, and business associations.

The next section presents our design propositions. To better illustrate the differences and to provide a more detailed discussion about the components of the CIMO-logic, we have chosen 6 main design propositions from our project (2 for each social interaction mechanism), presented into two different versions/interpretations of what can be the CIMO-logic components.

3.2 Version 1 of the CIMO-Logic

In Version 1 (Fig. 1), each design proposition comprises the same context (C), together with a proposed intervention (I), following one of the identified generative mechanisms (Information Sharing, Collaboration, Collective Action - M_{IS}, M_C, M_{CA}), to produce particular outcomes (O_{IS}, O_C, O_{CA}).

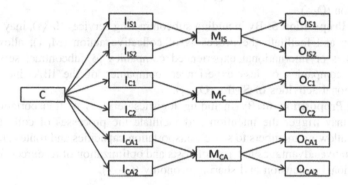

Fig. 1. Version 1 of the CIMO-logic

The general form of the design propositions Version 1 is $(C, O) \rightarrow (I, M)$. The interpretation[1] is *"to achieve outcome O in context C, enact intervention I to trigger mechanism M"*.

The 6 design propositions for Version 1 are:

The context (C) for all design propositions is *the improvement of the internationalization processes of SMEs with the support of DPs managed by IBAs* (this is the design context):

- **Design Proposition 1:** By managing and supporting the whole information life-cycle (information sources, information acquisition, information dissemination, and information utilization) (I_{IS1}), may trigger the intention and facilitate the processes of information sharing (M_{IS}), resulting in CNs of SMEs to have a more efficient and effective access, processing, and utilization of valued internationalization information (O_{IS1}).

---

[1] This is a rigid interpretation. In a real case this is fuzzy e.g., "I might trigger M" or "to achieve O, I is probably a good way".

- **Design Proposition 2:** By including a digital market observatory with market sheets, prospective reports and market studies (I_{IS2}), may trigger the intention and facilitate the processes of information sharing (M_{IS}), enabling to analyze, systematize, discuss and make available relevant information on emerging international markets that may be priority targets for the sector (O_{IS3}).
- **Design Proposition 3:** By developing roadmaps that are a combination of skills mapping (competences available in the IBA's members) and foresight (future trends, future requirements, potential partnerships, prospective markets and competences needed) (I_{C1}), may trigger the intention and facilitate the processes of collaboration (M_C), improving the provision of market intelligence services by the IBA and potentiate different types of collaborations (O_{C1}).
- **Design Proposition 4:** By having a marketplace for the placement of offers and market opportunities from foreign entities and clients (I_{C2}), may trigger the intention and facilitate the processes of collaboration (M_C), fostering matchmaking processes and allow users to apply and pursue new opportunities for international expansion (O_{C2}).
- **Design Proposition 5:** By including subcontracting services (I_{CA1}), may trigger the intention and facilitate the processes of collective action (M_{CA}), allowing large companies or international experienced companies to subcontract services from smaller companies or less experienced companies of the IBA, increasing the international activities of SMEs (O_{CA1}).
- **Design Proposition 6:** By including logistics services of transportation sharing (I_{CA2}), may trigger the intention and facilitate the processes of collective action (M_{CA}), allowing members to share transportation capacities and routes and promote collaborative advantages in terms of costs and optimization of resources for a proper international expansion and sharing economy (O_{CA2}).

3.3 Version 2 of the CIMO-Logic

In the first version we have proposed different interventions, justified by the generative mechanisms of social interaction, and each of these interventions creates its specific outcome. However, a different interpretation can be achieved for the design propositions. In Version 2 (Fig. 2), the context (C) is the same, but now, our previous social interaction mechanisms represent three general outcomes that we want to achieve, i.e. the outcomes wanted for the proposed DP is to allow to increase and improve the social interaction structures of information sharing, collaboration, and collective action. Therefore, instead of having various outcomes, we now have three main general outcomes (O_{IS}, O_C, O_{CA}).

In Version 2, the proposed interventions (I) will trigger different mechanisms (M). After various iterations for the design propositions, we decided to introduce a new contribution and a new perspective for the CIMO-logic. Accordingly, to increase our understanding about the context under study, we opted for decomposing the mechanisms into two parts: (i) technical instruments (TI), which are the means and tools to facilitate the implementation of a proposed intervention; and (ii) social mechanisms (SM), which justify, and which are triggered by the interventions. In our view, this can contribute to obtain a more socio-technical perspective about the design propositions.

The general form of the design propositions in Version 2 is $(C, O) \rightarrow (I, SM) \vee (I, TI) \vee (I, SM \wedge TI)$. The interpretation is *"to achieve outcome O in context C, either enact intervention I to trigger mechanisms SM or TI or both SM and TI)"*.

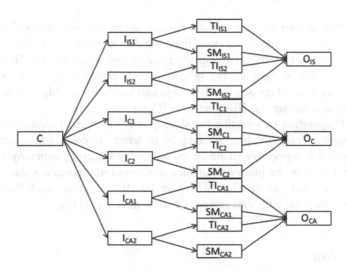

Fig. 2. Version 2 of the CIMO-logic

The 6 design propositions for Version 2 are (the context is the same of Version 1):

- **Design Proposition 1:** A more efficient and effective access, processing, and utilization of valued internationalization information (I_{IS1}), will enable managing and supporting the whole information lifecycle (information sources, information acquisition, information dissemination, and information utilization) (TI_{IS1}), as well as will promote discussion and knowledge sharing of opportunities (SM_{IS1}), improving the information sharing dimension of the CN of SMEs (O_{IS}).

- **Design Proposition 2:** Analyzing, systematizing, discussing and making available relevant information on emerging international markets that may be priority targets for the sector (I_{IS2}), will enable a digital market observatory with market sheets, prospective reports and market studies (TI_{IS2}), as well as will promote discussion and knowledge sharing on opportunities (SM_{IS2}), improving the information sharing dimension of CN of SMEs (O_{IS}).

- **Design Proposition 3:** Improving the provision of market intelligence services by the IBA and potentiating different types of collaborations (I_{C1}), will enable the development of roadmaps that are a combination of skills mapping (competences available in the IBA's members) and foresight (future trends, future requirements, potential partnerships, prospective markets and competences needed (TI_{C1}), and will improve the technical reputation of the IBA (SM_{C1}), leading to more collaboration-intensive activities in the IBA (O_C).

- **Design Proposition 4:** Enacting matchmaking processes and allowing SME users to apply and pursue new opportunities for international expansion (I_{C2}), will develop a marketplace for the placement of offers and market opportunities from foreign entities and clients (TI_{C2}), and will develop the reputation of the IBA as trusted broker (SM_{C2}), leading to more collaboration-intensive activities in the IBA (O_C).
- **Design Proposition 5:** Incentivizing large companies or international experienced companies to subcontract services from smaller companies or less experienced companies of the IBA for increasing the international activities of SMEs (I_{CA1}), will increase the use of the platform subcontracting services (TI_{CA1}), as well as will increase trust levels between the IBA large and small firms (SM_{CA1}), increasing the joint activities among the IBA members (O_{CA}).
- **Design Proposition 6:** Enacting the sharing of transportation capacities and routes and promoting collaborative advantages in terms of costs and optimization of resources for a proper international expansion and sharing economy (I_{CA2}), will increase the use of the platform logistics services of transportation sharing (TI_{CA2}), as well as will increase trust levels between the IBA large and small firms (SM_{CA1}), increasing the joint activities among the IBA members (O_{CA}).

4   Discussion

Looking at the case applications of the CIMO-logic from the literature (Table 2), it is possible to see that this framework has been applied in different research contexts, which shows its applicability for example in managing processes or in the design of information systems. Regarding the CIMO components, it is clear in all studies that the context (C) is the one that provides no room for doubts in terms of its meaning. Each study addresses a specific problematic context, following a certain research objective. Likewise, the component of the outcome (O) does not appear to create difficulties in terms of interpretation. The outcomes in those studies are defined according to the result of the proposed interventions.

Nevertheless, the same does not happen when we are analyzing the components of the interventions (I) and the mechanisms (M). So, let's first recall the definitions of those CIMO components (Table 1). Interventions are defined as purposeful actions or measures proposed by someone to solve a problem or need, and that will influence the outcomes. These proposed actions can take the form of a product, a process, a service or an activity. Mechanisms are then triggered by the intervention, by explaining why the intervention will produce a certain outcome.

Analyzing the case applications from the literature, most of the proposed interventions are in fact actions proposed by the research team to solve a problem. However, while some studies define more general interventions for their design propositions such as "*establish a team*" [21] or "*plan for lean and quality*" [22], others try to be more specific in their proposed interventions, with examples such as "*tracking composites of several products*" [20] or "*building a common space representation*" [19]. In the case of Hellstrom et al. [16], the CIMO-logic was used for the purpose of a research synthesis (looking at previous literature), rather than to develop design propositions. Thus, in this case it is not clear what are the actions or measures that the researchers want to propose, originating interventions that stand more like an explanation of a factor instead of a purposeful action.

In our case study we made an effort to be specific with the interventions for our design propositions, by defining particular features for DPs, demonstrated by examples such as *"managing and supporting the whole information lifecycle..."*, *"having a marketplace for the placement of offers..."* or *"including logistics services of transportation sharing"*. Nonetheless, we are also aware that to be more rigorous, an additional effort should be made by us and by future studies to be as specific as possible with the interventions in the design propositions, in order to facilitate the understanding from the users and targets for the proposed interventions, as well as to reduce ambiguities among the research community.

After that comes the mechanisms, which in our opinion is the CIMO component that generates more problems in terms of interpretation and understanding. Again, mechanisms in CIMO are used to support the idea that a certain intervention will produce a determined outcome, or, in other words, mechanisms offer an understanding of why an intervention happens. The six case applications from the literature present very different interpretations and perspectives for the mechanisms in the CIMO-logic. To exemplify, in some cases the mechanisms are considered as specific tools *"design for Six Sigma, SIPOC analysis"* [22], or actions *"managing investment and risk"* [23]; *"creating a small entrepreneurial focused team"* [21].

During the development of our design propositions, we had difficulties to clearly define this component of the CIMO-logic. Those difficulties were also justified by the lack of a more agreed and unified version of this framework in the literature. That is why we chose to present in this paper two different versions and interpretations for the design propositions (in fact, additional versions could have been defined): (i) the first one considering our generative mechanisms as the social interaction structures of information sharing, collaboration and collective action, which in our view help to justify the outcomes of the proposed interventions; and (ii) the second version, where we introduce a new view for this particular framework, by dividing the generative mechanisms into technical instruments and social mechanisms, to obtain a more sociotechnical perspective about the design propositions.

The design propositions from our case study could be used by IBAs, researchers and practitioners for the design and development of more effective collaborative DPs as socio-technical systems for supporting SME internationalization. By explicitly defining each component of the CIMO-logic, we believe that having the design propositions defined in this way can become the proposed interventions more clear and transparent for the potential users and stakeholders.

We can conclude this discussion by arguing that the application of the CIMO-logic is very much subject and dependent of the context and of the view of each design or research team. In our view, each component of the CIMO-logic needs to be clearly defined and explicitly presented when developing the design propositions. In addition, the connections between each CIMO component need to be well justified to make sense for both researchers and practitioners. Another important aspect is to increase the number of studies that can apply the CIMO-logic, in order to have a good progress on its discussion and evolution as a prescriptive method, as well as to contribute for making this framework well established and well framed in terms of research.

5 Conclusion

This paper aims to contribute to better design CNs by exploring the CIMO-logic approach. By showing and discussing both examples from the literature and from our own work, we believe that we have produced important insights for the future development of a prescriptive research framework supporting researchers in using the CIMO-logic for the design of CNs and cognitive systems mediated by DPs.

We hope that this study can help clarify each component of the CIMO-logic, to allow for further applications of this framework in different research contexts, and to help future studies in developing more rigorous design propositions, as innovative DSR artifacts. This study can also be further extended by performing a systematic collection and analysis of the previous literature of CIMO, with the aim of trying to obtain a more agreed and unified version for future exploitation.

Acknowledgments. This research was funded by the Portuguese funding agency, Fundação para a Ciência e a Tecnologia (FCT), through the Ph.D. Studentship SFRH/BD/110131/2015. It was also supported by the Project "TEC4Growth - Pervasive Intelligence, Enhancers and Proofs of Concept with Industrial Impact/NORTE-01-0145-FEDER-000020" financed by the North Portugal Regional Operational Programme (NORTE 2020), under the PORTUGAL 2020 Partnership Agreement, and through the European Regional Development Fund (ERDF).

References

1. Spagnoletti, P., Resca, A., Lee, G.: A design theory for digital platforms supporting online communities: a multiple case study. J. Inf. Technol. **30**, 364–380 (2015)
2. Bellini, F., D'Ascenzo, F., Dulskaia, I., Savastano, M.: Digital service platform for networked enterprises collaboration: a case study of the NEMESYS project. In: Borangiu, T., Drăgoicea, M., Nóvoa, H. (eds.) IESS 2016. LNBIP, vol. 247, pp. 313–326. Springer, Cham (2016). https://doi.org/10.1007/978-3-319-32689-4_24
3. Carneiro, L., Soares, A., Patrício, R., Azevedo, A., Pinho de Sousa, J.: Case studies on collaboration, technology and performance factors in business networks. Int. J. Comput. Integr. Manuf. **26**, 101–116 (2013)
4. Sebastian, I., Mocker, M., Ross, J., Moloney, K., Beath, C., Fonstad, N.: How big old companies navigate digital transformation. MIS Q. Exec. **16**, 197–213 (2017)
5. Costa, E., Soares, A., Sousa, J.: Information, knowledge and collaboration management in the internationalisation of SMEs: a systematic literature review. Int. J. Inf. Manag. **36**, 557–569 (2016)
6. de Reuver, M., Sørensen, C., Basole, R.C.: The digital platform: a research agenda. J. Inf. Technol. **33**, 124 (2018). https://doi.org/10.1057/s41265-016-0033-3
7. Hevner, A., Chatterjee, S.: Design Research in Information Systems: Theory and Practice. Springer, New York (2010). https://doi.org/10.1007/978-1-4419-5653-8
8. Hevner, A., March, S., Park, J., Ram, S.: Design science in information systems research. MIS Q. **28**, 75–105 (2004)

9. Vaishnavi, V., Kuechler, W.: Design Science Research Methods and Patterns: Innovating Information and Communication Technology. CRC Press, New York (2015)
10. Peffers, K., Rothenberger, M., Tuunanen, T., Vaezi, R.: Design science research evaluation. In: Peffers, K., Rothenberger, M., Kuechler, B. (eds.) DESRIST 2012. LNCS, vol. 7286, pp. 398–410. Springer, Heidelberg (2012). https://doi.org/10.1007/978-3-642-29863-9_29
11. Gregor, S., Hevner, A.: Positioning and presenting design science research for maximum impact. MIS Q. 37, 337–355 (2013)
12. van Aken, J.: Developing generic actionable knowledge for the social domain: design science for use in the swamp of practice. Methodol. Rev. Appl. Res. 2, 9–25 (2015)
13. van Aken, J.E.: Design science: valid knowledge for socio-technical system design. In: Helfert, M., Donnellan, B. (eds.) EDSS 2012. CCIS, vol. 388, pp. 1–13. Springer, Cham (2013). https://doi.org/10.1007/978-3-319-04090-5_1
14. Denyer, D., Tranfield, D., van Aken, J.: Developing design propositions through research synthesis. Organ. Stud. 29, 393–413 (2008)
15. Brouwer, P., Brekelmans, M., Nieuwenhuis, L., Simons, R.: Fostering teacher community development: a review of design principles and a case study of an innovative interdisciplinary team. Learn. Environ. Res. 15, 319–344 (2012)
16. Hellström, M., Tsvetkova, A., Gustafsson, M., Wikström, K.: Collaboration mechanisms for business models in distributed energy ecosystems. J. Clean. Prod. 102, 226–236 (2015)
17. Holmstrom, J., Tuunanen, T., Kauremaa, J.: Logic for accumulation of design science research theory. In: 47th Hawaii International Conference on System Sciences, pp. 3697–3706 (2014)
18. van Aken, J., Chandrasekaran, A., Halman, J.: Conducting and publishing design science research: Inaugural essay of the design science department of the Journal of Operations Management. J. Oper. Manag. 47–48, 1–8 (2016)
19. Pascal, A., Thomas, C., Romme, A.G.L.: An integrative design methodology to support an inter-organizational knowledge management solution. In: International Conference on Information Systems (2009)
20. Holmström, J., Främling, K., Ala-Risku, T.: The uses of tracking in operations management: Synthesis of a research program. Int. J. Prod. Econ. 126, 267–275 (2010)
21. van der Kroft, T.J.: Innovation Strategies for the BoP: New Venture Development at Philips (2010)
22. Madu, C.N., Kuei, C.-H.: Disaster relief supply chain quality management (DRSCQM). Int. J. Qual. Reliab. Manag. 31, 1052–1067 (2014)
23. Krause, W., Schutte, C.: Developing design propositions for an open innovation approach for SMEs. S. Afr. J. Ind. Eng. 27, 37–49 (2016)
24. Costa, E., Soares, A., Sousa, J.: On the use of digital platforms to support SME internationalization in the context of industrial business associations. In: Handbook of Research on Expanding Business Opportunities with Information Systems and Analytics, pp. 1–25. IGI Global, Hershey (2018)
25. Costa, E., Soares, A., Sousa, J.: Institutional networks for supporting the internationalisation of SMEs: the case of industrial business associations. J. Bus. Ind. Mark. 32, 1182–1202 (2017)
26. Costa, E., Soares, A., Sousa, J., Jamil, G.: Information management for network transformation in industrial enterprises associations: the case of the internationalization process. In: Jamil, G.L., Soares, A.L., Pessoa, C.R.M. (eds.) Handbook of Research on Information Management for Effective Logistics and Supply Chains, pp. 415–436. IGI Global, Hershey (2017)

Development of a Collaborative Platform
for Closed Loop Production Control

Ben Luetkehoff$^{(\boxtimes)}$, Matthias Blum, and Moritz Schroeter

FIR at RWTH Aachen University, Production Management,
Campus-Boulevard 55, 52074 Aachen, Germany
{lh,bl,sch}@fir.rwth-aachen.de

Abstract. In today's turbulent market, the way data are used in production is one of the key aspects to maintain or increase a manufacturing company's ability to compete. Even though most companies are aware of the advantages of collecting, analyzing and using data, the majority of them do not exploit these fully. Thus, IT systems and sensors are integrated into the shop floor in order to deal with the current challenges, leading to an overwhelming amount of data without contributing to an improvement of production control. Because of developments like digitization and Industry 4.0, there is an innumerable amount of existing research focusing on data analytics, artificial intelligence and pattern recognition. However, research on collaborative platforms in traditional production control still needs improvement. Therefore, the main goal of this paper is to present a platform based closed loop production control and to discuss the relevant data. The collaborative platform represents the basis for a future analysis of high-resolution data using cognitive systems in order for companies to maximize the automation of their production. A use case at the end of the paper shows the potential implementation of the findings in practice.

1 Introduction

Manufacturing companies no longer only produce products – they also produce data. Industry 4.0 and the Internet of Things are some of the reasons for the immense increase in data collection on the shop floor. However, simply collecting various amounts of data is not enough. Ideally, the data collected are used to improve the production processes by reducing and controlling the growing complexity. In fact, a full exploitation of the generated data is necessary for an improvement of production control by analyzing the collected data, finding patterns and returning drawn conclusions into the system [1, 2]. The goal of the research project "Intelligent Production Control" (iProd) is to use the data produced on the shop floor and along the order execution process, collect it on a shared platform and use Artificial Intelligence to recognize patterns and use the results to control the production [3].

A support system, such as the one being developed in the research project, is necessary to support agile processes [4] and because of the limited capabilities of employees when it comes to the detection and eliminations of disturbances [5]. Collaborative data platforms represent a high value for companies as long as more than one use it. This means that the

L. M. Camarinha-Matos et al. (Eds.): PRO-VE 2018, IFIP AICT 534, pp. 278–285, 2018.
https://doi.org/10.1007/978-3-319-99127-6_24

more users adopt and contribute to a platform, the more valuable it becomes [6]. This is relevant in the big picture because most big data analyses are based on inflexible heuristic optimizations and static analyses. However, companies still need to put a lot of effort into the development of a self-learning closed loop production control that eliminates deviations and disturbances independently [7, 8]. The first step into that direction is the collection and storing of relevant data from the shop floor and IT systems used for the order processing.

The goal of this paper is to develop and present the idea of a collaborative platform-based closed loop production control by demonstrating how to collect relevant data. The analysis of the data is supposed to enable companies to improve their order processing processes in the end.

First, we outline the motivation of the paper and give a short overview of the relevant state of the art. Building on the state of the art, we discuss the relevant requirements before we show the application of the concept within a use case of one research partner. To conclude we summarize the findings and discuss the future research.

2   Motivation for the Collaborative Platform

A constantly rising flood of data already is and will be unavoidable in the future. The question that arises is which data to collect and how to handle it [9]. Since data is automatically collected, it should be made use of. However, there are "various challenges related to accessing and managing all relevant data [...]" [10]. The problem is the storing of information on different levels and systems in a company, leading to a heterogeneous landscape and a difficulty in gaining knowledge from the data.

A solution to the problem where to store and how to handle data are collaborative data platforms. Data platforms represent a high value to companies as long as more than one use them. This means that the more users adopt and contribute to a platform, the more valuable it becomes to each user.

Collective intelligence is defined as "an emergent property from synergies among three elements: (1) data knowledge; (2) software; (3) experts and others with insight that continually learns from feedback to produce just-in-time knowledge for better decisions than any of these elements acting alone" [11].

Therefore, the motivation for this research is to gain knowledge from data generated by different companies, use a collaborative platform to analyze the data and feed it back to the companies to support the experts.

3   State of the Art

In this section, the basics of production control are reviewed and the basic principles of platforms, data collection, IT systems and their application in production planning and control are discussed.

In general, there are two important differences between open loop production control and closed loop production control, i.e. feedback mechanisms. The advantage of closed loop production control is an increased reaction speed when disturbances occur [12].

Just like in control theory, the production represents the closed loop controlled system (see Fig. 1 below) whose actuating variables can be derived from the production [13].

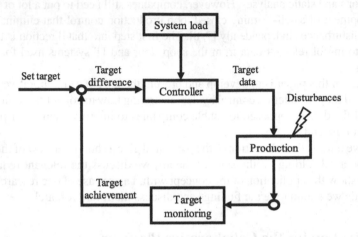

Fig. 1. Production control [13]

Industry platforms are products, services, or technologies developed by one or more companies, and which serve as a basis for a larger number of companies to "build further complementary innovations and potentially generate network effects" [6]. When looking at software companies such as Microsoft or SAP, platforms are becoming more and more popular in many fields. This may be because a high amount of data can be processed in a short period. Moreover, platforms can be considered as a "growing set of complementary innovations" and advantages come along when they are used [6].

In companies many heterogeneous IT systems exist that are supposed to manage the production planning and control. Two of the main systems for this task are Enterprise Resource Planning (ERP) and Manufacturing Execution Systems (MES) [14]. Research on closed loop production control, which means adding an additional feedback loop to the open loop production control, is found in several publications [7, 15, 16]. However, since they are mostly based on discrete-event simulation, they require a lot of manual effort and the automation of said models has solely been discussed theoretically [17].

The data from the production needs to be up-to-date and interpretable by machines [2]. Part of the information is the production data (e.g. sensor data) itself and their data points, which is necessary to filter by relevance. In order to do this, a domain-specific information model needs to be developed. Domain Specific Languages (DSL) and Open Platform Communication (OPC) are necessary to model complex automation systems such as the proposed platform [18]. They are supposed to improve the monitoring and control of systems in production [19].

Overall, platforms are becoming more and more popular in many fields because of the possibility to transfer a high amount of data in a short period. Moreover, the necessary data for a closed loop production control can nowadays be generated and analyzed. However, existing approaches and products neglect the fact that the data from one system may not be enough and the platforms need to be fed by more than just one IT-System in order to generate reliable results.

4 Requirements

There are four basic requirements for the proposed concept to establish a collaborative platform. The first element (A) presents the process of data collection in general and describes which actuating variables to collect from the production and where this data can be captured. The second element (B) describes the data platform with of the collected data. Steps (C) and (D) deal with finding methods to analyze data and recognize pattern as well as the recirculation of the results into the system. This paper focusses on the first two elements since the last two elements are still being researched and will be published later.

(A) Data collection
Before uploading data to the platform, it needs to be collected throughout the different enterprise levels of a company. Within the framework of this paper, the considered levels will be the shop floor, the Manufacturing Execution System (MES) and the Enterprise Resource Planning (ERP) (see Fig. 2).

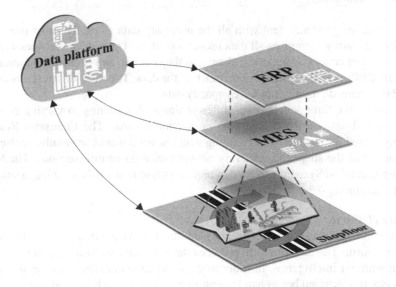

Fig. 2. Data exchange and access between enterprise levels and the data platform

The basis for a real time closed loop production control is high-resolution *shop floor data*. Part of the relevant data is manufacturing, energy consumption and production data. The production data can be machine data (and tool data) or process and quality data that originates from sampling, measuring and testing data [20]. Moreover, smart object data is collected on the shop floor by using systems such as Real Time Location

Systems (RTLS). Shop floor data is available close to real time, meaning that data is generated every minute, second or millisecond.

The *ME-System* exchanges data with the ERP-system regarding the management level [21] and receives and processes, among other things, data from the shop floor. Data that an MES is able to record can either be internal or external [20]. The ME-system is able to check the collected data, e.g. from the shop floor, for plausibility, which can contribute to guaranteeing high data quality (Table 1).

Table 1. Internal and external data sources in ME-Systems [20]

Internal sources	External sources
Finely planned production	Goods receipt slips, vendor and customer information
Orders, process data, process information	Information from other systems participating in quality assurance
Material status, claim information, additional inspection	CAD, PLM, and smart objects
Requirements due to special circumstances	Order data from the data of ERP/PPS production orders
Personnel qualifications	

ERP Systems generally deal with all the necessary data along the order processing. Therefore, it mainly comprises all data related to orders. The borders between the three enterprise levels cannot be separated clearly, as they overlap and exchange information – especially ERP and ME-Systems share much of the data. The main difference is the fact that ERP-systems do usually not have capacity data.

Moreover, the three levels cover different timescales leading to varying effects of the transferred data on the closed loop production control. The Enterprise Resource Planning is used for production scheduling within several weeks or months, whereas the time horizon of the shop floor can vary between minutes or milliseconds. The Manufacturing Execution System is located in between those two levels, enabling a supply of information among them [21].

(B) Data platform

The data collected from the three systems mentioned above are transferred to the collaborative platform. The data platform provides the basis for real-time pattern recognition through artificial intelligence. In order to draw valuable conclusions from the data, a filter needs to be applied beforehand to ensure that only data whose evaluation will lead to significant results is generated and uploaded. Depending on the companies in focus and their production processes, the data may vary. There are multiple ways of implementing a new data platform, depending on each company's preferences regarding data sharing, local accessibility and provision of data for others.

Possible implementation potentials would be a cloud solution if the company shares collected data and analyses with other companies with access to the platform. An in-house solution could be implemented if the platform is only applied within one company or if the company demands private access to collected and analyzed data (Fig. 3). Within the range of this paper, a cloud solution is used, as several companies are accessing and contributing to the platform. The established collaborative data platform operates acts as a decision support system.

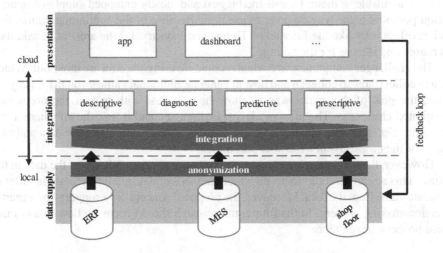

Fig. 3. Cloud vs. in-house platform solution

5 Use Case

The company in focus produces foils and foil products (e.g. plastic bags) in three shifts with around 50 employees. Because of its relatively small size and standardized processes, the sales team can accept and loosely plan orders based on the remaining capacity in production and customer order specifications. Roughly two weeks before the start of production, the production manager reviews the planned orders and manually adjust them to fit the schedule based on the given constraints. Currently, a lot of manual planning and implicit knowledge of the production manager is required, especially when deviations occur.

In order to reduce the manual planning effort in production, the collective platform is supposed to analyze the relevant data and assist the management by generating response strategies and giving decision support. The necessary data already mostly exists in the ERP-System with ME-functionalities:

- Order information, such as delivery date, quantity and recipe
- Production status, such as capacity, workload, personnel, material
- Machine specific information, such as producible products

The manual effort was necessary because machine specific information has been part of the production manager's implicit knowledge and not shared with the system. Since this is of vital importance for the production planning, this data had to be formalized and introduced into the system.

6   Conclusion and Further Research

In today's turbulent market, manufacturing companies need to make use of every resource available to them. One of the biggest and mostly untapped supply of optimization potential is the way companies use data. Because of the continuing digitization and developments like the Internet of Things and Industry 4.0 the amount of said data increases and is there for the taking.

The challenges companies face when it comes to using the data are threefold: Which data to collect, how to collect it and how to generate additional value through its analysis. Thus, the goal of this paper was to show how to deal with two of the previously mentioned challenges. The relevant data was discussed and it was shown where it can be found. Secondly, the concept of a platform as a means to collect the data and as a basis for the necessary analysis was introduced.

However, there is still a lot of research necessary to make full use of the data in the future. This research should focus on which methods of data analytics to use in order to generate value from the data. Moreover, the proposed concept only supports the experts' decision-making process. In the future, the research should focus on how to automate these processes even more.

Acknowledgement. The European Regional Development Fund (ERDF) funded the presented research. The authors would like to thank the European Regional Development Fund for the kind support and making this research possible.

References

1. Kropp, S.K.: Entwicklung eines Ereignismodells als Grundlage der Produktionsregelung. In: Schriftenreihe Rationalisierung, 1st edn., vol 137. Apprimus, Aachen (2016)
2. Schuh, G., Blum, M.: Design of a data structure for the order processing as a basis for data analytics methods. In: Portland International Conference on Management of Engineering and Technology (PICMET), Honolulu, pp. 2164–2169 (2016)
3. Luetkehoff, B., Blum, M., Schroeter, M.: Self-learning production control using algorithms of artificial intelligence. In: Camarinha-Matos, L.M., Afsarmanesh, H., Fornasiero, R. (eds.) PRO-VE 2017. IFIP, vol. 506, pp. 299–306. Springer, Cham (2017). https://doi.org/10.1007/978-3-319-65151-4_28
4. Camarinha-Matos, L.M., Afsarmanesh, H., Fornasiero, R. (eds.): Collaboration in a data-rich world. IFIP, vol. 506. Springer, Cham (2017). https://doi.org/10.1007/978-3-319-65151-4
5. Meier, C.: Echtzeitfähige Produktionsplanung und -regelung in der Auftragsabwicklung des Maschinen- und Anlagenbaus, 1st edn., Wissenschaft, vol. 117. Apprimus, Aachen (2013)
6. Gawer, A., Cusumano, M.A.: Industry platforms and ecosystem innovation. J. Prod. Innov. Manag. **31**(3), 417–433 (2014). https://doi.org/10.1111/jpim.12105
7. Hamann, T.: Lernfähige intelligente Produktionsregelung. Informationstechnische Systeme und Organisation von Produktion und Logistik, vol 7. GITO, Heidelberg (2008)
8. Hauptvogel, A.: Bewertung und Gestaltung von cyber-physischer Feinplanung, 1. Aufl. Produktionssystematik, vol 6. Apprimus Verlag, Aachen (2015)
9. Schuh, G., Blum, M., Reschke, J., et al.: Der Digitale Schatten in der Auftragsabwicklung. ZWF **111**, 48–51 (2016)

10. Kassner, L., Gröger, C., Mitschang, B., et al.: Product life cycle analytics – next generation data analytics on structured and unstructured data. Procedia CIRP **33**, 35–40 (2015)

11. Glenn, J.C.: Collective intelligence and an application by the millennium project. World Futures Rev. **5**(3), 235–243 (2013). https://doi.org/10.1177/1946756713497331

12. Wiendahl, H.-P.: Betriebsorganisation für Ingenieure, 8., überarb. Aufl. Hanser, München (2014)

13. Wiendahl, H.-P.: Fertigungsregelung: Logistische Beherrschung von Fertigungsabläufen auf Basis des Trichtermodells. Hanser, München (1997)

14. Kletti, J., Schumacher, J.: Die perfekte Produktion: Manufacturing Excellence durch Short Interval Technology (SIT), 2nd edn. Springer, Heidelberg (2014). https://doi.org/10.1007/978-3-662-45441-1

15. Simon, D.: Fertigungsregelung durch zielgrößenorientierte Planung und logistisches Störungsmanagement. iwb Forschungsberichte, vol. 85. Springer, Heidelberg (1995). https://doi.org/10.1007/978-3-662-07197-7

16. Zetlmayer, H.: Verfahren zur simulationsgestützten Produktionsregelung in der Einzel- und Kleinserienproduktion. iwb Forschungsberichte, vol. 74. Springer, New York (1994). https://doi.org/10.1007/978-3-662-10769-0

17. Selke, C.: Entwicklung von Methoden zur automatischen Simulationsmodellgenerierung, vol. 193. Utz, München (2005)

18. Fowler, M.: Domain-specific languages: description based on print version record. In: A Martin Fowler Signature Book. Cover Addison-Wesley Signature Series. Addison-Wesley, Upper Saddle River (2011)

19. Goldschmidt, T.: Towards an infrastructure for domain-specific languages in a multi-domain cloud platform. In: Cabot, J., Rubin, J. (eds.) ECMFA 2014. LNCS, vol. 8569, pp. 242–253. Springer, Cham (2014). https://doi.org/10.1007/978-3-319-09195-2_16

20. VDI R: 5600, Manufacturing Execution Systems. Verein Deutscher Ingenieure (2007)

21. Kletti, J.: MES - Manufacturing Execution System: Moderne Informationstechnologie Zur Prozessfähigkeit Der Wertschöpfung. Springer, Dordrecht (2006). https://doi.org/10.1007/3-540-28011-1

Reducing Information Load to Enhance Collaborative Awareness Thanks to a Pre-selection of Information

Audrey Fertier[1]([⊠]), Aurélie Montarnal[1],
Anne-Marie Barthe-Delanoë[2], Sébastien Truptil[1],
and Frédérick Bénaben[1]

[1] Centre Génie Industriel - Université de Toulouse - IMT Mines Albi,
Toulouse, France
audrey.fertier@mines-albi.fr
[2] Laboratoire de Génie Chimique - Université de Toulouse - CNRS,
INPT - UPS, Toulouse, France

Abstract. There is a need for collaboration support systems, suited to crisis management, able to sustain collaborations in ever more unstable environments. The organizations involved in a crisis response need support in limiting information overload by accessing information suited to their current needs. The collaboration support system proposed in this paper uses a Common Operational Picture (COP), supported by a Geographical Information System (GIS), that consists of information selected according to (i) the on-going collaboration phase, and (ii) the level of commitment within the collaboration of the current user. Additionally, to validate the proposed classifications, the paper demonstrates how the pre-selection can be applied to support crisis collaborations, operating under high stress and high information load.

Keywords: Collaboration · Crisis management · Common Operational Picture
Information overload · Model driven engineering

1 Introduction

When gathered inside one room, the partners of a collaboration can directly access large amounts of information [10], enabling them to enhance their collaborative awareness. They can identify common goals, critical partners, or share accurate information.

Because the collaborations tend to extend their geographical reach, they can-not communicate as easily as before. To help them, [19] recommends the use of a common *artifact* to support cooperative activities that can be both individually conducted and interdependent. The main goal of the *artifact* is to reduce the complexity of collaborations, including the complexity of their information system due to:

- The amount of information in our daily lives is continually increasing and is multiplied by existing information systems [11], while our brains can only process a limited amount of complex information;

© IFIP International Federation for Information Processing 2018
Published by Springer Nature Switzerland AG 2018. All Rights Reserved
L. M. Camarinha-Matos et al. (Eds.): PRO-VE 2018, IFIP AICT 534, pp. 286–294, 2018.
https://doi.org/10.1007/978-3-319-99127-6_25

– Each partner must be able to access a part of the collaborative awareness adapted to their business and their level of responsibility;
– Information shared within a collaboration comes from heterogeneous sources, and each has an expiration date before which it must be used.

These three issues are particularly true during a crisis situation where the collaboration aims to respond to every risk and consequences due to the disaster [12, 15, 20]: the crisis cells have to face high information load and high time pressure, within complex communication channels, while the collaboration can easily breakdown due to heterogeneous experiences, information accesses and comprehensions.

To support the partners in managing the information available within the collaboration, we proposed a *collaboration support system* able to select information according to (i) the on-going collaboration stage and (ii) the level of commitment of the current user, in order to give each user access to a suited Common Operational Picture (COP), supported by a Geographical Information System (GIS).

A COP is, as defined by [16], an operational picture shared by several partners during a particular operation. Its goal is to enable a shared Situation Awareness (SA) within the collaboration. In this case, the term SA can be defined as a model of the environment surrounding the collaboration [9]. This COP can be displayed through the use of a GIS. According to [16], such an information system is a powerful tool to support SA, in particular during crisis situation where almost all relevant information is spatial.

Our goal is to strengthen collaborative awareness in order to enhance the agility of the collaboration (defined in [2]) in the face of new threats or opportunities. The collaboration support system described in this paper includes:

– A meta-model, as defined by [7], to enable a unified approach of interoperability, and its models modelling the collaborative situation.
– A GIS that takes the role of a COP to communicate information from the system to the user;
– An automatic classification by collaboration stages to filter information according to the current phase of the collaboration;
– An automatic classification by partner roles to filter the information according to the place of the user in the collaboration.

Section 1 presents the *collaboration stages* and the *partners roles* classifications that are used to select the information to be displayed on the COP. Section 2 proposes to validate these two classifications by using them in case of a very specific type of collaboration: a crisis collaboration.

2   The Use of a COP to Enhance Collaborative Awareness

The Fig. 1 illustrates how the collaboration support system, proposed in this paper, operates to adapt its COP to is current user and to the current stage of the collaboration. The design of the system involves the definition of a meta-model, several partners' roles and several collaboration's stages, that have to be common to every collaboration type:

- The *meta-model* (defined in [7]) is used to homogenize and organize available information in models. Such a meta-model, dedicated to collaborations, is described in [3].
- The *role* is used to select information, according to the need of the partner, using the collaboration support system.
- The *stage* is used to select information over time.
- The *logs* are stored to enable future improvements of the collaboration support system.

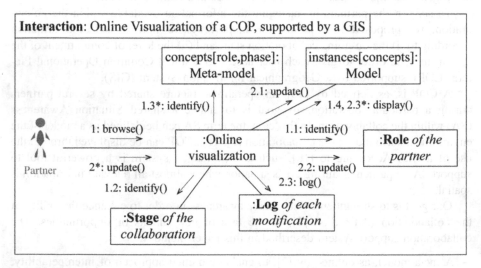

Fig. 1. A communication diagram, in Unified Modelling Language (UML) that illustrates how each partner of a collaboration can use the COP interface of the collaboration support system to enhance their collaborative awareness

a. The partners classification to ensure confidentiality

The work of [21], followed by [5], enabled us to identify three partner roles, inspired from the maturity levels of collaborations and described in Table 1. By default, the system does not share information of higher responsibility levels, with lower responsibility levels:

A partner P1, with a role R1
can reach information shared by a partner P2, with a role R2
If only R1 ≥ R2

Furthermore, during an "update()" operation (cf. Fig. 1), a partner can set the *default responsibility level* of information that he adds to the system. A *federated partner* can, for example, decide to make its newly added information visible to one, several, or all, *open partners* (cf. Table 1).

Table 1. The partners classification by partner roles, defined in this paper

Role of a partner	Definition of the paper
Communicating partner	A partner that exchanges and shares information with the collaboration
Open partner	A communicating partner that shares business services and system functionalities with the collaboration
Federated partner	An open partner that takes part in the collaborative process, and shares the collaboration's goals

b. The collaboration classification to filter the displayed information

Two previous research works [3, 22] have enabled us to identify five main collaboration stages that are described below in Table 2. Each collaboration stage comes with its own information needs

Table 2. The collaboration classification by stages, defined in this paper

Stage of the collaboration	Definition of the paper
Perception (Pr)	When each partner gathers information to improve their situation awareness of the collaboration
Comprehension (Cp)	When each partner learns how to adapt its information or its outputs to the other partners
Understanding (Ud)	When new information is inferred from the information shared between several partners
Convergence (Cv)	When common goals are identified, solutions are proposed, a solution is chosen and a collaborative process is designed
Monitoring (Mg)	When the partners adapt their solution, while the collaborative process runs

The Table 3 shows how the concepts of one collaboration meta-model (from [3]) can be classified. For example, the partners of a collaboration need to learn about each other at the beginning of the collaboration during the perception stage (cf. Table 2). Conversely, the goals of the collaboration are set during the convergence stage, when everyone SA is good enough to support this decision.

The classifications are used to identify the "default information" to be first displayed on the COP, for one given user:

If a partner needs additional information,
the system does not refer to the collaboration classification,
but only to the partners classification that manage responsibility levels

To sum up, the pair *<collaboration stage, user role>* enables the generation of a view of the model, suited to the current collaborative situation, in order to feed the COP displayed by the GIS. The Fig. 2 shows how information is selected according to the need of the user. This follows the recommendations of Mica Endsley [9] about *goal-directed task analyses.*

Table 3. The concepts of the meta-model [3], labelled with the five collaboration stages, according to their level of usefulness

Concepts from [3]	Definition of the paper, inspired from [3]	Pr	Cp	Ud	Cv	Mg
Partner	A partner of the collaboration	x	–	–	–	–
Environment Component	Anything composing the environment of the collaboration, that can be mapped in the COP	x	–	–	–	–
Characteristic	Feature due to the particular environment of the collaboration that could generate opportunities or threats	x	–	–	–	–
Capacity	Capacity One partner's capability, that can be used in the collaborative process	x	x	x	x	x
Objective	A goal of, at least, one of the partner	–	–	x	x	x
Performance indicator	An indicator that measures the performance of one capability, given a goal	–	–	–	x	x
Process	A process that invokes and orders capabilities according to conditions and events	–	–	–	–	x
Fact	An event witnessed by, at least, one of the partner	–	–	–	–	x

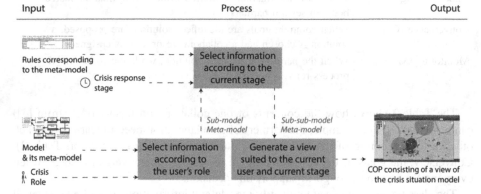

Fig. 2. The process enabling the collaboration support system to generate views suited to both the responsibility level of its user and the current collaboration stage

3 The Case of Crisis Collaboration

In the aftermath of a disaster, a crisis response requires the collaboration of numerous, heterogeneous partners, under high stress and high time pressure [18]. This paper unfolds the scenario of a 100-year flood provided by the ANR GéNéPi project. It allowed for the interview of many practitioners often involved in crisis collaborations.

The results, recorded in specifications [17], underlines the issues still faced by practitioners during crisis responses:

- Much of the information available is unclear, outdated or unreliable, and only the partners with high expertise can get by;
- The diagnosis of the impacted territory and the analysis of the vulnerable assets at stake remains difficult;
- Due to the number of partners involved, it is hard to take into account all possibilities of response process, and even harder to find the optimal response process.

The collaboration support system proposed in this paper can support them in dealing with:

- The issues due to the instability of the crisis, thanks to the COP that display the information contains in a model that can be continuously updated, as in [1];
- The issues faced during the understanding phase, thanks to the capacity of the COP to enhance collaborative awareness, as underlined by [4, 6];
- The issues due to information overload thanks to the collaboration and partners classifications, as described in Sect. 1.

In order to enable the collaboration support system, illustrated in Fig. 2, to generate views of crisis situations, the classifications of collaboration stages and partners' roles dedicated to crisis collaboration still need to be defined.

a. The partners classification adapted to crisis collaboration support
In France, in case of a 100-year flood, the organization involves four different responsibility levels [8]

- Local level;
- County level;
- Zonal level;
- National level.

The hierarchies in place, corresponding to the crisis partners' roles, impose a dedicated information management. For example, a prefect (county level), aiming to communicate to the press, needs to know about the number of people without electricity supply in the county. Conversely, the power supplier (local level), aiming to ensure the continuity of their network, needs to know the exact locations of cut points on their network.

b. The collaboration classification adapted to crisis collaboration support
Like the collaboration stages proposed in this paper, several crisis collaboration phases have been defined over time. Among the first to distinct four phases were Rosenthal and Kouzmin [18]: "Crises [...] may be considered in terms of circular processes involving *mitigation* and *preparation*, *response* as well as *recovery and rehabilitation*". Inside the *response phase*, a French official document [14] recognizes five more phases:

– The *confirmation* of the alert (Ca): "Is there a disaster? What is its scale?";
– The alert (Al): "What are the concerned organizations that will take part in the collaboration?";
– The characterization of the crisis (Cc): "Where are the assets vulnerable to the consequences of this crisis?";
– The evaluation phase (Ev): "Where are the damaged assets? Where are the threatened assets?";
– The *follow-up phase* (F l) that consists of "thoughtful actions" to anticipate long-term consequences.

All the concepts from a meta-model dedicated to collaborative crisis management, as the one described in [3], can be linked to these crisis response phases. The obtained table (an extract is given in Table 4), along with the meta-model from [3], is used by the collaboration support system instead of the Table 2 suited to all kind of collaboration.

Rationally, the links (•) from Table 3, can easily be applied to the crisis concepts of Table 4 because they all inherit from one concept of Table 3. For example, information concerning a new event, useful during the *evaluation phase* of a crisis, are also useful during the *monitoring phase* of the collaboration, because an event is considered as a fact.

Thanks to these new crisis collaboration response phases, and new crisis partners' roles, a collaborative support system, as the one presented in Fig. 2, can select the information to be displayed to its user according to their relevance, and therefore decrease information load of the partners involved in a crisis situation.

Table 4. Some crisis concepts from [13], labelled with the five crisis response phases from [14], according to their usefulness

Concepts from [13]	Parent concept from [3] (cf. Table 3)	Ca	AL	Cc	Ev	Fl
Danger	Characteristic	x	–	–	–	x
Actor	Partner	–	x	–	–	–
Good	Environment component	–	–	x	x	–
Event	Fact	–	–	–	x	–
Response	Process	–	–	–	–	x

4   Conclusion

This paper offers to use a collaboration support system to display relevant information, via a Common Operational Picture (COP) based on a Geographical Information System (GIS) and describing the collaborative situation.

To further limit information overload and to take into account the different responsibility levels involved, the paper proposes two classifications, dedicated to collaborations:

- The *collaboration classification* to adapt the COP to the current collaboration stage that is either the perception, the comprehension, the understanding, the convergence or the monitoring stage.
- The *partners classification* to adapt the view to the goal of the current user. It consists of three categories: communicating, open or federated partners.

To extend the proposed classifications, we have checked that these solutions, dedicated to collaborations, apply to crisis collaborations: collaboration in highly unstable environment, under high-stress and time pressure.

Acknowledgements. This work would have not been possible without the GéNéPi project research team, or the computer engineers team from the industrial engineering center of IMT Mines Albi.

Funding Sources. This work was supported by the French National Research Agency, through the GéNéPi project funding (program: Resilience and crisis management [DS0903] 2014; project ID: ANR-14-CE28-0029).

References

1. Barthe-Delanoë, A.M., Bénaben, F., Carbonnel, S., Pingaud, H.: Event-driven agility of crisis management collaborative processes. In: Proceedings of the 9th International ISCRAM Conference, Vancouver BC, Canada (2012). http://www.iscram-live.org/ISCRAM2012/proceedings/124.pdf
2. Barthe-Delanoë, A.M., Truptil, S., Bénaben, F., Pingaud, H.: Event-driven agility of interoperability during the Run-time of collaborative processes. Decis. Support Syst. **59**, 171–179 (2014). http://www.sciencedirect.com/science/article/pii/S0167923613002868
3. Benaben, F., Montarnal, A., Truptil, S., Lauras, M., Fertier, A., Salatge, N., Rebiere, S.: A conceptual framework and a suite of tools to support crisis management, Hawaii (2017). https://scholarspace.manoa.hawaii.edu/bitstream/10125/41178/1/paper0029.pdf
4. Björkbom, M., et al.: Localization services for online common operational picture and situation awareness. IEEE Access **1**, 742–757 (2013)
5. Bénaben, F.: Conception de Système d'Information de Médiation pour la prise en charge de l'Interopérabilité dans les Collaborations d'Organisations. thesis, Institut National Polytechnique de Toulouse, October 2012. https://hal-mines-albi.archives-ouvertes.fr/tel-01206234/document
6. Bunker, D., Levine, L., Woody, C.: Repertoires of collaboration for common operating pictures of disasters and extreme events. Inf. Syst. Front. **17**(1), 51–65 (2015)
7. Bézivin, J.: On the unification power of models. Softw. Syst. Model. **4**(2), 171–188 (2005). https://doi.org/10.1007/s10270-005-0079-0
8. DSC: Organisation de la réponse de sécurité civile. Technical reports (2004)
9. Endsley, M.R.: Design and evaluation for situation awareness enhancement. In: Proceedings of the Human Factors Society Annual Meeting, vol. 32, pp. 97–101. SAGE Publications, Los Angeles (1988). http://journals.sagepub.com/doi/abs/10.1177/154193128803200221
10. Jongsawat, N., Premchaiswadi, W.: A study towards improving web-based collaboration through availability of group awareness information. Gr. Decis. Negot. **23**(4), 819–845 (2014). https://doi.org/10.1007/s10726-013-9349-3
11. Karlsson, M.: Challenges of Designing Augmented Reality for Military use (2015)

12. Klein, G., Feltovitch, P., Bradshaw, J., Woods, D.: Common ground and coordination in joint activity. In: Organizational Simulation, vol. 44, pp. 139–185. Wiley (2005). http://www.jeffreymbradshaw.org/publications/Common_Ground_Single.pdf

13. Lauras, M., Truptil, S., Bénaben, F.: Towards a better management of complex emergencies through crisis management meta-modelling. Disasters **39**(4), 687–714 (2015)

14. Le Cedre: ORSEC Zonal et départemental, disposition spécifique POLMAR/Terre (2015)

15. Lee, J., Bharosa, N., Yang, J., Janssen, M., Rao, H.R.: Group value and intention to use — A study of multi-agency disaster management information systems for public safety. Decis. Support Syst. **50**(2), 404–414 (2011). http://www.sciencedirect.com/science/article/pii/S0167923610001776

16. Luokkala, P., Nikander, J., Korpi, J., Virrantaus, K., Torkki, P.: Developing a concept of a context-aware common operational picture. Saf. Sci. **93**, 277–295 (2017). http://www.sciencedirect.com/science/article/pii/S0925753516304647

17. Renou, T., Dolidon, H.: Cahier des charges à l'origine du projet GéNéPi. Technical report, CEREMA & IDETCOM, Loire Moyenne (2015)

18. Rosenthal, U., Kouzmin, A.: Crises and crisis management: toward comprehensive government decision making. J. Public Adm. Res. Theory **7**(2), 277–304 (1997). https://academic.oup.com/jpart/article-abstract/7/2/277/957517

19. Schmidt, K., Simonee, C.: Coordination mechanisms: Towards a conceptual foundation of CSCW systems design. Comput. Support. Coop. Work (CSCW) **5**(2–3), 155–200 (1996)

20. Shen, M., Carswell, M., Santhanam, R., Bailey, K.: Emergency management information systems: Could decision makers be supported in choosing display formats? Decis. Support Syst. **52**(2), 318–330 (2012). http://www.sciencedirect.com/science/article/pii/S016792361 1001552

21. Touzi, J., Benaben, F., Pingaud, H., Lorré, J.P.: A model-driven approach for collaborative service-oriented architecture design. Int. J. Prod. Econ. **121**(1), 5–20 (2009). http://www.sciencedirect.com/science/article/pii/S0925527309001005

22. Warner, N., Letsky, M., Cowen, M.: Cognitive model of team collaboration: macro-cognitive focus. Proc. Hum. Fact. Ergon. Soc. Annu. Meet. **49**(3), 269–273 (2005). https://doi.org/10.1177/154193120504900312

Information Systems Integration

On Reliable Collaborative Mobility Services

A. Luis Osório[1(✉)], Luis M. Camarinha-Matos[2], Hamideh Afsarmanesh[3],
and Adam Belloum[3]

[1] ISEL - Instituto Superior de Engenharia de Lisboa,
Instituto Politécnico de Lisboa, and POLITEC&ID, Lisbon, Portugal
lo@isel.ipl.pt
[2] Faculty of Sciences and Technology and CTS-Uninova,
NOVA University of Lisbon, Caparica, Portugal
cam@uninova.pt
[3] University of Amsterdam (UvA), Amsterdam, The Netherlands
{h.afsarmanesh,a.belloum}@uva.nl

Abstract. Current approaches for development of collaborative business process automation, when requiring the participation of multiple stakeholders, lack proper formalization in terms of the required informatics systems landscape. Existing solutions depend on specific technology strategies and do not offer a suitable model for the fast-growing collaborative services. In this paper, we present the concept of an open informatics system of systems (ISoS), as a holistic framework that can be applied to a European wide payment system for collaborative multi-modal mobility services. To illustrate how the ISoS framework could be applied in practice, we consider the payment service to support public transports, motorway and bridges tolling, payment in parking lots, bicycle renting and payment in a fueling station, all under a single contract. While each participating organization (any infrastructure operator) is free to adopt any applicable technology, the proposed ECoNet collaboration infrastructure is aimed to support a multi-supplier (open) informatics system technology landscape. Based on results from previous research, the paper introduces a strategy to allow effective and reliable EU wide collaborative mobility services.

Keywords: Complex informatics systems · Collaborative networks
Collaborative services · Distributed systems · Integrated system of systems

1 Introduction

Collaborative services have been gaining importance, namely because of key decisions of the European Commission aiming to push increased competitiveness to enhance value for the European Union. The recent SEPA[1] directive will make it possible from the beginning of 2018 for any company to offer services based on client's direct debit authorization. This initiative opens the possibility for payment of new collaborative

---

[1] Single euro payments area (SEPA) initiative and direct debit payments legislation, SEPA Direct Debit (SDD).

© IFIP International Federation for Information Processing 2018
Published by Springer Nature Switzerland AG 2018. All Rights Reserved
L. M. Camarinha-Matos et al. (Eds.): PRO-VE 2018, IFIP AICT 534, pp. 297–311, 2018.
https://doi.org/10.1007/978-3-319-99127-6_26

services, offering European citizens a single contract to pay the use of any European mobility-related infrastructure. Such collaborative multimodal mobility services consider payments in any infrastructure, under a single contract and potentially offered by competing providers. This leads to a business scenario in which the European Citizens are free to select a collaborative mobility services provider (CMSP). An example of a provider can be the Via-Verde company [24], already offering collaborative mobility services in Portugal. The utilization of the infrastructures, e.g. riding a tram, is somehow validated based on mobile technologies [8] (QRCode, NFC/Bluetooth, WiFi), smart cards, biometrics or other authentication/validation mechanisms. To make this scenario clear, we consider that any company acting as a service provider must implements a CMSP reference model, being regulated by mobility authorities. The purpose of a CMSP is to offer collaborative mobility services for citizens, whose payment is made under a unique contract as shown in Fig. 1. The mobility authorities or regulators have the responsibility to audit the quality of the offered services and verify if providers are following the contracting policies. Banks provide direct debits from client's accounts, based on explicit debit authorizations. Furthermore, the banks manage the money transfer from a CMSP to the Collaborative Mobility Infrastructure Operators (CMIO) partners (the payments for the utilization of facilities), as direct debits, under the SEPA initiative.

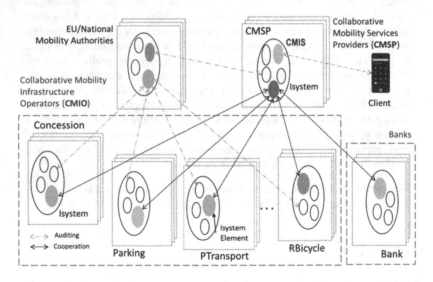

Fig. 1. Collaborative mobility services providers (CMSP)

Handling services offered by more than one stakeholder presents main challenge, since this implies coping with a diversity of processes and technology cultures in need of cooperation [31]. This means that even if citizens (clients) only "see" the multimodal mobility service provider, they in fact, interact with different collaborative mobility infrastructure operators (CMIO) when they travel throughout Europe. This scenario suggests a complex design, operation, and coordination of a composition of services provided by diverse infrastructure operators, banks, mobility regulators and other stakeholders such as call-centers. Consequently, the CMSP companies face high risks, since the required informatics systems, e.g. the core Collaborative Mobility Informatics System (CMIS), to support billing, invoicing, reporting, analysis and forecasting, customer's assistance, and other functions, face complex integration challenges. Operation and management of the involved computational transactions need to be under an integrated coordination system providing reliable business process automation. Additionally, the possibility of scaling up the number of clients and the increasing dependency of businesses from diverse technologies used by the involved parties, make the architecture of a supporting infrastructure, as well as its operational management, complex [3].

In this position paper, the main purpose is to further extend on our previous work in this field, proposing a flexible and scalable infrastructure for an open informatics systems landscape, addressing the CMSP business vision. This infrastructure targets:

(i) An open technology architecture where the involved computational elements are substitutable, as a strategy to reduce technology dependencies, and

(ii) A unified open collaborative platform, as a strategy to reduce the current complex web of adapters (or mediation systems) linking diverse technology systems of each participating business partner.

The aimed contribution is therefore to propose both, a novel informatics technology infrastructure for CMSP business companies, and a strategy to computationally tie the business and regulator partners under the common collaborative networked organization model [6]. This proposal also assumes a commitment to Collaborative Regulation strategies as discussed in the context of the International Telecommunication Union (ITU) that are established as the 5th generation regulations for sustainable citizen benefit, addressed by the connected digital society [18].

The paper builds on top of previous research on Informatics System of Systems (ISoS) framework [26] and the Cooperative Enabled System (CES) [22] to address reliability in an ambitious validation scenario, and with enhanced requirements. For the Collaborative Networks dimension, we extend the previously proposed Enterprise Collaborative Network (ECoNet) platform [27], contributing for reliability, creation of adaptive ties among partners, and providing a reference implementation of the ISoS framework.

In Sect. 2, we present the state of the art related to reliable informatics systems architecture and development strategies for collaborative networks. In the Sect. 3 we discuss the proposed Collaborative Mobility Services Provider scenario for the application of the ISoS model, and the ECoNet framework for structuring the cooperation among informatics systems of the participating stakeholders in order to offer collaborative mobility services. Discussing the conclusions and further research in Sect. 4 we presents the created value and lessons learned.

2 State of Research and Trends

In this sector, we are still in the era of "islands of automation" where the huge standardization efforts made along the last decades remain insufficient [26]. It is interesting to analyze the strategy that has been followed by well-known companies like Amazon, Google, Facebook, LinkedIn, Netflix, that have grown fast on the web and are today the main contributors to interesting open source developments. This strategy seems adequate to induce novel approaches in the market (competition under unified approaches), aiming to reduce dependencies and costs. The highly reliable Apache Kafka messaging system, originally developed by LinkedIn and later incubated as an Apache project [14, 34], is an example of such dynamics. Moreover, there is an interesting discussion about dependencies, based on an empirical look at Amacon.com that points to the potential weaknesses of complementing business partners which use platforms to ground their businesses [36]. The conclusion identifies the platform leaders as those active on finding added value, and making partners appear to depend on such sharing of the distribution network, e.g. for the case of Amazon online shop. The above work also mentions situations related to the sharing of technology platforms (Microsoft/Netscape or Apple/App providers) where it seems to be a trend for platform owners to control partners, putting them in a weaker position by indirectly controlling their business. In the purposed scenario, the collaborative mobility services provider is potentially the "powerful node" in the mobility network. Empirical evidence from the Via-Verde case confirms this [24] as well as the development of alternative payment services by members of this network to avoid sharing costs. The Via-Card payment system developed by one of the Portuguese concessionaires, in competition with the Via-Verde service, demonstrates that the management of value in such collaborative networks is a complex endeavor, founded on discussions centered around the risks of collaboration [17].

Furthermore, there is also a recurrent discussion about vendor lock-in regarding the dependencies from cloud service providers [2]. For instance, the mOSAIC system includes an open API to expose what the authors reference as the application (informatics system), making it independent of a specific cloud provider. They further research on common services like discovery, brokering, matchmaking, interoperability, and compositions of services from multiple cloud providers. While challenging, the approach seems to weaken the cloud customers' side, by lacking an analysis of how complex informatics systems shall be structured. In fact, from an interesting survey of web related technologies [15], the main question to address is how to make reliable complex distributed systems, made of existing and upcoming technology diversity, and from the rapidly evolving science and technology. Such fast-evolving dynamics makes it difficult to establish a vendor-agnostic strategy [26]. The interesting survey in [29] identifies several vendor lock-in dependencies from acquisitions by the Information Technology department of the Dutch Tax and Customs Administration (DTCA). A partnership with the suppliers is proposed as a strategy to reduce dependency, in the research classified as a monopoly. These suggestions are aligned with another report on next-generation IT operating models, where collaboration with suppliers is also suggested [20]. The proposed approach is interesting, but in our understanding of the problem it requires more than a change in the relationship between customers and suppliers. The complexity of developing integrated distributed informatics system requires a novel modularity abstraction able to manage the existing tensions among collaborating stakeholders and their specific technology systems that is supporting critical business processes through complex critical systems.

As discussed in [26], existing standards have proved insufficient for an open informatics system. In spite of the importance of the service-oriented architecture (SOA) paradigm for system development, a composition of software and cyber-physical parts into a consistent modular construct, is lacking. The open OSGi specification with its modularity framework and declarative and remote services specifications [9] while important is only one among many de facto adopted specifications. A more recent trend in some approaches involves micro-services. In a report from NIST, a microservice is defined as a "... *basic element that results from the architectural decomposition of an application's components into loosely coupled patterns consisting of self-contained services that communicate with each other using a standard communications protocol and a set of well-defined APIs, independent of any vendor, product or technology*" [13]. This is in fact an architectural style sharing most of the motivations of the SOA principles. One exception however is for the vendor independence, meaning that technology dependencies are the main motivation for this more recent rebranding of service-oriented modularity. In fact, and as far as the business processes, services, and governance models viewpoints are concerned, there is a need to apply a modularity strategy to reduce technology dependencies. In spite of contributions from the ITIL standard, as a structuring and coordination strategy for IT resources, and COBIT, as a reference governance framework for the IT, the multi-vendor aspect remains an open issue, as discussed in [35]. The question is how to formalize complex technology system setups? The approach is not exclusive to the structuring of software parts that implement services of a system. It is more on how minimal (atomic) they are as computational responsibilities, potentially with multiple suppliers, and how they are composed to establish systems, which in our research are addressed as informatics systems (Isystems) or software-centric systems [26].

An interesting comparison of governance/coordination strategies adopted by SOA and micro-services (µservices) is discussed in [7], positioning SOA towards a centralized orchestration and µservices towards a distributed choreographic model. One problem, however, is the diversity of semantics as an obstacle for a sustainable lifecycle management of complex informatics systems. Our understanding is that the differences among SOA and µservices are not so relevant to our addressed challenge. The challenge is how to name and structure, with a precise semantics (developing a formal model), the growing complexity of informatics system under a coordinated collaborative multi-supplier network of providers of sub-systems, as well as their development, maintenance, and operations services.

Fault tolerance in distributed systems and communication infrastructures is also a key recurrent topic. The Critical Information Infrastructures, for long addressed by the network and distributed systems community, raise the need for robust abstractions. For instance, the statement "*we lack a reference architecture of 'modern critical information infrastructure'...*" in [28] remains a valid point. In fact, no effective formal framework models failures in a collaborative networked organization informatics infrastructure.

The question is, how to guarantee that no client has ever to face a failure situation preventing a validation of a payment for a mobility service, somewhere in a public transport in the EU space? For domains involving a large number of distributed elements supporting critical services (as it is the case of the collaborative multimodal mobility services), many of them are dependable from the point of view of the communication infrastructure, operating systems/virtualization, and middleware, as discussed in [10]. Furthermore, the design of fault tolerance mechanisms for reflective middleware components, with modification of the software architecture at runtime, is proposed and discussed in [30]. However, for our discussed problem domain, such a strategy seems difficult to apply, since we address the cooperation among system elements under diverse implementations, different models and technologies, and operations and management responsibilities.

3   The Proposed Approach

The proposed CMSP business case is a challenging scenario. For this context, our approach considers elementary computational responsibilities as parts of an informatics system (commonly referred as software elements or software systems). By system's definition, each element can itself be an informatics system (Isystem), following a decomposition of complexity till manageable elements. One question is what these final atomic elements should be. In our model, they are the Cooperation Enabled Systems (CES) [22]. These atomic elements, viewed as services in an SOA perspective, can be considered as μservices since they model and operationalize a suite of multi-technology computational services. According to our model, a CES is always under the responsibility and is part of an informatics system (Isystem). The model does not restrict a CES as an informatics system since, according to the ISoS model [26], an informatics system can have a single CES, the CES_0 responsible for supporting the I-system concept. As discussed in the mentioned paper, the informatics technology landscape of an organization made of Isystems (Isystem$_0$, Isystem$_1$, Isystem$_2$, ..., Isystem$_n$; for $n > 0$), includes a meta-Isystem$_0$ with the responsibility of governance of the overall technology landscape. Under this model, any Isystem must cooperate with the Isystem$_0$ of the organization where it is being deployed to get access to all existing services it is supposed to use (integrate with; dynamic adaptation/interoperation). As a simple example, let us consider users' profiles to manage user's authentication and access rights implemented by a single Isystem$_i$. Therefore, we propose the development of further research efforts, answering the requirements of the CMSP scenario, adopting both ISoS and the Enterprise Collaborative platform (ECoNet) [27] as an open specification and open source initiative. The adoption of the ISoS framework and ECoNet with its Enterprise Collaboration Manager (ECoM) Isystem aims at facilitating the adherence of the mobility infrastructure operator, as depicted in Fig. 2.

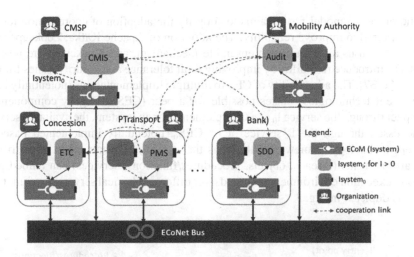

Fig. 2. The CMSP business based on the ECoNet collaborative platform

The adherence of infrastructure operators is one of the main obstacles for the implementation of the CMSP collaborative business. Even if the current approach requires the development of specific adapters which are difficult and costly to develop and maintain, this move leads to a perception of the added advantages and openness to the risks of the required changes.

The proposed modeling approach based on both ISoS and ECoNet requires however further research to answer the CMSP requirements. One key issue for the success of the CMMP concept is the ability to scale fast for a complete adherence of infrastructure operators at European level. If the model succeeds, any EU citizen is allowed to access any infrastructure with an offered collaborative multimodal mobility service. On the other hand, in case of success, the CMSP Isystems landscape becomes very complex and critical since a failure without a formal acceptable recovery mechanism can compromise the CMSP business. The ECoNet and ISoS models, based on an open specification and reference implementation, are expected to facilitate the development of both informatics systems and the necessary collaborative contexts (CoC) [23, 27] potentially offered by multiple stakeholders. It is in the interest of CMMP, authorities, and citizens that the business model scales fast under a competing model with the expectation of better services and fair prices.

From the informatics engineering viewpoint, one main contribution is the technology independence and adaptive modularity framework offered by the CES abstraction. However, even if CES is not used to structure an Isystem, a supplier is even able to comply with the ISoS framework. The proposed approach establishes multiple adherence levels with the objective of making easier a shift from the current development culture (legacy) to an effective lower grained multi-supplier model. As suggested in [26], existing informatics systems, e.g., an ERP can wrap the current implementation and offer an equivalent I_0 service that is supposed to be implemented by the CES_0 element of an Isystem. On the other hand, the legacy ERP can access any other Isystem through the I_0 service of the $Isystem_0$.

The proposed model further aims to simplify the adoption of coordination mechanisms required to improve reliability. The adoption of Apache Kafka, Zookeeper with its Zab consensus algorithm with ensemble mechanism, and blockchain are research options to introduce reliability by improving fault tolerance and security issues for CES element [1, 37]. The adaptability of CES to multiple implementations (potentially based on different technologies) makes possible for a peer (CES or legacy component) to introspect through the service I_0 of a CES element. For an Isystem, the available services are accessed through the I_0 service of its CES_0, potentially implemented based on different technology frameworks. It means that a CES, as a composite of distributed software elements (threads, objects, procedures/functions, services) can embed more than one execution environment scattered over different physical servers (for fault tolerance), as depicted in Fig. 3.

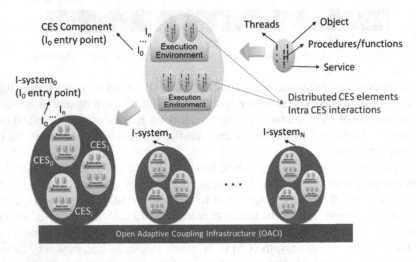

Fig. 3. A detailed view of ISoS and CES elements

The CES components can be running on-premises on local computer systems or in the cloud. Further research is needed to make CES abstraction redundant by extending the model to support the deployment in a network of computers and this way able to offer fault tolerance capabilities. The approach generalizes an initial restriction to CES elements, making, in this way, possible to develop reliable atoms of an Isystem, as depicted in Fig. 3 for a CES component. Furthermore, the Open Adaptive Coupling Infrastructure (OACI) is nothing more than the effective interactions among the multi-services and multi-technology CES elements. In fact, as discussed in [26], through I_0 any CES or any Isystem through its CES_0, can cooperate with any other CES by accessing the required service endpoint.

Illustrative Examples of Potential Application. The proposed ISoS framework can contribute to accommodate evolving "technology cultures" by encapsulating legacy products into CES abstractions. As an example, and related to the referenced SINCRO project, a cinemometer supplier can make available its product as a CES element by implementing the I_0 service, making in this way possible for a peer element to introspect the required interfaces and the supporting technology frameworks. A business challenge like the proposed CMSP needs to assume the state of the art is not ready if competing (multi-supplier) technology solutions are required. The same is happening for several innovative application domains like smart cities, "digital" enterprises (Industry 4.0), digital healthcare, digital public services, where new intelligence services expect to make easier and "green" the citizen's life.

Such holistic endeavors put challenging research questions to the informatics and systems engineering area on how to construct such complex ecosystems under a competition regulated market. Similar to the CMSP scenario, they require a higher or even new integrated approach for the intra-organization domain and reliable networked organization mechanisms for a streamlined collaboration under complex business and technical interactions. The CMSP business is not too different from the logistics single window for a door-to-door freight track, and trace worked in the MIELE project that identified the need of a formal structuration of the networked organizations perspective through the proposed ECoNet platform [27]. It is a step further in understanding how processes, data, computing, and coordination or management models can contribute to an open informatics systems landscape.

The recognized dependencies that are supporting the digital transformation in almost all application domains require sound independent market approaches towards agnostic technology and services provision. The scientific community has here a responsibility, in cooperation with open initiatives, to contribute to realizable approaches to be adopted by the market under regulation (conformity certification mechanisms) validation processes. One possibility is to promote tighter coordination between standardization and research efforts towards more open products and services (pluggable into multi-supplier setups). It requires the adoption of promising open specifications and open source led by large user organization, e.g., the interesting case of Google's Kubernetes (embedding Docker) as an interesting framework to manage complex deployments on multiple computing nodes (on-premises or cloud) of reliable informatics systems [32]. It is worthwhile to note that this research only refers the fact that the Kubernetes platform includes an additional rte container engine (beyond docker) suggesting the need for standardization, as the unique threat in the discussed Strengths, Weaknesses, Opportunities, and Threats (SWOT) analysis. If we want the research community to take the lead of a business processes and technology agnostic approach to CMSP and similar challenges, there is a needed for a strategy to induce productization dynamics based on valuable reference implementations, developed under open specifications and open source models. These valuable reference implementations can work as mechanisms (tools) for the scientific foundation of the formulated hypothesis.

4   Foundations and Value Creation

One expected added value of this proposal is the possibility (facilitation) for smaller technology and service companies to participate in the development of the upcoming complex informatics systems. The vision of a competitive public procurement based on certified CES elements as building blocks of Isystems is challenging. Its feasibility is partially proven based on the experience with the Portuguese National vehicle speed enforcement network (SINCRO) where suppliers were invited to adhere to a common framework (interfaces) for local cabinets and cinemometers (cyber-physical elements).

Some Lessons Learned. From previous projects showing a clear gap between theoretical models and the real world, it could be observed that value is often not directly viable by a number of reasons like the lack a business driver, the different perceptions of value, etc. For instance, in the case of the ITSIBus model [24], the system concept was never suggested to be adopted by suppliers because of the risk to induce a rise in costs.

The need for higher integration levels and reliable enterprise informatics systems has been for long discussed under the complementary perspectives of business and technology. In some cases, this discussion uses different terms and concepts, depending on the background of the contributors. The case study of the adoption of unified enterprise architecture by the Norwegian higher education sector is an interesting example of the difficulty to establish an integrated business and information and technology vision [21]. It is common research practice to address the automation of business processes to establish specific strategies, e.g., the eRIM framework that proposes an automation strategy for the electronic civil construction requirements [12]. The proposed framework in the mentioned work addresses domain-specific issues based on a SOA architecture but without a clear modularity framework able establish a clear separation between the problem domain and the technology strategy to address it under a well-founded model. The need for a new generation of enterprise information systems, guided by an enterprise engineering perspective, is discussed in [11] as a research approach that might take some time to be adopted by the market. A continuous alignment of business and IT is guaranteed by evolving from model-driven engineering to a continuous alignment based on meta-modeling and human-interpretable graphical enterprise architecture and machine-interpretable enterprise ontologies. In this and another paper with common authors, the emphasis is put on enterprise architecture/ontology and the potential of the Zachman's two dimensions enterprise model for the upcoming challenges [16]. This business/IT perspective lacks, however, an analysis of the need to structure the technology landscape aiming to be prepared to answer such modeling and meta-modeling levels under agnostic competitive technology offerings. Furthermore, the model proposed by those authors also lack the collaborative dimension, since organization's technology landscape needs to cope with critical processes at collaborative networks level. We believe that a balanced, holistic approach to business and informatics engineering addressing the complexity of large and distributed informatics system of systems is needed. Based on our research we envisage that enterprise engineering shall evolve to collaborative enterprise engineering under formal constructive models able to scale under dependability in order to ensure a sustainable move to the collaborative digital era. There is a need to consolidate emergent Collaborative Network models like the ARCON reference model [5, 6] towards vendor-agnostic informatics systems for the critical collaborative processes dependent on heterogeneously distributed technology landscapes. The proposed CES, ISoS, ECoNet [25], emerged based on real-world scenarios, contributing to reliable and open informatics systems for collaborative networks, thus potential contributions for the realization of ARCON (meta-modeling framework).

Towards an Implementation Roadmap. Similar to other initiatives, an open source and open specifications initiative needs to be developed to make available validated implementations of ISoS components and a reference implementation of the ECoM with collaborative contexts for the exchange of data and coordination information among CN members, in addition to other ECoNet platform components. Starting from the prototype developed in the MIELE project, the challenge is to invite informatics systems development companies to support the initiative with the advantage of being them suppliers of supporting products and services. The proposed open innovation model seems to differ from the long-studied open innovation a from company viewpoint [4]. However, the value identified in [33] from the Brisa research investments under an open innovation strategy, make us believe that open source dynamics have the potential to speed-up and scale an effective adoption of the proposed theoretical models. The Brisa company is a highway concessionaire with public responsibility, assuming the investment as a strategy to reduce acquisition costs, reduce the risks to implement new services, and promote product innovation. The strategy is to make available an enhanced version of the ECoMsgExchange reference implementation as a version downloadable through business partner companies with a minimal set of features. The idea is to challenge partners to use the validation demo to establish a multitenant Virtual Collaboration Context with business partners and share messages and files [27]. The main purpose is to strengthen valuable synergies between user organizations and regulators on promoting open specifications validated through reference implementations under open source dynamics, with the participation of product and services companies. From previous experience, it is difficult to manage the perception of value by end-organizations, product and service suppliers and also regulators. However, also from previous projects, we observed that given the perception about the *de facto* fast trend for business digitalization and the need for total integration, both intra and inter organizations, consensus about open specifications is an imperative trend. The Advanced Metering Infrastructure (AMI) is another interesting research area, questioning the need for common water and environment sensors technology [19] that partially corroborates the proposed strategy.

Therefore, the proposed CMSP and similar holistic scenarios (the trend) put some novel research questions that need an answer before business adopts them, since citizens expect them to ensure their legitimate rights. However, given the fierce pressure from the market to offer new business services and given the panoply of technologies, in many cases without proper coordination, there is a risk for our holistic initiative. The scientific community can play here a leading and mediating role by designing approaches and maintaining a continuous research agenda grounded on a conformity certification role (on behalf of public interests). Such a strategy is needed to achieve a generalized multi-supplier technology and services landscape for the fast-coming digital world, under a competent regulation.

5   Conclusions and Further Research

The proposed strategy is a step further towards the construction of a model for the complex informatics systems for collaborative networks contexts. The discussed mobility scenario is challenging enough to illustrate the diversity of paradigms from low-level computational services to the collaborative business processes level, under a holistic approach. The CMSP business operators face a risky business since potentially millions of users depend on the reliability of distributed elements from infrastructures and informatics systems and processes from a diversity of organizations around Europe.

With the proposed research direction, based on a partially validated strategy, we aim to contribute to the feasibility of managing a diversity of issues under common formal models. The proposed strategy considers both the intra-organization and the collaborative networked organization's dimension. For the collaborative dimension a specialized Isystem, developed under an open specification and conformity certification process, is adopted. The ECoM Isystem is responsible for managing the relationships between the organization as a node of a collaborative network and its business partners. The ECoNet system was validated as a pilot in the European MIELE project and is adopted by the proposed collaborative multimodal scenario to formalize data and coordination exchanges among multimodal collaborative mobility services provider business partners.

We identify a number of open challenges at different levels for such complex endeavor. The following four levels are considered: (i) *infrastructure elements* (validators at public transport, vehicle classification, license plate recognition, gate in a parking lot, etc.), (ii) organizations' *Isystem landscape* (commonly referenced as IT), (iii) Organization's users and partners business *processes and services* (also commonly referenced as IT), and (iv) the *collaborative network* dimension, managing business relationships, trust, and risks. For each of these dimensions we identify further research challenges:

i.   *Infrastructure elements* – How to guarantee that a citizen always has a mechanism to authenticate and make the payment in any infrastructure, even when without a specific credential (mobile, card) or some element of an Isystem in the validation path fails;
ii. *Isystem landscape* – How to coordinate the substitution of an Isystem, e.g., the Isystem that manages toll payments;
iii. *Processes and services* – How to coordinate local specific processes (including changes in local policies) with collaborative commitments, e.g., change of already paid multimodal reservations;
iv. *Collaborative network* – How to manage business risks among networked stake-holders considering that each member has different investment levels in the quality of processes and technology.

Based on the experience from previous partial results, it is expectable that further consolidation of the proposed models, namely the development of reference implementations under an open source and open specifications communities, will help to understand further weaknesses and help to improve formal models. The proposed CMSP scenario is a quite complex one, requiring further validation and adherence, from both collaborative multimodal service providers (CMSP) and infrastructure operators, aiming to evolve for vendor-agnostic technology landscapes. It is also of paramount importance the adherence of technology providers to discuss and contribute to the proposed models, making them prepared to participate in competitive tenders.

Acknowledgments. This work has been partially supported by Galpgeste and BP Portugal through the research project Horus, by the Administration of the Port of Lisbon and Leixões through the MIELE project, the A-to-Be (Brisa Innovation and Technology), and ANSR (National Road Security Authority) through the SINCRO project. Partial support also from the Center of Technology and Systems – Uninova, and the Portuguese FCT-PEST program UID/EEA/00066/2013.

References

1. Ailijiang, A., Charapko, A., Demirbas, M.: Consensus in the cloud: Paxos systems demystified. In: 2016 25th International Conference on Computer Communication and Networks (ICCCN), pp. 1–10, August 2016
2. Amato, A., Cretella, G., Di Martino, B., Tasquier, L., Venticinque, S.: Semantic engine and cloud agency for vendor agnostic retrieval, discovery, and brokering of cloud services. In: Al-Saidi, A., Fleischer, R., Maamar, Z., Rana, O.F. (eds.) ICC 2014. LNCS, vol. 8993, pp. 8–25. Springer, Cham (2015). https://doi.org/10.1007/978-3-319-19848-4_2
3. Balalaie, A., Heydarnoori, A., Jamshidi, P.: Microservices architecture enables devops: migration to a cloud-native architecture. IEEE Softw. **33**(3), 42–52 (2016)
4. Birkinshaw, J.: Reflections on open strategy. Long Range Plann. **50**(3), 423–426 (2017). Open strategy: transparency and inclusion in strategy processes
5. Camarinha-Matos, L.M., Afsarmanesh, H., Ermilova, E., Ferrada, F., Klen, A., Jarimo, T.: ARCON reference models for collaborative networks. In: Camarinha-Matos, L.M., Afsarmanesh, H. (eds.) Collaborative Networks: Reference Modeling, pp. 83–112. Springer, Boston (2008). https://doi.org/10.1007/978-0-387-79426-6_8
6. Camarinha-Matos, L.M., Afsarmanesh, H.: Towards a reference model for collaborative networked organizations. In: Shen, W. (ed.) BASYS 2006. IFIP AICT, vol. 220, pp. 193–202. Springer, Boston (2006). https://doi.org/10.1007/978-0-387-36594-7_21. On reference models for collaborative networked organizations. Int. J. Prod. Res. **46**(9), 2453–2469 (2008)
7. Cerny, T., Donahoo, M.J., Trnka, M.: Contextual understanding of microservice architecture: current and future directions. SIGAPP Appl. Comput. Rev. **17**(4), 29–45 (2018)
8. Couto, R., Leal, J., Costa, P.M., Galvão, T.: Exploring ticketing approaches using mobile technologies: QR codes, NFC and BLE. In: 2015 IEEE 18th International Conference on Intelligent Transportation Systems, pp. 7–12, September 2015
9. Cuadrado, F., Dueas, J.C., Ruiz, J.L., Bermejo, J., Garcia, M.: An open source platform for the integration of distributed services. In: 22nd International Conference on Advanced Information Networking and Applications - Workshops (AINA Workshops 2008), pp. 1422–1427, March 2008
10. Garcia-Valls, M., Casimiro, A., Reiser, H.P.: A few open problems and solutions for software technologies for dependable distributed systems. J. Syst. Archit. **73**, 1–5 (2017)
11. Hinkelmann, K., Gerber, A., Karagiannis, D., Thoenssen, B., van der Merwe, A., Woitsch, R.: A new paradigm for the continuous alignment of business and it: combining enterprise architecture modelling and enterprise ontology. Comput. Ind. **79**, 77–86 (2016)

12. Karim Jallow, A., Demian, P., Anumba, C.J., Baldwin, A.N.: An enterprise architecture framework for electronic requirements information management. Int. J. Inf. Manag. **37**(5), 455–472 (2017)
13. Karmel, A., Chandramouli, R., Iorga, M.: Nist definition of microservices, application containers and system virtual machines. Technical report, NIST - National Institute of Standards and Technology (2016)
14. Kreps, J., Narkhede, N., Rao, J.: Kafka: a distributed messaging system for log processing. In: Proceedings of 6th International Workshop on Networking Meets Databases (NetDB), Athens, Greece (2011)
15. Lampesberger, H.: Technologies for web and cloud service interaction: a survey. Serv. Oriented Comput. Appl. **10**(2), 71–110 (2016)
16. Lapalme, J., Gerber, A., Van der Merwe, A., Zachman, J., De Vries, M., Hinkelmann, K.: Exploring the future of enterprise architecture: a Zachman perspective. Comput. Ind. **79**, 103–113 (2016)
17. Macedo, P., Camarinha-Matos, L.M.: Value systems alignment analysis in collaborative networked organizations management. Appl. Sci. **7**(12), 1231 (2017). https://doi.org/10.3390/app7121231
18. Maddens, S.: Building blocks for smart societies in a connected world: a regulatory perspective on fifth generation collaborative regulation. Technical report, ITU, Regulatory and Market Environment Division, BDT (2016)
19. McHenry, M.P.: Technical and governance considerations for advanced metering infrastructure/smart meters: technology, security, uncertainty, costs, benefits, and risks. Energy Policy **59**, 834–842 (2013)
20. Mercer, S., Everson, P., Cox, T.: The next generation of it operating models - 6 key themes for the CIOs. Technical report, Deloitte (2014)
21. Olsen, D.H., Trelsgard, K.: Enterprise architecture adoption challenges: an exploratory case study of the Norwegian higher education sector. Procedia Comput. Sci. **100**, 804–811 (2016). International Conference on ENTERprise Information Systems/International Conference on Project MANagement/International Conference on Health and Social Care Information Systems and Technologies, CENTERIS/ProjMAN/HCist 2016
22. Osório, A.L., Camarinha-Matos, L.M., Afsarmanesh, H.: Cooperation enabled systems for collaborative networks. In: Camarinha-Matos, L.M., Pereira-Klen, A., Afsarmanesh, H. (eds.) PRO-VE 2011. IFIP AICT, vol. 362, pp. 400–409. Springer, Heidelberg (2011). https://doi.org/10.1007/978-3-642-23330-2_44
23. Osório, A.L., Camarinha-Matos, L.M., Afsarmanesh, H.: Enterprise collaboration network for transport and logistics services. In: Camarinha-Matos, L.M., Scherer, R.J. (eds.) PRO-VE 2013. IFIP AICT, vol. 408, pp. 267–278. Springer, Heidelberg (2013). https://doi.org/10.1007/978-3-642-40543-3_29
24. Osório, A.L., et al.: Open multi-technology service oriented architecture for "Its" business models: the ITSIBus Etoll services. In: Camarinha-Matos, L.M., Afsarmanesh, H., Ortiz, A. (eds.) PRO-VE 2005. IFIP AICT, vol. 186, pp. 439–446. Springer, Boston (2005). https://doi.org/10.1007/0-387-29360-4_46
25. Osório, A.L.: Towards vendor-agnostic IT-System of IT-Systems with the CEDE platform. In: Afsarmanesh, H., Camarinha-Matos, L.M., Lucas Soares, A. (eds.) PRO-VE 2016. IFIP AICT, vol. 480, pp. 494–505. Springer, Cham (2016). https://doi.org/10.1007/978-3-319-45390-3_42
26. Osório, A.L., Belloum, A., Afsarmanesh, H., Camarinha-Matos, L.M.: Agnostic informatics system of systems: the open ISoS services framework. In: Camarinha-Matos, L.M., Afsarmanesh, H., Fornasiero, R. (eds.) PRO-VE 2017. IFIP AICT, vol. 506, pp. 407–420. Springer, Cham (2017). https://doi.org/10.1007/978-3-319-65151-4_37

27. Osório, L.A., Camarinha-Matos, L.M., Afsarmanesh, H.: ECoNet platform for collaborative logistics and transport. In: Camarinha-Matos, L.M., Bénaben, F., Picard, W. (eds.) PRO-VE 2015. IFIP AICT, vol. 463, pp. 265–276. Springer, Cham (2015). https://doi.org/10.1007/978-3-319-24141-8_24

28. Veríssimo, P., Neves, N.F., Correia, M.: CRUTIAL: the blueprint of a reference critical information infrastructure architecture. In: Lopez, J. (ed.) CRITIS 2006. LNCS, vol. 4347, pp. 1–14. Springer, Heidelberg (2006). https://doi.org/10.1007/11962977_1

29. Sjoerdstra, B.: Dealing with vendor lock-in, June 2016. http://essay.utwente.nl/70153/1/Sjoerdstra_BA_BMS.pdf

30. Stoicescu, M., Fabre, J.-C., Roy, M.: Architecting resilient computing systems: a component-based approach for adaptive fault tolerance. J. Syst. Archit. **73**, 6–16 (2017)

31. Pham Thi, T.T., Dinh, T.L., Helfert, M., Leonard, M.: Modelling collaborative services: The COSEMO model. CoRR, abs/1704.03740 (2017)

32. Truyen, E., Van Landuyt, D., Reniers, V., Rafique, A., Lagaisse, B., Joosen, W.: Towards a container-based architecture for multi-tenant saas applications. In: Proceedings of the 15th International Workshop on Adaptive and Reflective Middleware, ARM 2016, pp. 6:1–6:6. ACM, New York (2016)

33. Urze, P., Abreu, A.: Knowledge transfer assessment in a co-innovation network. In: Camarinha-Matos, L.M., Xu, L., Afsarmanesh, H. (eds.) PRO-VE 2012. IFIP AICT, vol. 380, pp. 605–615. Springer, Heidelberg (2012). https://doi.org/10.1007/978-3-642-32775-9_60

34. Wang, G., Koshy, J., Subramanian, S., Paramasivam, K., Zadeh, M., Narkhede, N., Rao, J., Kreps, J., Stein, J.: Building a replicated logging system with apache kafka. Proc. VLDB Endow. **8**(12), 1654–1655 (2015)

35. Wiggers, P., Armes, D., Engelhart, N., McKenzie, P.: SIAM: Principles and Practices for Service Integration and Management. Van Haren Publishing (2015)

36. Zhu, F., Liu, Q.: Competing with complementors: an empirical look at amazon.com. Harvard Business School Working Paper, No. 15-044, December 2014. 2015:15468, 01 2015

37. Zupan, N., Zhang, K., Jacobsen, H.-A.: Hyperpubsub: a decentralized, permissioned, publish/subscribe service using blockchains: Demo. In: Proceedings of the 18th ACM/IFIP/USENIX Middleware Conference: Posters and Demos, Middleware 2017, pp. 15–16. ACM, New York (2017)

A Plug and Play Integration Model for Virtual Enterprises

Juan D. Méndez[1(✉)], Ricardo J. Rabelo[1], Fabiano Baldo[2],
and Maiara H. Cancian[3]

[1] Department of Automation and Systems Engineering,
Federal University of Santa Catarina, Florianopolis, SC, Brazil
juand.mendez28@gmail.com, ricardo.rabelo@ufsc.br
[2] Department of Computer Science,
Santa Catarina State University, Joinville, SC, Brazil
fabiano.baldo@udesc.br
[3] Estacio University, SC401 Road km 1, Florianopolis, SC, Brazil
maiara.cancian@estacio.br

Abstract. Systems integration is a key issue to be faced when supporting Virtual Enterprises (VE) execution. However, it is very complex regarding the dynamic composition, autonomy and large distribution of its members as well as the high heterogeneity of IT and business processes' models used by them. It has been realized by many works in the literature that SMEs should have some preparedness, including at the IT level, in order to create a feasible solution for them to get onboard and agilely interoperate in real VEs. This work intends to overcome some drawbacks of current approaches for that, proposing a model where VE partners can more easily get into a VE when it is created (*plug*) so that the VE can be executed seamlessly during its operation (*play*) and dissolution (*unplug*), including the support of some level of semantic interoperability. A prototype has been implemented, and results are discussed.

Keywords: Virtual Enterprises · Service Oriented Architecture
SOA · Systems integration · Semantic interoperation · Ontologies
Enterprise Service Bus · ESB

1 Introduction

Virtual Enterprises (VE) are increasingly becoming a net-working pattern to boost companies' agility. Bearing in mind that one of the fundamental VE's properties is that the transactions between its members should be predominantly done via computer networks [1], systems integration becomes a cornerstone issue.

Broadly, VE integration means allowing companies (and their computing systems) to be seamlessly and agilely tied up and to interoperate so as to more effectively support the execution of the involved VE's business processes [2].

This scenario imposes considering some tough aspects in terms of systems integration, like as [2, 3]: the dynamic, temporary and simultaneous belonging of companies to different VEs throughout their life cycles; the massive use of computing

L. M. Camarinha-Matos et al. (Eds.): PRO-VE 2018, IFIP AICT 534, pp. 312–324, 2018.
https://doi.org/10.1007/978-3-319-99127-6_27

networks required to support the communication between VE members regarding the collaborative and sharing natures of the work; companies are geographically distributed and independent, adopting different IT, business process (BP) models, terminologies and working methods; the different governance rules imposed to each VE; and the different security domains to be crossed by the BPs' transactions.

Dealing with all these aspects is very complex. EU Research projects, like PRODNET, DAMASCOS, CrossWork, ATHENA, ECOLEAD and COIN[1], have addressed them in the last two decades providing comprehensive frameworks that embrace the entire VE life cycle at variable levels of depth, although being naturally restrained by the advances of IT and Internet in the time. In order to decrease the problem complexity, some assumptions have been usually made, such as [2–4]: companies are 'somehow' already and properly IT-enabled to participate in a VE; VE members adopt the same integration technologies as well as BP models and terminologies; in practice, once the VE is created it does not change its composition; and they basically do not handle the VE dissolution phase. Besides that, they are either theoretical or too general when trying to propose solutions to face those assumptions, or they implement some solutions using approaches that ended up leaving VE partners' integration a not so agile and seamless process [3].

This paper is not another wide framework like those ones. Instead, it focuses on the VE integration part, approaching it in a different way towards decreasing the mentioned assumptions. Its contribution is represented by a so-called *plug & play* model, where VE partners (i.e. their IT systems) can more easily get into a VE when it is created (*plug*) so that the VE can be executed seamlessly during its operation (*play*) and dissolution (*unplug*), including some level of semantic interoperability.

The model conception and its implementation rely on SOA (*Service Oriented Architecture*) [5], open IT and BP standards, integration patterns, and on ESB (*Enterprise Service Bus*). A software prototype has been implemented to evaluate the proposed model in a controlled environment and results are presented and discussed.

This paper is organized as follows. Section 1 has introduced the problem and the objectives of the work. Section 2 summarizes the main outcomes of related works. Section 3 presents the proposed plug & play model. Section 4 describes the implemented prototype and the achieved results. Section 5 presents some preliminary conclusions and the next main steps of this work.

2 Literature Review

There are different definitions for systems integration and interoperation. In this work the following ones were adopted: *systems integration refers to the ending goal of making a global system architecture to work united and completed, involving coordination, coherence and uniformization. Systems interoperability refers to a means to achieve integration, endowing systems with the ability to exchange/use parts (data, and*

---

[1] https://www.cordis.europa.eu/project/rcn/35881_en.html, 53702_en.html, 71382_en.html, 72762_en.html, 74487_en.html, 85550_en.html.

functionalities or services) of another system without loss or distortion, aiming at mutual understanding within a loosely-coupled federated environment [3].

As mentioned before, a number of works have been addressing systems integration and interoperation in networked organizations (as VEs). They basically set up a (sometimes complex) wrapper, using different IT, and a communication layer over SMEs' systems to make them interacting via a common, predefined and mostly proprietary BP model, with almost none semantic interoperability support, and with quite low means for VEs to indeed work as a dynamic network in a more agile process of get-in and get-off from the VE throughout its life cycle [2–4, 8, 9].

In terms of approaches to tackle semantic interoperability in SOA and/or ESB-based environments, the following ones can be highlighted.

Schratzenstaller *et al.* [6] proposed the creation of a single ontology to support semantic interoperability in VEs without the need to annotate the partners services' interfaces. An ESB is used and enriched with the ontology, but the entire process should be done manually, non-automatically, including partners' identification and the configuration of their services' references and the equivalent payload terms in the ESB. They do not support at all the VE dynamics and partners unplugging.

Zhu [7] developed a prototype to enhance the ESB with semantic mediation. A central ontology is created representing the proprietary enterprise's vocabulary, whose concepts are considered in the services' payloads. Services' descriptions are annotated based on these concepts using SAWSDL for SOAP web services, and ontologies for REST services are created using WSMO Lite (a W3C submission for semantic descriptions). All the mappings between the services payload's terms and the enterprise vocabulary are predefined and manually set up. Once this is done, the prototype can do the mediation between different payloads in run time. This work has considered just one company, and not a VE and the related issues.

Shi *et al.* [8] proposed an ontology-driven integration framework for heterogeneous systems based on SOA. It is divided into three main modules: integration control, service bus and system integration. A hybrid ontology architecture is used to reduce the high coupling and the number of mappings between ontologies. All mappings are carried out manually. This work has considered a hypothetic BP model as well as a generic company scenario, and not a VE and the related issues.

Khalfalla *et al.* [9] proposed a two-phase model to ensure semantic interoperability in a cloud based platform, enabling collaboration within networked organizations in the aerospace industry. The model uses a central ontology to support semantic interoperation, which serves as a major reference in the collaboration. In the first phase (off-line) a sort of actions are performed: creation of the reference and mapping ontologies, the publishing of enterprises systems' APIs as web services considering their native data models, and the creation of rules to make the conversion and mapping between the these models and the reference ontology. The second phase (on-line) allows companies collaboration using those rules and a transformation service that automatically executes the transformations between the different companies' data models. As this scenario focuses on data exchange, without considering the coordinated execution of BPs, ESB is not used. Although this scenario has comprised networked organizations, they did not support a truly VE.

3 The Plug & Play Integration Model

A fundamental assumption in the proposed model is that all VE members belong to a long-term alliance of type VBE (*Virtual organization Breeding Environment*) [1], which is intrinsically grounded on trust, resources sharing, members' autonomy, common working principles and whose members have the willingness to collaborate.

The model's design principles have tried to follow some elements of advanced visions on integration of VBE- and VE-like networks involving SMEs, which include [4, 10, 11]: open, non-intrusive, scalable, loosely-coupling and service-oriented architectures, plug & play collaboration infrastructures, and integration at the design time and at the run-time as well. Considering these principles, the model was designed to support the integration of companies' systems in VEs so that they can be called to execute the required VE's BP activities (considering semantic interoperability) and hence the VE can seamlessly operate and further be dissolved. For that, the model splits the VE integration process into three major phases:

   I. *Plug-in* phase: preparation phase executed when a member is recruited by a VBE and its systems should be prepared to work with when VEs were created.
  II. *Play* phase: the phase where VBE members are selected to participate in VEs and their systems are integrated and interoperate in order to execute the required VE's BPs. Considering the VE reference framework proposed in [2], this phase assumes that activities as VE planning, partners' search and selection, negotiation and contracting have already and somehow been done.
  III. *Unplug* phase: the phase where VE members' systems are logically disconnected from the VE when a given member leaves it.

Considering the VBE life cycle stages [14], the *plug-in* phase is executed in the *VBE creation* stage, (*ICT Setup* and *Member population* steps). The *play* phase is executed when the VE is created (VE *creation* stage) and operated (VE *operation* and *evolution* stages). The *unplug* phase is executed in the *evolution* or *dissolution* stages.

The model relies on two basic approaches regarding its design principles and goals: the use of reference models for BP modeling and of service orientation (SOA) as the underlying basis for systems implementation.

BP reference models, like *EDIFACT, Rosettanet* and *ebXML*, have been used by companies since many years as a "*lingua franca*" to reduce semantic interoperability problems in the transactions between business partners. In this work the UBL (*Universal Business Language*) open BP reference model supported by OASIS [12] has been adopted as its BPs are devised to support supply chains, which is a type of network quite close to VEs. UBL 2.2 is composed of 68 processes, each of them having activities and data structures to be exchanged when they are executed.

This does not mean that all VBE members must have to adopt it. UBL is internally used in the model's architecture as a meta-model which all transactions between VE members are converted and based on. Actually, the model's architecture is open to work with any BP reference model, be it standard or proprietary. It is up to the VBE organization, or even to the VE, to decide about which BP model is to be adopted.

Service Oriented Architecture (SOA) has been increasingly used to deliver interoperable, flexible and loose-coupled solutions [4]. Although SOA is technology independent, some open standards have been developed to implement its concepts, as *Web Service, SOAP, WSDL* and *BPEL*, from W3C[2], which are used in the model internal implementation. In the same way, VBE members' systems do not have to adopt them at all as the model's architecture is open to support multiple technologies. This flexibility is granted by another technology, the ESB. The ESB (*Enterprise Service Bus*) acts as a computing infrastructure that provides secure and reliable communication involving heterogeneous and loose-coupling environments.

However, ESB commercial software do not handle semantics. In order to overcome this, ontologies have been considered as the most suitable approach [4, 6]. The proposed model supports the OWL and OWL-S[3] semantic web technologies, delivering the UBL ontology to represent the information that is exchanged within the VE and the ones representing the native semantics of each VE member in its systems.

3.1   The *Plug-in* Phase

This is an off-line and very preliminary phase, fundamentally related to companies' IT preparedness, which is one of the pre-conditions for their participation in VEs [1, 10]. IT preparedness involves many aspects, as processes and IT governance, legacy systems integration, software maturity, security and supporting hardware [2, 10].

This work assumes that all this is somehow and previously dealt with by the own companies when they are accepted to be members of a given VBE [1, 14]. This also means that companies should handle hiding their organizational and cultural heterogeneity when they decide to work in a VBE/VE and share common working principles [1]. Besides that, and regarding the adopted SOA approach, it is also assumed that their systems are duly wrapped and exposed as software services, implemented in different technologies (as *web services* and *REST*), in order to be further accessed by VBEs' and VEs' related client applications [10].

Therefore, the core goal of the plug-in phase is to make VBE members 'ready to participate' in VEs once they are created.

Still in this phase, as a step related to the semantic interoperability, each company's service is semantically annotated and mapped against the respective UBL BP's activities ontology. This also considers the different services granularities (to be considered when the systems are wrapped) and implementation technologies. Companies' systems can keep working using their proprietary BPs, terminologies and data models. However, if a legacy system uses a proprietary protocol or it is not exposed as a service, a wrapper has to be built up to enable it getting into the VBE. For example, if a given VE member deals with logistics (to send some product's parts to another member) its logistic legacy system has to be wrapped as a service (with its interface) respecting the activities of the *shipping* UBL BP.

---

[2] https://www.w3.org.

[3] https://www.w3.org/Submission/OWL-S and www.w3.org/TR/owl2-overview.

Wrapping legacy systems as services (or more modern ITs) and adopting given BP models to leverage higher interoperability is actually a common practice in companies when doing business. What the model proposes is a configurable, open and standard-based integration connector, a "plug", bridging the companies' internal models and the VBE e VE computing infrastructure, so preserving companies' heterogeneity. This also means that companies can use different "plugs" enabling them to make business with other networks.

Three steps have been devised to support this process, illustrated in Fig. 1.

i. The construction of the UBL-based OWL ontology. This step is supported by the *Automatic Ontology Creation module*, which is used by the VBE IT administrator to feed it with the vocabulary's XML/XSD schemas and returning the equivalent OWL ontology. This ontology will be used in further steps to establish mappings with the messages exchanged by the VE members' systems and to resolve the mediation between different data models at runtime.

ii. Once the global vocabulary is defined the next step is taking every company's single service (previously wrapped), describing it semantically using OWL-S [15] and registering it in the VBE services repository. This action is performed by the IT manager of each company.

iii. The last step refers to use the created semantic descriptions of each service to extract information about the services' *payloads* and to further map it against the UBL Ontology. This is supported by the *semi-automatic mapping module*.

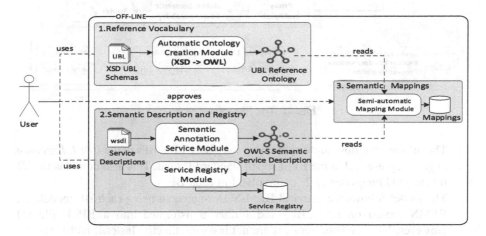

Fig. 1. The Plug-in phase steps

This topology, which combines one central ontology (the UBL one) and the many other ones (representing the members' services), considers the performance benefits in the mediation process as showed in [16].

3.2   The *Play* Phase

It is an on-line phase. It is executed to support each company (its systems) to get dynamically, logically and temporarily integrated and interoperate within the VE computing environment once it is selected to be a VE member.

It is important to highlight that plenty of VEs can be created simultaneously and that a given company (i.e. its systems) can get into several VEs simultaneously too.

This phase is executed in three moments: (1) when the company is selected for a VE (*creation stage*); (2) when other companies are selected to get onboard to the VE due to extra activities not initially planned and then the VE should be recomposed (*evolution stage*); and (3) when a given VE member does not accomplish its duties and one or more new members should get onboard to replace it (*evolution stage*).

Three steps are also involved to support this process, as illustrated in Fig. 2.

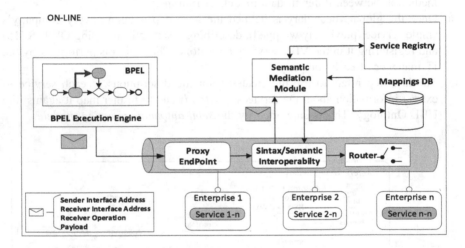

Fig. 2. The Play phase steps

i. The information flow starts by running the given VE's BPs in the *BPEL Execution engine*, represented in the BPEL open standard format. This also contains the VE members (*Enterprises 1, 2 ...*) involved in each BP.

   The model follows the classical BPM-SOA approach, being each BP modeled in BPMN (based on e.g. UBL) and further transformed into a BPEL file [5]. However, VE members' services are not invoked directly. Instead, BPEL invokes the ESB (see Fig. 2), which makes the services invocation themselves.

ii. The model exposes a proxy (*integration endpoint*) in the ESB infrastructure, which receives all the invocations made by the *BPEL Execution engine*. Those invocations have information containing: the *payload* (information sent in proprietary format and data model of the sender member); the address of the source and the receiver services' interfaces; and the operation to be invoked in the receiver party. There is only one ESB for the entire VBE. The ESB allows the dynamic, logical and "temporary" integration as well as the binding, communication and execution of companies' services associated to the several VEs' BPs while preserves the different implementing IT of companies' systems.

iii. Once the integration endpoint receives an incoming message from the *BPEL Execution engine,* it passes it to the *semantic mediator service.* It uses the sent interfaces' addresses to query the *mappings database* looking for the necessary mappings to transform the source payload into the receiver data model. Once the mappings are received the necessary protocol/format transformations of the message are managed by the *ESB.* The ESB uses the received interface address and operation name to invoke it, following the router integration pattern provided by the *ESB* so completing the communication between VE members while supporting syntactic and semantic interoperability.

The ESB setting up and configuration as well as the services instantiation, semantics treatment and services invocation for each VE are performed automatically, dynamically and transparently to the users and companies.

3.3 The *Unplug* Phase

It is also an on-line phase. It happens in two situations: (1) when the VE member accomplishes its duties (during the VE operation or evolution stages) and naturally leaves the VE (in the VE dissolution stage); and (2) when a given VE member has some problems to accomplish its duties and should leave the VE after a sort of general analyses (during the VE operation stage).

The VE Coordinator should update the VE plan in the situation 2 according to the results of the new partners' selection process (step *i* of the *Play* phase). The VE's BPEL file is automatically reconfigured.

VE dissolution is a topic not much covered neither in practice nor in the literature. Several complex issues, at different types, are actually involved when a VE member leaves a VE, especially in the situation 2. Besides legal issues (also considering that a VE should be kept operational until all the legal obligations have been fulfilled), it is necessary to handle logistics and other aspects related to the physical parts that were being produced. There are also some tough IT problems. For example, when a given member is producing its parts, its software services are also in execution and have some associated state memory. From the services technology point of view, replacing a VE member by one company (or even by more than one) would also mean to pass the same state memories to the new members' services, which is very complex.

None of these issues are currently supported by this presented model. However, besides the provided support for that BPEL reconfiguration and for that logical disconnection of the VE member's services, this model simplifies the problem, supporting a replacement of one member by only one, assuming that this replacement will imply that the involved services are no longer held to any process.

4   Implementation and Preliminary Assessment

This section presents the VE scenario and computing prototype that was implemented to qualitatively assess the proposed integration model.

All the model's artifacts were implemented using SOAP, web services and Java language, and deployed in a local network and controlled environment.

Related to VE members' services, plenty of services were implemented in a simple way also using those ITs to simulate the VBE members' services in this current version of the prototype. The use of web services is not a limitation at all as the model is able to handle multiples technologies thanks to the ESB capabilities.

In the *Plug-in* phase, a key issue that had to be faced was the one related to ontologies, the conversion of XSD/XML to RDF/OWL. There are many approaches for that [17] and the one developed in [18] has been chosen and implemented as it has fit best the requirements of the intended model.

A second implemented artifact was the *semantic annotation service*, which generates compliant OWL-S ontologies from a WSDL description. The work developed in [19] was modified and implemented as a service. This artifact generates the process model, the grounding and profile ontologies that store all the necessary information to get the service description, data model and implementation details.

The third artifact was the *Ontology Matcher Service*. It is responsible for automatically finding the semantic equivalence between services' terms (from the companies' data models) and the respective terms in the UBL ontology. There are also some approaches to tackle this, as in [20–22]. The *Agreement Maker Light* matcher [23] was chosen regarding the desired level of precision and execution time for the model. It was also modified and wrapped as a service.

The result of all this process is a set of mappings. Considering the complexity involved in matching problems [23] ontology mappings can have some imprecision. Given that the quality of this mapping is crucial for the proper functioning of the whole model, the mappings are not immediately set up for being used. Instead, each company's IT manager is assisted with an interactive GUI to make the final checking (and corrections) of the suggested mapping of each service against the UBL ontology.

In the *Play* phase, the given VE's BPs are modeled in BPMN and further converted to BPEL 2.0 following the WS-BPEL standard. The BPEL process is deployed using the execution engine supported by *Apache ODE*[4] orchestrator. It invokes the integration endpoint, which is exposed as a SOAP service in the chosen message infrastructure (supported by *MULE ESB*[5]) and that is responsible for managing the messages exchange between VE members. The members' services are registered using *jUDDI*[6] service registry (that supports UDDI 3.0 standard), and the ontology mappings are stored in a MySQL database.

In order to evaluate the proposed model and the semantic mediation approach, a scenario has been devised and modeled in BPMN using UBL, as showed in Fig. 3.

---

[4] http://ode.apache.org/.

[5] https://www.mulesoft.com/platform/soa/mule-esb-open-source-esb.

[6] https://juddi.apache.org/.

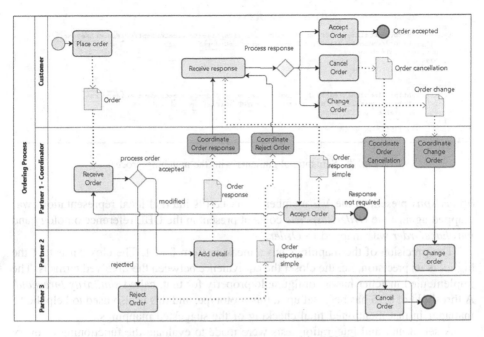

Fig. 3. Ordering process expressed in BPMN

The scenario refers to a hypothetic customer who asks for a given product close to a given VBE's company. This product is basically composed of three parts, being one part produced by this company. This company then triggers the process of VE creation, ending up by forming the following VE: this company ('Partner 1') as the *VE Coordinator* and which interacts with the customer; and 'Partner 2' and 'Partner 3', which manufacture the other two product's parts. These two partners should send their parts directly to Partner 1 for the final assembly once they are finished.

This scenario is associated to the UBL process *'Ordering Process'* (one of the 68 BPs of the standard), which has a number of sub-processes and internal activities. A number of documents are also needed to be exchanged within this process and, in the case of a VE, different partners are responsible for executing some of the sub-processes. Due to space restrictions, Fig. 3 only shows one part of the *Ordering Process*, covering the acceptance and rejection of the business request. Many BPs will be normally involved in a 'real' VE regarding its full life cycle and the BP's needs of the customer order in place.

From the execution point of view, the way the model treats one VE and one UBL BP is exactly the same than as for many VEs and multiple BPs.

This scenario assumes that services are made available by the involved companies (the *plug-in* phase). Several different services were implemented using different data models so as to better test the mediation process in each BP transaction.

Figure 4 presents an excerpt of the results of this process. The example shows two mappings established between the ontology (representing the ordering SOAP service of *Partner 2* ('E2')) and the UBL reference ontology. It can be observed that the concept

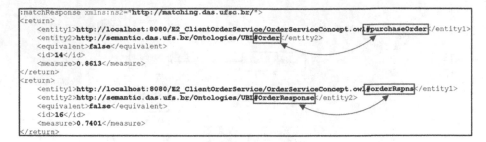

```
:matchResponse xmlns:ns2="http://matching.das.ufsc.br/">
<return>
    <entity1>http://localhost:8080/E2_ClientOrderService/OrderServiceConcept.owl#purchaseOrder</entity1>
    <entity2>http://semantic.das.ufs.br/Ontologies/UBL#Order</entity2>
    <equivalent>false</equivalent>
    <id>14</id>
    <measure>0.8613</measure>
</return>
<return>
    <entity1>http://localhost:8080/E2_ClientOrderService/OrderServiceConcept.owl#orderRspns</entity1>
    <entity2>http://semantic.das.ufs.br/Ontologies/UBL#OrderResponse</entity2>
    <equivalent>false</equivalent>
    <id>16</id>
    <measure>0.7401</measure>
</return>
```

Fig. 4. Semantic alignments with the matching process

orderRspns present in the VE member's service (its internal local representation) was mapped against the *OrderResponse* concept present in the UBL reference ontology and *purchaseOrder* was mapped to *Order*.

The precision of the mappings has a measure from 0 to 1. The closer it is to 1 the higher is its precision, i.e. the closer the equivalence between the involved terms is. The implemented matcher has a configurable property for that, called *similarity threshold*. A threshold of 0.95 has been set up in this prototype, and this is also used to help the IT manager in that mentioned final checking of the suggested mappings.

A set of unit and integration tests were made to evaluate the functioning of every implemented module and of the model as a whole, i.e. if it supported the right VE operation, allowing VE members to seamlessly and automatically communicate with each other about BP-related transactions regarding syntactic and semantic differences.

5   Conclusions

This paper has presented a contribution towards a more agile integration of companies to VEs and their systems' interoperation.

It is represented by a three-phase model that, respecting the VBE and VE life cycles, helps companies in their IT preparedness, their integration and operation in VEs, and their unplugging from them.

The model was devised based on state-of-the-art design principles, like being open, low intrusive and service-oriented. To be highlighted the strong use of IT and BP open standards as well as of integration patterns in all the involved actions.

Important to mention that, once companies' systems are made available (in the *plug-in* phase), all the VE operation is executed automatically (unless given BPs' activities are designed to request human intervention) and transparently, dynamically (allowing companies to enter and to leave a VE and automatically respecting the VE's plan), using open and standard-based IT and BP model but preserving companies' autonomy and their IT heterogeneity. VBE members can also come and go but this is transparent for the plug & play model's execution.

The developed prototype could show the potential of the proposed approach and of the semantic mediation techniques used.

Although the whole model is open to handle multiple technologies thanks the use of an ESB, only W3C IT standards were used in this prototype. Yet, although UBL has been adopted as the internal BP reference for the basics of systems interoperability, the model is open to support any other BP model.

The model tries to contribute to mitigate interoperability problems at three levels [13]. At the *technical* (or syntactical) level, it handles the existence of different systems and services, using different data formats and data integration middleware (e.g. ESB), and their access from disparate systems. At the *semantic* level, the meaning of the exchanged data and messages are automatically recognized and further processed via reference data and ontologies. At the *organizational* level, there is a BP alignment and the automated processing of its workflows through the use of common services-based architecture (e.g. SOA). No concrete contributions are provided to the fourth and upper level, the *legal* interoperability.

Next main short-steps of this research are: (i) supporting semantic description of REST services; (ii) stressing the prototype in scenarios composed of plenty of simultaneous EVs, BPs and companies (i.e. services) in a distributed and less controlled computing environment; (iii) the analysis and implementation of how security needs can be expressed as non-functional requirements when modeling BPs at the BPM/BPMN level and be automatically and properly interpreted and dealt with by the ESB; and (iv) the integration of the implemented model with an almost finished module to support resilience at runtime of SOA-based VE systems.

References

1. Camarinha-Matos, L.M., Afsarmanesh, H.: Collaborative networks: a new scientific discipline. J. Intell. Manuf. **16**(4–5), 439–452 (2005)
2. Rabelo, R.J., Gusmeroli, S.: The ECOLEAD collaborative business infrastructure for networked organizations. In: Camarinha-Matos, L.M., Picard, W. (eds.) PRO-VE 2008. ITIFIP, vol. 283, pp. 451–462. Springer, Boston, MA (2008). https://doi.org/10.1007/978-0-387-84837-2_47
3. Romero, D., Vernadat, F.: Enterprise information systems state of the art: past, present and future trends. Comput. Ind. **79**, 3–13 (2016)
4. Panetto, H., Jardim-Goncalves, R., Romero, D.: New perspectives for the future interoperable enterprise systems. Comput. Ind. **79**, 47–63 (2016)
5. Draheim, D.: Service-oriented architecture. Business Process Technology: A Unified View on Business Processes. Workflows and Enterprise Applications, pp. 221–241. Springer, Heidelberg (2010). https://doi.org/10.1007/978-3-642-01588-5_8
6. Schratzenstaller, W.M.K., Baldo, F., Rabelo, R.J.: Semantic integration via enterprise service bus in virtual organization breeding environments. In: Nguyen, N.T., Trawiński, B., Fujita, H., Hong, T.-P. (eds.) ACIIDS 2016. LNCS (LNAI), vol. 9622, pp. 544–553. Springer, Heidelberg (2016). https://doi.org/10.1007/978-3-662-49390-8_53
7. Zhu, W.: Semantic mediation bus: an ontology-based runtime infrastructure for service interoperability. In: IEEE 16th International Enterprise Distributed Object Computing Conference Workshops, pp. 140–145 (2012)

8. Shi, K., Gao, F., Xu, Q., Xu, G.: Integration framework with semantic aspect of heterogeneous system based on ontology and ESB. In: Proceedings of the 26th Chinese Control and Decision Conference, pp. 4143–4148 (2014)
9. Khalfallah, M., Figay, N.: A cloud-based platform to ensure interoperability in aerospace industry. J. Intell. Manuf. **27**, 119–129 (2016)
10. Picard, W., Paszkiewicz, Z., Gabryszak, P., Krysztofiak, K., Cellary, W.: Breeding virtual organizations in a service-oriented architecture environment. In: SOA Infrastructure Tools - Concepts and Methods, pp. 375–396 (2010)
11. Dehbokry, S.G., Chew, E.: Toward a multi-disciplinary business architecture reference model for SMEs. In: Proceedings of the 23th European Conference on Information Systems (2015)
12. OASIS: Universal Business Language Version 2.2 (2018). http://docs.oasis-open.org/ubl/UBL-2.2.html
13. EIF, European Interoperability Framework: Towards Interoperability for European Public Services, European Commission (2011)
14. Romero, D., Galeano, N., Molina, A.: A virtual breeding environment reference model and its instantiation methodology. In: Camarinha-Matos, L.M., Picard, W. (eds.) PRO-VE 2008. ITIFIP, vol. 283, pp. 15–24. Springer, Boston, MA (2008). https://doi.org/10.1007/978-0-387-84837-2_2
15. France Telecom, University of Maryland, NIST, Nokia, Stanford Univ., Toshiba: OWL-S: Semantic Markup for Web Services, in www.w3.org/Submission/OWL-S/
16. Abadi, A., Ben-Azza, H., Sekkat, S.: An ontology-based framework for virtual enterprise integration and interoperability. In: International Conference on Electrical and Information Technologies (ICEIT 2016), pp. 36–41 (2016)
17. Hacherouf, M., Bahloul, S.N., Cruz, C.: Transforming XML documents to OWL ontologies: a survey. J. Inf. Sci. **41**, 242–259 (2015)
18. Yüksel, M.: A Semantic Interoperability Framework for Reinforcing Post Market Safety Studies. Ph.D. thesis, Middle East Technical University (2013)
19. Paolucci, M., Srinivasan, N., Sycara, K.: Towards a semantic choreography of web services: from WSDL to DAML-S. In: Proceedings of the International Conference on Web Services (ICWS' 2003), pp. 22–26 (2003)
20. Banouar, O., Raghay, S.: Comparative study of the systems of semantic integration of information: a survey. In: Proceedings of the12th International Conference of Computer Systems and Applications, pp. 1–8 (2015)
21. Liu, H., Cutting-Decelle, A.-F., Bourey, J.-P.: Use of ontology for solving interoperability problems between enterprises. In: Camarinha-Matos, L.M., Boucher, X., Afsarmanesh, H. (eds.) PRO-VE 2010. IAICT, vol. 336, pp. 730–737. Springer, Heidelberg (2010). https://doi.org/10.1007/978-3-642-15961-9_86
22. Achichi, M., et al.: Results of the ontology alignment evaluation initiative 2017. In: Proceedings of the16th International Semantic Web Conference, pp. 61–113 (2017)
23. Faria, D., Pesquita, C., Santos, E., Palmonari, M., Cruz, I.F., Couto, F.M.: The agreement maker light ontology matching system. In: Meersman, R., et al. (eds.) OTM 2013. LNCS, vol. 8185, pp. 527–541. Springer, Heidelberg (2013). https://doi.org/10.1007/978-3-642-41030-7_38

Assessment of IS Integration Efforts to Implement the Internet of Production Reference Architecture

Günther Schuh, Jörg Hoffmann[✉], Martin Bleider, and Violett Zeller

FIR e. V. at RWTH Aachen University, Aachen, Germany
{Guenther.Schuh,Joerg.Hoffmann,Martin.Bleider,
Violett.Zeller}@fir.rwth-aachen.de

Abstract. As part of a collaborative network, manufacturing companies are required to be agile and accelerate their decision making. To do so, a high amount of data is available and needs to be utilized. To enable this from a company internal information system perspective, the Internet of Production (IoP) describes a future information system (IS) architecture. Core element of the IoP is a digital platform building the basis for a network of cognitive systems. To implement and continuously further develop the IoP, manufacturing companies need to make architecture-related decisions concerning the accessibility of data, the processing of the data as well as the visualization of the information. The goal of this research is the development of a decision-support methodology to make those decisions, taking under consideration the evaluated IS integration effort. Therefore, this paper describes the allocation of IS functions and identifies the effort drivers for the respective IS integration by analyzing the integration possibilities. Conclusively this approach will be validated in a case study.

Keywords: Internet of Production · Information systems
Information system architecture · Information systems integration
IS-architecture of manufacturing companies · Agile and learning companies

1 Motivation and Challenges

Realization of *Industrie 4.0* concepts drive manufacturing companies to the implementation of central, real-time use of data [1]. For this reason, they need to use information from different information systems (IS) and an increasing number of devices necessary for handling and processing the huge amount of data [2]. The real-time use of data is a key enabler for companies to join collaborative networks [3, 4]. However, establishing a central data pool is associated with extensive effort within the company [3]. This is, because data is often not available in sufficient quality or even not accessible neither inside nor outside the company. Previous approaches like centralized ERP or PLM systems did not adequately meet all existing requirements in practice. In addition, they struggle to meet new requirements introduced through machine learning and cognitive system approaches. Therefore, new approaches have been developed to facilitate an integration layer for the companies' information sources. Concepts such as SOA or MISE [4] require

© IFIP International Federation for Information Processing 2018
Published by Springer Nature Switzerland AG 2018. All Rights Reserved
L. M. Camarinha-Matos et al. (Eds.): PRO-VE 2018, IFIP AICT 534, pp. 325–333, 2018.
https://doi.org/10.1007/978-3-319-99127-6_28

a total rebuild of a companies' IS architecture [5]: the integration is a challenge due to heterogeneous data, differing system models and unclear responsibilities inside the companies [6]. For that reason, especially small or medium sized manufacturing companies dread to implement such concepts. In particular, companies are missing an approach on how to measure the effort for implementation and how to deduce decisions to take.

Recent publications suggest a platform based approach as a future IS architecture for manufacturing companies [5, 7, 8]. In such an architecture, existing IS remain mostly untouched and a new platform-layer is implemented on top of them. A model explicitly addressing manufacturing companies is the *Internet of Production* (IoP) [8]. Those models are well described concerning the future IS architecture layout, but they are missing concrete descriptions on how companies should implement them: what decisions they should take, and what functionality they should implement in which layer. To increase their practical value, the process of IS function integration decisions will be explained in this paper, addressing the research question: *How can architecture decisions regarding the integration of IS functionalities into the IoP be structured, systematically made and necessary changes planned accordingly?*

2   Fundamentals

2.1   Internet of Production Reference Architecture

The approach of the IoP enables companies to quickly initiate data-based decisions and change processes, thus enabling the company to be part of a collaborative network. The reference architecture describes the aggregated product life cycle from development to the use of a product (Fig. 1). The horizontal layers represent the collected data, the assisting systems and the applications that support the developer, the manufacturer and the customer in each period. The central *Middleware+* layer receives heterogeneous raw data from different sources or distributed systems and creates *Smart Data* based on various

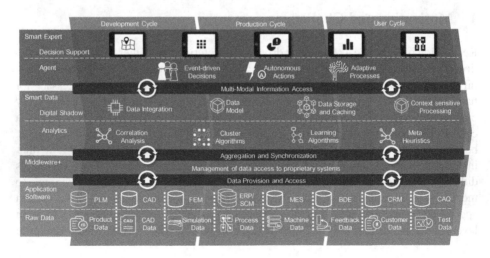

Fig. 1. Internet of production reference architecture [8]

algorithms. This data with a high content of information provides the basis for the digital shadow, which describes a digital real time reflection of the reality. Users can have access to the data models via *apps* and software-based *agents* can use the smart data for automatic decision-making. By sending back the data to the middleware and application software, it is possible to achieve continuous synchronization, which ensures consistency and avoids conflicting data sets. The IoP is described in more detail in [8, 9], the single layers are described in more detail in Sect. 3.

2.2 IS Integration

An IS is an aggregation of socio-technical subsystems with the purpose of supporting management and operational decision making as well as providing means of information and communication [10, 11]. Methods of IS integration management can be utilized to achieve the goal of a consistent IS architecture [12]. Therefore four integration objects can be classified: IT strategy, IT organization, IT landscape and stakeholders [12, 13]. For the basic paths it can be distinguished between horizontal (across different divisions, but on one architecture level) and vertical integration (within one division, but over different architecture levels) [14].

Nowadays most IS architectures involve three different layers: data layer, processing layer and presentation layer [15]. Common integration technologies are the use of middleware and the Enterprise Application Integration (EAI) concept. Middleware offers standard interfaces for data exchange, but lacks in flexibility in a business process oriented integration. EAI offers a separation from business process logic and interface programming in a way that development and maintenance efforts are low [13].

Main drivers of effort for IS integration can be subdivided in: Complexity of the IS project [12], legal guidelines [13], quality guidelines on the basis of certain attributes such as functionality, reliability, usability, efficiency, maintainability and portability of an IS integration and erroneous planning and conception of an IS integration. These categories may overlap partly, for e.g. the portability affects the complexity as well as the quality guidelines of an IS project. Effort can be displayed in seven requirements, which are speed of integration, minimization of integration expenses, minimization of integration risks, potential for synergies, technology innovation, protection of investment, and minimization of archiving effort [13].

2.3 IS Architecture Decisions Today

Transformation towards vertical and horizontal integration, in order to realize a consistent data processing is a key topic in the context of *Industrie 4.0* [16] and the collaboration within manufacturing networks [3]. The respective IS architecture decisions nowadays are influenced by the concepts of service-oriented architectures (SOA) and micro services. Even though a modular design of the architecture leads, due to uncoupling and reuse, to less IT complexity, a complete implementation of SOA in manufacturing companies is not feasible [9]. As described, the IoP represents a clear target architecture for manufacturing companies to fulfill the corresponding requirements. This paper will outline the path of transforming towards an IoP architecture and provide a method to systematically conduct related decision.

3   Mapping of IS Functionalities Within the IoP Layers

The high structural complexity of collaborative networks and the related IS architecture can be managed by pre-structuring reference models [17]. Still, on the company level the transformation towards and adaptation of this pre-structuring model, the IoP, must be managed with low effort and high velocity. A function-based approach taking into account a defined set of effort drivers will enable companies to do so.

For the integration of IS functionalities, the functional blocks need to be separated from the process or use case [18] and based on the users' requirements further detailed into functional modules, so these modules can be located to the current IS architecture layers [2, 19]. To derive a detailed description of the IoP layer for this purpose, existing IS architecture layer models have been analyzed (see Fig. 2). The aspects of the different models with different focus have been combined with the specific aspects of the IoP to enable the goal of a quickly initiating change processes. The result is the following description of the IoP layer:

Raw data contains data storage functionalities including the databases of the core IS, collection of sensor data, machine data and asset data.

Application Software contains the functionalities regarding data generation and transformation within core IS, connectivity of physical assets to core IS and functionalities regarding data based control of assets.

Middleware+ contains all functionalities regarding the communication and routing of data between the different layer and core IS, including the scheduling of communication, modeling of communication channels, data defect detection (regarding data format), transformation of data in further processable format and asset management of data sources.

Analytics contains all logical functions processing data of at least two separate data sources or two separate core IS. This includes a logical data defect detection, historical analysis, formation of performance indicators, prognosis and simulations.

Digital Shadow combines analyzed data to case-specific sets of information containing all relevant information. Thus, the layer contains the respective data models, storage of the aggregated information and access management of agents to the information.

Agents autonomously combine information. This layer contains business decision rules and connects information objects of different layer.

Decision Support represents the user interface to the decision maker. It contains the data entry point for information searches, the mapping of information to business processes and all visualization functionalities.

Additionally to the layer descriptions, general decision rules are necessary:

- Adaptation of core IS shall be minimized to only configurations. Extensive specific adjustments or fast and close to the customer developments are implemented in different IoP layers. Exceptions are changes requiring secure and safe development (e.g. regulatory changes).

- Data processing and storage that can be performed within the same core IS should remain within this IS.
- Sensors preprocessing the data shall be directly connected to the middleware+ layer. Basic sensors should remain connected to a core IS or raw database.

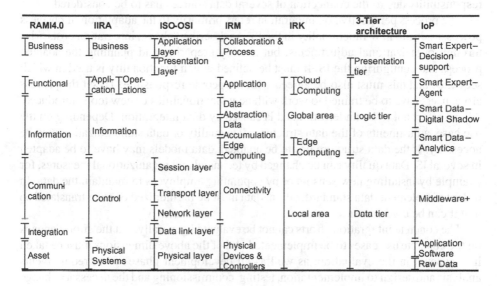

RAMI4.0	IIRA	ISO-OSI	IRM	IRK	3-Tier architecture	IoP
Business	Business	Application layer / Presentation layer	Collaboration & Process		Presentation tier	Smart Expert–Decision support
Functional	Appli-cation / Oper-ations		Application	Cloud Computing		Smart Expert–Agent
			Data Abstraction	Global area	Logic tier	Smart Data–Digital Shadow
Information	Information		Data Accumulation			Smart Data–Analytics
			Edge Computing	Edge Computing		
Communi-cation	Control	Session layer				
		Transport layer	Connectivity			Middleware+
		Network layer		Local area	Data tier	
Integration		Data link layer				Application Software
Asset	Physical Systems	Physical layer	Physical Devices & Controllers			Raw Data

Fig. 2. Analysis of existing IS layer models (based on [20–25])

4 Assessment of Integration Measures

In this research, integration refers to adapting a part of the IS architecture to enable new functions (see Sect. 3). This can be done through *programming* of new functionality, development of *interfaces* between IS, or *introduction* of new software. Doing so, integration costs are incurred at four integration dimensions. In these dimensions, integration costs can arise both as a one-off expense and as running costs, such as license costs. However, this article focuses on the one-off costs.

In the technical dimension, development costs depend on the properties of the existing IS. Interfaces must be adapted to link data sources, and effort depends on the degree of standardization of the IS to be connected. Proprietary interfaces require more effort than standardized interfaces such as OPC-UA. If the interface has to be capable of real-time operation, technical outlay for fail-safe operation is created by means of redundant systems. In programming, the effort depends on the basis on which new functions are implemented. If the development environment of the digital platform is used, which enables e.g. visual scripting, development is less complex than when implementing proprietary development without the use of frameworks. In the simplest case, functionality can be implemented by just configuring an IS.

From an organizational point of view, effort can range from a simple task assignment to an employee, to a reorganization, depending on the scope of the change. An effort driver is the required adjustment speed. If fast adaptations are often required, an IT of two speeds should be introduced. Process adaptations are often directly linked to the integration of new functions, which in turn generate effort through training and learning in the reorganization of departments. Also the necessary reorganization of the data responsibility due to the connection of several data sources has to be considered.

The process perspective on integration refers primarily to the adaptation of business processes due to new functionality in the IS. As described above, integration costs arise through organizational adjustments, but also by preparing and planning the adapted process and configuring the IS. It must be defined which functionality is used in which sequence and this must also be agreed with the people responsible. To set the process alive, users have to be trained to work with new functionalities or new tools introduced.

An effort not to be underestimated is caused by data integration. Depending on the use case, adjustments of the data structure, data quality or data standardization may be necessary: If the data structure has to be adapted, data models may have to be adapted in several IS. Data quality can be changed by technical and organizational measures, for example by installing new sensors or by appointing employees to maintain the data. In order to implement data standardization, data must be harmonized or even translated so that it can be used across systems.

The concrete integration efforts cannot be evaluated generally, but the effort depends on the concrete use cases to be implemented. All of the above dimensions must be taken into account in the evaluation, as well as all development phases from requirements analysis and design to implementation, testing, commissioning and the necessary change management.

5   New Approach on Architecture Decisions

The core objective is to integrate functionalities into a central platform, still using standardized core IS and no longer to implement everything in individual systems or focus on in-house developments. The whole decision process applies to adding new functionalities into the IoP but also transforming the current IS architecture to an IoP-like architecture. The following seven steps describe the application of the approach:

1. Create a detailed description of the use case/process to be implemented
2. Gather internal objectives that the integration needs to match based on company and IT strategy
3. Detail the use case into functional blocks and further into functional modules
4. Compare needed functionalities with existing functionalities
5. Derive possible technical integration scenarios regarding all additional functionalities and interfaces within the IoP (based on Sect. 3)
6. Quantify the integration efforts for each relevant scenario (based on Sect. 4)
7. Decide on integration scenario.

6   Case Study: Weight Prediction for Product Development

An electric car company develops a small and light electric city car. The company has only been founded three years ago. As a start-up, it facilitates agile development methods unlike in traditional OEMs with conventional development processes. Still, decision makers in the company need to have real-time transparency on the development status - in case of the examined company: especially on the car's weight. Therefore, the company needs to summarize and visualize the data from the IS within the development cycle of the IoP, including data from suppliers throughout the collaborative supply chain. One specific goal is to forecast the weight change during development phase. The development of an app to enable the desired transparency is only on part of the companies' IT strategy to implement the IoP infrastructure.

The necessary functionality for this case ranges from data modelling to aggregate the needed data, evaluation and prognosis of the weight status, to visualization of the CAD data. Parts of the required functionality exist, e.g. visualization in the PDM system. However, there is no cross-system evaluation. Therefore, the company had several integration scenarios: (1) Development of a specific adaptation of the PDM system, (2) integration of the function into the existing IoT platform, and (3) implementation of an in-house development. Since scenario 3 requires significantly more effort in development, because it is not based on any existing technology, two options remain. The company evaluated the development costs for programming the PDM in comparison to the cost to implement interfaces to the IoT platform and build an app on its basis. Therefore, they detailed their requirements and compared it to the existing functionality: e.g. the PDM system is capable of *storing the data* in the correct structure, in the IoT platform, *apps* can be built on basis of existing templates. Taking in account the strategy of the company to build more such apps in future, the one-off cost of implementing an interface between IoT platform and PDM can be rated lower. Hence, the company has opted for scenario 2.

7   Summary

After summarizing the state of the art concerning IS integration and IS architecture decisions, this paper introduces a method on how to map IS functionalities into the IoP. It gives an overview of integration measures to be taken into consideration, and introduces an approach on how to decide on IS architecture changes. Still there is further work to be done: Especially the monetary calculation of implementation costs has not been covered in this paper, but will be part of future research. The work has so far focused on the manufacturing industry, though other industry sectors such as logistics and service providers suffer similar challenges. Thus, the concepts in this paper should be transferred to other industries.

References

1. Kagermann, H.: Chancen von Industrie 4.0 nutzen. In: Vogel-Heuser, B., Bauernhansl, T., ten Hompel, M. (eds.) Handbuch Industrie 4.0 Bd.4. SRT, pp. 235–246. Springer, Heidelberg (2017). https://doi.org/10.1007/978-3-662-53254-6_12
2. Li, F., Zhang, P., Huang, H., Chen, G.: A model-based service-oriented integration strategy for industrial CPS. In: Wan, J., Humar, I., Zhang, D. (eds.) Industrial IoT 2016. LNICST, vol. 173, pp. 222–230. Springer, Cham (2016). https://doi.org/10.1007/978-3-319-44350-8_22
3. Brettel, M., Friederichsen, N., Keller, M., Rosenberg, M.: How virtualization, decentralization and network building change the manufacturing landscape. Int. J. Mech. Aerosp. Ind. Mechatron. Manuf. Eng. **8**(1), 37–44 (2014)
4. Benaben, F., Mu, W., Boissel-Dallier, N., Barthe-Delanoe, A.-M., Zribi, S., Pingaud, H.: Supporting interoperability of collaborative networks through engineering of a service-based Mediation Information System (MISE 2.0). Enterp. Inf. Syst. **4**, 1–27 (2014)
5. Schuh, G., Hoffmann, J., Gruber, M., Zeller, V.: Managing IT complexity in the manufacturing industry. An agenda for action. J. Syst. Cybern. Inform. **15**, 61–65 (2017)
6. Yang, Y., Yin, C., Li, X. (eds.): A XML based information integration for field layer, MES and ERP. In: 2017 5th International Conference on Enterprise Systems (ES) (2017)
7. Lu, Y., Cecil, J.: An Internet of Things (IoT)-based collaborative framework for advanced manufacturing. Int. J. Adv. Manuf. Technol. **84**, 1141–1152 (2016)
8. Schuh, G., et al.: Change Request im Produktionsbetrieb. In: Brecher, C., Klocke, F., Schmitt, R., Schuh, G. (eds.) AWK Aachener Werkzeugmaschinen-Kolloquium 2017, pp. 109–131. Apprimus, Aachen (2017).
9. Stich, V., Hoffmann, J., Heimes, P.: Software-definierte Plattformen. Eigenschaften, Integrationsanforderungen und Praxiserfahrungen in produzierenden Unternehmen. HMD **55**, 25–43 (2018)
10. Bagad, V.S.: Management Information Systems. Technical Publications, Pune (2008)
11. Krcmar, H.: Informationsmanagement. Springer Gabler, Berlin (2015). https://doi.org/10.1007/978-3-662-45863-1
12. Dern, G.: Integrationsmanagement in der Unternehmens-IT. Systemtheoretisch fundierte Empfehlungen zur Gestaltung von IT-Landschaft und IT-Organisation. Vieweg+Teubner, Wiesbaden (2011)
13. Guggenberger, J.M.: Aufbau und Ablauf einer IT-Integration. Phasenmodell und Vorgehenskonzept unter Berücksichtigung rechtlicher Aspekte. Gabler Verlag, s.l., Wiesbaden (2010)
14. Kaib, M.: Enterprise Application Integration: Grundlagen, Integrationsprodukte, Anwendungsbeispiele. Springer, Wiesbaden (2002). https://doi.org/10.1007/978-3-663-07913-2
15. Abts, D., Mülder, W.: Grundkurs Wirtschaftsinformatik. Eine kompakte und praxisorientierte Einführung. Springer Vieweg, Wiesbaden (2017). https://doi.org/10.1007/978-3-658-16379-2
16. Schuh, G., Anderl, R., Gausemeier, J., ten Hompel, M., Wahlster, W. (eds.): Industrie 4.0 Maturity Index. Die digitale Transformation von Unternehmen gestalten. Utz, München (2017)
17. Kandjani, H.: Reducing the structural complexity and transaction cost of collaborative networks using extended axiomatic design theory and virtual brokerage. Concurr. Eng. **22**, 320–332 (2014)
18. Müller, J.: Workflow-Based Integration. Springer, Dordrecht (2006). https://doi.org/10.1007/b138228

19. Ma, C., Wang, J.: Enterprise information management system integration based on internet of things technology. Manag. Eng. **22**, 12–15 (2016)
20. DIN: Referenzarchitekturmodell Industrie 4.0 (RAMI4.0). Beuth, Berlin (2016)
21. Industrial Internet Consortium: The Industrial Internet of Things. Volume G1: Reference Architecture (2017)
22. Leimeister, J.M.: Einführung in die Wirtschaftsinformatik. Springer Gabler, Wiesbaden (2015). https://doi.org/10.1007/978-3-540-77847-9
23. Green, J.: The Internet of Things Reference Model, Chicago (2014)
24. Heidrich, M., Luo, J.J.: Industrial Internet of Things: Referenzarchitektur für die Kommunikation, München (2016)
25. Alt, R., Puschmann, T.: Digitalisierung der Finanzindustrie. Grundlagen der Fintech-Evolution. Springer Gabler, Heidelberg (2016). https://doi.org/10.1007/978-3-662-50542-7

Collaborative Business Strategies

Business Impacts of Technology Disruption - A Design Science Approach to Cognitive Systems' Adoption Within Collaborative Networks

Katri Valkokari[1]([⊠]), Tuija Rantala[1], Ari Alamäki[2],
and Katariina Palomäki[1]

[1] VTT, Technical Research Centre of Finland, PL1306, 33101 Tampere, Finland
{katri.valkokari, tuija.rantala,
katariina.palomaki}@vtt.fi
[2] Haaga-Helia Applied Sciences, Ratapihantie 13, 00520 Helsinki, Finland
ari.alamaki@haaga-helia.fi

Abstract. Digitalisation and data are stated to be significant drivers of change, technology disruption, and new business. The purpose of this study is to explore the business impacts of technology disruption, more specifically the adoption of cognitive systems within collaborative networks through a design science approach. In accordance with design studies, the relevance of the research results and the research quality are evaluated against the practices of seven companies that participated in the research process. At the crossroads of technology and business disruption the two main dimensions illustrate: (1) the technical complexity of cognitive systems adapted from conventional data utilisation to learning cognitive systems and (2) the broadness of business impacts from a company's internal processes to changes in ecosystems.

Keywords: Technology diffusion · Collaborative networks · Design science
Cognitive systems · Big data analytics · Business ecosystems

1 Introduction

Disruptive technologies not only enhance technological possibilities, but they also allow and force actors to experiment with alternative innovative processes and arrangements at several levels from societal changes at macro level to human behaviour at micro level [1, 2]. The new generation of data-driven business and cognitive systems are changing the way companies manage and operate their business processes [3], but the impact is not equal in all phases and levels of value chains. The advancements in cognitive systems create new business opportunities for some companies while others suffer from losing current traditional business opportunities. In this networked business setting of our study, collaborative cognitive systems have a broad meaning of an interconnected system of humans, data processes and artificial intelligence agents across company borders. For example, cognitive systems are replacing manual work processes through artificial intelligence applications, but they also open new markets

L. M. Camarinha-Matos et al. (Eds.): PRO-VE 2018, IFIP AICT 534, pp. 337–348, 2018.
https://doi.org/10.1007/978-3-319-99127-6_29

for data integration and data-enabled novel services. Although the potential business impacts of cognitive systems are surrounded by tremendous hype emphasizing the vast opportunities, empirical research is scarce. Design science was, therefore, a natural choice for the research approach of our study, to bridge the gap between theoretical discussion and practical challenges related to technology disruption and systemic change. Furthermore, the area of collaborative networks is by nature multi-disciplinary as well as interdisciplinary, it can enhance a more holistic understanding of the technology diffusion at stake, as has been pointed out regarding the similar hype around the concept of Industry 4.0 [4].

Understanding the systemic change required for technology diffusion is simultaneously an engrossing academic research question and a practical challenge for all actors involved in data-driven business and cognitive systems. The technology disruption in this study is examined especially from the perspective of new business creation through data utilization/data-driven business. In this study, we recognized four categories that illustrate the impact of cognitive systems adoption based two main dimensions of technology and business disruption: (1) the technical complexity of the cognitive system adopted and (2) business impacts from companies' internal processes to changes at ecosystems.

2 Design Science Approach

In management studies, a design science approach is often linked to other qualitative approaches, such as action research, participatory case studies, academia–industry partnership, and constructive approaches. They all share the aim of joint problem solving and bridging between theory and practice. In this study, the research process was based on the design science framework (see Fig. 1). According to it, *build and evaluate* are the key research activities in design science. In this joint problem solving process between the practitioners and the researchers, constructs (or concepts) form a vocabulary for the problem solving and a model presents relationships among constructs. The challenge of construction building in this study was the need to combine a variety of theories and concepts from business management and information technology.

	Build	Evaluate	Theorize	Justify
Constructs				
Model				
Method				
Instantiation				

Fig. 1. Design science research process in this study introduced by March and Smith 1995 [5].

This kind of approach also suggests that research is not just about understanding and explaining issues and phenomena but also about changing them [6] and affecting creation of new ideas and innovation. Therefore, a joint project (or process) of researchers and practitioners – companies or other organisations – and close cooperation throughout the problem solving are necessary in such a research setting. In the other words, through the practical case studies, the practitioners and the researchers strove to jointly build and evaluate the design science research artefact, a framework for business impacts of cognitive systems (Fig. 2). The methods in design science refer to a set of steps and an instantiation operationalizes these constructs, models and methods, i.e. they are the realization of the jointly built artefact in its environment.

In Table 1, we present the research process covered in this paper. The build column includes exploration of discussion related to technology and business disruptions – and more specifically the literature on cognitive systems and collaborative networks (Sect. 3 of this paper). The evaluation column covers the methods by which the constructs and models have been evaluated with the practitioners through an iterative process (Sect. 4).

As Table 1 indicates, our study is in the early phases of theorizing and justifying the research outcomes, although the joint problem solving process started a year and half ago. This is mainly due to the challenging research setting at the crossroads of several theoretical concepts, i.e. multi-disciplinary and interdisciplinary approaches have been needed. Therefore, both practitioners and researchers participating in the research process have different backgrounds from business development to data analytics. And time is needed to find key concepts, shared language and make sense of meanings of the concepts, i.e. making the vocabulary together.

3 Constructs: Making the Vocabulary for Practical Problem Solving

3.1 Technology Diffusion and the Challenge of Systemic Change

By far one of the greatest disruptions seems to be digitalization and the Internet. And this transformation is driven by two major forces: the new technological possibilities and the fast changing market demands [4]. Such disruptive technologies, by definition, disrupt existing social institutional arrangements as they challenge and revolutionize the way business is conducted, competition in the market place as well as human interaction in a society. In other words, their diffusion requires a systemic change from macro to micro level [1, 2]. Companies have had to particularly tackle the question of what they can do to avoid displacement brought on by technological disruption [8], as new technologies demand new kinds of business capabilities and often businesses may even have to learn to move away from the logic of action which they are used to. The question is multifaceted. First, new technologies and the accompanied new business models utilizing them require that companies have the kind of competencies they do not yet have. Secondly, companies must learn away from the present industry paradigms, i.e. logic of action, within their business environment. And thirdly, the radical change in business operations requires interlinked changes of companies' customers and partners' businesses. In other words, collaborative or networked innovations are needed.

Table 1. Summary of the key research activities of the design science process in this study.

	Build	Evaluate	Theorize/Justify
Constructs	Find key concepts for cognitive systems and business impact in ecosystems through	Investigating the practical challenges in business development	Barriers – the challenge and opportunity taxonomy ([7]: ISPIM conference paper)
Model	Define the factors for technology and business disruption (Workshop)	Framing for business impacts of cognitive systems' adoption	A framework presented in this paper
Method	Interviews (22), literature review, and one workshop	Two workshops	

3.2 Big Data, Artificial Intelligence and Cognitive Systems

Big data has various definitions, because research in the big data area is quite novel [9, 10] and academic research focuses on data analytic tools rather than business impacts. Big data can be described, for example, as "a collection of large and complex data sets, which are difficult to process using common database management tools or traditional data processing applications." [11]. There are typically three features – volume, variety and velocity – that characterize big data [12]. Thus, business data is typically consisting from both big and non-big data. Furthermore, it is often exclusive in containing non-disclosure agreements, but firms are realizing the strategic importance of investing in insight based decision-making and value co-creation [3].

The ability to capture, store, aggregate and analyse data for extracting intelligence is vital for strategic decisions [13] and there is a variety of different means for data processing. Similarly to big data, artificial intelligence (AI) also has several definitions. AI can be defined, for example, as an ability that a digital computer or computer-controlled robot can use to complete tasks that are commonly associated with intelligent beings. Thus, the scenarios of the future impact of AI technologies and their potential vary from a utopian to dystopian world [14], which is typically in case of broader disruptions causing significant uncertainty.

Cognition, both natural and artificial, is about anticipating the need for action and developing the capacity to predict the outcome of those actions. *Collaborative cognitive systems* have been defined as systems where there are intelligent agents that assist humans in their cognition [15]. In this networked business setting collaborative cognitive systems have the broader meaning of an interconnected system of humans, data processes and artificial intelligence agents across company borders. Regarding the technology disruption, we have positioned these three concepts – big data, artificial intelligence and cognitive systems – in a continuum describing the intensity of technology change in this study. This is in-line with the well-known continuum presented in the DIKW (data, information knowledge, wisdom) - model (for a summary of the DIKW - concept see, for instance [16]).

3.3 Business Ecosystems/Collaborative Networks

In the current networked business environment cooperative actions and decisions are not made in a centralized way [17]. Therefore, the full potential of a data-rich world can be captured in collaboration with a variety of external actors, i.e. collaborative networks (CN), as access to and integration of third-party big data sources is required to explore changes in this business environment [18].

Our study approached "collaborative cognitive systems" from the meso (organisational) level. The concept of collaborative network organisations (CNOs) highlights that there is an organisation encompassing shared governance rules as well as the participants' activities, and roles, whereas the concept of virtual organisation breeding environment (VBE) represents the more loosely coupled co-operation setting found with a bundle of organisations. Thus, long-term co-operation agreements and interoperable infrastructure are also mentioned as a 'base' for breeding environments [12].

Anyhow, the practitioners were more familiar with the concept of business ecosystems. Therefore, in order to help the joint sense making we preferred to use the concept of *business ecosystems* to capture a dynamic, temporary, continuously changing, hyperconnected, and networked assemblage that emphasize the need for collaborative system level choice. Through the ecosystem approach, collaborative networks are defined as autonomous, geographically distributed, and heterogeneous [19]. It highlights that even in collaborative networks each network member has its own reasons to collaborate.

4 Practical Evaluation of Constructs and Models - Methods for Joint Problem Solving

Through a design science approach, we explored the business impacts expected from the adoption of cognitive systems within collaborative networks, i.e. business ecosystems. First, to set the scene and understand the practical problems the researchers conducted semi-structured interviews (typically more like discussions) with the key persons of the seven companies participating in the process (Table 2). Five of the companies (A - D and G) have a main business model linked to traditional domains (healthcare, manufacturing, automation and recruitment), whereas three (E, F and H) focus on services related to data processing through Big Data analytics and AI technologies. The role of these three firms was to support the others in envisioning the change and opportunities arising. Thus, company H only took part in the workshop phase of the process.

These discussions highlighted that the companies are actively considering how to benefit from technology disruption and grab the opportunities enabled by new technologies. Or on the other hand, they have to think of what they can do to avoid displacement brought on by technological disruption. The interviewees stated that the

Table 2. Case companies and interviews.

Case company	Industry	Size	Experience in big data utilization	Number of interviewees
A	Healthcare	Large	Experienced	6
B	Manufacturing	Medium-sized	Beginner	3
C	Automation	Large	Experienced	2
D	Manufacturing	Large	Beginner	6
E	Data processing	Start-up	Advanced	2
F	Data processing	Large	Advanced	1
G	Recruiting & staffing (services)	Large	Experienced	2
H	IT consulting and services	Small	Experienced	–

question of technology disruption is multifaceted. First, utilizing new technologies and the accompanying new business models require that companies have the kinds of competencies they do not yet have. Secondly, companies must learn away from the present industry paradigms, i.e. logic of action within their business environment. And thirdly, the radical change in business operations requires interlinked changes of companies' customers and partners' businesses. In other words, collaborative or networked innovations are needed to grasp the emerging opportunities.

This kind of approach also proposes that research is not just about understanding and explaining the phenomena but also about changing them [6] and participating in the creation of new ideas and innovation. Therefore, a joint project (and process) of researchers and practitioners – companies or other organisations – and close cooperation throughout the problem solving are necessary in such a research setting. Therefore, at the first workshop (see Table 3) – concurrently with one-to-one discussions – researchers and practitioners set the scene together, i.e. a joint understanding of the state-of-the-art and *build* together the constructs and models for making sense and understanding the key factors of this technology and business disruption. The second workshop went deeper in understanding the challenges of the creation of new data-driven business and discusses on different constructs (i.e. variety of data sources and analytics tools) and the taxonomy created [7]. This resulted in the grounding for the third workshop, where researchers and practitioners utilized the business impacts framework (presented in the next section) in order to *evaluate* the systemic changes related to technology disruption.

Table 3. Workshops.

Workshops	Actors	Participants	Discussion topics	Content	Date
1. Set the scene (vocabulary and constructs)	5 companies (A, B, D, E, H) and 3 research organizations	14	The content of each case, feedback and finding synergies	Case presentations and joint discussion	7.6.2017
2. Understanding challenges of new business creation through big data utilization	4 companies (A, D, E, H) and 3 research organizations	12	Challenges of new business creation through big data utilization and achieving feedback for presented categorization	Presentation of interview results, individual assignment, joint discussion based on individual assignments	21.11.2017
3. Business impacts and roles in data-driven business	2 companies (D, E) and 3 research organizations	8	The business impacts of big data utilization and the different roles for creating business from it	Presentation of research findings, joint discussion (individual assignments …)	8.2.2018

5   Business Impacts Framework - Illustrating the Four Categories

At the crossroads of technology and business disruption the two main dimensions illustrate changes in: (1) the technical complexity of cognitive systems adopted as a continuum from big data, artificial intelligence and collaborative cognitive systems (Sect. 3.2) and (2) business impacts from companies' incremental improvement of internal processes to systemic changes at ecosystems (Sect. 3.3).

The framework (Fig. 2) contains four categories. The first two categories, the process change and the role change in the value chain, describe the more company specific impact of data utilization. Therefore, a company may accelerate its own performance through traditional data mining or even change its role in the value chain, when utilizing more intelligent data systems. The last two categories, the competition environment change and the significant turning point of the market and emerging ecosystems, describe the more ecosystem specific impact of data utilization. Therefore, the data utilization may have an influence on the competition environment or even disrupt the market and enable new ecosystem emergence.

The framework was utilized to identify the level of cognitive systems adaptation and to demonstrate its impacts on a company's internal processes and the surrounding ecosystems through two dimensions (vertical and horizontal). In the following four sub-sections typical company perspectives related to these categories are highlighted through quotations. Most of the quotations are from the five companies currently operating in traditional sectors, as they perceived the change to be more concrete. The two companies, who had their competence in data processing, supported others in foreseeing the in-coming changes and opportunities provided by technology.

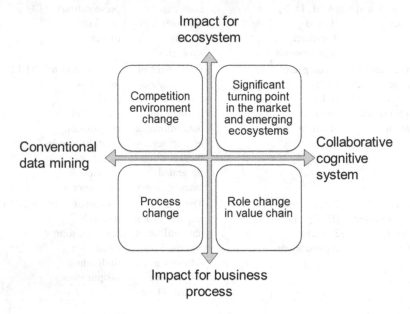

Fig. 2. Business impacts framework.

The following quotation from the entrepreneur of company E illustrates how he was challenging the other companies to start with analysis of the strategic importance of knowledge and data processing tools: *"from the company perspective, the management group or on the management level, they should be capable of formulating what is wanted out of data. ... it's a combination of many kinds of know-how. But nothing happens unless the management group has an understanding of what is wanted out of the data."*

5.1   Process Change

In the first of the identified categories, the impact of big data affects the business processes within the organization. Apart from the two data processing companies (E and F), the other five companies (A - D and G) recognized that the process change is a typical impact from utilizing big data in business development. The following quotation from the customer service, communications and marketing manager of company B represents a typical example: *"With data, you are able to understand the customer better. It also helps the way we develop our processes, so that we concentrate on the right things. So, it guides our own development measures....We can automatize the way we work, and then also create savings, and thus offer more competitive pricing."*

5.2   Role Change

In the second of the identified categories, the impact of big data or artificial intelligence on the business processes within the organization, only a few of the participating companies had actively been processing the possibilities to change their role in value chains, i.e. both B and D are transforming from product-based businesses to services, while the others already had more service-oriented business models. One example of such consideration is provided by corporate social responsibility director of company B: *"We have analysed the news feed, and recognized trends such as where we are going, what is happening beneath, and this is something that customers see a remarkable added value in. The comments we have received is that we are the first component manufacturer that talks about future... it's not like we have all the answers about the future, but we are starting the discussion. And this gives an impression to customers that this is something that we manage... and we have translated it to "common language" so that everyone can seize on it... So, analysing and data and trying to think how you can serve customers with it, that alone can add competitiveness."*

5.3   Competition Environment Change

In the third of the categories, the impact of big data on the business ecosystem level, all of the companies have recognized that these digital technologies have caused or will cause significant changes in their business environment. The following quotation from the business development manager of company D states that decision-makers need new tools for understanding the turbulent business environment: *"I think it gives an opportunity to recognize new things, which is important because being aware is essential to the management. Decision-makers need to understand how the world is changing and why it is so."* Thus, not all of them had an active or reactive perspective on these in-coming changes. In the following quotation a business intelligence manager from company C highlights how they are looking for external data sources and analytics to gain a better understanding of the business environment: *"A part of the data that we buy are analyses on the future development of the business field. We aim to buy these from many providers. We don't really make this kind scenario work by ourselves. We also follow and analyse our competitors, and if we see that a competitor is making a new move and there is something happening, we try to figure out what it means for us. For example, if a competitor is being sold, we try to figure out what it means for us, in the short-term and in the long-term."*

5.4   Ecosystem Change

Finally, in the fourth category, the impact of cognitive systems on the business ecosystem level, one of the companies stated that they have a clear vision of how to make new business enabled by AI technologies, as the following quotation from the research and clinic director of company A presents: *"In the future we can sell these insights [that we get from data]. And we can also use this data as a tool in political discussions... From data, we can see what will happen and we can quantify it, which makes observations a political argument in these discussions."*

Similarly, the business intelligence manager of company C described how technology development opens possibilities to renew both processes and thinking, at ecosystem level: *"The reality is that, like I said, decisions are made intuitively, but utilising data may bring out and verify things that have been assumed... so with data we can break those harmful, intuitive beliefs so changes can be made to the established practices... a machine could present us the fresh, unlocked way of thinking."*

To sum up, the practitioners had a strong belief that the business ecosystems were changing significantly. The following quotation from the service director of company G highlights this well: *"I believe that when we catch data and knowledge flows, and are able to manipulate the data with powerful tools such as AI solutions, we can make really big changes and make an impact."*

6 Discussion About Making Sense of the Business Implications of Cognitive Systems

Disruptive technologies may propel the emergence of and experimentation with new and alternative innovation paradigms [3], and collaboration networks [4, 18]. However, their business impacts are complex and multi-faceted and seldom simply positive or negative. Furthermore, the sense-making process within these dimensions seems to be broken up to technology- and business-oriented tracks, both in practice and at academic discussions.

Also, it was quite typical in the participating companies that big data utilisation or the possibilities of Artificial Intelligence had been considered by persons responsible for IT systems, AI technologies or business intelligence. In other words, the clear connection to business development was still limited and or focused on collecting and analysing customer data. The quotation of the entrepreneur from company F highlights how a joint understanding and continuous discussion is needed for success: *"this is not an IT project, this is not an HR project, this is a management group's project."*

The framework (Fig. 2) also supported the shared sense-making between the technology- and business-oriented persons (both researchers and practitioners) as it helped to build a joint vocabulary for the level of changes. For example, as the DIKW (data, information knowledge, wisdom)-model was well known it also supported understanding of the impact of different technologies from big data on cognitive systems. Thus, the practical examples show that the new way to manage and operate business processes through and with data-driven cognitive systems disrupts existing markets, change value chains or only affects the operative capability of companies. For example, adopting gene data in the healthcare services opens new bio-banking markets whereas improving analyses of customer behaviour through big data impacts the internal operative effectiveness only at the level of the marketing department.

In some business areas, cognitive systems are creating new business opportunities or even new markets for technology and service providers. The companies need new technological applications and services when adopting cognitive systems. The way in which companies adopt new cognitive systems impacts either their business processes or entire ecosystems. For example, companies may adopt the cognitive systems by improving quality control or customer satisfaction through deploying advanced data analytics instead of manual excel sheets. In this way, the adaptation of cognitive systems is changing the existing business processes within the organization, but its impact on the entire ecosystem is low. The use of cognitive systems is not reshaping new markets but it is only improving the way in which companies operate business processes. The adoption of cognitive systems in creating new business has an effect at the level of ecosystems as we have seen in the gene data-based biobank business or in marketing, where cognitive systems predict consumer behaviour in e-commerce.

To sum up, the level of impact on the business ecosystem mainly depends on the business needs that the companies are solving, ranging from the effects on emerging ecosystems to the effects for conventional process improvement. Additionally, the impact is not similar for all players in the same business ecosystem, which reveals changes in the roles of service and technology providers.

7 Conclusions

The managerial implications of this study consist of clarifying the scattered concepts around cognitive systems and a framework for understanding the business impacts. Theoretical contributions indicate how the design science approach is a suitable method for addressing ill-structured managerial problems of technology and business disruption. Regarding joint problem solving, the specific challenge in this study was the need to combine a variety of theoretical concepts – as well as the practical know-how – from the business management and information technology areas.

Design science is more traditionally utilized in information systems fields [20] and therefore, also the practitioners with Information technology background were more familiar with the approach. In management and business studies, design science holds a steady but minor position on the side lines of mainstream descriptive studies – there are some examples in operations management [21] and on-going discussion also within the collaborative networks research community. Thus, a design science approach can also be linked to several other qualitative approaches, which all share the aim of joint problem solving and bridging between theory and practice. These kinds of needs are definitely increasing in the area of business research as the business environment is highly turbulent and technological hype is commonplace.

Acknowledgments. The authors would like to thank the BIG (Big data – Big business) project and all its parties, as well as Business Finland (the Finnish innovation funding, trade, investment, and travel promotion organization) for their support of this study.

References

1. Geels, F.W.: From sectoral systems of innovation to socio-technical systems: insights about dynamics and change from sociology and institutional theory. Res. Policy **33**(6–7), 897–920 (2004)
2. Valkokari, K., Paasi, J., Rantala, T.: Managing knowledge within networked innovation. Knowl. Manag. Res. Pract. **10**(1), 27–40 (2012)
3. Chang, R.M., Kauffman, R.J., Kwon, Y.: Understanding the paradigm shift to computational social science in the presence of big data. Decis. Support Syst. **63**, 67–80 (2014)

4. Camarinha-Matos, L.M., Fornasiero, R., Afsarmanesh, H.: Collaborative networks as a core enabler of industry 4.0. In: Camarinha-Matos, L.M., Afsarmanesh, H., Fornasiero, R. (eds.) PRO-VE 2017. IAICT, vol. 506, pp. 3–17. Springer, Cham (2017). https://doi.org/10.1007/978-3-319-65151-4_1
5. March, S.T., Smith, G.F.: Design and natural science research on information technology. Decis. Support Syst. **15**(4), 251–266 (1995)
6. Burke, W.: Organization Change: Theory and Practice. SAGE Publications, Thousand Oaks (2002)
7. Rantala, T., Palomäki, K., Valkokari, K.: Challenges of creating new B2B business through big data utilization. In: The ISPIM Innovation Forum, Boston (2018)
8. Christensen, C.M.: The Innovator's dilemma: When New Technologies Cause Great Firms to Fail. Harvard Business School Press, Boston (1997)
9. Sivarajah, U., Kamal, M., Irani, Z., Weerakkody, V.: Critical analysis of big data challenges and analytical methods. J. Bus. Res. **70**, 263–286 (2017)
10. Frizzo-Barker, J., Chow-White, P.A., Mozafari, M., Ha, D.: An empirical study of the rise of big data in business scholarship. Int. J. Inf. Manag. **36**(3), 403–413 (2016)
11. Sabarmathi, G., Chinnaiyan, R., Ilango, V.: Big data analytics research opportunities and challenges: a review. Int. J. Adv. Res. Comput. Sci. Softw. Eng. **6**(10) (2016)
12. Hashem, I.A.T., Yaqoob, I., Anuar, N.B., Mokhtar, S., Gani, A., Khan, S.U.: The rise of 'big data' on cloud computing: review and open research issues. Inf. Syst. **47**, 98–115 (2015)
13. Sanders, N.R.: Big data driven supply chain management: a framework for implementing analytics and turning information into intelligence. Pearson Education, Upper Saddle River (2014)
14. Makridakis, S.: The forthcoming Artificial Intelligence (AI) revolution: its impact on society and firms. Futures **90**, 46–60 (2017)
15. McNeese, M.D.: New visions of human-computer interaction: Making affect compute. Int. J. Hum Comput Stud. **59**(1–2), 33–53 (2003)
16. Hey, J.: The data, information, knowledge, wisdom chain: the metaphorical link. Intergov. Oceanogr. Comm. **26**, 1–18 (2004)
17. Bernus, P., Noran, O.: Data Rich – But Information Poor. In: Camarinha-Matos, L.M., Afsarmanesh, H., Fornasiero, R. (eds.) PRO-VE 2017. IAICT, vol. 506, pp. 206–214. Springer, Cham (2017). https://doi.org/10.1007/978-3-319-65151-4_20
18. Paajanen, S., Valkokari, K., Aminoff, A.: The opportunities of big data analytics in supply market intelligence. In: Camarinha-Matos, L.M., Afsarmanesh, H., Fornasiero, R. (eds.) PRO-VE 2017. IAICT, vol. 506, pp. 194–205. Springer, Cham (2017). https://doi.org/10.1007/978-3-319-65151-4_19
19. Camarinha-Matos, L.M., Afsarmanesh, H.: Collaborative Networks: Reference Modeling. Springer, New York (2008)
20. Gregor, S., Hevner, A.R.: Positioning and presenting design science research for maximum impact. MIS Q. **37**(2), 337–355 (2013)
21. Holmström, J., Ketokivi, M., Hameri, A.-P.: Bridging practice and theory: a design science approach. Decis. Sci. **40**(1), 1540–1559 (2009)

A Modeling Framework to Assess Strategies Alignment Based on Collaborative Network Emotions

Beatriz Andres[1(✉)], Filipa Ferrada[2,3], Raul Poler[1],
and Luis M. Camarinha-Matos[2,3]

[1] Research Centre on Production Management and Engineering (CIGIP),
Universitat Politècnica de València (UPV), Calle Alarcón, 03801 Alcoy, Spain
{bandres, rpoler}@cigip.upv.es
[2] Faculty of Sciences and Technology and Center of Technology
and Systems - UNINOVA, Nova University of Lisbon,
Campus de Caparica, Caparica, Portugal
[3] Uninova Institute, Centre of Technology and Systems, Caparica, Portugal
{faf, cam}@uninova.pt

Abstract. The Collaborative Networks (CN) discipline has been largely studied in last decades, addressing different problems and proposing solutions for the robust establishment of collaborative processes, within the enterprises willing to collaborate. The main aim of CN research is, therefore, to generate approaches that enable creating effective relationships in the long term, to achieve stable and agile alliances. The concept of alignment among the CN partners has been considered since the beginning of CN research. Nevertheless, novel perspectives of study in CN, such as the consideration of collaborative emotional states, within the CN, have been introduced in recent years. This paper connects the research area of strategies alignment and the CN emotion models. Accordingly, a modelling framework to assess strategies alignment considering the emotional environment within the CN is proposed. The modelling framework allows representing how the enterprises emotions affect in the selection and alignment of formulated enterprises' strategies.

Keywords: Collaborative Networks · Strategies alignment
Collaborative network emotions · System dynamics

1 Introduction

Research works on the Collaborative Networks (CN) discipline has been increasing since its appearance, proof of this is the wide variety of articles published in the area [1]. As a result, a wide range of knowledge is available in the context of CN. This knowledge has been summarized in [2], through a taxonomic approach that gathers relevant collaborative processes, as well as models, guidelines and tools designed to support their proper execution. The proposed approaches, contributing to the research area of CN, encompass collaborative processes from strategic to tactical and operational decision-making. The strategic decision-making level includes the following

© IFIP International Federation for Information Processing 2018
Published by Springer Nature Switzerland AG 2018. All Rights Reserved
L. M. Camarinha-Matos et al. (Eds.): PRO-VE 2018, IFIP AICT 534, pp. 349–361, 2018.
https://doi.org/10.1007/978-3-319-99912-6_30

collaborative processes: coordination mechanisms design, decision system design, network design, partners' selection, partners' coordination and integration, performance management system design, product design, and strategy alignment. At the tactical decision-making level, the proposed approaches deal with contracts' negotiation, coordination mechanisms management, demand forecast, knowledge management, operations planning, performance management and measurement, costs and profits sharing, uncertainty management, etc. Finally, the collaborative processes at the operational decision-making level refer to information exchange management, interoperability, inventory management, lot sizing, order promising process, process connection, and scheduling.

The notion of alignment has been present since the origins of the CN discipline. This term is related with the integration and complementation of resources and capabilities of the different enterprises participating in the CN [3]. The main aim of the alignment is to achieve long term and sustainable collaborative relationships. In this regard, some authors have associated the idea of alignment with gaining better performance levels [4]. Accordingly, the alignment of CN partners has been studied in different areas, including value systems alignment [5] and strategies alignment [6, 7].

Moreover, recent research in the discipline of CN is moving towards the need to provide socio-technical systems capable of recognizing the social and organizational complexity of the CN environment. In this direction, "human-tech" friendly systems resorting to cognitive models of human factors such as trust or emotion are being introduced. For instance, the collaborative emotion (C-EMO) modelling framework proposed in [8], adopts and integrates some models from the human psychology, sociology and affective computing areas. It consists on applying the emotional processes of humans to the CN context, creating the notion of "emotion" in CN and providing mechanisms to estimate the CN's and the organization's "emotional states" giving, in this way, support to decision-making processes.

In this context, this work is guided by the following research question *"What would be a suitable framework to adequately support companies on modelling, assessment and resolution of the strategies alignment process from a collaborative perspective, considering the companies' collaborative emotional context?"*. In this line, the work presented in this paper, proposes a modelling framework for the assessment of strategies alignment having into account the emotional state of the collaborative environment and a simulation methodology based on system dynamics to model the inherent collaboration complexity. The proposed approach connects the research areas of collaborative enterprises' strategies alignment and the emotion models.

The remainder of this paper is organized as follows: Sect. 2 introduces the system dynamics simulation method, well regarded to model complex systems. Section 3 presents an overview and a relational view of the strategies alignment and the C-EMO models. Section 4 presents a modelling framework to assess the collaborative enterprises' strategies alignment regarding the emotional state. Section 5 includes a numerical example to provide an intuitive insight of the developed modelling framework and the derived simulation results. The work is concluded in Sect. 6, where future research lines are also identified.

2 System Dynamics Simulation Methodology in CN

The reason why analytical models are sometimes difficult to apply in complex systems, and particularly to CN, is because mathematical formulae can be very complicated and interfere with finding a solution in a reasonable time [9]. In this regard, simulation methods are more fruitful when dealing with CN, considering their capability of modelling suitable degrees of realism of the CN and attaining accurate system's description. CN are characterized by being complex systems formed by a diversity of autonomous and heterogeneous organizations, which are geographically distributed, and that collaborate to better achieve common or compatible goals [10]. This definition is analogue to the characterization of complex systems in system dynamics (SD) simulation methods: (i) decentralized nature, in which the system's behaviour arises from the self-organization of its components without these being controlled by any extrinsic entity to the system, (ii) the presence of loops of causality and nonlinear feedback, and (iii) the fact that it contains several self-contained units that can interact, evolve and adapt their behaviour to changes in the environment [11].

Moreover, with SD simulation, researchers can model and simulate interactions among different sub-systems leading in this way, to the overall system behaviour [12]. SD results in a different approach of the traditional if-then-else simulation methodologies; as such, it has been applied in many research fields, such as supply chain management and performance [13, 14], healthcare economic evaluation forecasting [15], biomedical sciences [16], partners selection [17], climate monitoring and water resource management [18], predicting social trends like technology adoption [19], and market changes forecasting [20].

Typically, SD simulation methods have been also applied jointly with multi-agent systems (MAS), with the aim of developing models in which a group of agents, individually and explicitly represented, interact in an environment in which certain variables evolve following a dynamic pattern [21].

3 Background

This section provides a brief overview of the strategies alignment model (SAM) and the C-EMO modelling framework. The adopted modelling approaches are given in both cases. An integrated view of both presented models is given, aiming at highlighting the associated theoretical body of knowledge with the intention of proposing a modelling framework to assess the strategies alignment considering CN emotions, as later described on Sect. 4.

3.1 Strategies Alignment Model

Let us consider that two enterprises, a distributor (e_1) and a manufacturer (e_2) in a CN, each one defines two objectives (o_{ix}) and formulates two strategies (S_{is}). Each objective has an associated KPI to measure its performance. For instance, e_1 defines o_{11}: *Increase product sales by 10%*, and o_{12}: *Reduce product costs by 30%*; and formulates S_{11}: *Invest 0.5 m.u on marketing activities*, and S_{12}: *Carry out negotiations with other manufacturers to reduce purchase costs.* Similarly, e_2 defines o_{21}: *Increase the profit by 15%*, and o_{22}: *Reduce the amount of product that cannot be sold by 100%*; and formulates S_{21}: *Use different distribution channels to sell the product in other markets*, and S_{22}: *Buy a machine to manufacture derivative products, reprocessing the product that cannot be sold (that is, low cost product).* With this example it can be seen that S_{12} is not compatible with S_{21}, because S_{12} is dedicated to establishing new relationships with other manufacturers, which will imply reduction of the benefit defined in o_{21}. In addition, if e_1 conducts negotiations with other manufacturers (S_{12}), the o_{22} will be negatively influenced. Moreover, the activation of S_{21} has a negative influence on o_{11}, defined to increase sales of the product; and the o_{12} defined to reduce the costs of the product. Considering the above, S_{12} and S_{21} are identified as non-aligned strategies, if they are activated at the same time. On the other hand, S_{11} and S_{22} are considered as aligned strategies since they have a positive influence on the achievement of the defined objectives.

Carrying out collaboratively the strategies alignment process allows considering all objectives of the companies in the CN when deciding which strategies are the best to activate, achieving greater levels of adaptability, agility and competitiveness.

The SAM model [6] allows to formally represent the influences that the strategies activated in a company have on the performance indicators (KPI) defined to measure the achievement of the objectives, in all the CN companies. It will allow to model (i) the intra-enterprise influences, that is, the influences that the strategies formulated in a company have on the objectives defined in the same company; and (ii) inter-enterprise influences, that is, the influences that the strategies formulated in a company have on the objectives defined in the other companies of the CN.

SAM's main objective is to identify, amongst all defined strategies, those that have a higher level of alignment. SAM calculates the improvement or worsening of the KPIs when a strategy is activated. Thus, the developed model supports companies in making decisions regarding the number of strategy units (u_S_{is}) to be activated, and the time when these strategies must be activated (ti_S_{is}) in order to maximize network's performance, (KPI_{net}). Let's suppose that the strategy defined is, S_{is}: *Buy machines (at maximum 3)*; translating this strategy to one unit of strategy, u_S_{is}: *Buy 1 machine*; the activation of one unit of strategy (u_S_{is}) has the associated cost of buying one machine (i.e. $S_{is}\_mu = 10000$ m.u.).

In order to model the process of strategies alignment, a set of five objects have been defined: (i) set of networks, $net = (1,..., NET)$; (ii) set of enterprises i forming the network, $i = (1,..., I)$; (iii) set of objectives x defined by each enterprise, $x = (1,..., X)$; (iv) set of key performance indicators (KPIs) k to measure the level of objectives' achievement, $k = (1,..., K)$; and (v) the set strategies s formulated by each enterprise in order to achieve the objectives, $s = (1,..., S)$. The influence that one strategy formulated by an enterprise i (S_{is}) has on a particular KPI defined by an enterprise i to measure the objective x_i (KPI_{ixk}) is modelled through the function $f\_inf\_S_{is}\_KPI_{ixk}$ (see Fig. 1). This function, is a piecewise function that depends on the time [$f_1(t)$]. For modelling $f\_inf\_S_{is}\_KPI_{ixk}$ a normalised horizon is used as the unit ($H = 1$) and the duration parameters are distributed in this H of time: (i) $d_1\_S_{is}$, delay, time period between the initial time of activation of S_{is} (ti_S_{is}) and the time when the KPI_{ixk} is started to be influenced by the activated S_{is}; (ii) $d_2\_S_{is}$, time period between when S_{is}

starts to influence the KPI_{ixk} until the maximum level of influence is achieved ($inf\_S_{is}\_KPI_{ixk}$); (iii) $d_3\_S_{is}$, time period in which S_{is} is exerting the highest influence ($inf\_S_{is}\_KPI_{ixk}$) on the KPI_{ixk}; (iv) $d_4\_S_{is}$, total duration of S_{is}; (v) ti_S_{is} identifies the starting point of activation of the S_{is} and allows modelling that not all the strategies are activated at the same time. Accordingly, the SAM allows identifying and assessing the strategies that are aligned and positively influence the objectives defined by all the network enterprises; enabling the increase of the network KPI.

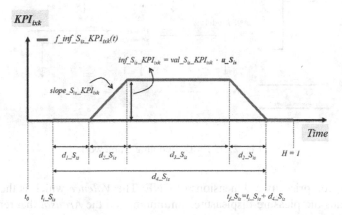

Fig. 1. Curve ($f\_inf\_S_{is}\_KPI_{ixk}$) that models the influence of S_{is} on the KPI_{ixk}

3.2 C-EMO Modeling Framework

The Collaborative Emotion modeling framework (C-EMO), [22] represents a system that appraises emotions of CN members with different skills and characteristics and reasons about the way emotions affect those members and the entire collaborative environment. It gives support to the notion of emotions in the context of a CN and is grounded on the theories of human-emotion found in psychology and sociology. C-EMO comprises the concepts of CNE (collaborative network emotion), IME (individual member emotion) and ANE (aggregated network emotion) and assumes the modeling of any typology of CN. C-EMO is built using object-oriented models providing two main constructs (IME and ANE models), each comprising its attributes and their relationships, as presented in Fig. 2: (i) *Individual Member Emotion (IME model)* for appraising the emotion of each CN member individually and examining the effects this emotion has on both the CN member behavior and the CN environment; and (ii) *Aggregated Network Emotion (ANE model)* for estimating the overall emotion present in the CN and examine the effects such emotion has on the network environment and on its members.

The theories that give support to the C-EMO are adapted from the theories of human emotion and consist of a combination of the dimensional theory and the components of emotion from the appraisal theory. The former is based on the Russel's circumplex model of emotion [15] which facilitated a good adaptation from the human model to the organizational model, through its well-defined structure for representing

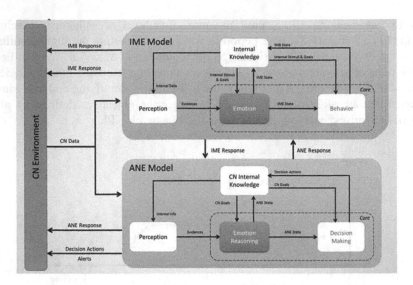

Fig. 2. C-EMO modeling framework

emotions. It comprises two dimensions of CNE: The *Valence* which is the dimension that represents the pleasure-displeasure continuum, and the *Arousal* that represents the level of activation, novelty and expectation of the emotional stimuli. Hence, CNEs can be defined with positive or negative valence and high or low arousal, and the emotions that are proposed to describe the "emotional states" of CN members are **excitement** (*val>0, aro>0*), **contentment** (*val>0, aro<0*), **frustration** (*val<0, aro>0*) and **depression** (*val<0, aro <0*). The four components of CNE which are based on the Scherer's [23] components of emotion, are: cognitive or appraisal component, feeling component, motivational component and expression component. Both the IME model and the ANE model building blocks represent the four CNE components.

3.3   Integrated View of SAM and C-EMO

The diagram of Fig. 3 represents in a schematic way, an integrated view of the two approaches used in this paper, SAM and the C-EMO. Both approaches are linked through the degree of impatience $\left(\alpha_i^{Sis}\right)$, which is the output data of the C-EMO and is used as an input data of the SAM. Parameter α_i^{Sis} is widely explained in Sect. 4, but roughly speaking, the degree of impatience is the extent of rapidness into which the enterprise is willing to obtain the maximum level of KPI_{ixk}. The α_i^{Sis} is generated in the IME model of the C-EMO, which is modelled in the *Emotion* element using the SD method. Values of α_i^{Sis} near 0 indicate that the enterprise i is more patient to obtain the expected level of KPI_{ixk}, when the strategy S_{is} is activated. Parameter α_i^{Sis} is an input to the SAM and is used through translating α_i^{Sis} in time units (t_S_{is}), when the S_{is} is activated. Moreover, SAM calculates the $t_m\_S_{is}$, which is the **actual time when the maximum level of the KPI_{ixk}** is achieved, being S_{is} activated. In order to consider the impatience emotion in SAM, the proposed extension of SAM considers the comparison between the t_S_{is} (obtained from α_i^{Sis}) and $t_m\_S_{is}$. Accordingly, if the time in which the enterprise i is willing to achieve the maximum level of KPI_{ixk} is higher than the real time in which the maximum level of the KPI_{ixk} is achieved ($t\_S_{is} > t_m\_S_{is}$), then the strategy S_{is} is activated; and therefore, aligned with all the $KPIs$ defined by each of the CN partners, and with the impatience emotion of all the CN partners. Otherwise, when $t\_S_{is} < t_m\_S_{is}$, the S_{is} will not be activated. Finally, the extended SAM, will allow to identify the amount of extra monetary units that the enterprise i can invest in each strategy Sis, in order obtain in a quicker way the maximum level of KPI_{ixk}, and comply with the condition $t\_S_{is} > t_m\_S_{is}$. It is assumed that, the higher amount of extra monetary units invested implies a lower time needed to obtain the maximum level of KPI_{ixk}. Thus, if the enterprise is very impatience (higher values of α_i^{Sis}), this is translated in a lower t_S_{is}, therefore more extra monetary units will be need to invest.

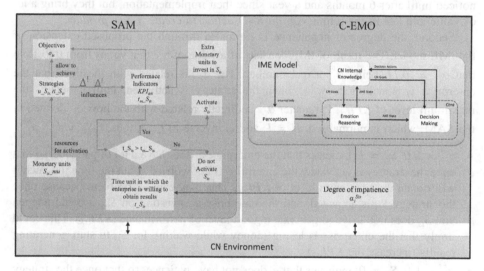

Fig. 3. Integrated view of SAM and the IME model of the C-EMO modelling framework

4   Modelling Framework

The proposed modelling framework uses as a base the SAM model, extending it for the consideration of emotions when a strategy is collaboratively activated between partners of a CN. The C-EMO modelling framework, as previous described, considers gathering all the affective states from two variables Valence and Arousal. Accordingly, the IME can be understood as a linear combination of these two dimensions and the emotional state of an enterprise is described as $ei(t) = <Vi(t),Ai(t)>$. The IME, therefore depends on the time. Following the CNE dimensional approach, there is one possible active emotion for each circumplex quadrant: excitement, contentment, frustration and depression. In order to connect both models, the IME model of C-EMO and SAM, a new combination of valence and arousal is introduced in order to define the patience and impatience emotions. In the same way, the IME model, via its system dynamics model, is adjusted to comprise the new modelling parameters and appraise the new emotions. The emotion impatience, is then used as an input to the extended SAM. The degree of impatience is related with the time unit, in which each CN partner is willing to achieve the maximum level of KPI_{ixk}, when a particular strategy S_{is} is activated.

First, it must be stated that strategies can be defined at short, medium or long term: (i) short term (ST): actions that are designed with the aim of obtaining immediate results, between one day and, at the most, one month; *e.g. an advertisement campaign in the media*; (ii) medium term (MT): actions to remain active without despairing in short-term action or falling into the passivity of the long term; *e.g. collaborative distribution, through contacting related distribution companies and reaching an agreement to cross-ship products to open a wider distribution channel and attract potential customers in the short term*; and (iii) long term (LT): actions designed and conceptualized with a vision for the future, whose positive results do not begin to be noticed until after 6 months and a year since their implementation, but they bring a lot of value and last in the future; *e.g. an R+D action to create a new product.*

Second, the degree of impatience is estimated through the proposed extension of the IME model. The result of IME consists of a value of α_i^{Sis} that varies from 0 to 1, so that $\alpha_i^{Sis} = [0,1]$; being α_i^{Sis} a real number. The α_i^{Sis} is related with the time that the enterprise e_i is willing to wait, when the strategy is activated, until it obtains the maximum level of KPI_{ixk}. Parameter α_i^{Sis} is directly related with the horizon defined in the SAM, which is normalised, $H = 1$, and is inverse to t_S_{is}; thus, $t\_S_{is} = 1 - \alpha_i^{Sis}$:

- $\alpha_i^{Sis} = 0$ ($t\_S_{is} = 1$) indicates that the enterprise e_i does have a lot of patience, so that once the strategy is activated, the enterprise is not worried about the time in which it will obtain the maximum level of KPI_{ixk}. This may cause a problem because once the strategy S_{is} is activated, and the enterprise is investing on S_{is}, it could happen that S_{is} does not arrive to generate a good level of performance (KPI_{ixk}). This could imply that the enterprise is losing money while waiting for S_{is} to start generating results (increase the KPI_{ixk}).
- $\alpha_i^{Sis} = 1$ ($t\_S_{is} = 0$) indicates that e_i does not have patience, so that once the strategy is activated, the enterprise is willing to obtain the desired results immediately. It is characterised by the fact that the enterprise does not see the results, of the activated strategy, immediately, and stops the investment. This may cause a problem because it could happen that the results (achieve the higher level of KPI_{ixk}) are going to be visible in a near time, but not immediately. The enterprise can lose the investment, but if it would wait a little bit, the results could start to be visible, and the maximum level of the KPI_{ixk} could be achieved.
- $0 < \alpha_i^{Sis} \leq 0.5$ ($1 > t\_S_{is} \geq 0.5$) means that e_i is not as passive as when $\alpha_i^{Sis} = 0$.
- $0.5 < \alpha_i^{Sis} < 1$ ($0.5 > t\_S_{is} > 0$) means that e_i is not as restlessness and impetuousness as when $\alpha_i^{Sis} = 1$.

Finally, the degree of impatience of each enterprise e_i (α_i^{Sis}) is also defined according to the three types of strategies (ST, MT and LT). C-EMO models the degree of impatience in a specific enterprise depending on the type of strategies defined at the short, medium and long term. It could happen that the enterprises are less patience when formulating short term strategies, because they manifest quickly their results; and the enterprises are more patience when formulating long term strategies, because the results need more time to be reflected in the KPIs:

- $\alpha_i^{Sis\_ST}$: degree of impatience when e_i formulates S_{is} in the short term;
- $\alpha_i^{Sis\_MT}$: degree of impatience when e_i formulates S_{is} in the medium term;
- $\alpha_i^{Sis\_LT}$: degree of impatience when e_i formulates S_{is} in the long term.

In order to answer the research question presented in Sect. 1, the SAM is extended by considering the following flow diagram (Fig. 4); the shadowed squares mark the proposed extensions. The notation and formulas (Table 1), which relate the emotion perspective with the SAM are also described.

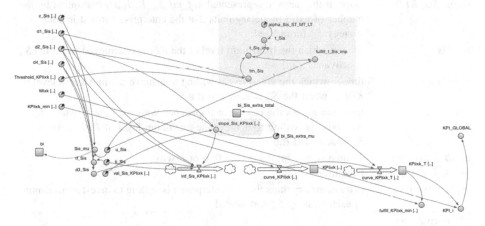

Fig. 4. Extended SAM: flow diagram

The parameter $bi\_Sis\_extra\_mu$ acts as a new decision variable of the SAM, identifying the number of extra monetary units that enterprise i has to invest in each formulated strategy S_{is}, apart from the budget initially defined. The slope of function $f\_inf\_S_{is}\_KPI_{ixk}(t)$ is higher because it is multiplied by the extra budget used ($bi\_Sis\_extra\_mu$); therefore, more quickly reaches the maximum level of KPI_{ixk}. But also, as the enterprise invests more money for the activation of the strategy S_{is}, the maximum level of KPI_{ixk} also increases. In the extension of SAM it is considered that the relation between the $bi\_Sis\_extra\_mu$ and the KPI_{ixk} is $1:1$. When the strategy S_{is} has a positive influence in the KPI_{ixk}, the more extra money invested in a particular strategy ($bi\_Sis\_extra\_mu$), the higher level of KPI_{ixk} is reached. If the influence is negative, the higher extra money invested, the lower level of KPI_{ixk} is reached. The extended SAM also includes the restrictions related with the parameters $bi\_Sis\_extra\_total$ and t_Sis_imp, which must be positive, and the parameter $fulfill\_t\_Sis\_imp$, which must be equal to 1.

Table 1. Nomenclature and SD formulation

Nomenclature	
Parameter	Definition
bi_Sis_extra_mu	number of extra monetary units that the enterprise i invest in each strategy S_{is} formulated
alpha_Sis_ST	degree of impatience when the strategy S_{is} is characterized by being for the short term [0,1]
alpha_Sis_MT	degree of impatience when the strategy S_{is} is characterized by being for the medium term [0,1]
alpha_Sis_LT	degree of impatience when the strategy S_{is} is characterized by being for the long term [0,1]
u_Sis	units of strategy S_{is} activated
Dynamic variable	Definition
slope_Sis_KPIixk	slope of the ramp in represented in $f\_inf\_S_{is}\_KPI_{ixk}(t)$ multiplied by the number of extra monetary units that the enterprise i invest in each strategy S_{is} formulated
tm_Sis	time in which the maximum level of the KPI_{ixk} is achieved when the S_{is} is activated (t.u.)
t_Sis_imp	time in which the enterprise is willing to achieve the maximum level of KPI_{ixk}, when the S_{is} is activated (t.u.)
t_Sis	time that relates the degree of impatience with the time in which the enterprise is willing to achieve the maximum level of KPI_{ixk}, when the S_{is} is activated (t.u.)
fulfill_t_Sis_imp	1 when (t_Sis_imp*u_Sis)>=0; 0 otherwise
Stock variable	Definition
bi_Sis_extra_total	extra monetary units that the enterprise i is willing to invest at maximum in each strategy S_{is} formulated
SD Formulation	
bi_Sis_extra_total = bi_Sis_extra_total - bi_Sis_extra_mu	
slope_Sis_KPIixk = ((1+bi_Sis_extra_mu) · u_Sis · val_Sis_KPIixk [dimension_KPIixk])/ d2_Sis.get(index_Sis)	
tm_Sis = d1_Sis.get(index_Sis) + d2_Sis.get(index_Sis)	
t_Sis_imp = t_Sis-tm_Sis	
t_Sis = 1-alpha_Sis_ST	
fulfill_t_Sis_imp = ((t_Sis_imp*u_Sis)>=0) ? 1:0	

5 Case Study

An example is presented with the main aim of illustrating the proposed approach. This example considers two enterprises (e_1 and e_2), each one defining two objectives (e_1:o_{11} and o_{12}; e_2: o_{12} and o_{22}): (i) o_{11}: Increase the product sales by a 10%; (ii) o_{12}: Reduce the costs of the product by a 5%; (iii) o_{21}: Increase the enterprise profit by a 15%; (iv) o_{22}: Reduce the quantity of product that cannot be sold by 100 %. The achievement of the objectives is measured through the KPI_{ixk}. In order to achieve the objectives, each enterprise formulates two strategies (e_1: S_{11} and S_{12}; e_2: S_{21} and S_{22}), with different levels of application: (i) S_{11}: Increase the marketing activities on the product (ST); (ii) S_{12}: Conduct negotiations with the manufacturing partner to reduce purchasing costs (LT); (iii) S_{21}: Open new distribution channels to spread out the product in other markets (MT); (iv) S_{22}: Product promotions (ST). The input data gathered directly from the enterprises is stored in Table 2, in which the data related with the strategies durations and costs can be seen as well as the values of influence $val\_S_{is}\_KPI_{ixk}$ estimated by each enterprise and the budget.

Table 2. Input data

Enterprise 1 $b_1 = 3$

														kpi $_{111}$		kpi $_{121}$	
S_{11}	u_S_{11}	?	ti_S_{11}	?	c_S_{11}	2	d_1_S_{11}	0,05	d_2_S_{11}	0,01	d_4_S_{11}	0,6	w$_{111}$	0,5	w$_{121}$	0,5
	b1_S_{11}_extra_mu	?	alpha_S_{11}_ST	0,1	b1_S_{11}_extra_total	10							Threshold_kpi$_{111}$	0,2	Threshold_kpi$_{121}$	0,1
													val_S_{11}_kpi$_{111}$	0,8	val_S_{11}_kpi$_{121}$	-0,01
S_{12}	u_S_{12}	?	ti_S_{12}	?	c_S_{12}	3	d_1_S_{12}	0,2	d_2_S_{12}	0,03	d_4_S_{11}	0,5	val_S_{12}_kpi$_{111}$	0,3	val_S_{12}_kpi$_{121}$	0,7
	b1_S_{12}_extra_mu	?	alpha_S_{12}_MT	0,9	b1_S_{12}_extra_total	10							val_S_{21}_kpi$_{111}$	-0,1	val_S_{21}_kpi$_{121}$	-0,3
													val_S_{22}_kpi$_{111}$	0,3	val_S_{22}_kpi$_{121}$	0,2

Enterprise 2 $b_2 = 6$

														kpi $_{211}$		kpi $_{221}$	
S_{21}	u_S_{21}	?	ti_S_{21}	?	c_S_{21}	6	d_1_S_{21}	0,1	d_2_S_{21}	0,02	d_4_S_{21}	0,75	w$_{211}$	0,5	w$_{221}$	0,5
	b2_S_{21}_extra_mu	?	alpha_S_{12}_LT	0,6	b2_S_{21}_extra_total	10							Threshold_kpi$_{211}$	0,3	Threshold_kpi$_{221}$	0,15
													val_S_{21}_kpi$_{211}$	0,7	val_S_{21}_kpi$_{221}$	0
S_{22}	u_S_{22}	?	ti_S_{22}	?	c_S_{22}	5	d_1_S_{21}	0,05	d_2_S_{21}	0,01	d_4_S_{21}	0,5	val_S_{22}_kpi$_{211}$	0,2	val_S_{22}_kpi$_{221}$	0,8
	b2_S_{22}_extra_mu	?	alpha_S_{22}_ST	0,95	b1_S_{22}_extra_total	10							val_S_{11}_kpi$_{211}$	0,3	val_S_{11}_kpi$_{221}$	0,4
													val_S_{12}_kpi$_{211}$	-0,2	val_S_{12}_kpi$_{221}$	-0,3

Two scenarios are compared for the validation of the SAM using C-EMO. Scenario 1 uses data of Table 2, and enterprise 2 identifies an $alpha\_S22\_ST = 0,95$. In scenario 2 the enterprise 2 reduces by 0,05 the degree of impatience, so that $alpha\_S22\_ST = 0,9$. Results (Table 3) with the initial input data (scenario 1) show that the S_{11} and S_{21} must be activated in one unit, providing a KPI of the network equal to 2,6315. The solution in scenario 2, shows that the S_{11} and S_{22} must be activated in one unit, giving a KPI of the network equal to 3,927; a 37% higher than in the scenario 1. Therefore the proposed approach, allows to support the CN enterprises, advising that slight differences in the degree of impatience could change the activation of aligned strategies increasing on higher values of enterprise and network KPIs.

Table 3. Results

	u_S_{11}		u_S_{12}		u_S_{21}		u_S_{22}		KPI$_1$		KPI$_2$		KPI$_{net}$	
Scenario 1	u_S_{11}	1	u_S_{12}	0	u_S_{21}	1	u_S_{22}	0	KPI$_1$	0,907	KPI$_2$	4,356	KPI$_{net}$	2,6315
Scenario 2	u_S_{11}	1	u_S_{12}	0	u_S_{21}	0	u_S_{22}	1	KPI$_1$	3,479	KPI$_2$	4,375	KPI$_{net}$	3,927

6 Conclusions

A connection between two relevant approaches in the scope of CN discipline is presented, aiming at proposing a new modelling framework to support companies on modelling, assessment and resolution of the strategies alignment process considering their collaborative emotional state. Both approaches are based on SD simulation method. An integrated view diagram relating SAM and C-EMO models is proposed. It starts with the calculation of the degree of impatience within the IME model of C-EMO. The degree of impatience is translated in time units and serves as an input to SAM, which identifies the strategies to be activated accordingly and computes the extra monetary units to be invested in the strategies execution in order to accelerate obtaining the maximum level of KPI_{ixk} monetary.

Future work will rely on extending the proposed approach, from a decentralized perspective. Accordingly, future developments will pass by jointly using system dynamics and agent-based (AB) simulation methodologies. With the introduction of AB, the proposed approach will work at two levels, (i) at the CN level, modelling the complex system as a collection of autonomous decision making entities called agents, and; (ii) at the individual level, where each agent individually evaluates its situation and takes decisions following a set of rules that are modeled with the system dynamics method.

References

1. Camarinha-Matos, L.M.: Collaborative networks in industry and the role of PRO-VE. Int. J. Prod. Manag. Eng. 2(2), 53–57 (2014)
2. Andres, B., Poler, R.: Models, guidelines and tools for the integration of collaborative processes in non-hierarchical manufacturing networks: a review. Int. J. Comput. Integr. Manuf. 2(29), 166–201 (2016)
3. Bititci, U., Martinez, V., Albores, P., Parung, J.: Creating and managing value in collaborative networks. Int. J. Phys. Distrib. Logist. Manag. 34(3/4), 251–268 (2004)
4. Carbo, B.: Align the organization for improved supply chain performance. ASCET Proj. 2, 244–447 (2002)
5. Macedo, P., Camarinha-Matos, L.: Value systems alignment analysis in collaborative networked organizations management. Appl. Sci. 7(12), 123 (2017)
6. Andres, B., Poler, R.: A decision support system for the collaborative selection of strategies in enterprise networks. Decis. Support Syst. 91, 113–123 (2016)
7. Andres, B., Macedo, P., Camarinha-Matos, L.M., Poler, R.: Achieving coherence between strategies and value systems in collaborative networks. In: Camarinha-Matos, L.M., Afsarmanesh, H. (eds.) PRO-VE 2014. IFIP AICT, vol. 434, pp. 261–272. Springer, Heidelberg (2014). https://doi.org/10.1007/978-3-662-44745-1_26
8. Ferrada, F., Camarinha-Matos, L.M.: A system dynamics and agent-based approach to model emotions in collaborative networks. In: Camarinha-Matos, L.M., Parreira-Rocha, M., Ramezani, J. (eds.) DoCEIS 2017. IFIP AICT, vol. 499, pp. 29–43. Springer, Cham (2017). https://doi.org/10.1007/978-3-319-56077-9_3

9. Campuzano, F., Mula, J.: Supply Chain Simulation. A System Dynamics Approach for Improving Performance. Springer, London (2011). https://doi.org/10.1007/978-0-85729-719-8
10. Camarinha-Matos, L.M., Afsarmanesh, H.: Collaborative networks: a new scientific discipline. J. Intell. Manuf. **16**(4–5), 439–452 (2005)
11. Vicsek, T.: Complexity: the bigger picture. Nature **418**(6894), 131 (2002)
12. Sterman, J., Richardson, G., Davidsen, P.: Modelling the estimation of petroleum resources in the United States. Technol. Forecast. Soc. Chang. **33**(3), 219–249 (1998)
13. Vlachos, D., Georgiadis, P., Iakovou, E.: A system dynamics model for dynamic capacity planning of remanufacturing in closed-loop supply chains. Comput. Oper. Res. **34**(2), 367–394 (2007)
14. Campuzano-Bolarín, F., Mula, J., Peidro, D.: An extension to fuzzy estimations and system dynamics for improving supply chains. Int. J. Prod. Res. **51**(10), 3156–3166 (2013)
15. Barton, P., Bryan, S., Robinson, S.: Modelling in the economic evaluation of health care: selecting the appropriate approach. J. Heal. Serv. Res. Policy **9**(2), 110–118 (2004)
16. Eldabi, T., Paul, R.J., Young, T.: Simulation modelling in healthcare: reviewing legacies and investigating futures. J. Oper. Res. Soc. Spec. Issue Oper. Res. Heal. **58**(2), 262–270 (2007)
17. Andres, B., Poler, R., Camarinha-Matos, L.M., Afsarmanesh, H.: A simulation approach to assess partners selected for a collaborative network. Int. J. Simul. Model. **16**(3), 399–411 (2017)
18. Gohari, A., Mirchi, A., Madan, K.: System dynamics evaluation of climate change adaptation strategies for water resources management in central Iran. Water Resour. Manag. **31**(5), 1413–1434 (2007)
19. Fishera, D., Norvell, J., Sonka, S., Nelson, M.J.: Understanding technology adoption through system dynamics modeling: implications for agribusiness management. Int. Food Agribus. Manag. Rev. **3**, 281–296 (2000)
20. Lyneisa, J.M.: System dynamics for market forecasting and structural analysis. Syst. Dyn. Rev. **16**(1), 3–25 (2000)
21. Borshchev, A., Filippov, A.: From system dynamics and discrete event to practical agent based modeling: reasons, techniques, tools. In: The 22nd International Conference of the System Dynamics Society (2004)
22. Ferrada, F.: C-EMO: A Modeling Framework for Collaborative Network Emotions Doctoral dissertation, Nova University of Lisbon, Portugal (2017). https://run.unl.pt/handle/10362/26857
23. Scherer, K.R.: Emotions are emergent processes: they require a dynamic computational architecture. Rev. Philos. Trans. R. Soc. Biol. Sci. **364**(1535), 3459–3474 (2009)

Adaptive Sales & Operations Planning: Innovative Concept for Manufacturing Collaborative Decisions?

Jean-Baptiste Vidal[1], Matthieu Lauras[2(✉)], Jacques Lamothe[2], and Romain Miclo[3]

[1] University of Orléans, IUT, Orléans, France
jean-baptiste.vidal@univ-orleans.fr
[2] IMT Mines Albi, Industrial Engineering Department, Albi, France
{matthieu.lauras,jacques.lamothe}@mines-albi.fr
[3] AGILEA Conseil, Toulouse, France
romain.miclo@agilea.fr

Abstract. By definition, *Supply Chain Management* includes a huge number of collaborative decision processes. In a manufacturing environment, the Sales & Operations Planning (S&OP) process is often used to support strategic and tactical decisions such as recruitment, investment on machines or subcontracting. S&OP was invented in the eighties when collaboration issues between and within companies were radically different from what obtains today. Many rules and opportunities that are important for manufacturing collaborative decisions have changed but not in this process. Recently, the Demand Driven Institute has developed the *Demand Driven Adaptive Enterprise* system that includes an innovative process called Adaptive S&OP. The purpose of this paper is to develop a structured comparison between the traditional S&OP and the new Adaptive S&OP, to objectively characterize their differences, and to highlight points of vigilance regarding future Adaptive S&OP implementations. Based on this analysis, some suggestions for future research works are made.

Keywords: Manufacturing collaborative decisions
Sales & Operations Planning · Adaptive Sales & Operations Planning
Comparison framework · Supply Chain Management
Demand Driven Adaptive Enterprise

1 Introduction and Research Question

Sales & Operations Planning is probably the most popular collaborative process for supporting strategic and tactical decisions in manufacturing environment. Designed more than 30 years ago, this process is regularly enriched and criticized in the Supply Chain literature [6]. Notably, scholars point out that this process is not necessarily applied as it should be and not necessarily adapted for the current organizational networks, which have changed a lot during the last decades. Parallelly, some authors have recently suggested some new paradigms and approaches to manage material flows within and between companies. This is essentially the case of what is called *Demand*

L. M. Camarinha-Matos et al. (Eds.): PRO-VE 2018, IFIP AICT 534, pp. 362–374, 2018.
https://doi.org/10.1007/978-3-319-99127-6_31

Driven Adaptive Enterprise system [12]. In this system, one of the pillars is called Adaptive Sales & Operations Planning (AS&OP) and the authors affirm that this can address the limits and weaknesses of the current S&OP processes. The purpose of this research is to compare the traditional S&OP process with this new AS&OP process in order to know whether AS&OP is a really innovative contribution for collaborative decisions in a manufacturing environment. The objective of this analysis is also to highlight some points of vigilance on AS&OP that should be further studied.

The paper is divided into four complementary sections. The first one discusses some key points in the literature on this topic. The second one develops a structured framework that can be used to compare processes in terms of both objective and coordination issues. The third section develops a discussion based on these comparisons while the last section gives a rapid conclusion on this research work.

2 Background

2.1 Manufacturing Collaborative Decisions

Managing a manufacturing plant entails making decisions at different levels: strategic, tactical and operational. For decades, decision-makers use the Manufacturing Resource Planning (MRP II) system to support their decisions [16]. This system is a cascading planning system that offers a set of planning process for each decision level. Regarding the strategic and tactical levels, MRP II is executed through the Sales and Operations Planning (S&OP). This was made to support collaboration between the different stakeholders of a company (finance, sales, production, logistics, supply, etc.) regarding decisions such as recruitment, investment on machines or subcontracting. Definitively, MRP II and S&OP have brought benefits to companies during decades. But these tools seem now to become obsolete as the economic rules and environment have drastically changed [13]. Consequently, there has emerged recently from the corporate world a fundamental rethinking of the MRP II logic – a rethinking that draws on elements of developments such as Lean Systems and Theory of Constraints to improve the overall performance of manufacturing operations and collaborative mechanisms. This rethinking has resulted in a new approach – Demand Driven Adaptive Enterprise [12].

2.2 "Sales & Operations Planning"

Richard C. Ling [4] is recognized by academics and practitioners as the father of S&OP in the late 1980s. Since his first model of the process [5], S&OP was popularized by practitioners through the exchanges of best practices in the supply chain community such as APICS. The APICS defines S&OP as *"A process to develop tactical plans that provide management the ability to strategically direct its businesses to achieve competitive advantage on a continuous basis by integrating customer-focused marketing plans for new and existing products with the management of the supply chain. The process brings together all the plans for the business (sales, marketing, development, manufacturing, sourcing, and financial) into one integrated set of plans"*. This definition underlines the collaborative nature of S&OP so that all the company's functions generate an aligned business plan.

Practitioners tried to standardize this process in order to implement it in different business activities. Figure 1 shows the five-step common approach accepted as traditional in business activities [6]. The goals of S&OP are easy to understand, but practitioners in many different companies failed to totally implement this process or did not achieve the expected competitiveness in their markets.

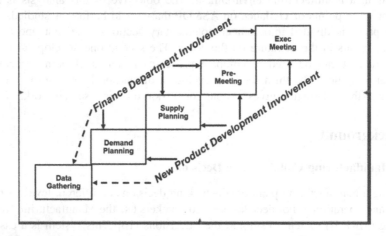

Fig. 1. S&OP model for practitioners [6]

Considering S&OP at the supply chain level, Fig. 2 shows a model used during APICS Annual Event 2017. Main boxes fit the Wallace model [6], but they are now detailed and linked to the long-term business objectives. This underlines the idea of practitioners to keep original methodology.

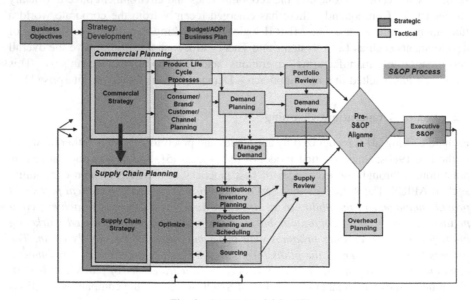

Fig. 2. S&OP Model by [7]

According to several recent literature reviews [2, 8, 9], the interest of academics for S&OP has grown since 2000. These literature reviews show two important points:

- The complexity of the S&OP process is a reality. Multiple extensions of the original model were proposed and there is now needs to build a common framework for comparison.
- Despite growing research activity, there is a requirement for fine granulometry studies for academics as well as for practitioners.

It is possible to understand that there are multiple reasons for failure when S&OP is implemented. Despite many improvements and the identification of diverse and numerous success factors [10], S&OP remains a difficult process to implement [3]. The gap between expected and actual benefits is big [11]. However, practitioners still need answers to their vital problem: balancing supply capabilities with market expectations and needs at a strategic level while generating profit. In an environment where the variety and complexity of products is growing, the time to react is very low, supply chains and markets are spread around the world and customer requirements are very strong, it is more and more difficult to achieve success with the implementation of S&OP. With this new environment, S&OP was kept with its initial structure, without major modification. Academics and Practitioners continue to extend and refine the theoretical vision of S&OP with the aim of identifying the reasons for the failures in reality or the difficulty of reaching a high level of maturity in its implementation: recent research works show that it seems necessary to carry out practical and theoretical studies including contextual impacts [9, 11].

2.3 "Adaptive Sales & Operations Planning"

In 2017, the Demand Driven Institute (DDI) created a new approach called *Demand Driven Adaptive Enterprise* - DDAE [12] based on three major processes:

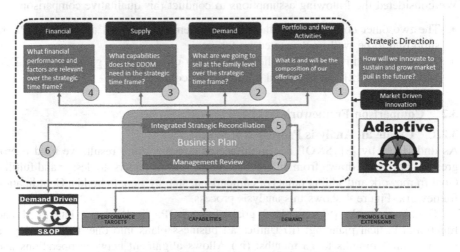

Fig. 3. Model AS&OP by Demand Driven Institute

- Demand Driven Operating Model (DDOM) at the operational level;
- Demand Driven Sales & Operations Planning (DDS&OP) at the tactical level;
- Adaptive Sales and Operations Planning (AS&OP) at the strategic level.

DDAE (the evolution of the first concept DDMRP create by DDI) proposes an integration of multiple approaches such as Lean, Theory of constraint and MRP II. [13] shows that this integrated approach works at the operational level but the demonstration at the strategic level is yet to be done. As the first and second processes have just been assimilated by first practitioners, DDI introduced in 2017 the third AS&OP process (see Fig. 3) as a new way to formalize and use the S&OP philosophy.

3   Research Questions and Proposal

3.1   Research Questions and Assumptions

Today the number of DDAE practitioners is low in proportion to those practicing S&OP but the interest of the practitioner community is high. Although the concept of DDAE is recent, there are studies on operational parts of the DDAE model like DDMRP [13], but none of them is based on AS&OP. As the research on S&OP is rich [8], as much on the mastered aspects as on those that are yet to be developed, it seems logical to try to compare S&OP and AS&OP by relying on the major features already studied on S&OP. The corpus of knowledge on DDAE is beginning to be accessible on this subject, through trainings and conferences proposed by the DDI and its global affiliates [12]. Based on this material, we propose in this paper to study the potential of this new collaborative approach by answering two simple research questions:

RQ1: Is AS&OP really a novelty compared to traditional S&OP?
RQ2: Which priority aspects of AS&OP should be studied in future academic research works for supporting efficiently the first implementations?

We considered the following assumptions to conduct this qualitative comparison:

- The two other components of the DDAE system (i.e. DDOM and DDS&OP) are supposed to be well implemented on the field.
- The study is limited to the public DDAE body of knowledge gathering from DDI white papers [12] and dedicated trainings and conferences.

3.2   Comparison Framework

3.2.1   Create an Analysis Process

As underlined by [8], S&OP is a multifaceted concept. As a result, we used a progressive approach, drawn from different academic journal papers, to design and fulfill a Goal framework and adding points of comparison, step by step, to build a Coordination framework. Figure 4 shows this analysis process.

Goal-framework: [8] records 5 goals for S&OP: (i) Produces integrated and functional tactical planning; (ii) Unifies all business plans into one; (iii) Develops a vision from 3 months to 18 months; (iv) Allows alignment between operations and strategy; (v) Generates values and drivers of the company's performance. We will use

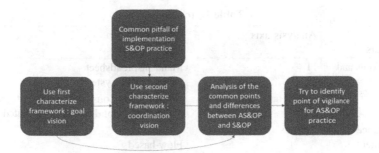

Fig. 4. The process of analysis and synthesis proposed in this paper

them to compare S&OP and AS&OP. Coordination-framework: four elements will be used to build it to make a comparison between S&OP and AS&OP: (i) literature search synthesis framework [8] (ii) Coordination of S&OP framework [2] (iii) the classical pitfalls of implementing S&OP in the real world [6, 14] (iv) feedback from a dozen S&OP implementation experts. The coordination-framework described by [2] defines six principal coordination mechanisms. They are selected to constitute our *constructs* defined as point of views that are traditionally used by academics and practitioners to describe S&OP concepts: (i) S&OP organization; (ii) S&OP Process; (iii) S&OP Tools and Data; (iv) Performance management; (v) Strategic alignment; (vi) S&OP culture and leadership. For each *construct*, we selected the most convincing *analysis axis* to make our comparison on the basis of relevant information mainly from [2, 8]. In the same way, for each *analysis axis*, we have associated a *criterion* with 2 or 3 differentiating levels of characterization (Table 1).

Table 1. Criteria on S&OP Coordination

Coord. Constructs	Analysis axis	Criteria
S&OP organization	Stakeholders	All internal service except finance
		All internal service included finance
		All internal service included finance and external suppliers
	Ritual meeting	Sporadic and informal meeting
		Regular meeting or upon request according to event
S&OP Process	Formalization	High Level (Macro vision)
		Detailed Level (Micro)
	Links between activities	Linear
		Nonlinear interconnected
	Outcome	Plan production only
		Plan sales, production, investment not integrated
		Plan sales, production, investment integrated

(continued)

Table 1. (*continued*)

Coord. Constructs	Analysis axis	Criteria
S&OP Tools and Data	IT	Manual/Spreadsheet Dedicated IT system
	S&OP data requirement	Numbers/No Consolidation/No integration Numbers consolidated and integrated
Performance management	Metrics	Cost-based Flow-based Production-based
	KPI's	Used to perform internal performance only Used Internal and for Firm Performance, effectiveness of the S&OP Process
Strategic alignment	Vertical alignment/tactical reconciliation	Disconnected Effective reconciliation
S&OP culture and leadership	Rewarding and incentives	Functional incentives with no integration Collaborative S&OP enhances integration
	Top management ownership	Low participation of executives High participation of executives
	Change management	Top-down approach Bottom-up approach

The S&OP concept was created nearly 40 years ago. With the contributions of the practitioners and academics, a theoretical and practical (rather rich) vision of S&OP can be spread out according to several stages of maturity [15]. Nevertheless, a large number of companies are struggling to go beyond a low maturity stage [3]. To compare S&OP and AS&OP, three distinct levels of S&OP have been identified as a reference: low maturity level of theoretical S&OP, high maturity level of both theoretical S&OP and practical S&OP. Practical S&OP means the concrete practices observed through the implementation of S&OP on the knowledge acquired from the feedback of a dozen S&OP implementation experts. Table 2 shows the complete characterization framework.

Table 2. Coordination-framework gap analysis

Construct	Analysis axis	Low Maturity Level S&OP theoretical	High Maturity Level S&OP theoretical	S&OP practice	High Maturity Level AS&OP theoretical
S&OP organization	Stakeholders	All internal services except finance	All internal services, included finance and external suppliers	All internal services except finance	All internal services, included finance and external suppliers
	Ritual meetings	Sporadic and informal meetings	Regular meeting or		Regular meetings or

(*continued*)

Table 2. (*continued*)

Construct	Analysis axis	Low Maturity Level S&OP theoretical	High Maturity Level S&OP theoretical	S&OP practice	High Maturity Level AS&OP theoretical
			upon request according to event		upon request according to event
S&OP Process	Formalization	High Level (Macro vision)	High Level (Macro vision)	High Level (Macro vision)	High Level (Macro vision)
	Cycle	Linear	Linear	Linear	Non- Linear Interconnected
	Outcome	Plan sales, production, investment not integrated	Plan sales, production, investment integrated	Plan production only	Plan sales, production, investment integrated
S&OP Tools and Data	IT	Manual/Spreadsheet	Dedicated IT system	Manual/Spreadsheet	Dedicated IT system
	S&OP data requirement	Numbers/No Consolidation/No integration	Numbers consolidated and integrated	Numbers/No Consolidation/No integration	Numbers consolidated and integrated
Performance management	Metrics	Cost-based	Cost-based	Production-based	flow-based
	KPI's	Used to perform internal performance only	Used Internal and for Firm Performance, effectiveness of the S&OP Process	Used to perform internal performance only	Used Internal and for Firm Performance, effectiveness of the S&OP Process
Strategic alignment	Vertical alignment/tactical reconciliation	Disconnected	Effective reconciliation	Disconnected	Effective reconciliation
S&OP culture and leadership	Rewarding and incentives	Functional incentives with no integration	Collaborative S&OP enhance integration	Functional incentives with no integration	Collaborative S&OP enhance integration
	Top management ownership	Low participation of executives	High participation of executives	Low participation of executives	High participation of executives
	Change management	Top-down approach	Bottom-up approach	Top-down approach	Bottom-up approach

To study S&OP practices we used classical pitfalls reported by practitioners about S&OP [6, 14] that have been classified in our selected points of view:

- S&OP organization: The strategic players of the company think that only the supply chain and the production are concerned by this process; the meeting monthly loses its meaning in the eyes of the main actors: no decisions made, short-term management only, too much details, search for the culprit; no integration of suppliers' or customers' vision;
- S&OP Process: lack of formal processes about S&OP meeting, no formal approach to link tactical and strategic decisions;

- S&OP Tools and Data: product life stages are not considered, lack of data accuracy or gathering;
- Performance management: the actors focus on the short-term objectives and do not consider the possibility of taking important decisions regarding the future of the business. They focus on only one goal: "establish a demand forecast instead of other key issues concerning S&OP";
- Strategic alignment: Strategy alignment is dysfunctional as it is not shared between company functions;
- S&OP culture and leadership: The S&OP team does not try to avoid conflict neither to monitor the efficiency of the S&OP process and to improve the company.

3.3   Gap Analysis

3.3.1   Goal-Framework

Through the test-one, AS&OP principles [12] seem to cover all the different points that are usually identified in a traditional S&OP. We conclude that an AS&OP can be assimilated to a type of S&OP as academics and practitioners usually describe it.

3.3.2   Coordination-Framework

On this dimension, the comparison was done based on data available in [12] for the AS&OP, in [2, 3, 8, 9] for the theoretical S&OP and in [6] and our knowledge acquired by interviews with dozens of S&OP implementation experts for the practical S&OP. Table 2 shows the results.

4   Discussion and Research Agenda

4.1   Comparison Between High Level Maturity S&OP and aS&OP

First of all, we compare the result between the column "high maturity level" and AS&OP. We observe two discordant elements in this comparison: S&OP Process and Performance Management. The other ones are not discriminating.

The first difference refers to the non-linearity of the AS&OP process as described in [12]. Figure 5 shows that the processes (1.) portfolio and new activities, (2.) demand, (3.) supply and (4.) financial, are considered together to accomplish an (5.) integrated strategic reconciliation. Practitioners [4] who originally introduced S&OP recommended to have a cross-functional process with interconnections between all services. This was broken in [6] with the introduction of the pre-meeting step (iv) and the linearization of steps i, ii and iii. AS&OP finally suggests coming back to the initial approach. The traditional linear approach of S&OP has made this concept understandable for a wide range of companies but it has also led to set-up failures such as the lack of interest of some of the strategic players concerned other than production and sales. Indeed, a lot of information useful for the coordination of this process is established in a non-linear way, requiring more complex round trips than the present model, with coordination to be agile and permanent between the services. The non-linear matrix vision of the AS&OP model can potentially be a best way to success in this coordination point of view, enabling the departments concerned to better find their

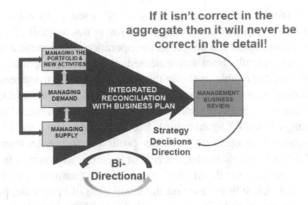

Fig. 5. Evolution of S&OP by Dick Ling (APICS Event 2016)

place according to their real operating rhythm. It is also a difficulty that will have to be overcome particularly in terms of practical organization.

AS&OP are mainly flow-oriented (i. working capital, ii. contribution margin, iii. customer base). DDI practitioners think that the most important thing is to use relevant information at each level. In that sense, they are inspired by Theory of Constraints and Lean Management philosophy to opt for a flow vision rather than a cost approach.

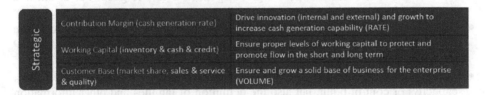

Fig. 6. AS&OP Strategic KPIs [12]

The goal of S&OP is to help the coordination of a company's services to make both strategic and tactical decisions for the success of the company. The problem of choosing indicators to drive this process is an important research topic. Traditionally, the practitioners focus on the optimization of the resources until they see only the problem of the capacity versus demand. This constitutes a problem because it ends up concerning only the services of the production and the sales. Consequently, there generally is a disengagement from other departments, with ultimately a malfunction of the S&OP process. Also, the choice of AS&OP specific KPIs (see Fig. 6) seems to be a major asset to ensure the success of its implementation.

4.2 Comparison S&OP Practices Vs AS&OP

Let's now compare the results between the columns practical S&OP and AS&OP. The idea is to test the ability of the AS&OP approach (as a whole DDAE) to be implemented efficiently in the field by avoiding the conventional pitfalls of traditional

S&OP. About performance management, AS&OP used a flow-based metrics as highlighted by DDAE implementation experts. This is not a detail. They explain that the flow approach makes sense to people at the operational and tactical levels (DDOM and DDS&OP have actually been implemented in several companies). In the early stage of AS&OP, this can enable to obtain the adherence of top management from each department including sales and finance. A general (success of S&OP culture and leadership) disinterest is a major reason for the failure of stakeholders' integration and the lack of meetings (S&OP Organization). S&OP Process, data and IT (S&OP tools and data) are required to optimize business profit (performance management) [2]. Regarding the A&SOP process model, the risk of failure is as much as in S&OP. But it seems necessary to try to detail this model, for example on the link with DDS&OP. Similarly, A&SOP is based on the simulation of optimistic, pessimistic and median strategic scenarios, and this requires a dedicated IT, which does not completely exist yet. These links and specificities can make AS&OP and S&OP approaches successfully reach a high stage of maturity.

4.3   Point of Vigilance

DDI experts on AS&OP develop analogies with the concept of S&OP in a grid at different levels of maturity [12]. On the basis of our understanding we can make some recommendations for both scholars and practitioners as a set of points of vigilance.

- For S&OP, the formalization of a global point of view is good, but to allow a successful implementation, developing a detailed approach will be a plus;
- Little information is given by DDI on how to make all the steps, from 1 to 6 (see Fig. 3). The implementation of the S&OP process is already difficult, the AS&OP model of flows needs to be clarified/explained;
- Step 6 links AS&OP and DDS&OP. The positioning of buffer (stock, time, capacity) or control point, but also the definition of families and other information required by the DDS&OP process also needs to be clarified specifically such as to achieve a successful implementation of the vertical alignment between AS&OP and DDS&OP;
- Regarding S&OP tools and data, they need to be supported with relevant data that require dedicated software. Studying and developing these software and decision support systems seem to be mandatory. Otherwise, the AS&OP may have unrealistic goals (to carry out long-term simulations of optimistic, pessimistic and median scenarios);
- Concerning performance management, more studies on the benefits and limits of this choice of metrics (i. working capital, ii. contribution margin, iii. customer base) can be done in order to demonstrate their value, compared to existing flow-based metrics.

5   Conclusion and Further Research

In this paper, we focused on decision support processes for strategic collaborative manufacturing activities. We argued that usual approaches are based on tools that were developed a long time ago and which seem not to be relevant anymore. At the same time, new proposals have recently appeared on the market to address this issue, but no scientific study has been developed to assess their benefits and limits.

Therefore, we have presented and discussed in this paper a structured comparison between the S&OP and AS&OP concepts. Our findings show that in terms of goals, AS&OP and S&OP are quite similar. But on the issue of coordination, AS&OP includes real and significant novelties compared to the traditional S&OP approach and has a better potential for success However, lack of scientific studies on DDAE, DDMRP and especially on AS&OP allow us making only partial conclusions on the real benefits of AS&OP. Given that our results can be considered as preliminary, further research is still needed.

An extension of this research might consist in improving the framework of the analysis, which allowed only a comparison with a large mesh as well as including additional criteria as analysis axes. [9] for instance showed the relevance of including finer study parameters to better understand the concept of S&OP and consequently of AS&OP. Another perspective could be on an objective assessment of AS&OP implementation (the first ones are ongoing and not yet finished) results compared to those of S&OP. We could, in view of the craze of practitioners for DDAE, take advantage of the future experiences to study in more depth the specifics of AS&OP. Lastly, future research works should consist in developing a kind of AS&OP maturity model that end-users can use to improve their performance.

References

1. Hadaya, P., Cassivi, L.: The role of joint collaboration planning actions in a demand-driven supply chain. Ind. Manag. Data Syst. **107**(7), 954–978 (2007)
2. Tuomikangas, N., Kaipia, R.: A coordination framework for sales and operations planning (S&OP): synthesis from the literature. Int. J. Prod. Econ. **154**, 243–262 (2014)
3. Grimson, J.A., Pyke, D.F.: Sales and operations planning: an exploratory study and framework. Int. J. Logist. Manag. **18**(3), 322–346 (2007)
4. Ling, D., Coldrick, A.: Breakthrough Sales & Operations Planning: How we developed the process, p. 39 (2009). http://dickling.net/breakthrough-sop/
5. Ling, R.C., Goddard, W.E.: Orchestrating Success: Improve Control of the Business with Sales & Operations Planning. Wiley (1989)
6. Wallace, T.F.: Sales and Operations Planning: The How-To Handbook. Steelwedge Software (2008)
7. APICS 2017 | APICS Event. http://www.apics.org/credentials-education/events/event-landing-page/2017/10/15/default-calendar/apics-2017
8. Tavares Thomé, A.M., Scavarda, L.F., Fernandez, N.S., Scavarda, A.J.: Sales and operations planning: a research synthesis. Int. J. Prod. Econ. **138**(1), 1–13 (2012)
9. Kristensen, J., Jonsson, P.: Context-based sales and operations planning (S&OP) research: a literature review and future agenda. Int. J. Phys. Distrib. Logist. Manag. **48**(1), 19–46 (2018)

10. Lapide, L.: Sales and Operations Planning Part I: The Process, p. 3 (2004)
11. Jonsson, P., Holmström, J.: Future of supply chain planning: closing the gaps between practice and promise. Int. J. Phys. Distrib. Logist. Manag. 46(1), 62–81 (2016)
12. Demand Driven Adaptive Enterprise (DDAE): The Demand Driven Institute - World Leader in Demand Driven Education. https://www.demanddriveninstitute.com/demand-driven-adaptive-enterprise-m
13. Miclo, R.: Challenging the Demand Driven MRP Promises: A Discrete Event Simulation Approach. Ph thesis, Ecole nationale des Mines d'Albi-Carmaux (2016)
14. APICS: CPIM - Certified in Production and Inventory Management | APICS (2016)
15. Jansson, J., Åberg, F.: Sales and operations planning in the process industry: A diagnostic model (2014)
16. Wight, O.: The executive's guide to successful MRP II, vol. 6. John Wiley & Sons (1995)

Industry 4.0 Support Frameworks

Awareness Towards Industry 4.0: Key Enablers and Applications for Internet of Things and Big Data

Myrna Flores[1,2(✉)], Doroteja Maklin[2], Matic Golob[2],
Ahmed Al-Ashaab[3], and Christopher Tucci[1]

[1] École Polytechnique Fédérale de Lausanne, College of Management,
Odyssea Building, 1015 Lausanne, Switzerland
{myrna.flores, christopher.tucci}@epfl.ch
[2] Lean Analytics Association, Via Colombei 22, 6914 Carona, Switzerland
{doroteja.maklin, matic.golob}@lean-analytics.org
[3] Cranfield University, Building 50, Cranfield, Bedfordshire MK43 0AL, UK
a.al-ashaab@cranfield.ac.uk

Abstract. The fourth Industrial revolution promises to increase productivity, flexibility and automation of internal business processes integrating value chains and supporting companies to design and offer novel services based on the availability of data enabled by different technologies. As a result, companies are investing great efforts to understand in which way Industry 4.0 technologies could be deployed to leverage their current operations and deliver a more competitive value proposition to existing and new customers. In this context, the objectives of this paper are: (1) to provide the findings from a research project which aimed to capture the awareness from companies about Industry 4.0, (2) identify which are the key enablers for the successful implementation of Internet of Things (IoT) and Big Data and (3) propose further suggestions about research needed to facilitate the development Collaborative Networks towards Industry 4.0.

Keywords: Industry 4.0 · Internet of Things · Big Data · Survey
Collaborative networks

1 Introduction

The fourth Industrial revolution, also referred to as Industry 4.0, follows previous industrial revolutions which occurred from the 18th century to date. Norbury (2015) and Gilchrist (2016) highlighted certain challenges associated with the three previous revolutions, such as: (1) An increase in complex products; (2) Shorter innovation cycles; (3) Volatile markets and (4) The incapability of human efforts to handle the complexity of present industrial processes and systems.

The term "Industry 4.0" was coined in Germany at the Hannover Messe in 2011 and since then it has become more and more popular; nevertheless, for several, it still remains a buzzword. It comprises several technologies as Internet of Things (IoT), Big Data, Artificial Intelligence, Virtual Reality, 3D Printing, Cyber Security to name a

© IFIP International Federation for Information Processing 2018
Published by Springer Nature Switzerland AG 2018. All Rights Reserved
L. M. Camarinha-Matos et al. (Eds.): PRO-VE 2018, IFIP AICT 534, pp. 377–386, 2018.
https://doi.org/10.1007/978-3-319-99127-6_32

few. Their application targets the improvement of internal operational efficiencies and to create new business models offering new data driven services focusing on providing novel customer experiences. Many consulting companies offer their services to support firms applying these latter enabling technologies for what many refer to as "Digital Transformation".

Although there has been an explosion of interest about Industry 4.0 in the last years, still most companies are at the very beginning of their digital transformation journeys. In this context, the aim of this research was to understand the level of awareness in companies about its benefits and business impact and which do they consider are the main implementation enablers for Internet of Things (IoT) and Big Data. The research project followed a structured research methodology as shown in Table 1.

Table 1. Research Methodology

Identify	Define the research questions and unit of analysis
Learn	Conduct a state-of-the-art literature review
Explore	Develop a structured online survey and collect data
Analyze	Analyze the survey results
Diffuse	Develop research publications and whitepapers

In the first phase, the research questions were defined as follows:

(1) **How do companies envision and understand Industry 4.0?**
(2) **Which are the main enablers to implement IoT and Big Data?**

During the *Learn* phase, a literature review was carried out and the offers of top-ranked consulting companies were searched to have a better understanding of their services towards Industry 4.0. In the *Explore* phase, a survey was designed and conducted to obtain the trends, challenges, potential applications and enablers related to Industry 4.0. Figure 1 shows some of the companies that participated in the survey. In the *Analyze* phase data was examined and in the diffuse phase a detailed report with all the findings was distributed to companies together with scientific publications.

Fig. 1. Some of the participating companies in the survey (Aug to Sept 2017)

2 Internet of Things and Big Data

2.1 Internet of Things

A combination of two words, "internet" and "things", which are the building blocks that make up the phenomenon called the Internet of Things (IoT). The "things" aspect was well-captured by Chaouchi, et al. (2013): "things or objects are described as a set of atoms; the atom is the smallest object in the Internet of Things". Some examples of items that can be connected to this are: Buildings, Machines, Industrial Plants, Assets, Vehicles, Transport Units, Containers, Devices, People, and Animals.

The IoT can be defined as the extension of the internet of physical things in such a way that sharing, processing and utilizing data is possible at the same time as interaction with human beings and the virtual world is, with value creation being the end product (Atzori et al. 2010; Khodadadi, et al. 2016).

The Internet of Things consists of four important components: (1) Connectivity: RFID technology and Wireless Sensor Networks (WSNs) appeared in 100% of the literature that was reviewed; (2) The middleware which acts as a platform through which heterogeneous devices can communicate with each other; (3) Cloud computing which is an important factor ensuring real-time access to and storage of big data generated between devices; and, (4) Data analysis, since a large amount of the data generated will be analyzed.

2.2 Big Data

On the other hand, the term Big Data (BD) has become a real buzzword even though it is not a new concept. Big data refers to large data sets that are impossible to manage and process using traditional data management tools due to their volume and speed of creation. Valuable information and in-sights are obtained when big data are collected and analyzed (Akoka, Comyn-Wattiau and Laoufi 2017).

Gartner (2012), Kwon and Sim (2013) and McAfee and Brynjolfsson (2012) defined Big Data in terms of 3Vs: (a) Volume, referring to the massive amount of data that utilizes huge storage; (b) Velocity, representing the high frequency or speed at which data are created and transferred; (c) Variety, as data comes from a large variety of different sources, dimensions and formats of data. In other words, big data can be structured or unstructured.

Some authors/practitioners went beyond this definition by adding a fourth V, which stands for Value, to point out the importance of obtaining economic benefits from data (IDC 2017; Forrester 2012). Furthermore, White (2012) introduced a fifth V, which stands for Veracity, to emphasize the importance of quality data and the reliability of the sources of data.

On the other hand, Big Data Analytics (BDA) use advanced techniques to obtain useful patterns/insights from an enormous amount of data (Matsunaga, Brancher and Busto 2015).

3   Survey and Findings

The survey designed for this research consisted of 27 questions distributed in four sections: (a) Awareness about Industry 4.0, (b) The Internet of Things, (c) Enabling technologies, and (d) Talent. It was sent by email to 2500 companies and it was intensively promoted in Social Media (LinkedIn, Facebook and Tweeter).

In total 76 individuals located in 25 countries and working in a variety sectors provided a response. The distribution of responses per country, also shown in Fig. 2, was as follows: United Kingdom (16), Spain (12), Mexico (8), France (5), Switzerland (4), Italy (4), USA (4), Sweden (2), India (2), Slovenia (2), Taiwan (1), Belgium (1), Colombia (1), Hungary (1), Serbia (1), Turkey (1), Germany (1), Vietnam(1), Brazil (1), Latvia(1), The Netherlands (1), Nigeria (1), Australia (1), Portugal (1) and 3 were unknown. Figure 3 shows the different sectors.

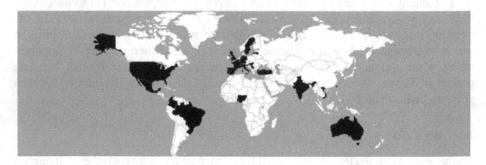

Fig. 2. Countries represented in the research (N = 76)

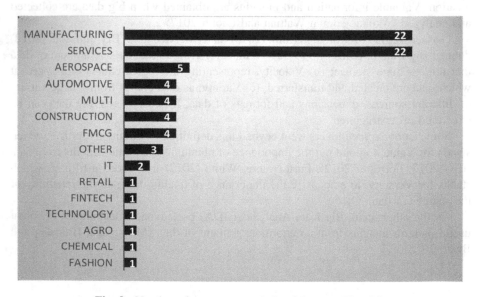

Fig. 3. Number of responses per industrial sector (N = 76)

The first question addressed the definition of Industry 4.0. The proposed definition was:

"The next industrial revolution involves the integration of the physical world and the digital world and it is driven by the four disruptions below:

1. The impressive rise in data volumes, computational power and connectivity
2. The emergence of analytics and business-intelligence capabilities
3. New forms of human-machine interaction such as touch interfaces and augmented-reality systems
4. Improvements in transferring digital instructions to the physical world, such as advanced robotics and 3-D printing".

The survey results observed in Fig. 4 show that 65% of the respondents agreed with the definition mentioned above. Another 20% agree with the definition but would add further details, including AI decision-making and the cultural transformation required and 15% either do not have an opinion or disagree.

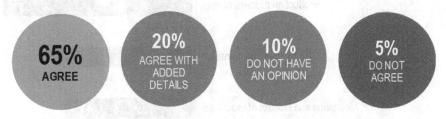

Fig. 4. Opinion about the Industry 4.0 definition (N = 71)

In terms of implementation strategy and commitment, as observed in Fig. 5, only 17% of the companies already have a fully implemented strategy.

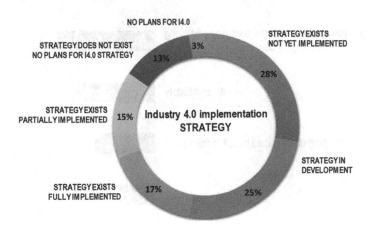

Fig. 5. Current status of an Industry 4.0 Implementation Strategy (N = 72)

3.1   Key Enablers and Applications for Internet of Things (IoT)

(a) **Have business focus:** An increase in efficiency is considered as the main driver for companies to implement the IoT in their processes (57%), followed by predictions for cost savings (47%) which would result from its implementation. 45% of the respondents state that decision making is optimized when using the data gathered and analyzed, while 43% support that the flexibility of the processes is increased.

(b) **Define a leading role:** 47% do not have the role of Chief IoT Officer in their organigram.

(c) **Be clear on the industrial application:** The top 3 applications of the IoT are: 63% in the production process to support the real-time process control, 47% to gather data and make informed decisions on predictive maintenance and 43% to monitor and control machines. Interestingly, the activities related to develop new services is still low. Figure 6 consolidates the results about the different applications.

Fig. 6. Main industrial Applications for Internet of Things (IoT) (N = 72)

3.2   Key Enabler and Applications for Big Data

According to the analysis, the major enabler for big data are the employees' mindset and skills. Figure 7 consolidates the most relevant skills identified in this research. The majority of the respondents built Data Analytics knowledge internally, either by educating existing employees or hiring talents. The position of internal data scientist is present in 57% of the organizations and 18% of the organizations still outsources the data analysis task due to the lack of talent.

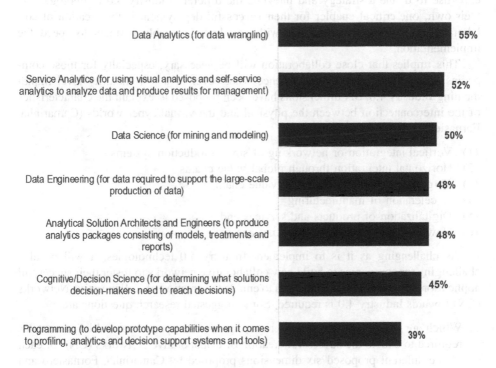

Fig. 7. Skills required to support big data analytics functions (N = 73)

In terms of applications, Big Data is seen as a supporting technology enabling optimized decision making (55%) and helping to increase efficiency (50%) and productivity (43%). The survey respondents report that Big data is most often used to enable predictive maintenance (50%), monitor production processes (43%) in real and near real time and to perform performance measurements (43%). Big data analytics is also used as a tool to capture and identify customer requirements through marketing (30%) as well as for the supply chain integration and traceability of goods in and out of the company in 27% of the cases. Only 20% of the respondents use big data to support marketing for dynamic pricing and marketing to explore new markets. In 64% of the responses, Big Data implementation was carried out by internal teams; 23% hired external consultants.

4   The Creation of Collaborative Networks Towards Industry 4.0

Industry 4.0 is mainly characterized by an increasing digitalization and interconnection of manufacturing systems, products, value chains, and business models which require a convergence of different technologies. Additionally, these latter systems will also need to interface with humans, in particular employees and customers with different skills and demands. Considering that most companies still do not count with the vital expertise to define a strategy and integrate the different Industry 4.0 technologies on their own, one critical enabler for their successful deployment is the creation of collaborative networks or ecosystems with key knowledgeable partners to speed the implementation.

This implies that close collaboration will be necessary, especially for those companies that have no previous experience whatsoever or a low maturity level implementing Industry 4.0. Six dimensions have been proposed to explain the characteristics of the interconnection between the physical and the virtual/cyber worlds (Camarinha, Fornasiero and Afsarmanesh 2017):

(1) Vertical integration or networking of smart production systems
(2) Horizontal integration through global value chains
(3) Through-engineering across the value chain
(4) Acceleration of manufacturing
(5) Digitalization of products and services and
(6) New business models and customer access

As challenging as it is to implement Industry 4.0 technologies, it will be also challenging for companies to build new collaborative networks to foster their successful application. Therefore, further research to enable the creation of Collaborative Networks (CN) towards Industry 4.0 is required. Some suggested research questions are:

a. Which are the drivers, challenges, risks, frameworks, processes and business rules required to enable the successful creation of Collaborative Networks (CN) for each of the different proposed six dimensions proposed by Camarinha, Fornasiero and Afsarmanesh (2017): towards Industry 4.0?
b. Which guidelines could be proposed to support the search and selection of partners towards a successful creation of CN for Industry 4.0?
c. Which are the change management approaches to inspire other companies to join collaborative networks? Are there any unsuccessful cases? Which are the root causes for their failure?
d. Which are they key roles required? Will the broker role orchestrating the network be required?
e. How to identify the strategic relationships organizations need to create and which collaborative networks are already available for them to join?
f. What factors could hinder the raise and evolution of collaborative networks to co-create new digital services?
g. Which soft and hard skills are required by employees to improve their collaborative culture to co-develop novel solutions towards Industry 4.0?

5 Conclusions

This paper presents the insights gained through literature review and a survey answered by 76 practitioners from different industrial sectors in 25 countries. The findings revealed that there is a good level of awareness about Industry 4.0 among the participating companies. Only 10% reported they are not aware of the topic. The rest of them confirmed to have an understanding of the definition and the benefits Industry 4.0 brings.

Participants agreed that Industry 4.0 technologies first demand a business case, which should be periodically reviewed. There is a latent and confirmed need for new skills and workers have to be trained to be prepared for this revolutionary change. Practitioners recommended an evaluation of its impact on the organization, the training, new talent acquisition, the culture and the processes change requirements. These latter changes should be kept in mind when planning the transformation in order to gain the expected benefits.

Last but not least, as most companies do not count with the vital expertise to define and deploy a strategy integrating the different Industry 4.0 technologies on their own, it is expected a fast emergence of new collaborative networks. Therefore, further research is required to enable organizations envisioning such digital transformation. This paper includes a list of key research questions that need to be addressed to support organizations to be successful during their Industry 4.0 journeys.

Acknowledgments. The authors thank Angelo Parentini (2017) and Oluwaseyi Omoloso (2017) two master degree students at Cranfield University for their valuable contribution.

References

Akoka, J., Comyn-Wattiau, I., Laoufi, N.: Research on big data – a systematic mapping study. Comput. Stand. Interfaces **54**, 105–115 (2017)

Atzori, L., Lera, A., Morabito, G.: IoT: a survey. Comput. Net. **54**, 2787–2805 (2010)

Camarinha-Matos, L.M., Fornasiero, R., Afsarmanesh, H.: Collaborative networks as a core enabler of Industry 4.0. In: Camarinha-Matos, L.M., Afsarmanesh, H., Fornasiero, R. (eds.) PRO-VE 2017. IAICT, vol. 506, pp. 3–17. Springer, Cham (2017). https://doi.org/10.1007/978-3-319-65151-4_1

Chaouchi, H., Bourgeau, T., Kirci, P.: Internet of Things: from real to virtual world. Next-Generation Wireless Technologies, pp. 161–188. Springer, London (2013)

Forrester: The big deal about big data for customer engagement business: Leaders Must Lead Big Data Initiatives To Derive Value (2012). http://www.forrester.com/ Accessed 28 May 2017

Gartner: Big Data (2012). https://research.gartner.com/definitionwhatis-big-data?resId = 3002918&srcId = 1-8163325102. Accessed 28 May 2017

Gilchrist, A.: Industry 4.0: the Industrial Internet of Things. Apress, New York (2016)

Harvey, C.: 50 Top Open Source Tools for Big Data (2016). http://www.datamation.com. Accessed 02 Jun 2017

IDC: Data Age 2025: The Evolution of Data to Life-Critical. Don't Focus on Big Data; Focus on the Data That's Big (2017). http://www.idc.com. Accessed 01 Jun 2017

Khodadadi, F., Dastjerdi, A.V., Buyya, R.: Internet of Things: an overview. Internet of Things: principles and paradigms, pp. 3–23. Elsevier, España S.L. (2016)

Kwon, O., Sim, J.: Effects of data set features on the performances of classification algorithms. Expert Syst. Appl. **40**(5), 1847–1857 (2013)

Matsunaga, F.T., Brancher, J.D., Busto, R.M.: Data mining techniques and tasks for multidisciplinary applications: a systematic review, Revista Eletrôn. Argentina-Brasil Tecnol. Inform. Comun. **1**(2) (2015)

McAfee, A., Brynjolfsson, E.: Big data: the management revolution. Harv. Bus. Rev. **90**(10), 61–68 (2012)

Norbury, A.: Industry 4.0 – Vision to Reality (2015). https://ukmanufacturing2015.eng.cam.ac.uk/proceedings/Industry4.0AN10715.pdf

Omoloso, O.: Internet of Things (IoT) towards Industry 4.0. Unpublished master's thesis, Cranfield University, UK (2017)

Parentini, A.: Big Data and Analytics. Unpublished master's thesis, Cranfield University, UK (2017)

White, M.: Digital workplaces: vision and reality. Bus. Inf. Rev. **29**(4), 205–214 (2012)

A Framework to Support Industry 4.0: Chemical Company Case Study

Daniel Cortés Serrano[1]([✉]), Dante Chavarría-Barrientos[1], Arturo Ortega[2],
Belén Falcón[2], Leopoldo Mitre[2], Rodrigo Correa[2],
Jaime Moreno[2], Rafael Funes[2], and Arturo Molina Gutiérrez[1]

[1] Product Innovation Research Group, Tecnologico de Monterrey,
School of Engineering and Science, Mexico City, Mexico
{a01655708,dante.chavarria,armolina}@itesm.mx
[2] LOVIS, Mexico City, Mexico
{arturo.ortega,belen.falcon,leopoldo.mitre,rodrigo.correa,
jaime.moreno,rafael.funes}@lovis.email

Abstract. The concept of Industry 4.0 corresponds to a new way of organizing the production of goods, taking smarter decisions based on environmental variables and optimizing available resources. However, there is still a journey to carry out the implementation of this concept with current technologies. To make this transformation of the industry, it is necessary to characterize the Industry 4.0 concept, adopt a strategic thinking, and acquire skills, aptitudes, and attitudes. Enterprise reference models can help in orchestrating the change, however, the relationship between existing reference models and Industry 4.0 needs further clarification. Thus, this paper proposes a framework that links a reference model with the Industry 4.0 concept. Furthermore, a tool for the instantiation of the framework is proposed to provide practical approach. And the results of implementing the proposed framework are presented in a case study.

Keywords: Industry 4.0 · Cyber-Physical Systems · Industrial Internet of Things
Enterprise Operating System · Cognitive systems

1 Introduction

Today, enterprises need to be designed according to customer requirements, optimize available resources, become agile and respond to market changes in intelligent manners [1]. Enterprises are immersed in their context and operation. Monitoring continues changes over environmental variables are expected to adopt new strategies. To make smarter decisions it is necessary to create Collaborative Networks of Cognitive Systems which could exploit new technologies such as Big Data, Industrial Internet of Things, Advanced Robotics, Artificial Intelligence, Hyperconnectivity, Cloud Computing, Cybersecurity, Additive Manufacturing and Cyber-Physical Systems [2]. With the application of this technologies, an enhance their reactive and proactive capabilities are expected [3, 4]. Sensing technology is now a reality and adaption of these sensors to

© IFIP International Federation for Information Processing 2018
Published by Springer Nature Switzerland AG 2018. All Rights Reserved
L. M. Camarinha-Matos et al. (Eds.): PRO-VE 2018, IFIP AICT 534, pp. 387–395, 2018.
https://doi.org/10.1007/978-3-319-99127-6_33

obtain real-time data is proving a competitive advantage to enable context and knowledge-based decision making [5].

Virtues of Industry 4.0 were planned to respond a need in the production of goods [6], the concept has been expanded to planning, supply chain logistics, product development, and services, though. Company's value chain facilitates the flow of information from the physical world to business decisions in real time with these technologies. Within Industry 4.0 vision, each company need to identify every part of the enterprise which could contribute to data system taking advantage of different information extracted by different sensors measuring either environment or own resources [7] and decisions would be based on current information, considering the total behavior of the enterprise. Thus, transitioning from conventional factories into Smart Factories and creating a Collaborative Network (CN).

Even CNs are part of the transition towards Industry 4.0 enterprises, there is still missing references on how to accomplish it. This paper aims at that purpose introducing a framework and a successful case study from a Chemical Sector Company where Enterprise Operating System designed is implemented and virtues of Industry 4.0 have to yield them. The Paper organizes as follows, Sect. 2 describes the relationship between CNs and Industry 4.0. Then, Sect. 3 describes framework and EOS as a solution and methodological approach towards Industry 4.0. Then, Sect. 4 presents an applied case study. Finally, Sect. 5 provides conclusions and future work.

2   Industry 4.0, Collaborative Networks and Reference Models

Industry 4.0 proposes the use of technology and connections to generate a system capable of obtaining data from the environment to make smart decisions. According to [8] principles that lead to Industry 4.0 are (1) interconnection: ability of machinery to communicate with people through networking, (2) information transparency: capability of information systems and CPS to create virtual copies of the physical world into digital models aided by sensors, (3) decentralized decisions: enable cyber systems to come up with decisions to complete intended goals and (4) technical assistance: ability of the system to support human decisions through different indicators.

On the other hand, Smart Factories are environments where hardware and software interact throughout sensors and actuators interconnected in real time and enable manufacturing relevant information anytime anywhere.

Therefore, Industry 4.0 would not be possible if connection among different areas is omitted in facilities design, that is, if there is no communication and information shared, there would not be possible to generate Smart Factories [9, 10] where humans are decision makers instead of operators. Cyber-Physical Systems (CPS) integrate computing and communication capabilities enabling networking from hardware and software with human beings [2]. In fact, CNs are enablers for Industry 4.0, where every technology acquired must contribute data generation for better decisions [3].

Nonetheless, even there are technological advantages that enable Industry 4.0, there are also factors that have limited the progress of the fourth industrial revolution, among them, uncertainty is a recurring theme that has reduced the inclusion of various technological systems. Thus, the main obstacles to become part of Industry 4.0 are [11, 12]:

- The lack of digital culture and adequate training.
- Resistance to change.
- The absence of a clear vision of digital operations and the leadership of senior management.
- A confused knowledge of the economic benefits of investing in digital technologies.
- Reliability of digital security.

Reference models aim of being reused for different but similar application scenarios [13], enabling minimize obstacles, recognition of capabilities required and clarifying new opportunity areas for revenue increase. A structured vision of technology when instantiating reference models allows identifying information flow and risks involved. An instantiation is done to generate the proposed framework.

3 Proposed Framework

CNs are enablers of the fourth industrial revolution because all principles of Industry 4.0 are related. On the other hand, reference models tackle the main obstacles to adopt Industry 4.0. In recent years, Sensing, Smart and Sustainable System (S^3) [14] has been a conceptualized model of how decision must be taken in enterprises, products must be developed, cities must be planned, and the world must be conceived taking advantage of available technological resources. In that sense, the fourth industrial revolution could be achieved by Smart Factories applying S^3 principles aided by CNs (View Fig. 1).

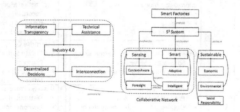

Fig. 1. Collaborative Network conceptual model.

Sensing and Smart principles from S^3 Systems are correlated with Interconnection from Industry 4.0, that enables a Collaborative Network where machines from Smart Factories are capable of providing real-time internal or environmental information in order to make decisions making it more automated.

Not only S^3 system has offered a start point for Smart Factories, but also, it has been conceived from five viewpoints defining a reference model. S3-RM also has been instantiated, activities and tools are provided for its application in different contexts in [15].

Thus, Smart Factories developed in the context of Industry 4.0 require to monitor functions, Yusuf has proposed five components to measure in order to accomplish that purpose [16]:

- Enterprise Resource Management (ERM): obtains the status of resources in a dynamic way.
- Enterprise Process Management (EPM): executes and coordinates business processes defined by internal processes.
- Enterprise Information Management (EIM): coordinates, protects and supports the exchange of information between the resources connected to the system.
- Presentation Management (EP): consists of a series of services that provide information in real time on commercial resources feed the system through the exchange of information, which allows better control.
- Interoperability Management (IM): is a series of services that provide the mapping of heterogeneous resources to operate them.

Enterprise Operating System (EOS) concept emerged as a solution to monitor ERM, EPM, EIM, EP, and IM, it was put into practice in the last decade [17], however, the objectives and concepts that it seeks are older. The concept appeared at the end of the 1980s, in the form of an integrated infrastructure within CIMOSA [18] architecture. S^3-RM has been used to define EOS solution according to five viewpoints proposed [17] as shown in Fig. 2.

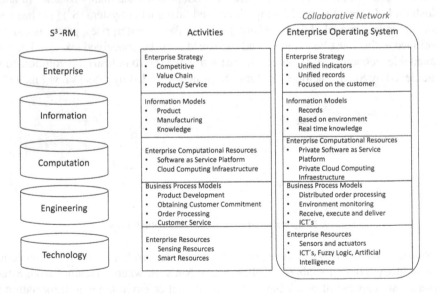

Fig. 2. Enterprise Operating System solution

All activities presented for EOS solution are also a Collaborative Network, due to the fact that every viewpoint is satisfied using shared resources in a system. Therefore, EOS solution also conceived as a Collaborative Network is able to lead into Smart Factories (an S3-System) through S^3-RM which leads into Industry 4.0. All five viewpoints aim at covering four pillars of Industry 4.0. Gathering information from different areas promoting decentralized decisions is achieved by enterprise strategy and business process model. Virtualizing reality to accomplish information transparency and interconnection is achieved by information, computation and technology resources. Thus, the proposed framework is presented in Fig. 3.

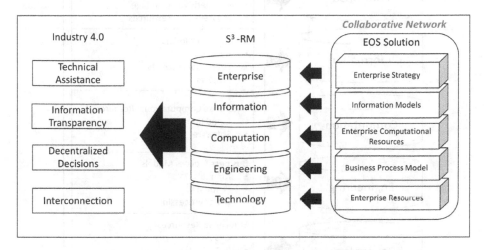

Fig. 3. Reference Framework, EOS Solution as Industry 4.0 catalyst

According to Fig. 3, all information collected in real time by EOS aims to establish a long-term vision for the enterprise, search for dynamic solutions, unify records, optimize value creation focused on customers and decision making of firms. EOS solution is then a Collaborative Network between human beings and CPS, but above all else, between its environment which could also create CNs between enterprises, providers, clients and different entities.

4   Case Study

LOVIS enterprise (https://www.lovis.com/en) has developed a complete EOS solution based on CNs between areas of the enterprise. One of his clients, a Chemical Sector Company which belongs to the automotive sector, had an ERP developed to its measure, however, the growth of the company and its diversification have caused that it is no longer a viable option without a considerable investment. The company has grown larger over the years and the complexity of its activities has adapted more efficiently to EOS solution by LOVIS.

The adoption of this system has allowed a CN inside the company which allows better control of resources, real-time knowledge of the system and a more detailed interaction of the areas that make up the company. Even reluctant to change from the company due to the large investment in ERP solution, EOS benefits were presented causing the company to adopt a newer solution as shown in Fig. 4. Five Viewpoints were considered for a company to transition into EOS using S³-RM.

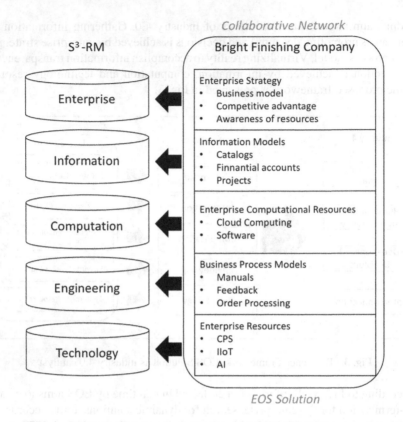

Fig. 4. Reference Framework, Instantiated for Bright Finishing company

Enterprise Viewpoint, aided by digital operation and management lead the company to *Flexibility*. The company started its activities and took control in a traditional way until the acquisition of a customized ERP system, however, the complexity of its activities and processes led them to look for other alternatives that would allow flexibility in the production lines. EOS solution (View Fig. 4) allowed to face these difficulties, flexible structure allowed the incorporation of different product lines and the materials used in each stage of the process.

Technology Viewpoint allowed the company to acquire *Reconfigurability*. Due to the type of system that was available, the areas were seen as modules, this changed with the implementation of newer system, making them more flexible and reconfigurable, since all the information that is processed communicates with the rest of areas and allows to identify vulnerable points in the production line, once identified the areas of opportunity, it is possible to reconfigure the system to optimize the lines, but above all adapt it to the growth of the plant. Therefore, introducing cloud services and higher cybersecurity, with business activities carried out in Mexico and the United States it was necessary that the information handled is available, be able to adapt to changes regarding business policies and monitor activities anywhere.

Engineering viewpoint was covered making use of *Digitalization*. The manufacturing company of the automotive sector performed the processes in a traditional way, and although computer records were kept all phases of the process were optimized and digitized with the newer acquisition, economic benefits are presented due to resource administration. Today, the company relies on the IIoT to track resources, as well as the reprocessing of parts, which existed and a paper control was carried out. After the implementation, transactions have been made online using Cloud Computing, which allows verifying at all times the pieces that make up the process and their status along the value chain. The level of follow-up of the raw material had been a particularly complex subject, due to the flexibility that this system allows, it has been solved in its entirety and allows to carry out other activities such as accounting, financial and organizational strategies for future productions.

Information and computation viewpoint allowed *Smartisation* in the company. The level of smartness of the company has been gradually increasing, currently, the sensors that allow monitoring the production process are integrated into the daily activities of operators and the same production line, training is one of the most important programs for the company nowadays. In order to carry out the monitoring in real time, sensors and verifiers have been implemented in all the stages in order to know the current status and what has been done. Thus, when it is necessary to know the current situation of the company, it is enough to consult the EOS register and it is possible to take actions that improve the current situation. Knowing what happens in real time within the company has allowed delegating, detailed scheduling of deliveries, disposition of resources and cash flows. Thus, the integration of the EOS solution solves the basic management activities for the organization.

Adopted technologies were mostly IIoT, CPS, Cloud Computing and Data Analytics, transforming a traditional company into a Smart Factory and developing a CN among areas which have allowed:

- Real-time information at all levels.
- Production programming, supply.
- Consumption.
- Costs.
- Expenses (including travel expenses).

In terms of security, covering all main obstacles that lead into Industry 4.0:

- Restrictive costs, authorization is needed to request more inventory.
- Lots identified, does not allow mixing if it is not part of the process.
- Complete traceability of the pieces.
- Control of the mixtures used.
- Flexibility, security, and implementation.
- Real-time data management with information protected by high-performance servers and security standards.

In the future, the company seeks full control of its activities in both nations, responding to the changing needs of customers more efficiently, minimizing any delay contemplating supplies and suppliers within the system, responsiveness and flexibility, to provide a solution to problems more accurately with the knowledge of the business; improve the cost analysis, to offer better prices in real time and differentiate from the rest of the competitors with its response capacity.

5   Conclusion

EOS solution has proven to be a system that allows it to be adapted into companies from different sectors creating a collaborative network that could transcend other entities, thus, it offers a gradual transition to the Industry 4.0 of its clients, connection among areas of the company.

The contributions to Industry 4.0 offered are:

Innovation. In the logistic process by incorporating all areas of the business, in the production part to be able to monitor the entire production chain and verify its status continuously. In the services offered, to include both suppliers and customers within the system giving a more precise answer to the needs processed by cognitive system with real knowledge of the environment, increasing Reconfigurability.

The technologies that the system uses are essentially sensors and CPS, as well as the IIoT and Cloud Computing to monitor information in real time from anywhere, increasing Digitalization. Not only, all the users of EOS have their information available, through different security protocols, data protection is guaranteed, but also, Flexibility for enterprises are increased due to the lack of hardware for storing information.

For the implementation of the LOVIS EOS in a company, it is required to know in detail the operation of the same, thus, locating points of information that flow and that are necessary for the optimal functioning of activities. Information Transparency ensures that the information reflected corresponds to reality, status verification points and restrictions of the physical world. Taking advantage of the IIoT to use real-time measurements of the interconnected process and Big Data to optimize resources and the cycles of them. In addition, by not being a rigid system, allows the expansion of the company, both vertically and horizontally. Thus, EOS solution is a viable option for any size of company which offers a complete transformation of how activities are carried out in an organization, either for the production of goods or the supply of services, transforming a traditional process into a more flexible, reconfigurable and intelligent one.

EOS has provided benefits when it is compared to traditional enterprise applications, implemented in more than 27 industry sectors and in less than twelve months without operational interruptions, providing a Return of Investment (ROI) of at least 100% during the first year of operations [16]. Thus, it is proven as a system that contributes to the formation of companies within Industry 4.0 creating cognitive systems from collaborative networks.

Acknowledgments. The development of this work was carried out in conjunction with the company LOVIS and CONACyT funds, giving the corresponding authorship to both organizations.

References

1. Weichhart, G., Molina, A., Chen, D., Whitman, L.E., Vernadat, F.: Challenges and current developments for sensing, smart and sustainable enterprise systems. Comput. Ind. **79**(Supplement C), 34–46 (2016). https://doi.org/10.1016/j.compind.2015.07.002
2. Herterich, M.M., Uebernickel, F., Brenner, W.: The impact of cyber-physical systems on industrial services in manufacturing. Procedia CIRP **30**(Supplement C), 323–328 (2015). https://doi.org/10.1016/j.procir.2015.02.110
3. Camarinha-Matos, L.M.: Collaborative networks: a mechanism for enterprise agility and resilience. In: Mertins, K., Bénaben, F., Poler, R., Bourrières, J.-P. (eds.) Enterprise Interoperability VI. IESACONF, vol. 7, pp. 3–11. Springer, Cham (2014). https://doi.org/10.1007/978-3-319-04948-9_1
4. Dilberoglu, U.M., Gharehpapagh, B., Yaman, U., Dolen, M.: The role of additive manufacturing in the era of industry 4.0. Procedia Manuf. **11**(Supplement C), 545–554 (2017). https://doi.org/10.1016/j.promfg.2017.07.148
5. Zezulka, F., Marcon, P., Vesely, I., Sajdl, O.: Industry 4.0 – an introduction to the phenomenon. IFAC-PapersOnLine **49**(25), 8–12 (2016). https://doi.org/10.1016/j.ifacol.2016.12.002
6. Ferreira, I.A., Alves, J.L.: Low-cost 3D food printing. Ciência & Tecnologia dos Materiais **29**(1), e265–e269 (2017). https://doi.org/10.1016/j.ctmat.2016.04.007
7. Oussous, A., Benjelloun, F.-Z., Ait Lahcen, A., Belfkih, S.: Big data technologies: a survey. J. King Saud Univ. - Comput. Inf. Sci. (2017). https://doi.org/10.1016/j.jksuci.2017.06.001
8. Hermann, M., Pentek, T., Otto, B.: Design principles for industrie 4.0 scenarios. Paper presented at the 2016 49th Hawaii International Conference on System Sciences (HICSS), 5–8 January 2016
9. Lucke, D., Constantinescu, C., Westkämper, E.: Smart factory - a step towards the next generation of manufacturing. Paper presented at the Manufacturing Systems and Technologies for the New Frontier, London (2008)
10. Weiser, M.: The computer for the twenty-first century, pp. 94–100. Scientific American, September Issue (1991)
11. Schröder, C.: The Challenges of Industry 4.0 for Small and Medium-sized Enterprises (2016)
12. Varghese, A., Tandur, D.: Wireless requirements and challenges in Industry 4.0 (2015)
13. Becker, J., Delfmann, P.: Reference modeling: Efficient information systems design through reuse of information models (2007)
14. Chavarría-Barrientos, D., Camarinha-Matos, L.M., Molina, A.: Achieving the sensing, smart and sustainable "everything". In: Camarinha-Matos, L.M., Afsarmanesh, H., Fornasiero, R. (eds.) PRO-VE 2017. IFIPAICT, vol. 506, pp. 575–588. Springer, Cham (2017). https://doi.org/10.1007/978-3-319-65151-4_51
15. Chavarria-Barrientos, D., Batres, R., Perez, R., Wright, P.K., Molina, A.: A step towards customized product realization: methodology for sensing, smart and sustainable enterprise. In: Afsarmanesh, H., Camarinha-Matos, L.M., Lucas Soares, A. (eds.) PRO-VE 2016. IFIPAICT, vol. 480, pp. 327–339. Springer, Cham (2016). https://doi.org/10.1007/978-3-319-45390-3_28
16. Yusuf, Y.Y., Sarhadi, M., Gunasekaran, A.: Agile manufacturing: The drivers, concepts, and attributes. Int. J. Prod. Econ. **62**(1), 33–43 (1999)
17. Chavarria-Barrientos, D., Chen, D., Funes, R., Molina, A., Vernadat, F.: An enterprise operating system for the sensing, smart, and sustainable enterprise. IFAC-PapersOnLine **50**(1), 13052–13058 (2017). https://doi.org/10.1016/j.ifacol.2017.08.2004
18. International Council on Systems Engineering: INCOSE Systems Engineering Handbook: A Guide for System Life Cycle Processes and Activities (2015)

Collaborative Design of Warehousing 4.0 Using the Concept of Contradictions

Dmitry Kucharavy[✉], David Damand, Marc Barth, and Ridha Derrouiche

EM Strasbourg Business School, Université de Strasbourg HuManiS (EA 7308),
61 Avenue de la Forêt-Noire, 67085 Strasbourg Cedex, France
dzmitry.kucharavy@etu.unistra.fr

Abstract. The general context of this paper is the strategic planning of distribution centre warehouses. The idea is to anticipate changes in the warehouse based on objectives and issues generally linked to market (e.g.: electronic trade, etc.) and environmental developments (e.g.: last-mile logistics, etc.). Planning requires overcoming the consequences of the choices made as well as their interactions. To inform and justify projected technological choices, it is crucial to identify and understand design rules which are often contradictory. Problems arise out of contradictions! To support strategic planning, the decision-making aid proposed in this paper consists of extracting and formalising all problems in the form of contradictory design rules.

Keywords: Warehousing systems · Strategic planning · Technology forecasting Evolution of warehousing · Cartography of contradictions

1 Introduction

To a large extent, the logistics costs of warehouses are determined during the design phase [1]. As a general rule, based on a functional description, the warehouse design phase consists of choosing a layout and associated technologies of the four core activities (receiving, storage, order picking and shipping), as well as a planning mode for the operations related to these activities [2, 3]. Changes in this functional description are primarily correlated with the rapidly evolving market [4]. The emergence of new consumption patterns, such as e-commerce for example, is likely to impose the introduction of new dedicated storage technologies, involving substantial investment and high financial risks to boot.

As a result, it is imperative to plan and control the strategic evolution of logistic warehouses. Strategic planning decisions, generally characterised by a 10 to 15 year timeframe, relate to the determination of the general policies and plans for the use of the resources of the future warehouse [5].

In some cases, these evolutions can be promptly addressed via planned decisions; the activities associated with the decision are execution activities [6]. Conversely, when there are no decisions relating to the new situation, a problem solving activity is required.

L. M. Camarinha-Matos et al. (Eds.): PRO-VE 2018, IFIP AICT 534, pp. 396–405, 2018.
https://doi.org/10.1007/978-3-319-99127-6_34

These unscheduled decisions are more difficult to examine as they involve a wide-ranging body of knowledge (endogenous and exogenous to the warehouse). This body of knowledge is often contradictory.

Research projects undertaken in warehousing design primarily focus on endogenous warehousing parameters [7, 8]. Few projects simultaneously factor in endogenous and exogenous parameters. The warehouse of the future depends on environmental developments. Market demands, limitations and trends bring about operational, technological and organisational innovations and changes [4]. This context raises two research questions. First question: what are the key characteristics for strategic decision-making in terms of warehousing design? Second question: how to define a systematic method for identifying key warehousing design parameters?

This paper proposes a contribution to the first question only. The expected contribution is the formalisation of a number of generic design rules (means/effect) using an adapted language [7]. The expected nature of design rules is contradiction.

The paper is structured as follows. Section 2 presents the theoretical framework. Section 3 presents the methodological framework to identify and extract generic design rules. Section 4 presents an industrial application by a 3PL logistics provider. Finally, Sect. 5 concludes this paper and outlines research prospects.

2   Literature Review – Theoretical Framework

A warehouse can be represented as a storage tank [9]. It has a buffer function in light of the variability and uncertainty inherent in the supply chain. Its life cycle includes three major stages: design and construction; operation, development and reorganisation; decommissioning or reprocessing. To consider conceptual design on a 5 to 10 year timeframe in terms of organisational architecture and processes, a reliable vision of the demands, limitations and trends of the future warehouse is needed [4]. The strategic decision relating to warehouse evolution must take account of the dynamic changes of the activities and functions, as well as the specific characteristics of the system's life cycle [10].

Strategic decision-making in warehousing design is linked to the following generic questions:

- What are the achievable and unachievable performance levels?
- Is it necessary to modify the condition of the existing system?
- What is the effect of decision criteria on the new situation?
- What are the most significant decision criteria in terms of system performance?
- When decision criteria cannot be modified simultaneously, in what chronological order should these criteria be modified?
- Etc.

The traditional approach in the design phase consists of inventing, creating possible alternatives from which to choose. The rational decision-making model [11, 12], is a 6-step process [13]: 1. define the problem; 2. identify decision criteria; 3. weight the criteria; 4. develop alternatives; 5. assess alternatives (rule if criterion=… then alternative=…); 6. choose the best alternative. This model is a sequential and logical structuring of the information to be analysed [5, 14]. The multi-criteria approaches generally undertaken [6] help select the best solution or the optimal solution from a broad range of solutions, the YES-NO type alternative being one particular case as part of a more general case. When alternatives are incompatible with the decision criteria values, a position must be taken in relation to these contradictions.

This paper hypothesises that the problem solving process during the design phase involves the identification of one or more contradictions resulting from the new decision context (e.g. market developments). Consequently, contradictions are the expression of a problem by consequences of the choices made, but obviously at least two opposing consequences are required for a problem to arise. By expressing the cause-and-effect relationships between means and performance, the contradiction identification process reveals the rules used. This helps clarify conflict areas, but also and most importantly the reasons for projected technological choices.

To advance the decision-making process towards a choice of technological solution, literature proposes several technological forecasting methods. Initial significant research dates back to the early 20th century [15–17]. The primary purpose of these methods is to provide a consensual view of the future technological situation [18]. A review of scientific journals, institutional reports and publications [19–21] highlights methodological advances in terms of technological forecasting for socio-economic and technological levels, rather than for the technological level itself. The major improvements identified by the methods used to forecast technological changes relate to a combination of existing techniques and models, and the refinement of existing methods [22, 23]. The exponential increase in the number of publications, institutions and researchers involved in forecasting and the development of technological forecasting methods in the past five decades has yielded a multitude of techniques and methodologies [24].

After reviewing the current practice of long-term technological forecasting methods, these methods can be classified into four categories [25]:

(1) phenomenological models (for example time series data extrapolations, regressions),
(2) intuitive models (for example the Delphi method, structured and unstructured interviews),
(3) monitoring and mapping (for example by reviewing the literature and sources published, scenarios, mapping of existing information),
(4) and finally, the causal models used in this paper to analyse warehousing system evolution rules.

The next chapter describes the method based on causal models.

3 Research Methodology

The research-intervention method selected relies on the "Researching Future" method (technological forecasting method) [26, 27]. This method combines maps of contradictions [28] with S-curves of logistics functions [29, 30]. The research method follows the methodological triangulation principle. Triangulation is often used in management sciences. According to [31, 32], "triangulation should support a finding by demonstrating that independent measures of it agree with or, at least, do not contradict it". Denzin [33] highlighted three types of triangulation: the use of different data sources (time, space, persons); the use of different researchers; the simultaneous use of different methods.

To obtain the map of contradictions, the "Researching Future" method used in this paper connects the principles of the following methods:

- the "System Operator" model from the Theory of Inventive Problem Solving - TRIZ [34],
- the "Contradiction" model derived from TRIZ is developed to model networks of problems within OTSM-TRIZ [35],
- S-curves [30],
- technology substitution models are used to measure the time and capacity of evolution and substitution processes [36, 37],
- interpretation patterns of the knowledge obtained from the DITEK model [38].

The contradiction representation language is illustrated in Fig. 1.

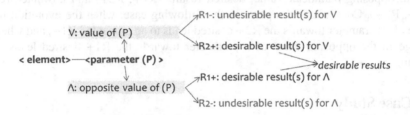

Fig. 1. Contradiction description model.

An example of contradiction is described in Fig. 2 corresponding with the following interrogation:

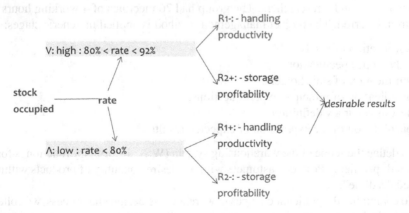

Fig. 2. Example of contradiction: *handling productivity* = number of (parcels or pallets)/hour; *storage profitability* = (storage turnover/m^2)/cost per m^2 of the storage surface area

In the <distribution centre> *system*, the *trend* <significant flow heterogeneity> encounters a *barrier* <storage profitability>.

The semantics used are as follows:

- *Element* – everything (tangible or intangible) used in a combination to form a whole or a unit,
- *System* – group of elements interacting with each other, linked and interdependent, performing a certain function as part of a super-system.
- *Trend* – change in a system characteristic over a long period.
- *Barrier* – limitation of resources (e.g., space, time, energy),
- *Parameter* – characteristic of an element which can be acted upon,
- *Result* – consequence of an action due to the value of a parameter (e.g. desired result); every indicator has a measurable value, measurement unit – standard required to measure an indicator.

The following syntax is used:

Contradiction – model to describe a problem through the description of a conflict of interest. The contradiction model includes an element, a parameter, a parameter value and an opposing parameter value, desired results (R1+, R2+) and unwanted results (R1−, R2−). Contradiction appears in the following case: when the evolution in the value of a parameter towards the R2+ desired leads to an unwanted R1−, and when the change in the opposing value of a parameter towards the R1+ desired leads to an unwanted R2−.

4   Case Study

Intervention research is conducted in a French 3PL. Their turnover in 2016 was €2.045 billion. The scope of the study consists of 25 warehouses. Customers are mainly from the agri-food, retail and healthcare industry.

A working group was assembled. The group includes 6 individuals, respectively 3 experts in 3PL and 3 researchers. The group had 26 meetings of 4 working hours over a 12-month period. The project management method is applied in generic stages:

- identification of needs,
- study scope specification,
- identification of stakeholders,
- consolidation of principal expert questions,
- analysis accuracy definition,
- consolidation of the expression of expected results.

To define the scope of the warehousing system (WS), the primary function is formulated and specified: "Provide customers with the desired quantity of products within the desired deadline".

To comprehend significant changes in warehousing design and process, we collected chronological data on the surface area of the LP's warehouses (m^2). As the built-up surface and expected values are confidential information for the LP, no actual figure will be presented. The partial results of the study are presented in Figs. 3 and 4. The S-curves obtained help position the current WS in relation to its life cycle. S-curves are developed on the basis of 25 WSs spread over 13 countries.

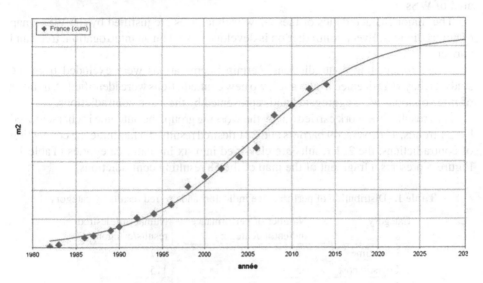

Fig. 3. Example of changes in the surface area of WSs built in France in m^2 (Tm = 2005.5; Δt = 30.1; Rsquare = 0.993)

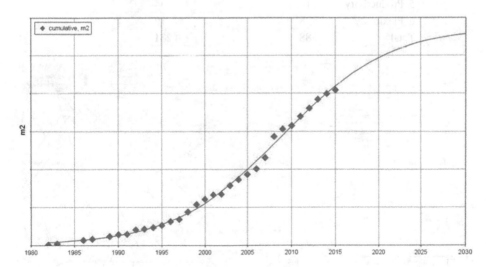

Fig. 4. Changes in the surface area of WSs built worldwide in m^2 (Tm = 2008.9; Δt = 27.2; Rsquare = 0.996)

The increase in the surface area of existing WSs in France should stop by 2020 (Fig. 3). At global level, it is estimated that saturation will be reached by 2022. New warehousing technologies should drive revenue growth without increasing the surface area of WSs.

The major characteristics of these new technologies are justified by the WS's map of contradictions. Every contradiction is developed based on an interrogation, trend and barrier.

When formulating contradictions, certain interrogations were excluded from the study as they were deemed irrelevant. Two new contradictions were identified. A number of interrogations were aggregated and represented by the same contradictions.

As a result of the work carried out by the working group, the outcome is characterised by: 21 trends, 48 drivers, 49 barriers and 281 desired results. To facilitate the connection of contradictions, the 281 results are classified into six indicator categories (Table 1). Figure 5 presents a fragment of the map of the 58 resulting contradictions.

Table 1. Distribution of performance indicators and desired results by category.

Category	Number of performance indicators/category	Number of desired results/category
1. Lead-time	6	37
2. Logistic cost	35	115
3. Investments	15	43
4. Delivery method	8	33
5. Productivity	16	34
6. Flexibility	8	19
Total	**88**	**281**

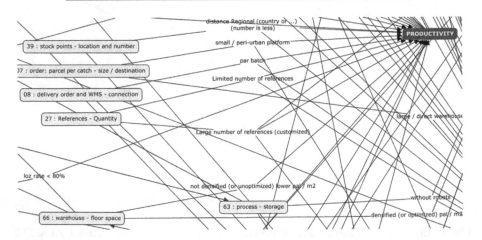

Fig. 5. Extract from the map of 58 contradictions

To achieve a definitive description of the most significant contradictions (in terms of changes in the WSs), the direct links between the contradictions formulated must be examined. This activity is under review.

The map of contradictions represents the conflicts of interest between seven major players (Fig. 6). The number of most significant contradictions concerns the logistics provider and the industrial producer, who are therefore the key players in the change process.

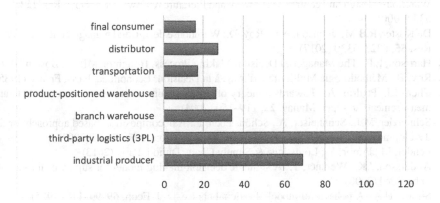

Fig. 6. Number of connections classified by stakeholder

5 Discussions and Prospects

The issue dealt with in this paper is as follows: "what are the key characteristics for strategic decision-making in terms of warehousing design?". The result is the definition of a map of ware-housing system contradictions. Problems are represented in the form of contradictions for identifying major future WS characteristics. The result achieved is described by a map of 58 contradictions. These contradictions are obtained by linking 281 desired results (e.g. location of the ware-house) with 88 performance indicators (e.g. delivery times, etc.) classified into 6 categories (e.g. logistics cost, etc.). These contradictions concern 7 stakeholders (e.g. end user, distributor, etc.). The concept of contradiction is pertinent for initiating issues pertaining to the strategic evolution of WSs.

The results obtained only allow for partial generalisation, as the scope of application is characterised by 25 WSs from the agri-food, retail and healthcare industry. The prospects of this study are the prioritisation of contradictions and the development of a systematic method designed to identify contradictions.

Acknowledgments. This study was funded by FM Logistic Corporate SAS. We wish to thank the members of FM Logistic who generously devoted time to this study.

References

1. Roveillo, G., Fulconis, F., Paché, G.: Vers une dilution des frontières de l'organisation: le prestataire de services logistiques (PSL) comme pilote aux interfaces. Logistique Manag. **20**(2), 7–20 (2012)
2. Gu, J., Goetschalckx, M., McGinnis, L.F.: Research on warehouse operation: a comprehensive review. Eur. J. Oper. Res. **177**, 1–21 (2007)
3. Rouwenhorst, B., Reuter, B., Stockrahm, V., van Houtum, G.J., Mantel, R.J., Zijm, W.H.M.: Warehouse design and control: framework and literature review. Eur. J. Oper. Res. **122**, 515–533 (2000)
4. De Koster, R.B.M., Johnson, A.L., Roy, D.: Warehouse design and management. Int. J. Prod. Res. **55**, 6327–6330 (2017)
5. Harrison, E.F.: The Managerial Decision-Making Process. Houghton Mifflin, Boston (1995)
6. Roy, B.: Méthodologie Multicritère d'Aide à la Décision. Economica, Paris, France (1985)
7. Chen, I.J., Paulraj, A.: Towards a theory of supply chain management: the constructs and measurements. J. Oper. Manag. **22**, 119–150 (2004)
8. Schnetzler, M.J., Sennheiser, A., Schönsleben, P.: A decomposition-based approach for the development of a supply chain strategy. Int. J. Prod. Econ. **105**, 21–42 (2007)
9. Fender, M., Pimor, Y.: Logistique & Supply Chain. Dunod, Paris (2013)
10. Andersson, J.K., Wemnér, T.: A strategic decision-making model for supply chain - a void to be filled (2008)
11. Simon, H.A.: A behavioral model of rational choice. Q. J. Econ. **69**, 99–118 (1955)
12. Hastie, R., Dawes, R.M.: Rational Choice in an Uncertain World: The Psychology of Judgment and Decision Making. Sage, Thousand Oaks (2010)
13. Robbins, S.P., Judge, T., Tran, V.: Comportements organisationnels. Pearson Education, Paris (2014)
14. Robbins, S.P., Judge, T., Breward, K.: Essentials of Organizational Behavior. Prentice Hall, Upper Saddle River (2003)
15. Ayres, R.U.: Technological Forecasting and Long-Range Planning. McGraw-Hill Book Company, New York (1969)
16. Linstone, H.A., Turoff, M.: Delphi: a brief look backward and forward. Technol. Forecast. Soc. Change **78**, 1712–1719 (2011)
17. Martino, J.P.: Technological Forecasting for Decision Making. Elsevier Publishing Company, New York (1972)
18. Kostoff, R.N., Schaller, R.R.: Science and technology roadmaps. IEEE Trans. Eng. Manag. **48**, 132–143 (2001)
19. Roper, T.A., Cunningham, S.W., Porter, A.L., Mason, T.W., Rossini, F.A., Banks, J.: Forecasting and Management of Technology. John Wiley & Sons Ltd., New York (2011)
20. Armstrong, J.S.: Principles of Forecasting: A Handbook for Researchers and Practitioner. Kluwer Academic Publishers, Boston (2002)
21. Grübler, A.: Technology and Global Change. International Institute of Applied System Analysis. Cambridge University Press, Cambridge (2003)
22. Glenn, J.C., Gordon, T.J.: Futures Research Methodology. Version 2.0 (2003). http://www.millennium-project.org/millennium/FRM-v2.html
23. Miranda, L.C.M., Lima, C.A.S., Piedade, R.: On trends and rhythms in scientific and technological knowledge evolution: a quantitative analysis. Int. J. Technol. Intell. Plan. **6**, 76–109 (2010)
24. Slupinski, M.: Technology Forecasting – State of the Art Update/Deliverable 2.3 FORMAT Project, Milan, Italy (2013)

25. Cascini, G., et al.: FORMAT - building an original methodology for technology forecasting through researchers exchanges between industry and academia. Procedia Eng. **131**, 1084–1093 (2015)
26. Kucharavy, D., De Guio, R.: Technological Forecasting and Assessment of Barriers for Emerging Technologies (2008). http://hal.archives-ouvertes.fr/hal-00282751/en/
27. Kucharavy, D.: Combination of contradictions based approach and logistic curves models for strategic technological forecasting. In: Global TRIZ Conference 2013, Seoul, Korea (2013)
28. Kucharavy, D., De Guio, R., Gautier, L., Marrony, M.: Problem mapping for the assessment of technological barriers in the framework of innovative design. In: 16th International Conference on Engineering Design, ICED 2007. Ecole Centrale Paris, Paris, France (2007)
29. Modis, T.: Technological substitutions in the computer industry. Technol. Forecast. Soc. Change. **43**, 157–167 (1993)
30. Modis, T.: Natural Laws in the Service of the Decision Maker: How to Use Science-Based Methodologies to See More Clearly further into the Future. Growth Dynamics (2013)
31. Miles, M.B., Huberman, A.M.: Analyse des données qualitatives. De Boeck Supérieur (2003)
32. Rothbauer, P.: Triangulation. SAGE Encycl. Qual. Res. Methods **1**, 892–894 (2008)
33. Denzin, N.K.: The research act: a theoretical orientation to sociological methods (1978)
34. Altshuller, G.S., Williams, A.: Creativity as an Exact Science: The Theory of the Solution of Inventive Problems. Gordon and Breach Science Publishers (1984)
35. Khomenko, N., Yoon, H.: OTSM-TRIZ as a response to the request from the specialized and interdisciplinary problem situations. In: Korea TRIZCON 2010, p. 16 (2010)
36. Marchetti, C., Nakicenovic, N.: The dynamics of energy systems and the logistics substitution model. Int. Inst. Appl. Syst. Anal. Res. Rep. **79–13**, 71 (1979)
37. Modis, T.: Predictions - 10 Years Later. Growth Dynamics, Geneva, Switzerland (2002)
38. Grundstein, M.: Three postulates that change knowledge management paradigm. In: Hou, H.-T. (ed.) New Research on Knowledge Management Models and Methods, pp. 1–22. InTech (2011)

Health and Social Welfare Services

The Robot Who Loved Me: Building Consciousness Models for Use in Human Robot Interaction Following a Collaborative Systems Approach

Adamantios Koumpis[✉], Maria Christoforaki, and Siegfried Handschuh

Fakultät für Informatik und Mathematik, Universität Passau, Passau, Germany
{adamantios.koumpis,maria.christoforaki,
siegfried.handschuh}@uni-passau.de

Abstract. We build on the results of our MARIO project to support the benefit of informing research taking place in the area of development of human consciousness models for use by robots to facilitate human robot interaction with research results from the area of collaborative systems. The main outcome of such a research would be a software model of a robot assistant that might offer functionality and features of a 'virtual coach' with an in-built evolution capability.

Keywords: Human-robot interaction · Consciousness modelling
Distributional semantics · Surrogate (virtual) objects
Data curation of semi-structured and unstructured data

1 Introduction

We shouldn't see the future as black. On the other hand, our daughters may be thousands of miles away from us – and our partners either dead or on a cruise ship in the Caribbean. So we are 'home alone' – but in contrast to the (now rather old) movie hero that was 8 years old, we are 80+. Luckily, we are not totally alone as we have a robot that lives with us. The robot follows our routine and for some few days now is spotting that:

- We are missing meals
- We are not taking any calls
- We are not leaving home
- We skip exercises and avoid taking our medication

Is it depression? Is it loneliness? Is there something that the robot should do to help? In the European Horizons2020 MARIO project (www.mario-project.eu) we have been building Apps that would help the robot entertain persons with dementia. But we haven't thought about reaching a higher level, namely of equipping the robot with the necessary consciousness model that will help it become a self-starter in many everyday situations that a human might operate well. There is surprisingly much research work and bibliography in the area of collaborative systems, some of which also relevant to elderly care, that can be of direct value and use in the area of human robot interaction. In this paper we aim to make clear the need for synergies between the two areas.

© IFIP International Federation for Information Processing 2018
Published by Springer Nature Switzerland AG 2018. All Rights Reserved
L. M. Camarinha-Matos et al. (Eds.): PRO-VE 2018, IFIP AICT 534, pp. 409–416, 2018.
https://doi.org/10.1007/978-3-319-99127-6_35

By January 2018 our European research project MARIO (www.mario-project.eu) came to its end. In MARIO we introduced a humanoid care robot to help and facilitate interactions with persons with dementia – an all in all difficult 'target' group [1]. However, and going one level deeper in the project and its research agenda, we were addressing the difficult challenges of loneliness and isolation in older persons with dementia through innovative and multi-faceted inventions delivered by service robots. The effects of these conditions are severe and life-limiting. They burden individuals and societal support systems. Human intervention is costly but the severity can be prevented or mitigated by simple changes in self-perception and brain stimulation mediated by robots. In [2] is stated that until the present, 'loneliness is being treated as a symptom of mental health problems; however, for elderly (aged 60 years and above), loneliness has become a disease in itself. There are epidemiological, phenomenological, and etiological reasons to say that'.

What we have identified during the project lifetime and both as result of our research activities, but also as result of our interactions with patients, their relatives and the carers, is that there is well identifiable space which may have been treated as a blindspot as of today and which concerns the area of modelling of human consciousness mechanisms to govern the robot. Human consciousness in our context refers both to the robot that may need to build some primitive 'consciousness' to support its interactions with the humans in the form of empathy or affection, but also from the side of the human user so that in case of loss of abilities due to dementia or some other reason, they will be assisted for a variety of functions and tasks.

This means that while in MARIO project we mainly cared about offering interventions, there is need for some new research that will analyse human consciousness mechanisms, identify their main features, and identify the border between human consciousness and unconsciousness to support reasoning, learning and adaptation to varying emotional and behavioural patterns, conditions and preferences.

The main outcome of such a research would be a software model of a robot assistant that might offer functionality and features of a 'virtual coach' with an in-built evolution capability. At a first level, such a capability should be based on routine tasks and some initial relevant physiological and behavioural data; over time it should become more specialised to reflect the particular needs and preferences of each individual older person.

In [3], the authors pose a rhetoric question, asking whether it is 'possible to devise a general architectural principle that might lead an artificial agent to exploit what is called consciousness in human beings and various animals?', stating also that 'in a scientific and technological context, whatever formulation of consciousness one opts to consider, consciousness should not come at the end of the day as an addition to an otherwise working description of a physical system'. For such a 'working description of a physical system' it is that the authors of [4] recognize that one has to look into the construction of agent-oriented design processes, and more specifically what the authors call 'the definition of the best way to create ad-hoc agent oriented design processes'. In this respect, the development of consciousness as a multi agent system would, following the authors' argumentation line, require 'great efforts in learning and using an existing design process' and the main idea of the approach taken is one has to include in the design process also the system metamodel.

In [5] the author reports about the advances made in the IT industry in the area of machine reading, to avoid the term distant reading introduced by Moretti in [6] and which has been in the last years mainly focused on the 'reading' of literature, and what was considered as one of artificial intelligence's holiest grails for many years. What is interesting and relevant to our context here is a remark that one of the interviewed researchers (Ernest Davis, a New York University professor of computer science and AI researcher) provided, namely that this (: machine reading) is 'technically an accomplishment, but it's not like we have to begin worshipping our robot overlords', adding what epitomizes most successfully the point we take in our research namely that 'When you read a passage, it doesn't come out of the clear blue sky: It draws on a lot of what you know about the world'.

2   The Main Idea

The idea of approaching real world objects through knowledge graphs automatically created from multimodal information sources is, at least to our knowledge from the literature, uncommon. However, what might be a more uncommon idea is the case of automatically building and populating human consciousness models with the use of knowledge graphs.

Knowledge discovery from digital big multimodal data can be done effectively by employing techniques like machine learning (such as Deep learning, SIFT), distributional semantics in NLP e.g. for text mining purposes and semantic augmentation (use of domain specific formal ontologies) [7].

However, and in order to facilitate the modeling of human consciousness, such an approach can be seen as a process where studying the actual artefact (i.e. the human consciousness) is replaced by studying a latent (virtual) object consisting of a dense network of related information. This latent object is produced from secondary sources, namely digital or digitised images and texts or other modalities, where the image or the text is used as an interface to the latent object, to which the human user has no access to.

We see a similarity with the case of an art historian studying artefacts from images and catalogues or essays, or a medical doctor trying to identify pathogenies from medical images and test data. In both cases the form of information can be:

- structured data (e.g. data from a collections management system records or medical test results)
- unstructured text (e.g. free text description of an artefact)
- images (e.g. digital or digitized images of museum objects, or CAT scans)
- formalized domain knowledge existing in bibliography and in the experience of the person examining the material

These sources constitute already a limiting approach to the true nature of the object as such, since they constitute already 'processed' knowledge, thus eliminating facets of it (e.g. same as 2D images provide us with information about the form of an object from a certain perspective only, textual descriptions offer information only deemed important by the author of the document, etc.).

Moreover, the application of algorithms in these already secondary sources are perceived as black boxes, thus giving the domain experts no transparent results to construct an argumentation supporting their research.

3 The Need for a Collaborative Systems Perspective

There is a qualitative difference between the term *need* and this of a *necessity*; though both words are pretty close, denoting some similar condition, the difference between them lies on the prioritization, as while for a need there is an absolute demand, the necessity also relates to a craving without which a person manages to survive.

Our main position in this position paper is that there is a well identifiable space for research to take place in the following years that will aim to support the field of human-robot interaction and in particular the area of content-creation with research that will be, at a first level informed, and at a further level building on the work of collaborative systems. Work conducted and reported in [8, 9] is of direct relevance in a variety of ways as we shall be able to indicate below, where we see a great potential in the collaboration and the synergies for future research with the help of the PRO-VE community.

In [10], the authors state that 'in order to have a robotic system able to effectively learn by imitation, and not merely reproduce the movements of a human teacher, the system should have the capabilities of deeply understanding the perceived actions to be imitated'. In our context, we need to combine all existing knowledge patterns and information sources that may be considered as relevant to a situation that our MARIO robot may encounter, while also relate them or, if more appropriately, match them with a situation that the robot may have just or recently encountered with a human user, like this of holding a conversation on a family matter (planning for the visit of a relative or need to have some medical tests). To this aim we take a holistic approach that combines bottom-up and top-down approach. In particular:

- bottom-up approach that is based on the employment of Big Data analytics techniques to explore what may in the future constitute some potentially relevant patterns by having access to a vast pool of online media resources like social media, internet discussion forums, blogs, etc. that are relevant to the discussion topic between the human and the robot, as well as a
- top-down approach that takes as starting points existing patterns or instances of past interactions between the robot and the human in the recent past, and check for their relevance.

As one may expect, the superiority and the longer term sustainability and value of our approach relates to the combination of both bottom-up and top-down approaches. Only the top-down would result into yet another 'spell-checker'; only the bottom-up would result into an endless crawling of the Web where patterns might be ignored even if they would exist because they couldn't be identified using the current information. Same as in crime forensics where DNA profiling may have been used after several years to identify individuals by characteristics of their DNA, our tools shall offer the capability to store patterns that will be identified after some time, when some increased information will have been collected. This is an important feature of our approach.

Further to this, complementary and potentially relevant patterns will be identified by means of algorithms in statistical analysis and machine learning for sentiment extraction and social network analysis (Bottom-Up-Approach). In particular, this approach has the potential to uncover hitherto unknown patterns in the source data and therefore enable the construction of new hate speech categories related to a specific field and knowledge base. The outcomes of both approaches will be united in a consistent, unified formal knowledge representation, to allow both for an extended and improved understanding of the subjects of investigation and for a long-term, versatile reusability of the collected data. At our group we have developed data-driven methods for data-driven decision making, recommendation and contextual suggestion engines, using and/or developing algorithms for classification, clustering, rule extraction and sentiment analysis.

To the above one may find an instance of the problem of origins and first cause or what we usually call as a chicken and egg situation. We have been all educated to use in relational data and database modeling as this has been typically the prevailing paradigm that was also driven by the structure of available data for many years now. The key question that has been driving the development, the research and the business there and is also used as the main design theme is: *"What answers do I have?"*

However, today's problems and challenges as well as modern data and database modeling (what is also usually called as 'NoSQL') is typically driven by application-specific access patterns, i.e. the types of queries to be supported. So the main question and also the main design theme here is: *"What questions do I have?"*

It is for this reason that collaborative systems are relevant and highly necessary to consider as an enabling technology for all future developments in the areas of intelligent systems and in particular for the area of human robot interaction.

One should be able to intuitively see the difference and also the parallels we see with the modelling of human consciousness. As an example we can imagine a library with all sorts of books – the books that a person may have read in their lives. We are all aware of the Dewey system – or as it is properly called: the Dewey Decimal Classification. This is an ideal role model example on why people came up with the concept and the idea of relational databases. And, by the way, this is a system that started being shaped back in the 1870s.

However, if one imagines that our driver is **not** to find:

- if a book exists in our library or
- who has borrowed it,
- who is the publisher,
- when it was published or
- other similar 'relational' questions,

but:

- anything about the contents of the books,
- anything that might be unexpected, unplannable, impossible or even at some point to consider as unworthy to even model when building our 'neat and cute' relational database reality,

it is in this case, ***where we don't know which possible questions we have***, where the need for adopting a collaborative systems approach comes on stage.

There is always a risk with the quality of the information acquired from unknown sources – a good example for this relates with the case of fake news. If the consciousness model for our case relies on any type of lesser value content such as the case of fake news, it is obvious that this will affect the quality of the model as such. To this problem, however, we can take a similar stand to the one we take in real life: not all people build their consciousness on the same sources or may be able to exhibit some evidence-based consistency in the way their consciousness models are built. But it is therefore that a CN-based approach would increase the value of the end system, as the aggregate results of such a consciousness model that comes as outcome of the collaboration amongst can will tend to be more accurate than any single entity alone. This collaboration aspect should be not mistakenly related to with crowdsourcing that is rather the process where knowledge is obtained from the public at large through a system of invitations and incentives [12, 13].

3.1   A Word on Ethics

The ethics work during the MARIO project provided an innovative, integrated approach to addressing ethical issues in robot design, research and implementation, addressing the entire development process of the project [11]. As developed within the project lifetime, the ethics framework we developed provided a new comprehensive review of relevant interdisciplinary literature with relevance for understanding ethical concerns regarding the use of care robots, a useful contribution to the field of the ethics of care robots. In addition, its findings informed the approach to data management in the project.

On the basis of the MARIO ethics framework, a set of innovative practical tools in the form of five ethics checklists were developed to guide ethical practice for different stakeholders in robot development, research and implementation. These were tested by different stakeholders, who found them to be helpful practical tools for their respective practice areas. An "ethical encountered issues" form was employed during the pilots, to capture evidence on the incidence of actual ethical issues that stakeholders encountered during trials. These indicated that careful implementation was required, but that users generally tolerated the robot well and distress was rare.

These tools have the potential to be employed in different care robot projects, and the ethics tools and experiences from the project will be published to make them available to the international robot community, contributing to the development of a solid evidence base of ethical concerns in care robotics, which, if those results remain as positive as during the MARIO project, is likely to facilitate wider societal acceptance of the use of care robots in the care setting. It is interesting in this context to take into account that in [14] the authors identify in relation to service robots a problem related, amongst others, with loss of control from the side of the elderly person due to robot monitoring and the interventions that the latter undertake within their daily activities and routine. This is true at a great extent, and same as the (feeling of a) loss of privacy and the (feeling of) infantilisation. However, one has to admit that the benefits of such a technology equal out at a great extent all potential drawbacks.

4   Conclusions

Developments in the addressed area of modeling human consciousness in computable and computer-processable forms are still in a fluid form. This poses a challenge for bringing together a corpus of research that has taken and is still taking place in the area of collaborative systems to identify and, if possible, also seize challenges that will change the way we perceive our idea for the use of robots in everyday tasks. The result of a robot intelligence will not anymore rely on its 'hardwired' intelligence but, with use of sentiment analysis and deep learning technologies, their capabilities to extract information from a variety of modalities and media including videos, images, natural language, as well as structured data and then automatically transform them into 'actionable information' by means of deploying them in their interactions with the human users.

It is worth to mention here that in the MARIO project, as well as in the context of the present paper, we refer to robots that act as an extension of humans offering to them a symbiotic perspective, so these are not what one would consider as 'truly autonomous robots'. However, the aim to model aspects of the human consciousness is dual namely on the one hand to replicate it in robots, while on the other hand to help robots extend and complement the consciousness of people with decaying cognitive ability.

From our research expertise it is evident that we promote the idea of exploiting developments in the areas of semantic technologies and statistical based natural language processing to facilitate the task of building data-driven models of body consciousness that will be possible to be easily populated with big data acquired from a variety of sources. Furthermore, we are able to see that the improvements to be made will seriously lag behind the needs that exist if our research shall not be informed and enriched with the perspective taken in the area of collaborative systems.

Human intelligence is in all its aspects and manifestations such a system, consisting of a variety of entities and artifacts, demonstrating also characteristics of autonomy as well as synergy, geography is also of importance with the ability to take advantage of geographical distribution as well as of geographical concentration, while last but not least, heterogeneity is also a key term as it affects all levels like the culture, the socio-economic context, or even the daily (operational) routines.

It may seem like a novelty to think of a future with networks of collaborating robots that are working together to offer a service to an individual. However, and while from a technology stance this may be a novelty, from an organizational point this is not at all: currently, and for the care to an old person, there may be their children that will interact with the physicians and the nurses. In the future, all these interactions may take place in an automated fashion by robots that will live with us same as the MARIO robot does with the persons with dementia.

Acknowledgements. This work was supported in part by a grant from the European Union Horizons 2020 – the Framework Programme for Research and Innovation (2014–2020) under grant agreement 643808 Project MARIO "Managing active and healthy aging with use of caring service robots".

The authors would like to our thanks and appreciation to the two anonymous reviewers that provided us with good advice and input to our ideas and thoughts.

References

1. Casey, D., et al.: What people with dementia want: designing MARIO an acceptable robot companion. In: Miesenberger, K., Bühler, C., Penaz, P. (eds.) ICCHP 2016, Part I. LNCS, vol. 9758, pp. 318–325. Springer, Cham (2016). https://doi.org/10.1007/978-3-319-41264-1_44
2. Tiwari, S.C.: Loneliness: a disease? Indian J. Psychiatry **55**(4), 320–322 (2013)
3. Manzotti, R., Chella, A.: Physical integration: a causal account for consciousness. J. Integr. Neurosci. **13**, 403 (2014)
4. Seidita, V., Cossentino, M., Chella, A.: A proposal of process fragment definition and documentation. In: Cossentino, M., Kaisers, M., Tuyls, K., Weiss, G. (eds.) EUMAS 2011. LNCS (LNAI), vol. 7541, pp. 221–237. Springer, Heidelberg (2012). https://doi.org/10.1007/978-3-642-34799-3_15
5. Harwell, D.: AI's ability to read is hailed as milestone, but there's still long way to go, originally published 21 January 2018. https://www.seattletimes.com/business/ais-ability-to-read-is-hailed-as-milestone-but-theres-still-long-way-to-go/. Accessed 3 May 2018
6. Moretti, F.: Distant Reading, London, Verso (2013)
7. Efson Sales, J., Freitas, A., Davis, B., Handschuh, S.: A compositional-distributional semantic model for searching complex entity categories. In: Proceedings of the Fifth Joint Conference on Lexical and Computational Semantics, pp. 199–208 (2016)
8. Baldissera, T.A., Camarinha-Matos, L.M.: Towards a collaborative business ecosystem for elderly care. In: Camarinha-Matos, L.M., Falcão, A.J., Vafaei, N., Najdi, S. (eds.) DoCEIS 2016. IFIP AICT, vol. 470, pp. 24–34. Springer, Cham (2016). https://doi.org/10.1007/978-3-319-31165-4_3
9. Camarinha-Matos, L.M., Rosas, J., Oliveira, A.I., Ferrada, F.: Care services ecosystem for ambient assisted living. Enterp. Inf. Syst. **9**(5–6), 607–633 (2015)
10. Chella, A., Dindo, H., Infantino, I.: Anchoring by imitation learning in conceptual spaces. In: Bandini, S., Manzoni, S. (eds.) AI*IA 2005. LNCS (LNAI), vol. 3673, pp. 495–506. Springer, Heidelberg (2005). https://doi.org/10.1007/11558590_50
11. Felzmann, H., Murphy, K., Casey, D., Beyan, O.: Robot-assisted care for elderly with dementia: is there a potential for genuine end-user empowerment? The Emerging, Oral presentation to the Policy and Ethics of Human Robot Interaction Conference (2015). http://dx.doi.org/10.13025/S8SG6Q
12. Prpić, J., Shukla, P.: Crowd science: measurements, models, and methods. In: Proceedings of the 49th Annual Hawaii International Conference on System Sciences, Kauai, Hawaii. IEEE Computer Society (2016)
13. Gerber, E.M., Hui, J.: Crowdfunding: Motivations and deterrents for participation. ACM Trans. Comput. Hum. Interact. (TOCHI) **20**(6), 34 (2013)
14. Sharkey, A., Sharkey, N.: Granny and the robots: ethical issues in robot care for the elderly. Ethics Inf. Technol. **14**(1), 27–40 (2012)

Services Evolution in Elderly Care Ecosystems

Thais A. Baldissera[✉] and Luis M. Camarinha-Matos

Centre Technology and Systems – UNINOVA, Faculty of Sciences
and Technology, NOVA University of Lisbon, Caparica, Portugal
{tab, cam}@uninova.pt

Abstract. The aging process typically requires personalized care services for each individual. In this context, a collaborative elderly care ecosystem can support the provision of integrated services that may combine contributions from multiple providers. Through composition of services a personalized solution, tailored to the individual customer, respecting her/his requests, preferences, lifestyle, and constraints, can be achieved. An additional issue the ecosystem must deal with is the problem of evolution, as individual's care needs are not static over time. Consequently, the care services need to evolve accordingly to keep the elderly's requirements satisfied. This process of services' adaptation is challenging since many services can be dependent on each other, and there are various constraints that need to be observed before adaptating and enacting new services. In this paper, we exploit socio-technical aspects of service adaptation in the context of elderly care ecosystems. Starting with a service personalization method previously proposed, we introduce various cases of evolution of elderly care services in response to new requirements. The method considers customer's inputs and suggests evolution plans based on the MAPE-K methodology. An application example is then introduced to illustrate the approach.

Keywords: Elderly care ecosystem · Service evolution
Service Composition and Personalization · Collaborative networks

1 Introduction

The world's elderly population has been increasing at an impressive rate in the last decades. By 2050, it is estimated that seniors over 80 will represent an increase of 205% in relation to 2017 [1]. In various parts of the world, elderly will exceed the number of adolescents, which calls the attention for the aging process in our society [1, 2]. With aging, extra care needs are required to safeguard seniors and increase their life quality. In this process, each individual elderly may require specific assistance (e.g., care and help) depending on his/her life setting, involved relatives, health status, preferences, and constraints. Thus, a care service may be perfectly adequate for an individual and extremely purposeless for another.

In this context, the need for creating personalized (respecting preferences, limitations, living context) and evolving services becomes crucial with the changing conditions of the senior [3]. For instance, when moving to a new address, new care needs are identified, when some care need becomes obsolete or when the involved persons,

© IFIP International Federation for Information Processing 2018
Published by Springer Nature Switzerland AG 2018. All Rights Reserved
L. M. Camarinha-Matos et al. (Eds.): PRO-VE 2018, IFIP AICT 534, pp. 417–429, 2018.
https://doi.org/10.1007/978-3-319-99127-6_36

financial constraints, etc., change there is a need to find the best {service-provider} pairs for the new context.

Addressing this challenge, this paper proposes a method to adapt services to evolving needs in the context of an Elderly Care Ecosystem (ECE) [4] focusing on supporting collaborative multi-stakeholder services. The remainder of this paper is structured as follows: Sect. 2 describes the motivation scenario; Sect. 3 presents a brief overview of ICT and Aging projects; Sect. 4 presents the relevant information available in ECE; Sect. 5 describes the solution ({service, provider} pair) personalization and composition method (the SCoPE method) and Sect. 6 introduces the SEvol method to evolve customer's solution in accordance with new requests and changes in life context. Finally, in Sect. 7 conclusions and directions for future work are presented.

2 Motivating Scenario

In order to guide the presentation of the proposed approach, let us consider a motivating scenario. Anna is an 82-years old, retired woman that lives alone, and suffers from hypertension, has cognitive disabilities, and movement constraints. Three years ago, she had an accident, and since then her health is under monitoring in her smart home which is equipped with various sensors and smart devices. Examples of some of these devices are automatic doors and windows opening devices, instantaneous 112 and her son callers, light switches, remote controllers for multimedia devices, smart bracelet which sends information to her doctor's central desk about her blood pressure and movements during the day, etc. In addition, her son (John) takes her to physical therapy twice a week. Anna had an assistant to clean and cook, but as in the last medical appointment, the doctor gave her a specific diet because her blood tests revealed a beginning of diabetes, Anna and her son decided to buy ready meals at a company specialized in diets for people with diabetes. John is also worried because he was assigned by his company to attend a training course abroad with one-month duration. This will change Anna's therapy routine because he will not be able to take his mother to therapy during this period. As such, a transport service to take Anna to treatment will be contracted.

3 Some Projects on ICT and Aging

Recent progress on technological devices and infrastructures creates the opportunity for new classes of services for elderly people [5]. This trend is reflected in a large number of research initiatives on ICT and aging during the last decade. This is clearly illustrated by an analysis of 190 projects started since 2001 as part of ICT and Aging agenda of European framework programs [6].

Figure 1 shows the distribution of projects in terms of developed services. From the 190 projects, 168 consider a simple provider and 22 consider collaborative providers in the four life settings defined by the BRAID - Bridging Research in Ageing and ICT Development - roadmap project [7]: Independent living, health and care, occupation in life, and recreation in life.

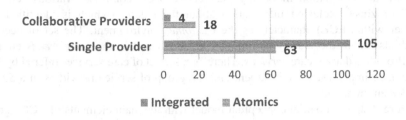

Fig. 1. Projects in the aging domain – mode of service provision

The older projects from 2001 to 2008 had focused on services by single providers. The concern was to meet the maximum service level by the same provider. The AMIGO project [8] – Ambient Intelligence for the Networked Home Environment - was one of the first addressing collaborative providers with integrated services in 2004. Although AMIGO was not specifically for aging solutions, the project suggested solutions for independent living that were promising and followed by other projects. Since 2009, projects aimed at single providers continue but a large project aimed at elderly health, the EMOTION-AAL [9] project, effectively focused on services delivered through various providers in the context of Europe. The aim of EMOTION-AAL is to develop an integrated healthcare concept for elderly people in rural areas in Europe. In this project an integrated solution for the elderly was developed based on seamless inclusion of social services and new technologies in rural areas, named "The Emotional Village". The project includes intense support for self-care and prevention and assistance to carry out daily activities, health and activity monitoring, enhancing safety and security.

Since 2010 to 2015, 21 other projects have been funded, which focus on collaborative providers. Of these projects, 18 deliver atomics services such as INCLU-SIONSOCIETY, MYLIFE, HOST, SAAPHO, CARE@HOME, LILY, MEDIATE, CARERSUPPORT, OSTEOLINK, AWARE, GO-MYLIFE, JOIN-IN, HELASCOL, ANIMATE, GIVE&TAKE, ELDERS-UP!, SPONSOR and ACTGO-GATE, for independent living, occupation in life, and recreation in life. The other 3 develop integrated services, CARE4BALANCE, AAL4ALL and T&TNET projects, all with greater focus on independent living. This analysis points to a potential market expansion, especially in the areas of occupation in life and recreation in life. Other projects are in progress (starting in 2016) and more details about each project can be seen in [6].

4 Elderly Care Ecosystem

An Elderly Care Ecosystem (ECE) shall include various elements, namely the seniors (customers) profile and their current care needs, available care services, service providers entities, among others [4, 10, 11].

From the information modelling perspective, ECE comprises various "environments" or zones. Relevant information about the elderly (which is identified as a customer within ECE) characterizes the *Customer* environment. The set of needs of individuals within the elderly community is established in the *Care Needs* environment. Providers deliver care *services*. Therefore, the set of care services offered by ECE is organized in a *Service* environment and the group of service providers in a *Service Provider* environment.

Figure 2 shows a partial conceptual model with the main elements of ECE (a more detailed ECE model is presented in [10]). The *Customer* and *Service* are linked by *Request,* representing the customer's demand and preferences. *Coverage* represents the connection between *Service* and *Care_Need* describing the coverage level of the covered care need taxonomically organized in a *Care_Needs_Taxonomy*.

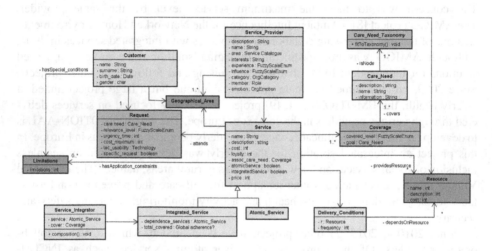

Fig. 2. ECE partial conceptual model

Limitations, *Geographical_Area* and *Resource* indicate *hard restrictions* which can limit the availability of a service (or service provider) to a specific customer. For instance, if the service provider does not cover the customer's location, or if the customer has a special condition (e.g., Alzheimer disease) and the service presents application constraints for this situation, or even if the customer has a need for a resource (e.g., tablet, wi-fi internet, caregiver) which she/he does not have for the operation of the service, etc., then such constraints need to be taken into account.

A service might have conditions of delivery (*Delivery_Conditions*) based on parameters, for instance, needed resources (e.g., a bracelet) and frequency (e.g., three times a week). These parameters can change the business process regardless of service provision.

In the collaborative networks domain, an atomic service is represented by a single business service and an integrated service indicates a composition of atomic services. In our model, a service can be atomic (*Atomic_Service*) or integrated (*Integrated_Service*). A *Service_Integrator* entity is responsible for the composition of integrated services.

5 Service Composition and Personalization

In the elderly care domain, personalization involves the analysis of the senior's life context. The organization responsible for delivering care and assistance services (in our case, the ECE) identifies specific requirements for the customer's context and builds (or composes) a service solution to fit the needs.

In a previous work, the SCoPE (Service Composition and Personalization Ecosystem) method was proposed to support the process of composing and personalizing services in a collaborative network environment for elderly care.

SCoPE (see Fig. 3) is based on three main steps: *(i) scope filtering* - responsible for matching and excluding {service, provider} pairs based on the care need taxonomy, (ii) *adherence calculation* – resulting in the first rating of {service, provider} pairs based on adherence multidimensional matrix for a specific customer, and *(iii) service composition and ranking* - using strategies for service composition and offering a list of potential solutions.

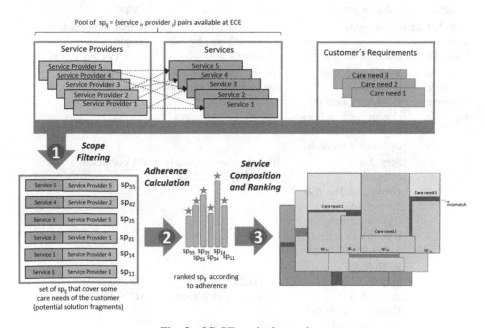

Fig. 3. SCoPE method overview

In *Scope Filtering* (step 1), available services (and corresponding providers) that cover some of the customer's care needs are identified, excluding those that are unsuitable due to geographical restrictions, special conditions, unavailable resources, and other hard constraints. The {service, provider} pair must guarantee that the service attends some customer's care needs, ensuring a proper personalization and adapting to the feedback received from both the ECE, the VO partners, the customer and her/his relatives, certifying in this way a current service personalization.

The *Adherence Calculation* (step 2) identifies personal customer's requests and characteristics for service adherence evaluation taking into consideration cultural differences, religious constraints, social aspects, place of living, etc.

Adherence represents a compatibility relation between the individual customer and a solution fragment sp_{ij} (service s_i and respective provider p_j) and it is calculated by estimating four coefficients: *Closeness (CL)*, *Partial Adherence (PA)*, *Adherence (AD)*, and *Global Adherence (GA)*. *CL* is represented by a multidimensional matrix of the "proximity" between customer's requests and the features of the {service, provider} pair fragment. *PA* is an intermediate computation that refines the closeness based on criteria's weights ponderation. Finally, *AD* represents the resulting adherence according to the service's coverage level to each care need, and *GA* represents the adherence considering all care needs together.

Table 1 summarizes the *adherence calculation* process, including the goal, inputs, and outputs for each step.

Table 1. Steps of adherence calculation process

Adherence calculation process		Input	Output
Step 1. Criteria's weights definition **Goal.** Define criteria's weights		Decision-making criteria selected by the customer	Vector of normalized weights: $W = \{w_1, w_2, \ldots, w_{cri}\}$
Repeated for each fragment sp_{ij}	**Step 2.** Closeness Calculation **Goal.** Calculate the closeness of each sp_{ij} fragment against the customer's requests	sp_{ij} fragments features and customer's requests	*Closeness* vector: $CL = \{cl_1, cl_2, \ldots, cl_{cri}\}$
	Step 3. *PA* calculation **Goal.** Calculate the *Partial Adherence (PA)*, combining criteria's closeness and criteria's weights ponderation	$W = \{w_1, w_2, \ldots, w_{cri}\}$; $CL = \{cl_1, cl_2, \ldots, cl_{cri}\}$	*PA* coefficient
	Step 4. *AD* vector calculation **Goal.** Calculate the *Adherence (AD)* combining the *PA* and the service coverage level about the customer's individual care needs	*PA* coefficient; Customer's care needs (CA); Service Coverage Level regarding the care need	*AD* vector $AD = \{ad_1, ad_2, \ldots, ad_{ca}\}$
Step 5. GA matrix Calculation **Goal.** Calculate the *Global Adherence* (all care needs together) and build the solution fragments and care needs mapping		*AD* vector	*GA* multidimensional matrix

Service Composition and Raking (step 3) uses strategies for achieving a personalized result. Traditional methods for service composition involve human judgments and frequent step-by-step interaction with the customer and service provider (a kind of service co-design). In our approach, we keep the human decision, but mainly for the final stage where the best solutions have already been found easing decision making. The service composition process can then proceed using the group of sp_{ij} fragments that have a reasonable *adherence* level. Various alternative composition methods can be considered, for instance with the purpose of adherence's maximization, number of services minimization or maximization, balanced number of providers, etc.

In the end, a customer's solution is presented through a vector representing the corresponding service and provider fragments (sp_{ij}) and their *adherence* (*ad*) to each care need k, the *Global Adherence* (*GA*) and cost of the solution, and the relation between adherence and cost. For instance, considering Anna's scenario described above, she has four available solutions to choose as described in Table 2 (in our application example). Solution 1 presents the best adherence (*GA*), but the highest cost-benefit ratio is representing by solution 2. Through the human interaction process, Anna will then choose her preferred solution.

Table 2. Anna's personalized solutions

Solutions	To *bloodPressure* care need				To *homeSafety* care need				Global approach		
	sp_{ij}	ad	cost	ad/cost	sp_{ij}	ad	cost	ad/cost	GA	Cost	Ranking: GA/cost (%)
Solution 1	sp_{51}	0.767	200€	0.383	sp_{22}	0.927	40€	2.317	**0.847**	240 €	0.770
Solution 2	sp_{64}	0.639	75€	0.852	sp_{64}	0.791	75€	1.055	0.715	75 €	**0.953**
Solution 3	sp_{11}	0.728	100€	0.728	sp_{21}	0.782	30€	2.607	0.755	130 €	0.581
Solution 4	sp_{51}	0.767	200€	0.383	sp_{21}	0.782	30€	2.607	0.774	230 €	0.337

6 Service Evolution Process in ECE

For each new context change, the ECE broker analyses the situation (in collaboration with the relevant stakeholders) and adapts the service to fit that context. In other words, the service solution evolves to cope with the new life stage. Under this perspective, the notion of evolutionary service [12–14] means that the provided service adapts to the senior's needs, and to any changes that affect the senior's life context.

Based on the *MAPE-K* framework [15], this section presents a self-adaptive system approach for service evolution into ECE. After the *SCoPE* process, the customer is assisted by a personalized solution (*customer's solution*). This solution represents the initial knowledge K: the current service(s) and provider(s) which attend the customer's requirements. Figure 4 illustrates this approach, which we call SEvol.

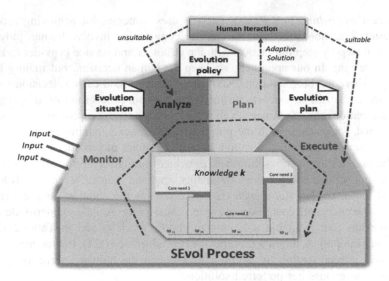

Fig. 4. Service evolution process – *SEvol*

The following phases are considered:

- *Monitor* phase receives a set of *inputs* which can come from several sources, for instance, from the customer and his/her family, or from the ECE, mainly represented by VO coordination, ECE management, or service provider. In this paper the main triggers of SEvol are those coming from the customer.
- *Analyze* phase verifies if the current solution covers the new requests. If the current solution is unsuitable to cope with the environment changes, the *Analyze* function indicates the goals not covered by the solution (evolution situation) which will be the focus of the *Plan* function.
- The *Plan* phase considers the customer as unique, respecting his/her preferences and lifestyle and historical information available in ECE, and plans the solution evolution aiming a minimum of disturbance. With the designed evolution plan, the customer is contacted (*human iteration*). If she/he accepts the proposed solution, the *execute* phase starts, otherwise the process goes back to the *analyze* phase with the customer's feedback.
- The *Execute* phase is the responsible for finalizing the evolution process (implementation of evolutionary solution). Notice that the evolution should not be considered a new personalization since it does not seek the better possible results from scratch, but instead seeks a satisfactory solution with the least possible disturbance to the customer (that is already used to the specific characteristics of current solution).

6.1   Evolution Plan

The evolution (or adaptation) is based on customer's inputs. We consider as primary inputs to the evolution process: (a) the identified new care need, (b) identification that a care need is no longer present, or (c) identification that service changes the delivery conditions.

The proposed service evolution strategy into ECE is based on composition (or decomposition in case of fragment removal) of the current solution or the parameter change of delivery conditions. For each situation, the detailed strategy is presented below.

6.1.1 Situation (a): Adding a Care Need x

The newly added care need should be connected to customer's solution; therefore, adding a new care need implies the adaptation of the integrated service and provider fragments. It is possible to classify this adaptation into two categories:

- (a1) Identifying (in the current solution) a service and provider fragment that covers the new care need (the solution is not changed).
- (a2) Adding a new service and provider fragment that cover the new care need.

In general, when a care need is added, the current solution is not prepared to attend this care need. So the process should identify if the current solution satisfies the new care need. If so, the process ends. Otherwise, the service and provider fragments which cover the new care need x are identified in order to extend the current solution (based on adherence resulting from SCoPE process).

Figure 5 shows (at a high level) the sequence of adaptation the new customer request.

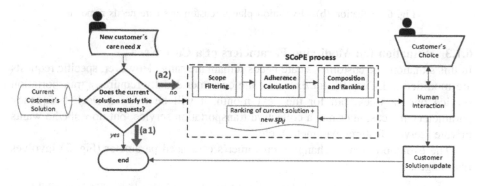

Fig. 5. Situation (a) - Evolution plan for customer's care need addition.

6.1.2 Situation (b): Removing a Care Need x

This removal should not affect the current solution for other care needs. So, two strategies are considered:

- (b1) Removal of {service, provider} pair that covers the x care need.
- (b2) Change of {service, provider} pair that jointly covers x and other care needs (for instance a care need y).

The immediate removal of a {service, provider} pair fragment can only be done if it is exclusively attending the *x* care need. Otherwise, the fragment that is attending care need *y* (that is covered by the same solution fragment) can be updated if there is a better service adherence to *y*. This process can be repeated when other care needs also are covered by the same fragment. A workflow of the evolution plan to customer's care needs removal is illustrated in Fig. 6.

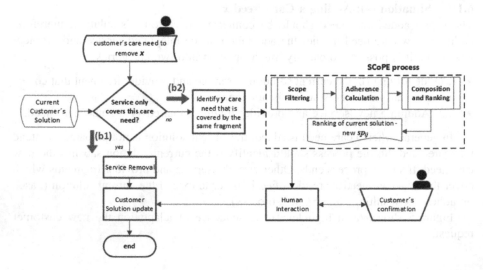

Fig. 6. Situation (b) - Evolution plan to customer's care needs removal

6.1.3   Situation (c): Modifying Parameters of a Care Need

In this situation, the customer's care needs remain the same. However, specific requests are modified in ECE [10], for example, the customer usually requires a transportation service once a week, but for the next month, it will be twice a week (frequency parameter); the customer had a collective transportation service, but now she/he wants private (service features parameter), etc.

The evolution plan to change a customer's care need parameter (Fig. 7) involves two stages:

- (c1) Identify the parameter which should be changed checking if it is available in the current solution.
- (c2) Find a {service, provider} pair available that attends the new parameter.

6.2   Evolution Planning Application

Each situation of the evolution plan is exemplified taking into account the solutions shown in Table 2 (Sect. 4). Let us imagine that Anna has chosen the solution 3 (sp_{11}, sp_{21}) two/three years ago, and now she also needs the transportation service (newly identified care need *n*), and the solution will evolve. In the first analysis, sp_{21} service covers the *homeSafety* care need, but the ECE verifies that it is also available for

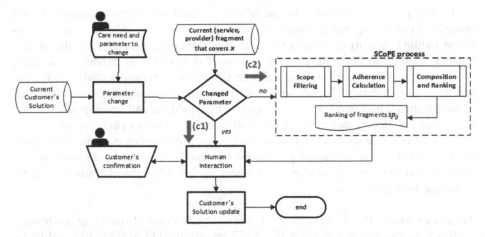

Fig. 7. Evolution plan for customer's care need parameters change

transportation services covering the new request and representing a (a1) evolution plan. The solution is the same with new aggregated values (*GA, Cost, and Ranking: GA/Cost (%)*). On the other hand, if the current solution is solution 2 (sp_{64}), a new {service-provider} pair would have to be found to compose the solution representing a (a2) evolution plan.

The same solution 3, in the (b) situation that removes the care need m (for instance, Anna no longer needs *bloodPressure* care need) the sp_{11} pair is removed from the current solution representing a (b1) evolution plan. However, considering solution 2, sp_{64} pair covers both care needs (*bloodPressure* and *homeSafety*) and cannot be immediately removed (b2 situation).

In the last evaluation plan, a parameter of service needs to be changed, for instance, Anna measures the tension once a day, but now she needs three times a day, *frequency* parameter is modified (c1 evolution plan), or if it is not possible, a new service is found to replace the existing one.

7   Conclusions and Future Work

One of the most significant challenges of ageing population will be to ensure sustainability, while guaranteeing proper care for elderly without creating a heavy burden on younger age groups, both in cost and life dependency. Collaborative technologies represent a significant impeller to active ageing mainly through a collaborative business ecosystem which, on the one hand, offers new business opportunities to service providers who work together and can evolve their business, as well as the elderly who can meet demands through personalized and always up-to-date services.

In this context, an Elderly Care Ecosystem has the potential to provide an environment where personalized and evolutionary solutions might increase customer's satisfaction, allow costs and risks sharing and strengthen providers' business.

In this paper, an overview of the SCoPE method highlights its support to the process of composing and personalizing services. Further, we propose a service evolution method (SEvol) to support the adaptation process (evolution) of current customer's solution to new requests. This proposal is intended to provide an adaptive system that can work well with an ECE framework to service personalization, composition, and evolution. In this sense, its validation depends on the acceptability, appropriateness, and feasibility of the approaches, models, and developments within the domain of elderly care ecosystem in collaborative networks environment.

As part of future work, we intend to further detail the service evolution conceptual model, examine from the market perspective how the ECE can be built (or composed) from the existing service providers and actors, and validate the algorithms used for prototype implementation.

Acknowledgment. This work has been funded in part by the Center of Technology and Systems (CTS – Uninova) and the Portuguese FCT-PEST program UID/EEA/00066/2013, and by the Ciência Sem Fronteiras Program and Instituto Federal Farroupilha (Brazil).

References

1. Kearney, A.T.: Understanding the Needs and Consequences of the Ageing Consumer. The Consumer Goods Forum (2013). https://www.atkearney.com/documents/10192/682603/Understanding+the+Needs+and+Consequences+of+the+Aging+Consumer.pdf/6c25ffa3-0999-4b5c-8ff1-afdca0744fdc. Accessed 10 Oct 2017
2. Bureau, P.R.: World population data (2017). http://www.worldpopdata.org/index.php/map. Accessed 05 Oct 2017
3. Baldissera, T.A., Camarinha-Matos, L.M.: Services personalization approach for a collaborative care ecosystem. In: Afsarmanesh, H., Camarinha-Matos, L.M., Lucas Soares, A. (eds.) PRO-VE 2016. IFIPAICT, vol. 480, pp. 443–456. Springer, Cham (2016). https://doi.org/10.1007/978-3-319-45390-3_38
4. Baldissera, T.A., Camarinha-Matos, L.M.: Towards a collaborative business ecosystem for elderly care. In: Camarinha-Matos, L.M., Falcão, António J., Vafaei, N., Najdi, S. (eds.) DoCEIS 2016. IFIPAICT, vol. 470, pp. 24–34. Springer, Cham (2016). https://doi.org/10.1007/978-3-319-31165-4_3
5. Camarinha-Matos, L.M., Ferrada, F., Oliveira, A.I., Rosas, J., Monteiro, J.N.: Integrated care services in ambient assisted living. Paper presented at the IEEE 15th International Conference on e-Health Networking, Applications and Services (Healthcom 2013), Lisbon, pp. 197–201 (2013)
6. AAL-Europe: Active and assisted living programme (2001). http://www.aal-europe.eu/
7. Camarinha-Matos, L.M., Afsarmanesh, H., Ferrada, F., Oliveira, A.I., Rosas, J.: A comprehensive research roadmap for ICT and ageing. Stud. Inf. Control **22**(3), 233–254 (2013). https://doi.org/10.24846/v22i3y201301
8. Georgantas, N., et al.: Middleware architecture for ambient intelligence in the networked home. In: Nakashima, H., Aghajan, H., Augusto, J.C. (eds.) Handbook of Ambient Intelligence and Smart Environments, pp. 1139–1169. Springer, Boston (2010). https://doi.org/10.1007/978-0-387-93808-0_42
9. Maier, H.-O.: EMOTION-ALL (2010). http://www.aal-europe.eu/projects/emotionaal/

10. Baldissera, T.A., Camarinha Matos, L.M., DeFaveri, C.: Designing elderly care ecosystem in collaborative networks environment. In: IEEE International Conference on Computing, Networking and Informatics, Ota, Lagos, Nigeria (2017). https://doi.org/10.1109/iccni.2017.8123818

11. Camarinha-Matos, L.M., Rosas, J., Oliveira, A.I., Ferrada, F.: Care services ecosystem for ambient assisted living. Enterp. Inf. Syst. 9(5–6), 607–633 (2015). https://doi.org/10.1080/17517575.2013.852693

12. O'Grady, M.J., Muldoon, C., Dragone, M., Tynan, R., O'Hare, G.M.: Towards evolutionary ambient assisted living systems. J. Ambient Intell. Humaniz. Comput. 1(1), 15–29 (2010)

13. Hong, J., Suh, E.-H., Kim, J., Kim, S.: Context-aware system for proactive personalized service based on context history. Expert Syst. Appl. 36(4), 7448–7457 (2009). https://doi.org/10.1016/j.eswa.2008.09.002

14. Brown, A., Johnston, S., Kelly, K.: Using service-oriented architecture and component-based development to build web service applications. Rational Software Corporation (2002)

15. IBM: An architectural blueprint for autonomic computing. IBM White Paper (2006). https://www-03.ibm.com/autonomic/pdfs/AC%20Blueprint%20White%20Paper%20V7.pdf

Towards a Cognitive Linked Public Service Cloud

Santiago Salem[1(✉)], Adegboyega Ojo[2(✉)], Elsa Estevez[1,3(✉)], and
Pablo R. Fillottrani[1,4(✉)]

[1] Department of Computer Science and Engineering,
Universidad Nacional del Sur, Bahía Blanca, Argentina
salem_santiago@hotmail.com, {ece,prf}@cs.uns.edu.ar
[2] Insight Centre for Data Analytics,
National University of Ireland Galway, Galway, Ireland
adegboyega.ojo@insight-centre.org
[3] Institute for Computer Science and Engineering (UNS–CONICET),
Bahía Blanca, Argentina
[4] Comisión de Investigaciones Científicas de la Provincia de Buenos Aires,
Tolosa, Argentina

Abstract. Cognitive computing applications are steadily growing across sectors and increasingly considered for adoption in government for transforming public services. Semantic technologies have been identified as one of the enabling technologies for cognitive computing capabilities. This paper describes some foundational efforts for the deployment of ontological semantics-driven cognitive capabilities in delivering a family of public services. First, we present an application profile for the Core Public Service Vocabulary extending the core vocabulary into a rich domain ontology – Social Welfare Service Ontology. Second, we use the Social Welfare Service domain ontology to as a basis for the design of a Linked Public Service Cloud. The proposed Cloud comprises a detailed description of concrete instances of social welfare services and links (relationship) between such services. By linking services across linked public service clouds associated with different public administrations, like different municipal governments, we demonstrate how cognitive capabilities supporting citizen requests could be realized through reasoning and propagation of information over semantic networks of public service clouds.

Keywords: Linked data · Cognitive applications · Linked public service cloud
Ontologies · Semantic technologies

1 Introduction

Whole-of-Government (WoG) and Networked Governance approaches are increasingly adopted in public administrations to enable collaboration across agency boundaries and with third-parties parties for access to external resources and rapid innovation. These approaches require for support shared and connected information and technology infrastructure across and beyond government. For instance, in Networked Governance, public technological platforms that are able to connect citizens and other external parties to

© IFIP International Federation for Information Processing 2018
Published by Springer Nature Switzerland AG 2018. All Rights Reserved
L. M. Camarinha-Matos et al. (Eds.): PRO-VE 2018, IFIP AICT 534, pp. 430–441, 2018.
https://doi.org/10.1007/978-3-319-99127-6_37

government agencies (e.g. social media platforms) are critical for enabling interaction. In the context of the WoG, shared services and service catalogs describing and relating services exemplify enabling infrastructure for joined-up and coordinated service delivery.

With the recent upsurge in interest in Artificial Intelligence, Cognitive computing, Big Data Analytics, governments like the private sector have begun to seriously explore how to effectively harness these disruptive technologies in building smarter services and infrastructure that are able to respond better to citizens needs. Evidence of this interest is captured in [1] where the potential applications areas of Cognitive computing in the public sector were articulated.

Cognitive computing aims to mimic the human process of knowing and problem-solving and decision making based on the perception and understanding of concepts. Cognitive systems offer four main capabilities [1, 2]: (1) *understanding* - the process of comprehending different types of data, like pictures and text; (2) *reasoning* - the process of inferring a conclusion based on information that has been previously analyzed; (3) *discovery* – reading and identifying patterns over huge amount of data in faster ways than humans can do; (4) *learning* - acquiring knowledge from different sources helping to reduce mistakes in future decisions. Given their valuable capabilities, cognitive computing applications are steadily growing across sectors and increasingly considered by governments for transforming public services. As it is explained knowledge-workers use 2.5 h per day looking for information and such time could be reduced by 50% using appropriate cognitive applications [3].

Cognitive systems employ different techniques and tools to extract information from unstructured sources using Natural Language Processing techniques. One of the main challenges in NLP is related to semantics. Semantics enables defining concepts (i.e. their meaning) and the existing relations between them. To formally represent semantics, ontologies provide a mechanism for specifying and capturing the knowledge of a specific domain in machine-readable form. Consequently, semantics and ontologies play an important role in cognitive systems because they facilitate some tasks of NLP; enabling cognitive systems to understand and reason, as human beings do, facilitating the understanding of concepts by computers.

In this paper, we demonstrate the centrality of semantics and ontology in enabling cognitive capabilities in shared government information and service infrastructure. Specifically, we show how cognitive capabilities in public service cloud infrastructure underpinned by an ontology of social welfare public services can enhance government efficiency and contribute to improving the delivery of public services to citizens. In this context, the public service ontology enables two cognitive features: (1) acts as the memory or internal knowledge base and (2) affords the mechanism for reasoning to solve problems such as service eligibility decisions and discovery of relevant services for the government customer – the citizen.

The rest of this paper is structured as follows. Section 2 introduces cognitive technologies and their usage in government. Section 3 presents an ontology for welfare public services and explains cognitive capabilities offered by the ontology. Section 4 builds the concept of cognitive linked service cloud based on the capabilities offered by the ontology introduced in Sect. 3. Section 5 explains scenario for the usage of such tools in collaborative government networks. Finally, Sect. 6 discusses and concludes the paper.

2 Cognitive Technologies in Government

The term *Cognitive Technologies* was coined various decades ago and despite the regular appearance of new technologies which makes such technologies to vary and progress in a steady way, the term remains actual and relevant. In particular, the development of cognitive technologies was initially envisioned in the 1978 Practical Aspects of Memory Conference [4]. Later, in 1995, the Ontario Institute for Studies in Education defined them as those that transcend typical human cognitive limitations like memory [5]. A recent definition explains that they refer to technologies that directly or indirectly affect learning, retention, remembering, reasoning, and problem-solving [4]. Currently, cognitive technologies are applied to many issues of our daily life. For instance, such technologies are used by software applications providing us information about the conditions of our daily trips to commute from one place to another; to keep track and remind us about our appointments and planned events; to inform us about weather conditions; and to detect if an illegal transaction was conducted by a given customer; among other examples.

Government is a main application area for cognitive technologies. In particular, new innovative and smart services, such as personalized, anticipated, context-aware and context-intelligent services [6] can be delivered and their delivery can be improved through the use of cognitive technologies. For example, [7] introduces a chatbot[1]-based prototype for assisting users in retrieving and analyzing open data in a friendly way. Chatbots are developed using a combination of various technologies, like pattern matching, parsing, artificial intelligence, machine learning and ontologies [7]. Another technology, text mining is utilized for analyzing textual data provided in the form of opinions or complaints by the public in government systems to detect improvement areas in service delivery [8, 9]. In addition, a service ontology has been enhanced with a semantic approach to support various usage contexts and scenarios for public services. In this case, the proposed solution contributes to improving the level of automation of the discovery and composition processes of public services [9].

3 Semantics-Driven Cognitive Capabilities in Welfare Service Management

This section presents the conceptual framework used for defining the vocabulary (Sect. 3.1), the ontology for public services, in particular, the ontology for welfare public services (Sect. 3.2) and its formalization through an ontology authoring tool (Sect. 3.3).

---

[1] A chatbot is a computer program able to maintain a conversation with a user, either through text or voice.

3.1   Conceptual Framework

The framework identifies main concepts related to the delivery of public services. The model is based on previous studies [10–14] which identify and describe common concepts for the provision of seamless public services. Figure 1 synthesizes the concepts that are later extended for the specific case of Welfare Public Services.

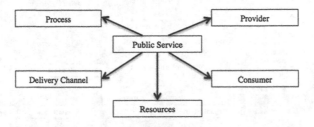

Fig. 1. Conceptual model

Terms included in the conceptual model are explained as follows: *Public Service* – is a service performed for the benefit of the public, especially provided by a non-profit organization; *Provider* – is the entity responsible for providing the service; *Consumer* is an individual that receives the public service; *Resources* – comprises all assets and other resources used for providing the service; *Delivery Channel* – refers to the means used by the provider to deliver the public service to the consumers; and *Process* – comprises all the activities necessary to produce as final output the provision of the public service to the consumers.

3.2   Vocabulary and Ontology Design

Local governments use different approaches to describe their public services. This refers both, to the terms of the vocabulary but also to how much details they include in such descriptions. In addition, service descriptions are usually provided using free narrative forms and in the same government unit, they highly differ in the way they are written.

One of the tasks of this research was to identify and understand the vocabulary that captures common concepts and features of social welfare services. To address this challenge, we conducted a survey among representatives of two local governments in Buenos Aires Province, Argentina - Bahía Blanca and La Plata. The survey was carried out online, implemented using an open source tool (LimeSurvey), and also through an offline version implemented in Microsoft Word. It was conducted during June-July 2017 in Bahia Blanca, and during September–October 2017 in La Plata. The collected answers were related to 20 welfare public services.

Based on the conceptual –framework described before, the services identified through the survey, and the interactions with representatives of both municipal governments, we defined an initial set of vocabulary terms (see Fig. 2). Using the set of terms, the second step was to extend the vocabulary based on local and sectorial features and also extending it using the Core Public Service Vocabulary – CPSV (see Fig. 3), an ontology that captures key concepts about public services, like for example, related to the legal basis for the provision of the service, contact point and opening hours, the output delivered by the service and other data.

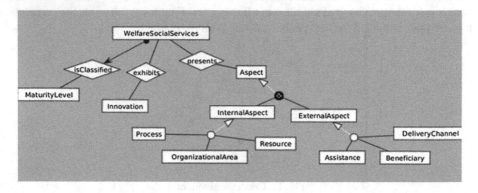

Fig. 2. Welfare public services – Initial vocabulary

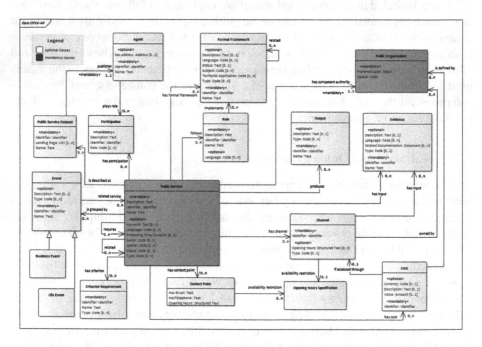

Fig. 3. Core public service vocabulary

Considering that cognitive systems need to have all concepts defined with formal semantics and machine-readable descriptions of the services for proper understanding, we design an ontology in the next step. The proposed ontology captures common concepts – e.g. *Assistance*, *Beneficiary*, *Maturity Level* and attributes required for the complete description of a Welfare Public Service, including aspects that are of special interest for the back-office and front-office applications and processes.

The ontology up to the third level is presented in Fig. 4 and the object properties in Table 1. Each of the concepts included in the ontology is explained as follows. *Welfare-SocialServices* – represents any welfare public service provided by a local government and is an extension of the Public Service defined in the Core Public Service Vocabulary; *Category* – represents the specific type of the service provided –possible values are: unemployment, teenagers, pregnant, elderly people, and furthermore. *MaturityLevel* – refers to the service maturity level. Possible values include: informational, interactive, transactional and connected. *Innovation* – refers to the type of innovation applied by the service. Possible values include those in [6]; *Aspect* – depicts a feature of a service. It could be internal or external; *InternalAspect* corresponds to any service feature that is not visible to the public; *ExternalAspect* refers to any service feature visible to the public; *Process* - comprises the activities performed by the service provider. It could be *ApplicationProcess* or *DeliveryProcess*. *ApplicationProcess* - refers to all the activities that should be done when an individual decides to enroll in a welfare public service. *DeliveryProcess* - corresponds to all the activities that should be completed to bring the benefit to the beneficiary. *ElegibilityCriteria* - comprises all the requirements that the individual must fulfill to become a beneficiary. *OrganizationalArea* – identifies the government organizational unit response for the service provision; *Resourse* – refers to any kind of resource used for producing and delivering the service. It could be human, financial, technical or organizational. *Human* – refers to all the people that is involved in the process. *Financial* – refers to the money received to provide the service and it could come from the national, province or local government. *Technical* – comprises any kind of technical device or equipment used for the business process underpinning the service provision. *Organizational* – refers to the strategy and plans that are followed for the service provision and delivery. *Assistance* – identifies the type of benefit received; *Beneficiary* – represents the service recipient. It could be a household or a person. *Household* – refers to a whole family or group of individuals that live in the same house and receive a benefit. *Person* – refers to an individual; and *Delivery* – comprises the channels used to deliver a service and the specific range of time in which the service will be available. *DeliveryChannel* – refers to the means used to deliver the service. *DeliveryDate* – comprises the

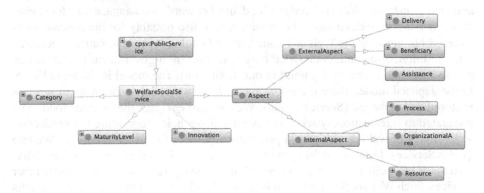

Fig. 4. Core public service vocabulary application profile for welfare services

date when the service was delivered for the first time and when will be finished, and data on how periodically the assistance is delivered to the beneficiaries.

Table 1. Welfare public services vocabulary – Object properties.

Object property	Domain	Range	Is inverse of
hasCategory	WelfareSocialService	Category	isCategoryOf
isClassified	WelfareSocialService	MaturityLevel	classifiedBy
Exhibits	WelfareSocialService	Innovation	exhibitedBy
Presents	WelfareSocialService	Aspects	belongsTo
hasDeliveryDate	Delivery	DeliveryDate	isDeliveryDateOf
hasDeliveryChannel	Delivery	DeliveryChannel	isDeliveryChannelOf

3.3 Implementation

After defining the ontology, we formalize it through a software tool. For this, we used Protégé, a well-known ontology editor that has the advantage of being free and open-source. The formal definition of the ontology enables to more rigorously describe each public welfare services, and to publish more reliable data as open data through the local government portal.

4 Cognitive Linked Service Cloud

This section presents the evolution of the developed ontology through a Welfare Service Cloud (Sect. 4.1), to a Cognitive Welfare Service Cloud in which the cognitive features are enacted in a specific application context (Sect. 4.2).

4.1 From Welfare Social Ontology to Welfare Service Cloud

Based on the Welfare Public Service Ontology defined in Sect. 3, each agency can define instances of such ontology with the different welfare public services that they deliver. With such instantiations, a public administration jurisdiction (e.g. local or state authority) can have a Welfare Service Cloud, in other words, a data space used for storing all the services described using the ontology. It is also possibly for the concrete individuals or instances of the Welfare Public Service Ontology to be automatically acquired through information extraction (NLP based process) from government public service portals (we shall return to this point in our discussion). The model is shown in Fig. 5. In the depicted model, there is a government cloud, where information about services is stored and managed (Service Cloud). We can also envisage the service cloud to be integrated to information systems in government agencies supporting the production and delivery of welfare services. In particular, a subset of such services is the Welfare Public Services. Data stored for each of the services can be linked – e.g. services delivered to the same citizen (shown as internal links in the figure) or services related to other services. Such Welfare Service Cloud is accessed and managed by all government units or entities of the same public administration, who are the providers of the services in the cloud.

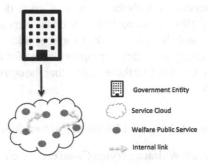

Fig. 5. Welfare service cloud

4.2   From Welfare Service Cloud to Cognitive Linked Service Cloud

Adding one more layer of integration, we may consider linking the Welfare Service Clouds managed by local governments. This is realised by linking ontologies in two or more Welfare Service Clouds. For instance, service clouds in two different local authorities could be linked by relating similar or equivalent services in the different clouds. This integration further strengthens the cognitive capability potentials of the Service Clouds and enables governments to deliver seamless services regardless the public administration jurisdiction that are involved. By linking the welfare service clouds it would be possible to have access to significant amount of data, and through cognitive systems, to produce data supporting evidence-based public policies. A schema of this concept is shown in Fig. 6.

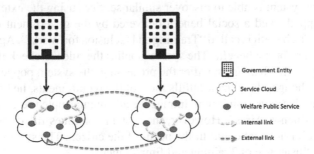

Fig. 6. Cognitive linked service cloud

5   Scenarios for Exploring the Cognitive Linked Service Cloud

The objective of this section is to explain the process for using the cognitive linked service cloud and to present a concrete scenario illustrating its potential.

5.1 Process

The Welfare Public Service that each government entity delivers is described using the Core Welfare Public Service Vocabulary. Each of such description constitutes an instance of the ontology that is stored in the Welfare Service Cloud. The ontology enables linking services, and the use of linked services allows government entities to improve their service delivery and opens up opportunities for developing new applications that can take advantage of it, like those supporting the delivery of seamless services or evidence-based policy-making.

5.2 Scenario - Decision Making and Discovery of Services in Inter-linked Clouds

As explained in Sect. 4, each Welfare Service Cloud can have internal and external links to similar services. To demonstrate the importance of such links and of having the welfare services documented in the Welfare Service Cloud, consider a citizen looking for information about services. He uses the Government Mobile App that provides an interface to query the Welfare Service Cloud of his local government. He is unemployed and wants to know if he is eligible for the unemployment benefit that his local government is delivering[2]. The program is called "Insurance for Training and Employment". The aim of the program is to help unemployed people to acquire new skills so they can apply for a new job. The program also provides advice for finishing previous studies. The citizen ticks the requirements that he fulfilled and with that information, using existing rules and internal linked data in the cloud, for instance, enabling to check the applicant´s education, history of previous works, and previous services received from this program, the system exploiting its cognitive capabilities is able to determine whether the applicant is eligible for the benefit or not.

  The citizen still has some doubts. He will be moving to Buenos Aires in the next three months and wants to know if there is some similar benefit in that city. Using the mobile app, the system is able to discover similar services using the external links (see Fig. 7). The app showed a social benefit delivered by the government of the City of Buenos Aires. The benefit is called "Training and Inclusion for Work"[3]. Again the citizen ticks for applying for the benefit. The system applies the rules to check if the citizen is eligible to receive that benefit and after the processing, the system popped up that he is not eligible. Although, the citizen fulfills most of the requirements, he does not satisfy the requirement that says "minimum, immediate and uninterrupted residence of 2 years in the City of Buenos Aires". However, the system continues the discovery process searching for a service that could fit the needs of the citizen. The system found a third service called "Insurance of Training and Employment"[4].

---

[2] Government of Municipality of Bahia Blanca, government website for employment. http://www.bahia.gob.ar/empleo/ (visited 14-07-2018).

[3] Government of Municipality of Buenos Aires, government website for employment, http://www.buenosaires.gob.ar/desarrollohumanoyhabitat/economiasocial/programafit   (visited 14-07-2018).

[4] Argentinean National Government, Capacity-building portal, https://www.argentina.gob.ar/acceder-al-seguro-de-capacitacion-y-empleo (visited 15-04-2018).

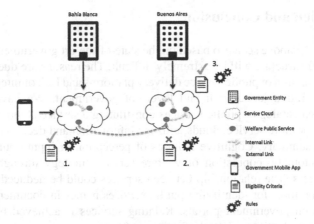

Fig. 7. Scenario proposed

The benefit provides training and financial help for persons who are actively looking for a job. The requirements are the following: (1) being over 18 years old; (2) in case of being under 25 years old, having the studies of the secondary school finished; (3) being unemployed and being actively looking for a job; (4) being a permanent resident in the country; (5) having a national identity document; (6) being in the group of unemployed persons and (6) not receiving another assistance or benefit from the National, Provincial or local Governments, except those granted to veterans of the Malvinas war. The citizen ticked the requirements he fulfilled and then the system process that data taking into account the rules presented and validating the information using external links of the clouds. The system showed to the citizen that he is able to receive the benefit.

In the scenario defined above, we can see two important cognitive capabilities, discovery and reasoning. Discovery is the process of searching through huge amount of data in faster ways that humans can do. The links that exist between services, let the system discover similar services that could be stored in the same Welfare Service Cloud or it could be stored in an external cloud. If this task should be done manually, it would be slower than using the system, the employee should search over all the social services, understand them and decide if they are or not similar. This process is done faster than a human being could do. Furthermore, the capability of reasoning is also present in the scenario. Reasoning is the process of arriving to a conclusion after analyzing information that is served as an input. When the citizen wants to know if he or she is eligible for certain social service, the system is the responsible of taking into account the socio-economics characteristics of the citizen and, using the existing rules, it is able to reason and decide if the citizen could apply to a specific social service. In this scenario, we are helping in the process of decision making, making it easier and faster than if should be done by humans.

6   Discussion and Conclusion

Implementing the above scenario based on the state-of-the-art government information and service infrastructure will be extremely difficult. The reasons are due to the nature of the implementation of public service delivery platforms and lack of integration across public administration jurisdiction and levels of government. We have shown that through a linked catalog of public services constituting a service cloud and the cross-linking of two or more service clouds, citizens information and decision needs can be better met. In summary, Cognitive features of perception or input could be realized through the automatic population of welfare service ontology through information extraction process. The relationship between services could be deduced using named entity extraction tools for identifying public services names in documents describing public service on government portals. Relating services is achieved by linking the uniform resource identifiers (URIs) of services. The reasoning is enabled through the rules in the welfare service ontology and problem-solving is made possible by combining the reasoning capability with access to sources of citizen information through interfaces provided by government information systems.

We can thus argue that semantic technologies play an important role in cognitive systems. We defined the concept of Welfare Service Cloud and extended it to Cognitive Linked Service Cloud, where semantics helps to understand the meaning of the services described. However, we note that semantics and ontologies need to be supported with text-mining techniques such other natural language processing tools for realizing semantic-driven cognitive capabilities in real applications like the scenario described in Sect. 5. We conclude that integrating the semantic web with requisite complementary technology can deliver cognitive capabilities for networks of collaborative systems.

In our view, the contributions of this work are: (a) illustrating how an ontology serves as a foundational component of a cognitive system; (b) providing a concrete scenario and use case for the application of semantics-driven cognitive systems in government collaborative networks; and (c) development and implementation of an application profile for the Core Public Service Vocabulary Application for the domain of Social Welfare Services. We believe that our concept of Cognitive Linked Service Cloud concept has major implications for regional initiatives such as the European Single Market where European citizens freely moving across borders of European nations still require access to services in their home countries.

References

1. W. and S. & Analytics: Your cognitive future Part I: The evolution of cognitive (2015)
2. Beetz, M., Buss, M., Wollherr, D.: Cognitive technical systems — what is the role of artificial intelligence? In: Hertzberg, J., Beetz, M., Englert, R. (eds.) KI 2007. LNCS (LNAI), vol. 4667, pp. 19–42. Springer, Heidelberg (2007). https://doi.org/10.1007/978-3-540-74565-5_3
3. Tahamtan, N.: How Semantic Technologies Enable Domain Experts to Steer Cognitive Applications (2017)
4. Walker, W.R., Herrmann, D.J.: Cognitive Technologies, Essays on the Transformation of Thought and Society. McFarland & Company, Inc., Jefferson (2005)

5. Greening, T.: Building the constructivist toolbox: an exploration of cognitive technologies. Educ. Technol. **38**(2), 23–35 (1998)
6. Bertot, J., Estevez, E., Janowski, T.: Universal and contextualized public services: digital public service innovation framework. Gov. Inf. Q. **33**(2), 211–222 (2016)
7. Porreca, S., Leotta, F., Mecella, M., Vassos, S., Catarci, T.: Accessing Government Open Data Through Chatbots. In: Garrigós, I., Wimmer, M. (eds.) ICWE 2017. LNCS, vol. 10544, pp. 156–165. Springer, Cham (2018). https://doi.org/10.1007/978-3-319-74433-9_14
8. Surjandari, I., Megawati, C., Dhini, A., Hardaya, I.B.S.: Application of text mining for classification of textual reports: a study of Indonesia's national complaint handling system. In: Proceedings of the International Conference on Industrial Engineering and Operations Management, pp. 1147–1156 (2016)
9. Narinam, D.: Analyzing text-based user feedback in e-Government services using topic models. In: Proceedings - 2013 7th International Conference on Complex, Intelligent, and Software Intensive Systems, CISIS 2013, pp. 720–725 (2013)
10. Ojo, A., Janowski, T., Estevez, E.: A composite domain framework for developing electronic public services. In: SETP, pp. 234–241 (2007)
11. Ojo, A., Janowski, T., Estevez, E.: Domain models and enterprise application framework for developing electronic public services. In: Proceedings of the 6th International EGOV Conference, pp. 157–164 (2007)
12. Janowski, T., Ojo, A., Estevez, E.: Rapid development of electronic public services – software infrastructure and software process, Technology, pp. 294–295 (2007)
13. Janowski, T., Ojo, A., Estevez, E.: Rapid development of electronic public services – a case study in electronic licensing service. Architecture, pp. 292–293 (2007)
14. Estevez, E., Fillottrani, P., Janowski, T.: From e-Government to seamless government. In: Conf. Collab. Electron. Commerce. Technol. Res. (CollECTeR Iberoamerica 6–9 Novemb. 2007), pp. 269–280 (2007)

Cognitive Services for Collaborative mHealth: The OnParkinson Case Study

Patricia Macedo[1,2(✉)], Rui Neves Madeira[1],
and Luis M. Camarinha-Matos[2]

[1] ESTSetúbal, Instituto Politécnico de Setúbal, Setúbal, Portugal
{patricia.macedo, rui.madeira}@estsetubal.ips.pt
[2] Faculty of Sciences and Technology and Center of Technology
and Systems - UNINOVA, Nova University of Lisbon,
Campus de Caparica, Caparica, Portugal
cam@uninova.pt

Abstract. Nowadays, there is a huge demand for personalized health services. The evolution of cognitive systems technology combined with the hot trend of the mobile apps market became an important driver for personalization in the health field. One of the challenges concerns providing credible information about health issues tailored to each end-user. In this direction, this paper aims to present a cognitive services model in order to support the building of cognitive-based collaborative networks to provide tailored health information through appropriate interfaces. The discussion regarding the integration of the services is based on the experience acquired with the implementation of the OnParkinson mobile app, which is a case study integrating the IBM Watson cognitive services.

Keywords: mHealth · Cognitive computing · Collaborative networks
Parkinson's disease · Watson · Personalization · Mobile computing

1 Introduction

The healthcare field is adopting the use of mobile devices to provide innovative healthcare services. Mobile health (mHealth) solutions are developing very fast and since a few years it became "the new edge of healthcare innovation" [1]. This new approach does not intend to replace the health professionals, but rather to include them in the process as a supporting element and a manager [2]. mHealth is changing the way the health professionals are now engaging in their daily work but, on the other hand, these new solutions depend on their acceptance by healthcare customers (e.g., patients and caregivers). mHealth solutions should meet the users' specific needs and interests in order to become truly integrated into their everyday lives, thus being a major vehicle for their involvement in their healthcare process. The future of healthcare should be one in which the healthcare customer will be involved, which is what s/he has always wanted to be [3], getting an accurate picture of the many factors that affect her/his health. Moreover, health customers are more likely to stick with mobile apps recommended by professionals resulting in a higher involvement in their healthcare [4]. The aforementioned points work as a driver to a new model of health professional-patient collaboration.

L. M. Camarinha-Matos et al. (Eds.): PRO-VE 2018, IFIP AICT 534, pp. 442–453, 2018.
https://doi.org/10.1007/978-3-319-99127-6_38

Nowadays, people generate large amounts of health-related data, from mHealth apps and personal fitness trackers to electronic medical records and clinical research [5]. However, a big part of these data are underutilized or discarded and the vast majority of healthcare customers do not even have access to their data, but they want personalized, transparent, integrated, and high-quality care [5]. mHealth solutions are likely to allow the collection of data that can contribute to improving evidence-based practice and research, creating conditions to "deliver highly personalized healthcare in general and suitable intervention for patients to manage their chronic conditions in particular" [6]. The integration of cognitive computing into healthcare systems can now help to cope with health data that were previously "inaccessible", producing a high impact on the healthcare field. The adoption of cognitive computing services brings the model to a new level of collaboration, namely between people and technology with the goal of transforming healthcare on a global scale [5, 7].

The combination of mHealth with cognitive services that understand, reason, and even learn, may help people expand their knowledge base, improving professionals' productivity, while deepening and redefining a patient's path to better health. Besides the obvious application on clinical and decision making support, a major focus of cognitive computing has been around the user experience, being applied to "help with patients' understanding of their conditions, how they can manage their condition and treatment, and potential consequences of procedures" [5]. Motivated by these perspectives, this paper presents a model towards the integration of cognitive-based services into mHealth solutions in order to bring them closer to the patients and their caregivers, leveraging the collaboration with the health professionals, while providing tailored information through appropriate interfaces (see Fig. 1).

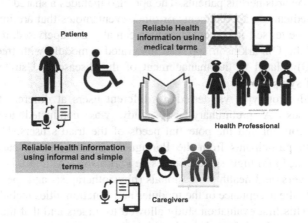

Fig. 1. Personalized cognitive mHealth apps provide tailored information.

This work is based on the experience obtained with the implementation of the OnParkinson mHealth solution, which constitutes a case study based on the usage of IBM Watson cognitive services. Starting from a study of the needs of the triad "people with Parkinson's Disease (PD), their caregivers and health professionals",

ONParkinson appeared with the focus on the empowerment of this triad to help both patients and caregivers to better manage PD.

The paper is organized as follows. Section 2 presents the OnParkinson solution. Section 3 introduces a brief overview of relevant cognitive platforms and the services that can be used and integrated into a mHealth solution to help finding knowledge pertinent to support health consumers' clinical issues. The experience obtained with the integration of IBM Watson services into OnParkinson is detailed in Sect. 4, while Sect. 5 proposes a model for the integration of cognitive services and discusses the notion of a distributed health-related community as a collaborative cognitive system. Finally, conclusions and future work are presented in Sect. 6.

2   The OnParkinson mHealth Solution

The OnParkinson mHealth solution [8] is a platform, in which a mobile app is the main interface to provide patients and their caregivers with self-management capabilities to help them feel empowered in their ability to find strategies in a more informed and collaborative way (see Fig. 2). The platform includes a server that contains a central repository where all data are stored. The platform also intends to optimize therapy outside the clinical context, with remote support from the health professionals, providing them with an exclusive Web interface, which works as a complement to the mHealth app. The Web app integrates a more complete and interactive dashboard than the mobile interface, allowing better monitoring and remote support of the therapy outside the clinic context. An essential feature of this Web app is an interface through which the health professional can add new therapeutic exercises to create programs based on them towards her/his patients. The app also includes a shared "calendar" with reminders of medication, appointments or other events/notes that are important to the user, enabling a better self-management, which can also be supervised, if required. The first version of the OnParkinson app also integrated a module with frequently asked questions (FAQ) related to the management of the disease and strategies for self-management of symptoms.

The mHealth prototype was tested by different users at different times and for different purposes. A preliminary user study was conducted to validate the OnParkinson's concept and the potential needs of the triad's users. User tests were carried out with participants from the Portuguese Parkinson's Disease Association (literally, Associação Portuguesa de Doentes de Parkinson - APDPk), including people with PD, caregivers, and health professionals (physiotherapists and speech therapists), in order evaluate the acceptance of the modules and functionalities included in this first version [8, 9]. This first evaluation study allowed to understand that the OnParkinson development was on the right path, with a high acceptance by the potential end-users. However, in order to improve the user experience and engagement, the app should provide personalized services. One of these required personalized services is to provide the users with reliable information about PD. The FAQ module was not enough for the users' needs, and a Question and Answer System that automatically answers questions asked in natural language about PD was required.

Fig. 2. OnParkinson mHealh solution.

The OnParkinson solution, developed within the MAiThE project [10], addresses two important societal challenges, which reflect the policy priorities of the Europe 2020 strategy. The challenge "Health, demographic changes and well-being", also included as one of the United Nations challenges for sustainable development 2030, is addressed since the project aims to develop personalized mHealth apps towards the specific needs of their end-users (patients, caregivers, and health professionals). A second challenge, "Europe in a changing world - Inclusive, innovative and reflective societies", is also addressed since the use of apps based on mobile devices naturally enhance the feeling of inclusion in citizens. In particular, they contribute to a more inclusive society by empowering individuals suffering from a pathology and their caregivers. These apps are expected to contribute to a more reflective society by engaging users and contributing to their awareness and understanding of the condition using personalized information.

3 Cognitive Technologies for Question and Answer Solutions

Cognitive technologies attempt to provide a way to reproduce aspects of human thinking, adding the ability to handle large amounts of information without bias [11]. Cognitive solutions use advanced reasoning, predictive modeling and machine learning techniques in order to: (i) search and analyze data from multiple sources, (ii) process natural language, (iii) integrate the feedback/knowledge of distinct users. Cognitive services offer computer vision, speech, translation, text analytics, and data analysis as cloud-hosted APIs. IBM Bluemix Cloud Platform [12], Google Cloud [13], Microsoft Azure [14] and Amazon AWS [15] are good examples of such hosted APIs.

A Question and Answer (Q-A) solution can use cognitive technologies in order to automatically answer a question posed in natural language [16]. The aim of a Q-A system is to deliver short, succinct, answers instead of overloading users with a large number of irrelevant documents. An intensive study of several Q-A systems can be found in [17].

Due to the fast development of cognitive services, it is becoming possible to implement a Q-A solution interconnecting distinct cognitive services. Examples of base services that can be useful to implement a Q-A solution include the following:

(i)   Cognitive Search: A service that enables to extract insights from large amounts of structured and unstructured data. It ingests, enriches, and indexes massive amounts of data from a variety of sources and offers a powerful query language as well as a natural language query capability to return contextualized, ranked answers at scale. For instance, the Watson Platform provides this service under the name of Discovery. This IBM and AWS platform does not offer this service directly; however they claim that they provide some services (Amazon Elasticsearch Service and Bing Web Search API) that allow implementing this feature [18].

(ii)   Chatbot: A service that provides components to build conversational bots. The Amazon platform solution offers the possibility to maintain a conversation using voice or text.

(iii) Speech to Text: A service that provides a way to transcribe human speech correctly. Google Cloud solution supports 120 languages and variants, while IBM Watson supports just seven languages. However, Watson allows customizing a recognition model to improve the accuracy of language and content.

(iv)   Text to Speech: A service that converts any written text into spoken words. IBM Watson supports seven distinct languages and 15 voices, while Google offers more than 30 voices, and Microsoft more than 70 voices.

(v)   Translation: A service that offers a dynamic translation of text between language pairs. Some of these solutions allow customization. For instance, Watson supports three types of customization: forced glossary, parallel phrases and corpus-level customization; and Microsoft enables customers to build a translation system tuned to their terminology and style, using the translator hub.

(vi)   Natural Language Processing: A service that allows applications to understand what a person wants in their own words. Usually, it uses machine learning to allow developers to build applications that can receive user input in natural language and extract meaning from it. This service is usually integrated into the implementation of chatbots, directly or indirectly. Watson Assistance is an example where this service is offered. This feature is not offered by Azure, but tutorials are available to use LUIS in Boot Framework to build a chatbot (see [19] as an example).

Table 1 summarizes the services provided by various platforms of Cognitive Services.

Table 1. Cognitive service from IBM, Amazon, Google and Microsoft.

Platform	Cognitive Search	ChatBot	Speech To Text	Text To Speech	Translation	Natural language Processing
IBM Blue Mix Platform (Watson)	Discovery	Assistance	Speech-To-Text	Text-To-Speech	Language Translator	Natural Language Understanding
Google Cloud		Hangouts Chat	Google Speech	Text-to-Speech	Google Tradutor	Cloud Natural Language
Microsoft Azure		Bot Framework	Bing Speech	Bing Text to Speech	Translator Text	(LUIS) Language Understanding
Amazon AWS		Lex	Transcribe	Polly	Translate	Comprehend

4 The Experience with Watson Services

The IBM Bluemix Cloud Platform was selected as the provider of the cognitive services required to implement the Q-A function on the OnParkinson solution. One of the requirements concerning the Q-A feature was to provide a speech user interface, i-e., a patient would be able to put her/his questions orally and listen to the answer. As the OnParkinson solution has been firstly developed for the Portuguese market, the solution should provide interaction in the Portuguese language. Another important issue was the supported programming languages, since we were adding the new module into an existing mobile app. IBM Bluemix Cloud Platform supports Java, node.js, and PHP programming languages. Moreover, Watson services had already been used with success in health research projects [5, 20, 21], which gave us some confidence.

The following IBM Watson Services were used and integrated into the OnParkinson platform: (i) Text to speech; Speech to text, and (iii) Discovery module (see Fig. 3). The Discovery service is the core of the Q-A solution, which allows searching both private and public documents whose response will be attributed through Watson's cognitive reasoning process. The reasoning system should be trained for more accurate results.

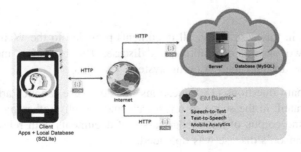

Fig. 3. The OnParkinson's architecture integrating Watson services.

The Q-A function on the OnParkinson app is called Ask. This feature includes the possibility to write or dictate a question. The obtained results can be read, or the user can opt to listen to the reading of the documents (see Fig. 4). The main element to make the Q-A function available is the Watson-Discovery Service. However, the performance of the system depends on: (i) the corpus of knowledge, where the Discovery will look for the answer, and (ii) the "training" of the Discovery system. As explained before, the Discovery System uses reasoning techniques to look for a suitable answer to the question made. In the case of the healthcare field, the delivered information should be reliable, since we are in a very sensitive area, where incorrect or inappropriate information may compromise patient's safety.

Fig. 4. OnParkinson's mobile interfaces: Ask Button; Post Question (oral, or written); Receive answers.

Therefore, in this case study, all documents provided to the Watson system were selected by two experts on Parkinson's disease. The following methodology was applied in order to train the reasoning system:

- A set of main questions (180 questions in Portuguese) about Parkinson's disease was elaborated, in the scope of a research study in physiotherapy.
- To create the corpus of knowledge, a set of documents with relevant information about Parkinson's disease was uploaded.

- The 180 questions were used to question Watson twice. In each iteration, the 180 questions were made and, for each question posted, the system retrieved a set of relevant documents with information that, according to the reasoning system, answer it. The expert scored each retrieved document according to the degree of fitness to the question posed (where a score of 5 indicates maximum relevance).

The "training" process must be performed directly in the Bluemix platform. Initially, the Retrieve and Rank service was used instead of the Discovery service, which allowed to score the answer directly by the end-user, but that service is no longer available.

The end-user testing regarding the ASK function has not yet been performed, since the system tests and the tests with the expert during the training process show that the information retrieved for some pre-defined questions is not satisfactory. From the analysis performed, and comparing with previous studies from other researchers [21–23], the poor performance achieved with Watson Discovery may be in the low amount of information loaded into Watson and in the small number of training iterations. Another relevant issue is that the implemented solution does not offer information tailored to each end-user, according to the user profile. Information for a patient should be presented differently from that presented to a health professional. Moreover, in order to have the Reasoning System tuned, both patients and caregivers, as well as health professionals, should be able to score the obtained answers.

5   Collaborative Cognitive Services Model

From experience with the Watson Services in implementing a system that provides tailored information, a set of services were identified as mandatory. In Fig. 5, the ASK process is modeled using BPMN 2.0.

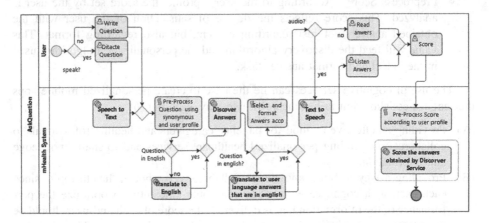

Fig. 5. Ask a question process as a model for tailored information.

The model represents the tasks performed by the user, and the ones executed by the mHealth system. The mHealth tasks are divided in:

1. Cognitive External Tasks – Tasks where cognitive computing is used. Preferably, these tasks are implemented using external services like the ones provided by one of the platforms referred in Sect. 3.

   - Speech To Text – In case the user chooses to dictate the question instead of typing, a service to convert speech to text is called.
   - Translate to English – In order to increase the search space, the question is translated into English.
   - Translate to User Language – The answers obtained that are not in the user language are translated.
   - Discover Answers – The question is submitted, and a set of answers is obtained. To increase the search space, if the user has a language other than English, two questions are sent, one in English and one in the user's language.
   - Score Answers – It is used to give feedback about the relevance of the answers retrieved by Discover Answers. The score value is used by the machine learning algorithm (of cognitive search service) to improve its performance.

2. Internal Tasks – Tasks implemented directly on mHealth System. Although these tasks are not called cognitive tasks, some of them apply techniques commonly used in cognitive computing, such as reasoning and clustering.

   - Preprocess Questions – This task makes a preliminary treatment to the original question. According to the user profile, the question is "rewritten" in order to make it more standard. Some words are translated, to avoid foreign words and dialect words.
   - Select and format answers - According to the user's profile, an answer is composed and formatted. (For example, if the user belongs to the short answer profile, the answers is shortened).
   - Preprocess Score - According to the user's profile, the score set by the user is analyzed. This score reflects the degree of satisfaction of the user with the obtained answer, not just regarding content, but also regarding format. This value will feed the discovery algorithm and the personalization algorithm used in the Select and format answer task.

The use of cognitive services can be the base to create personalized mobile apps that engage collaboration in healthcare in two ways (see Fig. 6):

(A) Providing an effective method for patients, caregivers and health professionals to collaborate on building personalized healthcare services and to share knowledge and information.

(B) Providing a way to build knowledge collaboratively about a health topic, since each user, as a cognitive entity, can contribute efficiently to optimize the performance of the information that is delivered (the score of each end-user should be pre-processed to obtain the general score that feeds the machine learning algorithm).

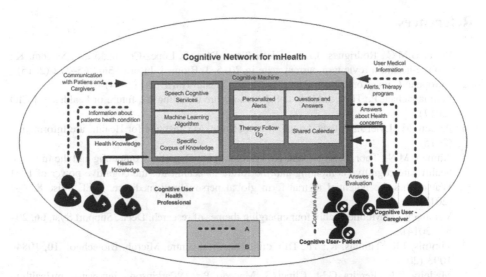

Fig. 6. Cognitive-based collaborative network for healthcare.

In fact, we can go further and consider users and the mHealth platform as being part of a cognitive-based collaborative network for healthcare [24, 25], providing an hybrid-augmented intelligence in which the end-users and the cognitive computing based apps are cognitive entities, which work collaboratively to improve health services and create knowledge.

6   Conclusion and Future Work

The study presented by this paper aims to (i) analyze how cognitive services can be integrated into mHealth solutions to provide end-users with tailored information through appropriate interfaces and interaction, and (ii) provide a model to support a collaboration engagement in healthcare, where knowledge about health is built collaboratively between end-users and cognitive computing based apps.

The cognitive services model is proposed following the experience obtained with the integration of Watson cognitive services into the OnParkinson mobile solution. The model identifies which services should be integrated in order to have a cognitive-based tailored Q-A system. Moreover, the model defines a set of "internal tasks" that must be implemented to provide personalized information. Another relevant issue, which was identified with the experience of using Watson, is the importance of the scoring process in order to fine-tune the machine learning algorithm. How the score of each end-user should be pre-processed before being "injected" into the machine learning algorithm is still an open issue in our research. Further developments aim to better explore the notion of a distributed health-related community as a collaborative cognitive system.

Acknowledgments. This work has been partially supported by the Center of Technology and Systems (CTS) – Uninova, and the Portuguese FCT-PEST program UID/EEA/00066/2013.

References

1. Silva, B.M.C., Rodrigues, J.J.P.C., de la Torre Díez, I., López-Coronado, M., Saleem, K.: Mobile-health: a review of current state in 2015. J. Biomed. Inform. **56**, 265–272 (2015)
2. European Comission: Green Paper on Mobile Health (mHealth) (2014)
3. Padmanabhan, P.: How unlikely collaborations are changing the future of healthcare | CIO (2017)
4. Aitken, M., Lyle, J.: Patient Adoption of mHealth. MS Institute for HealthCare Information (2015)
5. Ahmed, M.N., Toor, A.S., O'Neil, K., Friedland, D.: Cognitive computing and the future of health care cognitive computing and the future of healthcare: the cognitive power of IBM Watson has the potential to transform global personalized medicine. IEEE Pulse **8**, 4–9 (2017)
6. Varshney, U.: Mobile health: four emerging themes of research. Decis. Support Syst. **66**, 20–35 (2014)
7. Timmis, J.K., Timmis, K.: The DIY digital medical centre. Microb. Biotechnol. **10**, 1084–1093 (2017)
8. Madeira, R.N., Pereira, C.M., Clipei, S., Macedo, P.: ONParkinson – innovative mHealth to support the triad: patient, carer and health professional. In: Oliver, N., et al. (eds.) MindCare/FABULOUS/IIOT 2015-2016. LNICST, vol. 207, pp. 10–18. Springer, Cham (2018). https://doi.org/10.1007/978-3-319-74935-8_2
9. Pereira, C., Macedo, P., Madeira, R.N.: Mobile integrated assistance to empower people coping with Parkinson's disease. In: ASSETS 2015 - Proceedings of the 17th International ACM SIGACCESS Conference on Computers and Accessibility (2015)
10. Madeira, R.N., Macedo, P., Pereira, C., Germano, H., Ferreira, J.: Mobile apps to improve ThErapy-the health practitioner in your pocket knows you. In: ACM International Conference Proceeding Series (2017)
11. Chen, Y., Elenee Argentinis, J.D., Weber, G.: IBM Watson: how cognitive computing can be applied to big data challenges in life sciences research. Clin. Ther. **38**, 688–701 (2016)
12. IBM Watson Products and Services. https://www.ibm.com/watson/products-services/
13. Google Cloud Machine Learning at Scale | Google Cloud. https://cloud.google.com/products/machine-learning/
14. Cognitive Services | Microsoft Azure. https://azure.microsoft.com/en-us/services/cognitive-services/
15. Machine Learning at AWS. https://aws.amazon.com/machine-learning/
16. High, R.: The Era of Cognitive Systems: An Inside Look at IBM Watson and How it Works. IBM Corporation, Redbooks (2012)
17. Mishra, A., Jain, S.K.: A survey on question answering systems with classification. J. King Saud Univ. Comput. Inf. Sci. **28**, 345–361 (2016)
18. Strahan, B., Calhoun, J.: Create a Question and Answer Bot with Amazon Lex and Amazon Alexa | AWS Machine Learning Blog. https://aws.amazon.com/blogs/machine-learning/creating-a-question-and-answer-bot-with-amazon-lex-and-amazon-alexa/
19. Shang, E.: How to Build a Chat Bot Using Azure Bot Service and Train It with LUIS – Microsoft Faculty Connection. https://blogs.msdn.microsoft.com/uk_faculty_connection/2017/09/08/how-to-build-a-chat-bot-using-azure-bot-service-and-train-it-with-luis/
20. Gantenbein, R.E.: Watson, come here! The role of intelligent systems in health care. In: 2014 World Automation Congress (WAC), pp. 165–168. IEEE (2014)

21. Salvi, E., et al.: Exploring IBM Watson to extract meaningful information from the list of references of a clinical practice guideline. In: ten Teije, A., Popow, C., Holmes, John H., Sacchi, L. (eds.) AIME 2017. LNCS (LNAI), vol. 10259, pp. 193–197. Springer, Cham (2017). https://doi.org/10.1007/978-3-319-59758-4_20
22. Lally, A., et al.: Question analysis: how Watson reads a clue. IBM J. Res. Dev. **56**, 2:1–2:14 (2012)
23. Goel, A., et al.: Using Watson for Constructing Cognitive Assistants. Adv. Cogn. Syst. **4**, 1–16 (2016)
24. Zheng, N., et al.: Hybrid-augmented intelligence: collaboration and cognition. Front. Inf. Technol. Electron. Eng. **18**, 153–179 (2017)
25. Camarinha-Matos, L.M.: New collaborative organizations and their research needs. In: Camarinha-Matos, L.M., Afsarmanesh, H. (eds.) PRO-VE 2003. IFIPAICT, vol. 134, pp. 3–14. Springer, Boston, MA (2004). https://doi.org/10.1007/978-0-387-35704-1_1

Semantics in Networks of Cognitive Systems

Ontology-Based Semantic Modeling for Automated Identification of Damage Mechanisms in Process Plants

Andika Rachman[✉] and R. M. Chandima Ratnayake

University of Stavanger, 4036 Stavanger, Norway
{andika.r.yahya, chandima.ratnayake}@uis.no

Abstract. Damage mechanisms reduce the ability of equipment to deliver its intended function and, thus, increase the equipment's probability of failure. Damage mechanism assessment is performed to identify the credible damage mechanisms of the equipment; thereby, appropriate measures can be applied to prevent failures. However, due to its high dependency on human cognition, damage mechanism assessment is error-prone and time-consuming. Additionally, due to its multi-disciplinary nature, the damage mechanism assessment process requires unambiguous communication and synchronization of perspectives among collaborating parties from different knowledge domains. Thus, the Damage Mechanism Identification Ontology (DMIO), supported by Web Ontology Language axioms and Semantic Web Rule Language rules, is proposed to conceptualize damage mechanism knowledge in both a human- and machine-interpretable manner and to enable automation of the damage mechanism identification task. The implementation of DMIO is expected to create a leaner damage mechanism assessment process by reducing the lead-time to perform the assessment, improving the quality of assessment results, and enabling more effective and efficient communication and collaboration among parties during the assessment process.

Keywords: Ontology · Semantic model · Artificial intelligence
Damage mechanism · Automation · Cognitive system · Lean · Collaboration

1 Introduction

Damage mechanisms (DMs), such as corrosion and fatigue, relate to the process that diminishes the ability of process equipment to perform its intended function during operations [1]. DMs can lead to equipment failure and the release of hazardous substances, which is detrimental to the continuity of production and to the safety of personnel, society, and the environment [2]. Hence, DM assessment (DMA) becomes a critical task, to identify the relevant DMs in process equipment and to determine the appropriate mitigation technique and inspection method, in order to prevent catastrophic failure [3].

© IFIP International Federation for Information Processing 2018
Published by Springer Nature Switzerland AG 2018. All Rights Reserved
L. M. Camarinha-Matos et al. (Eds.): PRO-VE 2018, IFIP AICT 534, pp. 457–466, 2018.
https://doi.org/10.1007/978-3-319-99127-6_39

There are two main problems in performing DMA. The first is its tendency to be a time-consuming and error-prone task. The high number of items of equipment in a process plant and the complex interactions among factors that cause specific DM (e.g., material of construction and operating/environmental conditions) make DMA cumbersome and vulnerable to human error. Moreover, the DMA process highly depends on human cognition; thus, its results rely heavily on the assumptions, beliefs, and knowledge of the individuals who conduct the assessment [4]. Although industrial standards and company-specific guidelines exist to support the assessment [3], the lack of familiarity with these references may cause personnel to perform assessment based solely on their own knowledge and experience. Consequently, human biases and subjectivity are involved, causing the assessment results to vary from person to person.

The second problem concerns the multi-disciplinary nature of DMA domain knowledge. Various parties (e.g., materials/corrosion engineers, process engineers, contractors, etc.) collaborate on and contribute to the DMA process. However, there is a lack of methods which allow unambiguous communication and synchronization of perspectives among these collaborating parties. Consequently, different parties may develop their own terms to describe the same concept and semantic information [5], causing data mismatch and information inconsistency that hinder effective and efficient collaboration and information exchange [6].

The objective of this paper is to develop a DM identification ontology (DMIO) as a tool to tackle the aforementioned problems. The DMIO is an ontology-based semantic model that enables the conceptualization of DM knowledge in both a human- and machine-interpretable manner [7, 8]. Based on the DMIO, combinations of factors that affect the occurrence of certain DMs can be modeled into the Web Ontology Language (OWL) axioms and the Semantic Web Rule Language (SWRL) rules. This approach facilitates automated reasoning, to identify the relevant DMs based on the influencing factors and knowledge representation contained in the model. The application of DMIO is expected to create a leaner DMA process, by ensuring that the assessment is aligned with the specified guidelines, reducing the variability inherent in the assessment results, and reducing the overall lead-time to perform DMA.

Moreover, DMIO enables formalized communication within collaborating parties in the assessment process. DMIO provides structures for concepts in DMA domain knowledge that avoid semantic inconsistency and enable the effective and efficient collaboration of several disciplines and stakeholders in an overall DMA process [9]. It is a valuable tool for enabling unambiguous communication and the synchronization of perspectives among collaborating teams, as well as the interoperability and integration of tools and applications [10].

The remainder of this paper is organized as follows. Section 2 discusses the development process of DMIO. Sections 3 and 4 present the DMIO model and its implementation in Protégé. An illustrative example of DMIO implementation is given in Sect. 5 to demonstrate its utilization in a real case and to validate its functionality. Section 6 provides the discussion of the case study and Sect. 7 concludes the paper.

2 Development of Damage Mechanism Identification Ontology

The ontology construction process used in this research is adapted from Fernández-López, Gómez-Pérez and Juristo [11] (see Fig. 1). The main goal of the knowledge specification phase is to describe the purpose and scope of the ontology being developed [11]. The purpose of DMIO is to formalize DM knowledge in the process industries and to support automated DM identification. The scope of the ontology is static pressurized equipment (e.g., drums, filters, piping system, heat exchangers, etc.) in process plants. The DMA typically consists of three main steps: (1) data gathering, (2) DM identification, and (3) degradation rate estimation. The DMIO only covers the DM identification part of DMA.

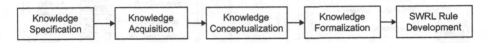

Fig. 1. The development process of DMIO

Knowledge acquisition involves identifying and elucidating relevant concepts in relation to the corresponding domain [11]. API 571 [12] and API 581 [1], the industrial standards that contain valuable concepts for identifying DMs in the process industries, are selected as the main sources for knowledge acquisition.

The knowledge acquisition step generates unorganized knowledge in the form of terms (e.g., instances, concepts, verbs, attributes) [13]. The knowledge conceptualization phase then arranges these terms into a structured model that describes the corresponding domain [11].

All the concepts and their associated relations, attributes, and instances from the knowledge conceptualization step are codified into a formal language in the knowledge formalization step. OWL, the standard language for ontology construction, is used to formalize the knowledge. This is supported by Protégé 5.2.0, an open-source software for building intelligent systems, based on OWL language [14].

SWRL is embedded to enable expressivity (i.e., rules and logic) in OWL [15]. In this study, the rules and logic established in SWRL are based on API 571. API 571 contains two main sections: (1) general DMs that are applied in all process industries and (2) DMs applied only in the refining industries. This study focuses only on the first section of API 571. In total, 39 DMs are coded into SWRL rules. In practice, API 571 is not used as the sole and final technical basis for DMA, but it is utilized in conjunction with the other related best practices and documentations [12].

3 The Taxonomical Structure of Damage Mechanism Identification Ontology

The DMIO represents the concepts, relations, attributes, and instances for performing DM identification in process plants. The DMIO, supported by OWL axioms and SWRL rules, becomes the foundation for automated DM identification in process plants. The visualization of DMIO is shown in Fig. 2. There are six main classes in the DMIO: the *Equipment* class, the *DamageMechanism* class, the *MaterialClass* class, the *Fluid-Stream* class, the *Unit* class, and the *Fuel* class.

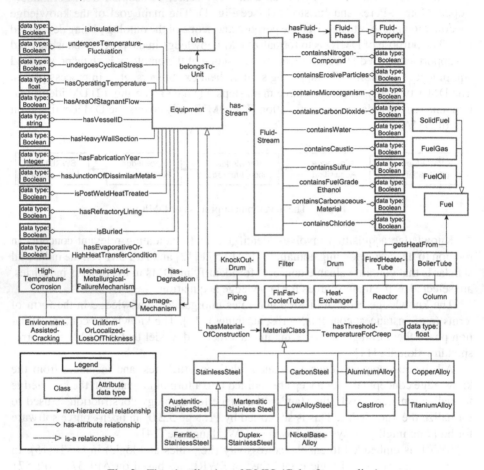

Fig. 2. The visualization of DMIO (Color figure online)

The *Equipment* class is central to the DMIO because the instances that undergo DMA comes from this class. The *DamageMechanism* class is related to the *Equipment* class through the *hasDegradation* property. The *DamageMechanism* class includes a set of damage mechanism types that affect equipment in the process plants, based on API 571. The *MaterialClass* is related to the *Equipment* class through *hasMaterialOfConstruction* property. The sub-classes of the *MaterialClass* represent the common material types used in the process plants.

The *FluidStream* class is connected to the *Equipment* class through *hasStream* property. This class embodies the actual fluid contained inside the equipment. The *Fluid-Stream* is also related to the *FluidPhase* class, to indicate the phase of the fluid stream. The *Unit* class, related to the *Equipment* class through *belongsToUnit* property, represents the process unit where the equipment is situated. This class is included in the ontology because the occurrence of some DMs (e.g., cooling water corrosion and boiler water condensate corrosion) is specific to certain units.

The *Fuel* class is related to two subclasses of the *Equipment* class (i.e., *FiredHeaterTube* and *BoilerTube*) via the *getsHeatFrom* property. The fired heater tube and boiler tube require heat energy to heat their fluid containment, and the energy source comes from fuel. The exposure of the fired heater tube and boiler tube to the emission and combustion products of the fuel can generate certain DMs, such as flue-gas dew-point corrosion and fuel ash corrosion. That is the reason the *Fuel* class is only related to *FiredHeaterTube* and *BoilerTube* subclasses.

In addition to class relationships, attributes are used to depict factors that can be expressed by literals (shown by the blue boxes in Fig. 2). These attributes are numerical concepts (e.g., operating temperature) or parameters that can be addressed by true or false value (i.e., Boolean data type).

Based on the DMIO, a set of SWRL rules, founded on API 571, are defined to identify the DMs. An example of a SWRL rule for one of the DMs is shown in Fig. 3.

Corrosion Under Insulation (CUI) of carbon steel description based on API 571:
CUI is a type of external corrosion that occurs on insulated piping, pressure vessels, and structural components, due to the presence of trapped water under the insulation. Insulated piping and items of equipment made of carbon steel and those that are in intermittent service or operate between $-12°C$ and $175°C$ are susceptible to CUI.

SWRL Rule for CUI of carbon steel based on API 571 description:
Equipment(?e) ^ hasMaterial(?e, ?m) ^ CarbonSteel(?m) ^ isInsulated(?e, true) ^ hasOperatingTemperature(?e, ?t) ^ swrlb:greaterThanOrEqual(?t, -12.0) ^ swrlb:lessThanOrEqual(?t, 175.0) -> hasDegradation(?e, CorrosionUnderInsulation)

Fig. 3. An example SWRL rule for corrosion under insulation (CUI) of carbon steel

4   Implementation in Protégé

The implementation of OWL-based ontology and SWRL into Protégé is described as a system architecture, shown in Fig. 4.

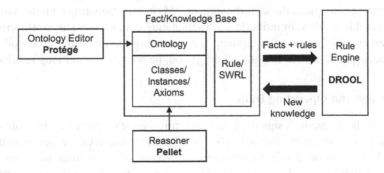

Fig. 4. Implementation environment of Protégé [16]

This system comprises four key components: (1) the ontology editor, (2) the reasoner, (3) the fact/knowledge base, and (4) the rule engine. Protégé serves as the ontology editor; i.e., it defines the ontology's classes, relations, attributes, axioms, and instances and puts them into a model that can be modified if necessary [16]. An excerpt of DMIO implementation in Protégé 5.2.0 is shown in Fig. 5.

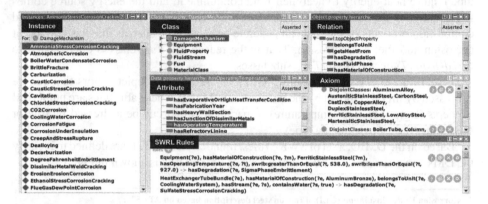

Fig. 5. An excerpt of DMIO implementation in Protégé

The reasoner provides the ontology editor with the capability to undertake automated classification and to check the consistency of the developed ontology [17]. In this study, Pellet is selected as the reasoner.

The fact/knowledge base contains the ontology and the SWRL rules. These facts and rules are passed to the DROOL rule engine, where they are combined and converted into new knowledge [16]. The generated new knowledge is then used to update the ontology.

5 Case Study: Identification of Damage Mechanisms in Fractionating Column in a Refinery

To demonstrate the utilization of DMIO and to validate its functionality in a real case, an illustrative example of the identification of DMs in a fractionating column in a refinery is given in this section. In refineries, a fractionating column is a part of the crude unit and is an essential piece of equipment for separating the incoming crude oil into its components parts, such as naphtha, light gas oil, heavy gas oil, and long residue.

5.1 Design and Operating Data

The schematic diagram, design data, and operating data of the fractionating column used as the case study are shown in Fig. 6. The fractionating column is not expected to undergo any cyclical stress or temperature fluctuation. No part of the column is buried, and no stagnant flow is expected inside it. The feed of the fractionating column is expected to contain some sulfur; other contaminants such as water and CO_2 are considered negligible. Components such as nitrogen compounds, caustics, chlorides, and ethanol are non-existent.

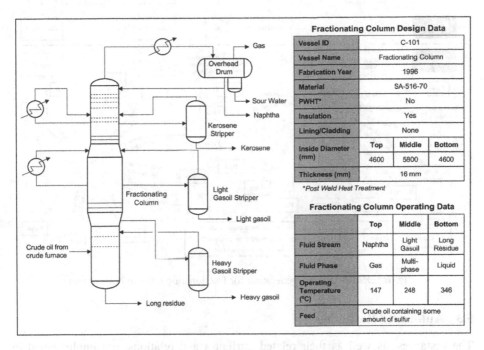

Fig. 6. The schematic diagram, design data, and operating data of the fractionating column

5.2 Instance Generation

Based on the aforementioned design and operating data, the instances related to DM identification for the fractionating column are generated. Because the fractionating column has different operating conditions in its top, middle, and bottom parts, three instances are generated for the fractionating column: *FractionatingColumnTop*, *FractionatingColumnMiddle*, and *FractionatingColumnBottom*. In this case study, only the *FractionatingColumnBottom* part is discussed.

The material of class construction of the fractionating column is SA-516-70. In the DMIO, the instances of the *MaterialClass* class are generalized, based on their general type. SA-516-70 is a type of low carbon steel, so it is modeled as a *LowCarbonSteel* instance under the *CarbonSteel* and *MaterialClass* class. An illustration of DMIO instances for the *FractionatingColumnBottom* is shown in Fig. 7.

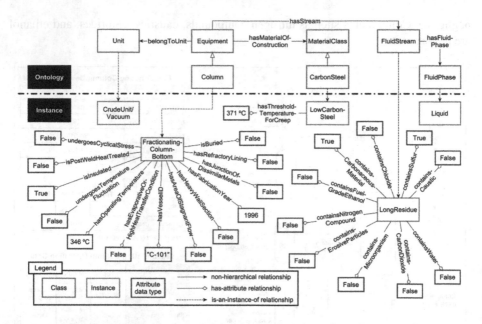

Fig. 7. DMIO instance generation for fractionating column bottom part

5.3 Automated Reasoning

The instances, as well as their related attributes and relations, are implemented in Protégé. To determine the credible DMs for the fractionating column, SWRL rules are evaluated by running the rule engine. Figure 8 depicts the asserted attributes and relations for the instance *FractionatingColumnBottom*. Based on the attributes, relations,

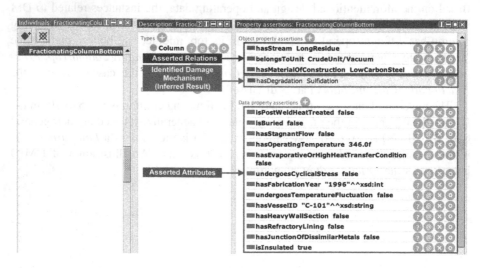

Fig. 8. The identified DM based on the automated reasoning for *FractionatingColumnBottom*

axioms, and SWRL rules, it can be inferred that *FractionatingColumnBottom* has *Sulfidation* as its credible DM.

6 Discussion

In the DMIO approach, the domain knowledge related to DMs is conceptualized into ontology classes, relations, attributes, axioms, and rules, in order to enable automated reasoning and the identification of DMs in processing equipment. Hence, the DMA process can reduce its reliance on the assumptions, beliefs, and knowledge of engineering personnel. The case study shows that the factors and constraints that influence the occurrence of DMs in the processing equipment are grounded on logic theory, such that semantic reasoning can be used to support the identification of credible DMs [16]. The case study only shows DMIO application on a processing equipment part. In practice, DMA is generally performed on thousands of equipment parts. This is the circumstance in which the benefits of DMIO will be more noticeable.

In manual DMA, the basis of performing DMA (i.e., assumptions, understanding, rules, etc.) is retained in the heads of personnel who perform the assessment. In contrast, DMIO provides an explicit documentation regarding the basis of performing DMA, which ensures the consistency and validity of the assessment results. Moreover, all concepts related to DMs are defined unambiguously and consistently in DMIO. This prevents data mismatch and inconsistency and, thus, improves collaboration and information exchange among parties involved in the overall DMA process.

This study focuses only on the DMs' definitions stated in API 571, but the ontology-based semantic modeling approach can also be used on the DMs' concepts defined by other guidelines. Furthermore, because DMIO's development is based on the knowledge acquired from API 571 and API 581, it is applicable to broad categories of process industries (e.g., refineries, petrochemicals, and oil and gas).

7 Conclusion

This study discusses the utilization of ontology-based semantic modeling to facilitate the automated identification of DMs in process plant equipment and to enable the unambiguous communication and synchronization of perspectives among collaborating teams involved in the overall DMA process. The DMIO is proposed to represent concepts, relations, attributes, and instances relevant to DM knowledge. Supported by OWL axioms and SWRL rules, the DMIO is the foundation for performing automated reasoning in identifying credible DMs in process equipment. To demonstrate the application of DMIO in a real case, a case study of DM identification in a fractionating column in a refinery is given. The proposed approach is demonstrated in Protégé 5.2.0, based on the knowledge acquired from API 571 and API 581. The result of this study is applicable within the scope of API 571 and API 581, which is the process industries.

This study proves that an ontological and semantic approach can be used to reduce the cognitive load of engineering personnel in performing DMA, reducing the human biases and subjectivity inherent in DMA, cutting the lead-time for performing DMA, and improving collaboration and information exchange among parties involved in the overall DMA process.

Acknowledgment. This work has been carried out as part of a Ph.D. research project at the University of Stavanger, funded by the Norwegian Ministry of Education and Research.

References

1. American Petroleum Institute: Risk-Based Inspection Methodology: API Recommended Practice 581, 3rd edn. American Petroleum Institute, Washington, D.C. (2016)
2. Singh, M., Pokhrel, M.: A fuzzy logic-possibilistic methodology for risk-based inspection (RBI) planning of oil and gas piping subjected to microbiologically influenced corrosion (MIC). Int. J. Press. Vessels Pip. **159**, 45–54 (2018)
3. American Petroleum Institute: Risk-Based Inspection: API Recommended Practice 580, 3rd edn. American Petroleum Institute, Washington, D.C. (2016)
4. Lintern, G.: The airspace as a cognitive system. Int. J. Aviat. Psychol. **21**, 3–15 (2011)
5. Frolov, V., Mengel, D., Bandara, W., Sun, Y., Ma, L.: Building an ontology and process architecture for engineering asset management. In: Kiritsis, D., Emmanouilidis, C., Koronios, A., Mathew, J. (eds.) Engineering Asset Lifecycle Management, pp. 86–97. Springer, London (2010). https://doi.org/10.1007/978-0-85729-320-6_11
6. Rajpathak, D., Chougule, R.: A generic ontology development framework for data integration and decision support in a distributed environment. Int. J. Comput. Integr. Manuf. **24**, 154–170 (2011)
7. Batres, R., Fujihara, S., Shimada, Y., Fuchino, T.: The use of ontologies for enhancing the use of accident information. Process Saf. Environ. Prot. **92**, 119–130 (2014)
8. Batres, R., et al.: An upper ontology based on ISO 15926. Comput. Chem. Eng. **31**, 519–534 (2007)
9. Kim, B.C., Jeon, Y., Park, S., Teijgeler, H., Leal, D., Mun, D.: Toward standardized exchange of plant 3D CAD models using ISO 15926. Comput. Aided Des. **83**, 80–95 (2017)
10. Rajsiri, V., Lorré, J.-P., Bénaben, F., Pingaud, H.: Knowledge-based system for collaborative process specification. Comput. Ind. **61**, 161–175 (2010)
11. Fernández-López, M., Gómez-Pérez, A., Juristo, N.: METHONTOLOGY: from ontological art towards ontological engineering. In: AAAI-97 Spring Symposium Series. American Association for Artificial Intelligence, Stanford University, EEUU (1997)
12. American Petroleum Institute: API Recommended Practice 571: Damage Mechanisms Affecting Fixed Equipment in the Refining Industry, 2nd edn. American Petroleum Institute (2011)
13. Lopez, M.F., Gomez-Perez, A., Sierra, J.P., Sierra, A.P.: Building a chemical ontology using methontology and the ontology design environment. IEEE Intell. Syst. Appl. **14**, 37–46 (1999)
14. Musen, M.A.: The protégé project: a look back and a look forward. AI Matters **1**, 4–12 (2015)
15. Horrocks, I., Patel-Schneider, P.F., Boley, H., Tabet, S., Grosof, B., Dean, M.: SWRL: a semantic web rule language combining OWL and RuleML. W3C Member Submission, vol. 21, p. 79 (2004)
16. Zhong, B.T., Ding, L.Y., Luo, H.B., Zhou, Y., Hu, Y.Z., Hu, H.M.: Ontology-based semantic modeling of regulation constraint for automated construction quality compliance checking. Autom. Constr. **28**, 58–70 (2012)
17. Zhang, S., Boukamp, F., Teizer, J.: Ontology-based semantic modeling of construction safety knowledge: Towards automated safety planning for job hazard analysis (JHA). Autom. Constr. **52**, 29–41 (2015)

Cognitive Based Decision Support for Water Management and Catchment Regulation

Ioan Petri[1($\boxtimes$)], Baris Yuce[2], Alan Kwan[1], and Yacine Rezgui[1]

[1] School of Engineering, Cardiff University, Cardiff, Wales, UK
{petrii,kwan, rezguiy}@cardiff.ac.uk
[2] College of Engineering, Mathematics and Physical Sciences,
University of Exeter, Exeter, UK
b.yuce@exeter.ac.uk

Abstract. The effect of climate change on water ecosystems include increased winter precipitation, severe floods, leading to fluctuations in stream flow in areas and affecting both fish survival and water supplies. Several methods exist for establishing projections of changes in precipitation with regards to river flows and water levels at the river-basin scale, but hydrological characteristics change remain difficult to predict. Ensuring optimization techniques for water systems becomes significantly important especially with the degradation of water ecosystems and increased risks for fish population.

On the other hand, water demand has increased in the recent periods with the population growth. Further changes in the irrigation water system demand are determined by climate change precluding the reliability of current water management systems and affecting on the water-related ecosystems.

To address these challenges real time water management and optimization strategies are required to facilitate a more autonomous management process that can address requirements for water demand, supply and ecosystem preservation.

We present a cognitive based decision system that performs river level prediction for water optimization and catchment regulation for preserving Usk reservoir ecosystem in South Wales. The research is conducted on the Usk reservoir in South Wales reservation that is seeking to preserve the ecosystem and for which we propose a more informed decision system for catchment regulation and water management. Our system provides five days river level prediction to regulate river levels by pumping from/to reservoirs and to create artificial spates during the salmon migration season and to coincide with periods of low river flow.

Keywords: Decision support · Cognitive systems · River prediction
Catchment management · Ecosystem preservation

1 Introduction

Research in water ecosystems has determined the need to use existing river catchment water supplies in a smarter way by having the ability to make decisions in real time. The objective is to address the decision making process involved in water management and catchment regulation by utilizing computer techniques and data analysis. This represents a key advantage for water resource coordination and process optimization by

© IFIP International Federation for Information Processing 2018
Published by Springer Nature Switzerland AG 2018. All Rights Reserved
L. M. Camarinha-Matos et al. (Eds.): PRO-VE 2018, IFIP AICT 534, pp. 467–477, 2018.
https://doi.org/10.1007/978-3-319-99127-6_40

employing data mining techniques on various sources of data. As data is continuously increasing, with sensors and meters broadcasting real time readings it is possible to devise scenario based optimization, where several hypothesis at the catchment level can be tested, results can be analyzed and understood and a decision can be determined in relation to requirements and constraints of stakeholders [1, 2].

There is a growing research interest on water management and ecosystem preservation that has been triggered by the changing conditions in climate, new urban strategies and increase in population. Such factors have led to the development of new businesses and technologies in the field of water management for addressing the complexity in the workflows associated with water and catchment regulation. Research has reported over time, variability and increased parameters for water demand and consumption which requires specialized methods for conducting optimization and informed decision at a catchment level. The field of water optimization and catchment regulation is large and complex; therefore regulation strategies and optimization are needed in order to address the water supply and demand requirements but also to address the degradation of the water ecosystems.

Cognitive systems have been intensively used for multi-objective optimization problems for facilitation analysis of different parameters and variables that may have an impact on a modelled phenomenon. Such systems require a data capture process from sensors and meters but also an expert computing infrastructure for conducting analysis [3, 4]. With such cognitive systems several interactions between the different sensors, devices, actuators, and controllers are facilitated, leading to the creation of "intelligent" collaborative decision systems which have embedded monitoring and controlling equipment and the potential to optimize various objectives along with operations and maintenance expenses [5, 6].

Cognitive based decision systems represent methods that use language processing mechanisms and machine learning techniques to simulate an existing reality and to assess potential risks that may be triggered in relation to monitoring parameters and studied objectives. Cognitive systems can be trained based on historical data by employing artificial intelligence algorithms and have the ability to mimic an existing system process and can facilitate behaviors, reasoning, adaptive reactions and an overall autonomy.

In this paper we present a prediction based cognitive system for decision support in water management and catchment regulation. The solution we propose is based on scenario modelling with artificial intelligence techniques for providing process management tools and to support informed decisions for users involved in the process on water resource preservation and regulation. Our system provides five days river level prediction to regulate river levels by pumping from/to reservoirs and to create artificial spates during the salmon migration season and to coincide with periods of low river flow. The described system supports collaboration of stakeholders in water management and facilitates integration of different knowledge systems greatly addressing the problem of catchment regulation.

The rest of the paper is organized as follows: In Sect. 2 we conduct a review of the state of the art from the field of water research; in Sect. 3 we present the approach and methodology of this study. We present the prediction system in Sect. 4 and we provide results and conclusions in Sect. 5.

2 Related Work and Approach

The recent research on water ecosystems and environment preservation aims at achieving a step change in water savings by applying and testing intelligent techniques for real time abstraction and discharge monitoring. There is an increased interest in creating an open, scalable, marketable and user-friendly system to optimize water resource management and replace the current licensing system. An innovative "just-in time" ability is required for creating substantial water savings, whilst also enhancing delivery on EU Water Framework Directive obligations. The objective on these researching attempts is to combine real time traditional catchment data with remote sensing to provide greater spatial assessment of catchment hydrological variability. Data systems development, predictive modeling and analysis are required in order to undertake and to test in catchments with farming, industrial and ecological stake-holders; and the regulatory viability developed with Natural Resources Wales.

The analysis presented in this paper are applied on the Usk river that has smaller abstractions for recreation and agriculture, but the test bed has been shown to be a robust model for constructing and testing scenario-based optimization. The mean annual daily water demand is around 200 Ml/day from the Usk where the River Usk also provides an important site for testing freshwater ecological requirements. Natural Resources Wales collaborate with the Usk and Wye Abstractors Group (and other organizations) to define the ecological flow requirements for ecosystem preservation. Although the Usk catchment is dominated by surface water supplies, groundwater plays a significant part in the water supply through boreholes – e.g. at Brecon. Groundwater factors needs to be considers and assessed when create a decision model. Transferability to other catchments and expansion to model conjunctive use schemes, such as SEWCUS (South East Wales Conjunctive Use System) are objectives to be addressed in order to achieve a smarter water management.

Several research studies on water optimization are seeking to devise a more intelligent water management system by conducting dependency analysis and mod-elling for water resources and corresponding mechanisms for adaptation, demand and response to changes. The results of these studies have provide useful insights for the water management domain and delivered an improved quality-of-services to respond to continuous increase of water demand. This study aims at designing and implementing a cognitive based system for water resources but also inform the work on water distri-bution networks where new parameters are relevant such as: topology, pressure control, leakage and resilience. The realisation of an intelligent system for water management should therefore take into consideration concepts from ICT, cloud and big data all connecting to data capture points supported with sensing capability and prediction in water level to facility water network management and regulation [7].

Prediction based cognitive systems use artificial neural networks for rainfall probability modelling and represents a key strategy to serve in the process of planning, utilisation and cording of water based workflows [8]. There are multiple data analysis and mining tools and techniques leveraging on artificial neural networks aiming at providing water projections and forecasting of events which have an associated probability of occurrence [9, 10]. Similar techniques are Support Vector Machine

(SVM) techniques, that are frequently used for undertaking hydrological modelling and address the increased complexity that is derived with the modelling and prediction process for water management [11, 12].

In this paper we present a prediction based cognitive system for river catchment regulation to assist users and stakeholder to collaborate in the process of decision management. We use the Usk reservoir (see Fig. 1) as a trial case utilising raw data captured from water stations sensing equipment and employ artificial neural networks techniques to forecast river level and flow for the stations part of the trial project. This cognitive system is then aimed to serve for a water decision system that can support actors involved in water business and ecosystem preservation to manage risk and conduct real time analysis for catchment regulation.

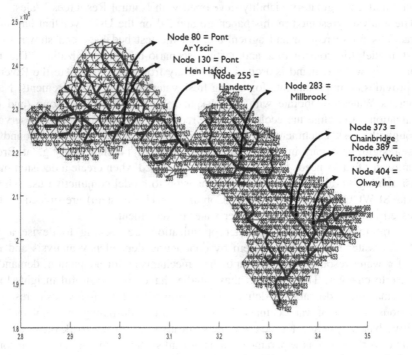

Fig. 1. The Usk reservoir model: Nodes identify stations that are part of our analysis: Pont ArYscir, Pont Hen Hafod, Llandetty, Millbrook, Chainbridge, Trostrey Weir, Olway Inn.

3   Methodology

The decision support cognitive system proposed in the paper utilizes artificial neural techniques to deliver five days forecasting in river depth and river flow for the Usk reservoir. We devise our system in multiple layers which interact and exchange data with the general objective of facilitating water management and ecosystem preservation.

3.1 Architecture

The architecture of the system is formed by three different layers which interact and facilitate data transfer and transformation from data capture layer to user decision support:

In the data capture layer, data is retrieved from the capture points identifying the seven stations within the Usk river. We have implemented a service that retrieves data based on hourly basis for the following stations: "PontArYscir", "Pont Hen Hafod", "Llandetty", "Millbrook", "Chain bridge", "Trostrey Weir", "Olway Inn".

The reading points at the station level broadcast periodical river depth values which are then transformed into equivalents river flow values by the prediction layer. To conduct the cognitive process weather data is also retrieved by a service that stores rainfall information associated with the reservoir from the UK Met Office weather service.

For the prediction layer we have implemented several modules: the Harbour module for station river data sets, the neural network module for prediction and the i-Depend module for dependency modeling module.

In the Harbour module, developed by Cambrensis (an industrial partner), we store the river depth datasets which is further used as an input for the prediction module. This module is formed of services that retrieve river data via an HTTP layer triggered on hourly intervals.

The artificial neural network (ANN) utilizes three main prediction objectives: river depth, river flow and rainfall. These objectives support the overall forecasting at the catchment level and are used to create a more informed decision making system for users (Fig. 2).

The i-Depend module enables a dependency modeling process and utilizes as inputs the results generated by the prediction model. An interaction between layers and modules alongside the overall architecture of the system are presented in Fig. 3. To support the functionality of the system for data analysis, forecasting and dependency modeling, a cluster based infrastructure is used.

The user layer facilitates direct interaction between users and the computer based system where several predictions and dependency modeling techniques are undertaken in relation to scenario data analysis for the catchment regulation. The web interface takes into account users profiles and preferences and enables users to access knowledge representation based on the previous analysis.

Users can create specialized use-cases based on agreed objectives to understand how the reservoir can evolve and to simulate river scenario projections that can inform decision and mitigate possible risks.

3.2 Modeling the Cognitive System with Artificial Neural Network

For the cognitive system we consider an ANN (Artificial Neural Network) prediction function with inputs and pre-determined objectives such as: $f(a) : Ia \rightarrow Ra$, where Ia : $[d_i, r_i]$ represents the input of the ANN system (d_i is the river depth of node n_i, where node n_i is a station s_i from the reservoir), r_i identified the rainfall of node n_i and $Ra \rightarrow [p_d, p_f, p_r]$ represents the results associated with the prediction engine (p_d is the

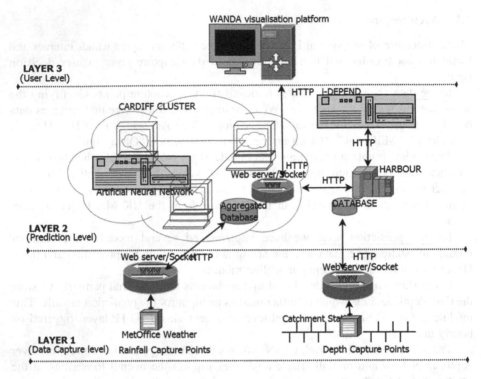

Fig. 2. The cognitive based decision support system architecture; The system includes: (i) the data capture layers used to fetch river data, (ii) the artificial neural network layer used to predict river flow and river depth and (iii) the user layer for presenting the results of the prediction for decision makers.

predicted depth for n_i, pf is the predicted flow for n_i, p_r is the predicted rainfall). The set of input values I_a is formed of readings recorded at the station level whereas R_a determines the output for the prediction engine identifying river depth, river flow and rainfall.

The development of the ANN system identifies several stages in relation to training and calibration. The artificial neural network involves calibration stages where a cost function is utilized for increasing the accuracy of the forecasting process. The training is performed over multiple rounds and multiple historical datasets which are prepared and pre-processed to serve into the prediction process. The ANN has been configured to return the river depth, river flow and rainfall for the sever stations within the Usk reservoir as illustrated in Fig. 3.

Several ANN models have been tested to find the best configuration on both Visual Studio platform and MATLAB. For C++ Based Fast ANN (FANN) models we have used: (i) Standard Backpropagation - where the weights are updated after each training pattern and (ii) Advanced batch training - not use the learning rate (default training algorithm). For MATLAB based ANN models we have used: (i) Conjugate Gradient Backpropagation with Powell-Beale restarts and (ii) Gradient Descent Backpropagation.

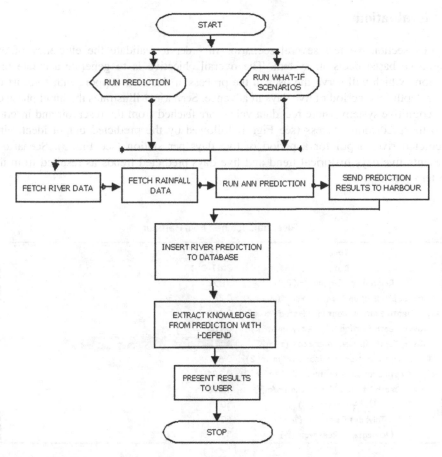

Fig. 3. The overall cognitive based decision system workflow: This workflow identifies: scenario definition phase to support the prediction, data capture phase with (i) river data and (ii) rainfall data, prediction deployment and user interfacing with results.

The elaboration of the ANN module consisted in multiple training rounds where 80% of the stored datasets have been utilized while the remaining 20% was utilized for the testing phase. With the training and calibration process the results accuracy of the ANN has been identified in value of 93% for all the selected objectives: river depth, river flow and rainfall. A challenge in the ANN development process was the quality of data and fluctuation of the recorded values to which we have applied different normalization techniques which led to an improvement in the overall results. In total the resulted ANN performance for one step ahead prediction of river depth, river flow has been indentified in average of 93%. An exception is the rainfall which has been recorded with an accuracy of 89%.

4 Evaluation

In this section we test several scenarios in order to validate the efficiency of our cognitive based decision system. The overall objective is to generate accurate predictions which will serve the user in the process of decision support with forecast on river depth for a period of five days in advance. Scenario 1 illustrates the input phase on the cognitive system where real data values are fetched from the reservoir and inserted into the prediction process (see Fig. 4) followed by the predicted output identifying predicted river depth for a period of five days per station (see Fig. 5). Scenario 2 presents five days historical trend and five days predicted trends as resulted from the system (see Fig. 6).

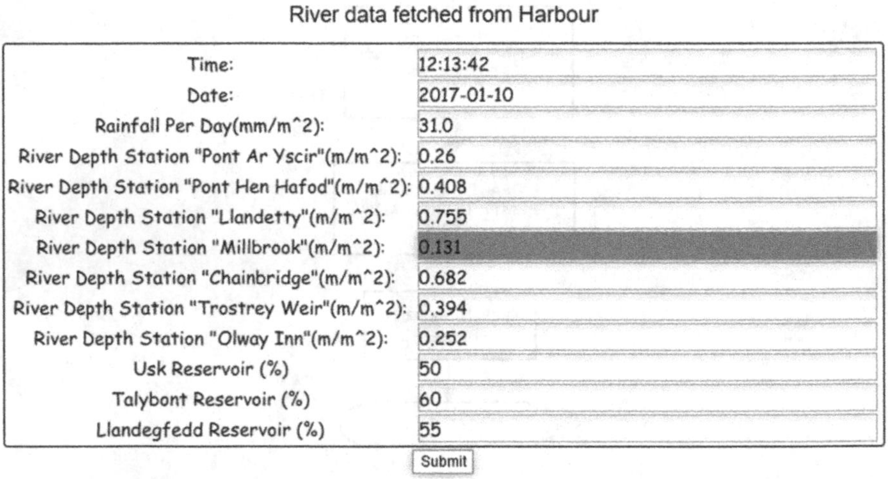

River data fetched from Harbour

Time:	12:13:42
Date:	2017-01-10
Rainfall Per Day(mm/m^2):	31.0
River Depth Station "Pont Ar Yscir"(m/m^2):	0.26
River Depth Station "Pont Hen Hafod"(m/m^2):	0.408
River Depth Station "Llandetty"(m/m^2):	0.755
River Depth Station "Millbrook"(m/m^2):	0.131
River Depth Station "Chainbridge"(m/m^2):	0.682
River Depth Station "Trostrey Weir"(m/m^2):	0.394
River Depth Station "Olway Inn"(m/m^2):	0.252
Usk Reservoir (%)	50
Talybont Reservoir (%)	60
Llandegfedd Reservoir (%)	55

Submit

Fig. 4. The data capture phase within the prediction based cognitive process: Several scenario variables are retrieved and used as input for the prediction phase. These variables are of two types: (i) river based variables and (ii) system based variables.

4.1 Scenario 1: Overall Catchment River Level Prediction

This scenario investigates the impact of river depth as a mean to monitor the evolution of the Usk reservoir in the determined evaluation interval of five days. With data retrieved from the capture points at the station level and rainfall recorded with a services dedicated for the MetOffice UK, the system determines trends for river depth for an interval of five days.

As reported in Fig. 4, there are several variables that we consider in the overall scenario development phase which after rounds of modeling, training and forecasting can provided the evolution of river depth for the monitored stations. In Fig. 5 we present the results of the scenario reported in Fig. 4, with predicted values for all stations and a graphical comparison of the predicted river depth and actual river depth.

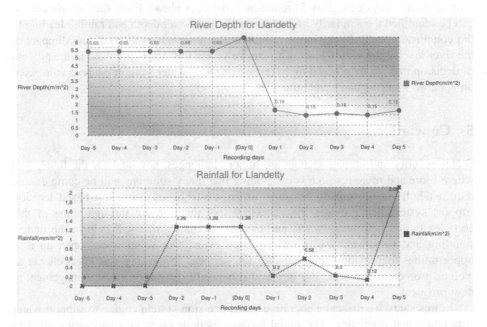

Type of parameter(mm/m^2)	Value
Initial Rainfall	31.0

Type of Parameter(m/m^2)	[Initial River Depth]	[Day 1 Prediction]	[Day 2 Prediction]	[Day 3 Prediction]	[Day 4 Prediction]	[Day 5 Prediction]
River Depth Station Pont Ar Yscir	0.26	6.1089	0.5523	0.1736	0.1833	0.2438
River Depth Station Pont Hen Hafod	0.408	0.6107	0.6542	0.3234	0.2747	0.2997
River Depth Station Llandetty	0.755	6.2587	2.3928	0.7108	0.5873	0.6916
River Depth Station Millbrook	0.131	3.8261	0.3336	0.1573	0.1531	0.2027
River Depth Station Chainbridge	0.682	1.1865	5.4420	3.5638	2.7568	2.3763
River Depth Station Trostrey Weir	0.394	7.0770	2.3800	1.6960	1.5445	1.4157
River Depth Station Olway Inn	0.252	5.6093	2.9953	2.1567	1.9466	1.8426

Fig. 5. The output of the decision process; identifying initial river depth and initial rainfall together with the predicted values for river depth, on five days forecast interval for all seven stations within the Usk reservoir.

Fig. 6. Station based prediction with historical river depth and rainfall: In this illustration Llandetty station is presented for five days historical and five days forecast. [Day 0] represents the current day whereas [Day –5, Day –1] is a five days historical period and [Day 1, Day 5] represents five days in future.

It can be observed that the cognitive system is based on the ANN engine and can support simulation of various what-if scenarios where possible events at the river level and at the weather level can be identified and impact can be determined for a period of five days in future. Such scenario based simulation can prove to be extremely efficient for users involved in the process of decision management at the river level and can lead to more informed strategies and coordination of a water ecosystem.

Figure 4 illustrates the input of the simulation where variables have been selected after sensitive analysis of the overall repository of historical data. These historical data have informed the modeling process of the ANN which has returned the forecasted values for station river depth as illustrated in Fig. 5.

4.2 Scenario 2: Station River Depth Prediction

This scenario focuses on per station evaluation of the river depth in order to provide a more concise and focused evaluation. On a station level the user is more interested in determining shorted intervals evolution of the river depth in relation to variables that can impact such river depth projections independently to other stations. Using a similar methodology as in the multiple stations context, Fig. 6 illustrates past, current and future river depth trends for river depth and rainfall on a per station basis. The analysis are conducted on the intervals [Day −5, Days 5], where [Day 0] is today, [Day −5] represents five days ago, [Day 5] represents five days ahead. From the experiments, it can be identified the similarity in fluctuation between river depth and rainfall leading to the conclusion that a change in the rainfall at the reservoir level has a direct impact of the river level at the station level. This can be utilized by actors involved in the process of decision making by proceeding to release or retain water from/in the reservoir based on specific water management strategies.

5 Conclusions

Water security and climate change are major challenges, now and for the future and where more and more research is concluding that many solutions will be complex and require a holistic approach. In this paper we have established a cognitive based decision support system that provides the necessary tool that can cut through some of this complexity and help users to test and evaluate scenarios that will help in the under-standing and visualization of a water related event. Our solution can open up new opportunities to provide additional decision services to existing customers/clients as well as promoting and using this new and enhanced expertise on water management to new prospects.

In this study we present a cognitive based decision system engine to support water simulation and prediction. The initial analysis is undertaken at a per-station level to understand the impact of rainfall at the level of a station and to study various relevant scenarios which can inform the implementation of strategic decisions at the catchment level. The Usk reservoir has represented an extremely dynamic pilot project where multiple variables are involved and multiple objectives need to be assessed in order to create a more informed water management process based on a cognitive evaluation supported by ANN algorithms. Such development at the catchment level can be of impact to manage water resources and to address the set of factors associated with the process of water management and catchment regulation.

Acknowledgments. This work is part of the Innovate UK Water Security Project: "Developing a Real Time Abstraction & Discharge Permitting Process for Catchment Regulation and Optimized Water Management", grant number: 504460.

References

1. McCann, J.A., et al.: Optimized water demand management through intelligent sensing and analytics: the WISDOM approach (2014)
2. Adarsh, S., et al.: Appropriate data normalization range for daily river flow forecasting using an artificial neural networks. In: Hydroinformatics in Hydrology, Hydrogeology and Water Resources, pp. 51–57. International Association of Hydrological Sciences Publication, UK (2009)
3. Petri, I., Diaz-Montes, J., Zou, M., Zamani, A.R., Beach, T.: Distributed multi-cloud based building data analytics. In: Kecskemeti, G., Kertesz, A., Nemeth, Z. (eds.) Developing Interoperable and Federated Cloud Architecture, pp. 1–398. IGI Global (2016). https://doi.org/10.4018/978-1-5225-0153-4
4. Yuce, B., Li, H., Rezgui, Y., Petri, I., Jayan, B., Yang, C.: Utilizing artificial neural network to predict energy consumption and thermal comfort level: an indoor swimming pool case study. Energy Build. **80**, 45–56 (2014). ISSN 0378-7788
5. Robles, T., et al.: An Internet of Things-based model for smart water management. In: 28th International Conference on Advanced Information Networking and Applications Workshops (WAINA), Victoria, pp. 821–826 (2014). https://doi.org/10.1109/waina.2014.129
6. Kumura, T., Suzuki, N., Takahashi, M., Tominaga, S., Morioka, S., Ivan, S.: Smart water management technology with intelligent sensing and ICT for the integrated water systems. Special Issue on Solutions for Society - Creating a Safer and More Secure Society (2015)
7. Tadokoro, H., Onishi, M., Kageyama, K., Kurisu, H., Takahashi, S.: Smart water management and usage systems for society and environment, Hitachi Report, pp. 164–171 (2016)
8. Dimitri, P.S., Khada, N.D.: Model trees as an alternative to neural networks in rainfall-runoff modelling. Hydrol. Sci. J. **48**(3), 399–411 (2003)
9. Vapnik, V.: The Nature of Statistical Learning Theory. Springer, New York (1995). https://doi.org/10.1007/978-1-4757-3264-1
10. Schlkopf, B., Smola, A., Williamson, R., Bartlett, P.: New support vector algorithms. Neural Comput. **12**, 1207–1245 (2000)
11. Liu, Y., Pender, G.: Carlisle 2005 urban flood event simulation using cellular automata-based rapid flood spreading model. Soft. Comput. **17**(1), 29–37 (2013)
12. Wang, W.C., Chau, K.W., Cheng, C.T., Qiu, L.: A comparison of performance of several artificial intelligence methods for forecasting monthly discharge time series. J. Hydrol. **374**(3–4), 294–306 (2009)

Achieving Smart Water Network Management Through Semantically Driven Cognitive Systems

Thomas Beach[(⊠)], Shaun Howell, Julia Terlet, Wanqing Zhao,
and Yacine Rezgui

School of Engineering, Cardiff University,
5 the Parade, Roath, Cardiff CF243AA, UK
{beachth, howellsk, terletj, zhaow3,
rezguiy}@cardiff.ac.uk

Abstract. Achieving necessary resilience levels in urban water networks is a challenging proposition, with water network operators required to ensure a constant supply of treated water at pre-set pressure levels to a huge number of homes and businesses, all within strict budgetary restrictions. To achieve this, water network operators are required to overcome significant obstacles, including ageing assets within their infrastructure, the wide geographical area over which assets are spread, problematic internet connectivity in remote locations and a lack of interoperability between water network operator ICT systems. These issues act as key blockers for the deployment of smart water network management technologies such as optimisation, data driven modelling and dynamic water demand management. This paper presents how the use of a set cognitive analytic smart water components, underpinned by semantic modelling of the water network, can overcome these obstacles. The architecture and underpinning semantics of cognitive components are described along with how communication between these components is achieved. Two case studies are presented to demonstrate how the deployment of smart technologies can improve water network efficiency.

Keywords: Smart water networks · Semantics · Resilience · Cognitive systems

1 Introduction

Urban water systems are responsible for abstracting, treating and delivering clean water. They also collect, transport, treat and release waste water. These systems, are among the most critical of a nation's infrastructure and are complex systems, spread over a wide geographical area, utilising ageing assets. These systems are operated under tight financial constraints, while also operating at near capacity. This increasing demand on water resources requires more efficient water management. The ability to intelligently monitor water networks and analyze real time information is one way to enable better management of the conflict between water demand and provision [1].

To overcome these issues, the water sector is undertaking a transformation using smart systems with water networks augmented with smart technologies having been noted to promote efficacy, efficiency, and resilience in water infrastructure [2, 3]. A big

© IFIP International Federation for Information Processing 2018
Published by Springer Nature Switzerland AG 2018. All Rights Reserved
L. M. Camarinha-Matos et al. (Eds.): PRO-VE 2018, IFIP AICT 534, pp. 478–485, 2018.
https://doi.org/10.1007/978-3-319-99127-6_41

part of these systems is the use of technology such as sensors, analytics software, and decision support tools. However, there are obstacles to deploying these smart technologies within water networks; (a) the decentralised structure of water networks where assets are managed and monitored by local technicians, with limited central monitoring/control, (b) the wide geographical area over which assets are spread, (c) problematic/expensive internet connectivity in remote locations, and (d) a lack of interoperability between water network operator ICT systems [4].

In overview, current systems to support the usage of these smart technologies are lacking in integration between sensors/actuators, analytic tools and, furthermore, lack the ability to contextualise the large amount of data collected from urban water systems in a way that promotes scalability, reliability, portability and future adaptability.

The objective of this research is to determine if the use of a cognitive systems approach overcomes the obstacles faced by water network management systems, and, secondly, if the use of semantics is an appropriate way of storing and contextualizing data within and about this system, thus improving interoperability. Thus, this paper presents a water management system augmented using cognitive software components, underpinned by a semantic model of the water network. The key novelty of this work is the application of cognitive system to large-scale water network management and, secondly, the utilization of semantics to contextualize; (a) data regarding the physical water network and (b) the structure of the cognitive system managing this network. The systems performance and novelty will be demonstrated by describing how these components can improve the performance and efficiency of water network operation.

The remainder of this paper will be structured as follows; Sect. 2 will present key background, Sect. 3 will present the overall architecture of a smart water network management system, focusing on the cognitive system components. Section 4 will provide an overview of the semantic model that underpins this management system. Section 5 will present two case studies demonstrating the functionality of this approach. Finally, Sect. 6 will conclude the paper.

2 Background

This section will provide a brief introduction to the two key topics discussed in this paper; (a) urban water systems, (b) their conceptualisation through semantic modelling and (c) the use of cognitive systems to manage physical assets in real world systems.

2.1 Urban Water Systems

Urban water systems can be defined as all processes and artifacts pertaining directly to the delivery of potable water to users and the safe removal of both foul and surface waters. The major processes of urban water systems include: (a) **water abstraction:** the extraction of water from a source, (b) **water treatment:** the purification of water, (c) **water distribution:** the process of distributing potable water from treatment plants to consumers, (d) **water usage:** utilization of water, (e) **wastewater collection:** collection and conveyance of wastewater to wastewater treatment plants and (f) **wastewater treatment and discharge:** the removal of contaminants.

2.2 Semantic Modelling

For software and humans to use data, they must derive knowledge from the data i.e. for a person to use a temperature to decide about what to wear, they must know that 'the temperature' is referring to an air temperature according to a specific unit of measurement. These semantics are typically implicit; a person can implicitly derive knowledge from a temperature with ease. In a software context, this translates to a developer evaluating the implicit semantics of data when building an application. To solve this problem of implicit semantics a semantic model can be used.

A semantic model describes the objects in a domain, and the relationships between them, in a machine interpretable manner. The use of semantic models can overcome the need for explicit integration of semantics within specific applications, reducing the time and cost necessary to develop these applications and resulting in applications that are portable and interoperable with other software components [4]. Semantic modelling has already seen significant use in the smart construction and smart cities fields [5]. However, other than recent work by the authors in [4] very little modelling widely adopted, or standardised in the water sector.

2.3 Cognitive Systems

Cognitive systems are systems of software components that exhibit cognitive ability. More specifically, these are components that can adapt their operation through their perception of the system in which they are deployed [6]. Cognitive systems are often described as being stateful, with the ability to perceive and contextualize the system in which they are deployed, and adaptable, possessing the ability to adapt their behavior to changing conditions. Cognitive systems have already seen considerable utilization in the management of the built environment. They have been utilized to manage power demand within smart grids [5] using a system of cognitive home gateways. They have also been utilized to add intelligence to the built environment, through intelligent spaces/zones/buildings and districts [7]. Finally, cognitive systems have been utilized in the smart cities context [8] to provide a cognitive management framework to show why and when objects in a smart cities system need to be connected, to enhance existing services and applications. However, despite this, the use of cognitive systems in the smart water field is rare, with their usage restricted by the slower pace of smart technology deployment currently encountered in this domain [4].

3 Smart Water Network Management

Our cognitive smart water network management system is a multi-layer event based systems featuring a series of cognitive edge services. As described previously, this system exhibits cognitive functionality to overcome issues commonly faced in the smart water field i.e. (a) the decentralised structure and wide geographical area of water networks, (b) problematic/expensive internet connectivity, and (d) lack of interoperability. The key cognitive aspects of the system are the ability of each edge service to independently manage itself, its communication and the analytical tasks it performs, based on characteristics that are specified within the semantic model. The system is broken down into two layers, core and edge. The core components operate over the entire urban water system and are generally hosted and operated centrally by water network operators. The edge components consist of a series of cognitive edge services, each of which is located at distributed locations within the water network and is responsible for managing aspects of the water network in that local area. Physically these edge services can be deployed on a variety of hardware from standard desktop computers, to custom made gateway boxes (left of Fig. 1) to small integrated controllers (right of Fig. 1).

Fig. 1. Edge service deployment methods

The detailed architecture of the system is shown in Fig. 2 and is now described in more detail:

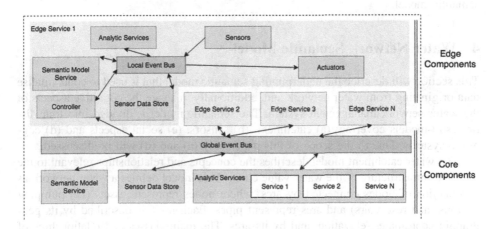

Fig. 2. Water network management architecture

Core Components: There are several core components; (a) a global event bus - responsible for distributing events to all other system components and edge services, (b) a sensor data store that archives all events from the message exchange, thus providing an historical record of all sensor readings, actuations and other event traffic, (c) a semantic model service - responsible for providing a virtualized representation of all aspects of the urban water system, through the use of the systems semantic model, and (d) a series of analytic services that perform analysis and generate new knowledge.

Edge Components: At the edge the system consists of a series of independent services that each consist of several components; (a) a local event bus - responsible for distributing events to all other components within the edge service, (b) semantic model service – that provides access to the semantic model, (c) a sensor data store that stores all data within the edge service, (d) a series of analytic services that act on the data stored within the edge service, (e) sensors/actuators within the water network that are connected to the edge service, and (f) a cognitive controller – that manages the operation of the edge service.

Communication between all components utilizes the common 'vocabulary' provided by the semantic model. This ultimately provides a common interface for software components to share data through that enriches sensed data with context and meaning. Additionally, edge services exhibit cognitive behavior through the cognitive controller's ability to intelligently manage adaptable analytic services. Each analytic service is problem specific, but the cognitive controller is a generic component that manages edge services based on characteristics specified in its semantic model. The key functionalities of the controller are to manage; (a) communication between the edge and core services, (b) the upload/download of event data between edge and core services and (c) invocation of the analytic services. Thus, the cognitive controller is the key enabler in overcoming issues of problematic/expensive internet connectivity in remote locations within water networks, by intelligently managing the use of the available internet connectivity following a set of characteristics specified in the semantic model.

4   Water Network Semantic Model

This section will describe the underpinning semantic model that is used to contextualise data originating from water network and, additionally, manage the cognitive aspects of the water network management system. The semantic model is divided into four distinct sub-models covering; (a) catchment, (b) sensors, (c) social aspects and (d) cognitive systems. Due to the scope of this paper only (a) and (d) will be discussed.

The water catchment model describes the concepts and relationships relevant to the physical infrastructure of the water value chain. This model defines a water network as a collection of nodes connected by arcs, where nodes represent assets (i.e. pumping stations, and reservoirs) and arcs represent pipes. Each node is described by its geographic coordinates, elevation, and by its arcs. The main classes and relationships of the catchment model are illustrated in Fig. 3, in this figure arrows with solid heads represent relationships, arrows with hollow heads represent sub-types.

The cognitive system semantic model describes the structure of the water network management system itself, conceptualizing the make-up of the water network management system. This model describes the edge services present and the core analytic services that are currently deployed. This includes describing what analytic services, sensors, actuators are attached to each edge service, and the connectivity that is present between edge and core services. This includes the description of connectivity rules/restrictions, and data transfer aggregators that apply. Table 1 shows the various configuration options that are currently describable by the semantic model.

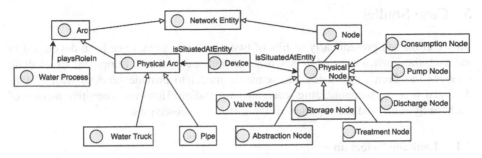

Fig. 3. Water catchment model

Table 1. Configurable properties for edge services.

Property	Description
Continuous	Service Execution - Services continually executed
Timed	Service Execution – Services executed at timed intervals
Event	Service Execution - Services executed based on received events
Connection	Service Execution - Services executed when connection to the core services exists
Availability	Connectivity Restriction - Edge service attempts to connect to core services whenever available
Timed	Connectivity Restriction - Edge service attempts to connect to core services at specified time interval
Priority	Connectivity Restriction - Edge service connects to core service to transmit high priority events whenever they are encountered. If no connection is available connection will be established as soon as available
Throttled	Connectivity Restriction - Data transmitted in each period will be limited
Connection Count	Connectivity Restriction - Number of connections in each period will be limited
All Updates	Connectivity Restriction - When connected to core services download all events received since last connection
Specified Updates	Connectivity Restriction - When connected to core services download all events matching a specified pattern received since last connection
High priority	Connectivity Restriction - When connected to core services download all high priority events received since last connection
Subsampling	Data Aggregator - Applies a specified subsampling method to the data over a given period i.e. transmit only hourly averages
Filtered	Data Aggregator - Filter out events that match a specified pattern from transmission
Presence	Data Aggregator - Transmit only the presence of specified events

5   Case Studies

This section will present early results of two case studies that have been developed to validate the applicability of this work. In both cases the development of analytic services has been eased using the semantic model to provide services with a standardized way of communicating/receiving information. However, cognitive aspects of each study differ and are reported in the following subsections.

5.1   Leakage Detection

This case study enables the detection of faults (such as leaks/pipe blockage) within a water network. The edge service in this case study is deployed at remote areas of pipeline where connectivity is either not guaranteed or costly. This edge service consists of two separate analytic services; a night flow service designed to detect smaller leaks and a burst detection service. To overcome communication issues this service will configure itself to produce and consume minimal data, reporting only detected leaks to the core and only receiving events that communicate updates to the semantic model (required to ensure it can correctly contextualize itself within the water network).

Night Flow: This is triggered on a timer when a flow reading taken near to 0200 is received. This service utilizes the water network semantic model to estimate the minimum night flow downstream of the point being monitored. If the measured night flow exceeds the estimated minimum flow by a significant amount, leakage is reported using a high priority even that is immediately communicated to the core services.

Burst Detection: The burst detection service is a simple data driven model that uses local sensor data to estimate the average flow at a given time of day. Whenever a new sensor reading is received, this service will update the data driven model with new sensor data, then, if the measured sensor data is significantly higher than the average for that time of day, a high priority leakage event is generated.

5.2   Data Driven Modelling:

This case study focuses on waste water pumping stations with combined sewer overflow tanks, many of which are in remote locations, thus data connectivity and costs are common issues. The goal of this case study is to use data driven models to predict the status of the overflow tank, and thus alert water network operators when it is expected to spill. Currently, water network operators can only detect a spill after it has occurred. This service consists of two analytic services that execute at timed intervals; a model updater and a predictor. To overcome connectivity issues this service will configure itself to connect to core services on a daily to transmit updated sensor data.

Model Update: This service updates the data driven model based on new data available from the water network. This service interrogates the existing data driven model on the edge service together with the water network catchment model to determine the data required to update the model to better reflect the current state of the water network. These data requirements are used to restrict the event updates downloaded from the core services. Once downloaded at the next timed connect the updated data is used to improve the existing data driven model.

Prediction: This service performs predictions using the data driven model at timed intervals. Should a prediction be produced that indicates the possibility of a spillage then this is communicated as a high priority event and the edge service will be immediately transmitted to the core services.

6 Conclusion

This paper has presented how the use of a set cognitive smart water software components, underpinned by a semantic model of the water network, are able to overcome obstacles to the adoption of smart technologies. These include the wide geographical area over which assets are spread causing problematic/expensive internet connectivity and the lack of interoperability between software systems.

These are underpinned by a semantic model, that provides superior interoperability between software components. This system also supports the deployment of cognitive services that can function intelligently independently of core systems components ensuring efficient and continuous operation of isolated components even when continual connectivity is not available or guaranteed. This paper has demonstrated the functionality of this approach through case studies showcasing how the water network management system can integrate analytic tools performing leakage detection and predictive modelling of the water network. In the future, more complex cognitive services must be developed to further validate the approach, current research directions include model predictive control of pumping and demand side management of domestic water usage.

References

1. Loucks, D.P., et al.: Water Resources Systems Planning and Management: An Introduction to Methods, Models and Applications. UNESCO, Paris (2005)
2. Kenny, D.: Smart Water Network Monitoring SBWWI Intelligent Networks. TaKaDu (2013)
3. Miller, J.M., Leinmiller, M.: Why Smart Water Networks Boost Efficiency. Schneider Electric (2014)
4. Howell, S., Rezgui, Y., Beach, T.: Water utility decision support through the semantic web of things. Environ. Model Softw. **102**, 94–114 (2018)
5. Barnaghi, P., Wang, W., Henson, C., Taylor, K.: Semantics for the internet of things: early progress and back to the future. Int. J. Semant. Web Inf. Syst. (IJSWIS) **81**(1), 1–21 (2012)
6. Thomas, R.W., Friend, D.H., Dasilva, L.A., Mackenzie, A.B.: Cognitive networks: adaptation and learning to achieve end-to-end performance objectives. IEEE Commun. Mag. **44**(12), 51–57 (2006)
7. Dounis, A.I., Caraiscos, C.: Advanced control systems engineering for energy and comfort management in a building environment—a review. Renew. Sustain. Energy Rev. **13**(6–7), 1246–1261 (2009)
8. Vlacheas, P., et al.: Enabling smart cities through a cognitive management framework for the internet of things. IEEE Commun. Mag. **51**(6), 102–111 (2013)

Collaborative Network for District Energy Operation and Semantic Technologies: A Case Study

Corentin Kuster[✉], Jean-Laurent Hippolyte, and Yacine Rezgui

BRE Trust Centre for Sustainable Engineering, Cardiff University, Cardiff, CF24 3AB, UK
kusterc@cardiff.ac.uk
http://www.cardiff.ac.uk/bre-trust-centre-sustainable-
engineering

Abstract. The growing interest toward renewable energies and alternative energy sources has led to the development of an increasingly complex district energy landscape with multiple agents and systems. In this new prospect, some frameworks such as USEF [1] or holonic multi-agent systems [2] propose new approaches, where, in the way of a Virtual Organisation Breeding Environment (VOBE) [3], diverse organizations cooperate on a long-term basis to run an energy system. This study focuses on the THERMOSS project, an EU-funded project that investigates the efficient operation of district heating and cooling networks, and demonstrates that such organisation can be integrated into the Collaborative Networks (CNs) paradigm. Additionally, a semantic approach is briefly introduced as a mean to support and improve data transfer and communication between the different entities of THERMOSS as a CN.

Keywords: Collaborative networks · District heating and cooling · Semantic

1 Introduction

Energy systems are changing with the current drive to reduce carbon emission from fossil fuelled energy sources. Indeed, energy planning is moving from centralized infrastructures to distributed systems where multiple renewable sources are integrated [1]. In this prospect, district heating systems are on the rise and a new management paradigm is emerging where network flexibility is key [4]. Demand-side management and demand-response approaches are deployed to fulfil multi-objective optimisation on energy cost, peak demand shaving, supply-demand matching and promote the use of renewable energy sources [4]. Such an approach relies on high-quality and extensive data, often in real or near-real time, placing data and information exchange at the core of the system [1]. The field is indeed moving toward a holistic and ICT (Information and communications technology) driven management of interdisciplinary and multi-agent systems and falls within the smart city movement [5]. Various parties pursuing a common purpose and leveraging a cyber-physical infrastructure make energy planning a form of collaborative network [3] (CN). Within a CN, autonomous, geographically

L. M. Camarinha-Matos et al. (Eds.): PRO-VE 2018, IFIP AICT 534, pp. 486–495, 2018.
https://doi.org/10.1007/978-3-319-99127-6_42

distributed, and heterogeneous entities join complementary sets of skills in order to achieve a common goal that would be difficult or costly with an individual approach [3]. Consequently, information exchange and interoperability between CN parties and software are prerequisites of an efficient implementation [2]. Some argue that heterogeneous data and communication protocols can be supported by semantic models [2, 5, 6] This paper presents the THERMOSS project as a collaborative network for smart district heating and cooling and introduces a semantic-driven approach for flexibility management of district heating and cooling. In a first part, the collaborative networks principles will be exposed and the new energy system paradigm will be described. THERMOSS will then be introduced and compared against collaborative networks theory. Ontology based systems are believed to be useful for the creation of a workable knowledge base for CNs [7]. Therefore, the ongoing efforts for the development of ontological data modelling are presented in a second part. Interoperability challenges will be introduced along with the ontologies considered to solve the issue within THERMOSS. Finally, the article will conclude on the benefits of such an approach as well as the future intended work in THERMOSS for its implementation.

2 Energy System as a Collaborative Network

In terms of organisation, certain complex systems would benefit from the added value of diverse entities that are not hold under the same well defined structure. This type of organisational structure has been theorised and formalised in the early 2000 by Camarinha-Matos and Afsarmanesh [8] as Collaborative Networks (CNs). Collaborative Networks are defined as a

> *"variety of entities (e.g., organizations and people) that are largely autonomous, geographically distributed, and heterogeneous in terms of their: operating environment, culture, social capital, and goals that collaborate to better achieve common or compatible goals, and whose interactions are supported by computer network"* [3].

The collaboration can take different forms depending on the duration, purposes, type of product and entities involved. Branches of CNs include [8]: virtual enterprise that is an alliance of enterprises formed to answer a business opportunity and communicate over computer network; virtual organisation that is in principle similar to virtual enterprises with the inclusion of non-profit organisation; virtual organisation breeding environment that is a virtual organisation relying on a "base" long-term cooperation agreement and interoperable infrastructure; e-science that coordinates resource-sharing and collaboration over a body of science; and a virtual laboratory that is a subset of e-science where the different research centres work together to solve a particular problem.

In a context where production is increasingly efficient and competitive, CNs are believed to achieve concurrency in operations, improve the workforce performance, effectively disseminate domain knowledge, reduce environmental impact, fast respond to needs and opportunities and be more innovative [7, 9]. Moreover, the growth in information and communication technologies (ICTs) supports the implementation of CNs by enabling distributed and heterogeneous systems and agents to share and communicate seamlessly [10]. CNs have already been considered in various areas such as:

- *manufacturing* for adaptive and responsive production [11];
- *construction* to better manage and coordinate large projects [12];
- *energy provider* for flexible and sustainable energy provision [13, 14].

The latter is particularly interesting in the current climate within the energy domain. Indeed, the energy system paradigm is changing due to the integration of distributed energy resources. It is moving from a centralized scheme where energy suppliers ensure the provision of energy from their own power plants to their end users, toward a distributed, bidirectional energy generation and distribution [1]. This new paradigm includes key aspects such as the integration of renewables, demand response, flexibility to reduce peak loads, system reliability, user becoming prosumers [15] etc. New stakeholder roles have appeared such as:

- *suppliers, balance responsible parties and producers* that need to ensure demand response and flexibility;
- *distribution network operators and distribution system operators* that must maintain network stability over peak loads and provide insightful information via the integration of smart meters;
- *transmission system operators* that must ensure energy flow balance against intermittent energy sources;
- *prosumers* that are partly producer and consumer and fully aware of the market and environmental concerns;
- *aggregators and energy service companies* that cumulate resource flexibility for a more reliable market and provide various energy related services such as maintenance or information services [1].

In this new prospect, initiatives have already been developed for the creation of distributed energy resources and its optimisation. An analogue situation can be observed in the heating and cooling sector where smart thermal grids are increasingly considered. This approach includes large scale and distributed renewable sources with well insulated distribution network, low temperature heat carrier and intelligent control and metering along with storage units that ensure cost effective and environmentally friendly energy supply [16]. THERMOSS is a European funded project that implements such innovative energy solutions for district heating and cooling (DHC) along with two decision support tools for a successful integration and optimisation: a sizing toolbox to facilitate DHC technology selection and integration; and an optimisation platform to control distributed energy resources and match need with demand. This study will focus on the latter.

Figure 1 shows THERMOSS structure diagram with a focus on the optimisation process. The different actors of the project are presented in the Social Agents group where their main contribution are allocated, namely optimisation developer, energy source provider, building and district manager and optimisation services provider. A colour code associates those contributions to physical and digital entities within the project. Additionally, the diagram presents the relationships between entities.

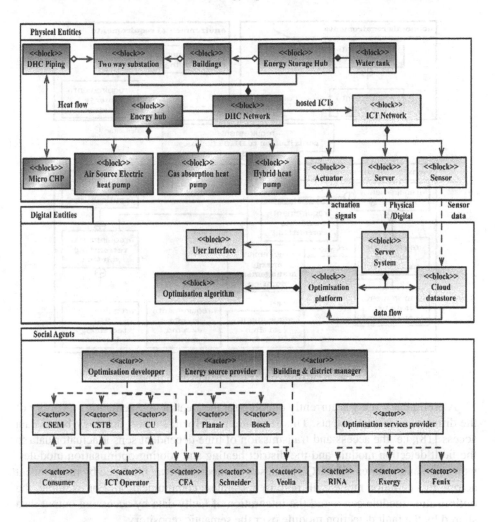

Fig. 1. THERMOSS SysML structure diagram: physical, digital entities and social entities.

Figure 2 shows the requirements that the project must fulfil collaboratively. This diagram formalized the economic, environmental and technical requirements that the project must fulfil and how they are linked together. According to the diagrams, on many aspects the THERMOSS project can be assimilated to a CN. Indeed, various entities are working together on the operation of a system that combines multiple domains for the completion of environmental, economic and technical objectives. Entities and requirements interconnections demonstrate the system dependencies and introduced a need for a collaborative approach. Table 1 refers to the 2016's Camarinha-Matos article [17] and shows how the THERMOSS project covers most aspects of a "collaborative smart grid".

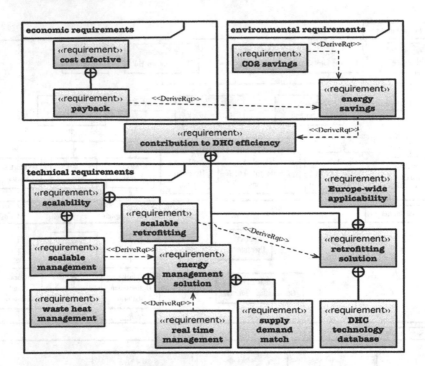

Fig. 2. THERMOSS SysML requirement diagram

A preliminary study is currently ongoing for the creation of a semantic repository of the different sites components. This semantic model will support ontology-based data access [18], i.e. the access and transmission of time-dependent sensor/actuator data to the fault detection module and the district heating and cooling optimisation modules, using semantic queries (SPARQL). Those two modules being managed by independent actors, this common model will help in a seamless communication. For example, the optimisation module can avoid the integration of faulty data by accessing output data shared by the fault detection module over the semantic repository.

Table 1. CN within THERMOSS (Sources for collaboration forms [17])

Catergories	Collaboration forms	Motivation	THERMOSS coverage	THERMOSS element
Value added services	Virtual organizations for service provision or long-term strategic networks/VO breeding environments	Providing services for energy cost and emissions reduction	✓	Optimisation services via the provision of optimisation platform and its algorithms
Energy market	Collaborative coalitions or virtual power plants	Smoothing peak demand via monetary incentives		
Customer engagement and behaviour change	Consortia of customers often relying on existing social network	Raising consumer awareness toward energy problematics to facilitate peak shaving		
Social smart grid	Dynamic consortia of consumers (a kind of collaborative cyber-physical system)	Dynamic monitoring for effective demand response and cost reduction	✓	Implementation of smart sensors that indirectly represent consumers
Energy management	Goal oriented consortia	Optimisation of energy demand-response and peak shaving	✓	Demand-Response and peak shaving optimisation with advanced control techniques for storing heat in the network
Infrastructure	Long-term networks of (smart) cyber-physical components, with self-organizing capabilities	Maintain and operate resilient, safe, and self-healing infrastructures	✓	Energy sources providers, district & building managers and ICTs operators jointly work on the implementation and maintenance of the infrastructures
Policy and roadmaps	Long-term strategic networks and goal-oriented virtual organizations	Ease collaboration between industry involved in energy infrastructure among them as well as customer		

3 Semantics for Interoperability Within THERMOSS

Interoperability is pivotal for collaborative networks, at a superstructural level, to homogenise information flows between heterogeneous organisations [19], but also, at an infrastructural level, to benefit from new cloud-based services [20]. More specifically, unifying semantic understanding throughout a collaborative network is key to overcome conceptual barriers, not only at the ICT level [10], but also at a higher level of abstraction [21, 22].

Ontologies are instrumental not only in:

- consolidating inter-enterprise knowledge [11];
- driving the design of services in lign with the Service Oriented Architecture paradigm [10]
- overarching heterogeneous data structures [23];
- but also, as exemplified in this paper, reconciling the semantics of multiple operational support tools (e.g. simulations, optimisation algorithms).

A key outcome of THERMOSS is the development of an optimisation platform and control system to balance energy supply within the heating network. The optimisation relies on data acquisition from sensors and control over actuators. There is therefore a need for the semantic representation of sensors and their readings as well as the different entities involved in data exchange and actuators. THERMOSS is currently investigating two ontologies as potential semantic basis:

- *W3C Semantic Sensor Network (SSN)* an OWL 2 ontology that defines capabilities and properties of sensors, their readings and the sensing process [24]. Based on the Dolce Ultra-Lite ontology (DUL), an upper level ontology, SSN and its core ontology SOSA (Sensor, Observation, Sample, and Actuator) are an extended version of the Observations & Measurements ontology [25] including sensors and their relationships. Physical sensors can be represented as *Sensing Device* that makes some *Observation*. An *Observation* is then link to an *Observed Property* (e.g. temperature) and a *Feature of interest* (e.g. air in the room 237). The output and its value are then represented by the *Sensor Output* and *Observation Value* classes. Additional classes allow the description of sensors networks (e.g. parent/child sensor relationships) and sensing processes (e.g. calculation method). Finally, even though locations, units, sensor hierarchy types were not included, they can be easily integrated via cross ontology object/data properties [26]. Several projects are currently using the ontology for application specific purposes [27–29].
- *Smart Appliances Reference Ontology (SAREF)* developed for semantic representation of smart appliances, including extensions for building and energy appliances. In SAREF, devices have a central role, being defined as "tangible object designed to accomplish a particular task in households, common public buildings or offices. In order to accomplish this task, the device performs one or more functions" [30]. Therefore, a temperature sensor is a device that is defined by its function "sensing" of "temperature" (*saref:SensorType*). Additionally, the device is related to a room or

space (*saref:BuildingSpace*). Finally, profiles are associated to devices and can be used for the optimisation of some properties such as energy for instance.

SAREF and SSN/SOSA differ in philosophy. While SSN remains abstract and can potentially describe any type of observation, SAREF is more industry oriented with concrete devices that serve well defined purposes. Semantic overlaps exist between the two ontologies such as *saref:Sensor* and *saref:Meter* are subclasses *sosa:Sensor*, *saref:Actuator* and *saref:Switch* are subclasses of *sosa:Actuator* or that *saref:Building-Space* can be seen as a subclass of *sosa:Platform* etc.

4 Conclusion and Future Work

Changing energy systems require changing organisational structures. Collaborative networks are believed to help in the establishment of virtual organisations in the energy sector where numerous entities from different domains collaborate to achieve a common goal. The EU funded THERMOSS project takes part in on-going efforts for the integration and management of renewable district heating and cooling heat sources. Focusing on the optimisation process within the project and supported by the literature, this paper has considered THERMOSS from the viewpoint of collaborative networks. Consequently, a key pre-requisite for THERMOSS as a collaborative network for energy balance optimisation is an efficient information exchange across domain and organisations. In this prospect, a semantic approach is considered with the use of a common ontology. Two ontologies have been addressed, the Semantic Sensor Network (SOSA/SSN) and the Smart Appliances Reference Ontology (SAREF) that have distinct approaches on the semantic representation of sensor networks within an urban environment and their readings. Future work would require the participation of the different partners of the project in a consultation through interviews and questionnaire. This iterative and participative process would then constitute a knowledge base across domains with relevant terminologies and identifies the overlaps with the existing ontologies. A more detailed methodology can be found in [5].

Acknowledgements. The research presented in this paper is financially supported by the Building Research Establishment (BRE) and the European Commission as part of the Horizon2020 THERMOSS (project Id: 723562).

References

1. USEF Foundation: USEF: the Framework specifications 2015 (2015)
2. Howell, S., Rezgui, Y., Hippolyte, J.L., Jayan, B., Li, H.: Towards the next generation of smart grids: semantic and holonic multi-agent management of distributed energy resources. Renew. Sustain. Energy Rev. **77**, 193–214 (2017)
3. Camarinha-Matos, L.M., Afsarmanesh, H.: Collaborative networks: a new scientific discipline. J. Intell. Manuf. **16**(4–5), 439–452 (2005)

4. Blaauwbroek, N., Nguyen, P.H., Konsman, M.J., Shi, H., Kamphuis, R.I.G., Kling, W.L.: Decentralized resource allocation and load scheduling for multicommodity smart energy systems. IEEE Trans. Sustain. Energy **6**(4), 1506–1514 (2015)
5. Hippolyte, J.-L., Rezgui, Y., Li, H., Jayan, B., Howell, S.: Ontology-driven development of web services to support district energy applications. Autom. Constr. **86**, 210–225 (2017)
6. Anda, M., Le Gay Brereton, F., Brennan, J., Paskett, E.: Smart Metering Infrastructure for Residential Water Efficiency: Results of a Trial in a Behavioural Change Program in Perth, Western Australia (2013)
7. Camarinha-Matos, L.M., Afsarmanesh, H., Galeano, N., Molina, A.: Collaborative networked organizations – Concepts and practice in manufacturing enterprises. Comput. Ind. Eng. **57**(1), 46–60 (2009)
8. Camarinha-Matos, L.M., Afsarmanesh, H.: Collaborative Networked Organizations. Springer, US, Boston (2004)
9. National Research Council: Visionary manufacturing challenges for 2020, visionary manufacturing challenges for 2020/committee on visionary manufacturing challenges, board on manufacturing and engineering design, commission on engineering and technology. In: Board on manufacturing and engineering design commission on engineering and technical systems (1998)
10. Rabelo, R.J., Gusmeroli, S., Arana, C., Nagellen, T.: The ecolead ICT infrastructure for collaborative networked organizations. IFIP Int. Fed. Inf. Process. **224**(3), 451–460 (2006)
11. Silva, N., Rocha, J.: VE Infrastructures Requirements for Cooperation and Knowledge Sharing. IFIP Int Fed. Inf. Process. **56**, 79–86 (2001)
12. Keller, M., Menzel, K., Scherer, Raimar J.: Towards a meta-model for collaborative construction project management. In: Camarinha-Matos, L.M., Afsarmanesh, H., Ortiz, A. (eds.) PRO-VE 2005. ITIFIP, vol. 186, pp. 361–368. Springer, Boston, MA (2005). https://doi.org/10.1007/0-387-29360-4_38
13. Allan, L., Menzel, K.: Virtual enterprises for integrated energy service provision. In: Camarinha-Matos, L.M., Paraskakis, I., Afsarmanesh, H. (eds.) PRO-VE 2009. IAICT, vol. 307, pp. 659–666. Springer, Heidelberg (2009). https://doi.org/10.1007/978-3-642-04568-4_68
14. Praça, I., Morais, H., Cardoso, M., Ramos, C., Vale, Z.: Virtual power producers integration into mascem. In: Camarinha-Matos, L.M., Afsarmanesh, H., Novais, P., Analide, C. (eds.) PRO-VE 2007. ITIFIP, vol. 243, pp. 291–298. Springer, Boston, MA (2007). https://doi.org/10.1007/978-0-387-73798-0_30
15. Rahimi, F., Ipakchi, A.: Demand response as a market resource under the smart grid paradigm. IEEE Trans. Smart Grid **1**(1), 82–88 (2010)
16. Lund, H., et al.: 4th Generation District Heating (4GDH). Integrating smart thermal grids into future sustainable energy systems. Energy **68**, 1–11 (2014)
17. Camarinha-Matos, L.M.: Collaborative smart grids – a survey on trends. Renew. Sustain. Energy Rev. **65**, 283–294 (2016)
18. Calvanese, D., Giese10, M.: The optique project: towards OBDA systems for industry (Short Paper)," OWL Exp. Dir. Work. OWLED, pp. 7–11 (2013)
19. Chituc, C.M., Toscano, C., Azevedo, A.L.: Towards seamless interoperability in collaborative networks. IFIP Int. Fed. Inf. Process. **243**, 445–452 (2007)
20. Petychakis, M., Alvertis, I., Biliri, E., Tsouroplis, R., Lampathaki, F., Askounis, D.: Enterprise Collaboration Framework for Managing, Advancing and Unifying the Functionality of Multiple Cloud-Based Services with the Help of a Graph API. In: Camarinha-Matos, L.M., Afsarmanesh, H. (eds.) PRO-VE 2014. IAICT, vol. 434, pp. 153–160. Springer, Heidelberg (2014). https://doi.org/10.1007/978-3-662-44745-1_15

21. Mulder, W., Rongen, P.H.H., Meijer, G.R.: Towards ontology-based CNO matching applied to squads. Collab. Networks Their Breed. Environ. **186**, 117–124 (2005)
22. Daclin, N., Chen, D., Vallespir, B.: Methodology for Enterprise Interoperability. IFAC Proc. **41**(2), 12873–12878 (2008)
23. Guevara-Masis, V., Afsarmanesh, H., Hertzberger, L.O.: "Ontology-Based Automatic Data Structure Generation for Collaborative Networks", in PRO-VE. Virtual Enterprises and Collaborative Networks **2004**, 163–174 (2004)
24. Compton, M., et al.: The SSN ontology of the W3C semantic sensor network incubator group. J. Web Semant. **17**, 25–32 (2012)
25. Cox, S.J.D.: Ontology for observations and sampling features, with alignments to existing models. Semant. Web **8**(3), 453–470 (2017)
26. W3C, "Semantic Sensor Network Ontology," 2005
27. Kharlamov, E., et al.: Ontology-based integration of streaming and static relational data with optique. In: Proceedings of the 2016 International Conference on Management of Data - SIGMOD 2016, no. ii, pp. 2109–2112 (2016)
28. Podnar Žarko, I., Broering, A., Soursos, S., Serrano, M. (eds.): InterOSS-IoT 2016. LNCS, vol. 10218. Springer, Cham (2017). https://doi.org/10.1007/978-3-319-56877-5
29. Atemezing, G., Corcho, O., Garijo, D., Mora, J., Poveda-Villalón, M., Rozas, P., Vila-Suero, D., Villazón-Terrazas, B.: Transforming meteorological data into linked data. Semant. Web **4**(3), 285–290 (2013)
30. Daniele, L., den Hartog, F., Roes, J.: Created in close interaction with the industry: the Smart Appliances REFerence (SAREF) ontology. In: Cuel, R., Young, R. (eds.) FOMI 2015. LNBIP, vol. 225, pp. 100–112. Springer, Cham (2015). https://doi.org/10.1007/978-3-319-21545-7_9

Dynamic Logistics Networks

Control Charts to Support Trust Monitoring in Dynamic Logistics Networks

António Abreu[1,2]($\boxtimes$), José Requeijo[3], J. M. F. Calado[1,4], and Ana Dias[1]

[1] ISEL - Instituto Superior de Engenharia de Lisboa,
Instituto Politécnico de Lisboa, Lisbon, Portugal
{ajfa,jcalado,asdias}@dem.isel.ipl.pt

[2] Centre of Technology and Systems, Uninova Institute, Caparica, Portugal

[3] UNIDEMI/SEM, Systems Engineering and Management, Lisbon, Portugal
jfgr@fct.unl.pt

[4] IDMEC-LAETA-IST-UL Lisboa, Lisbon, Portugal

Abstract. Nowadays, companies to be competitive must develop capabilities that enable them to respond quickly to market needs. According to some managers, the strategy is the development of dynamic logistics networks based on a collaborative environment. However, the absence of mechanisms to detect and even anticipate potential opportunistic behaviour is an obstacle to the proliferation of this way of working. The article aims to understand the role of trust to sustainability of collaborative processes. The paper begins by discussing the trust properties. It is then discussed how statistical control charts can be used to support the trust monitoring of each member within a collaborative ecosystem. The control charts' tools suggested in this paper are the Z control charts for trust level monitoring and the Zi capacity index. Finally, it is discussed how this approach can be applied to dynamic logistics networks within the context of a collaborative ecosystem.

Keywords: Trust · Logistic · Quality · Collaborative networks
Management

1 Introduction

Nowadays, in order to strengthen competitiveness, companies have to start learning to join forces in certain areas or competencies, and may wish to follow different paths in others, through the dynamization of intercompany relationships, giving rise to organizational models based on collaboration networks between companies [1].

With the rapid development of the technologies associated with the industrial revolution 4.0, in particular the information technologies and technologies associated with the Internet of Things (IoT), some authors defend the sustainability of new models which led to a proliferation of new designations such as the notion of virtual company/virtual organization, collaborative supply chain, Dynamic Supply Chain, Lean Supply Chain, among others [2–4]. Thus, the concept of dynamic logistics network should not be interpreted as a totally new model of cooperation, but as a process

© IFIP International Federation for Information Processing 2018
Published by Springer Nature Switzerland AG 2018. All Rights Reserved
L. M. Camarinha-Matos et al. (Eds.): PRO-VE 2018, IFIP AICT 534, pp. 499–511, 2018.
https://doi.org/10.1007/978-3-319-99127-6_43

of evolution of traditional logistics networks, induced by the development of technology. The concept of dynamic logistics network is related to a temporary network of companies, which is quickly formed to exploit a business opportunity in response to a market request and dissolves when its initial mission is achieved.

However, the relationships established between companies in a logistics network are not only relationships of buying and selling products or services, such as buying a book through a web page. A company is more than a set of products and services, these involve facets of a nature as diverse as cultural, legal, technological, organizational, geographic, economic, strategic, among others [5, 6].

Therefore, only having sufficiently consolidated knowledge can be implemented a set of principles and mechanisms that allow the sustainability of these new management models.

Thus, this article aims to contribute to characterize some of the relevant aspects that are the origin of the sustainability of dynamic logistics networks, seeking to find answers to the following questions:

- What is meant by the expression "the Enterprise E_i trusts Enterprise E_j?"
- What is the advantages of using statistical control charts for monitoring and control the trust levels of each of the dynamic logistics network members?

The paper is organized as follows. Section 2 describes the characteristics associated with trust. Section 3 presents a trust model for dynamic logistics networks. Section 4 presents some background about statistics process control needed to understand the authors' proposed approach. A case study is included in Sect. 5 to illustrate the application of the approach presented in the paper. Section 6 includes some concluding remarks.

2 Trust Properties

Based on the literature [7–10] can be identified a set of characteristics that are associated to trust, as following:

- Subjectivity – Trust reflects a subjective assessment of one enterprise in relation to other enterprises since different enterprises can assign different trust values to the same enterprise.
- Reduction of complexity – Under certain conditions trust can act as a mechanism to make processes more agile.
- Specific domain – The trust value is valid only in a specific domain. For each context under analysis, a trust value might be assigned to an enterprise. This means that an enterprise might have multiple trust values. As an example, the enterprise E_i trust on the enterprise E_j for the maintenance of an equipment but does not trust on its production capacity.
- Existence of memory – Various enterprises are able to identify past interactions in identical contexts with the same enterprises.
- Measurable – Trust can be measured through a scale where its limits are between total trust and total mistrust.

- Dynamics – The value of trust is dynamic and can increase or decrease. Its value depends on satisfaction degree resulting from past interactions among various enterprises.
- Nontransitive vs transitive – Trust itself is not transitive. As an example, if an enterprise E_i trust on an enterprise E_j and an enterprise E_j trust on an enterprise E_k, it is not mandatory that the enterprise E_i has to trust on the enterprise E_k.

However, if we admit that enterprises can make recommendations to other enterprises, then, through a recommendation mechanism, trust becomes transitive provided that the following conditions are met:

- The enterprise E_j explicit (recommend) the enterprise E_i that trust in the enterprise E_k.
- The enterprise E_i trust on the recommendations of enterprise E_j.
- The enterprise E_i have the possibility to evaluate the recommendations issued by the enterprise E_j without being subject to any kind of commitment.

3 Trust Model for Dynamic Logistics Networks

Considering that a dynamic logistics network can be understood as a cooperative process where the relations that are established are structured around social exchanges between the various agents (company - company relationship), which translate into transfer of resources, money flows, time, emotions, expectations and many other motivating elements, with the purpose of each of the enterprises seeking to achieve their business and/or social goals. Therefore, an enterprise only delegates a task to another enterprise when there is a trust threshold that compensates the risks.

Thus, in the proposed approach, the evaluation of the trust level of an enterprise E_j is a function of the following dimensions:

- Competencies – The enterprise E_i believes that the enterprise E_j has the knowledge and technology necessary to produce a certain expected result that will play a determining role in the success of its objective.
- Capability – The enterprise E_i believes that the enterprise E_j has the necessary resources to ensure that a given result is achieved according to the specifications defined.
- Resilience – The enterprise E_i believes that the enterprise E_j has robust processes and redundant resources that ensure the production of a given result even if a set of unforeseeable events occur.

If $T_{E_{ij},task_m}$ is designated as the enterprise trust value E_j to perform a task $task_m$ it follows that:

$$T_{E_{ij},task_i} = C_{E_{ij}}(task_m) \times CAP_{E_{ij}}(task_m) \times R_{E_{ij}}(task_m) \tag{1}$$

where:

$T_{E_{ij},task_m}$ - value associated with the trust assessment of the enterprise E_j to perform a $task_m$; this value belongs to the range $[0; 1]$.

$C_{E_{ij}}(task_m)$ - value associated with the competencies evaluation of the enterprise E_j involved in carrying out the task $task_m$; this value belongs to the range [0; 1].
$CAP_{E_{ij}}(task_m)$ - value associated with the resources evaluation of the enterprise E_j involved in carrying out the task $task_m$; this value belongs to the range [0; 1].
$R_{E_{ij}}(task_m)$ - value associated with the resilience evaluation of the enterprise E_j based on the processes and resources involved in carrying out the task $task_m$; this value belongs to the range [0; 1].

However, the existence of a positive trust value may not be sufficient for a given enterprise to trust on another enterprise to perform a particular task. Generally speaking, an enterprise E_i with a task $task_m$ to carry out, can take one of the following options:

- Seek to accomplish the task by itself;
- Delegate to another enterprise E_j the implementation of the task through a cooperation mechanism;
- Do nothing and give up the task.

In order to establish a logistics process between two enterprises it is necessary that there is a trust value that is acceptable to the enterprise that trust. Therefore, the following rule can be defined: When the trust value of an enterprise exceeds the Minimum Trust Value to Cooperate (MTVC), then the enterprise E_i can delegate on the enterprise E_j the execution of the task $task_m$.

Thus, the MTVC will play a role similar to the concept of lower specification limit (LSL) used in statistical quality control.

Although the determination of the minimum trust value is a subjective measure, in order to determine it, the following aspects must be taken into account:

- The enterprises, when they trust, delegate to another enterprise the performance of a certain task in order to seek to maximize their utility. The utility seeks to quantify in units of "useful" the gains that an enterprise E_i obtain by performing a certain task $task_m$. Thus, the utility of an enterprise E_i in the performance of a task $task_m$ in a certain time instant t is represented by $U_{E_i}(task_m)_t$. On the other hand, by normalizing utility values, these may vary in the range comprised between 0 and 10.
- Due to the difficulty in evaluating the impact of a task $task_m$, the term importance should be considered, since the scenario in which there is a task with great utility and of reduced importance is equivalent to the scenario of a task with a reduced utility and of great importance. This variable play two distinct but complementary roles. In the first place, importance seeks to quantify in a subjective way the multiplier effect of the expected gains resulting from the performance of a certain task. In the meantime, the importance reflects the possibility that an enterprise can change its preferences according to the market changes that may occur. That is, for an enterprise E_i the accomplishment of a task $task_m$ in the past could be of high importance while its realization in the present may be of minor importance. The importance of performing a task $task_m$ to an enterprise E_i at a given time t is represented by $I_{E_i}(task_m)_t$. On the other hand, by normalizing the importance values, these can vary in the range between 0 and 10.

In this context, the MTVC in the performance of a task will depend on the level of benefit associated with the task, that is, on the positive impact for an enterprise resulting from the accomplishment of a task, for the enterprise itself (self-benefit), or for another agent (benefit received), which can be measured in quantitative terms [11]. The quantification of benefits is given by the following equation:

$$B_{E_i}(task_m)_t = U_{E_i}(task_m)_t \times I_{E_i}(task_m)_t \qquad (2)$$

where:

$B_{E_i}(task_m)_t$ - value of the Benefit associated with the enterprise E_i resulting from the task $task_m$

$U_{E_i}(task_m)_t$ - value of Utility for enterprise E_i associated with the task $task_m$

$I_{E_i}(task_m)_t$ - Importance level of task $task_m$ for the enterprise E_i

Therefore, using the decision theory, the options described above can be represented in a decision tree as shown in Fig. 1. For the sake of simplicity and because of the option to do nothing and give up the task not be relevant to the analysis concerned, this option will not be considered.

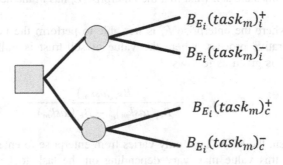

Fig. 1. Decision tree

Where:

$B_{E_i}(task_m)_i^+$ - benefit value of the enterprise E_i successful in accomplishing the task $task_m$;

$B_{E_i}(task_m)_i^-$ - benefit value of the enterprise E_i having failed to perform the task $task_m$;

$B_{E_i}(task_m)_c^+$ - benefit value of the enterprise E_i to be entrusted to complete the task $task_m$, to another enterprise and the enterprise performed the task successfully;

$B_{E_i}(task_m)_c^-$ - benefit value of the enterprise E_i to be entrusted to complete the task $task_m$, to another enterprise and this made the task unsuccessful.

Thus, an enterprise E_i should only entrust the performance of a task to another enterprise E_j when:

$$T_{E_i,E_j,task_m} \times B_{E_i}(task_m)_c^+ + \left(1 - T_{E_i,E_j,task_m}\right) \times B_{E_i}(task_m)_c^- \geq T_{E_i,E_i,task_m} \times B_{E_i}(task_m)_i^+ + \left(1 - T_{E_i,E_i,task_m}\right) \times B_{E_i}(task_m)_i^- \tag{3}$$

Then:

$$T_{E_i,E_j,task_m} \geq T_{E_i,E_i,task_m} \times A + B \tag{4}$$

where:

$$A = \frac{B_{E_i}(task_m)_i^+ - B_{E_i}(task_m)_i^-}{B_{E_i}(task_m)_c^+ - B_{E_i}(task_m)_c^-} \tag{5}$$

$$B = \frac{B_{E_i}(task_m)_i^- - B_{E_i}(task_m)_c^-}{B_{E_i}(task_m)_c^+ - B_{E_i}(task_m)_c^-} \tag{6}$$

$T_{E_i,E_i,task_m}$ - defines the self-trust that the enterprise E_i has in the accomplishment of the task $task_m$.

In the case where the enterprise E_i is not able to perform the task $task_m$, except through a cooperative process, where the value of self-trust is null, $T_{E_i,E_i,task_m} = 0$. Then, the MTVC is given as follows:

$$T_{E_i,E_j,task_m} > -\frac{B_{E_i}(task_m)_c^-}{B_{E_i}(task_m)_c^+ - B_{E_i}(task_m)_c^-} \tag{7}$$

As can be seen, the MTVC not only varies from enterprise to enterprise, as for the same enterprise, this value may vary depending on the task to be performed. For example, one of the factors that causes changes in the determination of the MTVC) is the relationship between $B_{E_i}(task_m)_c^+$ and $B_{E_i}(task_m)_c^-$. Therefore, the greater the value associated with failure $B_{E_i}(task_m)_c^-$ the bigger is the MTVC. In cases where the MTVC assumes a negative value, it means that trust is not a factor to be considered in the cooperation process.

4   Statistical Process Control (SPC)

All companies aim at the full satisfaction of their customers. This goal is achieved by increasing levels of trust between companies and their customers or business partners. Statistical methods play a key role in quality assessment, allowing, among other aspects, to evaluate whether a particular variable (product/service, process or other) completely satisfies the explicit needs, usually defined by a specification.

Statistical charts are valuable tools since they allow to distinguish between special causes and common causes of variation. The first developments were made by

Shewhart [12]. However, in order to meet the demands of today's world, several authors have been developing various types of charts [13]. When it is possible to conveniently estimate the process parameters, SPC is developed in two stages, Phase I and Phase II. In this context, the following methodology is suggested:

Phase 1

Taking into account the literature in this phase, the Shewhart chart is most appropriate for each product/service or characteristic [13, 14]. The upper control limit (*UCL*) and the lower control limit (*LCL*) of these charts, as well as the central line (*CL*), are determined through the formulas presented in Table 1.

Table 1. Control limits of Shewhart charts, in Phase 1 of *SPC*

Chart	LCL	CL	UCL
$\bar{X}$ (sample mean)	$\bar{\bar{X}} - A_2\bar{R}$ ou $\bar{\bar{X}} - A_3\bar{S}$	$\bar{\bar{X}}$	$\bar{\bar{X}} + A_2\bar{R}$ ou $\bar{\bar{X}} + A_3\bar{S}$
R (sample range)	$D_3\bar{R}$	$\bar{R}$	$D_4\bar{R}$
S (sample standard deviation)	$B_3\bar{S}$	$\bar{S}$	$B_4\bar{S}$
MR (moving range)	$D_3\overline{MR}$	$\overline{MR}$	$D_4\overline{MR}$

In the equations in Table 1 it is considered: $\bar{\bar{X}}$ – average of the samples means; $\bar{R}$ – average of the range samples; $\bar{S}$ – average of the samples standard deviations; $\overline{MR}$ - average of the moving ranges; being $A_2, A_3, B_3, B_4, D_3, D_4$ constants that depend on the sample size.

Phase 2 - Monitoring

After checking the stability and analysing the process capacity, in Phase 1 of the SPC, statistical process control is continued through its monitoring. This procedure is commonly referred to as SPC Phase 2. It follows, in this Phase, the application of the control charts Z and W, based on statistics Z and W calculated from statistics $\bar{X}$ (or X) and S (or R, or MR), respectively. Shown in Table 2 are the transformed Z and W for the different charts. The control limits of the charts Z and W are shown in Table 3.

Table 2. Statistics of Z and W charts

$Z_{\bar{X}}$ and W_s Chart	$Z_{\bar{X}}$ and W_R Chart	$Z_{\bar{X}}$ and W_{MR} Chart
$(Z_p)_{E_j} = \left(\frac{\bar{X}_p - \mu}{\sigma_{\bar{X}}}\right)_{E_j}$	$(Z_p)_{E_j} = \left(\frac{\bar{X}_p - \mu}{\sigma_{\bar{X}}}\right)_{E_j}$	$(Z_p)_{E_j} = \left(\frac{X_p - \mu}{\sigma}\right)_{E_j}$
$(W_p)_{E_j} = \left(\frac{S_p}{\bar{S}}\right)_{E_j}$	$(W_p)_{E_j} = \left(\frac{R_p}{\bar{R}}\right)_{E_j}$	$(W_p)_{E_j} = \left(\frac{MR_p}{\overline{MR}}\right)_{E_j}$

Table 3. Limits of control and centreline for Z and W charts

	$Z_{\bar{X}}$ and W_S Chart		$Z_{\bar{X}}$ and W_R Chart		$Z_{\bar{X}}$ and W_{MR} Chart	
	$Z_{\bar{X}}$	W_S	$Z_{\bar{X}}$	W_R	Z_X	W_{MR}
UCL	3	B_4	3	D_4	3	D_4
CL	0	1	0	1	0	1
LCL	-3	B_3	-3	D_3	-3	D_3

In the equations in Table 2 it is considered: $(\overline{X_p})_{E_j}$ - sample trust mean p for enterprise E_j; μ_{E_j} – trust mean relative to domain X for enterprise E_j; $(\sigma_{\bar{x}})_{E_j}$ - standard deviation of the sample trust means distribution for enterprise E_j; $(S_p)_{E_j}$ – sample standard deviation of the trust p for enterprise E_j; $(R_p)_{E_j}$ – sample range of the trust p for enterprise E_j; $(MR_p)_{E_j}$ – moving range of the trust p for enterprise E_j;

A relevant issue in the study of process performance in SPC Phase 2 is the definition of the periodicity of process capability analysis. Thus, it is suggested that this be done in real time, based on two normalized indexes Z_L and Z_U [14].

The analysis of the charts should reveal processes under statistical control, i.e. subject only to common causes of variation. The interpretation of Shewhart's charts is based on the existence of any non-random patterns, which may be detected by Norma ISO 8258:1991.

5 Potential Application

To illustrate the applicability of this methodology it is considered that there is a cluster of companies made up of four independent companies. Figure 2 shows the hypothetical matrix of competences.

	C1	C2	C3
E_1	X		
E_2			X
E_3	X	X	
E_4		X	X

Fig. 2. Competencies matrix

It is considered that, at a given moment, a customer Cl_1 contact the company E_1 for the production of several units of the product P.

According to the planning carried out by the company E_1 for the production of the product P the following competences are required:

$$P = C_1 + C_2 + C_3 \tag{8}$$

For the sake of simplification, it is not considered the possibility of another alternative process, which, using other competences, would also allow obtaining the product P with the same characteristics/functionalities.

Taking into account the defined context, the company E_1 will take a set of decisions and define the MTVC for each competency and for each of the companies, as shown in Fig. 3.

Competencies	Decision	MTVC		
		E_2	E_3	E_4
C1	Use internal resources	----	----	----
C2	Need for cooperation for not compromise other objectives		0,6	0,7
C3	Need for cooperation by not having C3	0,5		0,6

Fig. 3. Decisions of company E_1

In view of the decisions taken, the company E_1, recognizing the need for cooperation, announces, within the cluster, its needs in the competencies $C2$ and $C3$.

In order to select, at each moment, the best solution, i.e., the company that offers the best collaborative guarantees to the company E_1, the values of the level of trust that each company presented for the competences enunciated, $C2$ and $C3$ were determined during 15 periods. Considering the prior knowledge of trust of the companies E_2, E_3 and E_4 (i.e., the mean value and the dispersion value of each company for competencies $C2$ and $C3$, estimated values in the preliminary phase (Phase 1) of the statistical analysis of companies' processes) and based on the values of business trust at each moment, Z control charts were built to monitor the level of trust and performance of companies. The statistics that allow the construction of the charts are determined by the equations presented in Table 2.

These charts allow monitoring the trust level of companies in relation to competencies $C2$ and $C3$. This monitoring consists of verifying the stability of the processes (checking whether the standard of competence trust level is random) and detecting the existence of anomalous situations, characterized by values of the Z statistic that correspond to points outside the control limits of the chart. In addition, it was calculated the capability indices Z_L. This indicator, for a given competence ($C2$ and $C3$), gives indication of the suitability of each company to satisfy the minimum required level of trust.

The decision on the choice of the company to cooperate with the company E_1, for the period $p +1$, is taken on the basis of the information in the period p. The following criteria are established for the selection of the company that will collaborate with the company E_1:

1. Choose the company that has the highest absolute value of Z_i.
2. When the standard of trust of an enterprise presents special causes of variation (outside statistical control), it should not be selected for the next two instants (instants $p + 1$ and $p + 2$).

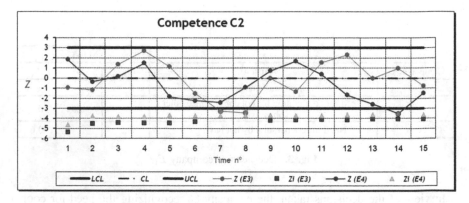

Fig. 4. Capability monitoring and analysis for the competence $C2$ of companies E_3 and E_4

Figure 4 shows the trust monitoring of companies E_3 and E_4 for the competence $C2$. The analysis of Fig. 4 leads to the following conclusions:

- Initially one should invest in partnership with the company E_3 (better value of Z_L), up to period 7 (1° criterion);
- For the company E_3, there are special causes in period 7 and period 8; thus, one should opt for the partnership with the company E_4 for periods 8, 9 and 10 (2° criterion).
- From the 11th period, since the company E_3 has a better value of Z_L than the company E_4, one should opt for the partnership with the company E_3.
- To register a special cause in period 14, referring to the company E_4, which does not influence the decision due to better value of Z_L for company E_3.

It is presented in Fig. 5 the trust monitoring of companies E_3 and E_4 for the competence $C3$. The analysis of Fig. 5 leads to the following conclusions:

- The processes relating to companies E_2 and E_4 (competence $C3$) are stable, i.e., there are no special causes of variation; so the decision on the choice of the company to cooperate with the company E_1 should be taken solely on the basis of the 1° criterion;

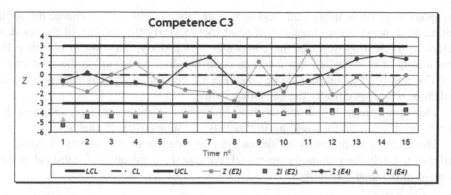

Fig. 5. Capability monitoring and analysis for the competence $C3$ for companies E_2 and E_4

- Initially one should invest in partnership with the company E_2 (better value of Z_L) up to period 10.
- For periods 11 and 12, since the values of Z_L for companies E_2 and E_4 are similar, the choice is indifferent, being the decision made based on other indicators in place of the level of trust;
- For the period 13 and following, one should opt for the partnership with the company E_4 (better value of Z_L).

With regard to competencies $C2$ and $C3$, the table presented in Fig. 6 summarizes the decision-making regarding the company that should be selected to collaborate with the company E_1.

Competence	1	2	3	4	5	6	7	8	9	10	11	12	13	14	15
C2	E_3	E_3	E_3	E_3	E_3	E_3	E_3	E_4	E_4	E_4	E_3	E_3	E_3	E_3	E_3
C3	E_2	E_2	E_2	E_2	E_2	E_2	E_2	E_2	E_2	E_2	E_2/E_4	E_2/E_4	E_4	E_4	E_4

Fig. 6. Decision-making on the collaborative process with companies E_2, E_3 and E_4 (choice of the company to collaborate with E_1, by period), concerning the competences $C2$ and $C3$

6 Conclusions

There seems to be a clear consensus that companies to survive have increasingly to establish "working together" relationships with other companies. In this context, the role of trust was discussed and a model was proposed to measure the level of trust between the various companies as support for the development of dynamic logistics networks.

The methodology proposed for the monitoring of trust presents a number of advantages that stand out: the perception of the evolution of the trust level of a company is possible using statistical techniques such as the control charts; the application of dimensionless charts Z is a good tool to verify the stability of the standard referring to the trust level of the companies under study, allowing in real time the monitoring of the standard that a certain company displays regarding the trust level.

The ability of a company to demonstrate a given competence is evidenced by an indicator, more specifically the capability index.

Decision-making based on statistical techniques such as those presented in this article, is more rigorous, avoiding in this way the subjectivity of analysis.

However, it is necessary to develop an application in real context in order to validate not only the proposed trust model, but also the application of statistical quality control in the trust monitoring.

Acknowledgments. This work was funded in part by the Center of Technology and Systems of Uninova and the Portuguese FCT-PEST program UID/EEA/00066/2013. And, it was also partially supported by FCT, through IDMEC, under LAETA, project UID/EMS/50022/2013.

References

1. Abreu, A., Camarinha-Matos, L.M.: An approach to measure social capital in collaborative networks. In: Camarinha-Matos, L.M., Pereira-Klen, A., Afsarmanesh, H. (eds.) PRO-VE 2011. IAICT, vol. 362, pp. 29–40. Springer, Heidelberg (2011). https://doi.org/10.1007/978-3-642-23330-2_4
2. Verdouw, C.N., Wolfert, J., Beulens, A.J.M., Rialland, A.: Virtualization of food supply chains with the Internet of Things. J. Food Eng. **176**, 128–136 (2016)
3. Simatupang, T.M., Sridharan, R.: The collaborative supply chain. Int. J. Logist. Manag. **13** (1), 15–30 (2002)
4. Jasti, N.V.K., Kodali, R.: A critical review of lean supply chain management frameworks: proposed framework. Prod. Plann. Control **26**(13), 1051–1068 (2015)
5. Abreu, A., Camarinha-Matos, L.M.: On the role of value systems and reciprocity in collaborative environments. In: Abreu, A., Camarinha-Matos, L.M. (eds.) PRO-VE 2006. IIFIP, vol. 224, pp. 273–284. Springer, Boston (2006). https://doi.org/10.1007/978-0-387-38269-2_29
6. Abreu, A., Camarinha-Matos, L.M.: Understanding social capital in collaborative networks. In: Ortiz, Á., Franco, R.D., Gasquet, P.G. (eds.) BASYS 2010. IAICT, vol. 322, pp. 109–118. Springer, Heidelberg (2010). https://doi.org/10.1007/978-3-642-14341-0_13
7. Axelroad, R.: The Evolution of Cooperation. Basic Books, New York City (1984)
8. Castelfranchi, C., Falcone, R.: Trust is much more than subjective probability: mental components and sources of trust. In: Proceedings of the 33rd Hawaii International Conference on Systems Sciences (HICSS 2000), Maui, Hawaii, USA (2000)
9. Gambetta, D.: Can We Trust, Trust? Trust: Making and Breaking Cooperative Relations, pp. 213–237. Electronic edition, Department of Sociology, University of Oxford (2000)
10. Chen, D., Chang, G., Sun, D., Li, J., Jia, J., Wang, X.: TRM-IoT: a trust management model based on fuzzy reputation for Internet of Things. Comput. Sci. Inf. Syst. **8**(4), 1207–1228 (2011)
11. Camarinha-Matos, L.M., Abreu, A.: A contribution to understand collaboration benefits. In: Camarinha-Matos, L.M. (ed.) BASYS 2004. IIFIP, vol. 159, pp. 287–298. Springer, Boston (2005). https://doi.org/10.1007/0-387-22829-2_30

12. Shewhart, W.A.: Economic Control of Quality of Manufactured Product. David Van Nostrand Company, Inc., New York (1931)
13. Montgomery, D.C.: Introduction to statistical quality control. Wiley, Hoboken (2007)
14. Pereira, Z.L., Requeijo, J.G.: Qualidade: Planeamento e Controlo Estatístico de Processos, Co-edição da Fundação da FCT/UNL e da Editora Prefácio, Lisboa (2008)

A New Approach for Supply Chain Management Monitoring Systems Adapted to Crisis

Quentin Schoen[1,2(✉)], Sébastien Truptil[1(✉)], Matthieu Lauras[1(✉)],
Franck Fontanili[1(✉)], and Aurélie Conges[1(✉)]

[1] IMT Mines Albi, Campus Jarlard, 81013 Albi Cedex 09, France
{quentin.schoen,sebastien.truptil,matthieu.lauras,
franck.fontanili,aurelie.conges}@mines-albi.fr
[2] Etablissement Français du Sang, Avenue de Grande Bretagne,
31027 Toulouse Cedex 03, France

Abstract. Sensitive products supply chain and supply chain facing crisis management share several aspects. In both cases, several decision makers have to choose the best options most of the time under pressure, often in emergency and need to access numerous information from the field. This shared monitoring aspect put forward the visualization need to consider in each decision all the crisis potential impacts. Unfortunately, for the transportation steps we focus on, the current transport management systems do not reach these requirements. In this paper, focusing on supply chains during crisis situations, we present a new monitoring system with adapted functionalities. The added value is a connection in real time and relevant way the data from the field to the information on a shared model used to make reliable decisions. We use the French Blood Establishment supply chain to illustrate the proposition.

Keywords: Monitoring system · Supply chain · Sensitive products
Collaboration · Real time

1 Introduction

The supply chain management, as any other field, may have to face with crisis situations. The Webster's New World College Dictionary defines it as "*a turning point in the course of anything; decisive or crucial time, stage, or event*". We find here the idea that a crisis is decisive for the future of the given environment [1] and must have consequences. This breaking point of a stable environment may affect all the actors in it, whatever their role is. Thus, according to [2] the crisis nature may be military, politic, economic, social, technical or humanitarian.

Another aspect to consider is the time. Indeed, a crisis may occur suddenly or progressively [3], depending on the triggering event(s). These/This event(s) may have severe impacts on the considering system/environment, depending on the environment's vulnerability and the consequences of these/this event(s). For instance, a truck crash is a sudden event whereas a vehicle stuck in traffic jam is more progressive. Depending

L. M. Camarinha-Matos et al. (Eds.): PRO-VE 2018, IFIP AICT 534, pp. 512–523, 2018.
https://doi.org/10.1007/978-3-319-99127-6_44

on the products inside (well protected or not, urgent or not), impacts may be important (valuable and/or sensitive products) or not (empty truck, not valuable products).

Being able to detect these events as soon as they happen and understand their impacts (current and potential) is one of the key elements to limit the crisis spreading and cascade effect. In order to reach this objective it is necessary to monitor the processes in real time and understand what is happening on the field. A decision support system fed with frequently updated, relevant and reliable information, would be able to help crisis units providing Common Operational Pictures (COP). The most reliable and relevant are the information provided quickly to the crisis unit, the highest are the chance to limit the impacts.

Proposal: In this situation, considering the supply chains transportation processes, our objective is to define a new way of monitoring them in crisis situation and in a larger extent a new way of monitoring sensitive products transports in general. In parallel, we describe a potential information system (IS) able to support this approach based on data collection and treatment. Our study perimeter is limited to the collection, treatment and decision support system abilities, focusing on transportation steps. The decisions broadcast to actors on the field and/or people able to concretely change parameters of the environment concerned by the crisis is out of our scope.

To reach this objective, we describe in the first section the concrete needs to respond to a crisis in supply chain. Focusing on the transportation steps, we describe in which extent Transport Management Systems could contribute to the crisis response in the second section. In the third one, a proposal is made in order to meet the described needs. Finally, we present a real use case based on our experience in the French Blood Establishment that deals with sensitive products.

2   Crisis Response from Supply Chain

2.1   A Response to the Crisis

Whatever are the prevention measures to reduce the system vulnerability and the preparation plans to anticipate the crisis management, a triggering event may happen. Thus, if we did not succeed in avoiding the crisis, it is necessary to be able to respond to it.

First, [2] defines the crisis response as "*special measures taken to solve problems caused by a crisis*". The objective is to stop the system deviation from the "normal" or "expected" state in order to implement a new stable one. One of the main problems concerns the variety of potential actors involved in a crisis response. In order to respond to it, they may have to collaborate, each one being responsible of its area of expertise and competencies. As [4] put forward, being able to make relevant decisions, under external and internal pressure, collaborating with people we are not used to work with is not an easy task. In order to achieve this objective of collaboration and relevant decision-making, a crisis unit may be defined during crisis preparation steps. The role of this crisis unit is to create a decision sharing and making environment. Each person involved is responsible of its domain (vertical aspect) and of the interface with the other ones (horizontal aspect), exchanging relevant information to coordinate the response.

Thus, one of the key issues is to collect data and share between stakeholders relevant and reliable information from the crisis state. As [5] put forward, many decisions are experience and knowledge based in each domain and not shared in a formalized way. In a dynamic and unstable situation, with potential emergency pressures, this must be a challenge to meet. In the following parts, we focus on this ability to obtain relevant and reliable information in the supply chain management.

2.2 Supply Chain Management Needs to Support Collaborative Crisis Management

In order to make relevant decisions based on reliable information about the supply chain, the stakeholders have different needs, described below, to make decisions.

Collect Relevant Data

The main objective of the supply chain management is to provide the required product, in the best state, at the right place, at the right time. During a crisis, the organization scheduled has to be reconsidered and the expected events may not happen. The environment evolves quickly in unexpected ways, the system is not stable and the consequences may be important. Thus, the decision makers may become blind quickly on their own processes. The first step to find a solution is to collect data from the field in order to follow the evolutions. These data are internal, from our own processes ("Where are my vehicles? In which state are my products?"), and external from the other factors which must affect our environment (weather, traffic, emergency services, lambda individuals, etc.).

Transmit and Exploit Reliable Data

After collecting data from the crisis state the next challenge is to transmit them to an appropriate IS and exploit them. In fact, the crisis IS has to deal with data from different sources, with different formats, putting forward different aspects of the crisis. The main challenge here is to be able to deal with these amounts of heterogeneous data, understand their meaning and build automatically relevant and reliable information. This step of data treatments allows reducing their volume and classifying them in order not to drown the stakeholders with raw data but provide required information based on them.

Encourage Exchanges Around a Shared Picture

Gathering all these information is most of the time not sufficient. Even if the information flow is understandable, these information are separated in lists, tables, and schemes, focusing on a domain. It is useful for each crisis unit stakeholders independently but does not encourage them to discuss. The information flow is reduced compared with the data flow but there is still a conceptual step to carry out in order to build a crisis situation overview. Creating a Common Operational Picture (COP) fosters the crisis unit members to work together from the same visualization of the crisis state; thus they understand others problematic and objectives. Moreover, this COP must be dynamic, updated frequently with new data based information, which contribute to follow and anticipate the situation.

Anticipate and Foresee to Support the Decision-Making

One of the key questions each stakeholder of a crisis unit is supposed to answer is: *"knowing the current situation, what is the expected one in a near future"*. The need to foresee the potential next events is a key element to make decisions and evaluate their impact before the implementation.

3   Inabilities of Transport Management Systems to Support Collaborative Crisis Management

In order to meet the needs we described above we could try to use existing systems that deal with transportation processes. These systems manage every day thousands of containers through the world and handle anomalies, consequences of unexpected and/or unwanted transportation events. We describe below their main functionalities, failures, and some logistic trends that should contribute to prevent Transport Management Systems (TMS) to meet these challenges.

3.1   Main Functionalities

The Transport Management systems are applications developed from the nineties which aim to provide «*"an enabling tool" for the safe and efficient operation of Freight Transport systems*» [6]. Progressively the TMS evolved due to the complexification of logistics operations on one part [7] and abilities of the computing systems and the Internet on the other part. Nowadays, these applications are most of the time proposed as Software as a Service (SaaS) through the Internet and functionalities have been split in blocks activated or not. Companies, either carrier or sender, which need TMS functionalities activate the ones they want in order to fulfill their needs. They pay a rent to access them and store their data in datacenters. Cloud computing technologies and SaaS approach offer the ability to Small and Medium Size companies to access to these technologies [8]. Thus, whatever is the number of actors involved in a supply chain, the interconnectivity becomes easier to reach through normalized systems like Application Program Interface (API) and Electronic Data Interchange (EDI).

The main functionalities TMS providers offer are: (i) pick-up and Delivery areas setup, (ii) rounds setup, (iii) clients and/or subcontractors setup, (iv) packages shipment, (v) transportation and customs documents creation, (vi) rounds optimization and simulation, (vii) packages transportation steps tracking, (viii) vehicles monitoring, (ix) freight market place, quotes and order, (x) finances, transportation billing, (xi) reverse logistic management, (xii) performance and anomaly management, KPI, (xiii) transportation fleet management, (xiv) mobile devices setup.

These functionalities cover a broad scope of the most common needs and are split in details in different blocks activated or not. However, in case of sensitive products transportation or crisis, these systems are not relevant enough.

3.2 Identified Problems in Case of Crisis

For almost 30 years, the logical approach used to design TMS was to consider containers as boxes defined by a list of parameters (sender, recipient, required transportation environment, weight, permissible transportation time, etc.) and gather them in vehicles. Next, tracking the vehicles (location, state) we track the containers. Nevertheless, this approach is not fully adapted and precise enough to crisis transportation management neither sensitive products supply chain.

In fact, these products are too important to be damaged/stolen/lost, because a priori necessary to reduce the damages and contribute to recover. We should be able to know exactly where is located each product and what its state is (temperature, humidity, shocks, etc.). Consequently, the TMS real time vehicles' tracking is not precise enough and *agility is limited*. Indeed, during a crisis, we have to be able to make relevant decisions based on reliable facts from the field. Seeing a vehicle as a *black box* do not usually allow to deviate one container among the others in case of unexpected event (urgent need on a site, container damage).

Moreover, we are not able to take advantages of the multimodality opportunities that still represent a complex step because of physical and computational *normalization lacks*. Thus, most of the time we do not take advantages of all the transportation means opportunities [8] but use one vehicle from the sender to the recipient whereas it might not be the most effective and efficient option.

Finally, optimization rounds and allocation, which aim to increase the efficiency, cannot be fed with other data than the available means from companies the sender knows or has a contract with. Car sharing and common transport availability are not tracked. Thus, these potential loads displacement are not used in the optimization algorithms. In case of emergency, TMS are able to take advantages of just *a part of all the available ability*.

These for the crisis and sensitive products supply chain management issues should be exacerbated, considering the upcoming logistic environment.

3.3 Upcoming Environment

In order to complete this analysis and anticipate future development we develop here some future logistic trends. Some of them may reinforce the TMS failures whereas some others could offer new opportunities in crisis management.

First, the product customization is increasing as [9] foresees it. Product configurations to reach the client needs improve the capability to customize the products. The problem is the potential uniqueness of each product. In case of damage on the container or theft during the transportation steps, it would be more complicated to replace the products by identical one. In case of crisis, it would be impossible to find quickly adapted and effective solutions without gathering reliable information in real time about the locations and states of every product and container. Moreover, the additive manufacturing development encourages this customization and last miles deliveries should increase [10]. Finally, traceability requirements in particular for cold supply chains would require too this somewhat real time monitoring systems.

Meantime, several technologies are about to offer new interesting possibilities in order to deal with crisis management. The development these last years of connected devices, the Internet of Things, allows to connect any object to the Internet [8]. The development of these powerful small devices represents a remarkable opportunity to collect and transmit data from the field easily and in real time. Cloud computing development has simplified the data storage and exchanges between these devices and people. The Software as a Service [11] way of thinking permits to offer an easy, flexible and relatively cheap access to interesting functionalities to any company. Combining these technologies, we are about to create a hyper-connected world in which the problem is not how to collect data but how not to be drown by them. As we describe it in the following sections, ability to deal with big data [12] issues, powerful data treatments like machine learning, process mining... allow exploiting these data in real time to extract relevant information. As for them, autonomous vehicle development [13] and «anytime, anywhere delivery model» should create in few years a capillary distribution network, connected to monitoring systems.

This state of the art of current TMS and the expected logistic environment shows these systems would not be relevant enough to deal effectively with supply chains, which are expected to be more and more sensitive to unexpected events and should require more and more collaboration. Therefore, *crisis management needs are spreading* and new opportunities to meet them are about to be available. A new supply chain management IS, able to deal with them, is proposed in the next section.

4 Proposal

4.1 Monitoring System

The approach we present here focuses on the containers (and products) to be transported, considering the vehicles as "potential load displacement". In fact, considering the hyper-connected and more collaborative world we are about to live in, it seems relevant to focus on the goods to be transported and not on the means as TMS do. As data are encapsulated and send on the network with switches and connections on the Internet, we can imagine that the normalized physical network would move physically and computationally normalized containers. This idea is very close from the Physical Internet philosophy developed by [14]. We describe below the main functionalities to address, summarized in the Fig. 1:

- *Container surveillance:* It is the ability to collect data about the container state, with tags in it or in its near environment, and to deduce relevant information from them. Topics like the physical and computational normalization, the container autonomy level and in which extent the decision support system is centralized or multi-agent based have still to be discussed.
- *Network analysis and surveillance:* While we gather data from the containers we have to gather data about all the available transportation means that are willing to load containers and their capabilities (destination, loading capacity, cost, etc.). Exploiting raw data from the field, we will be able to create reliable information about

the network. On the other part, the surveillance must provide information about the network state and prevent unwanted events. Delivery center expected capacity, weather, roadwork, are some of the parameters interesting to control in real time.

- *Container steering:* Gathering the previous functions it would be possible to route automatically the containers on the network, step-by-step. Defining containers allocation rules to the available transportation means around them would orientate the containers to the most suitable way. In this hyper-connected environment, the ability to take advantage of the best solutions would allow efficiency and effectiveness rise. Thus, the supply chain becomes able to respond almost automatically to any unexpected event.

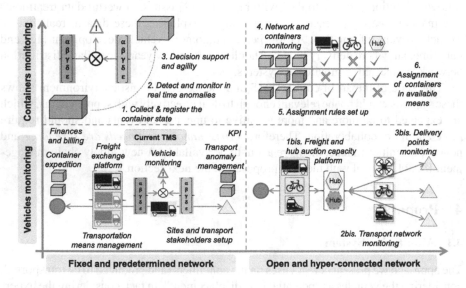

Fig. 1. Transportation monitoring systems evolution

Even if this kind of hyper-connected system may have problem in case of inability to collect enough relevant data from the field, it would meet the needs described above.

4.2 A New IS to Treat Big Data Issues

In order to meet the needs we described in the first section we have to design a IS able to cope with this upcoming technological environment.

Need 1: Collect Relevant Data

Whatever are the tags and technologies used to collect these data, if we want to be reactive and agile enough to reach the challenges described we need frequent updates from all of them. The Internet of Things development should allow data collection easily, from autonomous tags and sensors, mobile phones, camera, etc. Finally, we may produce too many data compared with what we really need. Thus, it brings big data constraints.

In fact, as [12] define it big data may be characterized by five variables: Volume, Velocity, Variety, Veracity, and Value.

Need 2: Transmit and Exploit Reliable Data

As the Fig. 2 shows it, the data flow has to be filtered through a homogeneity layer that deals with data variety [15]. After that, the data flow is split in two parts. The first one consists in data storage for a posteriori treatment and the second one in real time treatments. The database is used for two purposes. First, these data represent the raw material to define the rules used to understand the data flow. For instance, combining data values from a vehicle we can deduce its state and if it represents a problem. Moreover, with a machine-learning module complex rules based on experience will be deduced in order to feed the Complex Event-Processing (CEP) module, which aims to treat in real time the data flow. Secondly, registering crisis responses these data may provide proposition in order to respond to a new one whom aspects and parameters are very close from a previous one. Machine learning analysis will enrich reference models, which contribute to help for expected model simulations.

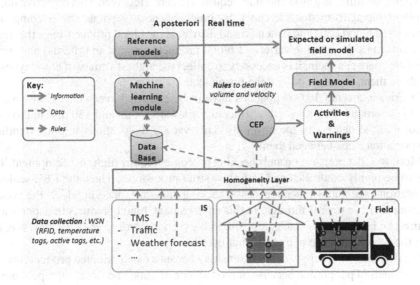

Fig. 2. Information system to support supply chain management during a crisis

Need 3: Encourage Exchanges Around a Shared Picture

The second part concerns real time data treatment in which the CEP will provide reliable and relevant information based on the data from the field. Thanks to the rules, activities and warnings will be modeled and feed the field model. This model is the Common Operational Picture the crisis unit is looking for.

Need 4: Anticipate and Foresee to Help the Decision-Making

Based on the previous crises and the current field situation it is possible to foresee the next steps. Databases register how the previous crises were solved with the potential solutions, their risks and impacts. Considering the pressure of crisis decision making this ability to foresee and simulate a decision would be a major improvement.

5   Use Case – The Blood Supply Chain

Based on the French Blood Supply Chain, we describe below the main advantages and benefits of the defined system. The advantage of this example is that the blood supply chain is itself a sensitive one, which implies a high level of surveillance in real time. Considering the products sensitiveness and the numerous transportation steps, any unexpected event may have impacts on the products and people who need them.

5.1   French Blood Establishment Products

The French Blood Establishment (FBE) is the only company in France allowed dealing with the blood supply chain. The main objective of the FBE is to be able to provide anywhere, anytime, any blood product required to cure a receiver. This objective implies to collect blood from donors, check its innocuousness, separate the 3 components (plasma, red blood cells and platelets) and distribute the blood products bags the nearest to the hospitals. Due to the variety of blood products (groups and rhesus) and incompatibilities between them, it is necessary to collect the highest variety of blood types and distribute them, the closest to all the hospitals.

In France, around 10.000 pouches have to be collected every day. Consequently, every year around 40.000 one day collection sites are set up and 130 distribution sites are located the nearest to the hospitals. This variety of locations implies significant transportation steps between them.

Moreover, the preparation and checking processes require high cost equipment. They have to be highly controlled and to follow strict procedures. Thus, the FBE settled 14 preparation sites and 4 innocuousness-checking sites in France in which the pouches and samples have to pass through. In this environment, blood products transportation is required, at least from the collection site to the preparation site and checking site, then from the preparation site to the distribution site.

Finally, the blood supply chain is sensitive because the distributed products are vital for thousands of people and because of product constraints. The storage temperature and the lifecycle are the two major constraints, which affect transportation steps. We summarize in the Table 1 these constraints:

Table 1. Lifecycles and storage temperature of the most common blood products

Products	Lifetime	Temperature
Whole blood	Less than 48 h	18–24 °C (0–24 h post swab)
Blood samples	Less than 48 h	2–10 °C (6–48 h post swab)
Platelets	5 days	20–24 °C shaken
Red blood cells	42 days	2–10 °C
Plasma	1 year	< −25 °C

This Supply Chain is a sensitive one due to the products value, their temperature and lifecycle constraints and the potential need as a matter of emergency of any product anywhere at any time. Any unexpected event may affect directly this supply chain; we develop briefly some of them in the following sub-section.

5.2 Unexpected Events

We can consider 4 main unexpected events that will affect the SCM. In the following situations, a crisis unit must be set up to find adapted solutions:

- A *massive accident/terrorist attack* raises suddenly the blood products needs in an area. This implies unexpected transports to be quickly organized.
- *Traffic jam* and/or *bad weather conditions* affect directly the transports (rounds and urgent ones). The temperature might be difficult to control if the transportation time is longer than expected.
- A *major problem on a site* (fire, flood, snow, inaccessibility, etc.) where high cost equipment shared between several sites and regions (samples checking) is located. This implies quick, adapted and efficient rerouting.
- In case of accident or attacks in which people are injured, the other people usually want to help and *give their blood*. In this situation, an unexpected rise of blood donation may affect the whole supply chain.

In order to respond to these crises, we describe in the next sub-section what would be the major improvements of the crisis management system described before.

5.3 Illustration

Considering this use case and the described unexpected events the Fig. 3 illustrates an ideal Common Operational Picture that would *foster and support collaboration* and help the FBE to make the best decision. Truck deviation to deliver products to the hospitals the nearest from the accident, urgent need on a site and real time truck stuck in traffic jam location are examples of this kind of abilities (cf. Fig. 3).

The major improvement of this kind of map is its ability to indicate on the same picture information used by all the stakeholders. This kind of *visualization contributes to share an understanding of the situation and make collaborative decision.*

Moreover, the truck on the left enlightened the added value of simulation to foresee the future system state. Based on machine learning analysis that feed reference models, the IS may provide an expected situation if we do not act and simulate impacts from a potential action.

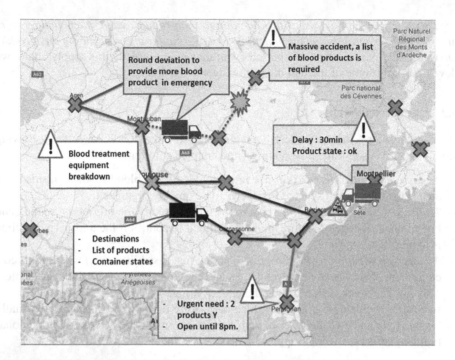

Fig. 3. Use case example of crisis management visualization

6   Conclusion

To conclude, considering the current and foreseeable inability of Transport Management Systems to meet the needs of sensitive products supply chain and crisis management, we propose a new way of designing a transport monitoring system, data based, and putting forward the visualization. This approach would represent an important added value for supply chain management. Considering the future deployments, we have to consider several challenges. First, in this kind of collaborative platform, keeping a clear visualization for stakeholders with enough relevant information without drowning them with unnecessary ones may be difficult. Secondly, the stakeholders may be reluctant to use this kind of systems because they may feel it reduces their autonomy. Finally, the whole system is data-based, consequently if some data are not available for any reason (communication issues, tags breakdown, etc.) the whole system may create an inaccurate picture.

Our next tasks are now to develop concretely this kind of IS and feed it with real time transportation data. These data may come from tracking systems and devices we will use directly inside the FBE containers. The main objective is now to experiment this proposition on the field, estimate its benefits in crisis situation and discuss its failures.

References

1. Lagadec, P.: La gestion des crises: outils de réflexion à l'usage des décideurs. Ediscience International (1991)
2. Devlin, E.S.: Crisis Management Planning and Execution. CRC Press, Boca Raton (2006)
3. Tomasini, R.M., Van Wassenhove, L.N.: Genetically modified food donations and the cost of neutrality: logistics response to the 2002 food crisis in Southern Africa. INSEAD Case, 604-024 (2004)
4. Lagadec, P.: Cellules de crise: les conditions d'une conduite efficace: gouvernements, ministères, entreprises, préfectures, administrations, municipalités, régions, médias, organisations internationales, organisations non gouvernementales, associations, syndicats. Les Éditions d'Organisation (1995)
5. Truptil, S.: Etude de l'approche de l'interopérabilité par médiation dans le cadre d'une dynamique de collaboration appliquée à la gestion de crise (Doctoral dissertation) (2011)
6. Giannopoulos, G.A.: The application of information and communication technologies in transport. Eur. J. Oper. Res. **152**(2), 302–320 (2004)
7. Marchet, G., Perego, A., Perotti, S.: An exploratory study of ICT adoption in the Italian freight transportation industry. Int. J. Phys. Distrib. Logist. Manag. **39**(9), 785–812 (2009)
8. Harris, I., Wang, Y., Wang, H.: ICT in multimodal transport and technological trends: unleashing potential for the future. Int. J. Prod. Econ. **159**, 88–103 (2015)
9. DHL. www.dhl.com/content/dam/downloads/g0/about_us/logistics_insights/dhl_logistics_trend_radar_2016.pdf
10. Boon, W., Van Wee, B.: Influence of 3D printing on transport: a theory and experts judgment based conceptual model. Transp. Rev. **38**(5), 556–575 (2018)
11. O'sullivan, D.: Software as a service: developments in supply chain IT. Logist. Transp. Focus **9**(3), 30–33 (2007)
12. Wamba, S.F., Akter, S., Edwards, A., Chopin, G., Gnanzou, D.: How 'big data' can make big impact: findings from a systematic review and a longitudinal case study. Int. J. Prod. Econ. **165**, 234–246 (2015)
13. Van Meldert, B., De Boeck, L.: Introducing autonomous vehicles in logistics: a review from a broad perspective (2016)
14. Montreuil, B.: Toward a physical internet: meeting the global logistics sustainability grand challenge. Logist. Res. **3**(2–3), 71–87 (2011)
15. Wang, T., Truptil, S., Benaben, F.: An automatic model-to-model mapping and transformation methodology to serve model-based systems engineering. Inf. Syst. e-Business Manag. **15**(2), 323–376 (2017)

An Approach for Surfacing Hidden Intentions and Trustworthiness in Logistics Resource Sharing Networks

Morice Daudi[1(✉)], Klaus-Dieter Thoben[2], and Jannicke Baalsrud Hauge[2,3]

[1] Faculty of Science and Technology, Mzumbe University, Mzumbe, Tanzania
dmorice@mzumbe.ac.tz
[2] Bremer Institut für Produktion und Logistik at the University of Bremen, Bremen, Germany
{tho,baa}@biba.uni-bremen.de
[3] School of Engineering, Technology and Health, KTH, Royal Institute of Technology,
Stockholm, Sweden

Abstract. Collaboration on sharing logistics resources aims to balance supply and demand of the idle, inefficiently, and underutilized resources. Although sharing is beneficial, many issues such as privacy, security, time, regulations, safety, biased reviews, and ratings hinder the sharing. Such problems procreate many uncertainties, which as a consequence, lead to low trust in sharing resources. Meanwhile, existing solutions such as trust and reputation mechanism, and online reviews and ratings incorporate the least consideration to monitor hidden intentions and behaviors of partners. Therefore, this paper proposes an approach to surface hidden intentions and trustworthiness of partners involved in sharing resources. The approach stands on cognitive principles to explore intentions and trustworthiness of suppliers and consumers of logistics resources. Application of the proposed approach is illustrated using industrial case extracted from ride-sharing platform.

Keywords: Collaboration · Intention · Trustworthiness · Resource sharing
Logistics networks · Cognitive systems · Prediction

1 Introduction

Collaboration in sharing resources is an approach to leverage multiple inefficiencies faced by individuals and organizations. It is a re-birth of traditional sharing, elevated by digital technologies. In logistics sector, for example, partners can share the vehicle trucks, warehouses, distribution centers, and machinery equipment [1–3] collaboratively. As well, human-beings are becoming part of shareable logistics resources because they provide the flexible workforce [4]. An overall goal of collaborative sharing is to balance demand and supply of idle and underutilized resources. Benefits of sharing resources include reducing costs and harms to the environment but also increase the efficiency of logistics services.

© IFIP International Federation for Information Processing 2018
Published by Springer Nature Switzerland AG 2018. All Rights Reserved
L. M. Camarinha-Matos et al. (Eds.): PRO-VE 2018, IFIP AICT 534, pp. 524–536, 2018.
https://doi.org/10.1007/978-3-319-99127-6_45

Efforts to share logistics resources encounter many difficulties, including tight regulations, perceived (existing) opportunism, and deceitful behaviors. Other impediments comprise the possibility of adverse outcomes such as theft, strangers, and intrusion of privacy [5]. On top of the outlined issue, the main impediment is the low level of trust. The little trust accrues from many sources including collaborative logistics processes and partner behaviors. In sharing resources, consumers need to trust that: supplier will deliver services according to reasonable standards; they will receive proper compensation in case of unmet expectations, and; their safety and security will be maintained [6]. Also, consumers need to trust the platform they use, as well as people they connect with [7]. Since sharing stands mainly on trust, its success has also to depend on building confidence and realistic expectations.

Similar to other forms of collaborative networks, resource sharing networks in logistics can rely on digital intermediating platforms. One goal of digital platforms is to reduce transactions costs incurred in intermediating suppliers and consumers. In particular, digital platforms facilitate and support: searching for partners; bargaining; reinforcing agreements and; evaluating (recommending) undertaken sharing transactions. Recommendation comprises mainly of reviews and ratings, which are used to generate reputation and trustworthiness. This paper acknowledges many works in literature, contributing on how to choose partners, enforce agreements, and evaluates (recommend) goods or services transacted.

Comparatively, partners' intention and trustworthiness featured in logistics resource sharing networks, as facilitated by digital platforms, rely also on reviews and ratings. One main drawback of such reviews and ratings is that some do not reflect reality. There are limitations, which feature in a perspective of biases [8, 9], low incentive to provide ratings, skewness towards positive rating, and unfair ratings [9]. There are many works in literature contributing to on how to improve limitations of online reviews and ratings (such as [10–13]). This paper, however, contributes to resolving this problem differently. The paper focuses on establishing a proposition that can complement some impediments in reviews and ratings. In particular, it proposes a cognitive approach that can surface hidden issues underlying logistics networks of sharing. The approach stands on cognitive systems to scrutinize patterns of suppliers and consumers of idle/underutilized logistics resources. The proposed approach provides headlights related to a party's intention and trustworthiness, which are difficult to realize under existing mechanics in online reviews and ratings.

The remainder of the paper consists of six sections. Section 2 describes and discusses shareable logistics resources, and trust in business relationships. Whereas Sect. 3 defines a methodology of the paper, Sect. 4 explains social behavior, intentions, and how they link to cognitive systems. Section 5 presents a proposed cognitive approach whose illustrative application appears in Sect. 6. The paper ends in Sect. 7 by providing concluding remarks and future works.

2   Trustworthiness in Sharing Logistics Resources

The present section describes and discusses resource sharing in logistics (Subsect. 2.1) as well as trust-building in networks supporting the sharing (Subsect. 2.2).

2.1   Resource Sharing in Logistics

One may categorize shareable resources in logistics as the physical, non-physical, and human assets. Sharing of the physical resources entails a joint usage of tangible assets such as the vehicles (trucks), warehouses, distribution centers, and machinery equipment [1–3]. Such infrastructures are potential to share because they frequently remain idle or underutilized. Additionally, sharing of the outlined infrastructures is beneficial because deploying them primarily on an individual basis is relatively difficult and expensive. The second category, non-physical resources, refer to intangible assets such as the data, information, supporting processes [14] and logistics services. Information, in particular, is a non-physical shareable resource [1, 2] that drives and makes logistics systems functional.

Partners may also share logistics services offered under cloud computing. The cloud computing services comprise of Platform as a Service (PaaS), Software as a Service (SaaS), and Logistics Business Process as a Service (BPaaS). The PaaS is a layer of clouds that provide vital services in the form of a framework that can be used to simulate various logistics scenarios [15]. Equally, the SaaS may, for example, offer shareable digital platforms to facilitate matchmaking among suppliers and consumers of shareable assets. Additionally, the BPaaS facilitates a bundling of several logistics cloud services from different vendors and suppliers, to produce a directly useable logistics turnkey application [16]. Moreover, sharing is seen to emerge in human resources. In recent years, skills and personal time seems offered through shareable modes under the facilitation of digital platforms [4]. For example, in the US, about 34% of the workforce work as freelancers, revealing that there is a fundamental shift in attitudes about flexibility in workforces [4].

2.2   Trust-Building in Resource Sharing Networks

Trust-building, especially in business relationships may be upheld by various processes, as well as determined using diverse perspectives. According to [17], development of trust in business relationships draws in the calculative, predictive, capability, intentionality, and transference processes. The predictive and intentionality processes appear to clarify and backup better the context of intentions and trustworthy, and; may contribute to understanding undisclosed intentions and trustworthiness of suppliers and consumers who share logistics resources. These processes are defined as follows. Trust-building under the [17]: predictive process relies on developing confidence by prognosticating a target's behavior on account of repetitive interactions, and; intentionality process requires evaluating motivations of the target. One can also express this motivation in the form of actions and intentions. In this context, therefore, a party can be trusted if its actions and intentions are perceived as benevolent by the perceiver [18]. Besides the trust-building processes, trust in business relationships also originates from specific determinants.

Trust in business relationships is determined by [19]: partners' social interactions; institutionalized processes and routines, and; supplier selection processes. These determinants feature mainly in digital platforms. From searching to evaluation, partners interact in many ways under the guidance of an intermediating company. The intermediating company is expected to have already ruled out processes and routines, which suppliers and consumers will follow. The supplier selection process, for example, can follow a widely used criterion such previous performance. Equally, suppliers may be selected depending on their track record of performance [19].

In the matter of structure, collaborative networks in which sharing networks befall undergo three phases, namely: selection, enforcement, and evaluation. The first phase requires both the supplier and consumer to exchange information concerning the supply and demand of shareable logistics resources. In this exchange, attributes of a specific resource, its conditions, as well as amount of demand have to be provided. Additionally, reputation and trust that can lead partners to share a resource depend fundamentally on previous reviews and ratings. In the second phase, subject to applied interactions protocols, the supplier and consumer bargain and agree to a deal that is to be transacted. Agreements to implement may benefit from the power of cyber-physical systems and internet of things especially in tracking progress. Different from previous phase, trust is built by anticipating outcomes to resource sharing transactions. One way to unveil this anticipation is to simulate particular sharing scenarios. In the third phase, operations on sharing logistics resources are completed. Upon completion, suppliers and consumers review and rate each other. Provided reviews and ratings constitute feedbacks to related transactions they had undertaken. The feedback also updates previous reviews and ratings.

3   Methodology

The present paper follows a methodology sequenced in three stages. First, the aspect of reputation and trust mechanisms underlying online transactions in e-commerce are adapted to constitute a basis of establishing intentions and trustworthiness in resource sharing networks. These aspects are then linked to cognitive systems in humans and later borrowed into a context of computational settings. The cognitive systems are further enriched by principles originating from social psychology theory, such as the theory of planned behavior. Since interactions of suppliers and consumers exhibit a social phenomenon, principles of social exchange are as well applied. Afterward, the cognitive approach to monitor interactions of suppliers and consumers is conceived. Finally, an illustrative application that draws from industrial cases is provided.

4   Reputation and Trustworthiness in a Cognitive Perspectives

This section discusses limitations of online trust mechanisms and strengthens a need to embed cognitive systems in digital platforms (Subsect. 4.1). Subsection 4.2 presents cognitive principles that guide conception of the cognitive approach.

4.1 Reputation and Trust in e-Commerce and Resource Sharing Platforms

E-commerce platforms enjoy the self-regulation (decentralized) and institutional (centralized) controls in safeguarding online sales and purchases. They also benefit intermediation, for example, to recover economic values (such as money) from incomplete or unfulfilled transactions. Besides the economic recovery, reputation and trust between trading partners are established using online reviews and ratings. Even though, as outlined earlier, such reviews and ratings suffer a range of deceitful manipulations. For example, authors in [20] emphasize that overall numerical ratings typically used in review systems may not ideally indicate satisfaction of customers. In regard to unfairness, common biases in user-generated online ratings include the simple bias, under-reporting bias, and sequential bias [8]. In spite of these challenges, yet there is a lack of a commonly agreed conceptual model to detecting deceitful manipulations [21] in reviews and ratings. Although reputation mechanisms in e-commerce carry limitations, still they can be adapted by digital platforms in resource sharing networks. Except that, such mechanisms need to be complemented with, for example, cognitive systems that monitor in background interaction activities of the suppliers and consumers. For this reason, this paper proposes an approach to complement such biased reviews and ratings.

For cognitive systems to detect susceptible intentions and trustworthiness from review and ratings, there must exist enabling environments. Enabling environments may be drawn by considering differences between transactions underlying e-commerce and sharing networks in logistics. Currently, this paper provides three differences. First, while e-commerce involves sales, purchases, and delivery of goods and services, resource sharing concerns a joint usage of logistics assets. Second, in e-commerce, products or services are purchased mostly once by the same individual for an extended period, while in resource sharing, the same resource can be re-shared by the same consumer in short period. Third, in e-commerce, the seller is mostly the trustee, whereas in resource sharing both supplier and consumer become trustor and trustee simultaneously[1].

In a context of outlined differences, resource sharing opens additional chance to examine whether reviews and ratings provided were manipulated or not. For example, if consumer rates the supplier positively, it is expected that he will prefer to share a resource with the same supplier when another opportunity unfolds. If this is missing in environments where supplier and consumer have all possibilities to re-share, it becomes a signal that previous reviews and ratings may have carried hidden intentions. In this case, therefore, one way to safeguard resource sharing in a context of digital platforms is to embed cognitive systems that can monitor in background interactions activities of suppliers and consumers. Expectedly, such cognitive systems have to provide hidden headlights regarding intentions and trustworthiness of both the suppliers and consumers.

4.2 Behavior and Cognitive Systems in Building Trust

Prediction as the trust-building process hinges on anticipating behaviors of a target. The anticipation may be unveiled by scrutinizing experience accumulated under repetitive

---

[1] Meaning that, trust is placed mostly in both the supplier and consumer.

interactions of actors. In digitally mediated interactions, the accumulation, processing, foreseeing, and understanding of intentions and trustworthiness can be attained using cognitive systems. Cognitive systems refer to the application of human-like character-istics to convey and manipulate ideas [22]. In computing arena, people refer to cognitive systems as cognitive computing. To its advantage, cognitive computing helps to illu-minate headlights that were previously invisible, thus, allowing people to make more informed decisions [23] as well as learning. In a standpoint of resource sharing networks, cognitive systems may assist to explore and discover partners' hidden intention and trustworthiness, which are difficult to unfold using programmable systems.

The models of social psychology may guide the ability to foresee, detect and under-stand the intentions and trustworthiness of partners. Towards this, the Theory of Planned Behavior (TPB) in [24] assumes that people do what they intend to do and do not do what they do not intend. Given this, intention sheds light on the possibility of actors to perform a particular action. The author [24] emphasizes further that the most immediate and vital predictor of a person's behavior is his/her intention to perform it. Usually, intentions unfold into behavior when people carry out their actions. Henceforth, behavior as a consequence of the intention is the manifest, observable response in a given situation concerning a given target [25]. The intention and behavior can be identified by patterns of interactions, for example, by monitoring actors' interaction activities [26] in the background. Even though, it is vital to take note regarding dynamics of intentions. The effects of time and new information drive dynamics of intentions [27]. One crucial issue in concern is about how to apply principles of social psychology to enrich cognitive computing to complement trust-building under aspects of intentions and trustworthiness. This application constitutes a foundation to the proposed approach.

Furthermore, trust-building, as enabled by cognitive systems, is also grounded in social exchange principles. According to [28], for all actions taken by persons, the more often a particular action of a person is rewarding, the more likely the person is to perform that action again. Meaning that partners with previous rewarding actions carry high possibility to re-engage in future resource sharing endeavors. Henceforth, by drawing from principles of intention and rewarding actions, this paper proposes an approach that can surface hidden intentions intrinsic in biased reviews and ratings. To exemplify this in brief, if one party rates another one positively, it is declaring its intention to engage in future resource sharing ventures. This intention can be confirmed or disconfirmed once another chance to re-share a resource unfolds.

5 Proposed Cognitive Approach

The proposed cognitive approach takes into account provisions discussed in previous sections. It mainly harnesses requirements on social behavior to rewarding actions, intention, as well as cognitive systems. Equally, the approach rests on the assumption that at least one previous interaction between specific supplier and a consumer exists. A related hypothesis is to foresee that interactions between the resource supplier and consumer will re-occur in future engagements. Meaning that the same consumer may re-share the same resource with the same supplier when another opportunity appears.

This assumption is distinct from e-commerce, where consumers can rarely re-purchase products or services (e.g., electronic equipment, fashion, and sporting goods) from the same seller.

In its current form, the cognitive approach focuses on collecting and measuring the following features. First, it measures a number of resources offered; acceptances and rejections made by suppliers and consumers, and; offers seen by supplier and consumer. Second, the cognitive approach also collects as well information related to externally influencing factors. For example, information related to capacity, quality and location of a resource, price (per time/space/slot), and in case of a vehicle truck, its origin, and destination. These features get analyzed to provide useful insights. Remaining part of the approach advances as follows.

The platform supporting sharing of logistics resources comprises of many suppliers and consumers (Fig. 1). A resource publicized by suppliers is made available to multiple consumers, and various suppliers can provide similar offers.

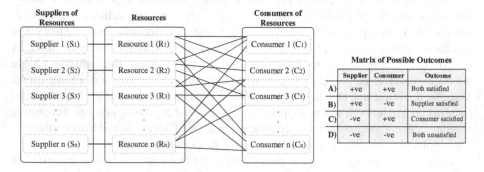

Fig. 1. Matching suppliers and consumers who share resources – a simplified view

Multiple offers enable consumers to access many options in searching and selecting a preferred supplier. For every possible search, the cognitive approach (system) records information about the resource, supplier, and consumer. It is worthy to note that, the supplier must have already described the resource in a manner desired, for example, by providing its capacity, location, price per time/space/slot, and in case of a vehicle truck, its origin, and destination. Afterward, interested consumers begin to interact with suppliers to negotiate a deal, and meanwhile; the system monitors in the background such interactions (Fig. 2). The system checks whether there exist supplier and consumer who had transacted earlier. If found, it checks again whether consumer C_x opts to transact with supplier S_x. The outcome is twofold: re-transacting or not. The choice to re-transact has to take into account that other influencing factors are held constant. Meaning that conditions (such as price which S_x declare) must be in a range that is similar or lower than those of remaining suppliers. Afterward, when supplier agrees to transact, the system rechecks a trend of the S_x to accept/bypass interested consumers, and similarly, the pattern of the C_x to take/reject offers from suppliers. For every termination or agreement reached, the system re-checks its stored history to draw helpful headlights. The check, mapping, and headlights to be derived are summarized in a matrix of possible outcomes (Fig. 1) as follows:

(a) Under normal circumstances, the expectation is that the two parties will re-transact. This expectation aligns to an attitude toward behavior (TPB), by which both the supplier and consumer had valued previous engagement positively. Equally, as per perceived behavioral control, consumer had previously perceived that the supplier has ability to perform a transaction (provide resource). However, if no party seems interested in re-transacting, and external factors are least influential, then it may imply that the previous reviews and ratings were unfair. The external factors constitute what the TPB refers to as control beliefs, which may facilitate or impede participation of supplier and consumer. Also, the implication rests on a principle that human-beings tend to repeat past rewarding actions while avoiding those costly ones. In addition, there might be an untold story that has to be unfolded between concerned supplier and consumer, which the reviews and ratings did not reveal;

(b) It is expected that consumer C_x will avoid to re-transact with supplier S_x because it was unsatisfied in prior engagements. Concordant to attitude toward a behavior (in TPB), consumer values negatively performance of the supplier by referring to previous engagements. Unlike the consumer C_x, the supplier S_x will be interested in re-transacting with consumer C_x because it valued previous engagement positively. However, if observed outcomes are beyond such expectations, then the reviews and ratings from one or both parties were possibly biased;

(c) Expectation along this outcome are similar to those in (b), except that this time the supplier S_x was unsatisfied;

(d) Since neither party was satisfied in previous engagements, it is expected that the supplier S_x and consumer C_x will not re-transact.

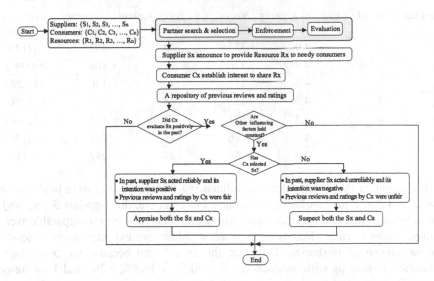

Fig. 2. A cognitive approach to surface hidden intention and trustworthiness

These headlights collected in a silent mode may later be published along with the supplier's and consumer's profile. The goal is to indicate intentions and trustworthiness of suppliers/consumers beyond those depicted in reviews and ratings.

6 Illustrative Application

Currently, the paper does not provide an empirical validation or evaluation of the proposed approach. It discusses illustrative example of the application of the cognitive approach. However, illustrating application by using industrial case is challenging due to lack of sharing practices, which entail likelihood of consumers to re-transact with the same supplier. As well, data about sharing scenarios involving assets such as vehicle trucks and warehouses is currently difficult to obtain. On account of this, the illustrative application is attained using ridesharing scenarios. The ridesharing offers an opportunity for suppliers and consumers of idle space in personal cars to re-share. Following this, one anonymous platform that offers ridesharing is used because suppliers and consumers of idle space in personal cars may attain a chance to re-share. The illustrative case study progresses as follows.

The list of suppliers offering shareable resources (idle spaces) between common source and destination areas is searched in the platform. A total of seven suppliers whose reviews exceed 100 are selected randomly. The selection seeks to ensure that, at least each supplier may have had a chance to re-share with the previous consumer. Afterward, analysis of the reviews is conducted to figure out consumers who have had ridesharing with the same supplier, at least, for more than once (Table 1). Equally, some years in which the supplier has been in business, its average rating, and ridings (sharing) are extracted.

Table 1. Summary of consumers' reviews and ratings on suppliers

Supplier	No. of years	Avg. rating	No. of sharing	Avg. sharing/ year	Consumers sharing	Consumers re-sharing
S_1	8	4.9	352	44	402	78 (19.4%)
S_2	4	4.8	116	29	106	0 (0.0%)
S_3	1	4.9	110	110	126	4 (3.2%)
S_4	5	4.9	221	44	154	8 (5.2%
S_5	4	4.9	171	43	122	2 (1.6%)
S_6	7	4.9	146	21	201	14 (7.0%)
S_7	7	4.4	256	37	247	28 (11.3%)

By assuming that other externally influencing factors (if any) were held constant; results in Table 1 may surface many issues. For example, the suppliers S_1, S_4, and S_5 had an almost equal number of average sharing (annually) as well as comparable average ratings. Under normal circumstances, such suppliers are expected to have scored a similar amount of re-sharing. However, this is different because the percentage of consumers re-sharing with suppliers S_1, S_4, and S_5 is 19.4%, 5.2%, and 1.6%, respectively. These results may convey an implication that many consumers evaluating the supplier S_1 had positive intention in their reviews and ratings.

In addition, it seems that reviews and ratings by such consumers of S_1 were mostly fair because many of them opted to re-share with their previous supplier. Correspondingly, the supplier S_1 appears to have exhibited behavior which is seemingly trusted by consumers. Unusual intention and trustworthiness appear in supplier S_2. Despite high average sharing per year, yet supplier S_2 had no any consumer opting to re-share with it, although its average rating is relatively high (4.8). The absence of re-sharing may imply that hidden intentions of consumers' reviews/ratings on the supplier S_2 were negative.

Further useful headlights may be derived by considering consumers who appeared to switch among suppliers. Towards attaining this, further analysis was undertaken to figure out if there exist resource consumers who have had ridesharing by more than one resource supplier (consumer shift). Figure 3 presents corresponding results. For example, out of 247 consumers who had ridesharing with supplier S_1; 8 had ridesharing with S_2; 10 had ridesharing with S_3; 11 had ridesharing with S_4; 6 had ridesharing with S_5, 10 had ride sharing with S_6, and; 10 had ridesharing with S_7.

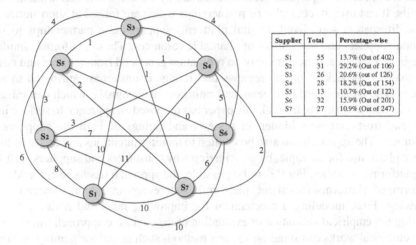

Supplier	Total	Percentage-wise
S1	55	13.7% (Out of 402)
S2	31	29.2% (Out of 106)
S3	26	20.6% (out of 126)
S4	28	18.2% (Out of 154)
S5	13	10.7% (Out of 122)
S6	32	15.9% (Out of 201)
S7	27	10.9% (Out of 247)

Fig. 3. Number of consumers who shift among suppliers

Assuming that customers prefer to attach themselves to a good supplier, results reveal that suppliers S_1 (13.7%), S_5 (10.7%), and S_7 (10.9%) managed to retain many customers. However, the situation is different to others, for example, supplier S_2 whose percentage of customers shifting to other suppliers is relatively large (29.2%). Under this circumstance, it seems that many consumers who have had ridesharing with supplier S_2 had no intention and trustworthiness to re-engage with that supplier, although their ratings were positive. This situation is different from supplier S_1 who had the highest number of consumers participating in ridesharing (Table 1) while having a low number of consumers who shift to other suppliers (Fig. 3).

As outlined before, these industrial cases have been provided to satisfy illustrative application of the cognitive approach. In view of this, used instances may contain limitations. For example, one flaw is that re-sharing in ridesharing may be affected many factors such as prices, date of travel, as well as the origin and destination. As far as the data used did not capture such issues, findings discussed in this section may be inconclusive. It might be that some consumers did not engage in re-sharing because their previous suppliers had changed, for example, common origins and destinations. Second, it may be that the offered ridesharing was unconducive to them, in terms of date and time of traveling, as well as price. If all these parameters had been captured since at beginning, it would help to enrich reported insights. It is suggested that these issues may be dealt with when undertaking empirical validation or evaluation of the proposed approach. Moreover, building on reported flaws, the present work do not compare its results to the state of the art. This is because data used in illustrative example lack some features. Correspondingly, extended evidence to justify selection of measurable features will be part of research works that succeeds the present paper.

7   Conclusion and Future Works

Collaboration in sharing logistics resources entails a joint usage of assets to attain mutual benefits. It can usually comprise of partnerships which are forged at short notice, and whose lifespan is short-lived. Digital platforms support these partnerships to inter- mediate suppliers and consumers of shareable resources. These platforms, similar to those in e-commerce, depend mainly on reputation generated from reviews and ratings. One major drawback of online reviews and ratings is unfairness attributed to many sources. The unfair (biased) reviews and ratings convey signals, which can misguide the individual to trust. To this end, this paper has proposed an approach to surface inten- tions and trustworthiness hidden in reviews and ratings of both the suppliers and consumers. The approach can also be applied to monitor intentions and trustworthiness among platforms, for example, by scrutinizing why consumers and suppliers shift from one platform to another. For this to be possible, the approach has to be embedded in a platform of platforms (regulator platform). Future research works extend to the following. First, modeling a mechanism for improving rates and reviews. Second, carrying out empirical validation or evaluation of the cognitive approach (mechanism). Such empirical works can stand on various methods such as serious gaming and multi- agent systems simulation.

References

1. Gci, Capgemini: 2016 Future Supply Chain. Serving Consumers in a Sustainable Way (2008). http://supplychainmagazine.fr/TOUTE-INFO/ETUDES/GCI_Capgemini-SC2016.pdf
2. Gorenflo, N.: The New Sharing Economy. Shareable Magazine (2010). https://www.shareable.net/blog/the-new-sharing-economy
3. Weinelt, B.: Digital Transformation of Industries: Logistics Industry (2016). http://reports.weforum.org/digital-transformation
4. Gesing, B.: Sharing economy logistics: Rethinking logistics with access over ownership. Troisdorf, Germany (2017). http://www.dhl.com
5. Buczynski, B.: Sharing is Good: How to Save Money, Time and Resources through Collaborative Consumption. New Society Publishers, Gabriola Island (2013)
6. Goudin, P.: The Cost of Non- Europe in the Sharing Economy. European Union, Brussels (2016). http://doi.org/10.2861/26238

7. Wosskow, D.: Unlocking the sharing economy: An independent review. Department for Business, Innovation and Skills, UK Government (2014). https://www.gov.uk/government/publications
8. Sikora, R., You, L.: Effect of reputation mechanisms and ratings biases on traders' behavior in online marketplaces. J. Organ. Comput. Electron. Commer. **24**(1), 58–73 (2014)
9. Josang, A., Ismail, R., Boyd, C.: A survey of trust and reputation systems for online service provision. Decis. Support Syst. **43**(2), 618–644 (2007)
10. Luca, M.: Designing Online Marketplaces: Trust and Reputation Mechanisms. Cambridge, MA (2006) http://www.nber.org/papers/w22616.pdf
11. Akoglu, L., Faloutsos, C., Chandy, R., Faloutsos, C.: Opinion fraud detection in online reviews by network effects. In: Proceeding of the 7th International AAAI Conference on Weblogs and Social Media, pp. 2–11. The AAAI Press, Palo Alto (2013)
12. Xu, C., Zhang, J.: Collusive opinion fraud detection in online reviews. ACM Trans. Web **11**(4), 1–28 (2017)
13. Mukherjee, S., Dutta, S., Weikum, G.: Credible review detection with limited information using consistency features. In: Frasconi, P., Landwehr, N., Manco, G., Vreeken, J. (eds.) ECML PKDD 2016. LNCS (LNAI), vol. 9852, pp. 195–213. Springer, Cham (2016). https://doi.org/10.1007/978-3-319-46227-1_13
14. Pomponi, F., Fratocchi, L., Tafuri, S.R.: Trust development and horizontal collaboration in logistics: a theory based evolutionary framework. Supply Chain Manag. Int. J. **20**(1), 83–97 (2015)
15. Schuldt, A., Hribernik, K.A., Gehrke, J.D., Thoben, K.-D., Herzog, O.: Cloud computing for autonomous control in logistics. In: 40th Annual Conference of the German Society for Computer Science, Leipzig, Germany, 27 September–1 October, pp. 305–310 (2010)
16. ALICE: Information Systems for Interconnected Logistics: Research & Innovation Roadmap (2014). https://www.etp-logistics.eu/wp-content/uploads/2015/08/W36mayo-kopie.pdf
17. Doney, P.M., Cannon, J.P.: An Examination of the nature of trust in buyer-seller relationships. J. Mark. **61**(2), 35–51 (1997)
18. Lindskold, S.: Trust development, the GRIT proposal, and the effects of conciliatory acts on conflict and cooperation. Psychol. Bull. **85**(4), 772–793 (1978)
19. Dyer, J.H., Chu, W.: The determinants of trust in supplier-automaker relationships in the U.S., Japan and Korea. J. Int. Bus. Stud. **31**(2), 259–285 (2000)
20. Racherla, P., Connolly, D.J., Christodoulidou, N.: What determines consumers' ratings of service providers? An exploratory study of online traveler reviews. J. Hosp. Mark. Manag. **22**(2), 135–161 (2013)
21. Hu, N., Bose, I., Koh, N.S., Liu, L.: Manipulation of online reviews: an analysis of ratings, readability, and sentiments. Decis. Support Syst. **52**(3), 674–684 (2012)
22. High, R.: The Era of Cognitive Systems: An Inside Look at IBM Watson and How it Works. International Business Machines Corporation (2012). http://www.redbooks.ibm.com/redpapers/pdfs/redp4955.pdf
23. Kelly, J.E.: Cognition and the future of knowing: How humans and machines are forging a new age of understanding (2015). https://www.research.ibm.com/software/IBMResearch/multimedia/Computing_Cognition_WhitePaper.pdf
24. Sheeran, P.: Intention—behavior relations: a conceptual and empirical review. Eur. Rev. Soc. Psychol. **12**(1), 1–36 (2002)
25. Ajzen, I.: Theory of Planned Behavior (2006). http://people.umass.edu/aizen/tpb.diag.html#null-link
26. Sherchan, W., Nepal, S., Paris, C.: A survey of trust in social networks. ACM Comput. Surv. **45**(4), 47 (2013)

27. Ajzen, I.: From intentions to actions: a theory of planned behavior. In: Kuhl, J., Beckmann, J. (eds.) Action Control. SSSSP, pp. 11–39. Springer, Heidelberg (1985). https://doi.org/10.1007/978-3-642-69746-3_2

28. Homans, G.C.: Social Behaviour: Its Elementary Forms (Rev. edn.). Harcourt Brace Jovanovich, Inc., New York (1974)

Collaborative Energy Services in Smart Cities

A Virtual Collaborative Platform to Support Building Information Modeling Implementation for Energy Efficiency

Ioan Petri[1(✉)], Ali Alhamami[1], Yacine Rezgui[1], and Sylvain Kubicki[2]

[1] School of Engineering, Cardiff University, Cardiff, Wales, UK
{petrii, alhamamia, rezguiy}@cardiff.ac.uk
[2] Luxembourg Institute of Science and Technology (LIST),
Esch-sur-Alzette, Luxembourg
sylvain.kubicki@list.lu

Abstract. There is increased interest in complying with the new regulations and policies associated with the climate change. In particular industries such as the AEC (Architecture, Engineering and Construction) industry seek to find new strategies and practices for facilitating sustainability but also new regulations to improve efficiency at the building level. Institutions and industrial bodies are now in the process of alignment with new legislative stipulations regarding carbon emissions with wider reflection into environment, social and economic models. At building level such strategies refer to decarbonisation and energy efficiency supported with data driven techniques enriched with virtual collaboration and optimization methods.

The increased interest of the research community in Building Information Modeling (BIM) has facilitated numerous solutions ranging from digital products, information retrieval, and optimization techniques all aiming at addressing energy optimization and performance gap reduction.

In this paper we present how a virtual collaborative system can be efficiently used for implementing BIM based energy optimization for controlling, monitoring buildings and running energy optimization, greatly contributing to creating a BIM construction community with energy practices. The solution described, known as energy-bim.com platform, disseminates energy efficient practices and community engagement and provides support for building managers in implementing energy efficient optimization plans.

Keywords: Virtual collaboration · Construction community
Building Information Modeling · Energy efficiency · Training

1 Introduction

Research studies have reported that global warming has a significant impact of the building sector and lead to the appearance of several stringent regulations and implementation rules imposed by European and National bodies in the field of energy and construction [1].

© IFIP International Federation for Information Processing 2018
Published by Springer Nature Switzerland AG 2018. All Rights Reserved
L. M. Camarinha-Matos et al. (Eds.): PRO-VE 2018, IFIP AICT 534, pp. 539–550, 2018.
https://doi.org/10.1007/978-3-319-99127-6_46

Recent researching attempts aim at providing a fundamental step change in facilitating efficiency at the building level through BIM training with a view to effectively address European energy and carbon reduction targets. There is an increased interest in promoting a well-trained world leading generation of decision makers, practitioners, and blue collars in BIM for energy efficiency and establishing a world-leading platform for BIM for energy efficiency training nurtured by an established community of interest [2]. Benchmarks exist at Europe-wide BIM trainings across the building value chain (including lifecycle and supply chain), highlighting energy efficiency linkages, as well as qualification targets, delivery channels, skills, accreditation mechanisms, while highlighting training gaps and enhancement potential.

With such a complex reality in the construction, Building Information Modelling (BIM) is paving the way to more effective collaboration process between actors involved in building lifecycle [3]. BIM facilitates a more data driven modeling and analysis of the built environment during its entire life cycle from concept design to decommissioning (Fig. 1). BIM brought the most transformative power into AEC/FM domain (Architecture, Engineering and Construction/Facility Management) during the last decade in terms of its fundamental life cycle and supply chain integration and digital collaboration [4]. BIM holds the critical key to revolutionize the construction industry, which is forecasted to reach over $11 trillion global yearly spending by 2020 [5]. Researching attempts aim to harmonize energy related BIM qualification and skills frameworks available across Europe with a view of reaching a global consensus through a BIM for energy efficiency External Expert Advisory Board (EEAB) [6].

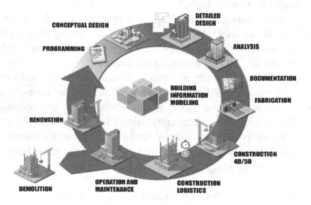

Fig. 1. BIM uses across building lifecycle: it presents the entire life cycle of projects from concept design to decommissioning.

This paper focuses specifically on using virtual collaboration to create a BIM community of professionals to enhance skills and enable BIM training and to enable in-depth analysis and gaps identification of skills and competencies involved in BIM training for energy efficiency. We have combined a number of different technologies such as semantic web, social networks, mobile applications towards a knowledge representation in order to address BIM for energy training and education.

Consultations and interviews have been used as a method to collect requirements and a portfolio of use-cases has been created to understand existing BIM practices and determine existing limitations and gaps in BIM training.

In Sect. 2, we will present background on collaboration and BIM training. Section 3 describes the proposed methodology and identified requirements. Section 4 presents the evaluation process and we conclude in Sect. 5.

2 Related Work

The building domain is extremely dynamic with knowledge and technical solutions evolving continuously, all related to a general objective of reducing energy in the building environment. Such performance management objectives have been also stipulated into the European Union regulation with particular emphasis on energy reduction, cost effective solutions and climate change strategies [6]. The dynamics of the construction market has been statically forecasted to grow in the next decade [7]. Countries such as UK have developed strategies to address these objectives: (a) 33% reduction in both the initial cost of construction and the whole life cost of assets; (b) 50% reduction in the overall time from inception to completion for new build and refurbished assets; (c) 50% reduction in greenhouse gas emissions in the built environment; (d) 50% reduction in the trade gap between total exports and total imports for construction products and materials [8, 9].

With the new technological developments it has become possible to address the energy demand, maximize the efficiency with optimization methods in building lifecycle and remove carbon footprint. This requires collaboration between various factors and actors involved in the process of construction and analysis of each building construction stage with identification of associated requirements and optimization objectives [10, 11].

To facilitate the development of performance management strategies for the built environment, companies and industrial organizations need to adhere to the digitalization process and to find new collaboration mechanisms involving virtual reality, community involvement and training strategies for roles and skills required for the construction process. BIM for energy represents a strategic field of research that industry seeks in adopting mainly focusing on the definition of levels for competencies and skills that are required within organizations.

Engagement with BIM practices has an implication on the organisation level but also represents a concept that actors involved in the construction industry need to understand. BIM represents a technology but is also referring to behaviours, culture, and set of values and experiences that can be identified in an institution in order to promote reliable construction and address sustainability.

3 Methodology

The research methodology proposed in this paper utilizes a methodology that is organized in two parts: (a) qualitative data analysis and (b) quantitative data analysis to elicit BIM training requirements for energy efficiency in the construction sector.

3.1 General Methodology

The requirements gathering studies employed extensive consultations including: (1) a user engagement instrument in the form of an online virtual collaborative platform to support with the requirement capture activity of the project while maximizing users' engagement by the creation of a community of practice around the theme of BIM for energy efficiency, (2) an online Europe-wide BIM use-case collection template and questionnaire (November 2017–February 2018) from which 38 best practice use-cases have been collected, (3) experts panel consultations in Europe comprising 1 workshop (c.**40** participants in total), (4) a series of 15 semi-structured interviews with key industry representatives (December 2017–February 2018), and (5) other focus meetings with project partners.

These consultation studies have been facilitated by an open community of users that share resources and experiences related to BIM energy training supported by **energy-bim.com.** The objectives of the consultations were to determine best practices, regulation awareness and gaps in BIM for energy efficiency domain and to determine a set of training requirements. The subsequent combined consultations explored stakeholders' knowledge, understanding, and behaviors, and helped identify key barriers to BIM applicability for energy efficiency. A number of **40** experts took part in the consultations (workshop), including: construction companies and practitioners, advisory groups, professional organizations, consultants, policy makers and education and training bodies.

The results of the use-cases and interview analysis are presented in Sect. 4. The detailed steps adopted in the methodology are as follows (see Fig. 2): (i) Adapt an existing web portal to carry out the study consultation while maximizing continuous engagement with our Expert panel and Community of Practice, (ii) Develop a Web Crawler that aggregated BIM related knowledge and stores it adequately to enable searches and authoritative URIs as input, (iii) Invite partners, expert panel members, and community of practice members to register on study portal to provide authoritative sources of information, (iv) Provide an implicit validation of the crawler, (v) Develop a framework to categorise all retained use cases using 2 dimensions, i.e. lifecycle (from Briefing to Recycling) and supply chain (i.e. Architects, Structural engineers, to blue collars), (vi) Develop a template to report selected use cases, implemented directly on the study portal. The template involves a field to categorise the use case for further retrieval, (vii) Filter and document all retained use cases on the portal, (viii) Generate the study requirements, (ix) Validate the requirements using our Expert Panel, (x) Community exposure by publishing the study use cases widely inviting people to register if they want to access study materials.

3.2 Supportive Virtual Community Platform for BIM Requirements Capture

To support with the methodology and create a dynamic community for capturing requirements for BIM training we have adapted and re-developed a web solution that provides integrated access to building information modelling (BIM) resources (Fig. 3).

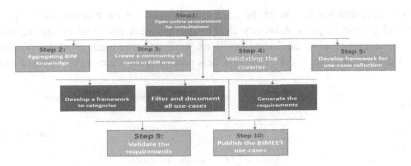

Fig. 2. General requirements methodology

This platform has a number of underpinning services and an ontology and has helped in the process of BIM training requirements for energy efficiency but also aims at solving the key issue of knowledge dissemination in, and stakeholder collaboration and engagement with, BIM practices and construction. The objective is to identify gaps and requirements as an initial phase but also to support with the project implementation phase in providing construction professionals with the necessary training to offer effective BIM expertise for energy efficient and low carbon solutions, while creating a virtual collaboration framework for BIM industry professionals (see Fig. 4).

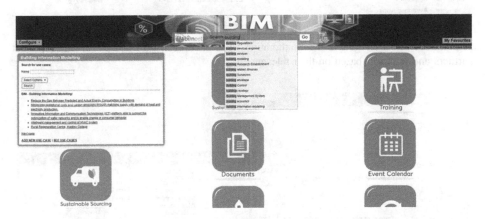

Fig. 3. The virtual collaboration platform interface: [www.energy-bim.com]

The Search Service: As part of the platform, we have implemented a search service that performs semantic searching on the BIM knowledge base from a set of authoritative URIs. The submitted BIM query has associated ontological artephacts that are then expanding in creating a framework of dependencies and concepts which have been developed based on a crawling process. The sources have been automatically retrieved and validated with support from the consortium of partners (see Fig. 4).

For testing and validation of the searching system, we have relied on the group of experts (External Experts Advisory Board) and partners involved in the requirement assessment phase, plus an increasingly expanding constituency as the platform is extended to further users. For collecting best practices use-cases in the field of BIM for

Edit Profile	Change Password	Change Search Preferences	Change Display Settings

Add New Site:

http:// [   ] ▼ [Add Site]

Site Name	Status	Number of Pages
My Sites:		
http://www.adveranda.com	Site not yet indexed ✗	
Core Sites:		
http://www.energysavingtrust.org.uk	Last updated:2012-11-01	3874 pages Reset
http://www.oneplanetproducts.com	Last updated:2012-11-01	171 pages Reset
http://www.ciria.org	Last updated:2012-11-01	1 pages Reset
http://www.ice.org.uk	Last updated:2012-11-01	3650 pages Reset
http://www.greenspec.co.uk	Last updated:2012-11-01	740 pages Reset
http://www.defra.gov.uk	Last updated:2012-11-01	8518 pages Reset
http://www.wrap.org.uk	Last updated:2012-11-01	207 pages Reset
http://www.carbontrust.co.uk	Last updated:2012-11-01	1991 pages Reset
http://www.bre.co.uk	Last updated:2012-11-01	35 pages Reset
http://www.bsria.co.uk	Last updated:2012-11-01	952 pages Reset
http://www.ihs.com	Last updated:2012-11-01	666 pages Reset
http://www.decc.gov.uk	Last updated:2012-11-01	685 pages Reset
http://www.architecture.com	Last updated:2012-11-01	6477 pages Reset
http://www.wholebuild.co.uk	Last updated:2012-11-01	480 pages Reset
http://www.rics.org/uk	Last updated:2012-11-01	348 pages Reset
http://eca.co.uk	Last updated:2012-11-01	44 pages Reset
http://www.cibse.org	Last updated:2012-11-01	1 pages Reset
http://www.buildingsmart.org.uk	Last updated:2012-11-01	16 pages Reset
http://www.labc.uk.com	Last updated:2012-11-01	1 pages Reset
http://www.ccinw.com	Last updated:2012-11-01	81 pages Reset
http://wales.gov.uk	Last updated:2012-11-01	0 pages Reset
Indexes Awaiting Approval:		
http://www.adveranda.com	Approve Index	Delete Index

Fig. 4. Sources Aggregation: The authorative URIs have been provided by BIMEET project partners and validated based on their relevance.

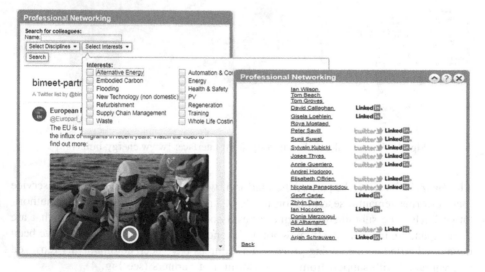

Fig. 5. Professional networking service: Presenting a searching results of individuals and experts in the field of BIM

energy a template has been designed and implemented and exposed online for users to submit their cases.

The Professional Networking Service: has been created on the hypothesis that social network activity is now increasing in relevance and useful insights can be drawn from analysis of such social network graphs. This service supports collaboration with Twitter and LinkedIn credentials and contributes to the process of knowledge creation for any BIM building project (Fig. 5).

4 Evaluation

In this section we present the evaluation of our collaboration process undertaken through the virtual platform in transferring knowledge between individuals and also automated gaps and skills identification in the field of BIM for energy. We present results of the requirement capture process, based on 6 months of work on collecting data and sources, as facilitated by the virtual platform and associated community followed by several requirements collected for the training process.

4.1 Use-Case Collection

The objective of this study is to demonstrate how virtual collaboration can support BIM based energy-efficient design, construction and building maintenance in many ways. In principal, BIM can boost and ease energy-efficient building on the basis of better data exchange and communication flows, and in practice for example by accelerating energy simulations and searching for beneficial solutions, supporting end users' involvement, requirement setting and commissioning, and by providing an opportunity for systematic maintenance management. Amidst the positive impacts brought about by BIM, AEC/FM industry can leverage BIM for greater energy efficiency in new designs as well as in retrofit and renovation projects. The study demonstrates the strengths of virtual BIM collaboration in energy-efficient building by collecting and providing use cases. Table 1 shows two examples of use-cases where life cycle applicability is aligned with eight work stages of RIBA plan of work 2013.

4.2 Platform Supported Use-Case Type Analysis

We have applied our automated analysis utilizing the web-platform on 40 use-cases collected from users in European countries. The results reported in this section present the distribution based on criteria such as: discipline, building type, impact, lifecycle stage.

Use-Cases Type Analysis: In this part we are interested in identifying what is the overall distribution of use-cases collected in relation to the use-case type. There are three types of use cases in this evaluation which are: (1) Research & Development, (2) Real world application and (3) BIM Guideline. As per the analysis, it can be observed that Research & Development covers a number of 17 use cases, and Real-

Table 1. BIM based best practice use-cases

Variables/use-cases	Use case 1	Use case 2
Title	Reduce the Gap between Predicted and Actual Energy Consumption in Buildings: KnoholEM project	BIM-based Parametric Building Energy Performance Multi-Objective Optimization
Use case type	Research & Development	Research & Development
Target discipline	Facility Management	Architectural Design
Target building type	Public	Domestic
Lifecycle applicability	In Use	Concept Design, Developed Design
Brief description	This study presents a novel BIM-based approach with the objective to reduce the gap between predicted and actual energy consumption in buildings during their operation stage [12]	An integrated system is developed for enabling designers to optimize multiple objectives in the early design process [13]. A prototype of the system is created in an open-source visual programming application - Dynamo, which can interact with a BIM tool (Autodesk Revit®) to extend its parametric capabilities
Impacts	The use of BIM has helped achieve a reduction of 25% energy compared to baseline figures	The use of a BIM model to generate a multiplicity of parametric design variations for simulated and procedural analysis is a viable workflow for designers seeking to understand trade-offs between daylighting and energy use

world application has 13 use cases and BIM guideline has only 1 use-case (at the time of writing this paper, additional ones are expected in this category) (see Fig. 6).

Target Discipline Analysis: The portfolio of use-cases is structured based on the target discipline. Figure 7 presents the distribution of use-cases based on the target discipline. Architecture design and Facility management discipline projects use BIM more frequently whereas structure engineer and mechanical engineer projects utilise BIM in a lower percentage. In the analysis we have used different target disciplines such as architecture design, facility management, structure engineer, mechanical engineer, and other.

Architecture designers are targeted by 29%, facility management by 25% whereas the structure and mechanical engineers are targeted by 16% and 14%, respectively.

Building Type Analysis: In this part we assess the use-cases based on the type of building project where BIM has been utilized. As reported in Fig. 8, the majority of projects are for public buildings whereas domestic, commercial and industrial building

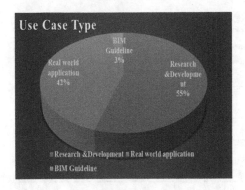

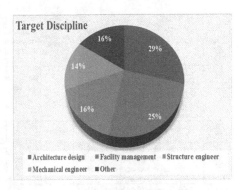

Fig. 6. Use-case type analysis of useBIM for Energy Efficiency

Fig. 7. Target Discipline analysis of use BIM for Energy Efficiency

seem less popular in adopting BIM. From the set of building types that we have used in our evaluation, the most popular are public buildings whereas domestic building, commercial building, and industrial building have lower percentage. As reported in Fig. 10, 65% of these use cases have applied BIM in public building, 17.5% in domestic building, and the rest of them in commercial and industrial buildings.

Lifecycle Stage Analysis: For the analysis, we have used RIBA stage life-cycles and this part aims at determining associated life-cycle stages of each BIM best practice use-case. Figure 9 shows that, 56% from the recorded projects use BIM for energy efficiency in the design stages in lifecycle of the project, whereas in-use stage identifies 13% in the lifecycle of the projects.

Target Discipline and Impacts: The first variable used for the analysis is the target discipline which we compare with the impacts to find the corresponding association between the target discipline and the impacts of use cases. Figure 10 shows that the majority of use cases that implement BIM for energy efficiency are associated with the facility management discipline. However, there are a number of use-cases that

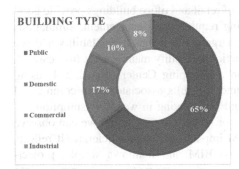

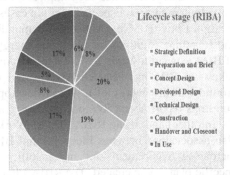

Fig. 8. Building type analysis of use BIM for Energy Efficiency

Fig. 9. Lifecycle stages analysis of use BIM for Energy Efficiency

No.	Use cases/ Target discipline	Architecture design	Facility management	Structure engineer	Mechanical engineer	Other	Impacts
1	Reduce the Gap Between Predicted and Actual Energy Consumption in Buildings						Reduction of 25% energy compared to baseline figures.
2	Minimizing operational costs and carbon emissions through matching supply with demand of heat and electricity production.						Leading to a 32% increase in profit and 36% reduction in CO_2 emissions.
3	Intelligent management and control of HVAC system						Up to 30% of Energy Saving Up to 30% Emission reduction
4	Friendly and Affordable Sustainable Urban Districts Retrofitting (FASUDIR) - Heinrich-Lubke housing area, Frankfurt, Germany						GWP reduction of 60%. Operational energy consumption reduction of 35%
5	Friendly and Affordable Sustainable Urban Districts Retrofitting (FASUDIR) - Budapest Residential District						Operational energy reduced by 35% and energy running costs reduced by 35%
6	An innovative integrated concept for monitoring and evaluating building energy performance (the gap between predicted and actual building energy performance is addressed by the project).						Achieve building energy performance
7	Parametric design of a shelter roof in urban context						Early BIM for parametric optimization through simulations
8	Building As A Service						Optimize energy performance in the application domain of non-residential buildings
9	Delivering highly energy efficient hospital centre						41% reduction in fabric loss heat, 29% reduction in carbon emissions,15% reduction in overall energy usage
10	Shopping Center using around half the energy of a typical development						50 % energy savings , 50 % savings in water consumption
11	Design of energy-efficient library with high architectural goals						Energy optimization results impacted for the building and HVAC design
12	Use of Optimization tool to compare hundreds of concepts energy efficiency before actual design						Use of Optimization tool has the potential to save money and time while directing to more optimal energy efficiency solutions.

Fig. 10. Relevance between target discipline and the impacts: This figure shows how the impact evolves with different disciplines.

implement BIM for energy efficiency methodology for multiple disciplines with great impacts on energy and water savings.

To this day, BIM has been implemented more and with more powerful results for some building types. Especially certain cases of retail and office buildings provide good examples how BIM has supported demanding requirement management, simulations and searching solutions for ambitious energy targets. For instance, availability and use of BIM data aid towards 25% of energy reduction in facility management (use case 1). Likewise, BIM has been effectively used in a Shopping Center (use case 4) using around half the energy of a typical development, results associated with commercial buildings report about 50% energy saving and 50% saving in water consumption.

In other hand, using RIBA Plan of Work for lifecycle applicability we can observe also associations between lifecycles and BIM impact on energy efficiency. It reflects increasing requirements for sustainability and BIM and it allows simple, project-specific plans to be created. The RIBA Plan of Work organizes the design process into different stages including briefing, designing, constructing, maintaining, operating and using building. According to these stages, various ways of use and levels of impact can be identified for the use of BIM for energy efficiency.

5 Conclusion

In this paper we present a virtual collaboration platform addressing the requirements elicitation phase for determining gaps and new strategies in delivering BIM training for energy efficiency. We have used a participative and incremental approach and involved the project's External Expert Advisory Board with a view to reach key stakeholder communities in order to help identify and then screen/analyse past and ongoing projects related to energy efficiency involving aspects of BIM. Our analysis and studies aimed at assembling evidence-based quantitative/measurable scenarios and use cases that demonstrate the role of BIM in achieving energy efficiency in buildings across the whole value chain. We have recorded a number of 38 best practices use-cases from the field of BIM for energy efficiency and conducted automated in depth-analysis to understand which are the gaps in BIM training and possible areas of improvement. These use-cases are published and maintained on the study platform (www.energy-bim. com) and accessible to potential users across Europe. The resulting evidence has been structured by stage and discipline, highlighting stakeholder targets ranging from blue collar workers to decision makers.

In future we are aiming at consolidating this community of BIM professionals that can share experiences and contribute to the development of building digitalization process with emphasis on BIM skills and competencies and associated training. We intend to create a framework for training BIM professionals for energy efficiency based on an assessment of desired skills and training objectives.

Acknowledgments. This work is part of EU H2020 BIMEET project: "BIM-based EU-wide Standardized Qualification Framework for achieving Energy Efficiency Training", grant reference: 753994.

References

1. European Commission: Challenging and Changing Europe's Built Environment A vision for a sustainable and competitive construction sector by 2030 (2005)
2. Thomson, D.B., Miner, R.G.: Building Information Modeling - BIM: Contractual Risks are Changing with Technology (2010)
3. Petri, I., Beach, T., Rezgui, Y., Wilson, I.E., Li, H.: Engaging construction stakeholders with sustainability through a knowledge harvesting platform. Comput. Ind. **65**, 449–469 (2014)
4. Eadie, R., Browne, M., Odeyinka, H., McKeown, C., McNiff, S.: BIM implementation throughout the UK construction project lifecycle: an analysis. Autom. Constr. **36**, 145–151 (2013)
5. Cummings, D., Blanford, K.: Global Construction Outlook: Executive Outlook (2013)
6. Petri, I., Kubicki, S., Rezgui, Y., Guerriero, A., Li, H.: Optimizing energy efficiency in operating built environment assets through building information modeling: a case study. Energies **10**, 1167 (2017)

7. Global Construction Perspectives and Oxford Economics: Global Construction 2030 A global forecast for the construction industry to 2030 (2015)
8. Magnier, L., Haghighat, F.: Multiobjective optimization of building design using TRNSYS simulations, genetic algorithm, and Artificial Neural Network. Build. Environ. **45**, 739–746 (2010)
9. Rezvan, A.T., Gharneh, N.S., Gharehpetian, G.B.: Optimization of distributed generation capacities in buildings under uncertainty in load demand. Energy Build. **57**, 58–64 (2013)
10. Rezgui, Y.: Harvesting and Managing Knowledge in Construction: From Theoretical Foundations to Business Applications. Routledge (2011)
11. Bryde, D., Broquetas, M., Volm, J.M.: The project benefits of Building Information Modelling (BIM). Int. J. Proj. Manag. **31**, 971–980 (2013)
12. Yuce, B., Rezgui, Y.: An ANN-GA semantic rule-based system to reduce the gap between predicted and actual energy consumption in buildings. IEEE Trans. Autom. Sci. Eng. **14**, 1351–1363 (2017)
13. Asl, M., Bergin, M., Menter, A., Yan, W.: BIM-based parametric building energy performance multi-objective optimization (2014)

Decentralised District Multi-vector Energy Management: A Multi-agent Approach

Joelle Klaimi$^{(\boxtimes)}$ and Meritxell Vinyals$^{(\boxtimes)}$

CEA, LIST, Laboratoire d'Analyse des Données et d'Intelligence des Systèmes,
91191 Gif-sur-Yvette, France
joelle.klaimi@cea.fr, meritxell.vinyals@cea.fr

Abstract. Despite its many advantages, the non-controllable and intermittent nature of renewable energy sources is adding further stress to the energy networks and hence, grid operators are often forced to curtail RES generation or to limit its further penetration in the most congested areas. Smart tri-generation districts (electricity, gas, heat) can be key to mitigate these issues and increase the renewable hosting capacity of the grid, provided their feature an optimal use of their energy conversion and storage capabilities. This paper presents a district energy management approach based on Multi-Agent System (MAS) that takes into consideration the tri-energyvectors (electricity, gas, thermal). The optimization problem is solved in a distributed way based on the Alternating Direction Method of Multipliers with the objective of minimizing district costs and preliminary results show the efficiency of our approach to achieve this objective.

Keywords: Multi-Agent Systems · Multi-vector energy management
Distributed optimisation · Energy conversion · ADMM

1 Introduction

In line with the energy and climate objectives, the share of energy generated from Renewable Energy Sources (RES) such as wind or solar energy is continuously growing, e.g. representing 30% in Europe in 2016[1]. Despite their many advantages, the intermittent and non-controllable nature of RES is adding further stress to the energy network and hence, grid operators are often forced to curtail RES generation or to limit its further penetration in the most congested areas. Smart tri-generation districts (electricity, gas and heat) can be key to mitigate these issues and increase the renewable hosting capacity of the grid, provided their feature advanced energy conversion and storage capabilities. Being equipped with boilers and heat pumps, the next generation of smart districts are capable of converting electricity into thermal energy, whereby excess energy can be stored thanks to their storage capacity. Analogously, power to gas technologies transforms the electricity into methane so that the latter can be reused (i.e. by a gas boiler)

---

[1] http://www.eea.europa.eu/data-and-maps/indicators/overview-of-the-electricityproduction-2/assessment.

© IFIP International Federation for Information Processing 2018
Published by Springer Nature Switzerland AG 2018. All Rights Reserved
L. M. Camarinha-Matos et al. (Eds.): PRO-VE 2018, IFIP AICT 534, pp. 551–559, 2018.
https://doi.org/10.1007/978-3-319-99127-6_47

or exported to a gas network. Unfortunately, even if these three networks are closely physically linked, different energy carriers are usually considered separately in energy management solutions, resulting in an under-optimal use of the capabilities of energy systems. Thus, there is the need of management algorithms which will ensure that the right conversion/storage method is chosen to avoid curtailment and maximise efficiency, taking into account all energy carriers. The optimal management of buildings has been commonly addressed by means of centralised approaches, which aggregate all needed information to make central decisions at a central controller. For example, Xiao *et al.* [1] proposed a novel approach that aims to reduce peak hours electricity consumption. In addition, some research papers used predictions in order to improve the quality of the proposed algorithms [2, 3]. However, the implementation of centralized approaches is typically not suitable for solving the multi-stakeholder district coordination due to the privacy and interoperability issues caused by a centralised optimisation strategy. In contrast, agent-based technology, which relies on dynamic, decentralised and hierarchical negotiation, is considered as a good solution for a smart grid communication because of the autonomy, reactivity, pro-activeness and collaborative capabilities of the agents [4]. For example, [5] proposes an agent that optimizes energy usage in commercial buildings by exploiting the flexibility of different occupants to hold event/meeting schedules. The work presented in [6] proposes a MAS-based control algorithm for building energy management system that is able to minimize energy costs while maximizing energy efficiency for all the energy zones using power system optimisations. Yuce *et al.* [7] presents a new scheduling algorithm for building energy management by using negotiation and optimisation algorithms. The proposed method requires (a) thermal energy modelling, (b) Artificial Neural Network (ANN) training, and (c) Genetic Algorithm-ANN (GAANN) based optimisation. This proposed algorithm integrates all building aspects: geo-metrical information, occupancy schedules, HVAC schedules and building materials details. Therefore, over the past years, some works have focused on designing new demand response schemes to better incentivise and coordinate the consumers. For example, in [8] authors formulated an energy consumption scheduling game, based on pricing tariffs which differentiate the energy usage in time and level. In order to minimize the peak-to-average ratio in aggregate load demand, the authors in [9] proposed to use a game theory for demand-side management. In the same context, a multi-party energy management model for smart buildings (integrating PV systems and automatic demand response) based on non-cooperative game theory is proposed in [10]. To address these challenges this paper proposes a MAS energy platform to optimise simultaneously the different energy flows of the district. In this context, this paper proposes the following contributions:

- We model the district multi-vector energy management problem by means of a multi-vector energy coordination network.
- We distribute this cooperative network among different agents and we use the ADMM algorithm as a coordination mechanism among these agents.
- We empirically evaluate our approach via simulations showing how the proposed approach can significantly reduce the district energy costs.

The rest of this paper is organized as follows. We first formulate the district multi-vector energy management problem as an energy coordination network (Sect. 2.1), we continue by presenting the optimisation algorithms (Sect. 2.2) and by describing some of the implemented agent models (Sect. 2.3). Finally, we present some simulation results (Sect. 3) and conclude (Sect. 4).

2 Distributed District Multi-vector Energy Management

The objective of district multi-vector energy management is to ensure an optimal use of energy at district-level. With this aim we propose to model the optimisation problem by means of an energy coordination network and solve it distributively using advanced optimisation schemes based on the ADMM algorithm. Our approach rely on predictions of consumption, RES and grid prices and performs a day-head optimisation providing the scheduling for the operations of the different district dispatchable devices (storages, converters, generator).

2.1 Multi-vector Energy Coordination Networks

Following [11], an energy coordination network consists of a set of terminals, T, a set of devices, D, and a set of nets, N. By definition, a terminal is defined as a connection that models the energy exchange between a (single) device and a (single) net. Thus, each terminal $t \in T$ is associated to an energy flow $p_t = (p_t(1), \ldots, p_t(H)) \in \mathbb{R}^H$, over a time horizon $H \in N^+$. A device is associated to one or more terminals (i.e. transfer points) through which it exchanges energy. For each device $d \in D$, d refers to: (1) the device; and (2) the set of terminals associated with the device itself. Furthermore, for all $\tau \in [1, H], p_t(\tau)$ is the energy consumed (if $p_t(\tau) > 0$, otherwise produced) by device d through terminal t, during the time step corresponding to τ. In this paper, we consider $p_d = \{p_d | t \in d\}$ as the set of all power schedules associated with a device d. Then, p_d can be associated with a $|d| \times H$ matrix. In addition to $|d|$ terminals, each device d is also associated with: (i) a cost function $f_n : \mathbb{R}|d| \times H \to \mathbb{R}$ that returns the operating cost of the device for a given energy schedule; and (ii) a set of constraints, C_d, that p_d should satisfy in order to be a viable planning. Nets are energy exchange zones which constrain the energy schedules to satisfy physical constraints (i.e. energy balancing). We use the same notation for nets as we do for devices: every net $n \in N$ has $|n|$ terminals, an objective function $f_n : \mathbb{R}|n| \times H \to \mathbb{R}$ and a set of constraints, C_n, that satisfy the energy balancing condition ($\sum_{t \in n} p_t(\tau) = 0, \forall \tau \in [1, H]$).

The global optimisation problem can be defined as follows:

$$min_{p \in \mathbb{R}^{|T| \times H}} \sum_{d \in D} f_d(p_d) + \sum_{n \in N} f_n(p_n) \tag{1}$$

$$\text{subject to } \forall d \in D : p_d \in C_d, \forall n \in N : p_n \in C_n$$

where $p = \{p_t | t \in T\}$ is the set of all terminal power schedules of the network. Here, the energy cooperation network model is extended to model multiple energy vectors. Let T be the set of all terminals in the multi-vector energy coordination network. Let $T_e \subseteq T$ be the set of terminals corresponding to the electrical network (i.e. those containing transfer of electric energy). Similarly, we define as $T_g \subseteq T$ and $T_h \subseteq T$ the set of terminals corresponding to the gas and heating network respectively. Figure 1 depicts a multi-vector energy network model for a generic district. Terminals corresponding to the heating flows (T_h) are represented as red lines, terminals corresponding to electricity flows (T_e) as blue lines and terminals corresponding to gas flows (T_g) as green lines. In a similar way, heating nets are represented by red squares, electricity nets by blue squares and gas nets by green squares. Devices are represented by circles (each with the colour of the network to which they form part or in two colours if they convert energy from one network to another). The district is composed of four houses (from left to right): one equipped with a power-to-heat (P2H) device (i.e. heat pump or an electric boiler) that is connected to the electricity network, two connected and heated by the district heating network (DHN), and one equipped with a domestic gas-to-heat (G2H) device (i.e. a gas-fired boiler) that is connected to the gas network. On the generation side, we have one device for each possible thermal generator, each linked to the DHN through a net. Some of these generators are single-terminal devices, such as the gas-fuelled boiler and the solar thermal panels. Others such as G2H or P2H are two-terminal devices, having each terminal in a different network. All the buildings are connected to the electrical network even if their thermal energy is not supplied by electricity since they will have at least some baseline electrical load and possibly some local production (PV).

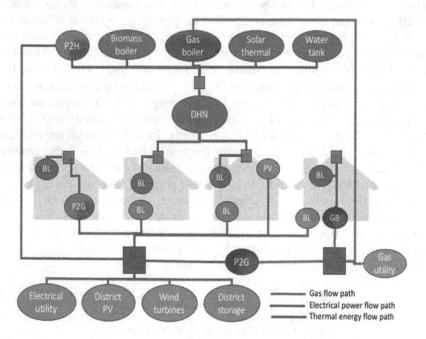

Fig. 1. Multi-vector energy network. (Color figure online)

Moreover, in addition to the electricity demand from the buildings, the electricity network is also connected to the heating network (through the P2H converter devices) and to the gas network (through the P2G device) which are seen as flexible loads. Unlike heating and electricity, for the gas network our focus is strictly on the P2G devices and consequently, buildings will only have a gas connection if they have a gas-fuelled boiler.

Finally, the electrical and gas network have each a device (i.e. the electrical/gas utility device) that models the connection with the respective utility through which each network is able to import/export energy from outside the district at the stipulated contract prices.

2.2 Optimisation Algorithm

The assumption taken here is that there are multiple actors involved in the multi-vector optimizer that, even if they agree on cooperating/coordinating, they are interested on keeping locally the control of their actions as well as any sensitive data regarding its internal business model, preferences, or assets. This will cover scenarios where for example the different energy carriers correspond to multiple independent entities. In this case the optimization will be carried out independently by the three different energy carriers. It can also cover scenarios in which the different prosumers as owners of their flexibility want to keep the control of their behind-the meter assets or they do not want to communicate their preferences to an external entity. Following [11], the optimization problem from Eq. 1 can be solved by a distributed iterative coordination protocol based on the ADMM. In more detail, given a scaling parameter ρ the ADMM algorithm follows the three steps below at each iteration $k + 1$:

The *device-minimization* step (i.e. parallelized among devices):

$$\forall d \in D, \quad p_d^{k+1} = argmin_{p_d \in C_d} \left(f_d(p_d) + \frac{\rho}{2} \left\| p_d - \dot{p}_d^k + u_n^k \right\|_2^2 \right) \tag{2}$$

The *net-minimization* step (i.e. parallelized among nets):

$$\forall n \in N, \dot{p}_n^{k+1} = argmin_{p_n \in C_n} \left(f_n(\dot{p}_n) + \frac{\rho}{2} \left\| p_n^{k+1} - \dot{p}_n + u_n^k \right\|_2^2 \right) \tag{3}$$

The (price) *scaled dual variables* update (i.e. parallelized among nets):

$$\forall n \in N, \quad u_n^{k+1} = u_n^k + \left(p_n^{k+1} - \dot{p}_n^{k+1} \right) \tag{4}$$

where u are the dual variables associated with the energy schedule p. The first step is achieved in parallel by all devices, and then the second and third step are achieved simultaniously by all nets.

2.3 Models of Device Agents

In this proposal, each device component is responsible for defining its local cost function and constraints as well as for implementing the *device-minimization* step (Eq. 2). The next subsections detail these local sub-problems and optimisation steps for the two main technologies that are focus of this paper: thermal energy storage systems and converters.

Thermal Energy Storage System. A thermal energy storage system is a one terminal device that models a water storage tank[2] which water temperature (ε) varies depending if it is taking in or delivering energy (i.e. if $p_s(\tau)$ is positive or negative) and should be kept within minimum and maximum temperature limits, i.e. $\varepsilon^{min} \leq \varepsilon(\tau) \leq \varepsilon^{max}$. Let ε^{init} be the initial temperature of the water storage, i.e. $\varepsilon(\tau) = \varepsilon^{init}$. At each time step $\tau \in [1, H]$ the water storage temperature evolves as:

$$\varepsilon(\tau) = \varepsilon(\tau - 1) - \eta_L(\tau) + \frac{\eta}{V \cdot D \cdot C} p_s(\tau) \tag{5}$$

where $C^{min} \leq p_s(\tau) \leq C^{max}, \eta \in]0, 1]$ is the heat exchange efficiency, V is the volume of the storage tank, $\eta_L(\tau)$ are the tank losses and D, C are respectively constants related to the density and the specific heat of water. To resolve the take into consideration all device constraints, we use a Dykstra projection algorithm [12]. We set up the output $y_{H,1}$ as a matrix of H values. We consider also a matrix $InitialCharge_{H,1}$ that takes into consideration all losses, then Eq. 6 presents the calculation of the initial charge at a timestep τ:

$$\text{Initial Charge}(\tau) = \frac{1}{\eta} \cdot \left(\varepsilon^{init} - \sum_{\tau=0}^{i} \eta_L(\tau) \right) \tag{6}$$

Converter. A converter is two-terminal device that transforms energy from one form (A) to another (B) such as converting electricity to heat. Electric boilers, gas boilers, heat pump and power to gas technology are modelled as converters devices. In this paper we use a simplified model for the converter which is based on three parameters: the minimum and maximum energy input (C^{min}/C^{max}) and the conversion efficiency factor ($\kappa \in (0, 1]$). Formally, the conversion equation for each time step $\tau = 1 \ldots H$ is defined as follows:

$$-p_B(\tau) = \kappa p_A(\tau) \tag{7}$$

where $C^{min}(\tau) \leq p_A(\tau) \leq C^{max}(\tau)$. For these constraints, the device-minimisation step can be computed analytically, as a projection on a hyperplane [13].

3   Verification of the Proposal Performance

Our simulations are carried out using JADE (Java Agent Development Framework) [14].

To show our proposal performance, we propose to simulate 2 scenarios with a time horizon H = 12. In the first scenario, we simulate separated networks (1 heating network, 1 electrical network and 1 gas network). The district electrical network is composed of 5 baseline loads, 3 renewable energy sources and a connection to the electric utility through which electricity can be imported/exported at fixed prices (varying between

---

[2] This paper considers only water storage.

0.12 and 0.33 €/unit for importing and fixed for 0.05 €/unit for exporting). The district heating network is composed of 5 baseline loads, 3 renewable energy sources, 1 thermal energy storage system and 1 generator with a price of 0.16 €/unit. The district gas network is composed of 5 baseline loads and one connection to the gas utility from which the district can import energy at the fixed price of 0.05 €/unit. In the second scenario, we connected all networks via converters (P2H, P2G and G2H with $\kappa = 0.8$, $C^{min} = 0$ and $C^{max} = 10$). As data for the baseline loads, we use the domestic unrestricted consumers Elexon load profile [15]. The data for renewable energy sources are retrieved from [16] and varies between 0 and 1.25. Thermal storage parameters are defined in Simulation parameters defined in [17] with $D = 1.7°c/h$, $V = 7570$ L, $C = 4.18$ kJ/Kg°c, $C^{max} = 90$, $C^{min} = 90$, $\varepsilon^{init} = 10°c$. Figure 2(a)–(c) shows the average cost per unit in both scenarios and for each network. First thing to observe is that for the heating network Fig. 2(b) the price per unit in the second scenario is zero since all the energy is produced either by heating RES or via converters imported from the other two networks. Instead, for the electrical network (see Fig. 2(a)) the cost of electricity for the

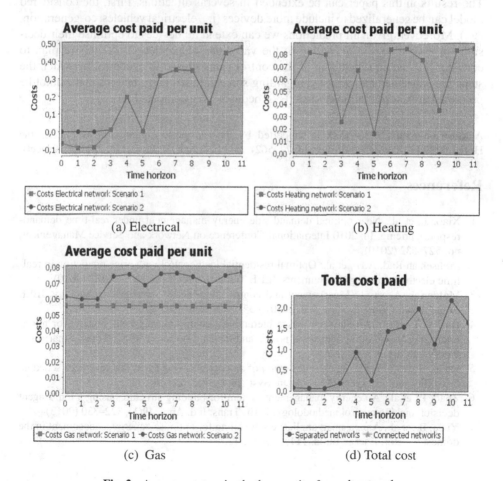

(a) Electrical

(b) Heating

(c) Gas

(d) Total cost

Fig. 2. Average costs using both scenarios for each network

first period is higher in the second scenario, since the excess of RES energy is exported to the heating network using the P2H converter and hence, the network does not receive the export price from the grid. Similarly, the cost per unit of the gas network is higher in the second scenario since the network exports through the G2H converter part of the energy. Figure 2(d) shows the total cost considering the three networks for the two scenarios. We observe here how there is a significant reduction on the district costs when optimising the three networks together.

4   Conclusions and Future Works

In this paper, we proposed a distributed energy management for an eco-district taking into consideration all energy vectors. We resolved the optimisation problem using ADMM and implemented it as a MAS. Using different experimental inputs and via simulations, we showed the accuracy and the performance of the proposed approach. The results in this paper can be extended in several directions. First, the considered model can be generalized to include more devices (i.e. electrical vehicles, co-generation, etc.). Moreover, given all predictions we can extend all devices to optimise their decisions at each time slot according to the variations of predictions. Then, we plan to consider a dynamic scheduling of the control using closed loop control by which the steps are scheduled and adjusted regarding some external perturbations that cannot be predicted at the original time when the schedules were computed.

Acknowledgments. This work is supported by the European Commission as part of the Horizon2020 THERMOSS (Project Id: 723562) and PENTAGON (Project Id: 731125) projects.

References

1. Xiao, J., et al.: Near optimal demand-side energy management under real-time demand-response pricing. In: 2010 International Conference on Network and Service Management, pp. 527–532 (2010)
2. Mohsenian-Rad, A.H., et al.: Optimal residential load control with price prediction in real-time electricity pricing environments. IEEE Trans. Smart Grid 1(2), 120–133 (2010)
3. Molderink, A., et al.: Management and control of domestic smart grid technology. IEEE Trans. Smart Grid 1(2), 109–119 (2010)
4. Bui, V.H., et al.: A multiagent-based hierarchical energy management strategy for multi-microgrids considering adjustable power and demand response. IEEE Trans. Smart Grid PP(99), 1 (2017)
5. Kwak, J., et al.: Tesla: an extended study of an energy-saving agent that leverages schedule flexibility. Auton. Agents Multi-Agent Syst. 28(4), 605–636 (2014)
6. Zhao, P., et al.: An energy management system for building structures using a multi-agent decision-making control methodology. IEEE Trans. Ind. Appl. 49(1), 322–330 (2013)
7. Yuce, B., et al.: Annga smart appliance scheduling for optimised energy management in the domestic sector. Energy Build. 111, 311–325 (2016)

8. Mohsenian-Rad, A., et al.: Autonomous demand-side management based on game theoretic energy consumption scheduling for the future smart grid. IEEE Trans. Smart Grid **1**(3), 320–331 (2010)
9. Nguyen, H., et al.: Demand side management to reduce peak-to-average ratio using game theory in smart grid. In: 2012 Proceedings IEEE INFOCOM Workshops, Orlando, FL, USA, 25–30 March 2012, pp. 91–96 (2012)
10. Ma, L., et al.: Multi-party energy management for smart building cluster with PV systems using automatic demand response. Energy Build. **121**, 11–21 (2016)
11. Kraning, M., et al.: Dynamic network energy management via proximal message passing. Found. Trends Optim. **1**(2), 73–126 (2014)
12. Tibshirani, R.: Dykstra's algorithm, ADMM, and coordinate descent: connections, insights, and extensions. In: Advances in Neural Information Processing Systems, vol. 30, pp. 517–528 (2017)
13. Parikh, N., Boyd, S., et al.: Proximal algorithms. Found. Trends R Optim. **1**(3), 127–239 (2014)
14. Bellifemine, F., Poggi, A., Rimassa, G.: JADE–A FIPA-compliant agent framework. In: Proceedings of PAAM, London, vol. 99, p. 33 (1999)
15. Elexon (2018). https://www.elexon.co.uk/
16. ausgrid (2018). http://www.ausgrid.com.au/
17. Farmani, F., et al.: A conceptual model of a smart energy management system for a residential building equipped with CCHP system. Int. J. Electr. Power Energy Syst. **95**, 523–536 (2018)

A Real-Time Energy Management Platform
for Multi-vector District Energy Systems

Muhammad Waseem Ahmad[1]([⊠]), Jonathan Reynolds[1], Jean-Laurent Hippolyte[1],
Yacine Rezgui[1], Michael Nikhil Descamps[2], Christian Merckx[3],
Jasper van Dessel[3], and Mathieu Lessinnes[3]

[1] BRE Centre for Sustainable Engineering, School of Engineering, Cardiff University,
Cardiff, CF24 3AA, UK
`{AhmadM3,ReynoldsJ8,HippolyteJ,RezguiY}@cardiff.ac.uk`
[2] Département Thermique Biomasse et Hydrogène, Commissariat à l'énergie atomique et aux
énergies alternatives, Chambéry, France
`Michael.Descamps@cea.fr`
[3] Tractebel Engineering SA, Boulevard Simon Bolivar, 34-36, 1000 Brussels, Belgium
`{christian.merckx,jasper.vandessel,`
`mathieu.lessinnes}@tractebel.engie.com`

Abstract. Management of increasingly complex, multi-vector, district energy
systems, operated by separate stakeholders, including prosumers, is a vital challenge to overcome in a fragmented energy landscape. The complex value chain
involved forms a cognitive virtual network with the shared objective to reduce
energy consumption, greenhouse gas emissions and maximise human comfort.
This paper will aim to illustrate the PENTAGON platform for integrated management of key stakeholder data to produce automatic, holistic and pre-emptive
decisions that ensure near-optimal management of a district energy system. The
PENTAGON platform architecture consists of five key modules including Smart
Connector to interface with existing District Energy Management Systems
(DEMS), a time series database, a prediction module, a multi-vector optimisation
module and a module ensuring the electric grid stability. Integration of these
distinct modules is achieved through an underpinning, shared, semantic description of the district components, sensors and scenarios. The ultimate goal of the
described platform is to achieve a step-change from static, reactive, rule-based
systems to an intelligent, adaptive, and pre-emptive control architecture that
makes new decisions based on perceived and predicted conditions.

Keywords: District energy management · ICT platform · Artificial intelligence
Multi-vector energy systems

1 Introduction

The existing building sector, one of the most substantial consumers of energy, contributes towards 40% of world's total energy consumption and 30% of the total CO_2 emissions [1]. Currently, most of the installed energy systems are based on fossil fuels, and

© IFIP International Federation for Information Processing 2018
Published by Springer Nature Switzerland AG 2018. All Rights Reserved
L. M. Camarinha-Matos et al. (Eds.): PRO-VE 2018, IFIP AICT 534, pp. 560–568, 2018.
https://doi.org/10.1007/978-3-319-99127-6_48

more focus on improving energy efficiency, integrating renewable energy sources and optimally managing energy systems is needed to meet national and international obligations. Decentralising energy infrastructure can also increase energy efficiency as it could reduce transmission losses and co-generation or tri-generation units could be utilised. The stochastic nature of renewable energy sources (e.g. wind and solar) increases the complexity in the management of a grid, as they introduce a level of uncertainty into energy supply systems. According to Reynolds et al. [2], the full potential of the smart grid can be utilised by increased interoperability, better energy management and forecasting of both supply and demand. Therefore, it is critical to holistically manage decentralised district energy systems and control a multi-vector energy system in an integrated manner.

Current energy management techniques in district energy systems are limited to relatively simple control mechanisms and don't consider the collaborative aspects of the domain resulting from the multiplicity of stakeholders and physical systems. Advances are needed in developing novel collaborative management and system modelling techniques, and development of management platform for the efficient operation of collaborative networks in energy systems. Mimicking human intelligence in software tools by managing the operation of collaborative networks in energy systems will not only provide better indoor environmental conditions but will also reduce energy consumption. This has enabled the development of complex collaborative systems inspired by human cognition, such as artificial neural networks, fuzzy logic, semantic web technologies, etc.

Our buildings and energy systems are equipped with a large number of heterogeneous devices, which mostly come from different vendors and use different communication protocols. To provide holistic management of energy systems, that are capable of tackling underlying heterogeneity, classification and description of different information within the decentralised energy systems and consumers are needed [3]. Semantic web technologies can improve the interoperability while reducing heterogeneity. These technologies (e.g., ontologies) can facilitate rapid exploration of information, i.e., it becomes easier to retrieve, correlate and integrate data by knowledge discovery, associating meaning to data and providing inter-relationships between modelled entities. The proposed energy platform leverages semantic modelling to allow interoperability of different data sources and provides an additional level of robustness to energy management of multi-vector systems. The rest of the paper is organised as follow. Section 2 details energy management platform along with its components; Smart Connector, prediction module, multi-vector optimiser and Smart Operation. In Sect. 3, we describe ICT architecture and interaction between different modules. Pilot site implementations are discussed in Sect. 4 and Conclusions are presented at the end of the paper.

2   PENTAGON Energy Management Platform

The functional architecture of the PENTAGON multi-vector flexibility management platform is depicted in Fig. 1. The district energy management system (DEMS) gathers measurements and communicates with the PENTAGON platform with the help of Smart

Connector. In this section, we will describe the functionality of software components of PENTAGON platform along with data flow.

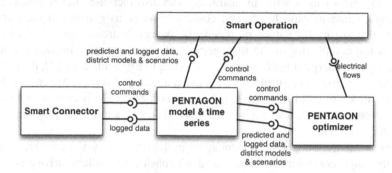

Fig. 1. PENTAGON component diagram

2.1 Definition of the Platform

- Smart Connector

Smart Connector acts as a translator, and collects data at every time step from the DEMS and organises it in a predefined structure. This data is then read and treated by other PENTAGON components. The Smart Connector also translates the optimal control actions (i.e., set-points calculated by the multi-vector optimiser) so that they can be interpreted and applied by the DEMS. The Multi-vector optimiser will always send an optimised solution over the next 24 h, however the Smart Connector will only communicate the next time step (15 min) of the solution and will store the remaining 24 h solutions until the new control actions are available.

- Prediction module

Predictive analytics play an important role in the management of multi-vector energy systems and serve as a core component of smart thermal and electrical grids. The PENTAGON prediction module will manage the prediction models and will forecast different variables. The variables of interest will include thermal and electrical energy demands and energy production from renewable energy sources. To train prediction models, different input features (e.g., outdoor weather conditions, time-related information, building occupancy, etc.) are tested to improve their performance.

- Multi-vector optimiser

Holistic management of decentralised district energy systems is the key to their success. Multi-vector energy networks (e.g., heat, gas and electricity) that were previously independently controlled are now required to be managed and controlled in an integrated manner as they have become more coupled (e.g. output of one systems is the input of second system). The PENTAGON multi-vector optimiser is responsible for computing control actions and set-points to minimise a defined objective function (e.g. minimise energy consumption/cost, increase occupants' comfort, etc.). The optimiser will exploit available flexibility within the district while satisfying the energy demand of the buildings. The optimiser will also consider the specific characteristics of conversion technologies to minimise the overall energy cost of the district while satisfying the systems' and networks' constraints. Internal simplified models will be used to effectively evaluate potential optimal solutions, dispatch, and define operational constraints. The computed power flow and set-point values will then be send to the Smart Operation and District Sever.

- Smart Operation

Smart Operation is a proprietary software tool from Tractebel that is used for the optimisation of an electrical distribution network in the presence of distributed energy resources (DERs) such as photovoltaic (PV) systems, wind turbines, electric vehicles (EVs), battery storage systems, etc. ensuring the adherence to grid constraints. Within PENTAGON, Smart Operation receives the forecasted consumption and production from PENTAGON prediction. It also receives the decisions taken by the PENTAGON multi-vector optimiser concerning the electric flexibility and the energy conversions. The later will not be changed in order to preserve the global equilibrium found by the multi-vector optimiser. Only the electric flexibility (state of charge of the batteries, curtailment or shedding) and the withdrawal from/injection to the grid can be re-evaluated by Smart Operation based on a more detailed model of the electric grid. To this aim, a multi-period AC Optimal Power Flow (AC-OPF) is run in which the electrical flows are optimised according to an objective function while respecting the grid constraints, e.g., voltage magnitude and current limits. Smart Operation will keep as much as possible the original dispatch schedule. If deviations are required, they will be minimized while at the same time being different enough to ensure the network security.

3   IT Architecture and Interaction Between PENTAGON Modules

3.1   Communication Between ICT Components

In the context of utility control infrastructures, European standardisation bodies recommend service-oriented architecture (SOA) [4], to facilitate the integration of:

- data services;
- functional logic services;
- and business logic services.

In an SOA, software functionalities are packaged in autonomous self-contained modules that operate independently from each other's state and context [5]. Figure 1 shows the main high-level components of the PENTAGON solution. The diagram points out the Application Programming Interface (API) that each module requires (half circles) and what other module is supposed to provide these interface (full circles). The district optimiser component uses the interfaces provided (1) by PENTAGON model component to retrieve relevant predicted data and to send thermal and gas network related commands, and (2) by the Smart Operation component to send optimised electrical flows.

The Smart Operation component uses the interface provided by the PENTAGON model component to send electrical network related commands, which are derived from the optimised electrical flows received from the district optimization component. The PENTAGON model component uses the interface provided by the district server to fetch the data measured in the district that are required for prediction. SOAs allow for complex yet flexible systems, individual components can evolve independently, assuming changes in interface specifications are kept to a minimum. The most common technique to implement interoperable SOA are web services. The PENTAGON platform has adopted the Representational State Transfer (REST) communicating architecture style. By definition, REST web services are lightweight and stateless [6], which can be regarded as a realisation of the SOA paradigm as it specifies how services are published, discovered, and consumed across the web [6].

3.2   PENTAGON Data Model

The PENTAGON data model is made up of different types of information: the topology of the different networks with associated parameters and the configuration parameters of the optimization problem (constraints and objective function). The information is managed by the PENTAGON-model. All the parameters, even those of the nonlinear model of Smart Operation, are part of the PENTAGON data model. None are managed in an external way by a module. Each of the considered test cases is fully represented by a database set and switching from one test case to another is thus automatic. The configuration of the model for each test case is provided in an Excel template, which is then loaded into the database. All parameters of the optimization problem (bounds, limits, prices, objective function type, constraints type, ...) are included in that template. The PENTAGON platform is therefore fully configurable in a very flexible manner. It is worth mentioning that the measurements transferred from the District Server are also registered in the PENTAGON data model.

The dynamics of the PENTAGON modules thus rely on an online transaction processing system composed mainly of:

- a database management system that is optimised for retrieval and/or update of semantic data and associated time-dependent data with respect to the complex domain-specific model and;
- the PENTAGON domain data model;

As shown in Fig. 2, PENTAGON's online transaction processing system drives interoperability with/within the platform, by maintaining consistent semantics throughout the whole PENTAGON stack. This consistency is delivered by systematic mappings between various representations. For instance, JSON objects exposed by the REST API align with the object models of the client libraries through automated code generation and the schema of the underlying (NoSQL) graph database aligns the object models through semi-automated object graph mapping. Modules using the platform (district optimisers, prediction modules, district gateways etc.) can have various degrees of coupling with the PENTAGON data model, from being loosely coupled by forging HTTP requests to retrieve/update data (e.g. a visualisation web application) to being tightly coupled by using the provided PENTAGON object model internally (e.g. the delegate application that connects to the District Server to retrieve time series values).

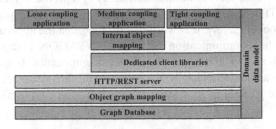

Fig. 2. PENTAGON online transaction processing system and possible degree of coupling

PENTAGON's domain model aligns and extends previous ontologies proposed by EU projects RESILIENT [7] and MAS2TERING [8]. In RESILIENT, an OWL [9] ontology formalised the socio-technical elements involved in district energy management systems, as well as their interrelationships [10]. The ontology was built on top of existing upper layer abstract ontologies, to achieve a two-fold representation of district energy systems, as systems of systems and as socio-technical networks. In the MAS2TERING [8], an ontology formalized the domain of flexibility management in smart energy systems [11]. The ontology aligns selected standards: the Universal Smart Energy Framework [12], OpenADR [13], Energy@home [14], and CIM [15].

3.3 Time Series Data Storage

In recently completed projects, RESILIENT [7] and MAS2TERING [8], the developed ontologies did not consider semantical features to represent time indexed data, observations from measurements and associated metadata. A number of existing semantic models that standardise the description of time series data, especially the data obtained from sensors and meters will be considered. Among these semantic models are;

- SensorML—SensorML is one of the OGC SWE information-encoding standards and provides models and encoding to represent any kind of process in sensors or post-processing systems [16].
- Semantic Sensor Network Ontology – This ontology is used to describe sensors, observation, and related concept. Domain knowledge (e.g., time, location of a sensor, etc.) are described and imported through other ontologies via OWL imports [17].
- SENML (Media Type for Sensor Markup Language) – This media type can be used in protocols (e.g., HTTP or CoAP) by sensors to send or configure measurements [18].

3.4 Security Requirements

PENTAGON project deals with sensitive data (i.e. information of energy consumption, etc.) and therefore user authentication will be employed to only allow authorised access.

All requests to any service will need the client to be authenticated, and will require users to enter their username and password. Communication security will be further enhanced by using the widely used secure communication HTTPS protocol. It consists of communication over HTTP within a connection encrypted by TLS (Transport Layer Security) or SSL (Secure Socket Layer). It is worth mentioning that the approach described here applied only to the communication between PENTAGON components. However, communication between third-party's services/components (e.g., DEMS, public weather services, etc.) and PENTAGON component might have to comply with different security policies (e.g., defined by district IT network administrators).

4   Project Pilot Sites and Implementation

PENTAGON proposes to implement a 2 step validation strategy that involves (i) live operations at limited scale on the experimental district heating network of CEA-INES (Chambery, France) and (ii) a wider assessment (low voltage and medium voltage level) of optimization capabilities based on simulations of the Blaenau Gwent district (Wales, UK). The experimental facility of CEA-INES is a scaled heating network with a set of heat generators, thermal storage, a network of pipes and valves, and heat consumers. On the heat production side, the facility includes a 300 kW gas boiler, a 100 kW absorption chiller, 300 m^2 of solar panels, and 50 kW heat pump is being deployed in the context of the project. On the consumption side, the energy is distributed to a thermal test rig, which can emulate building energy load in a flexible and reproducible way. This means that a given heat demand can be applied to the network, and heat production control variables can be tuned to satisfy the demand. In addition, thermal flexibility takes the form of a 40 m^3 water storage tank. The facility is managed and monitored by an instrumentation server that collects all data coming from sensors and actuators. The heat production units can be run in parallel or separately. The thermal storage provides flexibility to the system, and can be bypassed if required. A set of actuator valves are activated to choose between the different heat production units or to bypass the thermal storage. The building load is applied to the consumer heat exchanger using the building load profiles provided by PENTAGON-simulation.

The validation by simulations of the Blaenau Gwent district requires a heating network simulator and an electric network simulator. The heating network is simulated using the equation-based object-oriented language Modelica along with the simulation platform Dymola. The dynamic heating network model is based on detailed physical representation of the system by gathering component models that were previously developed and validated. The components models are taken from a CEA in-house Modelica library named DistrictHeating [19]. At the production plant level, the model enables the control of supply temperature and differential pressure, and takes into account heat propagation delays, heat losses, tube thermal inertia, and pressure losses. At the consumer level, the buildings are not explicitly modelled, but represented by their substation, which is the unit in which the energy is distributed from a high level to a low level. The substation is modelled as a system which includes a heat exchanger, a regulation valve, and an ideal controller. With this representation, building heat load temporal profiles can be used as inputs to the model. The electric network simulator is a multi-period load flow calculator which needs the power consumption and production of the different buildings and equipment. Those will be predefined based on historical measurements. The consumer side of the district (electric and heating energy consumption) will be modelled by using computational intelligence techniques (e.g., artificial neural networks, support vector machines, random forest, etc.). The models are capable of simulating complex building energy behaviour due to seasonal variations in weather conditions as well as system non-linearities and delays. The inputs of the models will be weather conditions, time related information, building occupancy, and past values of the variable.

5 Conclusions

This paper has introduced the PENTAGON platform for intelligent management of multi-vector energy networks. The platform consists of a collaborative network of modules coordinated through a shared, semantic understanding of the given energy networks. Vitally, the platform allows a paradigm shift from reactive, rule-based control to predictive, anticipatory control and management to attain energy and emissions reductions and maximise human comfort. This is achieved through a combination of real-time data retrieval and organisation through the smart connector, prediction of pivotal variables through leveraging artificial intelligence, deployment of advanced optimisation techniques and adjustment to real-time grid constraints though simulation all underpinned by a central, coordinating ICT infrastructure. Current energy management systems do not consider the collaborative aspects of the domain; PENTAGON platform uses semantic modelling to describe the district energy system to ensure interoperability and communication between ICT modules. Secure communication, one of the key element for real-time management of smart energy systems, will also be implemented as part of PENTAGON platform. The presented platform will be deployed and tested at two eco-districts.

References

1. Ahmad, M.W., Mourshed, M., Mundow, D., Sisinni, M., Rezgui, Y.: Building energy metering and environmental monitoring – a state-of-the-art review and directions for future research. Energy Build. **120**, 85–102 (2016)
2. Reynolds, J., Ahmad, M.W., Rezgui, Y.: Holistic modelling techniques for the operation optimisation of multi-vector energy systems. Energy Build., 1–31 (2018). https://doi.org/10.1016/j.enbuild.2018.03.065
3. Tomašević, N.M., Batić, M.Č., Blanes, L.M., Keane, M.M., Vraneš, S.: Ontology-based facility data model for energy management. Adv. Eng. Inform. **29**(4), 971–984 (2015)
4. CEN/CENELEC/ETSI.: Joint Working Group on Standards for Smart Grids, Final report (2011)
5. Papazoglou, M.P., Van Den Heuvel, W.-J.: Service oriented architectures: approaches, technologies and research issues. Int. J. Very Large Databases **16**, 389–415 (2007)

6. Sheng, Q.Z., Qiao, X., Vasilakos, A.V., Szabo, C., Bourne, S., Xu, X.: Web services composition: a decade's overview. Inf. Sci. **280**, 218–238 (2014)
7. CORDIS.: Coupling Renewable, Storage and ICTs, for low carbon intelligent energy management at district level. Publications Office of the European Union (2017). http://cordis.europa.eu/project/rcn/104392_en.html
8. CORDIS.: Multi-Agent Systems and Secured coupling of telecom and energy grids for next generation smartgrid services. Publications Office of the European Union (2017). http://cordis.europa.eu/project/rcn/192066_en.html
9. OWL Working Group.: OWL - Semantic Web Standards. Semantic Web Standards (2013). https://www.w3.org/2001/sw/wiki/OWL
10. RESILIENT consortium.: D2.4 – Architecture description of the information model for district energy management (2014)
11. Hippolyte, J.L., et al.: Ontology-based demand-side flexibility management in smart grids using a multi-agent system. In: IEEE International Smart Cities Conference (ISC2), Toronto, Italy, pp. 1–7 (2016)
12. USEF.: Usef Energy - Universal Smart Energy Framework (2017). https://www.usef.energy/
13. OpenADR Alliance.: OpenADR - Control Your Energy Future (2017). http://www.openadr.org/
14. Energy@Home.: Energy@Home – Home (2017). http://www.energy-home.it/SitePages/Home.aspx
15. IEC.: Energy management system application program interface (EMS-API)—Part 301: Common information model (CIM) base (2011)
16. Nengcheng, C., Hu, C., Chen, Y., Wang, C., Gong, J.: Using SensorML to construct a geoprocessing e-Science workflow model under a sensor web environment. Comput. Geosci. **47**, 119–129 (2012)
17. Semantic Sensor Network Incubator Group.: Semantic Sensor Net Ontology (2011). https://www.w3.org/2005/Incubator/ssn/wiki/Semantic_Sensor_Net_Ontology. Accessed 31 May 2017
18. Jennings, C., Shelby, Z., Arkko, J.: Media Types for Sensor Markup Language (SENML). IETF Trust (2012). https://tools.ietf.org/html/draft-jennings-senml-08
19. Giraud, L., Bavière, R., Vallée, M., Paulus, C.: Presentation, validation and application of the DistrictHeating Modelica library. In: Proceedings of the 11th International Modelica Conference, Versailles, France, pp. 79–88 (2015)

Cognitive Systems in Agribusiness

Towards Virtual Biorefineries

Michelle Houngbé[(✉)], Anne-Marie Barthe-Delanoë, and Stéphane Négny

Laboratoire de Génie Chimique, Université de Toulouse, CNRS, INPT, UPS,
4, allée Emile Monso – CS 44362, 31030 Toulouse Cedex 4, France
michelle.houngbe@inp-toulouse.fr,
{annemarie.barthe,stephane.negny}@ensiacet.fr

Abstract. A key challenge for the future, biorefineries are challenged by supply and demand variability. Indeed, biorefineries structures are traditionally centralised, with static processes where inputs and outputs are strictly defined and cannot be adapted (regarding quantity, quality, purity, etc.). This paper proposes a new approach where the process is decentralised to face the challenge of the agility of biomass processing. It leads defining virtual biorefineries, in which the stakeholders (farmers, industrials) are involved in a collaborative process, where they provide operation units as services and where existing plants and equipment are reused. The design of this collaborative biomass processing should also take into account functional and non-functional factors, such as the socio-economic context, weather conditions, etc. supported by information and communication technologies. Therefore, the biomass treatment process could be quickly designed and adapted, according to the detected changes of the ecosystem.

Keywords: Agility · Biorefinery · Collaboration · Industry 4.0
Model-driven engineering · Servitization

1 Introduction

Facing global environmental challenges, the development of biosourced products and energy are the cornerstone for a sustainable future, as stated by the European strategy for the bioeconomy [1]. In this same way, one of the French Energy Transition for Green Growth Act's goals is to increase the use of renewable energies to 32% of total energy consumption in 2030, where the biomass (and the biomass processing) will occupy a leading position [2].

Biomass is organic material that comes from plants and animals, and it is a renewable source of energy: wood and wood processing wastes, agricultural crops and waste material, animal manure, etc. Key player in the bio-based chemistry and energy, biorefinery is the "processing of biomass into a spectrum of marketable products and energy", as defined by the US Energy Information Administration [3] and Cherubini [4].

However, processing a living material like biomass is highly constrained by numerous hurdles like the biomass demand and supply irregularities, not only in terms of quantity and quality but also regarding producers' location and seasonality of the

L. M. Camarinha-Matos et al. (Eds.): PRO-VE 2018, IFIP AICT 534, pp. 571–580, 2018.
https://doi.org/10.1007/978-3-319-99127-6_49

production. Moreover, biorefinery is an extremely specialized and rigid system, whose structure is inherited from the oil-based refineries [5, 6].

The entire complex transformation of biomass into bioproduct is realized by one dedicated process (composed of four major unitary operations: pretreatment, fermentation, separation, purification), in one single facility involving one stakeholder. This centralized process is dedicated to a given input biomass and given output bioproduct(s) [7]. This is another hurdle to adapt the biorefinery to face variability and to set up plants. Finally, the biomass process treatment requires heavy initial financial investments and generates significant operating costs, whereas the variability of supply threatens the proper functioning of the biorefinery. The problem underlying these observations stems from the need to provide agility to biorefineries, both at the physical system and information system levels.

If agility is now a well known topic in the manufacturing industry (especially within the frame of Industry 4.0), it is surprisingly pioneering in the chemical process industry [8].

Thus, our goal is to answer to the following research question: How can biorefineries development be fostered with providing the required agility to cope with this unstable environment?

This article is organized as follows: Sect. 2 presents the state of the art about the agility of biorefineries. Section 3 develops the proposal of virtual biorefinery within the frame of the ARBRE project ("Agilité pouR les BioRaffineriEs", meaning Agility foR the BioRefineriEs) that aims at providing agility to biorefineries. Section 4 details a meta model of the virtual biorefinery, before concluding.

2   Agility of Biorefineries

We aim to provide agility to the biorefinery, which is for the moment a centralized and highly specialized system. Within the frame of the ARBRE project (2017–2021), the agility of a system is defined as "the capacity of a system to realize, in the shortest possible lapse of time (reactivity), the detection of its inadequacy to the environment in which it evolves and the execution of the necessary adaptation" [9].

In the biomass transformation literature, the agility of the process is not a primary concern. A few articles are interested in the topic but they remain at the chemical and technological levels. Agility is then seen as a flexible plant, where a reconfiguration of the process is achieved by switching equipment inside a single standalone plant. But, if we consider the biomass transformation process in the broader sense, being more than just the chemical process and including its environment (farmers, industrials, customers, etc.) it can be seen as a supply chain. Some research works study biorefinery design from the supply chain point of view, but they focus on the optimization (cost, energy) to design a centralized process [10, 11].

In the manufacturing industry, the needs to reduce costs and to maximize flexibility of the supply chain can be satisfied by calling to decentralized production systems and to inter-organizational collaboration strategy. These collaborations can lead to create Virtual Enterprise or Virtual Organization [12] made by several companies to reach one (or more) common objective(s). There is a few research works on the collaborative networks in the biomass processing area but the network is limited to only two stakeholders [13] and/or only consider the cost of the intermediate products transport to assess the feasibility of the decentralization [14]. The inherent constraints of the biomass treatment are not discussed, like the perishable nature of agricultural products, natural deterioration, crop seasonality, etc. to propose a relevant and realistic collaboration.

Moreover, the sustainability of the existing material, its reuse, its modularity and its ease of maintenance become major stakes (as underlined by the French strategy towards the bioeconomy [5]). In the manufacturing area, the servitization of companies is the transition from the sale of products towards the sale of integrated offers for products and intangible services [15]. Dahmani et al. [16] have studied the transition of a manufactured company towards a specific type of servitization: Product, Service, System.

The degree of servitization can also be raised until the level of service economy. The service economy was initially defined by Stahel [17] as the economy "[...] which optimizes the use or the function of goods and services, concentrates on the management of the existing wealth, in the form of goods, knowledge and the natural capital. The economic objective is to create the highest value in use possible during the longest possible time consuming the least material resources and possible energy". If servitization is not applied yet to the biomass processing industry, a bridge can be built between the servitization and cooperation economy (considered as the first level of the service economy). In France, one farmer out of two takes part into a cooperative association to share the use of equipment and thus share the investment in equipment and the hiring costs of the operators [18].

Agility also relies on the ability to ensure situational awareness [19]. Considering the high degree of connectivity of the agricultural sector (eFarming), the availability and the volume of exogenous data sources about weather conditions, territories (e.g. Open-Data), and the rise of new technologies producing amounts of data, there is a need for data, information and knowledge management to enhance situational awareness.

Moreover, Camarinha-Matos et al. [20] showed that collaborative networks are strongly affected in terms of structure, process and mechanisms by technologies from Industry 4.0, such as Big Data or Cyber Physical System. From the biomass processing point of view, Information and Communication Technologies (ICT) would support not only the characterization of the stakeholders (farmers, industrials, etc.) and their services but also the whole ecosystem (climate event, market event, etc.) to anticipate their consequences and react, either when designing or running the biorefinery.

Research works and projects conducted on supply chain agility and Industry 4.0 are applied to the manufacturing industries, and even institutions and administrations. But this is not the case for the biomass process industry where collaborative behavior and servitization, supported by ICT have never been established yet [10].

3   A Platform to Design and Monitor Virtual Biorefineries

Based on the previous observations, the French funded project ARBRE proposes to create a framework and a software platform to design and monitor virtual biorefineries.

First, the aim is, through a systemic approach, to model the biorefinery structure as a System of Systems where the chemical process is not performed on a single standalone unit anymore. With the servitization of the chemical plants, each unitary operation equipment would not only be reused for various processes (instead of being dedicated to a single transformation process), and this would allow the processing of various kinds materials and products, as well as a reconfiguration of the process according the variability (quality, quantity, demand, supply, etc.).

This lead us to define the concept of virtual biorefinery (Fig. 1) to provide the required agility to biomass processing: a collaborative process, involving the farmer, the facilities and the consumer, at both the physical and information system levels, which is built according the chosen chemical process and the chosen bioproduct and taking into account the context, the partners and their services and the performance. According to the objectives and the constraints, the role of the stakeholders can evolve.

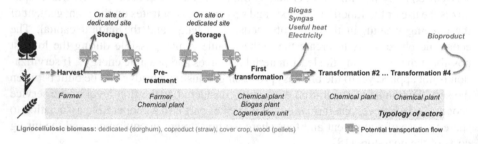

Fig. 1. The virtual biorefinery, as proposed in the ARBRE project.

The methodology of the ARBRE project is based on knowledge management and collaborative process design, following the methodology described in [21]. It will be

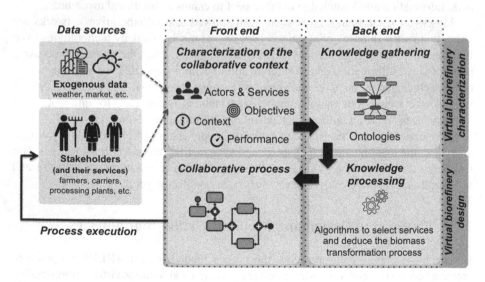

Fig. 2. The ARBRE software platform architecture, to design and monitor the virtual biorefinery.

implemented as a software platform, available to the stakeholders (Fig. 2). These ones will describe their services (from both functional and non-functional points of view) and their objectives on the platform. Exogenous data will be used to describe the environment.

Based on the gathered knowledge, collaborative opportunities for biomass processing and the associated chemical transformation process can be deduced. Then, mining the directory of available partners and their services, along with their functional and non-functional requirements, the collaborative process is deduced.

4 A Meta Model for Virtual Biorefineries

Designing the collaborative network to build the virtual agile biorefinery, whatever the type of biomass, requires to describe a generic collaborative process for biomass transformation and thus to gather relevant knowledge.

In other words, it is necessary to collect data and information about the collaborative virtual biorefinery system: actors and their services (e.g. {Farmer A}: {harvest straw/pace: 3 ha.h^{-1}}); collaborative objectives (e.g. produce biodiesel with straw); context (e.g. weather forecast, biomass physical properties and location, road network, etc.).

To achieve this, we will adopt a Model Driven Engineering approach, which enables to raise the level of abstraction among a complex and specific system (as the biomass processing) and experiment the virtual biorefinery, before designing it. The knowledge about the collaboration objectives, the actors, the services, the context, the threats and opportunities, and the performance will be represented as a meta model.

To this end, we will use the CORE meta model defined in Benaben et al. [22], as presented in Fig. 3 [23].

This meta model describes the main concepts of any collaboration, including objective, context, partners and performance. The interesting characteristic of this meta model is its ability to be specialized to fit with a given business domain. It has been successfully used into several research works and projects from crisis management [9] to trade exchanges [21].

Based on this CORE meta model, we propose to extend it into a meta model layer dedicated to the virtual biorefinery as envisioned in the ARBRE project.

The design of this first attempt of a meta model layer was supported by the literature and return of experience from industrial cases. For the moment, we focus on the context, partner and objective packages. The performance package will be studied in further works. Our proposal is shown and described below.

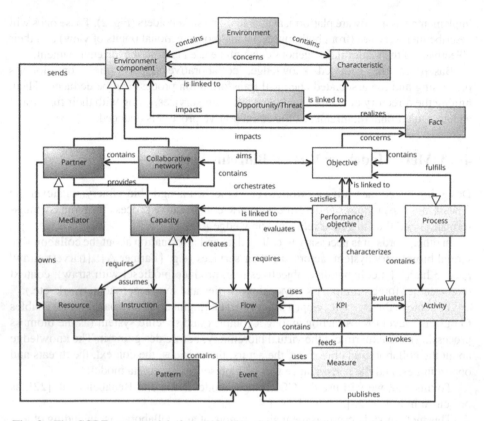

Fig. 3. The CORE meta model (from [22, 23]): Context (middle grey), Partners (dark grey), Performance (light grey), Objectives (white).

Context package
The *context* sets the characteristics of the collaboration environment (Fig. 4). The *deposit* is central in the context and inherits from the environment component concept from the CORE package.

First of all, the deposit contains the *biomass*, which is characterized by *biochemical and physical properties* (hygrometry, chemical composition, residual traces of plant protection products, etc.), which is related to the quality of the biomass, its *availability* relating to the volume and a *seasonality* which imposes the harvesting time.

Then, the deposit is located in a geographical *area* determined by a *climate* and a *topography* and where a *type* of *agriculture* (extensive or intensive agriculture, organic farming, etc.) is performed.

The *climate* impacts also the deposit according to the climate events (rainfalls, drought, storm, etc.). Other specialized elements compose the deposit.

Goods concern the required installations, as *roads*, to determine the accessibility to the deposit.

People represent the extended community who will be decisive regarding the social acceptability of the virtual biorefinery project.

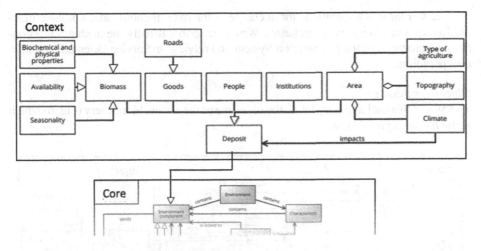

Fig. 4. Focus on the context package of the virtual biorefinery meta model.

Finally, the governing and decisional bodies settled on the deposit are represented by the *institutions* concept.

Partner package
The *partners* constitute the collaborative network (Fig. 5). Each *actor* inherits from the CORE partner concept and provides information about their capacity to realize a *service* according to their expertise and skills.

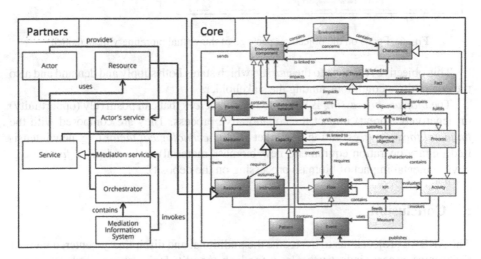

Fig. 5. Focus on the partners package of the virtual biorefinery meta model.

In a servitization context, their *resource* enables to characterize the *service* they will realize, according to an identified unitary operation, in the biomass processing.

The *mediator* is a specific actor in charge of the overall coordination of the collaboration, as a conductor in an orchestra. We can note that usually the mediator is a non-human actor, part of the Information System and relying on Service Oriented Architecture paradigm.

Objectives package
The aim of this package is to define the *objective* of the virtual biorefinery (Fig. 6) which is the *biomass processing*.

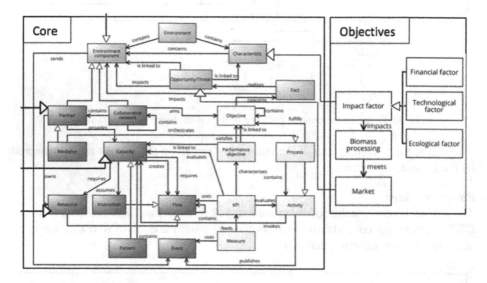

Fig. 6. Focus on the objectives package of the virtual biorefinery meta model.

This objective responds to the *market*, which states both supply and demand and also the competitive conditions among the stakeholders.

The *biomass processing* is linked to *impact factors* that can positively (opportunity) or negatively (threat) impact the collaborative process. They are composed with the *financial factor* (e.g. evolution of market price), *technological factor* (e.g. new intensified unitary operation equipment, new biomass material) and *ecological factor* (e.g. environmental impact of biomass processing on the deposit).

5   Conclusion

The ARBRE project aims to overcome the traditional and disciplinary-centered view of the biomass process industry that leads to a lack of agility facing changes, whatever their nature. The objective is to develop a virtual biorefinery framework, through a systemic view, enabling to: create synergies among the stakeholders (by using information and communication technologies), improve the efficiency of the dynamic of the collaborative network and enhance the interactions between the biomass processing stakeholders and the environment.

This paper has proposed a meta-model of a collaborative network dedicated to the biomass processing, taking into account the characteristics of this living material and its environment. This meta model is the cornerstone to design the virtual biorefinery envisioned by the ARBRE project. It will allow to collect and to process the necessary knowledge about the system, to support the deduction of the collaborative biomass processing and network of actors, and to monitor the virtual biorefinery.

This meta-model supports the modeling of a biorefinery seen as a collaborative network, adapted to the detected opportunities and to the characterization of the whole system (actors, context, etc.). In other words, it supports the modeling of an agile biorefinery. In addition to the acceleration of the set up of the biomass-processing infrastructure, this meta-model would also support the continuous monitoring of the biorefinery. If any element of the system evolves (actors, services, context, objective, performance), it would be possible to detect a deviation and to support decision-making facing the adaptation of the biorefinery to these new parameters.

Further works on this meta model will focus on refining it by adding the performance package (identifying the Key Performance Indicators) and assessing it on realistic industrial use cases of lignocellulosic biomass processing in the South of France area (provided by one of the project's partners).

Acknowledgments. These research works are funded by the French Research Agency (ANR) regarding the research project ARBRE [Grant ANR-17-CE10-0006], 2017-2021. ARBRE aims to develop French biorefineries as agile collaborative networks and supported by the Industry 4.0 paradigm. The authors would like to thank the project partners for their advice and comments regarding this work.

References

1. European Environment Agency: Innovating for Sustainable Growth: A Bioeconomy for Europe. European Union, Luxembourg (2012)
2. Assemblée Nationale, Sénat: LOI n° 2015-992 du 17 août 2015 relative à la transition énergétique pour la croissance verte (2015)
3. de Jong, E., Jungmeier, G.: Biorefinery concepts in comparison to petrochemical refineries. In: Industrial Biorefineries and White Biotechnology, pp. 3–33. Elsevier (2015)
4. Cherubini, F.: The biorefinery concept: using biomass instead of oil for producing energy and chemicals. Energy Convers. Manag. **51**, 1412–1421 (2010)
5. Le Déaut, J.-Y., Courteau, R., Sido, B.: De la biomasse à la bioéconomie: une stratégie pour la France. SENAT (2016)
6. Balan, V.: Current challenges in commercially producing biofuels from lignocellulosic biomass. ISRN Biotechnol. **2014**, 31 (2014)
7. Clark, J.H., Deswarte, F. (eds.): Introduction to Chemicals from Biomass. Wiley, Hoboken (2015)
8. Hossiso, K.W., Ripplinger, D.: The value of switching production options in a flexible biorefinery. Agric. Resour. Econ. Rev. **46**, 146–173 (2017)

9. Barthe-Delanoë, A.-M., Truptil, S., Bénaben, F., Pingaud, H.: Event-driven agility of interoperability during the run-time of collaborative processes. Decis. Support Syst. **59**, 171–179 (2014)

10. Yue, D., You, F., Snyder, S.W.: Biomass-to-bioenergy and biofuel supply chain optimization: overview, key issues and challenges. Comput. Chem. Eng. **66**, 36–56 (2014)

11. Feng, Y., D'Amours, S., LeBel, L., Nourelfath, M.: Integrated bio-refinery and forest products supply chain network design using mathematical programming approach - semantic scholar. In: Integrated Biorefineries: Design, Analysis, and Optimization, pp. 251–282. CRC Press, Boca Raton (2012)

12. Camarinha-Matos, L.M., Afsarmanesh, H., Garita, C., Lima, C.: Towards an architecture for virtual enterprises. J. Intell. Manuf. **9**, 189–199 (1998)

13. Kim, J., Realff, M.J., Lee, J.H., Whittaker, C., Furtner, L.: Design of biomass processing network for biofuel production using an MILP model. Biomass Bioenergy **35**, 853–871 (2011)

14. Bowling, I.M., Ponce-Ortega, J.M., El-Halwagi, M.M.: Facility location and supply chain optimization for a biorefinery. Ind. Eng. Chem. Res. **50**, 6276–6286 (2011)

15. Vandermerwe, S., Rada, J.: Servitization of business: adding value by adding services. Eur. Manag. J. **6**, 314–324 (1988)

16. Dahmani, S., Boucher, X., Peillon, S.: Industrial transition through product-service systems: proposal of a decision-process modeling framework. In: Camarinha-Matos, Luis M., Scherer, Raimar J. (eds.) PRO-VE 2013. IAICT, vol. 408, pp. 31–39. Springer, Heidelberg (2013). https://doi.org/10.1007/978-3-642-40543-3_4

17. Stahel, W.: The Performance Economy. Springer, Heidelberg (2010)

18. CUMA Chiffres clés, Edition 2017. Fédération Nationale des CUMA, Paris (2017)

19. Endsley, M.R.: Toward a theory of situation awareness in dynamic systems. Hum. Factors **37**, 32–64 (1995)

20. Camarinha-Matos, Luis M., Fornasiero, R., Afsarmanesh, H.: Collaborative networks as a core enabler of Industry 4.0. In: Camarinha-Matos, Luis M., Afsarmanesh, H., Fornasiero, R. (eds.) PRO-VE 2017. IAICT, vol. 506, pp. 3–17. Springer, Cham (2017). https://doi.org/10.1007/978-3-319-65151-4_1

21. Montarnal, A., Barthe-Delanoë, A.-M., Bénaben, F., Lauras, M., Lamothe, J.: Towards automated business process deduction through a social and collaborative platform. In: Camarinha-Matos, L.M., Afsarmanesh, H. (eds.) Collaborative Systems for Smart Networked Environments, pp. 443–451. Springer, Berlin Heidelberg (2014). https://doi.org/10.1007/978-3-662-44745-1_44

22. Bénaben, F., Lauras, M., Truptil, S., Salatgé, N.: A metamodel for knowledge management in crisis management. In: 2016 49th Hawaii International Conference on System Sciences (HICSS), pp. 126–135 (2016)

23. Macé-Ramète, G., Lamothe, J., Lauras, M., Benaben, F.: A road crisis management metamodel for an information decision support system. In: 2012 6th IEEE International Conference on Digital Ecosystems Technologies (DEST), pp. 1–5 (2012)

FIWARE Open Source Standard Platform in Smart Farming - A Review

Maria Angeles Rodriguez[1], Llanos Cuenca[2(✉)], and Angel Ortiz[2]

[1] School of Informatics, Universitat Politècnica de València,
Camino de Vera S/N, 46002 València, Spain
marodsa4@inf.upv.es
[2] Research Centre on Production Management and Engineering (CIGIP),
Universitat Politècnica de València, Camino de Vera S/N, 46002 València, Spain
{llcuenca, aortiz}@cigip.upv.es

Abstract. FIWARE is an open source platform for the deployment of Internet of Things (IoT) applications, driven by European Union and managed by FIWARE Foundation. Recently, FIWARE Foundation has launched his new product Agricolus, which focus on Smart Farming and it uses FIWARE infrastructure. Agricolus manages to bring Hardware and Software together in a decision-making process that support farming activities and offers a "plug and play" interface for precision agriculture. This is encompassed by the phenomenon of Smart Farming, which is a development that take advantage of the use of Information Communication Technologies (ICT) in the daily farm management. This review aims to gain insight into the state-of-the-art of FIWARE in Smart Farming and identify the components of Agricolus in comparison with essential FIWARE architecture.

Keywords: FIWARE · Agricolus · Smart Farming · Precision agriculture

1 Introduction

Recently, has been a growing interest in the use of new technologies, as Big Data and IoT, in areas with not many ICT influence such as agriculture. The application of technology represents an opportunity to improve current agricultural development, so new concepts like *Smart Farming* have been created to support agricultural production. Moreover, research and innovation in this field is being encouraged from the EU Framework Program named Horizon 2020. The term Smart Farming is linked to concept Precision Agriculture and is viewed as a hardware infrastructure for precision agriculture. Precision Agriculture is a term introduced in the 1980 [1] and refers to the management of agricultural plot by monitoring, data processing and intervention of crops [2]. Besides, it contributes to optimize the consumption of resources, eradicates farm epidemic, and provides the farmers an added value of decision making for exploitation daily operations and management [3].

In agriculture industry has been developed some farm IoT systems, for example, a remotely controlled farm that can be managed using mobile devices [4] or a wireless automation system by monitoring and collect crop data [5].

© IFIP International Federation for Information Processing 2018
Published by Springer Nature Switzerland AG 2018. All Rights Reserved
L. M. Camarinha-Matos et al. (Eds.): PRO-VE 2018, IFIP AICT 534, pp. 581–589, 2018.
https://doi.org/10.1007/978-3-319-99127-6_50

In this paper, we focus on the farm IoT systems developed with technology FIWARE [6]. FIWARE is an open standard platform that belong Future Internet Private Public Partnership (FI-PPP) program. This program aims to advance Europe's competitiveness in digital technologies, and in particular, to support a new European Cloud platform [7].

A recent example of farm IoT system created with open infrastructure FIWARE is *Agricolus*. Agricolus has been launched by FIWARE Foundation and developed by TeamDev on March 2018. This product manages to bring Hardware and Software together in a decision-making process that support farming activities and offers a "plug and play" interface for precision agriculture [8].

Therefore, the main contributions of this paper are: the literature update of components of FIWARE platform, the proposal of an actual review of FIWARE in Smart Farming explaining previous studies and its most reused FIWARE components, a description of the new product Agricolus and its architecture decomposed in FIWARE components.

For that, literature search related to this topic is carried out within well-known databases, such as ScienceDirect, Elsevier and others. The remainder of this paper is organized as follows. In Sect. 2, a review of components of FIWARE platform and a FIWARE overview in Smart Farming are detailed. A description of the new platform for precision farming called Agricolus is described in Sect. 3. The detail of the new platform Agricolus in its components FIWARE is proposed in Sect. 4. Finally, in Sect. 5 conclusions of this paper are exposed.

2   FIWARE in Smart Farming

FIWARE is present in many different sectors in Europe, for example, healthcare, telecommunications, environmental services, and recently agriculture. The key of FIWARE is to be an open architecture and a reference implementation of a service infrastructure, building upon generic and reusable building blocks, available through Application Program Interfaces (APIs) called Generic Enablers (GEs).

2.1   FIWARE Generic Enablers

The GEs offer a number of general-purpose functions, easing development of smart applications in multiple sectors, and they are grouped into functional groups. Below, we describe the most relevant GE implementations of components catalogue FIWARE divided by groups. For each GE the FIWARE Foundation provides their specifications and implementations with an open source license, which is included in the catalogue [10].

(1)   Services Ecosystem and Delivery Framework (SEDF): co-create, publish, cross-sell and consume applications or services.
   (i)   Business API Ecosystem (called Biz Ecosystem RI): offers support for selling apps, data, and services. Version: 6.4.0. Updated: 2017-12-20.
   (ii) Application Mashup (called Wirecloud): offers tools that allows users to create and run a web application front-end. Version: 6.4.2. Updated: 2017-11-01.

(2) Cloud Hosting (CH): provides computation, storage and network resources to manage services.
  (i) Application Management (called Murano): provides the basic support for hardware deployment management. Version: 5.4.3. Updated: 2016-11-03.
(3) Data/Context Management (DCM): easing access, gathering, processing, publication and analysis of context information at large scale.
  (i) Cygnus: Cygnus is a connector in charge of persisting sources of data in certain configured third-party storages. Version: 4.2.1. Updated: 2017-05-16.
  (ii) Publish/Subscribe Context Broker (called Orion): is an implementation of NGSI9 and NGIS10 with persistence storage. Version: - Updated: 2017-03-09.
  (iii) BigData Analysis (called Cosmos): is intended to deploy means for analyzing both batch and stream data. Version: 1.0.0. Updated: 2016-12-12.
  (iv) Complex Event Processing (called CEP): analyses event data in real time. Version: 5. Updated: 2016-08-07.
(4) Advanced middleware and interfaces to Networks and Devices (I2ND): build communication-efficient distributed applications, exploit advanced network capabilities and easily manage robotic devices.
  (i) Kiara Advanced Middleware: is a Java based communication middleware for applications. Version: 0.4.0. Updated: 2016-02-04.
(5) IoT Services Enablement (IoTSE): make connected things available, searchable, accessible, and usable.
  (i) Backend Device Management (called IDAS): connects IoT devices/gateways to FIWARE platform. Version: 7.1.3. Updated: 2018-02-12.
  (ii) IoT Discovery: allows context producers to register their IoT Objects in linked-data format. Version: 5. Updated: 2016-10-26.
  (iii) IoT Broker: is a middleware component enabling applications to retrieve information from IoT installations. Version: 6.4. Updated: 2018-01-17.
  (iv) IoT Data Edge Consolidation GE (called Cepheus): provides a common access in real time to data, for sensors. Version: 1.0.0. Updated: 2017-06-15.
(6) Security (SEC): make delivery and usage of services trustworthy by meeting security and privacy requirements.
  (i) Identity Management (called KeyRock): offers tools for administrators to support the handling of user functions. Version: 6.0.0. Updated: 2018-03-20.
(7) Advanced Web-based User Interface (AWUI): 3d &AR capabilities for web-based UI.
  (i) POI Data Provider: provides spatial search services and data on Points of Interest via RESTful. Version: 5.4. Updated: 2016-09-19.

When a software architect's develops a new agriculture solution or other kind of solution, it is not required to use all GE of the platform. The solution can use only the GEs that it demands for his case, because each GE of platform is independently.

2.2   FIWARE Generic Enables Used in Smart Farming

In previous studies of Smart Farming, some studies present solutions for precision agriculture using IoT platform of FIWARE [11–17] IoT platform as *&Cube* and *Mobius* [18] or ISOBlue [19]. In this paper, we focus in the studies based on used FIWARE:

Agri-IoT [11]: A semantic framework for IoT- based smart farming applications, which supports reasoning over various heterogeneous sensor data streams in real-time. Reused FIWARE GEs: IDAS and Cepheus.

SME Widhoc [12]: An application developed with the aim of reducing the amount of water necessary for irrigation tasks in real crops located in a semiarid area of the South of Spain. Reused FIWARE GEs: Orion, Cosmos, Cygnus and Wirecloud.

Testbed [13]: A testbed in a laboratory environment implemented to simulate different deployments and load conditions for analysis of an IoT use case scenario in the domain of precision agriculture. Reused FIWARE GEs: Orion, Cosmos, Cygnus, IoT Discovery and IoT Broker.

Cropinfra [14]: A comprehensive Internet-based networked crop production infrastructure to assist farmers to operate efficiently and fulfil farming demands using present and future technologies. Reused FIWARE GEs: CEP, Orion, Kiara Advanced Middleware, Business API Ecosystem, Wirecloud, IoT Broker and KeyRock.

FMS or Greenhouse [15–17]. A novel Business-to-Business collaboration platform from the agri-food sector perspective, which aims to facilitate the collaboration of numerous stakeholders belonging to associated business domains, in an effective and flexible manner. Reused FIWARE GEs: CEP, Orion, Kiara Advanced Middleware, Business API Ecosystem, Wirecloud, IoT Broker and KeyRock.

In these studies analysed, we can observe that Orion is the most reused FIWARE generic enablers, because it is reused in four out of five studies, followed by Wirecloud and IoT Broker that are reused in three out of five studies. Orion manage context information and is the mandatory component of FIWARE platform, Wirecloud displays data on dashboards and is essential for visualize context information, and IoT Broker is device interface and is key to retrieve information.

Other generic enablers such as Business API Ecosystem (seller of apps or services) or Kiara Advanced Middleware (communication middleware) are less reused because they aren't core generic enablers and are responsible of tasks that are outside the regular workflow of the context information (processing, analysis and visualization).

3   Agricolus - A New Platform for Precision Farming

In the agriculture-food sector, FIWARE Foundation has created an accelerator program called SmartAgriFood [20]. The SmartAgriFood accelerator is supporting Small and Medium-sized Enterprises (SMEs) developing smart services and mobile apps to be addressed in the agriculture-food sector. In particular, Agricolus, which has developed recently by TeamDev, is FIWARE IoT Ready certified and we can find in the official FIWARE Marketplace [21].

Also, TeamDev participates in other FIWARE programs like FIWARE iHubs network, being the provider of iHub Umbria (official iHub in Italy). The FIWARE iHubs programme supports local digital hubs to enrich their services, to build a network of tech-enabling communities and to encourage the formation of digital economy at a local level. iHub Umbria is based in building the community of local FIWARE developers and is the center dedicated to the adoption of FIWARE platform among local companies. This facilitates the creation of collaborative networks of developers-to-developers, developers-to-local companies, local companies-to-local companies to be more competitive together at local level [22].

TeamDev as member of SmartAgriFood accelerator, created Agricolus with the main motivation of to obtain real-time information about crops and farms. With this information, farmers are helped in the difficult process of making decisions about their agricultural production that they are faced daily.

This solution is a cloud applications ecosystem for precision farming with multiple purposes: disease awareness and forecasts, crop monitoring, decision support system for treatments and fertilizers, farm management and end to end traceability bringing valuable information to final users. In addition, it focuses entirely on the European market and, in particular, it concentrates on small, medium and large farms. For the moment, as recently launched, their first customers are Italian farmers and farmers associations who grow wine, olives, vegetables, oat, corn, and tobacco [23].

An example of implementation to this project is shown on Fig. 1. It is the deployment in some tobacco's crops located in different geographical regions of Italy (Veneto, Umbria e Campania). The recollected data provided by sensors installed in tobacco's crops are used to support decisions about agricultural operations like sowing

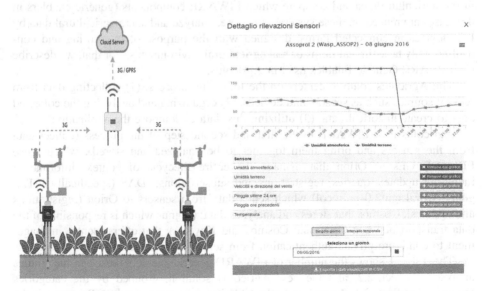

Fig. 1. Implementation example of Agricolus in tobacco's crops in Italy.

or harvest time, timing for treatments and predictive models to spread pests. All data converge in Agricolus suite for managing tobacco's crops and extract insight can guide cultivation techniques, essential to improve tobacco's quality [24].

Besides, Agricolus offers a Web application, which allows farmers to map fields combining external GIS (geographic information system) services and analyses information from crop management which stores in Agricolus platform. The web application shows a map with different types of geolocated crop and displays information about these crops (such as vegetation indices calculated or weather indicators) [8].

Likewise, to improve indicators information which shows on his Web application, Agricolus has integrate FIspace (another project that belongs to FI-PPP program) with his services. FIspace is a business-to-business (B2B) collaboration platform and aims at developing solutions to address the challenges in collaborative business networks, focusing on use cases from the agri-food or transport industries. It works like a social network, like LinkedIn or Facebook [25].

With FIspace the company can negotiate collaborations, manage intercompany business processes, exchange data or deliver and use value-added services; this is quite important to small or medium sized companies without enough technological resources. For instance, it only stores the links between business and the conditions for data sharing (never store the business data exchanged), with this programm will facilitate seamless B2B Collaboration, efficient developments of customized solutions with minimal costs and evolution of open business networks [25].

4 Components of Agricolus, a New FIWARE Architecture Use Case

In this paper, the main goal is to present systems developed with FIWARE technology in the agriculture area and compare which FIWARE components (generic enablers in this case) are reused on these systems; for store, analyze and share agricultural data by IoT devices in connected farms, designed with the purpose of monitoring and controlling daily tasks in real farms or real agricultural environments. For that, we describe the FIWARE Generic Enables used in Agricolus.

The Agricolus solution centers on the following process: (1) collecting data from several sources such as sensors and devices, (2) organizing and analyzing the collected data to create historical data, (3) utilizing this data to compose the application.

Agricolus uses FIWARE to the first and second step of the process (collect data from the sensors and bring them together to be analyzed and stored), which reuse FIWARE GEs as Orion that manage the entire lifecycle of context information including updates, queries, registrations and subscriptions; IDAS (specifically IoTAgent - UltraLight2.0 protocol) which sends data from sensors to Orion (registrations and updates); Cosmos that stores and analyzes data; Cygnus which is responsible of the data transport between Orion and Cosmos and KeyRock that offers identity management to configure private authentication from sensors and devices.

The Table 1 shows the number of FIWARE generic enablers reused in the studies analysed in Sect. 2.2, and the new Agricolus solution, grouped by the categories mentioned in Sect. 2.1. According to the table it can be noticed that DCM group is the most reused, because it is essential the data/context management for the IoT platform, for example Orion, Cygnus and Cosmos are core generic enablers in standard architecture FIWARE. Moreover, Orion is the star generic enablers, because it is reused in five out of six solutions and it seems essential for any IoT platform in Smart Farming.

Table 1. Number of FIWARE generic enablers reused in each group.

Smart Farm solution	SEDF	CH	DCM	I2ND	IoTSE	SEC	AWUI
Agri-IoT	0	0	0	0	2	0	0
SME Widhoc	1	0	3	0	0	0	0
Testbed	0	0	3	0	2	0	0
Cropinfra	2	0	2	1	1	1	0
FMS or Greenhouse	2	0	2	1	1	1	0
Total present applications	*5*	*0*	*10*	*2*	*6*	*2*	*0*
Agricolus	0	0	3	0	1	1	0
Total with Agricolus	*5*	*0*	*13*	*2*	*7*	*3*	*0*

5   Conclusions

This paper has identified the existing solutions in Smart Farming used by FIWARE and has compared FIWARE components (generic enablers) reused on these systems. Also, we have updated literature review of components of FIWARE platform and we have described a new platform for precision farming called Agricolus.

These solutions studied provide tools accessible to worldwide farmers and consumers too. These are good news for the agricultural sector, which can adopt these open technologies in their farms and create connected farms. By combining the FIWARE platform with other third-party developers as ArcGis (cartographic representation tools) that allowing the crop data to be visualized in maps in order to understand patterns and trends which improve the management farm.

To conclude, we observed that Publish/Subscribe Context Broker (implementation called Orion) belonging to DCM group, is the most generic enabler reused in solutions analyzed in Smart Farming, so data/context management can seem essential for any Smart Farming IoT platform. Therefore, FIWARE is a powerful open platform and it is a useful way to standardize the adoption of common interfaces in the IoT field in many different sectors in Europe as agriculture.

Acknowledgments. This research has been carried out in the framework of the project "Development of an integrated maturity model for agility, resilience and gender perspective in supply chains (MoMARGE). Application to the agricultural sector." Ref. GV/2017/025 funded by the Generalitat Valenciana.

References

1. Robert, P.C.: Precision agriculture: research needs and status in the USA. In: Stafford, J.V. (ed.) Proceedings of the 2nd European Conference on Precision Agriculture, Part 1, pp. 19–33. Academic Press, SCI/Sheffield (1999)
2. Ge, Y., Thomasson, J.A., Sui, R.: Remote sensing of soil properties in precision agriculture: a review. Front. Earth Sci. **5**(3), 229–238 (2011)
3. Sundmaeker, H., Verdouw, C., Wolfert, S., Pérez Freire L.: Internet of food and farm 2020. In: Vermesan, O., Friess, P. (eds.) Digitising the Industry - Internet of Things Connecting Physical, Digital and Virtual Worlds, pp. 129–151. River Publishers, Gistrup/Delft (2016)
4. Lin, J., Liu, C.: Monitoring system based on wireless sensor network and a SocC platform in precision agriculture. In: Proceedings of the International Conference on Communication Technology (ICCT), Hangzhou, pp. 101–104 (2008)
5. Kaewmard, N., Saiyod, S.: Sensor data collection and irrigation control on vegetable crop using smart phone and wireless sensor networks for smart farm. In: Proceedings of the International Conference on Wireless Sensors (ICWiSE), pp. 106–112 (2014)
6. FIWARE. https://www.fiware.org/
7. Future Internet Private Public Partnership (FI-PPP). https://www.fi-ppp.eu/
8. Agricolus. https://www.agricolus.com
9. FIWARE Generic Enablers. http://edu.fiware.org/
10. FIWARE Catalogue. https://catalogue.fiware.org/enablers
11. Kamilaris, A., Gao, F., Prenafeta-Boldu, F.X., Ali, M.I.: Agri-IoT: a semantic framework for Internet of Things-enabled smart farming applications. In: IEEE 3rd World Forum on Internet of Things, WF-IoT 2016, pp. 442–447 (2017)
12. López-Riquelme, J.A., Pavón-Pulido, N., Navarro-Hellín, H., Soto-Valles, F., Torres-Sánchez, R.: A software architecture based on FIWARE cloud for precision agriculture. Agric. Water Manag. **183**, 123–135 (2017)
13. Martínez, R., Pastor, J.Á., Álvarez, B., Iborra, A.: A testbed to evaluate the FIWARE-based IoT platform in the domain of precision agriculture. Sensors (Switzerland), **16**(11) (2016)
14. Pesonen, L.A., et al.: Cropinfra - an internet-based service infrastructure to support crop production in future farms. Biosys. Eng. **120**, 92–101 (2014)
15. Barmpounakis, S., et al.: Management and control applications in agriculture domain via a future internet business-to-business platform. Inf. Process. Agric. **2**(1), 51–63 (2015)
16. Kaloxylos, A., et al.: Farm management systems and the future internet era. Comput. Electron. Agric. **89**, 130–144 (2012)
17. Kaloxylos, A., et al.: A cloud-based farm management system: architecture and implementation. Comput. Electron. Agric. **100**, 168–179 (2014)
18. Ryu, M., Yun, J., Miao, T., Ahn, I.Y., Choi, S.C., Kim, J.: Design and implementation of a connected farm for smart farming system. In: 2015 IEEE SENSORS Proceedings, pp. 1–4 (2015)
19. Layton, A.W., Balmos, A.D., Sabpisal, S., Ault, A., Krogmeier, J.V., Buckmaster, D.: ISOBlue: an open source project to bring agricultural machinery data into the cloud, Montreal, 13 July–16 July 2014. American Society of Agricultural and Biological Engineers (2014)
20. SmartAgriFood. http://smartagrifood.com/
21. FIWARE MarketPlace. https://marketplace.fiware.org
22. FIWARE iHubs. https://www.fiware.org/community/fiware-ihubs/

23. Agricolus in FIWARE MarketPlace. https://marketplace.fiware.org/pages/solutions/2ec3c741ef4dd8f83bab4e83

24. Implementation example of Agricolus. http://www.libelium.com/increasing-tobacco-crops-quality-by-climatic-conditions-control/

25. FIspace. https://www.fispace.eu/whatisfispace.html

A Collaborative Model to Improve Farmers' Skill Level by Investments in an Uncertain Context

Ana Esteso[1(✉)], Maria del Mar E. Alemany[1], Ángel Ortiz[1], and Cecile Guyon[2]

[1] Research Centre on Production Management and Engineering (CIGIP), Universitat Politècnica de València, Camino de Vera S/N, 46022 València, Spain
aneslva@doctor.upv.es, {mareva, aortiz}@cigip.uvp.es
[2] Bretagne Development Innovation,
1bis Route de Fougères, 35510 Cesson-Sévigné, France
c.guyon@bdi.fr

Abstract. Some small farms are forced to waste a part of their harvests for not reaching the quality standards fixed by consumers. Meanwhile, modern retailers (MR) are interested in selling more quality products to increase their profits. MR could invest in a collaboration program so the small farmers could have access to better technologies and formation to increase the proportion of quality products. Unfortunately, the demand, the quantity of harvest, the proportion of harvest being of quality, and its increase with each investment are uncertain parameters. A fuzzy model considering these uncertainties is proposed to determine the investments that MR should made to maximize the profits of the supply chain in a collaboration context. A method to transform the fuzzy model into an equivalent crisp model and an interactive resolution method are applied.

Keywords: Agri-food supply chain · Farmer skills · Collaboration
Product quality · Fuzzy mathematical programming

1 Introduction

Quality standards imposed by end consumers forces some small farmers to throw away big amounts of products. This fact negatively impacts on the environment and the small farmers economies. If the proportion of quality products (QP) obtained in each harvest could be increased, this problem would be eliminated or mitigated. A high level of collaboration is necessary to ensure the quality of the agri-food products [1].

Recent papers propose models to empower small farmers through modern retailers' investments [2–8], but none of them considers the uncertainty of consumers' demand, quantity harvested, proportion of QP obtained from harvest, nor its improvement with each modern retailers' investment. If uncertainty is not considered, models will obtain solutions only applicable to situations in which all the data is known in advance. This paper aims to fill this gap by adapting the model [2] to the uncertain nature of these parameters. Methods to convert the fuzzy model into an equivalent crisp model [9] and a to select the best solution to implement in the AFSC [10] are employed.

© IFIP International Federation for Information Processing 2018
Published by Springer Nature Switzerland AG 2018. All Rights Reserved
L. M. Camarinha-Matos et al. (Eds.): PRO-VE 2018, IFIP AICT 534, pp. 590–598, 2018.
https://doi.org/10.1007/978-3-319-99127-6_51

The paper is structured as follows. Section 2 describes the problem addressed. Section 3 formulates the fuzzy model. Section 4 explains the methods used to solve the model and to select the solution to be implemented. In Sect. 5 these methods are applied. Conclusions and future research lines are drawn in Sect. 6.

2 Problem Description

The AFSC is responsible for the production and distribution of vegetables. It is comprised by small farmers (SF), farmer cooperatives (FC), modern retailers (MR), and consumer markets (CM). End consumers require vegetables with a minimum quality standard, however not all vegetables harvested by SF meet these standards. In fact, the quantity of harvest and the proportion of QP obtained in each harvest are uncertain. Once harvest is made, FCs classify the products into QP and non-quality products (NQP). FCs sell QP to MR, which are responsible of the QP distribution to CM. To reduce wastes, NQP are directly sold to CM at a very low price.

To increase the AFSC profits, more demand need to be covered with QP. For that, MR and SF can establish a collaboration program (CP). In this CP, MR would choose one or more SF and would give them funds with the objective to improve the quality of products. SF should use these funds to acquire new technologies, machineries and/or training. This will increase the proportion of QP to be harvested.

The CP sets three skill levels to which SF can belong according to the proportion of QP obtained in each harvest. When a MR funds one SF, the latter can improve the proportion of QP to be harvested and therefore SF can move up from one skill level to another. However, the improvement of the QP proportion is not known in advance to the fund application. MRs' investments cannot exceed the available budget for the CP.

A fuzzy model for deciding the investments to carry out to maximize the AFSC profits is proposed. The quantity of harvest, the proportion of it being of quality, the improvement of such proportion with each investment, and the demand are uncertain.

3 Fuzzy Model Formulation

The nomenclature employed to formulate the model is exposed in Table 1, where v refers to vegetables, c to the vegetables quality, i to SF, j to FC, k to MR, m to CM, t to periods of time, and FC_i to the set of SFs that belong to a particular FC j. The fuzzy model based on [2] can be presented as follows:

$$\max Z = \sum_v \sum_c \sum_i \sum_{j \in FC_i} \sum_m \sum_t \left(\sum_k Q_{ijkm}^{vct} + qm_{ijm}^{vct} \right) \cdot p_{ijm}^{vct}$$
$$- \sum_v \sum_c \sum_i \sum_{j \in FC_i} \sum_t q_{ij}^{vct} \cdot \left(dij_{ij}^{vt} + r_{ij}^{vt} \right)$$
$$- \sum_v \sum_c \sum_i \sum_{j \in FC_i} \sum_k \sum_t qk_{ijk}^{vct} \cdot djk_{jk}^{vt}$$

Table 1. Nomenclature

Parameters	
$\tilde{s}_i^{vt}$	Quantity of vegetable v harvested in SF i at period t
dij_{ij}^{vt}	Cost for distributing one kg of vegetable v from SF i to FC j at period t
r_{ij}^{vt}	Cost for producing one kg of vegetable v at SF i in FC j at period t
djk_{jk}^{vt}	Cost for distributing one kg of vegetable v from FC j to MR k at period t
dkm_{km}^{vt}	Cost for distributing one kg of vegetable v from MR k to CM m at period t
djm_{jm}^{vt}	Cost for distributing one kg of vegetable v from FC j to CM m at period t
p_{ijm}^{vct}	Price per kg of vegetable v with quality c from SF i through FC j in CM m at period t
pc^{vt}	Penalty cost for wasting or rejecting demand of one kg of vegetable v at period t
$\tilde{d}_m^{vt}$	Demand of vegetable v in CM m at period t
$\tilde{g}_{ij}$	Proportion of QP to be obtained at SF i in FC j
$\tilde{\beta}$	Improvement of the QP proportion with one skill level
h_{ij}^t	Cost of increasing one skill level of SF i in FC j at period t
L	Number of skill levels of CP
l_{ij}	Initial skill level of SF i at FC j
CPB	Budget for CP investments
Decision variables	
q_{ij}^{vct}	Quantity of vegetable v with quality c transported from SF i to FC j at period t
qm_{ijm}^{vct}	Quantity of vegetable v with quality c from SF i transported from FC j to CM m at period t
w_i^{vt}	Quantity of vegetable v wasted in SF i at period t
SL_{ij}^t	Current skill level for SF i in FC j at period t
qk_{ijkm}^{vct}	Quantity of vegetable v with quality c from SF i transported from FC j to MR k at period t
Q_{ijkm}^{vct}	Quantity of vegetable v with quality c from SF i in FC j transported from MR k to CM m at period t
rd_m^{vt}	Quantity of vegetable v demand rejected in CM m at period t
F_{ij}^t	Number of skill levels improved in SF i in FC j at period t

$$
-\sum_v \sum_c \sum_i \sum_{j\in FC_i} \sum_m \sum_t qm_{ijm}^{vct} \cdot djm_{jm}^{vt}
$$
$$
-\sum_v \sum_c \sum_i \sum_{j\in FC_i} \sum_k \sum_m \sum_t Q_{ijkm}^{vct} \cdot dkm_{km}^{vt} \tag{1}
$$
$$
-\sum_v \sum_t \left(\sum_i w_i^{vt} + \sum_m rd_m^{vt} \right) \cdot pc^{vt} - \sum_i \sum_{j\in FC_i} \sum_t F_{ij}^t \cdot h_{ij}^t
$$

Subject to:

$$
\tilde{s}_i^{vt} = \sum_{j\in FC_i} \sum_c q_{ij}^{vct} + w_i^{vt} \quad \forall i, v, t \tag{2}
$$

$$q_{ij}^{vct} \leq \tilde{s}_i^{vt} \cdot \left(\tilde{g}_{ij} + \tilde{\beta} \cdot SL_{ij}^t \right) \quad \forall i,j \in FC_i, v, c = 1, t \tag{3}$$

$$q_{ij}^{vct} \leq \tilde{s}_i^{vt} \cdot \left(1 - \tilde{g}_{ij} - \tilde{\beta} \cdot SL_{ij}^t \right) \quad \forall i,j \in FC_i, v, c = 2, t \tag{4}$$

$$q_{ij}^{vct} = \sum_k qk_{ijk}^{vct} \quad \forall i,j \in FC_i, v, c = 1, t \tag{5}$$

$$q_{ij}^{vct} = \sum_k qk_{ijk}^{vct} \quad \forall i,j \in FC_i, v, c = 2, t \tag{6}$$

$$qm_{ijm}^{vct} = 0 \quad \forall i,j \in FC_i, v, m, c = 1, t \tag{7}$$

$$qm_{ijm}^{vct} = 0 \quad \forall i,j \in FC_i, v, m, c = 1, t \tag{8}$$

$$qk_{ijk}^{vct} = \sum_m Q_{ijkm}^{vct} \quad \forall i,j \in FC_i, k, v, c, t \tag{9}$$

$$Q_{ijkm}^{vct} \leq qk_{ijk}^{vct} \quad \forall i,j \in FC_i, k, m, v, c, t \tag{10}$$

$$\sum_i \sum_{j \in FC_i} \sum_c \left(qm_{ijm}^{vct} + \sum_k Q_{ijkm}^{vct} \right) + rd_m^{vt} = \tilde{d}_m^{vt} \quad \forall m, v, t \tag{11}$$

$$\sum_i \sum_{j \in FC_i} \sum_t F_{ij}^t \cdot h_{ij}^t \leq CPB \tag{12}$$

$$\left(\tilde{g}_{ij} + \tilde{\beta} \cdot SL_{ij}^t \right) \leq 1 \quad \forall i,j \in FC_i, t \tag{13}$$

$$SL_{ij}^t = l_{ij} + \sum_{t_2=0}^{t} F_{ij}^{t_2} \quad \forall i,j \in FC_i, t \tag{14}$$

$$SL_{ij}^t = L \quad \forall i,j \in FC_i, t \tag{15}$$

$$\begin{array}{ll} F_{ij}^t, SL_{ij}^t & \text{\textit{INTEGER}} \\ q_{ij}^{vct}, qk_{ijk}^{vct}, qm_{ijm}^{vct}, Q_{ijkm}^{vct}, w_i^{vt}, rd_m^{vt} & \text{\textit{CONTINUOUS}} \end{array} \tag{16}$$

The model aims to maximize the profits obtained by the whole AFSC (1). For that, profits obtained when selling QP or NQP, as well as costs related to production, distribution, penalties for rejecting demand or wasting products, and investments in the collaboration program are considered.

The product balance at SF is set in constraint (2). Constraints (3) and (4) state the distribution of harvested product between QP and NQP respectively. Constraints (5) to (8) define the product flow between FC, MR and CM, ensuring that QP are only distributed through MR and NQP are directly served to CM. Product balance at MR is set in constraints (9) and (10). Quantity of demand being served and/or rejected is determined in constraint (11). Constraint (12) ensures that investments in the CP do not exceed the available budget for that purpose. The inability to obtain more QP than the quantity of harvested products is defined in constraint (13). Current skill level for each SF is calculated in constraint (14) and constraint (15) forces it to be lower than or equal to the maximum skill level of the program. Finally, constraint (16) sets the definition of variables.

4 Solution Method

First, the methodology proposed by Jiménez et al. [9] to transform a fuzzy model into an equivalent auxiliary crisp model is employed. The auxiliary MILP crisp model is comprised by the same objective function and constraints that the fuzzy model except for constraints (2–4), (11) and (13) that are replaced by constraints (17–23). We recommend readers to consult original source [9] for more information of this approach.

$$\left[\frac{\alpha}{2} \cdot \left(\frac{s_i^{vt1} + s_i^{vt2}}{2}\right) + \left(1 - \frac{\alpha}{2}\right) \cdot \left(\frac{s_i^{vt2} + s_i^{vt3}}{2}\right)\right] \geq \sum_{j \in FC_i} \sum_c q_{ij}^{vct} + w_i^{vt} \quad \forall i, v, t \quad (17)$$

$$\left[\frac{\alpha}{2} \cdot \left(\frac{s_i^{vt2} + s_i^{vt3}}{2}\right) + \left(1 - \frac{\alpha}{2}\right) \cdot \left(\frac{s_i^{vt1} + s_i^{vt2}}{2}\right)\right] \leq \sum_{j \in FC_i} \sum_c q_{ij}^{vct} + w_i^{vt} \quad \forall i, v, t \quad (18)$$

$$q_{ij}^{vct} \leq \left[\alpha \cdot \left(\frac{s_i^{vt1} + s_i^{vt2}}{2}\right) + (1-\alpha) \cdot \left(\frac{s_i^{vt2} + s_i^{vt3}}{2}\right)\right] + \left(\left[\alpha \cdot \left(\frac{g_{ij}^1 + g_{ij}^2}{2}\right) + (1-\alpha) \cdot \left(\frac{g_{ij}^2 + g_{ij}^3}{2}\right)\right] + \left[\alpha \cdot \left(\frac{\beta^1 + \beta^2}{2}\right) + (1-\alpha) \cdot \left(\frac{\beta^2 + \beta^3}{2}\right)\right] \cdot SL_{ij}^t\right)$$
$$\forall i, j \in FC_i, v, c = 1, t \quad (19)$$

$$q_{ij}^{vct} \leq \left[\alpha \cdot \left(\frac{s_i^{vt1} + s_i^{vt2}}{2}\right) + (1-\alpha) \cdot \left(\frac{s_i^{vt2} + s_i^{vt3}}{2}\right)\right] + \left(1 - \left[\alpha \cdot \left(\frac{g_{ij}^1 + g_{ij}^2}{2}\right) + (1-\alpha) \cdot \left(\frac{g_{ij}^2 + g_{ij}^3}{2}\right)\right] + \left[\alpha \cdot \left(\frac{\beta^1 + \beta^2}{2}\right) + (1-\alpha) \cdot \left(\frac{\beta^2 + \beta^3}{2}\right)\right] \cdot SL_{ij}^t\right)$$
$$\forall i, j \in FC_i, v, c = 2, t \quad (20)$$

$$\left[\alpha \cdot \left(\frac{g_{ij}^2 + g_{ij}^3}{2}\right) + (1-\alpha) \cdot \left(\frac{g_{ij}^1 + g_{ij}^2}{2}\right)\right] + \left[\alpha \cdot \left(\frac{\beta^2 + \beta^3}{2}\right) + (1-\alpha) \cdot \left(\frac{\beta^1 + \beta^2}{2}\right)\right] \cdot SL_{ij}^t \leq 1 \quad \forall i, j \in FC_i, t \quad (21)$$

$$\sum_i \sum_{j \in FC_i} \sum_c \left(qm_{ijm}^{vct} + \sum_k Q_{ijkm}^{vct}\right) + rd_m^{vt} \leq \left[\frac{\alpha}{2} \cdot \left(\frac{d_m^{vt1} + d_m^{vt2}}{2}\right) + \left(1 - \frac{\alpha}{2}\right) \cdot \left(\frac{d_m^{vt2} + d_m^{vt3}}{2}\right)\right] \quad \forall m, v, t \quad (22)$$

$$\sum_i \sum_{j \in FC_i} \sum_c \left(qm_{ijm}^{vct} + \sum_k Q_{ijkm}^{vct}\right) + rd_m^{vt} \geq \left[\frac{\alpha}{2} \cdot \left(\frac{d_m^{vt2} + d_m^{vt3}}{2}\right) + \left(1 - \frac{\alpha}{2}\right) \cdot \left(\frac{d_m^{vt1} + d_m^{vt2}}{2}\right)\right] \quad \forall m, v, t \quad (23)$$

The grade of feasibility for a particular solution is represented by α that is ranged from 0 to 1. All the fuzzy parameters follow triangular membership functions: $\tilde{s}^v_{ij} = \left(s^{v1}_{ij}, s^{v2}_{ij}, s^{v3}_{ij}\right)$, $\tilde{g}_{ij} = \left(g^1_{ij}, g^2_{ij}, g^3_{ij}\right)$, $\tilde{d}^{vt}_m = \left(d^{vt1}_m, d^{vt2}_m, d^{vt3}_m\right)$, $\tilde{\beta} = \left(\beta^1, \beta^2, \beta^3\right)$.

To select the final solution to be implemented in the AFSC, an interactive resolution method proposed by Peidro et al. [10] is followed. This method is comprised by three steps: (i) to solve the equivalent auxiliary crisp model for different values of α, (ii) to determine the satisfaction of decision maker for each α solution, and (iii) to select the α solution that better balances its feasibility and the decision maker satisfaction. For more detailed information of this approach, see [10].

5 Implementation and Evaluation

The model was implemented in MPL® 5.0.6.114 and solved by using Gurobi™ 7.0.2 Solver. A Microsoft Access Database is used to import input data and save decision variables values. The computer used for solving the model has an Intel® Xeon® CPU E5-2640 v2 with two 2.00 GHz processors, with an installed memory RAM of 32.0 GB and a 64-bits operating system.

The instance employed for solving the model is the extracted from [2] for the scenario with 120 periods of time and balanced demand-supply except for the fuzzy parameters. Data for s^{vt}_i, d^{vt}_m, g_{ij}, β [2] are used as the central values for the $\tilde{s}^{vt}_i$, $\tilde{d}^{vt}_m$, $\tilde{g}_{ij}$, and $\tilde{\beta}$ membership functions. The lower and upper limits for all functions are obtained by decreasing and increasing the central value by 10%.

The model has been solved for different grades of feasibility α. To evaluate each solution, two parameters have been selected: the total profits obtained by the whole AFSC (P) and the total quantity of quality products sold (QPS). As a second step, the decision maker specifies the aspiration level G and the tolerance threshold tt that is willing to accept for each evaluation parameter. This information is employed for identifying the membership function (24) that characterizes the satisfaction of the decision maker with each parameter result.

$$\mu_{\tilde{G}}(z) = \begin{cases} 0 & if\ z \le G - tt \\ \lambda \in [0,1] & if\ G - tt \le z \le G \\ 1 & if\ z \ge G \end{cases} \qquad (24)$$

In this case, the decision maker indicates that the aspiration level for P is 85,000 € although he would tolerate profits from 75,000 €. Similarly, the decision maker aspirate to sell 360,000 kg of QP although he would accept to sell at least 260,000 kg of QP. Using this data, the satisfaction grade for each parameter (μ_P and μ_{QPS}) and are calculated per solution (24). The global satisfaction level Λ for each α solution is determined as a weighted sum of the satisfaction of both evaluation parameters.

The satisfaction of a solution usually increases as the feasibility of the solution decreases. Thus, the solution that better balances the satisfaction degree and the feasibility degree will be selected for its implementation in the AFSC. To determine such balance, an acceptance index K is calculated for each solution as a weighted sum of the acceptation grade of the feasibility grade γ_α and the acceptation grade of the satisfaction grade γ_Λ. The acceptation grades for α and Λ are also determined by the membership function (24). The decision maker determines that the aspiration level for α is 0.7 although he would tolerate a α from 0.5. Similarly, he will tolerate Λ from 0.2 but sets the aspiration level for the Λ is 0.6. Results of the application of this interactive resolution method [10] are presented in Table 2.

Table 2. Interactive resolution method results.

α	$P(\text{€})$	μ_P	$QPS(kg)$	μ_{QPS}	Λ	γ_α	γ_Λ	K
0.0	87832.02	1.00	359113.23	1.00	1.00	0.00	1.00	0.50
0.1	86829.96	1.00	364062.82	1.00	1.00	0.00	1.00	0.50
0.2	86199.03	1.00	380605.81	1.00	1.00	0.00	1.00	0.50
0.3	84296.07	0.93	365272.20	1.00	0.96	0.00	1.00	0.50
0.4	82688.78	0.77	363798.77	1.00	0.88	0.00	1.00	0.50
0.5	81186.88	0.62	364107.60	1.00	0.81	0.00	1.00	0.50
0.6	**78914.08**	**0.39**	**316925.14**	**0.57**	**0.48**	**0.50**	**0.70**	**0.60**
0.7	75452.38	0.05	276434.09	0.16	0.10	1.00	0.00	0.50
0.8	68686.48	0.00	247245.82	0.00	0.00	1.00	0.00	0.50
0.9	62100.18	0.00	234247.68	0.00	0.00	1.00	0.00	0.50
1.0	55528.60	0.00	228194.37	0.00	0.00	1.00	0.00	0.50

The solution obtained with a grade of feasibility equal to 0.6 will be implemented in the AFSC as it has the most elevated acceptation index. In this solution, the MR invest to improve the quantity of QP in 90% of famers. Some farmers receive just one fund whereas other receive up to three funds. However, only the 67% of the budget for the CP is used. With these investments, the profits of the whole AFSC increases in a one per cent and the 85% of demand is fulfilled with QP. Thus, the presented model let MR know the number of funds to give to maximize the profits of the whole AFSC, and the specific farmers to which funds need to be given.

The solved model counted with 16,441 constraints and 12,000 variables, of which 9,840 were continuous variables and 2,160 were integer variables. The optimal solution has been found for all the α scenarios with an average resolution time of 1.44 s.

6   Conclusions

A model for empowering small-farmers through funds obtained by modern retailers' investments is proposed. It is considered that the quantity of harvest, the proportion of QP to be obtained from harvest, the improvement of this proportion through the collaboration program and the demand are uncertain parameters. A method to transform the fuzzy model into an equivalent crisp model [9] and an interactive resolution method [10] to select the solution to implement in the AFSC are employed.

To better represent the real behavior of AFSC, the proposed model could be extended by considering more sources of uncertainty existing in AFSC (e.g. economic data) [11]. In addition, the model could be adjusted to represent some real behaviors of consumers. For example, some consumers may not be willing to buy NQP although there is not enough QP to fulfill their demand. In such cases, some demand can be rejected while some NQP can be wasted. The model could also be extended by considering the perishability aspect of the products causing the loss of a proportion of QP and NQP along the entire AFSC. Finally, more realistic managerial and regulatory factors of AFSC as well as other aspects related with the consumers' behavior could be considered to better adjust the proposed model to real AFSC behavior.

Acknowledgments. The first author acknowledges the partial support of the Programme of Formation of University Professors of the Spanish Ministry of Education, Culture, and Sport (FPU15/03595). The other authors acknowledge the partial support of Project 691249, "RUC-APS: Enhancing and implementing Knowledge based ICT solutions within high Risk and Uncertain Conditions for Agriculture Production Systems", funded by the EU under its funding scheme H2020-MCSA-RISE-2015.

References

1. Zhao, G., Liu, S., Lopez, C.: A literature review on risk sources and resilience factors in agrifood supply chains. In: Camarinha-Matos, Luis M., Afsarmanesh, H., Fornasiero, R. (eds.) PRO-VE 2017. IFIP AICT, vol. 506, pp. 739–752. Springer, Cham (2017). https://doi.org/10.1007/978-3-319-65151-4_66

2. Esteso, A., Alemany, M.M.E., Ortiz, A.: Improving vegetables quality in small-scale farms through stakeholders collaboration. In: 12th International Conference on Industrial Engineering and Industrial Management (in Press)

3. Sutopo, W., Hisjam, M., Yuniaristanto: An agri-food supply chain model to empower farmers for supplying deteriorated product to modern retailer. In: Yang, G.C., Ao, S.I., Huang, X., Castillo, O. (eds.) IAENG Transactions on Engineering Technologies. LNEE, vol 186, pp. 189–202. Springer, Dordrecht (2013). https://doi.org/10.1007/978-94-007-5651-9_14

4. Sutopo, W., Hisjam, M., Yuniaristanto, Kurniawan, B.: A goal programming approach for assessing the financial risk of corporate social responsibility programs in agri-food supply chain network. In: Proceedings of the World Congress on Engineering 2013, pp. 732–736 (2013)

5. Sutopo, W., Hisjam, M., Yuniaristanto: An agri-food supply chain model for cultivating the capabilities of farmers accessing market using social responsibility program. Int. Sch. Sci. Res. Innov. **5**(11), 1588–1592 (2011)

6. Sutopo, W., Hisjam, M., Yuniaristanto: An agri-food supply chain model to enhance the business skills of small-scale farmers using corporate social responsibility. Makara J. Technol. **16**(1), 43–50 (2012)

7. Sutopo, W., Hisjam, M., Yuniaristanto: Developing an agri-food supply chain application for determining the priority of CSR program to empower farmers as a qualified supplier of modern retailer. In: 2013 World Congress on Engineering and Computer Science, pp. 1180–1184 (2013)

8. Wahyudin, R.S., Hisjam, M., Yuniaristanto, Kurniawan, B.: An agri-food supply chain model for cultivating the capabilities of farmers in accessing capital using corporate social responsibility program. In: Proceedings of the International MultiConference of Engineers and Computer Scientists, pp. 877–882 (2015)

9. Jiménez, M., Arenas, M., Bilbao, A., Rodríguez, M.V.: Linear programming with fuzzy parameters: an interactive method resolution. Eur. J. Oper. Res. **177**, 1599–1609 (2007)

10. Peidro, D., Mula, J., Jiménez, M., Botella, M.M.: A fuzzy linear programming based approach for tactical supply chain planning in an uncertainty environment. Eur. J. Oper. Res. **205**, 65–80 (2010)

11. Esteso, A., Alemany, M.M.E., Ortiz, A.: Conceptual framework for managing uncertainty in a collaborative agri-food supply chain context. In: Camarinha-Matos, Luis M., Afsarmanesh, H., Fornasiero, R. (eds.) PRO-VE 2017. IFIP AICT, vol. 506, pp. 715–724. Springer, Cham (2017). https://doi.org/10.1007/978-3-319-65151-4_64

Value Creation in Networks

Chinese Collaborative Software in Digital Transformation Era

Juanqiong Gou[✉], Nan Li, Wenxin Mu, Qinghua Liu, and Xiyan Lv

School of Economic and Management,
Beijing Jiaotong University, Beijing, China
{jqgou,17120615,wxmu,14241058,lvxiyan}@bjtu.edu.cn

Abstract. China is witnessing a large number of digital transformation cases, spearheaded by business model innovation but also by the emergence of systems that in one way or another to support collaborative network organizations. This paper establishes an analysis framework for collaborative management systems of dynamic organization, based on the literature review of digital transformation and collaborative management. It then analyzes the fitness of two existing and leading collaborative management software provided in the Chinese market. For each of the two systems, the paper specifies the system requirements and the applied modeling methods. The connotation of traditional collaborative software is extended in terms of collaboration goals, scope, content, and methods, as well as product innovation through cases analysis. Meanwhile, it gives direction for future collaboration system modeling.

Keywords: Collaborative network organizations
Collaborative management system · Collaborative Network

1 Introduction

Driven by the explosive spread and use of the Internet in industrial practices, there are a large number of organizational and management innovation cases in China. Digital transformation has, in turn, posed a huge challenge to the development of both applicable organization management theories and enterprise management systems. In recent years, the authors have conducted a large number of case studies and consulting works on digital enterprises and were involved in cooperative research together with software companies through being in charge of some smart campus construction projects. The authors have witnessed the timeliness of innovation in digital transformation, the great interest from the Chinese enterprises, and the urgent need to develop supporting software systems for enterprise collaboration. The cooperation with software companies also brought an in-depth understanding of the product design concepts and modeling methods, as well as the complexity and ambitions to generate new theories and models as well.

Through research and practice in European academic circles during the last two decades, Collaborative networked organizations (CNOs) was established as a study discipline. CNO studies primarily addressed all stages of the life cycle of dynamic goal-driven Virtual Organization (VO) networks, from supporting its formation and

L. M. Camarinha-Matos et al. (Eds.): PRO-VE 2018, IFIP AICT 534, pp. 601–611, 2018.
https://doi.org/10.1007/978-3-319-99127-6_52

configuration to its creation, operation, metamorphosis, and dissolution within the market and society [1]. When considering the distinct specificities of the Chinese business atmosphere, the authors specifically address a number of Chinese software industry that currently provides certain collaboration management systems to this market. The authors investigate whether and how the CNO discipline can provide some needed theoretical and system support for enterprise networking, which is currently lacking from the Chinese provided collaboration management systems, and thus can be used to enhance future product developments in these industries.

The method adopted by the article is a case study method. The case study method was chosen for two reasons. Firstly, the case study approach generates insightful stories rather than statistical information, and this permits a better understanding of organizational complexity from an insider's viewpoint [2]. Secondly, case studies enable the researcher to formulate a more holistic perspective on the studied phenomenon [3]. They are especially useful in exploring research areas that are theoretically less developed [4].

This paper selects two specific software enterprises. The research is based on a two-year study conducted in the two enterprises from 2016 to 2017. The focus of the study is on exploring the development and implementation of their system within the organizations and their customers. The data-collection methods employed in the study were: interviewing, on-site observation, and documentation. Especially the platforms are used in the real application of system development of the author's projects. All interviews were conducted on a face-to-face basis. Data were also collected from a range of documents, including letters, written reports, administrative memoranda. The latter was especially useful in case A for understanding the feedback from end users and their partners.

By using two case studies, the richness of the collaboration scenario is enhanced. The entrepreneurs of the two cases both have a background of the traditional enterprise system and then focus on the collaboration platform with different perspectives.

The case study is focusing respectively on business, organization, and management of collaborative research. For this purpose, based on the CNO theory, this paper first designs a framework for collaborative software analysis and research. Second, the cases are analyzed from the perspectives of their application scenarios, system requirements, modeling methods and their concerns for the future.

2 Literature Review

This part reviews the literature on digital transformation and collaborative management from the perspective of CNO theory.

2.1 Digital Transformation

The rapid development of digital technologies represented by cloud computing, analytics, mobile, social media, and the unprecedented interconnection and interoperability [5] are constantly changing the interactive interconnection of people, companies, governments, and surrounding communities. The new trend is the digital transformation, which has led to challenges and brought new opportunities for business model innovation [6].

Through the interconnection and intercommunication, a great deal of information has been generated, thereby deepening the improvement of business operations and all aspects of daily life. More enterprises begin to encapsulate the service capability based on the standard and form the API management mode for both internal and external consumption, which that will facilitate the rapid implementation of business and eco-environment interconnection at the business level [7]. Digital transformation has brought new opportunities for business model innovation [6]. The rapid development of mobile social networks takes full advantage of digital technologies to build out a global business ecosystem [8], so a new digital business model has begun to take shape.

Digital transformation is the result of the application of digital technology in all aspects of human society. It supports the creation and innovation of specific industries or fields, and this type of innovation breaks through the boundaries of traditional enterprises for new enterprises and moves to a broader ecology [9] in line with globalization environmental expansion.

2.2 Collaborative Management

A collaborative network (CN) is a network consisting of a variety of entities (e.g. organizations and people) that are largely autonomous, geographically distributed, and heterogeneous in terms of their operating environment, culture, social capital and goals, but that collaborate to better achieve common or compatible goals, and whose inter-actions are supported by computer network [10]. In today's society, collaborative networks manifest in a large variety of forms, including the production or service-oriented virtual organizations, virtual enterprises, dynamic supply chains, professional associations, industry clusters, professional virtual communities and collaborative virtual laboratories, etc. [11, 12]. Most forms of collaborative networks imply some kind of organization over the activities of their constituents, identifying roles for the participants, and some governance rules. Therefore, these can be called collaborative networked organizations (CNOs) [10].

Both formation and evolution of the CNO primarily involve dynamic reconfigu-ration of heterogeneous/autonomous resources, in response to the raised opportunities while being aware of the uncertainty of environmental dynamism. Based on [13], collaborative networks, such as virtual organizations, dynamic supply chains, profes-sional virtual communities, collaborative virtual laboratories, etc. are complex systems associated with uncertainties in dynamic business environments.

Research on CNOs and modeling of the dynamic organization, have defined two main organizational forms and management/governance models. The CNO theory includes two levels' management consideration, strategic(VBE)and tactical(VO)level, and the authors compare the two based on this literature, as shown in Table 1. The Virtual Organization (VO) and the Virtual Organizations Breeding Environment (VBE) are therefore established as the core distinguished classes with a number of subclasses addressing different dynamics and diversity of their business targets and management, as well as a wide variety of more specific organization examples [14, 15].

Table 1. Two different management mode in CNOs

		Goal	Organization operation
Short-term (VO)	Static	Identification of opportunities and goals	Formation of VO driven by the goal
	Dynamic	Execution, adjustment of goal	Dynamic coordination of members, resources and processes
Long-term (VBE)	Static	Convergence of long-term goal	Collaboration with the dynamic external environment
	Dynamic	Formation of strategic alliances, identification and integration of membership and resources, etc.	The evolving management of CNO

In the end, the introduced digital transformation and collaborative management theories provide strong theoretical basis for rapid development of the enterprise collaboration support software.

3   Case Analysis

This section will analyze the two cases. Firstly, it will describe the understanding of the demands or/and patterns of the organizational collaborative management in the initial stage of product design and the understanding of the digital transformation. Then their collaborative systems in the technical architecture and the CNO theory will be located.

3.1   Case Analysis of DAJIA

This part mainly describes the DAJIA company's understanding of the organizational management demand and its platform products in digital transformation era, analyzes the DAJIA modeling methods, and ultimately, discusses DAJIA from the perspective of CNO.

3.1.1   Analysis of Organizational Management Demand

DAJIA is a startup company that mainly adopts the method of customer-oriented management and operation to help traditional offline companies to carry out the digital transformation.

With social capital's adequacy and local government's aids This is the golden period for Chinese traditional industrial "digital transformation".; The advantages of traditional industries have also been steadily established, and the objective foundation of "Internet+" transformation is solid. So far, the Chinese economy is in a period of transition from a scarcity economy to a rich economic. The concept of customer consumption is greatly challenged, and consumption capacity and consumer demand are greatly upgraded. Products with high quality, high service, and cultural added value are increasingly recognized by consumers.

Chinese e-commerce has gone through two stages under the trend, which is the B2B (Business to Business) phase that indirectly benefits consumers and the C2C and B2C (Customer to Customer and Business to Customer) phase that directly reduce the selling price. With entering the omnidirectional digital transformation era, the third phase of e-commerce is O2O (Offline to Online or Online to Offline) business, which will be continually amplifying the traditional offline business market.

O2O business mainly includes two ways, online-to-offline and offline-to-online, in which there are Internet e-commerce companies and traditional brand companies as the main bodies. Table 2 show their advantages and disadvantages in digital transformation by comparing their differences in organizational management.

Table 2. Comparing the two main bodies of O2O business

	Internet e-commerce company	Traditional brand company
Brand influence	Platform influence	Brand influence
Offline service system	None	Very mature
The client system	The platform	A lot of regular customers
Service scenario	Informatization and fragmentation	Relatively complicated
Thought	Internet/community thought	Conventional thought that is not virally spread
The industrial chain	Different industry alliance	Independent industry
Business maturity	Low and cannot be marketable	Mature and can be marketable

Traditional enterprises, which possess many advantages such as high awareness of brand, offline customer service system and mature business, can expand their own brands and support off-line resource through virtual community platform. They may become a new Internet leader in the digital transformation. However, Internet e-commerce companies these days are mainly facing two difficulties. Firstly, it is too expensive to attract and sustain customer flow. Secondly, comparing with some largest intermediary platforms, like Alibaba, Taobao, Jingdong, therefore, most small and medium-sized e-commerce enterprises do not possess self-owned platform that can undertake cross-platform customer flow, which is a fatal issue.

Digital technologies can offer traditional brand retails new opportunities to attract customers online, which well quickly broaden the traditional offline business market. DAJIA, depending on the digital technologies, helps traditional enterprises in different industries with different collaborative platforms aiming their business demands, in which the enterprises can take on multiple customers and quickly gain benefit from them both online and offline. At the same time, DAJIA's platforms provide customers with full-cycle services, which can attract and sustain customer flow, broaden business operations, brand awareness and revenue for enterprises.

3.1.2 Enterprise Modeling Method

With the rapid development of IT technology and mobile Internet, the "scenario" has attracted wide attention from the business community [16], especially the Internet industry that defines the "scenario era" as the connection of everything following the IT (Information Technology) and DT (Digital Technology) eras. The so-called scenario thinking actually refers to a kind of service thinking based on the user scenarios, which is the human need and behavioural activities. User scenarios often appear in the system's interaction design field to represent stories about people and their activities to describe who will use the system to accomplish a task [17].

The products of DAJIA build a customer service scenario platform for customer community flow. The platform is mainly divided into three parts, as shown in Fig. 1, the introduction of customer flow, the operation of customer flow and the realization of customer flow. In introducing customer flow stage, the activity of introducing customer will be implemented on the community platform through scenario modeling, such as personalized interface, QR code, and promoters, etc., to increase new users and expand the community. Operation of customer flow is extracting existing scenarios (e.g. short texts) from social networks (e.g. WeChat, Weibo) to build a new scenario suitable for the transformation of traditional enterprises, in which customer traffic will be disseminated, converted, and tracked for retaining customers. Realizing customer flow is creating scenarios that generate consumer impulses to increase rebuys.

Fig. 1. Modeling Method of DAJIA

The core of modeling of DAJIA's products is collaborative scenario modeling based on user behaviour, so user behaviour is a focus of its attention. Scenarios for interactive design specifically divided into two levels [18]. The first level is an objective scenario, which is generally obtained through observation methods to reflect the user's status. This scenario is usually obtained by extracting user requirements before the system is established. The second level is the target scenario, which is a user scenario for solving design problems and requirements based on the first-level scenario. Specifically, user scenarios can be further subdivided into behavioural scenarios and interaction scenarios. The behaviour scenario mainly describes the user's behaviour flow, while the interaction scenario mainly refers to the scene in the interaction process between the user and the system. The former describes the story using the story version, and the latter uses the information flow chart, process story version and other tools to describe [19].

The collaborative scenario, based on user needs and behaviours, is used to represent the interaction and collaboration process of multiple subjects under a certain scenario.

3.1.3   Analysis Based on CNO

The customers of DAJIA are involved in the traditional enterprises, especially the traditional sales enterprises. The most typical representative is a woollen company, Jia Tehui. The company's ideal business model is to build China's largest weaving community. DAJIA helped it to activate customers who have accumulated over the years on Taobao, WeChat and Weibo, and realize its both online and offline channels to improve the profitability through creating a virtual community like VO by scenario modeling. In the virtual community, it provided a scenario-based e-commerce platform integrating shopping, community, high-quality content, and video course services. It freed itself from the exploitation of major e-commerce companies such as Taobao and created its own e-commerce platform, which recruited a number of woollen brands and formed the industrial chain of the weaving industry like VBE.

From the perspective of CNO management discipline, although the CNO theory emphasizes the dynamic and application of VO, it does not give a clear explanation for the specific organization and management within VO. DAJIA's customer service platform, like VO in the CNO theory, form a standardized VO exploiting scenario modeling, which pre-sets goals, tasks, and participants in the organization and implies a set of orderly management methods and scenario applications within VO. At the same time, the platform provides business analysis and membership management by System of Insight. The function, taking advantage of data analysis, can help users find potential partners and customers, which provides powerful data support for the formation of new VO in the future like VBE.

In the information system modeling of ARCNO [13], DAJIA's platform is more inclined to In-CNO perspective, while integrating shopping, community, high-quality content, and video course services in the platform. It uses scenario modeling to provide the role of customers in a full lifecycle scenario service, which free traditional companies from the exploitation of most famous e-commerce enterprises such as Taobao, Jingdong.

3.2   Case Analysis of SEEYON

This section will conduct a case analysis of SEEYON Company from the following three parts. The first part explains the understanding of the organizational management of SEEYON; the second part analyzes modeling method through products of SEE-YON; the third part discusses it by CNO theory.

SEEYON, founded in 2002, has been a focus in the field of collaboration management software for 16 years. It formed a complete product line, which is based workflow for collaborative organizations, from private to public clouds, from the Internet to the mobile Internet, from within the organization together to inter-organizational coordination. SEEYON is the NO.1 market share in China's collaboration management software market. It nearly has 50,000 government agencies and enterprise users, more than 5 million end users use SEEYON collaboration management software products and services every day.

3.2.1   Analysis of Organizational Management Demand

During the 16 years since establishment, SEEYON has been dedicated to continually developing collaborative management platforms and providing services for enterprises. At the same time, the organizational ecology of SEEYON continues to expand with the expansion of the company scale.

The collaborative management platforms of SEEYON focuses on the collaboration management of internal business processes based on "people-oriented" core conception and workflow to build a collaborative enterprise/organization, which is beneficial to improve supervision and control of people in the process of organization management and enhances the flexibility of organization in managing the uncertainty in the organization. In 2013, SEEYON launched a collaborative management platform named "V5" derived from "people-oriented" collaborative management conception, which provides the information collaboration within the organization. It includes five major aspects: portals, workflows, reports, platforms and AI. The application scenarios mainly include a certain scale, the pursuit of sustainable development of enterprises and government agencies, which demand focus on the administration, business team collaboration, business regulation, standardization, intensive management as the core.

When SEEYON's scale is becoming larger and larger these years, it will further expand its own ecological map and continue to enrich its own ecosystem to maximize the value of customers. The customers, such as Microsoft, Oracle, and Huawei, will all be included in SEEYON's ecological circle. SAP, the internationally renowned information service provider, has also joined SEEYON's ecological team to achieve collaboration management because SAP's customers need SEEYON to provide information portals and system integration services. It is deeply felt that only by SEEYON's own ability cannot help enterprises to complete the "Internet +" transformation and information portal integration, which requires industry chain partners working together to build a collaborative ecosystem. This ecosystem can respond to market competition and better serve customers and achieve industrial chain collaboration.

3.2.2   Enterprise Modeling Method

Because of the in-depth study of collaborative management and innovational development of collaborative management platform, SEEYON put forward enterprise architecture based on the collaborative technology platform, as shown in Fig. 2.

As the basic feature of the collaborative full-staff application, SEEYON integrated enterprise information portals, including PCs and mobiles, as shown in Fig. 2, realizing some key functions such as unified messaging, login and report. Then SEEYON's platform integrates much organization information such as office document, organizational performance, business process and knowledge management, which realizes communication and sharing of this information, target management, knowledge management and process management for wide organizational collaboration.

The digital platform is the engine of digital-driven enterprise transformation, especially as an information system that integrates staff and organizations. It collects, collates, and analyzes various data including management tasks, business processing, employee behaviour, and organizational processes, through the report centre to visualize

Fig. 2. Enterprise Architecture of SEEYON

data and information, which improves the operational efficiency of enterprises/organizations and realize data-driven business and data-driven enterprises.

3.2.3 Analysis Based on CNO

The collaborative platform of SEEYON is aimed to collaborate whole social and it has always served for the collaborative ecosystem. Together with customers, industry solution partners, ERP partners, system integration partners, product partners, etc., they have jointly promoted and achieved high-performance organizational management. Therefore, the collaboration in SEEYON is more on the VBE level [14]. However, the collaboration of VBE level is loosening and lack of management method in SEEYON's platform.

In the aspect of VO, SEEYON's products have been in the practice of the people-oriented concept. It gives full play to the group dynamic, which formed the custom quickly customized on-demand organization pattern and various business processes. SEEYON's integration of multiple products has formed internal and external inter-connections within the organization, but the organizational boundaries are still relatively clear. The company's products mainly form ad-hoc collaboration [1] through workflow, analyze behavioural performance, and help enterprise establish a dynamic task-driven management model through the workflow.

Although its collaborative management breaks the traditional rigid "best practice" in the past enterprise management and provides on-demand enterprise services to customers, it may face a new problem when the dynamic processes need to be optimized again.

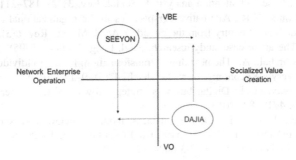

Fig. 3. Innovation in Business Model

4 Conclusion

The paper uses digital transformation and CNO theory to construct the main dimensions of dynamic organization collaborative modeling. Horizontal is the organizational evolutionary trend brought by digital transformation and vertical is the two forms of collaborative management model in dynamic organizational evolution, as shown in Fig. 3. Companies in internal management and companies providing social products have different development ways to building a collaborative platform. However, in the process of development, the understanding of the collaboration model and product demands of complex dynamic organizations gradually converges.

Based on the literature review of digital transformation and collaboration theories, the paper describes the connotation of the development of an organizational collaboration platform and the two directions of industrial development, as shown in Fig. 3. SEEYON, which is committed to corporate operation and management, has gradually begun to development mobile social product to create socialized value. DAJIA, which promotes social networking platforms, has added forms and process management and begun to pay attention to internal organization management.

The contribution to the theory of collaborative management and organization modeling represented by CNO is to map the theory and the actual needs of Chinese information system together. In the context of digital transformation, the two cases achieved a realistic analysis of the CNO theory and its value.

The digital transformation has brought many challenges to the field of information systems. The article provides a new perspective, namely the use of collaborative management theory and collaborative platforms to solve these problems. The collaborative management system will become an important type of information system, its connotation will continue to expand in terms of collaborative goals, scope, content, methods, etc. At the same time, the paper provides direction for modeling of collaborative management information systems through the case study.

References

1. Camarinha-Matos, L.M., Afsarmanesh, H.: A modeling framework for collaborative networked organizations. PRO-VE 2006. IFIPAICT, vol. 224, pp. 3–14. Springer, Boston (2006). https://doi.org/10.1007/978-0-387-38269-2_1
2. Mitchell, J.C.: Case and situation analysis 1. Sociol. Rev. **31**(2), 187–211 (1983)
3. Evered, R., Louis, M.R.: Alternative perspectives in the organizational sciences: "inquiry from the inside" and "inquiry from the outside". Acad. Manag. Rev. **6**(3), 385–395 (1981)
4. Stake, R.E.: The art of case study research. Mod. Lang. J. **80**(4) (1995)
5. Berman, S., Marshall, A.: The next digital transformation: from an individual-centered to an everyone-to-everyone economy. Strat. Leadersh. **42**(5), 9–17 (2014)
6. Emory University, et al.: Digital business strategy: toward a next generation of insights. MIS Q. **37**(2), 471–482 (2013)
7. Sawy, O.A.E., Pereira, F.: Digital business models: review and synthesis. Business Modelling in the Dynamic Digital Space. BRIEFSDIGIT, pp. 13–20. Springer, Heidelberg (2013). https://doi.org/10.1007/978-3-642-31765-1_2

8. Remane, G., Hanelt, A., Nickerson, R.C., Kolbe, L.M.: Discovering digital business models in traditional industries. J. Bus. Strat. **38**(2), 41–51 (2017)

9. Sawy, O.A.E., Pereira, F.: Business Modelling in the Dynamic Digital Space: An Ecosystem Approach. Springer, Heidelberg (2013). https://doi.org/10.1007/978-3-642-31765-1

10. Camarinha-Matos, L.M., Afsarmanesh, H.: Collaborative networks. In: Wang, K., Kovacs, G.L., Wozny, Michael, Fang, Minglun (eds.) PROLAMAT 2006. IFIPAICT, vol. 207, pp. 26–40. Springer, Boston (2006). https://doi.org/10.1007/0-387-34403-9_4

11. Camarinha-Matos, L.M., Afsarmanesh, H.: Collaborative networks: a new scientific discipline. J. Intell. Manuf. **16**(4–5), 439–452 (2005)

12. Camarinha-Matos, L.M., Afsarmanesh, H., Ollus, M.: Virtual Organizations Systems and Practices. Springer, Heidelberg (2005). https://doi.org/10.1007/b102339

13. Jamshidi, A., Rahimi, S.A., Ait-kadi, D., Ruiz, A.: A new decision support tool for dynamic risks analysis in collaborative networks. In: Camarinha-Matos, L.M., Bénaben, F., Picard, W. (eds.) PRO-VE 2015. IFIPAICT, vol. 463, pp. 53–62. Springer, Cham (2015). https://doi.org/10.1007/978-3-319-24141-8_5

14. Afsarmanesh, H., Camarinha-Matos, L.M.: On management of 2nd generation virtual organizations breeding environments. Annu. Rev. Control **33**(2), 209–219 (2009)

15. Afsarmanesh, H., Camarinha-Matos, L.M.: A framework for management of virtual organization breeding environments. In: Camarinha-Matos, L.M., Afsarmanesh, H., Ortiz, A. (eds.) PRO-VE 2005. IFIPAICT, vol. 186, pp. 35–48. Springer, Boston, MA (2005). https://doi.org/10.1007/0-387-29360-4_4

16. Zhang, J.: The age of the scenario era. ZheShang Mag. (12), 30 (2016)

17. Carroll, J.M.: Five reasons for scenario-based design. Interact. Comput. **13**(1), 43–60 (2000)

18. Wang, Y., Weifeng, H., Tang, J., Li, S.: Research on scenario theory in product interaction design. Packag. Eng. **38**(6), 76–80 (2017)

19. Zhao, W.: The application of scene story in user experience design. Design (9), 174–175 (2014)

Business Roles in Creating Value from Data in Collaborative Networks

Ari Alamäki[1]([✉]), Tuija Rantala[2], Katri Valkokari[2],
and Katariina Palomäki[2]

[1] Haaga-Helia University of Applied Sciences, Helsinki, Finland
`ari.alamaki@haaga-helia.fi`
[2] VTT, Technical Research Centre of Finland, Tampere, Finland
`{tuija.rantala,katri.valkokari,`
`katariina.palomaki}@vtt.fi`

Abstract. The present study investigates activities and actors' roles in how companies utilise and adopt big data and cognitive systems in their business processes. Based on the literature review, a qualitative analysis of 18 in-depth interviews with participants from six companies and a complementary review of five illustrative case companies, we identify five different roles to create business value or new business opportunities in the collaborative networks. Based on those business roles, we also identified activities and outcomes. This study contributes to the debate regarding business roles and activities and how companies create value in adopting data and cognitive systems in collaborative networks. For practitioners, the findings show that different data-driven business roles and opportunities exist in the collaborative networks. The business roles are not exclusive, and the same company can have several roles depending on the business case.

Keywords: Big data · Business roles · Cognitive systems
Collaborative networks · Value creation

1 Introduction

Data, a valuable form of capital, may enable new businesses and promote value creation for companies [1–3]. In collaborative networks, actors are interacting with each other for co-creating value, and they have different and supporting roles in value-creation processes. Thus, new ways to co-create value in collaborative networks create novel business opportunities for some companies to sell their data to other actors. Additionally, service providers could integrate others' data with their own to create analyses. Technology providers can develop new solutions to collect, manage and analyse data. All these examples point out that data may create new business opportunities. Managing data-driven businesses often requires inter-organizational collaboration where actors have a special role in data-centric value creation processes.

Data analytics is an essential activity in creating new knowledge in organizations. However, research on different value-creating roles in capturing business value from data analytics and cognitive systems from the viewpoint of collaborative networks is

L. M. Camarinha-Matos et al. (Eds.): PRO-VE 2018, IFIP AICT 534, pp. 612–622, 2018.
https://doi.org/10.1007/978-3-319-99127-6_53

scant. Moreover, most of the past research is rather conceptual or theoretical [4]. Thus, more research is needed to explain alternative roles of companies in creating new value by utilising data analytics and cognitive systems.

In solving the research gap, it is essential to focus on how data could create value for companies and their customers. New knowledge is more and more created in combination with human problem solving and cognitive computing. Today, it is a process where human needs and artificial intelligence are related. This study sought to investigate companies' activities and actors' roles in the utilisation and adoption of big data and cognitive systems in business processes. Through these roles, we studied how companies currently adopt data to create new value or business opportunities.

The paper is organised as follows. After this introduction, Sect. 2 reviews the essence of data, information, knowledge and business models. Section 3 describes the research method and data used in the study. After that, in Sect. 4, we present the five different business roles for creating new business through data utilization. The last section, Sects. 5 and 6, discuss the contribution of this study.

2 Knowledge-Intensive Business and Business Models

The research of inter-organisational value creation shows that companies are more dependent than ever on the effective knowledge management as it forms basics for new knowledge creation in collaborative networks [5, 6]. The cognitively processed outcome of information called knowledge has become a critical resource in inter-organisational exchange. As suppliers and customers depend on each other's knowledge resources more than ever [7], collaborative knowledge creation has become a critical competitive success factor for companies across industries. The increased need to promote new understanding through data analytics and knowledge management creates new business opportunities for several actors in collaborative networks [8].

In the following, we review the interrelationship of data, information and knowledge (Table 1). For understanding data-driven business models and business value in general, we need to understand the role of knowledge. Knowledge is a critical resource when companies extract business value from data in managing business practices and processes. It is also the refined mode of information needed in making complex decisions and in solving ill-defined problems. In fact, companies have always been dependent on knowledge that is a cognitively construed factual or procedural outcome that is created either by humans or cognitive systems [9].

Data represents a lower-level component from the business value perspective than does information and knowledge [10, 11]. For example, the Merriam-Webster and Cambridge dictionaries connect data to facts or information that can be easily delivered and managed by humans and computers. Data is the core component of information; it consists of bytes, numbers and symbols that humans or computers can re-structure or logically order the form of information. Unlike raw data, information can deliver meanings and messages. Information forms basics for knowledge that requires cognitive processing, unlike data and information. Although there is no consensus concerning the definition of information and knowledge, [12] they are strongly associated with reasoning, problem-solving and decision-making. For example, predictive

Table 1. Definitions of key concepts used in this study.

Key concept	Definition used in this study
Knowledge	Factual or procedural outcome of cognitively processed information. Its essence is often personal, contextual and situational "justified true belief" [12, 15]. Knowledge is the essential resource for managing, developing and evaluating business and technology practices and processes. Examples of knowledge are rules, methods, conclusions, diagnostics, advice, reviews, recommendations
Business model	The way in which company organizes its processes and businesses for creating business value in networks and ecosystems. Previous studies found the following data-related business models: data user, data supplier, data facilitator, data custodian, infomediary business, service provider, application provider [16–18]
Business role	The actual data utilisation related value-creating roles of actors and their positions in interorganizational interaction, where resource integration and value exchange take place
Data	Data, either small or big data, is the core component in creating new information and knowledge. It represents a concept lower than information and knowledge [10, 11]. Data provides value for business as "raw data", and it works as a building block in generating new knowledge. Examples of data are bytes, numbers or symbols that are easy to manage by cognitive systems and humans
Information	A structured form of data. It can be seen as a thing, process or personal information [15]. Information provides value for business in delivering facts from objects or phenomena. Examples of information are statistics, Excel sheets, memos, writings, lists, figures, tables

analytics and its recommendations assist marketing managers in timing their marketing campaigns to the most productive moments. Thus, cognitive systems can create new knowledge that helps companies make better decisions, solve problems and optimise processes. Data refined digitally to the mode of useful knowledge helps to develop and perform various practices and processes in organizations and ecosystems. This added value is essential as the level of business value directly relates to the meaningfulness and usefulness of knowledge.

For understanding how knowledge is managed in business processes, organizations and ecosystems, we adopt the knowledge management literature in classifying the levels of knowledge processes. In Carlile's [13, 14] knowledge management framework, knowledge is managed through sharing, interpreting and transforming knowledge. At the knowledge sharing level, existing knowledge is delivered across organizational boundaries. The category of knowledge interpretation adopts and modifies knowledge to the new context, and the category of knowledge transformation creates new knowledge and understanding.

In this study, the term business model describes how a company has organized its processes and businesses for creating business value for its customers or other stakeholders. Conversely, the business role of a company has a wider perspective in to the collaborative network and its influences. The business role better illustrates the actual role of an actor as a part of the collaborative network. It also shows the actors' positions in co-creating value through interorganizational interaction, where resource integration and value exchange represent the modern service-oriented approach to co-create value between actors. The actors are either resource suppliers, customers or customer's customers.

Although the research on data-driven business models and roles is scant, some research papers have covered data-driven business models. Schroeder [16] reviewed big data business models and classified business models in three main categories: data users, data suppliers and data facilitators. Data users are using data in decision making or integrating it into the products. Data suppliers are primarily selling data, and in the data infrastructure business model companies provide data-related infrastructure, consultancy or analytic services. Schroeder notes that there are dependencies between different business models. Janssen and Zuiderwijk [17] focused on infomediary business models in the data-driven business and recognized six sub-categories of solutions: single-purpose apps, interactive apps, information aggregators, comparison models, open data repositories, and service platforms. Thomas and Leiponen [18] classified big data business models in a literature review. As a result of the literature review, they recognized the following business models: data supplier, data manager, data custodian, data aggregator, application developer and service provider.

Unlike the studies above, our study recognises and reviews business roles from the business value perspective, i.e. how companies can create new business through utilising data. We emphasise both value for the company and value for customers, as it demonstrates interorganizational collaboration and business models taking place in collaborative networks. Value creation happens through resource integration processes where actors in different companies unite their resources and exchange value depending on their positions in the value chain [19]. Thus, the business value perspective provides a more comprehensive approach to analyse business roles as part of collaborative networks.

3 Methods

This study aimed to collect qualitative data from companies who are adopting data analytics in their business development, product development or new business creation.

The research approach this study uses is the case study, [20] as the aim was to develop a new understanding of the ways companies are adopting data in creating new business. We extended our research approach to the abductive qualitative research method, [21] as our goal is to build a new model that assists companies in identifying business opportunities and positioning themselves and their value-creating role in collaborative networks. The abductive research method enabled the researchers to build explanations and elaborate the conceptual model for combining literature review and empirical findings. Hence, the researchers simultaneously processed the prior literature and theories and the analysis of data gathered through empirical research and development work [21]. Using the iterative research process allowed for developing a deeper understanding of the empirical data being analysed while simultaneously contributing to the theory of new business creation in the realm of cognitive systems.

We collected data from in-depth interviews with company representatives and reviewing illustrative case examples. The interview data was collected during 2017 from 18 semi-structured theme interviews from six companies in the healthcare, manufacturing, staffing and data processing industries (Table 2). The case companies were in different development phases in terms of their experience in big data utilisation, and also in terms of their business models and new business creation.

Table 2. Interviews and interview data

Case company	Industry	Size	Experience in big data utilisation	Number of interviewees
A	Healthcare	Large	Experienced	5
B	Staffing	Large	Experienced	2
C	Manufacturing	Medium-sized	Beginner	2
D	Manufacturing	Large	Beginner	6
E	Data processing	Start-up	Advanced	2
F	Data processing	Large	Advanced	1

The interviews were audiotaped and transcribed to enable a qualitative content analysis. In the interview analysis, we applied codes with predefined coding categories, as our literature review formed our understanding of the levels of information processing and potential value in adopting data analytics in companies [22]. In addition to the interview data, the material from the additional illustrative cases was reviewed from the perspective of business roles and how they utilise big data analytics in their business. Thus, we used five illustrative cases to show examples how companies adopt the role in their business. We analysed data from web pages, articles, presentations, annual reports and marketing material.

4 Results

Based on our research findings, we identified five different business roles to show how companies are adopting data in creating new business opportunities. These roles relate to the provision enabling technologies for creating software and infrastructure business (technology provider), enriched data for creating new revenue (data refinery), analytics for creating new professional services (business analyst), data-driven applications for creating new service business (service provider) and value-added services for enhancing customer experience and purchase behavior (value catalyst). In the following, the five different business roles are described in more detail, and summarised in Table 3.

Provision of enabling technologies for creating software and infrastructure business (technology provider) is the first identified role. In this role, companies

Table 3. Actor roles, value creating activities and business value for customers

Actor's role	Value creating activity (actor's perspective)	Business value for customers
Technology provider	Enabling technologies for creating software and infrastructure businesses	Cognitive systems, analytic software and hardware solutions
Data refinery	Providing enriched data for creating new service businesses	Richer and qualified analytics
Business analyst	Supplying analytics for creating new professional services	Business insights
Service provider	Providing data-driven applications for creating new service business	Process improvements
Value catalyst	Delivering value-added services to enhance customer experiences and purchase behaviours	Enhanced customer experiences

design, produce and sell technological solutions to other companies. The following excerpt from interviews shows that the business model is built on technological competencies. *"...Sometimes we program almost on the hardware level, sometimes we can use standard SQL- and no-SQL-tools. Our development tool is programming language..."* (Founder of a software start-up). The excerpt shows how their role is technology provider in the ecosystem of cognitive systems. In addition to software solutions, these companies can also create value by enabling the collection of sensory data as part of physical artefacts. They create value for their own customers by providing, e.g., software products with advanced algorithms or IoT-type solutions. According to their value proposition, technology providers deliver technological software and devices that make it possible to collect, analyse and manage data. This business model is related to the Internet-of-Things (IoT) phenomena where IP-based sensors are connected to the conventional things. It enables service providers to collect usage data and remotely control and monitor physical devices or things. From a collaborative network perspective, technology providers need customers and service providers who embrace their software and infrastructure solutions.

Providing enriched data for creating new service business (data refinery) is the second identified role. The companies can sell datasets to other companies, who can combine it to their own datasets. They collect data, for example, from their own customer databases or production or delivery processes, but they do not only use it by themselves, but they also want to sell it to actors in their own ecosystem. Thus, they create value for other companies providing data for analysing processes. This business model focuses on the selling of data or data-focused services. A staffing company interviewee stated the following: *"We want to process the data and enrich it and offer it in different kinds of packages to different kinds of services. And we want to challenge our customer business fields to use their imagination about how we should package these big amounts of data that we now have so that companies are willing to pay for it. Either so that they collaborate with us and the data gives us competitive advantage, or* *that we will offer a new service in which our and our customers' data is used."* (Director of a staffing company).

This excerpt shows how companies can extract more value from conventional services by collecting data from their processes. For example, one media company in Finland has taken the courageous step of commercialising its anonymous customer data by offering data-refinery services [23]. The company's Finnish name, Rikastamo, broadcasts its value proposition, as this word means 'enricher' – a service that can help firms' enrich their own data by analysing and visualising them. Data refineries thus use technology providers' solutions and collaborate with business analysts and service providers who are typically their partners and customers.

Providing analytics for creating new professional services (business analyst) is the third identified role. In the third business role, companies can analyse their own or third party data for creating business insight. Thus, their value proposition promises new business insight that they sell to the actors. The following excerpt points out that companies use their own data in creating new services: *"...we are turning our operative model toward such [model] that we do not offer datasets, but we offer business insight based on those datasets, and then added-value increases"* (Director of a healthcare company).

The present excerpt reveals that service providers can begin to offer business analyst services instead of delivering only 'raw' data. Often these companies are categorised as professional service providers or business analysts, especially since industry expertise is needed to create business insights from datasets. Companies with large daily or monthly customer volumes collect client data as part of these firms' operative processes. Technology providers' advanced cognitive systems have even made data collection automatic, but companies need to deal with privacy and security issues so that they can utilise their data for commercial purposes. To this end, firms typically make use of data refineries and technology providers' services.

Providing data-driven applications for creating new service business (service provider) is the fourth identified role. The companies design services, either IoT applications or purely digital applications, that create value by advising customers in some special context. They collect and utilize data in creating real-time analyses that form basics for advises. Examples of this category are recommendation systems used in e-commerce and intelligent advisory systems used in industrial processes. In this role, service providers design and develop applications that utilize, e.g., a large amount of historical search and purchase history, identify the use segment, and then recommend products and services that best match the identified user profile in this user segment. The companies have also developed digital services where they combine their own data with customers' datasets and provide business insight to improve customers' operative processes, which is illuminated in the following comment by a staffing company representative: *"What we do is that we have built, for example, technologies with which we are able to handle data and offer it to customers in a form which they are interested in and which they see beneficial. Them giving us data creates added value. We work with it, add our own data into it and then package it to be used together, and so it* *brings us both added value and improves collaboration, management and decision-making".* (Director of a staffing company).

For example, the Internet of Things (IoT) has been applied by a welding company that offers its customers traceability through data systems. Welding machine manufacturer Kemppi Ltd. provides software modules that offer detailed data on everyone involved in welding processes [24]. From a collaborative network perspective, service providers thus work with technology and other service providers who participate in value co-creation by providing new services. Business analysts and data refineries may also offer other services that create business insights into how to improve processes.

Providing value-added services for enhancing customer experience and purchase behaviour (value catalyst) is the fifth identified role. Companies can also create value by sharing information as free to their customers. This role belongs to the category of loyalty programs, and its ultimate goal is to enhance customers' experience while they consume the companies' products and services. An interviewee from a manufacturing company describes the company's free data sharing as follows: *"We have analysed news feeds, and recognised trends such as where we are going, what is happening beneath, and this is something that customers see as a remarkable added value... And this gives an impression to customers that this is something that we manage... So, analysing and data and trying to think how you can serve customers with it, that alone can add competitiveness."* (Director of a manufacturing company).

This example shows that delivering data-related value-added services to customers can enhance customer experiences. The information concerning value-added services does not belong to the core product or service, but is, however, related to the process where consuming products or services takes place. From the business viewpoint, it enhances the customer experience by providing useful situational data. The data is collected from customers' usage processes. Thus, it does belong to the category of "reverse use of customer data". In their study, Saarijärvi et al. [25] show how several companies collect data from their customers; they return part of it as refined information, such as recipes based on food purchase history or household consumption history of electricity. This is known as "reverse use of customer data". The following excerpt shows how companies have also recognized the potential to improve customer experience by sharing information with customers: *"..it would be nice if we also could provide that, how would I say it in Finnish, solutions for customer experience and customer driven utilizing data ...we have issues that could be shared between customers as they have similar challenges..."* (Manager of a manufacturing company).

Companies can also share data freely on the public Internet. For example, KONE, a leading elevator manufacturer, has launched a public service where one can listen to how elevators "talk" to each other in their cloud centre. The public service illustrates how the elevators send sensory data to the cloud system, and how it returns data to the elevator that is connected to the cloud service [26]. Co-creating these services to enhance clients' experiences and purchase behaviours requires collaboration with other service providers, such as technology providers.

5   Discussion

Although the existing literature on data-driven business models [16–18] provides initial clues to valid categorisations, research on business roles and value-creating activities is still scant. Unlike previous research, the present study examined companies' roles in terms of business value and new business creation through data utilisation. These two perspectives provide a comprehensive approach to analysing companies' roles as part of collaborative networks. The present study's results contribute to filling the above-mentioned research gap by providing new findings on firms' roles in creating value from data-driven businesses. This research focused especially on actors' positions in interorganisational interactions in which resource integration and value exchange take place. Thus, our study contributes significantly to the on-going debate about data-driven businesses in collaborative networks [6, 8].

Based on empirical analyses, we identified five roles and value-creating activities concentrating on how to create value for customers. In addition, these roles collaborate with other roles depending on the business model applied. Each role has, therefore, its unique value-creating activities supported by other roles' activities. Companies can combine their datasets with other firms to produce richer analytics. The former companies can also analyse and visualise data to make them easier to share, facilitating service provider experts' adoption of data-based tools. In addition, these companies can also integrate resources to create new business insights. In this process, data analysts' results are integrated with the findings of service providers' industry experts, and new insights are generated. Value catalysts can create new value-added services by applying analytics and software solutions' results to existing digital or physical services. Some examples that fall into this category are IoT applications or mobile services that utilise external data sources.

Companies seldom create value alone in data-driven businesses. In these collaborative networks, actors integrate resources and exchange value based on these actors' business roles within networks. Firms collaborate to collect and manage data, analyse results, interpret findings and generate new knowledge. As a result, activities' potential value and cognitive systems' complexity naturally vary in business models. This is in line with the results of Carlile's [13, 14] research, which examined how actors engage in value sharing, as well as interpreting and transforming knowledge. Thus, companies are able to not only sell datasets but also help each other interpret data streams and analyse or create new business insights and recommendations.

These activities and business roles are not exclusive, and the same company can have several roles in the surrounding business ecosystem. In some cases, firms only sell 'raw data' to their partners. In other cases, these companies conduct analyses that produce business insights or license their algorithms to partners.

6   Conclusion

This study's results provide new insights into firms' roles and value-creating activities in data-driven business sectors. We identified five roles actors can play, each of which has value-creating activities that integrate with each other in collaborative networks.

The findings highlight that conventional service companies are also developing data-driven services. They are thus entering into new business ecosystems through roles that are new for these firms. The results show that companies seldom work alone when managing data and that value creation happens in networks in which firms have their own specialised role in integrating resources. These roles are not company specific although some companies specialise in specialised value-creating activities, such as software or consultancy. The findings reveal that large companies, especially, can play several different roles within corporations, so different business units may collaborate with each other to create new value for customers.

This study shows that practically any company can enlarge its business to include data management activities and become an actor in data-driven networks. However, firms must first identify processes in which data are created and managed. In addition, companies need to understand their business's position and opportunities in collaborative networks, as firms cannot suddenly start competing with their current loyal partners or customers. The present study's findings can, therefore, help practitioners identify new business opportunities that no one in their companies has recognised previously.

This study's most basic limitation is its reliance on a quite small number of interviews and company cases, which limits the results' transferability. Nonetheless, the findings provide a basic understanding of data-driven businesses' roles and value-creating activities. The present research raised questions concerning co-creation of network-based value propositions, which merit further examination. This study's results should also encourage researchers to explore empirically companies' value-creating activities in collaborative networks.

Acknowledgments. The authors would like to thank the BIG (Big data – Big business) project, all the parties behind the project, as well as Business Finland – the Finnish innovation funding, trade, investment, and travel promotion organization – for its support for this study.

References

1. Davenport, T.H.: How strategists use "big data" to support internal business decisions, discovery and production. Strategy Leadersh. **42**(4), 45–50 (2014)
2. Everelles, S., Fukawa, N., Swayne, L.: Big data consumer analytics and the transformation of marketing. J. Bus. Res. **69**, 897–904 (2016)
3. Frizzo-Barker, J., Chow-White, P.A., Mozafari, M., Ha, D.: An empirical study of the rise of big data in business scholarship. Int. J. Inf. Manag. **36**(3), 403–413 (2016)
4. Yoo, S., Choi, K., Lee, M.: Business ecosystem and ecosystem of big data. In: Chen, Y., Balke, W.-T., Xu, J., Xu, W., Jin, P., Lin, X., Tang, T., Hwang, E. (eds.) WAIM 2014. LNCS, vol. 8597, pp. 337–348. Springer, Cham (2014). https://doi.org/10.1007/978-3-319-11538-2_31
5. Kindström, D.: Towards a service-based business model: key aspects for future competitive advantage. Eur. Manag. J. **28**(6), 479–490 (2010)

6. Camarinha-Matos, L.M., Fornasiero, R., Afsarmanesh, H.: Collaborative networks as a core enabler of industry 4.0. In: Camarinha-Matos, L.M., Afsarmanesh, H., Fornasiero, R. (eds.) PRO-VE 2017. IAICT, vol. 506, pp. 3–17. Springer, Cham (2017). https://doi.org/10.1007/978-3-319-65151-4_1

7. Normann, R., Ramirez, R.: From Value Chain to Value Constellation: Designing Interactive Strategy. Harvard Business Review, Boston (1993)

8. Paajanen, S., Valkokari, K., Aminoff, A.: The opportunities of big data analytics in supply market intelligence. In: Camarinha-Matos, L.M., Afsarmanesh, H., Fornasiero, R. (eds.) PRO-VE 2017. IAICT, vol. 506, pp. 194–205. Springer, Cham (2017). https://doi.org/10.1007/978-3-319-65151-4_19

9. Alamäki, A.: A conceptual model for knowledge dimensions and processes in design and technology projects. Int. J. Technol. Des. Educ. (2017). https://doi.org/10.1007/s10798-017-9410-7. (advanced online publishing; in press)

10. Chen, M., et al.: Data, information, and knowledge in visualization. IEEE Comput. Graph. Appl. 29(1), 12–19 (2009)

11. Hey, J.: The data, information, knowledge, wisdom chain: the metaphorical link. Intergov. Oceanogr. Comm. 26, 1–18 (2004)

12. Gettier, E.L.: Is justified true belief knowledge? Analysis 23(6), 121–123 (1963)

13. Carlile, P.R.: A pragmatic view of knowledge and boundaries: boundary objects in new product development. Organ. Sci. 13(4), 442–455 (2002)

14. Carlile, P.R.: Transferring, translating, and transforming: an integrative framework for managing knowledge across boundaries. Organ. Sci. 15(5), 555–568 (2004)

15. Buckland, M.K.: Information as thing. J. Am. Soc. Inf. Sci. (1986-1998) 42(5), 351 (1991)

16. Schroeder, R.: Big data business models: challenges and opportunities. Cogent Soc. Sci. 2(1), 1–15 (2016)

17. Janssen, M., Zuiderwijk, A.: Infomediary business models for connecting open data providers and users. Soc. Sci. Comput. Rev. 32(5), 694–711 (2014)

18. Thomas, L.D., Leiponen, A.: Big data commercialization. IEEE Eng. Manag. Rev. 44(2), 74–90 (2016)

19. Vargo, S.L., Lusch, R.F.: From repeat patronage to value co-creation in service ecosystems: A transcending conceptualization of relationship. J. Bus. Market. Manag. 4(169), 169–179 (2010)

20. Eisenhardt, K.M., Graebner, M.: Theory building from cases: opportunities and challenges. Acad. Manag. J. 50(1), 25–32 (2007)

21. Dubois, A., Gadde, L.E.: Systematic combining: an abductive approach to case research. J. Bus. Res. 55(7), 553–560 (2002)

22. Strauss, A., Corbin, J.M.: Basics of Qualitative Research: Techniques and Procedures for Developing Grounded Theory, 2nd edn. Sage Publications, Thousand Oaks (1998)

23. Aller Media: How does data Refinery work? (2018). https://www.datarefinery.global/

24. Tapiola, S.: Adding value to every weld: the world's first modular toolbox for welding productivity and quality management. Kemppi ProNews 1(2014), 8–10 (2014)

25. Saarijärvi, H., Grönroos, C., Kuusela, H.: Reverse use of customer data: implications for service-based business models. J. Serv. Market. 28(7), 529–537 (2014)

26. Kone: Listen to machines talk (2018). http://machineconversations.kone.com/

Smart Tourism Destinations: Can the Destination Management Organizations Exploit Benefits of the ICTs? Evidences from a Multiple Case Study

Salvatore Ammirato[1], Alberto Michele Felicetti[1(✉)],
Marco Della Gala[2], Cinzia Raso[1], and Marco Cozza[3]

[1] Department of Mechanical Energy and Management Engineering,
University of Calabria, via P.Bucci, 87036 Rende, CS, Italy
{salvatore.ammirato,alberto.felicetti,
cinzia.raso}@unical.it
[2] Countryside and Community Research Institute, University of Gloucestershire,
Oxstalls Campus, Oxstalls Lane, Gloucester GL2 9HW, UK
mdellagala@glos.ac
[3] 3D Research srl, via Bucci, 45\C, 87036 Rende, CS, Italy
marco.cozza@3dresearch.it

Abstract. Recent developments of ICTs enable new ways to experience tourism and conducted to the concept of *smart tourism*. The adoption of cutting-edge technologies and its combination with innovative organizational models fosters cooperation, knowledge sharing, and open innovation among service providers in tourism destination. Moreover, it offers innovative services to visitors. In few words, they become *smart tourism destinations*. In this paper, we report first results of the SMARTCAL project aimed at conceiving a digital platform assisting Destination Management Organizations (DMOs) in providing smart tourism services. A DMO is the organization charged with managing the tourism offer of a collaborative network, made up of service providers acting in a destination. In this paper, we adopted a multiple case studies approach to analyze five Italian DMOs. Our aims were to investigate (1) if, and how, successful DMOs were able to offer smart tourism services to visitors; (2) if the ICTs adoption level was related to the collaboration level among DMO partners. First results highlighted that use of smart technologies was still in an embryonic stage of development, and it did not depend from collaboration levels.

Keywords: Destination Management Organizations · Smart tourism services
Multiple case studies

1 Introduction

The World Tourism Organization defined a Tourism Destination (TD) as "a physical space with or without administrative and/or analytical boundaries in which a visitor can spend an overnight. It is the cluster (co-location) of products and services, and of activities and experiences along the tourism value chain and a basic unit of analysis of

L. M. Camarinha-Matos et al. (Eds.): PRO-VE 2018, IFIP AICT 534, pp. 623–634, 2018.
https://doi.org/10.1007/978-3-319-99127-6_54

tourism. A destination incorporates various stakeholders and can network to form larger destinations" [1]. In the same report, the authors stated "to compete effectively, destinations have to deliver wonderful experiences and excellent value to visitors". The business of tourism is complex and fragmented and from the time that visitors arrive in the destination, until they leave it, the quality of their experience is affected by many services and interactions, including a range of public and private services, hospitality services, interactions with communities and environments.

Collaborative Networks represent a real opportunity for tourism operators of a TD to remain competitive in the aggressive global market [2]. With the establishment of a collaborative network in a TD, local tourism operators and tourists can be engaged in social relations and actively participate in continuous experience-based learning processes. Although in a TD live and operate many autonomous and heterogeneous entities, they all aim to achieve local tourism development and to increase their general competitiveness in respect to other TDs as common goal [3, 4]. Destination management calls for a coalition of different interests to work towards a common goal to ensure the viability and integrity of destinations "now, and for the future". A Destination Management Organizations (DMO) is the actor charged with strategic planning, managing, and organizing destination resources. To foster sustainable development practices in a destination, DMOs need to work closely with government agencies, local authorities, businesses, the tourism industry, and other destination stakeholders, to be effective in their role [5].

The role of a DMO should not rely just on marketing and management the destination. DMOs are required to reduce information asymmetries among stakeholders. In this vein, the massive adoption of ICT in many operational contexts related to the tourism experience is helping DMOs to operate as knowledge-based organizations [6].

Recent innovation in ICTs and their interconnections, combined with abilities to infer and reason on big data through artificial intelligence, have had a significant impact on tourism sector [8]. In particular, the sensor technology and the spreading of smartphones and ubiquitous technologies (RFID, NFC, BLE beacon and the Internet of Things - IoT) have enabled the collection, analysis and exchange, of real-time context-aware data, providing insights of digital and physical worlds [8]. In addition, use of web 2.0 and customer reviews on social media, have become important sources of information for both tourists and tourism operators. Tourists can use available information for their trip planning, while, service providers can use social media analytics tools for the tourists' digital footprint mining, with a value for their marketing activities [9]. The convergence of these technologies offers the potential to develop information systems able to supply tourists and tourism operators with information that is more relevant, and, in the end, to offer more enjoyable tourism experiences [10]. The adoption of such technologies, combined with the appropriate collaborative business models, support the rise of the *smart tourism destinations*, i.e. innovative tourist destinations built on an infrastructure of cutting-edge technologies and innovative organizational models, which supports the visitors' interaction with and integration into their surroundings, increasing the quality of their experience [11]. At the same time, *smart tourism destinations* enhance cooperation, knowledge sharing, and open innovation among service providers [12]. The combination of ICTs with collaborative tourism networks offers noteworthy opportunities to tourism destinations for internal business process re-engineering. It supports the provision of increasingly personalized tourist experiences and help tourism destinations to gain competitive advantage and to adopt sustainable development pathways [7, 13].

This paper reports main results of a multiple case studies research among five Italian successful DMOs. The study aims at investigating if selected DMOs are able to exploit the potentials of ICT. In other words, we investigate on the ability of a small sample of DMOs to exploit ICT potential in supporting the transformation of the respective managed destinations in real smart tourism destinations.

2 Theoretical Background

To favor the rise of a smart tourism destination, a DMO needs to become a boundary spanner between a collaborative network of local service providers and tourists. Its main role is to generate and disseminate information and knowledge [5]. A DMO able to reach this aim, lead its destination to become a Smart Tourism Destination. To support this transformation, a DMO has to provide services based on a variety of ICTs to both sides of its boundaries: the front end, meaning the ICTs useful to support the tourist 2.0, and the back end, meaning the set of technologies aimed at supporting the decisional and operational processes within the tourism destination [7, 14].

2.1 Front End: ICT at the Tourist 2.0 Side

From a visitor perspective, the availability of Web 2.0 tools and the provision of new personalised informative services can enrich a *tourism experience*. This is possible thanks to the spread of mobile devices. They enable the ubiquitous access to technologies including context-aware systems, augmented realities, autonomous agents searching and mining, ambient intelligence and recommender systems. For example, a tourist might be assisted with attractions, routes and tours recommendations, tourism services recommendations and personalized multiple-days tour planning. To provide these services it could be used a system able to reason and infer on context data. The system could use user location (extracted from GPS receivers, or through Wi-Fi, cell-id, RFID, etc.), time of day, current weather conditions and forecast, user profile information (in some case extracted from social networks), user constraints and preferences, attractions already visited, location and opening hours of POIs, collaborative user-generated content (e.g., comments, attractions ranking, photographs/videos [15]. The above-mentioned technologies can enrich each of the four phases of the so-called tourist 2.0 lifecycle, i.e. the sequence of activities that a tourist usually perform when lives a tourism experience [7]. The phase identified in [7] are dreaming (the emergence of a need, a desire to travel), planning (defining the details of the trip), experiencing (carry-out in-place tourism activities) and recollecting (remembering, memories of the in-place tourism experience).

In particular, for each stage of the lifecycle, we can give further examples related to the use of innovative ICTs. In the *dreaming* phase, tourists are looking for holiday ideas. At this phase, inspiration portals offer tools for sharing and searching geotagged multimedia contents and reviews, and enable tourists to get a virtual preview of the holiday [16]. In the *planning & booking* phase, tourists compose their holiday combining and booking transportations, accommodations, and services (excursions, events, etc.). At this stage, recommender systems and comparison web services allow online users to cope with the information overload [17]. In the *experiencing* phase, related with in-place tourism activities, context-aware systems, augmented reality and ambient intelligence, combined with the use of RFID, NFC, BLE beacon, sensors, actuators, mobile devices and the IoT, enrich the tourist experience [9]. The integration of these technologies enable the provision of services (maps, location-based services, recommender systems, etc.) affecting the way tourists 2.0 interact with the tourism destination. Recommender systems have become valuable for tourists, especially when they are able to reason and infer on data gathered from the context of the human-sensors interaction to assist users in their decisional processes [18]. They can supply tourists with highly accurate and effective tourist recommendations that capture usage, personal and environmental contextual parameters and respect personal preferences [18]. The *recollecting* phase is related to the tourist comes back home. Sharing services are used to recall tourist memories on visited places through photos, videos and stories and to give other prospective tourists tips on the experienced tourism destination.

2.2   Back Office: ICT at the DMO Side

From a business perspective, since the mid-nineties, ICTs have had a significant impact in the efficiency and effectiveness of tourism organizations and on their interactions with consumers. Web 2.0 and mobile ICTs support operations, business transaction and networking among partners in the tourism industry [12]. They enable operators to develop original ways to manage the tourism supply chains, the destination marketing and the relations with customers. Technological platform dynamically interconnecting stakeholders and exchanging real-time information on tourism activities, and social media represent important coordination mechanisms. They allow information and knowledge to flow more easily through networked actors operating in a tourism destination and more contextual data to be transmitted [19]. Moreover, the use of AI techniques, in particular artificial neural network (ANN) models, have become an essential tool for economic modelling and forecasting [20]. At the same time, the use of AI, information retrieval and natural language processing, lead to automatic discovery, analysis, and generalisation of tourism consumer views and opinions on tourism destination. Via the automatic recognition of semantic relationships between tourism product features and attributes, and consumer opinions and satisfactions, tourism organizations might control, evaluate and, eventually correct, their marketing strategies [21, 22]. Furthermore, big data analytics techniques for processing, modelling, and visualizing data, gathered during the whole tourist 2.0 life cycle, could generate more detailed information on visitors' spatial and temporal behaviour at the destination. Tourism organizations might exploit these information to formulate planning policy aimed at managing the tourist flows. They could reduce congestions in some areas, and encourage tourists to explore other less visited sites, or to buy less purchased services [23].

All the described technologies might improve the success of a tourism destination only in association with the appropriate social structure, and relationships among human actors and organisation in a tourist destination [7]. In particular, as regard tourism operators, as highlighted in [7], they may interact at four level of integration: *networking, coordination, cooperation, collaboration*; characterized by an incremental amounts of common goal-oriented risk taking, commitment, and resources sharing [24]. At the *networking* level, DMOs enable the information sharing among tourism service providers, who communicate one another for mutual benefit, but without a common goal. Tourism operators benefit from DMOs' communication and promotional activities, but each operator is responsible for his own services. The most common ICTs are inspiration portals [16], tourism services comparators [25], tourism social networks [17], and mobile and immersive technologies [7]. Moreover, DMOs, when equipped with analytics tools, share data on the market trends and users' perception of a destination to all the networked operators. At the *coordination* level, it is possible to observe a more organizational commitment. Members of the network, even if with different goals and using their own resources, align/alter their activities with the aim to achieve results more efficiently. To satisfy customers' needs, a tourism operator, thanks to the help of the DMO, might "extend" its business services, offering complementary services provided by other tourism operators. In addition to previous technologies, Destination Management Systems - DMSs become important. DMSs support automation of inter-organizational business process collecting into a single portal a variety of services provided by heterogeneous tourism operators located into a specific geographical area [26]. At the *cooperation* level, tourism operators share knowledge and resources to achieve compatible goals. The combined value is the addition of individual "components" of value generated by the participants in a quasi-independent manner. A DMO provides web-services to compose a customized tourism packages to tourists. At this level, in addition to the previous technologies, Tourism Dynamic Packaging Systems –TDPS are the most suitable solutions. They provide full automation through online applications; real-time update of travel product information; single price for an entire tourism package; guide consumers in the choice of products to add to the package, taking into account the compatibility with products previously added [27]. At *collaboration* level, all entities share risks, resources, responsibilities, and rewards to achieve a common goal. In this case, the DMO acts as the unique interface of the network. It allows customers to compose a tailored tourism package in a transparent way and it is responsible for its correct provision. At this level the planning and management process, is not only limited to packaging systems but regards many operative and supporting processes which are managed in a common way. In addition to TDPS, *Enterprise Resource Planning - ERP* technologies for networked tourism organizations represent an important tool to coordinate the network as a whole and to support the accomplishment of shared business processes.

3 Methodology

Considering the exploratory nature of this research, we approached it as a multiple case study [28]. According to Fink's suggestion [29] to use a small sample of population members, we selected a sample of convenience of five Italian DMOs, successful from an economic perspective. The focus on the specific country is justified by the leading role played by Italian tourism worldwide [30, 31].

In the scientific literature, there are plenty of studies related to the assessment of determinants of the economic "success" of a DMO. In [32, 33] exhaustive reviews on empirical studies and models to measure the success of DMOs are reported. The literature review highlights that success of DMOs and of TDs are strongly related. In this study, we defined a DMO as successful when it shows positive values on two indexes (the only two indexed on which scholars agree):

- Evolution across time of the number of presences and arrivals in the TD
- Evolution across time of the number of networked partners of the DMO.

To individuate the unit of analysis, we analyzed websites of Italian DMOs showing positive values on both indexes in the period 2014–2015. We retrieved website URLs searching specific keywords ("DMO", "destinazione turistica", "località turistica", "…", etc.) on the Google search engine. Information gathered from websites were then validated analyzing articles from newspapers and official papers published by refereed public associations (Italian chambers of commerce, the Italian ministry for Tourism and Cultural Heritage, Confturismo, Federalberghi, regional councilors of tourism, etc.).

Following Yin [28], we collected data by both a careful analysis of documentary sources and by the means of semi-structured interviews. Over the last three months of 2017, two researchers interviewed managers of each DMO. The questions asked during the semi-structured interviews were organized in four blocks: DMO's performances (economic data, visitors, tourist flows, etc.), DMO's members (type of service, number of structures, type of affiliation), DMO's services and ICTs adopted by DMO members.

4 Results

4.1 The Cases

Following Flyvbjerg's [34] suggestions, we choose the following critical case studies among Italian DMOs. We stipulated a "Non-disclosure agreement" with the DMOs we analyzed, whose names cannot be mentioned here without violating the anonymity of the case companies.

DMO A is a limited company providing organizational and administrative services to tourism related companies and it is responsible for the promotion, organization, management and coordination of tourism activities. Moreover, *DMO A* manages tourism services booking through its web portal. *DMO A* operates in a municipality that is a renowned winter and summer destination in the Alps, in the northern part of Lombardia Region. DMO's network consist of over 1,700 affiliated facilities (over 110 hotels, 90 restaurants, 2 trade associations, 1 museum, 8 travel agencies and many other suppliers of leisure activities).

DMO B is a public company operating in the tourism promotion of a metropolitan city in central Italy. The city attracts millions of tourists each year and it is famous for its culture, Renaissance art and architecture and monuments. *DMO B* manages 10 municipal museums and, through its web portal, it promotes tourism services, accommodation, facilities and restaurants. There is no a structured form of affiliation for tourism operators to *DMO B*. However, a loose form of partnership is envisaged for the operators who decide to join the service called "Card +", which allows tourists to obtain some benefits (e.g. discounts).

DMO C is a public consortium that aim to attract tourists and promoting conference and leisure tourism in a province located in the Veneto Region of Italy. The DMO consists of over 130 hospitality services, 45 restaurants and 4 suppliers of transport services. Furthermore, the DMO comprises 4 companies providing conference facilities, 3 companies specialized in organizing congresses, 2 destination management companies, 2 audio-visual service providers, and 2 providers of conference and interpreting services.

DMO D is responsible for promoting a province in the Piedmont Region as a tourist destination for leisure, sport, nature, culture, individual and group trips, conferences, conventions, incentive travel and business travel. The organizational network DMO D is made up of 3 trade associations, 2 suppliers of leisure activities, 12 incoming tour operators, 3 service providers, 1 hotel consortium, 55 municipalities. Moreover, the DMO gives visibility to all the accommodation facilities through its web portal.

DMO E is a public economic body of an autonomous region located on the north-eastern part of Italy. The mission of DMO E is to develop the regional tourism system cooperating with all active tourism operators and supplying them with guidelines to make promotional activities consistent. The DMO's network includes several tourist guide associations and tourism consortia, more than 20 incoming tourism agencies, 7 transport service providers, as well as museums, trade associations, public bodies and recreational activities providers. The DMO web portal gives visibility to all the accommodation facilities in the whole region. Moreover, these facilities can join the online booking service provided by DMO E, by paying a fee. To date, about 3,000 tourism services are accessible through the web portal, and about 1.170 of them can be booked thanks the booking service offered by DMO E.

The above-described Italian DMOs represent successful DMOs since the two indexes of success agreed in the extant literature are positive for all of them. The following table reports the success indexes for each case study. If compared with the growth rate of the Italian Tourist market in the same period (+4,4% evolution of arrivals in 2014–2015), it is noteworthy that all the sampled DMOs present higher values [35]. This reinforces the assertion that the five surveyed DMOs are successful (Table 1).

Table 1. The success indexes for each case study.

Indicators	DMO A	DMO B	DMO C	DMO D	DMO E
Evolution of the number of presences (2014–2015)	+ 9,35%	+ 2,47%	+ 3,50%	+ 8,84%	+ 5,11%
Evolution of the number of arrivals (2014–2015)	+ 5,85%	+ 6,10%	+ 5,95%	+ 5,61%	+ 4, 60%
Evolution of the number of networked partners (2014–2015)	Growth	Growth	Growth	Growth	Growth

4.2   Findings

The analysis of the case studies allowed us to identify ICT solutions adopted by the DMOs to support tourists during the whole tourism experience life cycle and to enable stronger interactions among tourism operators.

With reference to the *dreaming* phase, it emerges that all the analyzed DMOs use an inspiration portal to promote the destination. It allows tourists to have a preview of the territories, the cultures and the type of holiday they will experience. Moreover, DMOs are equipped with official pages and accounts on the main social networks (Facebook, Pinterest, Twitter, YouTube, Instagram, Google+). DMOs are very active on their social channels and constantly updated their content (in particular *DMO A* and *DMO E*, are characterized by a high degree of users' involvement). All the DMOs analyzed, except for *DMO C*, propose services they offer on interactive maps accessible through DMOs' web portals. Moreover, they offer content in different languages and include sections containing photo galleries, videos, brochures and multimedia guides.

For what concerns the *planning and booking* phase, the DMO websites provide sections dedicated to travel planning. *DMO A* allows tourists to book overnight stays, pre-packaged tourism solutions or customized tourism services. The portal offers the opportunity to make online payments. *DMO C* and *DMO E* allow tourists to book tourism services through external links or by filling-in an information request form. *DMO D* provides tourists with pre-packaged tourism services created by affiliated tour operators. The reservation can be made on *DMO D*'s web portal. *DMO B* provides only a "showcase website" allowing tourists to view a list of tourist services in the area. None of the analyzed DMOs proposes the use of advanced and dynamic tools for the creation of tourism packages like TDPS (Tourism Dynamic Packaging System). Although some DMOs adopt ICTs enabling tourists to buy pre-arranged packages online, only *DMO A* offers the opportunity to configure tourist packages but it post-pones the validation, acceptance and payment phases to be completed offline. Overall, other DMOs portals are configured as an exclusive "static" window of services and products and, therefore, are not able to support tourists in completing in an exhaustive way the planning and booking phase of their tourism experience.

Analyzed DMOs just barely support the *experiencing* phase. They do not provide any mobile app to assist tourist. Their websites give tourists the opportunity to obtain information on points of interest, events, tours, public transport, etc., but in the case of *DMO B* and *DMO C* the websites are not designed to be responsive, making it difficult for tourists to use them through smartphones, while they are involved in a tourism experience. None of the DMOs offers advanced services such as augmented reality, virtual reality, augmented experience through IoT technologies, guided site explo-ration, multimedia guides.

During the *recollecting* phase, the DMOs' websites do not offer a specific section devoted to tourist reviews, stories and memories, except for *DMO D*. Its website presents a specific section where it is possible to leave opinions and evaluations of some tourism products. *DMO E* examines conversations, comments and reviews on social media in order to detect and improve the "reputation" of the destination. *DMO A*, *DMO C* and *DMO D* use information from online review aggregators to evaluate customer satisfaction.

Overall, the ICTs adoption level for the analyzed DMO is not in line with the latest technological developments. DMOs sufficiently support the dreaming phase of tourist 2.0 lifecycle, while ICT-based services provided during the other phases are very poor. The lack or delay in the adoption of appropriate technologies during the tourist 2.0 lifecycle as a whole does not allow tourists to be involved in a real "augmented tourism experience".

By focusing on ICTs supporting interactions between DMOs and tourism operators, the study shows that *DMO A* manages operational processes through a DMS (Destination Management System), and institutional communications by using the restricted area of its web portal, social media, e-mail and collaborative working tools. *DMO D* manages operational processes via e-mail and thanks to a centralized platform with remote access for operators, while it circulates institutional communications by the means of collaborative tools, social media and e-mail. For all other DMOs, there are no significant back-office ICT solutions. Specifically, *DMO B* manages operational processes by e-mail or telephone, while institutional communications are distributed through the website, e-mails and phone calls; *DMO C* manages the operational processes by e-mail and telephone contacts, while institutional communications take place via e-mail or external collaborative working tools (for example Google Calendar).

Our analysis highlights that all the DMOs we studied use standard and, sometimes, obsolete tools to support interactions with network operators. They use basic ICTs such as e-mail, social media messaging and telephone contacts to circulate information. For the operational processes management, no DMO uses advanced ICT solutions such as TDPS (Tourism Dynamic Packaging System) or ERP systems (Enterprise Resource Planning). All the studied DMOs are limited in collaborative working tools.

With reference to the organizational aspects, it is possible to classify each DMO, on the base of its collaboration level as follows: *networking* for *DMO B*; *coordination* for *DMO C*, *DMO D* and *DMO E*; *cooperation* for *DMO A* (Table 2).

Table 2. Adequacy of front-end and back-end technologies.

	DMO A	DMO B	DMO C	DMO D	DMO E
Dreaming	☺	☺	☺	☺	☺
Planning / Booking	☺	☹	😐	😐	😐
Experiencing	☹	☹	☹	☹	☹
Recollecting	☹	☹	☹	😐	☹
Back-end technologies	😐	☹	☹	☹	☹
Level of collaboration	cooperation	networking	coordination	coordination	coordination

5 Conclusions

This study was the first of its kind and was based on a multiple case study approach. Since findings of the five cases are not expected to be widely generalizable, they contribute more substantially to the formulation of new hypotheses and to enable subsequent investigations according to other research designs.

In this paper we analyzed how the integration of technologies such as mobile devices, sensors and the IoT, combined with the evolution of artificial intelligence and semantic techniques to infer and reason on big data, have the potential to deeply impact on the tourism sector. We observed how the adoption of these new ICTs by collaborative networks of tourism services providers led by DMOs could bring tourism destination to become "smart", allowing tourists to be better able to enjoy their tourism experience long its whole life cycle. To understand the DMO's ability to offer smart tourism services to destination visitors and to find out any relation between adopted ICTs and the collaboration level among partners in a DMO, we then examined five case studies related to different successful DMOs operating in Italy. Results from the multiple case study show that the overall adoption rate of new technologies in the surveyed DMOs was very low. The five DMOs were using the appropriate ICTs to enhance the dreaming face of the tourism experience life cycle, but they were not supporting the other phase and in particular the experiencing one. Moreover, the DMOs we studied were not adopting most advanced technologies to foster the knowledge exchange and collaboration among their partners.

The success in terms of presences and number of networked partners in the 2014–2015 for the studied DMOs might be helped by the driving effect played by Italian tourism worldwide. Anyway, recent studies and analysis on tourist's preferences and needs have been highlighting the shift of the taste of tourists and their needs to search for more authentic and immersive experiences supported by ICTs. To keep continuing to compete and positively perform in the turbulent global market, and possibly to improve their successful performances, it would be worth for the examined DMOs to embrace the new technological development in the sector and to try to exploit the opportunities offered by the adoption of the most recent ICTs. DMOs could thus offer tourists better experiences supporting each phase of the tourism life cycle. At the same time, DMOs are asked to support collaboration among networked tourism service providers offering them systems able to collect, aggregate, analyze, infer and reason on data gathered during the whole tourism lifecycle. Only with such a reasoned approach to ICT adoption, DMOs could be better able to transform the TDs they manage into smart tourism destinations.

Acknowledgments. The research activity reported in this work is funded by MISE (Italian Minister of Economic Development) within the research project "SMARTCAL" (Project number F/050142/02/X32 – CUP B28I15000060008) as part of the "National Operational Programme for Research and Competitiveness 2014–2020".

References

1. Fabricius, M., Carter, R., Standford, D.: A Practical Guide to Tourism Destination Management. World Tourism Organization, Madrid (2007)
2. Afsarmanesh, H., Camarinha-Matos, L.M.: Future smart-organizations: a virtual tourism Enterprise. In: Proceedings of WISE 2000 – 1st ACM/IEEE International Conference on Web Information Systems Engineering, (Main Program), vol. 1, pp. 456–461. IEEE Computer Society Press, Hong Kong, 19–20 June 2000. ISBN 0-7695-0577-5
3. Loss, L., Crave, S.: Tourism breeding environment: business processes applied to collaborative networks in tourism and entertainment sector. In: Camarinha-Matos, L.M., Pereira-Klen, A., Afsarmanesh, H. (eds.) PRO-VE 2011. IFIPAICT, vol. 362, pp. 197–204. Springer, Heidelberg (2011). https://doi.org/10.1007/978-3-642-23330-2_22
4. Ammirato, S., Felicetti, A.M.: Tourism breeding environment: forms and levels of collaboration in the tourism sector. In: Camarinha-Matos, L.M., Scherer, R.J. (eds.) PRO-VE 2013. IFIPAICT, vol. 408, pp. 517–524. Springer, Heidelberg (2013). https://doi.org/10.1007/978-3-642-40543-3_55
5. Sheehan, L., Vargas-Sánchez, A., Presenza, A., Abbate, T.: The use of intelligence in tourism destination management: an emerging role for DMOs. Int. J. Tour. Res. **18**(6), 549–557 (2016)
6. Racherla, P., Hu, C., Hyun, M.: Exploring the role of innovative technologies in building a knowledge-based destination. Curr. Issues Tour. **11**(5), 407–428 (2008)
7. Ammirato, S., Felicetti, A., Della Gala, M.: Rethinking tourism destinations: collaborative network models for the tourist 2.0. Int. J. Knowl. Based Dev. **6**(3), 178–201 (2015)
8. Boes, K., Buhalis, D., Inversini, A.: Smart tourism destinations: ecosystems for tourism destination competitiveness. Int. J. Tour. Cities **2**(2), 108–124 (2016)
9. Gretzel, U., Werthner, H., Koo, C., Lamsfus, C.: Conceptual foundations for understanding smart tourism ecosystems. Comput. Hum. Behav. **50**, 558–563 (2015)
10. Gretzel, U., Sigala, M., Xiang, Z., Koo, C.: Smart tourism: foundations and developments. Electron. Mark. **25**(3), 179–188 (2015)
11. Lopez de Avila, A.: Smart destinations: XXI century tourism. In: ENTER 2015 Conference on Information and Communication Technologies in Tourism, Lugano, Switzerland (2015)
12. Wang, D., Li, X., Li, Y.: China's "smart tourism destination" initiative: a taste of the service-dominant logic. J. Destin. Mark. Manag. **2**(2), 59–61 (2013)
13. Buhalis, D., Law, R.: Progress in information technology and tourism management: 20 years on and 10 year after the Internet – the state of the eTourism research. Tour. Manag. **29**(4), 609–623 (2008)
14. Ammirato, S., Felicetti, A., Della Gala, M., Aramo-Immonen, H., Jussila, J.: Knowledge management and emerging collaborative networks in tourism business ecosystems. In: ECKM 2015 - 16th European Conference on Knowledge Management, Udine, Italy (2015)
15. Gavalas, D., Kenteris, M.: A pervasive web-based recommendation system for mobile tourist guides. Pers. Ubiquit. Comput. **15**(7), 759–770 (2011)
16. Not, E., Venturini, A.: Supporting users in organizing their vacation before, during, and after the travel. In: e-Review of Tourism Research (2010)
17. Mihajlović, I.: The impact of information and communication technology (ICT) as a key factor of tourism development on the role of Croatian travel agencies. Int. J. Bus. Soc. Sci. **3**(24), 151–159 (2012)
18. Gavalas, D., Konstantopoulos, C., Mastakas, K., Pantziou, G.: Mobile recommender systems in tourism. J. Netw. Comput. Appl. **39**, 319–333 (2014)

19. Del Chiappa, G., Baggio, R.: Knowledge transfer in smart tourism destinations: analyzing the effects of a network structure. J. Destin. Mark. Manag. **4**(3), 145–150 (2015)
20. Claveria, O., Torra, S.: Forecasting tourism demand to Catalonia: neural networks vs. time series models. Econ. Model. **36**, 220–228 (2014)
21. Akehurst, G.: User generated content: the use of blogs for tourism organisations and tourism consumers. Serv. Bus. **3**(1), 51–61 (2009)
22. Volpentesta, A.P., Muzzupappa, M., Ammirato, S.: Critical thinking and concept design generation in a collaborative network. In: Camarinha-Matos, L.M., Picard, W. (eds.) PRO-VE 2008. IFIPAICT, vol. 283, pp. 157–164. Springer, Boston, MA (2008). https://doi.org/10.1007/978-0-387-84837-2_16
23. Shoval, N.: Tracking technologies and urban analysis. Cities **25**(1), 21–28 (2008)
24. Camarinha-Matos, L.M., Afsarmanesh, H.: Collaborative networks: value creation in a knowledge society. In: Wang, K., Kovacs, G.L., Wozny, M., Fang, M. (eds.) PROLAMAT 2006. IFIPAICT, vol. 207, pp. 26–40. Springer, Boston, MA (2006). https://doi.org/10.1007/0-387-34403-9_4
25. Akoumianakis, D.: Ambient affiliates in virtual cross-organizational tourism alliances: a case study of collaborative new product development. Comput. Hum. Behav. **30**, 773–786 (2014)
26. Zanker, M., Fuchs, M., Höpken, W., Tuta, M., Müller, N.: Evaluating recommender systems in tourism — a case study from Austria. In: O'Connor, P., Höpken, W., Gretzel, U. (eds.) Information and Communication Technologies in Tourism, pp. 24–34. Springer, Vienna (2008). https://doi.org/10.1007/978-3-211-77280-5_3
27. Zach, F., Gretzel, U., Fesenmaier, D.R.: Tourist Activated Networks: Implications for Dynamic Packaging Systems in Tourism. In: O'Connor, P., Höpken, W., Gretzel, U. (eds.) Information and Communication Technologies in Tourism, pp. 198–208. Springer, Vienna (2008). https://doi.org/10.1007/978-3-211-77280-5_18
28. Yin, R.: Case Study Research and Applications: Design and Methods. SAGE Publications, Thousand Oaks (2017)
29. Fink, A.: The Survey Handbook, vol. 1. Sage, Thousand Oaks (2003)
30. Cuccia, T., Guccio, C., Rizzo, I.: UNESCO sites and performance trend of Italian regional tourism destinations: a two-stage DEA window analysis with spatial interaction. Tour. Econ. **23**(2), 316–342 (2017)
31. Ammirato, S., Della Gala, M., Volpentesta, A.P.: Alternative agrifood networks as learning communities: some issues for a classification model. In: Lytras, M.D., Ruan, D., Tennyson, R. D., Ordonez De Pablos, P., García Peñalvo, F.J., Rusu, L. (eds.) WSKS 2011. CCIS, vol. 278, pp. 293–300. Springer, Heidelberg (2013). https://doi.org/10.1007/978-3-642-35879-1_34
32. Bornhorst, T., Ritchie, J., Sheehan, L.: Determinants of tourism success for DMOs & destinations: an empirical examination of stakeholders' perspectives. Tour. Manag. **31**(5), 572–589 (2010)
33. Volgger, M., Pechlaner, H.: Requirements for destination management organizations in destination governance: understanding DMO success. Tour. Manag. **41**, 64–75 (2014)
34. Flyvbjerg, B.: Five misunderstandings about case-study research. Qual. Inq. **12**(2), 219–245 (2006)
35. UNTWO Annual Report (2016). http://cf.cdn.unwto.org/sites/all/files/pdf/annual_report_2015_lr.pdf. Accessed April 2017

Building Information Modeling

Innovative Enterprise Architectures
for Deploying Product-Service Systems in SME

João Vilas-Boas[1([⊠])] and João Simões[2]

[1] Business Research Unit (BRU-IUL),
Instituto Universitário de Lisboa (ISCTE-IUL), Lisbon, Portugal
jmvbs@iscte-iul.pt
[2] ROFF Consulting, Lisbon, Portugal
joao.rodrigues.simoes@roff.pt

Abstract. This exploratory research appreciates the conceptual adequateness of servitization business models for an Advanced Manufacturing Technology (AMT) SME in the Ornamental Stones (OS) cluster. It is argued for the inquiry process generated from the developed enterprise architecture (EA) as a significant research contribution to conduct fieldwork. The EA (theoretical contribution) was tested by gathering qualitative data from semi-structured interviews, unstructured observations and documentation. A discussion arose from empirical findings concerning the EA usefulness/usability to diagnose both the sponsor' state-of-the-art and needs (practitioner contribution). Primary stages of servitization found in the case might become advanced, if digital business platforms, Industry4.0 and collaborative networks (VBE/VO) are deployed. However, strong feelings of ownership in OS SME have constrained servitization progress and threatened cluster survival. Nevertheless, "mandatory" Building Information Modeling in Architecture, Engineering and Construction generates requirements for collaboration, promoting competitive advantage and enabling advanced servitization. Thus, innovative EA should anticipate/match future business requirements.

Keywords: Collaborative Networks (CN) · Enterprise Architectures (EA) Servitization/Product-Service system (PSS) · Business digitalization

1 Introduction

Neely [1] has been considering that manufacturers should move ahead pure manufacturing and offer services and solutions, delivered through their products. Therefore, servitization is one of the key strategic choices to create differentiation from competitors by offering value-added services [2] and so, by shifting from the products sale to a Product-Service System (PSS) [3]. Servitization has been mostly adopted by large manufacturers, e.g. Rolls-Royce with the "power-by-the-hour" solution [4], despite SME importance, representing ≈95% of existing businesses and employing ≈60% of private-sector workers [5]. Thus, a *first research question (RQ1) concerns the feasibility of PSS for SME, as well as for their Customers and Suppliers.*

L. M. Camarinha-Matos et al. (Eds.): PRO-VE 2018, IFIP AICT 534, pp. 637–649, 2018.
https://doi.org/10.1007/978-3-319-99127-6_55

The assignment and so, all the RQ concern an AMT SME in the OS cluster, the study scope. Therefore, the PSS concern an innovative business model regarding the equipment supplied by an AMT SME (the study sponsor) to the OS producers. However, the move to servitization and the offer of PSS generates huge managerial challenges that many companies are not yet prepared to deal with [6]. In addition, Romero et al. [7] have been arguing for Collaborative Networked Organizations as a growing trend in a highly competitive globalized economy, where collaboration is essential for business success. Thus, the ability of SME to address such a business model (BM) might increase, if they work with partners, in a win-win Collaborative Network (CN) relationship, since they do not appear to be prepared to deal with the consequent emerging managerial and technological challenges. Within this scope, a *second research question (RQ2) arises by questioning the ability of a CN to match the challenges imposed by servitization for SME.* In fact, Collaborative Organizations share core competencies and resources, for a better and quicker response to business opportunities [8].

On the other hand, Camarinha-Matos [9] also suggests that collaboration supported by Information and Communication Technology (ICT) enables SME to overcome geographic limitations and dispersion, by generating economies of scope and scale. So, a *third research question (RQ3) concerns the role of ICT in the adoption of servitization and in the creation and maintenance of a CN.*

CN supported by ICT appear to represent adjusted demands for the organizational structure of the research sponsor to enable the deployment of PSS business models. In fact, the sponsor is a SME with limited resources that develops Advanced Manufacturing Technology (AMT) for other SME from the Ornamental Stones (OS) Industry, being representative of the Cluster Portugal Mineral Resources Association (CPMRA). Moreover, the development of the decorative role for OS in the Architecture, Engineering and Construction (AEC) Industry has been placing new demands on the stones transformation, asking for a consumer attractive product. So, the sector leaders, which are Italian firms, compete on lower costs coming from high volumes, high product quality and, also, from their long-term reputation.

This means that the technological needs of OS SME might also be fulfilled by BM that enable customers to focus in their core business and to cut down an increasing capital investment by transferring equipment maintenance and machine update risks to the supplier. This deal become more appealing to SME, if technology customization and elimination of down times are added up, as well as their related maintenance costs, all included in a long-term pack of advanced services to be paid as a rent [10].

To sum up, this paper reports the exploratory development of a new Enterprise Architecture (EA) for a small machine tool manufacturer, based on a servitization strategy, organizationally supported by both a Collaborative Network (CN) and a Digital Business Platform (DBP). This model is made up of propositions that are statements deducted from the literature review, which define its theoretical contents. It also includes a schematic representation depicted by using a Data Flow Diagram (DFD) to outline the design of its relationships dynamics. Put together, this provides guidance to the design of a process of inquiry to operationalize a preliminary empirical test aiming at holistically discussing the usefulness of servitization on the sponsor case study.

Next sections are, as follows: (i) Conceptual Model Definition; (ii) Methodology; (iii) Empirical Findings from the Case Study; (iv) Discussion and, (v) Conclusions.

2 Definition of the Conceptual Model – Theoretical Propositions

Three propositions have arisen from an in-depth literature review. This was guided by concerns regarding the PSS feasibility for SME, the CN ability to fit servitization challenges and the ICT role in CN design, already expressed by the research questions.

Servitization stresses long term customer relationships and promotes innovation co-creation [11]. In *use-oriented and result-oriented services* the supplier owns the equipment, while the customer pays a long-term rent, getting rid of equipment responsibilities [12]. This enables the customer differentiation [13], supporting a sustainable competitive advantage based on a different way to deliver product functionality [4, 11]. Moreover, setting strategic alliances is a relevant way to overcome SME resources constraints [9], being a growing phenomenon in servitization [14]. In fact, collaboration and co-innovation in services open new paths to value creation [15]. Therefore, it is concluded that *PSS are feasible and desirable for SME, its Service Providers and Customers because there is a convergence of interest* (Proposition 1).

Moreover, business strategy and organizational structure are mutually dependent [16]. So, the increase in SME organization complexity introduced by servitization generates new needs for the structure [6, 13], a requirement for organizational change [17] and different relationships with the stakeholders [6, 13], as well as the adoption of new technologies [18]. A Virtual Organization (VO), which is based on networks that describe different relationships with external stakeholders [19] appears to be an interesting solution deserving to be detailed. A VO is a distributed, geographically dispersed, on-going, dynamic, temporary and self-restructured network of independent win-win partners supported by a common IT infrastructure that extends the internal organisation by cooperative processes facilitated by market coordination mechanisms and driven by demand, by sharing opportunities, information, cost and risk [20]. In fact, VO implementation leverages competencies, services and resources that are required to capture value, in order to overcome limits to growth imposed by rules and hierarchies [20]. In VO, the important process of partner selection might be conducted from the full population of organizations, which is not advisable, or from potential partners previously identified and prepared to collaborate that are grouped into a Virtual Organizations Breeding Environment (VBE) [21]. This is a long term association that includes an interoperable ICT, working rules and cooperation agreements, which assure the basic functioning of a CN [21]. To sum up, *Collaborative Networks through VO and VBE fit the challenges imposed by servitization for SME* (Proposition 2).

Technology is continuously changing the nature of products, processes, strategies, business models and competition [22], which might support the adoption of a PSS strategy [23] through an interoperable collaborative network. In fact, the new ICT requirements for the implementation of advanced services in servitization are illustrated by the four main topics, as follows: new ERP needs, Remote Repair Diagnostics and Maintenance Technology (RRDMT), Digital Business Platform (DBP) and Industry

4.0 (I4.0). For instance, in servitization there is a requirement for continuous data collection, treatment and processing [1] on a relational base that is out of the ERP scope (transactional). Moreover, RRDMT enable the identification and improvement of behaviour patterns that are critical to servitization, equipment remote control and repair customers needs and suppliers relationships [24]. In addition, a DBP is a common platform including several technologies targeting mutual development based on new digital business models that might enable SME to compete with big size companies [25]. As regards outputs, the DBP would share information concerning the PSS such as the equipment performance (e.g. availability, reliability), as well as service cost [26], linking the physical and virtual worlds.

Furthermore, an adequate EA [27] avoids ineffective strategy implementation by orienting the planning and design of IS/IT resources to match institutional objectives [28] and so, close the strategic gap [29]. In the EA context, the Business Architecture (BA) – e.g. servitization – is the strategic path used to orient the design of competitive business processes strategically aligned – e.g. VO/VBE – according to Gartner [29]. A digital platform allows a community of partners, providers and customers to share and enhance digital processes and capabilities for mutual benefit [29], which confirms DBP as an enabler of a VBE. In this way, different combinations of business models, leadership, talent, delivery and IT infrastructure platforms [29] might happen in a VBE ecosystem. Gartner [29] anticipates that 50% of BA will focus on DBP, until 2018. So, *ICT through a DBP, does enable the creation and maintenance of a CN* (Proposition 3, part I). Moreover, by pushing and enabling the ability of two or more systems to exchange and use information among them [30] technology demands an interoperability that is essential to the servitization business model. This interoperability requirements are placed at organizational level (business objectives and processes), semantic level (digital meaning of exchanged resource) and, at technical level (technology heterogeneity) [31]. In this way, *ICT is [also] an enabler of advanced services in servitization* (Proposition 3, part II), in addition to enable a VBE CN. Finally, it might be added that several elements of I4.0 [32] are present in the DBP. For instance, sensors, WiFi networks, and intelligent machines are generating huge amounts of data (big data) that might need to be stored in the cloud and transmitted across long distances requiring special requirements of Cyber Security. This configures an example of Industrial Internet of Things (IIoT), which might be completed by the generation of smart objects within a cyber-physical environment to enable remote monitoring and control of the production machines put together with both people and virtual/non-physical objects. To sum up, these propositions were deducted from an in depth literature review guided by the RQ, are part of the conceptual model, support the inquiry process and will be discussed with the data collected from the case study.

3   Methodology

This research aims at exploring the degree of fitness, adequateness and usefulness among PSS, CN and DBP, theoretically integrated as graphically depicted in Fig. 1. Therefore, a hypothetical-deductive approach was pursued by deducting a conceptual model, i.e. the Enterprise Architecture (EA), from a literature review that took place ahead of the field work. This model is not to be implemented but it is a core part of the developed process of inquiring supporting its conceptual development from the literature. Therefore, three propositions aiming at empirical cross-sectional discussion were deducted. Moreover, an organized and systematic process of inquiry to approach the state-of-the-art of servitization in the investigated case study was generated from the EA model [33] and so, from the deducted propositions. This innovative EA model promotes the building up of a supported answer to the research questions and so, of an organized path to pursue the research purpose. Its main dimensions are, as follows: (i) graphical expression by using a DFD approach (Fig. 1); (ii) detailed description of entities, activities and data flows by using a DFD approach [33]; and, (iii) generic interview guide deducted from the conceptual model description, to be customized according to each case situation [33]. This interview guide operationalizes the systematic inquiring process enabling that data to be collected match the research questions needs. Propositions will also be discussed during the research process aiming at "answering" the research questions. Its role is different from hypotheses that are quantitative and aiming at being either accepted or rejected. It is argued for this inquiring process as an innovative contribution to work into operations research.

In summary, the conceptual EA depicted in Fig. 1 represents a holistic approach to express a modern and updated strategic path for AMT SME in the OS cluster that makes explicit the disruptive role of the technological push. Therefore, a strategic reply was drawn in Activity 1 by matching the contextual threats and opportunities. Then, Activity 2 characterizes the structural configuration for enabling the chosen strategy. Finally, in Activity 3 adequate updated technological solutions are proposed based on the current status-of-the-art. The identified sub-activities process information, by transforming dataflows inputs into outputs. Thus, 40 dataflows were detailed from the literature [33]. In fact, they interconnect and transport information among sub-, inter- and intra-activities based on the analysis of the propositions coming from an in-depth literature review. As a consequence, a supported process of inquiry was theoretically designed, ahead of the fieldwork, a *sine qua non* condition for a deductive research [33]. Therefore, this framework enables the AMT SME to conceptually assess the requirements for a servitization business model, by holistically projecting its strategic vision of the business in the future, as regards the strategy itself, the organizational structure and the related technological requests. In this way, AMT SME may conceptually anticipate and discuss their future needs in terms of structure, business processes and resources that might be required to support the pursuing of a strategic servitization path towards their business goals.

At last, primary data were gathered by three semi-structured interviews at the sponsor and, completed by in loco observation and secondary data. Company directors from an innovative AMT SME with close academic relationships were interviewed. The interview guide was customized based on the conceptual model [33], according to [34] advices. However, some open questions were considered, in order to enable some exploration of relevant topics not included in the guide [34, 35]. A company site visit was run to better understand the business context, as well as to collect some data both secondary from documentation analysis and primary from unstructured observations. Then, source triangulation was pursued [34]. Finally, while construct validity was coming from a thorough literature review, reliability was assured by sending to the

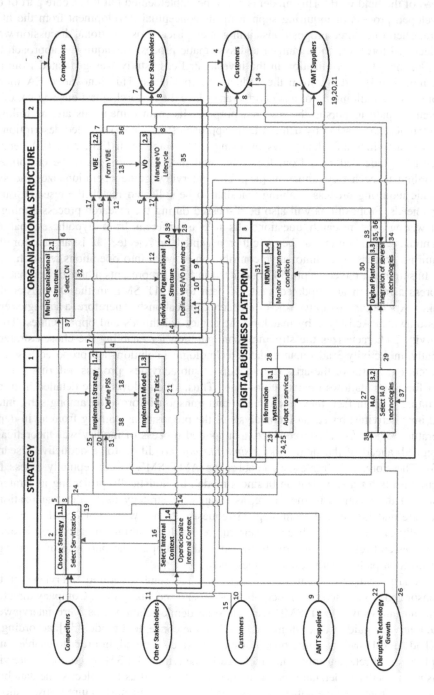

Fig. 1. Enterprise Architecture for AMT SME in the OS cluster [33].

interviewees copies of the notes, asking for their feedback and further correcting them. Since that the case study was purposefully selected, then the external validity of the results only concerns the chosen case, which is part of the CPMRA. Nevertheless, some analytical generalization [35] might even be possible, as further research.

4 Empirical Findings from the Case Study

The case sponsor is an international AMT SME with 20 years of existence. This *hidden champion* provides a service that is aiming at maximizing the customer return on investment by guaranteeing that the "machines are working at peak performance levels". They accomplish this commitment through (i) an on-line remote service, (ii) a global network of a highly skilled technical support staff, and by (iii) working together with the customer to optimize system and operator performance for greater productivity and quality. The case findings will be organized according to the developed propositions in Sect. 2, as follows.

Proposition 1: The case study firm develops horizontal technologies. It has already promoted innovation through cross-fertilization with the shoes industry, concerning the water jet cutting machines. Its main business model is oriented to product, despite a certain level of servitization having been offered as services associated to the products, as follows: (1) in sales – machine transportation, deployment on customer, customization, training and machine revision; (2) in maintenance – remote assistance during lifecycle at no cost; corrective maintenance, free for 2 years, for eliminating manufacturing defects, but paid to fix breakdowns. Despite this PSS stage being possible among SME customers, the risk is higher, because these companies, i.e. SME, are more fragile than long established big firms. However, one might still expect the AMT SME requirement for PSS to increase, depending on: the evaluation of business risk, specific marketplace demand, customer attitude towards machine use, relationships closeness, contractual conditions, customer assessment (education, training, use adequateness, maintenance concerns, etc.), geographic location, local partners typologies, etc. On the other hand, there are requirements for collaborative distributed structures (VBE) as an enabler of the implementation of Building Information Modeling (BIM) procurement, a concern that is currently being introduced in the AEC Industry (flow 11 in Fig. 1). In this way, either inter-client collaboration or client/supply chain collaboration or intra-SC collaboration in the OS are facilitated by a VBE/VO, which represents a new step in the cluster towards BIM introduction, according to our source. These requirements are also expected to facilitate the introduction of PSS supported by I4.0 initiatives, on both the manufacturers (OS SME) and OS customers sides, by bringing together partners to build up collaborative partnerships to address that threat. In fact, there is a convergence of interest on collaborative networks that might serve a threefold purpose, i.e. the new business models concerning the servitization of technology (AMT SME), the focus on the core business processes leaving out complex technologies for the experts (OS SME) and the partnerships to address BIM procurement (OS SME and OS customers). To sum up, it is argued for a convergence of interest between Customers and Service Providers that leverages the desirability of PSS for SME by supporting its feasibility.

Proposition 2: The decreasing of times-to-market of technological solutions introduced at higher rates, the increasing investment costs led by technological innovation and, the increasing complexity of both solutions and technology are reasons why the case company has chosen to pursue its own development together with other partners, such as AMT suppliers, Universities, Sectorial Technological Centers, Sectorial Associations and Customers. These consortia were formed to address mobilizing R&D projects, or other types of collaborative initiatives, e.g. innovative co-creation of technologies (AMT). This is the tested routing that will be used [36], once again, to reinforce the implementation of I4.0 within the context of a DBP that aims at supporting a collaborative network to enable an advanced PSS business model. In fact, challenges and requirements for this purpose are much broader, in both scope and scale, from the ones aiming at the focused development of AMT in equipment. In fact, the task is so huge that it might very well be impossible to address it as an independent firm. So, the new business model itself (servitization) will be dependent on a VBE from where VO will be formed to address the needs of a strategic Product-Service System configuration (e.g. flows 17, 13 in Fig. 1). To sum up, CN not only fit the challenges of servitization in the AMT SME, but they can simultaneously serve other purposes, such as the development of broader technological solutions by generating different VO from the same VBE, e.g. BIM procurement, as one interviewee stressed.

Proposition 3: The case study firm specially highlighted the role of ICT in the adoption of advanced services in servitization in several ways, as follows: (i) production – sensors, cameras and advanced proprietary software enabling digitalization and optimization of the cut profile to avoid defects and, also, to enable pattern matching; gathering production data to enable reliable production management, e.g. actual schedule, used materials, quality control, machine and operator times, set up times, down times, idle times, etc. (ii) maintenance – gathering, treating and processing massive amounts of data about equipment condition (e.g. energy consumption, oil leakages, equipment performance) through sensors, augmented reality and proprietary software enable remote maintenance. This means on time, cheaper and effective service, saving on travelling expenses. Moreover, progress in maintenance can be achieved by adequate software tools exploring the relationship between prognostics & health management technologies and, servitization [12], which might support the planning of the interventions of a CN of maintenance experts. The drawback concerns the "secrecy of clients' information" causing equipment to be off-line most of the time. On the other hand, data interoperability was mentioned as regards future requirements for BIM standards in procurement, despite many concerns of I4.0 already being addressed might also sustain this point. In addition, it looks that the involvement with the ICT support to CN (mezzo level) is not yet an institutional priority, perhaps because the company has mainly been focused in the development of advanced CNC machinery (micro level). However, it looks that is confirmed that ICT does enable the creation and maintenance of a CN through a DBP.

In fact, many of the current equipment features at the micro level are enablers of the digitalization required by CN, e.g. data interoperability, big data and related patterns, remote control, remote maintenance, specific proprietary software, standard CAD/CAM data formats, data security, real time operation, etc. So, the use of this equipment is a *sine qua non* condition for the deployment of CN (e.g. flows 35, 36, 37 in Fig. 1). Moreover, there appears to be an ongoing Digital Business Platform (DBP) under development, of which value/interest might be adequate for "different" CN, as far as their operating purposes require advanced manufacturing equipment; so, the same DBP is equally relevant to support; (i) either a new PSS business model for the AMT SME; (ii) or a servitization situation that enables OS manufactures to focus on their core business (OS SME); (iii) or, even, a new BIM business procurement model for OS SME and OS customers. Therefore, despite ICT is confirmed as an enabler of advanced services in servitization, the scope of the collaboration relationship supported by these equipment features appear to reach applications and uses far beyond the strict interest on a different business model (servitization) for AMT SME. Therefore, as regards the implementation of the CN, despite a VO aiming at this purpose might be formed from the emerging VBE, other VO with different purposes might also be formed (vide Fig. 2). To sum up, huge synergies might be achieved without a sharp increase in complexity, since different VO will address different purposes, despite being formed from a common VBE, the supporting CN. So, there is a requirement for an analysis at a macro level that sets the scene for a VBE in the OS, aiming at a broader purpose.

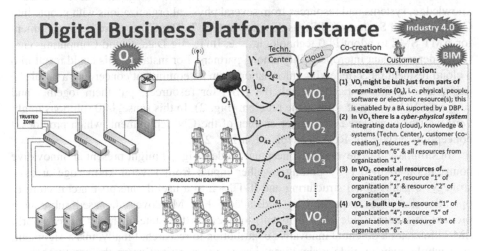

Fig. 2. Instance of a DBP supporting the formation of Virtual Organizations [36].

5   Discussion and Conclusions

The case study AMT SME belongs to the OS cluster, i.e. a set of organizations within the same specialization scope (OS), closely located, collaborating and achieving better results than isolated firms working on their own [37]. This is a different situation from belonging to a sector that is a grouping of companies put together for administrative or statistical purposes. The cluster behaves as a collaborative network constrained by a geographic area accomplishing the pre-requisites of PSS [38], since the delivery and contracting of services depend on the geographical relationship between customer and supplier [14]. On the other hand, one might conclude from Camarinha-Matos et al. [39] that the participation in a cluster in not enough for an advanced servitization strategy. In addition, Camarinha-Matos [9] refer to a VBE as a more feasible environment for service providing by being the preferable path to VO generation.

The major contribution of this research is the recognition of the emergence of VBE supported by DBP as relevant enterprise architectures to deploy collaborative networks as organic and flexible organizational structures that enable the development of innovative business models for SME, such as servitization (RQ2). In fact, a record of Past collaboration and good institutional relationships were found as significant enablers of a VBE (e.g. flow 12 in Fig. 1), where VO dedicated to the repairing services that are required by servitization might be bred. Moreover, other different VO might come out of the very same VBE to address different needs of the cluster (vide §4). Therefore, the VBE is supported by a DBP (e.g. flows 23, 33 and 12 in Fig. 1), which is essential for deploying PSS, as well as for developing an e-procurement strategy to implement a Building Information Modeling (BIM) approach in the AEC sector. To sum up, the empirical test of the proposed conceptual design of an Enterprise Architecture (Fig. 1) shows that PSS are feasible for both a SME and remaining stakeholders involved in the collaborative relationship (RQ1).

Furthermore, emerging VO might result from the integration of cloud data, knowledge, systems and resources from several physical organizations with people into Cyber-Physical Systems (CPS), as depicted in Fig. 2. Therefore, there is a requirement for AMT SME to adopt I4.0 technologies, i.e. IIoT, Big Data, Cloud Computing, etc., which demand data interoperability among partners. For instance, this could result into a cloud resident CPS (receiving information from an equipment concerning a problem) being able to automatically search the VBE for resources, put them together and suggest a VO aiming at solving the problem (Fig. 2). In this sense, I4.0 solutions might very well be considered as a major enabler of the CN deployment, which provides a conceptual answer for RQ3, as depicted in Fig. 2.

In summary, the developed conceptual model (Fig. 1) might present an innovative contribution to theory by putting together inputs from several knowledge areas – strategy, organizational structuring and IS/IT – into a useful enterprise architecture to operationalize PSS, expressed by a detailed DFD. Moreover, the used subsequent process of inquiry (vide [33] for detail) to question the state-of-the-art of real world SME illustrates a potential innovative contribution to research. Finally, this assignment, as a whole, may provide a significant innovative contribution to the practitioner, as regards the conceptual operationalization of routes to pursue the strategic objectives of a business model aiming at a servitization approach.

At last, it should be clear that the scope of this research was delimited by a conceptual approach. This is a legitimate researcher decision that was made by the start of the exercise. So, it is not a limitation to exclude the focus on implementation details or, even, on the specification of the technical solution. In addition, two significant limitations to servitization are going to be addressed next. First of all, in some markets, for some customers it might be difficult or unattractive to build up a VBE/DBP, because they miss the adequate conditions, such as the right partners or relationships, its internal social capital, money or knowledge to deal with business digitalization. This affects the offer of some advanced services of PSS. Secondly, the lack of open innovation in the OS SME generates strong feelings of ownership towards physical resources, capital, information and data that constrain collaboration and so, the progress of servitization, which might even provide a threat to the cluster survival. Therefore, hybrid business models are advisable for AMT SME looking for situational adaptation to different business contexts. Nevertheless, it should be added that "mandatory" progress towards BIM is expected in OS SME, due to the current trends in the AEC sector. This is going to generate strong requirements for VBE/VO, which will leverage competitive advantage and enable the servitization progress in AMT suppliers. To sum up the main recommendation for further work concerns studying a CN that implements a broader VBE to accommodate both current and anticipated future business requirements for the CPMRA, e.g. the INOVSTONE 4.0 initiative. Focusing on CN and digitalized business models might help SME to overcome both the organizational (structural, human and technical) and financial weaknesses that might constrain business development.

Acknowledgements. This research is supported by the INOVSTONE 4.0 Project, which is funded by *Portugal 2020*, within the scope of *Programa Operacional Competitividade e Internacionalização e Programa Operacional Regional de Lisboa*.

References

1. Neely, A.: The servitization of manufacturing: an analysis of global trends. In: Proceedings of 14th EurOMA, pp. 1–10. University of Ankara, Ankara, Turkey (2007)
2. Ahamed, Z., Kamoshida, A., Inohara, T.: Organizational factors to the effectiveness of implementing servitization strategy. J. Serv. Sci. Manag. **6**(2), 177–185 (2013)
3. Baines, T., Lightfoot, H., Benedettini, O., Kay, J.: The servitization of manufacturing: a review of literature. J. Manuf. Technol. Manag. **20**(5), 547–567 (2009)
4. Davies, A.: Moving base into high-value integrated solutions: a value stream approach. Ind. Corp. Change **13**(5), 727–756 (2004)
5. Gasiorowski-Denis, E.: The big business of small companies (2015). http://www.iso.org/iso/news.htm?refid=Ref1937. Accessed 22 May 2017
6. Oliva, R., Kallenberg, R.: Managing the transition from products to services. Int. J. Serv. Ind. Manag. **14**(2), 160–172 (2003)
7. Romero, D., Galeano, N., Molina, A.: Mechanisms for assessing and enhancing organisations' readiness for collaboration in CN. Int. J. Prod. Res. **17**(1), 4691–4710 (2009)
8. Camarinha-Matos, L., Afsarmanesh, H.: Elements of a base VE infrastructure. J. Comput. Ind. **51**(2), 139–163 (2003)
9. Camarinha-Matos, L.: Collaborative networked organizations: Status and trends in manufacturing. Ann. Rev. Control J. **33**(2), 199–208 (2009)
10. Baines, T., Shi, V.: A Delphi study to explore the adoption of servitization in UK companies. Prod. Plann. Control **26**(14–15), 1171–1187 (2015)
11. Tuli, K., Kohli, A., Bharadwaj, S.: Rethinking customer solutions: from product bundles to relational processes. J. Mark. **71**(3), 1–17 (2007)

12. Greenough, R., Grubic, T.: Modelling condition-based maintenance to deliver a service to machine tool users. Int. J. Adv. Manuf. Technol. **52**(9), 1117–1132 (2011)
13. Gebauer, H., Friedli, T.: Behavioral implications of the transition process from products to services. J. Bus. Ind. Mark. **20**(2), 70–78 (2005)
14. Baines, T.: Servitization impact study: How UK based manufacturing organisations are transforming themselves to compete through advanced services. ABS, Birmingham (2013)
15. Camarinha-Matos, L.M., Ferrada, F., Oliveira, A.I., Afsarmanesh, H.: Supporting product-servicing networks. In: Proceedings of 2013 International Conference on Industrial Engineering and Systems Management (IESM), Rabat, pp. 1–7 (2013)
16. Silva, J.: Restating a research definition in conformance to soft systems semantics. In: Proceedings of 16th EurOMA Conference, Sweden, 14–17 June 2009
17. Bustinza, O., Bigdeli, A., Baines, T., Elliot, C.: Servitization and competitive advantage: the importance of organizational structure. Res. Tech. Manag. **58**(5), 53–60 (2015)
18. Baines, T.: Exploring service innovation and the servitization of the manufacturing firm. Res. Technol. Manag. **58**, 9–12 (2015)
19. Reim, W., Parida, V., Ortqvist, D.: Product service systems (PSS) business models and tactics e a systematic literature review. J. Clean. Prod. **97**, 61–75 (2015)
20. Silva, J., Almeida, I.:. Collaborative networks as incubators of dynamic virtual organizations. Int. J. Manuf. Technol. Manag. **31**(1-2-3), 192–216 (2017)
21. Afsarmanesh, H., Camarinha-Matos, L.: A Framework for management of VO breeding environments. In: Camarinha-Matos, L., Afsarmanesh, H., Ortiz, A. (eds.) Collaborative Networks and their Breeding Environments, pp. 35–48. Springer, Boston (2005)
22. Porter, M., Heppelmann, J.: How smart, connected products are transforming competition. Harv. Bus. Rev. **92**(11), 1–23 (2014)
23. Reinartz, W., Ulaga, W.: How to sell service more profitable. HBR **86**(5), 90–96 (2008)
24. Baines, T., Lightfoot, H.: Servitization of the manufacturing firm: exploring the operations practices and technologies. Int. J. Oper. Prod. Manag. **34**(1), 2–35 (2013)
25. Manyika, J., Chui, M., Lund, S., Ramaswamy, S.: What's now and next in analytics, AI, and automation. McKinsey Global Institute (2017). http://www.mckinsey.com/global-themes/digital-disruption/whats-now-and-next-in-analytics-ai-and-automation?cid=other-eml-alt-mgi-mgi-oth-1705&hlkid=9a6016170fcb420f8a121a17c5a33c63&hctky=2399862&hdpid=8ce712f8-63e5-406f-bcdf-1cbc2c3f7d05#Table. Accessed 22 May 2017
26. Lightfoot, H., Baines, T., Smart, P.: Examining the information and communication technologies enabling servitized manufacture. Proc. Inst. Mech. Eng. Part B: J. Eng. Manuf. **225**(10), 1964–1968 (2011)
27. FEAPO.: Common perspectives on enterprise architecture. Federation of EA Professional Organizations. Architecture and Governance Magazine, 1–12 November 2013
28. Burton, B.: Digital business architecture - From strategy to guiding execution. Gartner (2017), https://www.gartner.com/webinar/3251017. Accessed 9 May 2017
29. Gartner: Gartner Says That by 2018, Half of EA Business Architecture Initiatives Will Focus on Defining and Enabling Digital Business Platform Strategies. Gartner Press Release (2017), http://www.gartner.com/newsroom/id/3660017. Accessed 7 April 2017
30. Geraci, A.: IEEE standard computer dictionary: Compilation of IEEE standard computer glossaries. IEEE Press (1991)
31. Pagano, P., Candela, L., Castelli, D.: Data Interoperability. Data Sci. J. **12**, 19–25 (2013)
32. Huxtable, J., Schaefer, D.: On servitization of the manufacturing industry in the RU. Procedia CIRP **52**, 46–51 (2016)
33. Simões, J.: Evaluation of innovative business models for SME: the servitization of the suppliers of advanced manufacturing technologies for the ornamental stones cluster. MSc thesis, Supervisor - João Vilas-Boas, IBS, ISCTE-IUL, Portugal (2017)

34. Saunders, M., Lewis, P., Thornhill, A.: Research Methods, 5ª edn. Pearson, Harlow (2009)
35. Yin, R.: Case Study Research: Design and Methods, 4ª edn. Sage Pub., Thousand Oaks (2009)
36. Silva, A., Vilas-Boas, J., Simões, J.: Definition of the mobiliser project INOVSTONE 4.0 Unpublished internal report Draft. Gestor do Inovstone 4.0 (2017)
37. Porter, M.: The five competitive forces that shape strategy. Harv. B. Rev. **86**, 79–93 (2008)
38. Williams, A.: Product service systems in the automobile industry: contribution to system innovation. J. Clean. Prod. **15**(11–12), 1093–1103 (2007)
39. Camarinha-Matos, L., Afsarmanesh, H., Ollus, M.: ECOLEAD: a holistic approach to creation and management of dynamic virtual organizations. In: Camarinha-Matos, L., Afsarmanesh, H., Ortiz, A. (eds.) Collaborative Networks and their Breeding Environments, pp. 35–48. Springer, Boston (2005)

Integrated Framework to Manage Building's Sustainability Efficiency, Design Features and Building Envelope

Tala Kasim[1(✉)], Haijiang Li[2], Yacine Rezgui[2], and Thomas Beach[2]

[1] School of Engineering and Applied Science, Aston University, Birmingham, UK
tala.kasim@yahoo.com
[2] School of Engineering, Cardiff University, Cardiff, UK
{Lih,rezguiy,beachth}@cardiff.ac.uk

Abstract. The construction industry is facing a challenge to move towards a more sustainable sector with energy-efficient buildings and sustainable design features. Building design and construction process are conditioned by numerous sustainability regulations and assessment measures. With the increasing use of building simulations, the potential of improving design features and promoting efficient construction has become a routine practice, starting at early stages of design and carried out throughout the life cycle of a building. Nevertheless, the construction process is currently lacking the presence of integrated systems that allow dynamic compliance checking of design features with building regulations using instant results from building simulation tools. Such integrated system requires access to regulatory compliance data and appropriate information exchange mechanism between building information model, regulatory requirements and building simulations tools. This paper will present an initiative for developing an integrated system that facilitates managing building performance dynamically through an appropriate information management process combining sustainability regulatory and building simulations with building information modeling. The paper will present a valid implementation results of compliance checking against some criteria of BREEAM assessment process. The quantitative analysis of the results revealed that more than 50% of compliance requirements cannot be fully automated and still requires users input. This is due to the fact that the IFC data model used for data extraction lacks a representation of certain domains of data.

Keywords: Regulatory compliance checking · Building simulations tools
Building information modeling

1 Introduction

The construction industry requires immediate and effective solutions to design sustainable and high-performance buildings to meet the needs of the 21st century (Everett et al. 2012). The use environmental assessment systems to evaluate building performance has

L. M. Camarinha-Matos et al. (Eds.): PRO-VE 2018, IFIP AICT 534, pp. 650–660, 2018.
https://doi.org/10.1007/978-3-319-99127-6_56

been widely implemented across the world to examine building compliance with sustainability requirements. These tools have been used during the design, construction and operation stages (Singh et al. 2012). However, the use of these tools has been criticized for being tedious and long processes. This is mainly due to the large amounts of data and information that need to be processed in order to undertake the assessment, further to the nature and the number of the performance criteria and their continuous increasing in details and complexity (Jaffe et al. 2005).

Although there are a plethora of environmental assessment methodologies (e.g., BREEAM and LEED) (Trusty 2000), however, the efforts needed in achieving the desired sustainable performance have often proved too expensive and time-consuming (Kibert 2008). There is still a gap in the provision of integrated systems that facilitate the assessment process in a simplified way. Hence, the construction industry needs an urgent fundamental cultural change in environmental assessment and compliance checking methodologies that allow lifecycle performance assessment in an integrated way (Lee and George 2013).

BIM technologies provide an opportunity to facilitate regulatory compliance checking process in an efficient way (Counsell 2012). The main characteristic of BIM is providing a digital representation of building information as a product of the modeling process. This information could be utilized in a smart way in order to undertake efficient processes, and regulatory compliance checking could be one of these processes (Jung and Joo 2011).

This paper presents an initiative of developing an integrated system that facilitates managing building performance dynamically through appropriate information management process by combining sustainability regulatory and building simulations with building information modeling. The availability of such will have significant advantages of promoting a more efficient regulatory compliance checking process.

2   Background

Many researchers and software vendors such as Autodesk have reported that BIM tools promote efficient sustainable construction through the availability of building information for compliance checking and simulation (Azhar et al. 2009). By using BIM as a design tool, an optimized design which meets regulatory requirements of sustainable construction could be achieved. This could be done when designers have access to a comprehensive set of information and knowledge in order to undertake compliance checking, such as building form, location, building components, materials and manufacturer information in addition to relevant technical systems. Since the use of BIM has only been mandated recently, research in the area of developing BIM integrated solutions has been growing. Hence, many researchers have been studying the integration between BIM and sustainability tools (Biswas and Tsung-Hsien Wang 2008). The aim of these research is to develop an automated assessment process Furthermore, there have been many practical attempts to consider sustainability assessment process as part of building design such as Bentley System's AECOsim Compliance Manager; "a project management and collaboration service to automate the LEED certification process for the United States Green Building Council's (USGBC)" (Bentley 2016).

There is a massive amount of sustainability analysis software tools. These tools are used to provide real-time indicators of building performance in line with sustainable construction agenda. Some of these tools are directly linked with environmental assessment methods, for example, IES<VE> for energy analysis has the features of checking compliance against part L of the English building regulations. IES<VE> also works parallel with LEED rating system. However, the process still lacks effective interoperability between BIM, regulatory requirements and building simulations tools (Crawley et al. 2001).

The integration between software tools requires an effective mechanism of information exchange. Currently, even within the BIM environment, different software use different data exchange format, as a result, direct integration is difficult to achieve. The most popular data exchange formats are Industry Foundation Classes (IFC) and gbXML and they both have their limitations; IFC does not include all of the information needed for sustainability compliance checking and gbXML is not comprehensive and it lacks lifecycle consideration and

With the increasing use of BIM, several tools have emerged for compliance checking and clash detection. One of the most popular tools is Solibri Model Checker (SMC). "Solibri has been designed to achieve continuous quality control for the build-ing model during its life cycle. Its functionality is based on an information take-off (ITO) capability, which allows users to collect information from the BIM, organize it, visualize it, read the IFC file, map it to its rules structure, and report results instantly. The information that can be checked with SMC includes areas and spatial calculations, the envelope of the building to be used for energy calculations, volumes, and quantities" (Kasim 2016). Many other systems also exist for design rule checking of examples; EDM Model Checker, and E-plan Check of the Singaporean CORNETE project Jotne Express Data Manager (Eastman et al. 2009)

All the previously reported compliance checking approaches used IFC models to facilitate information exchanging and processing, however, they are not using the full potential of the available information for automated comprehensive compliance (Salama and El-Gohary 2011). They only focused general features of building design within the architectural and structural design domain. These systems utilize a relatively simple form of rules of building geometry and special attributes to examine compliance checking (Khemlani 2002). For example, these tools proved efficient in checking access dimensions, wall thickness, doors sizes, and so on (Yang and Xu 2004). It can be concluded from literature review findings that BIM integrated solutions for sustainability checking is still in its early stages (Kasim 2013). Therefore, this paper presents the methodology that has been developed for a more comprehensive assessment process. The methodology presented in this paper aim at promoting an efficient integrated system for compliance checking which could be used iteratively to simulate the performance criteria against targeted regulations dynamically throughout the life cycle of building design and construction. This will facilitate compliance checking process as the design develops and building operates. In addition to providing designer with constant feedback on methods for optimized design with a desired building performance.

2.1 Regulatory Compliance

The field of sustainable engineering is facing the phenomena of increased numbers of regulations, building codes, and best practices. Furthermore, these regulations are growing massively in their volumes and complexity to meet the requirements of efficient designs, sustainable construction while reducing carbon footprints. Building codes and regulations cover a diverse range of aspects, falls under different categories with the aim of meeting the optimum functional requirements of building design while maintaining the environment. Hence, the categories of sustainable design regulations range from rules for promoting efficiency through energy and water consumptions, rules for sustainable logistics and supply chain management and rules for environmental protection through the choice of sustainable construction materials. There are significant differences between the global and national diverse building regulations, mainly in terms of their originality, historical development and the various emphasis on environmental issues. Nevertheless, the majority of these regulations share similar purposes and uses almost the same compliance checking methods and procedures.

The nature of these regulations can be described as either feature-based exigency or ward performance-based requirements; for instance, the assessment of energy efficiency is determined from both building design features such as (the choice of building materials, isolations, fittings and other specifications) the performance according to energy utilities.

The traditional methods by which compliance requirements are presented has been criticised for being inefficient by many researchers as in (Gupta and Dantsiou 2013); these criticisms have signaled a new way of thinking towards a dramatic change in setting up the regulations to meet the requirements of 21st century. These changes need to be done in line with the continuous changes in building design and operations processes which are becoming more ICT (information communication technology) oriented. (Rezgui and Medjdoub 2007) argued that in the face of such trends, design regulations, legislation and building standards, need to urgently comply with these conceptual challenges.

Despite the fact that achieving such conversions is limited by enormous amount of barriers, having regulatory- based IT infrastructure would have significant benefits for the long term of construction (Alavi and Leidner 1999). Some of these barriers are associated with the format of the current compliance requirements representation. Hence, an urgent transformation into logical expressions in a digital format is needed to replace the current textual representation of fragmented sets of information for compliance requirements. The transformation must be conditional to comply with automated extraction of information from regulations while preserving the same context in meeting compliance requirements. The main benefits of achieving such developments within the context of sustainable construction is the potential of applying verifiable smart compliance measurement procedures in assessing compliance with sustainable design requirements and achieving optimised design solutions.

In general, the way compliance with regulations is checked by comparing design features against compliance requirements based on the available data and information.

Then, a specific approach is used to evaluate the performance according to the nature of information and assessment criteria as follow:

(a) Data provided by building users such as operation status the number of occupants using the building, (b) Data obtained through the application of simple procedures and calculations based on existing data such as the calculations of volumes, areas, and enumerations, (c) Data obtained by using external applications such as numerical values of water and energy consumptions, and (d) information provided from external sources and GIS regarding external conditions such as weather and site conditions.

Although there are many tools that could massively facilitate the process through direct integration and smart intelligence, nevertheless, this integration has yet to be achieved.

3   Framework Development

The author has identified three major phases in order to achieve automated compliance checking of building performance. The initial phase comprise converting the textual complex format of regulatory into an explicit logical expressions which could support the automation. The second phase includes integrating external applications and building performance simulation tools with compliance checking tools. While in the final phase, having the regulatory requirements embedded into the compliance checking environment. By developing a framework based on these three phases, the process of compliance checking could become more efficient and transparent requires less efforts and investments. The phases of the framework developments are illustrated in Fig. 1.

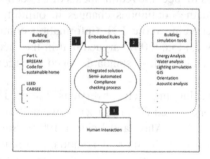

Fig. 1. Integrated system for compliance checking

Each phase has some challenges to limit the development of such integrated solutions. For example; in phase, compliance requirements in regulations and standards are described in textual documents that require human interpretation and processing. Therefore, they are not ready to be directly automated. While in line with phase 2, building performance simulation tools are criticised for their limited interoperability with the requirements of sustainable design specified by sustainability regulations. These two issues limits the achievement of the final phase of developing the integrated process of automated sustainability compliance checking. It can be summarised that most of the challenges are associated with information format and information exchange.

Nevertheless, the current evolution of Building information modelling technologies and data sharing regime has potentially intensified developing innovative solutions to streamline sustainability compliance checking.

3.1 Converting Textual Documents into Rules Using RASE

To develop the system, regulatory statements need to be described using logical decision spreadsheet. To do that, regulatory requirements were analysed and then re- written in a form of series of decision statements. Each of these statements has been placed in a cell within the decision spreadsheet.

One of the challenges was that regulatory statements are written in technical/legal language. They are designed for processing by professionals with experience in the domain and not ready for computer processing. Hence, additional stage was needed for separating the compliance requirements and their applicability to be further re-ordered into an applicable logical structure (Eastman et al. 2009b). For this purpose, RASE (Requirements, Applications, selection, and exemption) has been utilized in a process called "Marking Up". This process allows adding extra semantic information to the regulation.

Every single decision from compliance requirements assessment criteria has been re-written using RASE through the marked-up. The process involved identifying every 'objects', its 'properties' and 'requirements' for compliance as specified in the regulations. Once this process has been completed, a summary of all the required information to be extracted from the BIM model has been identified.

The software tool has been used to import the original textual statements from the standard document and regulations and to convert them to XML 'Extensible Markup Language' format. This is done by applying encoding format and applying a set of XML syntax to re-structures of the original sentence. This stage was followed by adding the four RASE operators; selection, application, exemption and requirements. Figure 2 demonstrates an example of regulation text that has been marked up with RASE using Require 1 tool AEC3 Ltd.

All framed walls, floors and ceilings not ventilated to allow moisture to escape shall be provided with an approved vapor retarder having a permeance rating of 1 perm (5.7 × 10–11 kg/Pa × s × m2) or less, when tested in accordance with the dessicant method using Procedure A of ASTM E96

Exceptions

1. In construction where moisture or its freezing will not damage the materials
2. Where other approved means to avoid condensation in unventilated framed wall, floor, roof and ceiling cavities are provided.

Fig. 2. RASE Application using Require 1 tool AEC3 Ltd.

"Requirement: Represents the criteria that are required to be true for a specific decision. It allows the specification of the decision to be made. The requirement statements

often start with obligation terms, such as *shall*, *must* and so on. A requirement or definition is highlighted in blue", as illustrated in Fig. 2.

"Application: Restricts the scope of the decision. The *applies* statement is highlighted in green in Fig. 2. The check applies to the filtered set of items, which are identified separately as an apply tag, for example, the apply tag may indicate that a decision applies to "external" doors only, or only to "Naturally Ventilated" rooms."

"Selection: The *select* statement is highlighted in purple in the example in Fig. 2. Each *select* statement serves to expand the scope of the decision. Often, a check contains a list of the selection of items to which it relates. There is a dictionary of phrases to define all of the terms used to describe the alternative items. A key feature is that each select statement increases the number of relevant items that are considered, for example, "walls", "floors" and "ceilings"."

"Exception: Specifies the cases to which the check does not apply. An exception is highlighted in orange on the previous example, illustrated in Fig. 2. The *exception* tag also filters the number of items within the scope of the decision" (Kasim 2015).

3.2 Rules Processing (Generation and Execution)

To execute the requirements for sustainability compliance checking, an open-source rule engine has been utilized namely the 'DROOLS rule engine' (Drools 2013).

An interim stage was required to convert the spreadsheet including the meta data into a format understandable by the rule engine. Therefore DRL (DROOLS Rule Language) (Community 2013) has been utilized to enable DROOLS rule engine to process the decision spreadsheets and the additional RASE meta-data that has been added to each individual cells within the generated decision spreadsheets.

The conversion from the spreadsheet to DRL is done by using a rule compiler which applies a series of logical formulas, the compiler works according to the decision spreadsheets and the RASE tags. The outcome of this process is a generated DRL ready for processing by DROOLS into an executable code where each individual cell in the decision spreadsheet is treated as a single rule. The process of rule execution is done in two steps: the first step is to determine if the rule is in scope, while the second step shows if the rule has been passed or failed. Figure 3 shows the logical formula which was used to process the rules. In Fig. 3, 'S1 and S2' represent the *"Select"* RASE Tags, 'E1, E2' represent *"Exception"* tags, ' A1, A2' represent the *"Applies"* tags and 'R1, R2' represent the *"Requirement"* tags.

For a rule to be applicable, it needs at least one selection, all applicability criteria and non of the exceptions must be met. to determine whether the rule has passed or failed, they are examined against meeting the requirements "R1" and "R2".

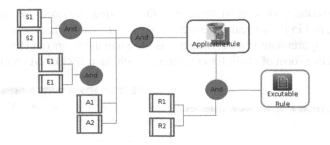

Fig. 3. Rules processing (Generation and Execution)

3.3 Mapping Regulatory Requirements to IFC Data Model

The main aim of using the rule engine is to examine the regulatory compliance of the BIM model. IFC data model has been used for this purpose as the standard data exchange format within Building information modeling environment. However, when IFC data model has been explores to examine the compatibility of data representation with the developed sets of rules, it has been determined that all the main building objects that were previously addressed for compliance are included in the IFC data model. Nevertheless, not all the pre-defined properties of these objects were necessarily fulfilling the requirements for compliance checking; it has been determined that there are still a plethora of characteristics and descriptive attributes to be added to the IFC data model to make it compatible with the compliance checking requirements. The availability of a comprehensive data model is important in order to establish a domain-compliant IFC that is ready for the undertaking automated compliance check.

It can be concluded at this stage that the rules engine is only capable for capturing the explicit data requirement directly from the IFC file. These limitations have motivated the author to seek alternative reasoning-based methods to extract more compliance requirements including the implicit requirements for compliance checking. A suggestion for using engineering ontologies has been considered for the aim of gathering the fragmented pieces of axioms from the IFC, in order to build domain ontology; It is not in the scope of this paper to discuss the compliance checking domain ontology, but such development can potentially facilitate extracting a wider range of information from an IFC model.

4   Implementation and Results Validation

Compliance checking system has been implemented in a real case scenario to examine its validity and efficiency. For this purpose, a previously generated BIM model of the design of a new development has been utilized. The case study design model has been provided by Skanska UK Ltd, where the development has been designed to achieve a BREEAM 'excellent' rating.

Figure 4 shows a screenshot of system implementation, in this figure, there is a window of user interaction and additional information requirements that need to be added before running the compliance check. Once added, the system scans the provided BIM model, and in the logical structured process, the system checks the model against compliance requirements (the decision tree is shown in the figure) and finally, the results are reported in a form of credit for compliance with each BREEAM criteria.

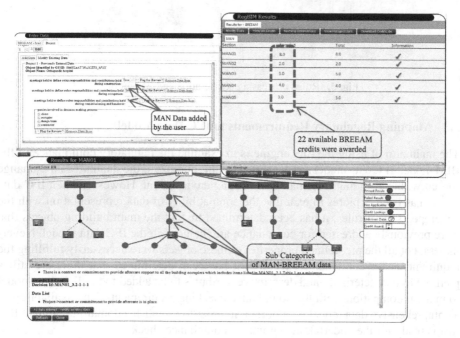

Fig. 4. System implementation results

5   Conclusion

The developed automated compliance checking process proof to have some limitations. Mainly, because the standard data format IFC lacks representations of all objects attributes needed for compliance checking. As a result, additional data is needed to enrich the current data model and to make it compatible with compliance requirements. When applying the process on a real case study for validation purpose. The process shows its validity and reliability and correct results were obtained as verified by a comparison with the traditional BRREAM assessment method.

The key feature of the developed approach is its ability to collect together the compliance information and use it directly as enrichment to the existing BIM model (IFC file). To this end, the developed system shows significant merits in terms of its ability to exploit a considerable amount of knowledge present in a BIM model, but interacting with assessors is still fundamental to close the loop of compliance checking as shown in Fig. 5. The quantitative representation analysis of compliance checking processes reveals that around half of the compliance requirements need to be addressed by the user and hence human interaction with the system is still required to add the missing domains of data to the IFC. Much of the required data is related to checks on supporting documentation i.e. contracts, and other documentations which are not within the scope of the current IFC.

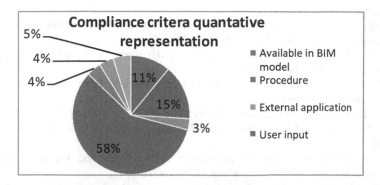

Fig. 5. Quantitative representation of compliance checking process

Nevertheless, even in these cases the system facilitates the compliance analysis by providing the user with the list of data that is needed for every decision. This enables the users to be able to visualise the effects of entered data on the final results.

The goal of user engagement is to provide additional pieces of information that can be helpful to proceed with running the compliance checking application automatically. To facilitate the user engagement, a user interface has been developed with a user-friendly interface. And to ensure that the information is consistent terminology and compatible with the rule engine requirements, additional features has been added to the user interface to constrain the data input process

Since the process still requires user engagement, the process is still not fully-automated. The next stage of the development will involve integrating the current outcome with building simulation tools to enrich the functionality of the semi-automated process. Although automating compliance checking is very difficult to achieve, but this development could open future opportunities for more coherent development to promote efficient compliance checking throughout buildings' life cycle.

References

Azhar, S., Brown, J., Farooqui, R.: BIM-based sustainability analysis: an evaluation of building performance analysis software. In: Proceedings of the 45th ASC Annual Conference (2009)

Bentley: AECOsim. 2016 Copyright Bentley Systems, Incorporated. Accessed October 2016

Biswas, T., Tsung-Hsien Wang, R.K.: Integrating sustainable building rating systems with building information models (2008)

Counsell, J.: Beyond Level 2 BIM, web portals and collaboration tools. In: 2012 16th International Conference on Information Visualisation, 2012, pp. 510–515. IEEE (2012)

Crawley, D.B., et al.: EnergyPlus: creating a new-generation building energy simulation program. Energy Build. **33**, 319–331 (2001)

Eastman, C., Lee, J.-M., Jeong, Y.-S., Lee, J.-K.: Automatic rule-based checking of building designs. Autom. Constr. **18**, 1011–1033 (2009)

Everett, R., Boyle, G., Peake, S., Ramage, J.: Energy Systems and Sustainability: Power for a Sustainable Future. Oxford University Press, Oxford (2012)

Hjelseth, E. Nisbet, N.: Capturing normative constraints by use of the semantic mark-up (RASE) methodology. In: CIB W78 2011 28th International Conference-Applications of IT in the AEC Industry (2011)

Jaffe, A.B., Newell, R.G., Stavins, R.N.: A tale of two market failures: technology and environmental policy. Ecol. Econ. **54**, 164–174 (2005)

Jung, Y., Joo, M.: Building information modelling (BIM) framework for practical implementation. Autom. Constr. **20**, 126–133 (2011)

Kasim, T.: BIM-Based Smart Compliance Checking to Enhance Environmental Sustainability. Ph.D. Cardiff University (2015)

Khemlani, L.: Solibri Model Checker. CADENCE-AUSTIN, pp. 32–34 (2002)

Kibert, C.J.: Sustainable Construction: Green Building Design and Delivery. Wiley, Hoboken (2008)

Lee, N., George, C.: Environmental Assessment in Developing and Transitional Countries: Principles, Methods and Practice. Wiley, Hoboken (2013)

Salama, D., El-Gohary, N.: Semantic modeling for automated compliance checking. J. Comput. Civ. Eng., 641–648 (2011)

Singh, R.K., Murty, H., Gupta, S., Dikshit, A.: An overview of sustainability assessment methodologies. Ecol. Indic. **15**, 281–299 (2012)

Singh, V., Gu, N., Wang, X.: A theoretical framework of a BIM-based multi-disciplinary collaboration platform. Autom. Constr. **20**, 134–144 (2011)

Kasim, T., Li, H., Rezgui, Y., Beach, T.: Automated sustainability compliance checking process. In: EG-ICE International Workshop on Intelligent Computing in Engineering Vienna, Austria (2013)

Trusty, W.B.: Introducing an assessment tool classification system. Adv. Build. Newslett. **25** (2000)

Yang, Q., Xu, X.: Design knowledge modeling and software implementation for building code compliance checking. Build. Environ. **39**, 689–698 (2004)

Meta-Standard for Collaborative BIM Standards: An Analysis of UK BIM Level 2 Standards

Mohamed Binesmael[✉], Haijiang Li, and R. Lark

School of Engineering, Cardiff University,
Queen's Building, 14-17 the Parade, Cardiff CF24 3AA, UK
{binesmaelm,lih,lark}@cardiff.ac.uk

Abstract. The nascent journey of the AEC (Architecture, Engineering, and Construction) industry toward a fully collaborative BIM (Building Information Modelling) maturity has resulted in the development of siloed standards. Whilst some countries lead the charge in BIM maturity level adoption, other countries are pressed to develop their own policies to minimise stagnation. This results in the unintended fragmentation of the AEC industry globally, and further enlarging the international collaboration rift within multinational firms. This article analyses key BIM standards and policies adopted in the UK based on a published 3C Meta-Standard framework. The disparity between the standards towards the Industry Foundation Classes (IFC) specification goals are highlighted to recommend adjustments where necessary. A 34% gap was found, particularly in the topic areas of object connectivity and the multiple disciplinary information capture. This study forms one of three key research elements in the pursuit of developing a dynamic and autonomous BIM platform, capable of delivering parameters between stakeholders involved in complex BIM projects.

Keywords: Meta-standard · Collaboration · BIM cognitive system
Building Information Modelling · BIM · Industry Foundation Classes
IFC · BIMNet

1 Introduction

To develop a cognitive system within the AEC (Architecture, Engineering, and Construction) industry requires an understanding of the relationships between stakeholders, the tools these stakeholders use, the standards by which they abide, and the data points that will be captured. The purpose of a cognitive system in the AEC industry is to facilitate the adoption of collaborative versions of Building Information Modelling (BIM), and allow for collaboration between humans.

The research herein will focus at analysing the standards perspective as standards highlight the necessary interactions between stakeholders, challenging how a collaborative network is designed. To self-assess standards and identify gaps in the current standards requires a framework of standard assessment, hence the 3C meta-standard framework will be utilised in the methodology of this study.

© IFIP International Federation for Information Processing 2018
Published by Springer Nature Switzerland AG 2018. All Rights Reserved
L. M. Camarinha-Matos et al. (Eds.): PRO-VE 2018, IFIP AICT 534, pp. 661–668, 2018.
https://doi.org/10.1007/978-3-319-99127-6_57

The UK Government mandated that public projects must be working at BIM Level 2 since 2016 with the aim of reducing public sector asset costs. BIM Level 2 requires the capture of data and documents electronically for project and asset information, as well as the use of a Common Data Environment (CDE) across disciplines for the handling of 3D geometrical and non-graphical data [1].

To achieve BIM Level 3, full collaboration across all disciplines is the necessary requisite alongside a central, shared project model [1]. To achieve full collaboration, interoperability must be prioritised by data standards to make data accessible across all platforms [2]. A bottom-up approach is being explored to ensure all stakeholders can easily be involved in the process from the outset. The difficulty with construction projects is that stakeholders are never the same and the dynamic relationships and information exchanges required between stakeholders often vary. A cognitive system that is able to develop, learn, and keep track of relationships for projects to suggest the best information exchanges therefore requires investigation to determine if it may solve the industry's woes.

2   Theory

2.1   State of the Art

The oft-cited BIM wedge (Fig. 1) developed by Mark Bew and Mervyn Richards [3] shows that the standards: *BS 1992:2007, PAS 1992-2:2013, PAS 1992-3:2014*, and *BS 1192-4:2014* fall below the threshold to achieve BIM Level 3. This study will focus on analysing these four documents against a high-level breakdown for *ISO 16739*, which is one of five basic methodology standards developed by buildingSMART International. *ISO 16739* outlines methods for exchange of relevant data through Industry Foundation Classes (IFC).

ISO 16739 was selected as the standard for testing the application of the 3C meta-standard framework, due to it being a key enabler to data interoperability.

The concept behind the methodology standards is to create a new digital language that is open and allows for structured information to be freely exchanged [4]. The goal of open standards is to steer industry towards collaboration and information exchange away from proprietary software, and therefore requires standardisation as a prerequisite [5]. The adoption of such standards can be further intensified through the effect of network technology, whereby the utility of users increases when another user adopts the standard [6]. A cognitive system that works in collaboration between people from all disciplines and software would instil this network technology across all stakeholders.

The UK is leading the charge in clearly defining standards and Publicly Available Specifications (PAS) required to achieve BIM Level 2. Countries worldwide are developing similar but incomplete mandates, such as a 10-part series for the *VDI 2552* in Germany; one published, two draft documents, and seven as ongoing projects. American standards are fragmented nationally across states, making it difficult to include them in the study scope. Norway leads in case studies of BIM adoption to high levels, however the mandate between levels is kept vague.

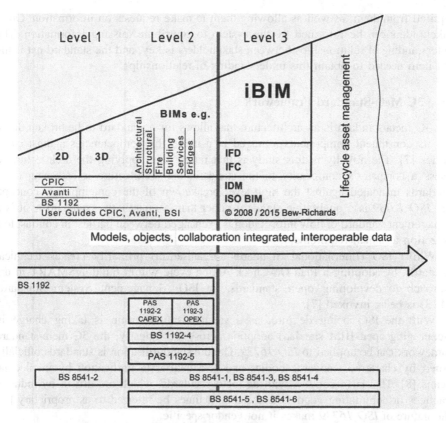

Fig. 1. BIM maturity levels (reproduced and cropped for detail from PAS 1192-5:2015)

This is an extensive list; therefore, the scope of this study is focusing on creating a 3C meta-standard framework to analyse the relevant UK BIM Level 2 documents, with the hope that future work can refine the framework process.

2.2 BIMNet Platform

Research at Cardiff University is underway to study the requirements of a cognitive system able to collaborate between processes, objects, and people under the envelope of standards. The application of this system will be first applied to the IFC for ports and harbours project which is one of five extensions underway of the IFC schema for infrastructure, as the current IFC schema focuses on buildings.

This study paves for the way for a standard net that interlinks standards. Next must be the analysis of relationships between stakeholders captured by a data exchange net. The knowledge utilised by these stakeholders will also need to be captured as a knowledge net. These nets interweave to form the BIMNet platform.

The BIMNet will be a cognitive platform for collaborative BIM, allowing stakeholders to know what information is available to them and what information is still required from them, as well as allowing them to make requests on information. Other stakeholders can be informed by the system to contribute missing information. The understanding of relationships between stakeholders is key, and the standard net is the first item needed to obtain this understanding of relationships.

2.3   3C Meta-Standard Framework

The 3C meta-standard is an architecture that allows for a standard to be broken down into its constituent components arranged in a matrix by competencies against capabilities [7]. The novelty in this study is that rather than applying the architecture to assess a company's conformity to the standard, the architecture is assessing other standards mandated against the high-level breakdown of the contemporary concept. The *ISO 16739* is a qualitative standard rather than a quantitative standard as it is a management standard of how information is exchanged between parties; in contrast to a collection technical requirement.

Whilst ISO (International Standards Organisation) primarily creates technical standards, by adopting a Plan-Do-Check-Action cycle within buildingSMART in the approach to developing open standards, an ISO Management System Standards (MSS) is being invoked [7].

With the ISO being de jure, as a standardisation group is taking charge in encouraging open BIM standard adoption across the industry, the 3C meta-standard framework can be applied to *ISO 16739*. De jure standardisation is standards officially issued by chartered standards bodies and is a deliberate unification by intellectual means [8]. This is in contrast with de facto standards, which are driven by industry practices or dominating vendors and can sometimes be referred to as proprietary [7]. The nature of *ISO 16739* makes it not vendor specific.

A multi-pronged approach to standard creation taking the best of both worlds could be achieved using PAS referenced in formal standards to allow for leading the market and quick adoption [9].

3   Methodology

The decision to analyse the UK BIM level 2 mandated documents was due to the EU approach to standardisation favouring development for interoperability over the USA approach which favours proprietary technologies [7], as well as clearly highlighted documents that pertain to BIM Level 2 adoption as a starting point. This makes the BIM Level 2 documents a good pilot for testing the 3C meta-standard approach as the UK aims for interoperability with BIM Level 3.

Whilst the BIM Level 2 suite of documents refers to eight documents to follow, only four were pertinent to the analysis. *PAS 1192-5:2015* complements these four documents (listed in chapter 2.1) however focuses on the security element of data exchange, and *PAS 1192-6:2018* layers on top of the four documents to discuss exchange of health and safety information for construction sites. Both are not in the scope of *ISO 16739*. The remaining documents (BS 8536-1:2015 and BS 8536-2:2016) make multiple references throughout their text to refer to the 4 documents listed prior.

3.1   3C Meta-Standard Framework Terms

The 3C meta-standard relies upon data to inform performance in the area being studied by the standard [7]. In this study this data is the evidence brought by the statements made within the BIM Level 2 documents.

The 3C meta-standard creates components by reformulating the standard statements into questions posed. These questions are placed within a matrix with the x-axis describing the competency to which it belongs, i.e. the "topics addressed and accounted by the standard" [7]. The y-axis of the matrix describes the capabilities of the standard, i.e. what is "analysed and assessed by the standard" [7].

Capabilities are further subdivided into a sub-taxonomy which contains three sub-subjects:

1. The need – the opportunity raised by the component,
2. The strategy – the approach introduced by answering the component,
3. The recommendations – how to achieve the target through the advice and directions provided by answering the component.

A final functionality termed Linkages, collects references made to other standards. The supra taxonomy consists of the components, competencies, and capabilities.

As this study is not focusing on developing a self-certification scheme, organising information by their properties and relations of data and knowledge is therefore not wholly required for this exercise [7]. This may be an approach that requires revision for analysing all national standards related to collaborative BIM.

3.2   3C Meta-Standard Framework Process

A process for developing the matrix had not been described in the referenced paper. The process followed for this study began by outlining all the necessary competencies in the x-axis. This was relatively simple to follow as it allows for the chronological completion of the standard.

Once the competencies were complete, a chronological approach was taken to reformulate each competency area into questions. These questions formed the components that filled the matrix intersecting with each newly introduced capability recommended by the standard. If a capability within the competency being analysed referred to another competency, a new component at the intersection of the capability and that competency was created.

This approach allowed for an organic growth of the matrix without backtracking through the standard or missing out components. Iterations of capability ordering were required at times to allow for visually connecting them.

4   Results

The high-level breakdown of *ISO 16739* resulted in the development of 41 competencies, measured by 29 capabilities, and 292 components intersecting the two axes (Fig. 2). These 292 components were applied to each of the four BIM level 2 documents being analysed. The analyses of the developed 3C meta standard against the four BIM Level 2 documents resulted in the majority of the components being addressed (Fig. 2). Components not addressed by these standards primarily included object connectivity and interdisciplinary topics.

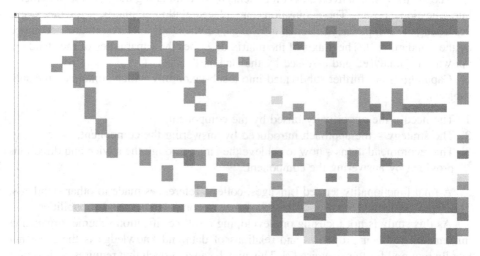

Fig. 2. Analysis of BIM Level 2 documents conforming to ISO 16739 3C Meta-Standard Framework Architecture. Green indicates at least one BIM Level 2 document adheres to the component. Lime green/yellow indicates at least one BIM Level 2 document partially adhering to the component. Red indicates no BIM Level 2 document adhering to the component. (Color figure online)

A detailed look at the components in Fig. 3 shows how the standard is reformulated as a matrix of closed questions to allow for simple self-evaluation. Once answered, the colour of the boxes automatically changes to create what's seen in Fig. 2.

Table 1 further divides the analysis into the separate document analyses that were conducted. It can be seen that *BS 1992-4:2014* contributes the majority of the components, covering at least 50% of the IFC specification. In total, it could be said that if a user adhered to the BIM Level 2 documents that they would be attaining 66% completion towards a collaborative BIM environment.

BS 1192:2007 covers the least out of the four documents analysed. This is not surprising as it predates the IFC4 specification which is the 2013 version of *ISO 16739*.

PAS 1192-2:2013 was a big leap in the number of components considered, which focused on information exchange for contracts, as well as responsibilities of actors. However, there was a lack of focus on objects and interoperability. The primary focus of this document covered the association and control competencies.

PAS 1192-3:2014 focused on the operation and management of assets and so contributed little to the IFC related elements.

	Association	Control
The need	Do you make reference to external or annotational information identified by a specific reference?	Do you describe requirements and constraints on objects?
The strategy	Do you include methods for physical composition and time-phased data?	Do you generalise controls into controlling cost, time, scope or quality?

Fig. 3. 3C Meta-Standard Framework Architecture: Detailed look at four components developed for ISO 16739. The upper axis forms the competencies, the left axis highlights the capabilities, with the intersection of the two forming the competency.

Table 1. Analysis of each of the four BIM level 2 documents independently and the overlapping total for 292 components in the matrix.

Standard Name	Yes	Partial	No	Linkages	% Yes	% Partial	% No
BS 1192 2007	26	6	260	2	9%	2%	89%
BSI PAS 1192-2 2013	90	13	189	3	31%	4%	65%
BSI PAS 1192-3 2014	47	6	239	2	16%	2%	82%
BS 1192-4 2014	146	12	134	1	50%	4%	46%
Total Overlapping	178	14	100	8	61%	5%	34%

BS 1192-4:2014 introduced COBie (Construction Operations Building information exchange) which dealt with many of the components raised by the IFC specification, from level 1 projects to a potential role within integrated BIM (UK Level 3), including some IFC entities.

5   Discussion and Conclusion

The 3C meta-standard framework is an engaging method of evaluating components of a standard. It simplifies the standard to a set of questions that users are required to answer through validating statements. The nature of the framework lends itself to self-validation and self-evaluation. Validation would require an expert panel workshop to discuss the developed matrix and compare answers.

Whilst most of the BIM Level 2 documents are PAS, the PAS process enabled the specification to rapidly be developed to fulfil the immediate need in the AEC industry. PAS *1192-2:2013* provided a leap in bringing on board the recommendations of *ISO 16739*. The development of *BS 1192-4:2014* as a British Standard was a good for leaping the industry toward the collaborative BIM vision. The gap remains in connecting all the disciplines as can be seen by the results. Whilst most of the capabilities were covered by the documents, the object connectivity and domain schema competencies lacked exposure. This allows for a BIMNet cognitive system to connect objects between the stakeholders of the various disciplines outlined in the domain schemas.

Future work will investigate applying the 3C meta-standard to other international and national standards such as Germany, China, and USA. Furthermore, a suite of 3C meta-standards could be developed for the remaining four basic methodology standards that cover processes, the mapping of terms, workflow coordination, and process translation, with linkages between them. Feedback for this study however is crucial to ensure further research is progressing in the right direction so that the BIMNet platform develops the right cognitive system for the AEC industry. The research question sought to analyse the mandated BIM Level 2 documents against *ISO 16739* which outlines the IFC specification for information exchange. A 34% gap was found, particularly in the topic areas of object connectivity and the multiple disciplinary information capture that is necessary if future collaboration for a BIM Level 3 system is to take place. This gap allows for a cognitive system such as the BIMNet platform outlined in this study to take hold.

References

1. BSI: FAQs | BIM Level 2. http://bim-level2.org/en/faqs/. Accessed 20 Apr 2018
2. Institution of Civil Engineers: State Of The Nation 2017: Digital Transformation (2017)
3. BSI: PAS 1192-5: 2015: Specification for security-minded building information modelling, digital built environments and smart asset management (2015)
4. BuildingSMART International: Open Standards - the basics - buildingSMART (2018). https://www.buildingsmart.org/standards/technical-vision/open-standards/. Accessed 20 Apr 2018
5. West, J.: Seeking open infrastructure: Contrasting open standards, open source and open innovation. First Monday (2007)
6. Heinrich, T.: Standard wars, tied standards, and network externality induced path dependence in the ICT sector. Technol. Forecast. Soc. Chang. **81**, 309–320 (2014)
7. Marsal-Llacuna, M.L.: The standards evolution: a pioneering Meta-standard framework architecture as a novel self-conformity assessment and learning tool. Comput. Stand. Interfaces **55**, 106–115 (2018)
8. Patzke, R., Schumny, H., Zisky, N.: Standardization aspects. Comput. Stand. Interfaces **19**, 249–256 (1998)
9. Stokes, A.V.: Who will standardise the standardisers: an analysis of the evolution of the standards-making process. Int. J. Med. Inform. **48**, 61–65 (1998)

Author Index

Printed in the United States
By Bookmasters

Printed in the United States
By Bookmasters